FEMALE AND MALE IN BORNEO: CONTRIBUTIONS AND CHALLENGES TO GENDER STUDIES

Edited by
Vinson H. Sutlive, Jr.

BORNEO RESEARCH COUNCIL MONOGRAPH SERIES

VOLUME ONE

BORNEO RESEARCH COUNCIL MONOGRAPH SERIES

Published by

THE BORNEO RESEARCH COUNCIL, INC.

Department of Anthropology
The College of William and Mary in Virginia
Williamsburg, VA 23185 USA

Series Editor: Vinson H. Sutlive, Jr.

Library of Congress Catalog Card No. 91-072229
ISBN 0-9629568-0-5
ISSN 1055-7792

Printed in the United States by
Ashley Printing Services, Inc.
Shanghai, VA

DEDICATION

This volume is dedicated to the men and women of Borneo, whose cultures have much to teach us about what it means to be human.

FEMALE AND MALE IN BORNEO
CONTRIBUTIONS AND CHALLENGES
TO GENDER STUDIES

THE BORNEO RESEARCH COUNCIL MONOGRAPH SERIES
VOLUME 1

PREFACE

The Borneo Research Council Monograph Series is devoted to continuing the rich tradition of scientific research on Borneo, and to the extension of knowledge about its people and their contributions to the full expression of what it means to be human.

The papers in this volume and others which will follow are based upon extended periods of fieldwork and ethnographic research. These papers amply demonstrate the productivity of ethnographic research and reject the caricature of anthropology as "interpretation" (Geertz 1973) or "emergent fantasy" (Tyler 1986:123), and find it ironic that the late Sir Edmund Leach, the scholar largely responsible for the modern era of anthropological research in Sarawak, in his last years perceived of ethnography as the writing of "fiction".

Anthropological generalizations and comparisons have largely ignored research results from Borneo. The numerous contributions of Bornean ethnography have included information about the developmental cycle of the family, the concept of the kindred, the nature of cognatic organization, property ownership, swidden cultivation, the nature of sultanates, and the function of headhunting. If considered, this research would require the reformulation of much anthropological theory.

The Borneo Research Council was founded in 1968 to promote scientific research in the social, biological, and medical sciences in Borneo. Among its purposes the Council has worked to permit the research community, interested government departments, and others to keep abreast of ongoing research and its results; to serve as a vehicle for drawing attention to urgent research problems; to coordinate the flow of information of Borneo research arising from many diverse sources; to disseminate rapidly the initial results of research activity; and to facilitate research by reporting on current conditions.

From its inception, the Council has worked cooperatively with the research institutions in Brunei, Sabah, Sarawak, and Kalimantan. The Council has helped integrate research results both from the various regions of Borneo and also from research originating in a variety of countries around the world.

The Council established the *Borneo Research Bulletin* for the rapid dissemination of research activities. The *Bulletin* is published semi-annually and is designed to appeal to scholars, government officials, laymen and amateurs, and businessmen.

Beginning in 1973, the Council has met in conjunction with the Annual Meeting of the American Anthropological Association, to share research results and raise issues concerning research problems. The Council chose to hold its meetings then because this was the one time when the largest number of members of the Council gathered in one place. And overseas members could at times make these meetings. In 1990, the first meeting of the Council in Borneo was held in Sarawak and was so successful that the Directors decided to establish a schedule of biennial meetings to be held in each of the states in turn.

The Monograph Series is the culmination of a decade of planning. Members of the Council have long been aware that there was a need to create a publication in which ethnographic data from Borneo might receive exposure beyond the Fellows and Members of the Council. This volume is based upon papers presented in an organized session of the American Anthropological Association in Chicago in 1987.

Within the next year, we anticipate publication of three other monographs. G. N. Appell is writing *The Analysis of Property Systems: Observational Procedures and Tree Ownership in the Societies of Borneo*. Robert Winzeler is editing papers from a 1989 program in a volume entitled *Spirit Mediums of Borneo*. And Michael Heppell is editing his dissertation, *Iban Social Control: The Infant and the Adult*, to incorporate comparative data from research on the Bidayuh.

Establishment of the series also is intended to encourage further research into the rapidly disappearing cultures of Borneo. Within the next decade, 70 to 80 percent of the rich cultural heritage of Bornean societies will be gone.

Many research problems still await study: The place of Borneo in human prehistory; the origins of Bornean hunter-gatherers; the introduction of rice cultivation; the evolution of a class system supported on swidden farming; the absence of social elaboration among interior and coastal societies practicing irrigated agriculture; and the impact of social change, especially development projects and urban migration.

We are pleased to inaugurate this monograph series which may be judged successful if it stimulates scholars and students of all professions to undertake research on the people of Borneo.

REFERENCES

Geertz, Clifford
    1973   The Interpretation of Cultures, New York, Basic Books

Tyler, Stephen
    1986   Post-Modern Ethnography: From Document of the Occult to Occult Document. In James Clifford and George E. Marcuse, eds., Writing Culture: The Poetics and Politics of Ethnography, Berkeley, University of California Press, pp. 122-140.

INTRODUCTION

Vinson H. Sutlive, Jr.
and
George N. Appell

The papers in this book describe human sexuality and gender[1] among a small sample of societies on the island of Borneo. Expressions of human sexuality vary widely among the 200 autonymic societies, which range in population from a few hundred persons to three-quarters of a million. Some are quite open about the subject, others circumspect and discreet.[2] The present work contains studies[3] of eight societies, with references to others. It does not deal with Chinese and Malays, who with others will be the subjects of future monographs on the same topic.

When we first read Donald Brown's statement that "little is known about human sexuality in Borneo" (p. 437), we disagreed. Here we concede Professor Brown's point. Although a considerable amount of information on human sexuality exists, as represented in this volume, the research results are preliminary, fragmentary, and raise many more questions than they answer.

Almost two decades ago, Wilhelm G. Solheim II (1972) observed that the archaeology of Southeast Asia is the least known in the world. What is true for the archaeology of the region is equally true for the ethnography.

LOCATING THE REGIONS
DESCRIBED IN THE MONOGRAPH

Appells & Doolittle Articles

Reece Article

BRUNEI

SABAH

Maxwell Article

Sutlive Article
(Sibu)

Kedit &
Winzeler
Articles

Crain
Article

Schneiders Article

SARAWAK

Davison, Sutlive
& Mashman
Articles

Drake
Article

Rousseau
Article

KALIMANTAN

Schiller Article

Yet the people of the region in general, and Borneo in particular, are not only as fascinating as any in the world but also crucial for the generation and testing of anthropological theory. Research on the prehistory, colonial and contemporary periods has contributed invaluable insights into varieties of human experiences, complementing and correcting the always incomplete record of human activities and achievements.

Paradoxically, many of the societies of Borneo have been studied extensively yet remain among the least known, even to students of the region of Southeast Asia. In *Gender and Anthropology* (Morgen, 1989), published by the American Anthropological Association, the paradox is obvious. The only studies of Bornean societies cited are those of Freeman (1970) and Tsing (1990). While numerous studies of sexuality and Bornean responses have been published over the past two decades (cf. G. N. Appell, 1966, 1969; L.W.R. Appell 1988; Brown et al. 1988; Freeman 1968, 1979; Graham 1988; Sather 1977, 1980; Sutlive 1977, 1979), none is included.

In her chapter on Southeast Asia in *Gender and Anthropology*, Aihwa Ong analyzes general characteristics of the gender systems for the region. Ong's summary for the region illustrates the almost complete omission of Bornean research and insights it provides for understanding human sexuality and gender distinctions. Contrary to her analyses, some Bornean societies emphasize opposition rather than complementarity, and authority based on gender rather than rank. While the status of women of Southeast Asia may be relatively high vis-à-vis women in other parts of the world, such as East and South Asia,[4] there are wide-ranging status distinctions among and between women of different societies within the region. Most women tend to work longer days, are much less mobile, have fewer choices in their activities, have greater responsibilities for their families, and are excluded from their society's system of prestige, with an obvious imbalance in rituals favoring males. Others enjoy advantage and privilege, more often because of a father's, brother's, or husband's position, in the acquisition of which women may be instrumental.[5]

Currently, differences between men and women are being exacerbated by technological and economic changes. The introduction of large chainsaws and outboard motors has created new opportunities for men that are unavailable to women.[6] In numerous instances, slightly skewed indigenous polities which have favored men have tilted even further, so that in state and national politics, men predominate with much greater authority. Technological and economic changes often have exacted a high price from women. Among urban migrants, indigenous women have fewer employment opportunities, and though there are some exceptions, educated women professionals generally are restricted by the well-known "glass ceiling".

As the papers in this volume describe, the realities and consequences of "genderfication" are much more complex than previous studies have indicated. With the rapid changes which are occurring among all the island's peoples, these papers are even more important because they provide baseline data against which comparisons of Borneo's societies may be made in future studies. They also complement and challenge many assumptions of gender studies.

On this point George Appell writes:

Research on the societies of Borneo offers a unique opportunity to cleanse many of the anthropological generalizations about society and human nature that are culturally contaminated from the presuppositions of our own cultural system and from cross-cultural research that is not yet truly cross-cultural (p. 114, this volume).

The misrepresentations of sexuality and culture in Samoan society by Margaret Mead (1928) and the recent refutation by Derek Freeman (1985) are too well-known to need discussion. On the basis of an interview with Mead's key informant (Frank Heimans 1988) and Freeman's most recent response to his critics, it is clear that Mead was told what the Samoan adolescents knew she wanted to hear and that she discovered what Boas sent her to find (Freeman 1991). The enduring effect of *Coming of Age in Samoa* has been the perpetuation of fictions of primitive promiscuity and titillating tales, reproduced in novels such as Irving Wallace's *The Three Sirens*.

From the papers in this volume, we may draw a number of generalizations about sex roles in Borneo:

- In all the indigenous cognatic societies women's roles are highly valued.[7]
- There is great variation in the use of sex roles as metaphors for other cultural domains among the peoples of Borneo.
- Ethnographies on Borneo societies almost totally neglect any description of socialization for sex roles.
- Strategies for the socialization of children for the roles of "female" or "male" are as diverse as Borneo's ethnic groups.
- Politics are generally in the hands of men, but not without input from women.
- In many of the societies unrestrained sex is viewed as detrimental to the social fabric and the relationship with nature and the supernatural.
- There is a realistic perception of the biological differences between men and women, women being considered physically less capable than men and in need of protection.
- Children are generally wanted and highly valued.

xiv

- There is considerable variation in attitudes and openness about sex, with some societies being entirely open, others more prudish.
- There is considerable variation also in the interlinkage and individuation of the drives of sex and aggression.
- Insofar as evidence is available rape does not occur within the societies represented in this volume.[8]

The Rungus and the Iban

Nine of the papers in this volume are based upon research in two societies, the Rungus and the Iban. We have arranged the first eight chapters to juxtapose materials on these two societies, the Rungus less affected by social change, and the Iban, more affected by it. In addition, there are significant differences between the Rungus and the Iban: in their socialization for the sex roles, in the division of labor, in attitudes towards menstruation and premarital sexual relations, in the individuation or interlinkage of sex and aggression in language, and in the manifestations of the tensions and resentments between men and women.

The Rungus

For the Rungus, Laura Appell argues that

. . . while the sex roles are not identical, they are equivalent and both behaviorally and ideologically they are of equal importance for societal functioning (p. 4).

Male and female roles are primarily balanced in the household economy. For each skill exhibited by a male, there is an equally important one possessed by the female (p. 10).

The division of labor based on age and sex is almost universal: Men and older boys perform the heavier tasks, whether of farming or housebuilding, women and older girls, the lighter, more tedious work, including a predominance of domestic chores.

In contrast with the Iban, the amount of time spent by Rungus men and women on domestic chores is fairly even, and attitudes towards sexual relations restrictive. Rungus men actually spend more time in their swiddens than do Rungus women, who stay in the longhouse to take care of young children. Following planting, Rungus men weed and guard the farms rather than travelling

xv

for headhunting or for healing, as is the case of the Iban. Different opportunities between Rungus and Iban for nurturance and for the development of a strong child-father relation are obvious.

Among the Rungus, girls of eight to nine years learn the ritual texts and after many years, may become a spirit medium.

A major value premise in Rungus society is that

". . . all sexual relations are potentially deleterious for the participants, as well as the rest of the society, the domestic animals, the
crops, and the land itself, unless properly entered into through
marriage [G.N. Appell 1976a:71]" (p. 9).

Unmarried males and females are required to remain apart; no contact or fondling is permitted, and "intentional physical contact with a girl on the part of a boy will be cause for litigation" (p. 18). Tensions between the sexes derive from (1) uxorilocal postnuptial residence and (2) conflict over use of the family's domestic animals. Rungus girls are expected to remain virgins until they are married, and to eschew any interest in sex. Even when married, girls may "shun the sexual advances of (their) spouse(s)" (p. 24), until they become accustomed to their husband.

Young Rungus women are taught to show no interest in men or in courtship itself. This apparent, or real, disinterest of young women in men extends into the relations of Rungus newlyweds, and a bride may literally (and physically) shun her husband until she achieves separation or divorce. At the other extreme are the Iban, among whom bachelors pay court to unmarried girls in the latter's family loft. If the girl responds favorably, a young man may intensify his advances.

Unlike some Native American and Circum-Mediterranean societies, there appears to be a much more relaxed attitude toward a girl's first menses. For the Rungus, as described by Laura Appell, menstruation is "an unmarked category both socially and culturally" (p. 29). The menstruating woman is not considered unclean or defiling, and no taboos attach to her during her period. Appell hypothesizes that the absence of menstrual taboos among the Rungus might be found in the social balance of male and female roles. Possible corroboration for this may be found by comparing the attitudes of the Rungus and Iban. With their biases which favor males, Iban describe a menstruating woman not only as "(be)coming bloody/cloth ['napkin'] (*datai darah/datai kain*) but also "(be)coming unclean" (*datai kamah*).[9]

xvi

Expectations for adolescent females and males vary widely. The tensions and resentments described for some societies, such as the Iban, are apparently absent among the Rungus. The Appells describe them as free from overtly sexual teasing and interpersonal violence. Thus, G. N. Appell reports that in using abusive language, men to men, or men to women, or women to men, or women to women, there is no utilization of any lexeme indicating sexual intercourse as a metaphor for physical aggression to the other.

> This form of verbal aggression just does not appear in the Rungus cognitive world (p. 76).

In his discussion of the interlinkage and individuation of the drives of sex and aggression, G. N. Appell raises several important questions about rape, viz.

> Is rape a universal feature of all human societies? Is it the product of the biological constitution of humans, or is it a product of sociocultural factors? This narrow focus on rape behavior limits our understanding of the social construction of the drives of sex and aggression.
>
> Furthermore, how do we define rape? Is rape a universal category applicable to the study of all societies? Or is it a category of the observer and therefore contaminated by the assumptions of his society so that it does not map adequately behavior in another society and may even distort the empirical evidence? (p. 59)[10]

Appell makes the important observation that among the Rungus the drives of sex and aggression are highly individuated, perhaps more so than in any society reported to date. He seeks an explanation in Rungus child-rearing behaviors. He concludes, however, that

> there appear to be no major child-rearing techniques that have relevance here, unless it is the permissive toilet training, which is not particularly unique, the process of weaning that occurs with the arrival of a subsequent sibling in which the father substitutes as the primary care-giver for this period, or the long-term physical contact between child and parent that arises from regularly carrying the child in a sarong close to the parent's body during the child's first two to four years (p. 112).[11]
>
> ... Thus, the only explanation ... for ensuring this segregation of the drives of sex and aggression is the overall pattern of jural

sanctions, rules of etiquette, and the background belief system. That is, models for and of behavior (p. 113).

Amity Appell Doolittle's study of *latah* among the Rungus and Robert Winzeler's research (below) on several Bornean societies, especially the Iban, provide further contrasts between relatively unacculturated and acculturated societies. *Latah* is learned behavior, characterized by echolalia (imitating the speech of another person), echopraxia (imitating the behavior of another person), or coprolalia (uncontrollable use of obscene language). Among the Rungus, latah is known as *obingsala*. After an extensive description of *obingsala*, and an examination of theories on latah by Hildred Geertz, Michael Kenny, Raymond Lee and R. C. Simons, Doolittle suggests

> a new theory to explain *obingsala* behavior which views the content as representing an anti-structural component and the recruitment of women to this role as a result of biological propensities (p. 146).

While Doolittle writes that *latah* behavior is exhibited only by Rungus women, she acknowledges that the Rungus know of men who do it "on purpose". The contrast appears to be a put-down of *latah* women, in that the latter "have no control over their behavior" (p. 127). From analysis of the content of the utterances such as "your vulva" or "your penis", it seems clear that the behavior is a socially acceptable way of expressing otherwise prohibited words.

Doolittle dismisses Kenny's hypothesis that *latah* is a way of symbolizing marginality and writes: " . . . (W)omen per se do not occupy marginal roles in Rungus society" (p. 144).[12] According to Doolittle, Rungus *latah* is a form of anti-structural behavior which is engaged in to help maintain the cultural boundaries, particularly in respect for another individual's personhood. While a woman *latah* may draw attention to herself, her behavior also functions to maintain the boundaries of the structure.

The Iban

The Iban are among the most aggressive and acculturated of indigenous Borneo societies.[13] Though described as "thoroughly egalitarian" by numerous ethnographers (cf. Freeman 1955:10; Sutlive 1988:3; Uchibori 1978:8), the Iban have been characterized by inequities between the sexes in responsibilities for family maintenance and farming, and in opportunities for travel and the acquisition of prestige. Freeman himself writes of the Iban that a woman's day is more equal than a man's day (1955:89),

and

Iban social life is dominated by male values . . . through the attainment of prestige in a series of exclusively male activities, the chief of these traditionally being in the cult of headhunting, which for the Iban, has long been a major obsession (1968:334).

There are some tasks Iban men will do, and others they just will not perform. Men help fell trees and perform the heavy work in farming, but weeding and guarding the fields fall to women, older men, and children. Men have been freer to travel in the "off-season", i.e., the period between planting and harvesting the rice.

While applicable to polity and access to some positions, the concept of "egalitarianism" has been extended uncritically and unjustifiably to other areas of Iban life. Women, as well as men, may represent their families in community meetings, may acquire and sell property, may engage a shaman for a healing ritual. Some women are dominant figures in their longhouses, but they are effectively excluded from warfare and the highly ritualized prestige system.

Julian Davison and Vinson Sutlive (Ch. 4) analyze headhunting and its attendant fertile field of symbolism. We attempt to analyze this central Iban ritual and the significance it holds for Iban men and women. Examining several well-known hypotheses, we conclude that headhunting and agriculture were symbolically linked to the seed-producing capacities of men,[14] and that references to "soul substance" or the equation of head with phallus (cf. Freeman 1979) introduce unnecessarily complicating variables. Iban mythology attributes the acquisition of the first rice seed to men (see Sutlive 1988:62-63), who still have the responsibility for replenishing the community's supply of seed as well as land for its planting.

Valerie Mashman and Richard Allen Drake analyze weaving as a parallel procedure for obtaining prestige for women (Chs. 5 and 6). Iban women have been the principal enculturators and in their weaving have perpetuated the rich symbolism of their culture. With all respect due the master weavers, however, this does not approximate the high regard and rewards of warriors or men who are successful in other activities.

Peter Mulok Kedit's analysis of the institution of *bejalai* ("travelling") (Ch. 7) and Winny Koster's study of prostitution (cf. Sutlive, Ch. 16, Appendix B) indicate the intensity of anger some Iban women have felt towards their travelling men. Women and children often suffer real deprivations because of the extended absences of men who choose to leave them for work or simply for adventure. Two of the women interviewed by Koster indicated that they were practicing prostitution to avenge themselves on their husbands.

It is important to note that travelling remains important among many, though by no means all, Bornean societies. Though increasingly women have opportunities for trips to Borneo's towns and cities, and some overseas, for the more mobile societies men still travel far more than women.

The initiate's journey or its equivalent, and the far greater opportunity for travel available to men, separates men from boys, and makes the adventurer more attractive as either suitor or husband (cf. Davison and Sutlive, this volume). From the equal privileges shared by headhunter and rhino hunter, it would appear that the critical feature in the making of a man is not headhunting per se. The demand of society is courage, not a specific act but the possession of a distinctive quality, by which the warrior or hunter is distinguished and through which the life of the group is secured.

This demand is described by David D. Gilmore in *Manhood* as

> . . . a moral instigation for performance . . . not just a call to aggression. . . A curious commonality is that true manhood is a call to nurturing. "Real" men are those who give more than they take, who . . . serve others by being brave and protective (1990:10).[15]

Gilmore's analysis of *Manhood* (op. cit.) provides insight into demands for performance by Iban men:

> . . . (W)hy the stress and drama of manhood? . . . (W)hy the trials and tribulations? Why must males be literally pushed into such displays of performance? . . . The key, I think, lies in the inherent weaknesses of human nature, in the inborn tendency of all human beings, male and female, to run from danger, to retreat from challenges, to return to the safety of the hearth and home. In psychoanalytic thinking, this tendency . . . is called psychic regression. It is defined as the tidal pull back toward the world of childhood, the pull back to the mother, the wish to return to the blissful, traumaless idyll of infancy (1990:10).

Unlike the egalitarian Rungus, a major concern among the Iban--to the point of constituting a type-anxiety for some members--is equity and justice, a concern which extends to relations between men and women. The concern is memorialized in proverb and aphorism: "Use the same measure for everyone" (Iban: *Adat para sagantang*) and "Don't have some climb the thorny cluster palm [*Oncosperma*] and others the areca palm" (Iban: *Anang menibong bepinang*). These apodictic statements express the anger[16] that Iban women have felt towards men who have abandoned them, who have forced them to assume major responsibilities for child rearing and provisioning of the family, and who have excluded them from acclaim and appreciation in virtually every ritual event. The sense of injustice or unfairness is stronger yet in those women are fully as intelligent and competent in the management of their affairs as any man.

In Robert Winzeler's survey of Sarawak societies (Ch. 8), he concludes that *latah* is related to gender, and that there are no *latah* men in the state. Further, *latah* occurs commonly among some societies and regions, but is absent in others. He raises important questions about the identification of *latah*--is it everywhere the same?--and the distribution of the behavior--how is it to be explained? Although the distribution might be explained by contact of other peoples with Malays, he observes that "there is almost certainly more to the distribution of *latah* in Sarawak than simple diffusion" (p. 324). Focusing on the Iban, he draws from Freeman's argument "that Iban women are intensively jealous of (their) men . . . " (p. 327), and the double standard for men and women in familial responsibilities, postmarital sexual morality, and opportunities for travel (cf. Heppell 1975; Kedit, this volume; Sutlive 1988:163-165). Winzeler concludes that *latah* behavior has been borrowed by some Iban women to vent their anger, to replace traditional rituals of social clowning and the ridicule of men, and to call attention to themselves.

Lun Dayeh

Other than Jay Crain's brief account (Ch. 9) of his family's experiences and the research of Heppell (op. cit.), to be published as a separate monograph in this series, we are unaware of any extensive ethnographic research which adequately describes how children become "men" or "women" in Borneo societies.

Building upon the early childhood experiences of his son Andy, who with his parents lived among the Mengalong Lun Dayeh, Crain describes the concerns of his host community about American child-rearing practices and Lun Dayeh efforts to ensure Andy's well-being and maturation. From his family's interactions with their hosts and hostesses, Crain analyzes

> Lun Dayeh notions of a dualistic cosmos . . . embodied in
> arguments about development, sexuality, and dangers of birds.
> By associating the dangers of separation, fornication, and nature,
> the Lun Dayeh both affirm and experience their unique ideology
> (p. 337).

The Lun Dayeh, as all of the societies in these studies, are strongly oriented toward community and against individualism. The former gives health and life, the latter, sickness and death. From birth, children are in constant sight and sound of others, and most are indulged any demand or desire. Through consistent and constant reminders, children are taught to behave in ways that are safe for the individual and society. The most important theme for the Lun Dayeh, and other Bornean groups, is the ambi-valence of human sexuality, which, if expressed in appropriate ways is enjoyable and constructive but, if unre-strained,[17] will be destructive not only of society but of nature itself.[18]

> (F)emales and males are complementary and interdependent.
> Females are naturally sexual; males learn about intercourse from
> females. Society involves distinctions between women and men
> to control the necessary but potentially destructive consequence
> of sexuality (p. 338).

The Selako

William and Mary Jo Schneider (Ch. 10) describe Selako models of the world and society as explicitly binary, with clearly discriminated domains for females and males.

> Gender roles and ideology among the Selako evidence a society
> where men are clearly awarded more prestige than women in
> subsistence, political, and religious spheres. . . Gender symbolism
> is important in food, dress, funerals, rituals of the annual cycle,
> and longhouse architecture (p. 362-3).

The Selako are concerned about sexuality and for its control. Social relations between unmarried Selako are difficult. Such difficulties are ameliorat-ed--or exacerbated--in dance contests which pit unmarried adolescent females against males. While the relatively high rank Selako women enjoy "should illuminate theory on the determinants of rank in human societies" (Ibid.), the rituals are heavily skewed in focus and performance in favor of men. The Schneiders describe an important distinction between "the conceptualization of sexuality . . . for which . . . (there exist) no behavioral reflexes . . . " (p. 360).

The Kadayan

In contrast with other societies in this sample, the Kadayans, analyzed by Allen Maxwell (Ch. 11), have no concept of gender equity, nor are they much concerned about the rights and responsibilities of either sex. Parity of the sexes is a meaningless equation among the Kadayan. Maxwell writes:

> One cannot argue that the Kadayan view males and females as being equal in either the "identity" sense or the "equivalence" sense of equality (see Spiro 1979:7-10). The Kadayan certainly do not view males and females as being "equal" in any strict sense of the term. They view them as different, but lack a developed ideology of the differences, which could intrude into everyday life to complicate routine tasks, especially those involving the economic cooperation and organization necessary in obtaining food by traditional means (p. 382).

Central Borneo

In Central Borneo, gender inequity is eclipsed by the class system. After considering the factors which limit gender inequality, Jérôme Rousseau (Ch. 12) describes the "transformations of the body, dress, rituals and other forms of behavior" which differentiate men and women.

> In daily life there is no great discrepancy between men and women, and no overall control of women by men . . . On the other hand, women are minorized at strategic moments of their lives (p. 406).

> In many cases, stratum ascription is of greater importance than gender differences. . . In central Borneo, while chiefs are usually men, some women occupied that position (p. 409).

Rousseau introduces a topic on great importance to gender studies, viz. women chiefs, but provides no information about it. This is a problem on which we urge further research.

The Ngaju

Drawing upon her own field research and the classic work of Hans Schärer, Anne Schiller (Ch. 13) analyzes the symbolism of the Ngaju, for whom "'male' and 'female' are exhaustive discriminations" (p. 418). The integration of Ngaju society employs a dynamic dualism seen clearly in rituals of marriage and death. Ngaju prefer marriage with a cousin to maintain balance between hierarchically-ranked moieties and protection of men and women from "*Hantuen* . . (bisexual) soulless, sanguisugent creatures characterized by amoral dispositions and promiscuous sexuality" (p. 429). Women are buried in coffins with hornbill ornamentation, symbolism otherwise reserved for men, and men are buried in coffins decorated like a watersnake, which symbolizes women. These most dangerous episodes of marriage (and parturition) and death also are most elaborated by Ngaju who affirm unity in patterned duality.

The Marks of Bravery

Tattooing is one of the marks of bravery among the interior tribes of Borneo.[19] But one of the most exotic, and least understood, marks of bravery is the insertion of penis pins, described by Donald E. Brown (Ch. 14). "In Borneo the surgery involves piercing the penis--much as one might pierce an earlobe--so that a pin can be worn in it" (p. 437). The more plausible explanations, none really very satisfactory, are given for this culture complex. The first suggests that the pins enhance the sexual pleasure of women. The second is that the pins are precautionary measures against *koro*, a folk disease in which the penis of an afflicted male shrinks into his body. The third describes the pins as a defense against the vagina dentata. And the fourth proposes that penis piercing is analogous to other forms of body piercing, performed to strengthen the body.

Although as Brown writes,

There is little consensus on the extent of pain and the risk of medical complications that penis pins entail for either men or women . . . (p. 439),

it is the editor's opinion that the complex is another test of masculinity, by which the pierced demonstrate further their capacity to withstand pain. From Brown's analysis and other sources, it seems extremely doubtful that the pins enhance sexual pleasure and that women insist on their men being pinned. If such urging has been forthcoming from women, one must wonder whether they actually receive greater sexual pleasure from the stimulation of the pin, or from a devious delight in knowing what the men were put through (or the other way around).[20]

Rule, Brittania

The most extreme attitudes towards gender--and race--reported in these papers is that of 19th century British colonists who had no concern for nor did they make any pretense of gender symmetry. They rationalized their administration of their subjects on the basis of European superiority in biological inheritance and intellect. In his description of Englishmen in 19th century Borneo, Robert H. W. Reece (Chapter 15) focuses on the first and second Rajahs of Sarawak and members of their staff, with the certain confidence of the natural superiority of Europeans over natives.[21]   Administrative officers and clerics, with their wives, strove to maintain their superior positions by keeping their subjects in their place. For some single officers there occurred "a subtle process of acclimatization" (p. 463), as native women who initially were thought "unattractive" underwent a remarkable transformation to things of beauty. Miscegenation was preferable to celibacy, though a threat to the pretenses of the small expatriate society.

Into the Modern World

In the final paper, Vinson Sutlive describes the movements of Iban into the city of Sibu, and consequences for female-male relations. Using Iban stories about the principal hero and heroine, Keling and Kumang, he illustrates that the fictional accounts are both factual and fanciful, and that Iban women have provided stability and continuity to Iban society while their men have been away performing deeds of derring-do. Rather than reducing differences in access and opportunity between the sexes, urban migration has exacerbated them. The relatively large number of prostitutes, the single largest category of women, demonstrates the differential rewards available.

Theoretical Approaches

Three approaches have informed the research and writing of the contributors to this volume: social anthropology, psychological anthropology, and history, with all the modifications and perturbations of each. These approaches are combined in several of the papers.

In those papers making use of social anthropological theory (William and Mary Jo Schneider [Selako], L.W.R. Appell and G.N. Appell [Rungus], Allen

Maxwell [Kadayan], Jérôme Rousseau [central Borneo], Anne Schiller [Ngaju], Julian Davison and Vinson Sutlive, Peter Kedit, Valerie Mashman, and Allen Drake [Iban]), female-male relations are analyzed from a structural perspective with familiar emphases upon complementarity and opposition, and differentiation of males and females. However, there is significant variation among Bornean societies, with the "egalitarian" Rungus and Iban, providing a contrast with the Selako and Kadayan, and with societies of central Borneo (cf. Rousseau, this volume) and Kalimantan among whom differences of hereditary rank eclipse gender distinctions.

In those papers using the concepts of psychological anthropology (Jay Crain [Lun Dayeh], Donald Brown on the penis pin, Amity Appell Doolittle and Robert Winzeler on *latah*) emphasis is given to the dynamics of personal and social relations. The authors give attention to the importance of differences in perceptions, of the normal—and not-so-normal--tensions of social life, of latent resentments and manifest hostilities between men and women.[22]

Questions for Future Research

Numerous questions arise from these papers and indicate the need for future research. We have listed some of the questions, though this list of questions is by no means exhaustive. Following the questions, Sutlive has provided partial and incomplete information based upon his research among the Iban and, where possible, has compared this information with other societies.

1.   To what degree is unrestrained sex threatening to various peoples of Borneo? Among the Penan? Among Islamic societies?

2.   How does enculturation for sex roles occur?

3.   There has been no reference in any of the literature to masturbation. This is a difficult subject to elicit data on, but we know nothing about this as yet.

4.   With the exception of L. W. R. Appell's (1988) study of the Rungus, there has been no investigation of the management of menstruation in Bornean societies and its cultural loading.

5.   What are the sociodynamics by which young men and young women get to know one another?

6.   What are the mechanisms by which marriages have occurred or have been arranged? How are these customs changing?

7.   Sexual jealousy is widespread throughout the societies of Borneo. There is yet to have been done a study that analyzes both the sociological and social psychological reasons for the unusual degree of sexual jealousy.

8.   What lessons may be learned about human sexuality from Bornean shaman?

9.   Does rape occur? If hostilities and resentments based upon gender exist among   Bornean societies and are not expressed in sexual violence, how are they resolved?

10.   How widespread and how frequent has been the practice of self-induced abortions? What has prompted women to abort?

11.   Are models of dualities with binary oppositions applicable to the indigenous societies of Borneo? Do these represent impositions from anthropology?

12.   To what extent are men and women free to travel?

13.   How are foreign media changing the attitudes and behavior of men and women in Borneo?

14.   How do women become chiefs (cf. Rousseau, this volume)? Among which societies? What is the extent of their authority?

Partial Answers from the Iban and Other Societies

How does enculturation for sex roles occur?

Little is known about the periods of early and middle childhood in Bornean societies. From the scant data which are available, however, there appear to be predictable regularities. Most parents want children, who are surrounded by nurturing and attentive adults.[23] As noted previously, there is little preference for either girls or boys.

Among the Iban, the few examples of children of neurotic parents provided by Heppell (op. cit.) are so exceptional as to be noteworthy. Children are in frequent contact with parents, other adults, or older siblings. They sleep suspended in sarongs from springs within sight and sound of the family and community. A whimper or cry elicits an immediate response with an embrace or food. As they hold infants, some adults fondle or stroke the children's genitals.[24]

By age three years, or at about the age when young children are developing their personal projective systems,[25] girls and boys begin to separate for the games each plays, girls participating in less aggressive activities, boys in games of challenge and chase.

Until about age five,[26] girls and boys swim and play naked either apart or together. There is no notion of immodesty, nor do adults show any concern about their unclothed children. By age five, however, children begin to show a sense of modesty they will maintain for life. Not only when males and females bathe at the river at the same time, but also when bathing with members of the same sex, no one ever exposes her or his genitalia.

Among more aggressive societies such as the Iban, early to mid-adolescence was the time for the initiate's journey. A fifteen- or sixteen-year old young man would organize a group of half-a-dozen to leave home for adventure. Young men were expected to go on such a journey which served a variety of functions: Prior to the suppression of headhunting, the journey was an occasion to collect one's first trophy. For men not inclined to headhunting, hunting rhinos provided an acceptable alternative. The journey also gave the adventurers a chance to reconnoitre unknown lands into which their group might move. If they returned with trophies, whether human or rhino, the initiates had the right to have their fingers tattooed with the distinctive and universally recognized design of the warrior. So marked, they were honored for life, and the subjects of adulation and honors at festivals.

What are the sociodynamics by which young men and young women get to know each other?

One of the traditional pan-Bornean proscriptions has forbidden heterosexual contact in public. Young men and young men, young women and young women, might hold each other's hands in public, but such misconduct between men and women has been unthinkable, even offensive. These restrictions are based upon an awareness of the dangers of unrestrained human sexuality. The awareness, which carries the full force of customary law, also prohibits unmarried couples, young or old, being together alone, apart from other members of the community. For the Kadayan, or at least Kadayan men, there is the conveniently shared belief "that, other things being equal, it would be the woman who would initiate a sexual encounter if the two were alone" (p. 381). According to social convention for most of the groups in this study, there could be only one reason why a man and woman would want to be alone.

Though public contact between men and women was forbidden, among groups such as the Kadayan and Iban there have existed numerous strategies for flirting and courting. One of these is a series of dance contests, in which " . . . young men and women compete with each other . . . by hurling the well-known Malay quatrains, or *pantun*, at each other" (Ibid.). Pairs of young women, one playing a gong, the other a drum, match verses with pairs of young men who move back and forth in patterned step. The quality of the verses is judged in part on the quality of the rhyme, in part on the use of double-entendre.[27] The audience whoops and yells with delight when one of the competitors sings a particularly lascivious verse. In one such contest which began about ten o'clock in the evening and lasted until about four the next morning, Sutlive observed two young women defeat all the men who came up against them.

Another strategy among the Iban has been socially-approved courting. In a much misunderstood practice, a young man visited an unmarried girl in the girl's family's loft, where first they talked, then pursued their amorous intentions. Contrary to the commonly held belief " . . . that pregnancies cannot result from a single act of sexual intercourse" (Beavitt 1967:408), the courtship patterns (*ngayap*) of the Iban not infrequently resulted in the girl's pregnancy. If one suitor was paying court, the girl's parents might press for marriage. However, if she had received more than one young man and none acknowledged paternity, she gave birth to the child for whom a pig was sacrificed. The bastard child was said to have been sired by the pig (*beapai ka babi*), and was prohibited from setting foot in other family's farms, lest he/she contaminate the soil.

Courtship patterns, justice for unmarried mothers and their children, and child support for mothers abandoned by husbands on *bejalai*, were topics of greatest concern for women participants during meetings held in Sarawak during the 1970s to codify customary law. In many cases, husbands cannot be found and, in those situations in which they can be found and fined, there have existed enormous disparities between political divisions in the amounts of settlements which can be exacted from the men.

A much more informal, and likely more common mode of flirtation is in the sexually implicit exchanges between unmarried men and women. Though this is rarely reported, possibly because it requires awareness of the use of euphemism, metonomy, synecdoche, and double entendre, verbal intercourse is permitted in public where physical contact is not. Travelling with a group of young men in the upper Sarikei River in the early 1960s, we met a group of young women travelling in the opposite direction. After the exchange of requisite greetings and pleasantries, the young men inquired about "the young girls' gardens", were their vegetables mature and ripe. One of the young men then offered to contribute an eggplant (*brinjal*) in their garden, a humorous suggestion of intercourse.[28]

A similar exchange occurred between one of my former female students and a young man who inquired about "the fruit of her trees". She replied that it was ripe and might fall soon, to which he enjoined that he would like to bring his harvest-pole to pick it. To which she wittily responded, "I doubt that your pole is long enough to 'take the fruit' from my tree."[29]

How have marriages been arranged, and are such arrangements changing?

Members of some of Borneo's indigenous societies have married in their early teens, sometimes by age 12 for young women, 15 for young men. With the exception of Muslims, polygynous marriages are exceedingly rare among indigenes (for exceptions see Sutlive 1988:176). In most traditional weddings the choice of a spouse is made by one's parents, seldom by the bride and groom. The selection was made on the basis of familiarity with and congeniality between the parents. In some societies, there was an effort to ensure that the man or woman came from an industrious family, one which did not carry the stigma of enslavement or any evidence of bad magic.

Traditional marriages, with the initiatives assumed by the parents, have been modified or replaced by educated and acculturated youth. A fundamental change in orientation has taken place. Rather than concern for the histories of the families, there is interest in the occupational future of the spouses. This is not to imply that all traditions have been abandoned, or that the parents do not play important roles in negotiating terms for their children's marriage. Rather, it is to observe that young people choose their spouses and enlist their parents in arranging for their wedding.

What lessons about human sexuality and gender are to be learned from the shaman?

Mashman writes that

It could possibly be argued that the existence of the manang in Iban society demonstrates the arbitrary nature of definitions of gender. The manang has no gender and both genders at the same time (Mashman, p. 242).

Among the Iban, not all young men had the courage to go on an initiate's journey. Whatever the reasons--fear, marginality, physical weakness--a few men in each river network refused the adventure. Tormented by conflict over the demands of society and their inabilities or unwillingness to comply, such men suffered rejection and ridicule. Whether such men were latently homosexual or bisexual is uncertain.[30] Shaman marry and have children, but are not inclined to acts of courage. Resolution to their conflict came in a culture-pattern dream, with a call to the office of shaman. Shaman go on journeys other men and women would not dare undertake. They do battle with enemies far more fearsome than those fought by warriors.

Though caricatured as unmanly and weaker, unable to compete in demanding physical acts and unwilling to join in initiates' journeys with other men, shaman may in fact be stronger--they generally are more intelligent--in their abilities to extricate themselves from their cultural milieu and resist the demands of their society. But whether stronger or weaker, it is certain that shaman are different from other men and, in those cases of women who take up the role, from other members of their sex.

Shaman, and other spirit mediums, are part of all Bornean societies, and will be the subject of a forthcoming volume in this series.

Does rape exist in all societies? in any indigenous Bornean society?

Sigmund Freud's association of "sex and aggression" has conjoined in popular usage these basic human drives like rice and curry, or fish and chips. To paraphrase the popular song, "Love and Marriage," you can't have one--sex--without the other--aggression. For example, Susan Brownmiller asserts that

from prehistoric times to the present rape has played a critical function . . . (of keeping) all women (emphasis added) in a constant state of intimidation, forever conscious of the knowledge that the biological tool must be held in awe for it may turn to weapon with sudden swiftness borne of harmful intent (quoted in Sanday 1975:5).

Among some Bornean societies, such as the Iban, the drives of sex and aggression appear to be inextricably interrelated. Men and women may tease and mock each other mercilessly.[31] The apparently innocent repartee of Kadayan and Iban youth described above masks very real hostilities and resentments

xxxi

which find outlets in the projective systems of Bornean societies. The most sexually overt Iban also are the most candid about the tensions between men and women. In the candid statement of Laja anak Sekudan, cousin of the late Tun Jugah:

> For us Iban, females are the enemy—is it the same for you white people? Are women your enemies? (Sutlive 1991, in press)

Female-male hostility is expressed in the response of an Iban in her interview with Dr. Winny Koster (Sutlive, Appendix B), when the former said she had taken to prostitution because she was angry with her husband.

Displacement, sublimation, projection, and probably denial, are defenses against anger and rage which, if vented against the real subjects of the feelings, would destroy or, at the very least, disrupt community life.

Strategies for handling gender-generated hostilities differ widely. By contrast, among the Rungus,

> there is no evidence that the females envy males, or vice versa, and there is no evidence of an underlying layer of aggression or antagonism with respect to the opposite sex as represented in mockery, jokes, overt statements, or the play of children (p. 88).

The societies of Borneo apparently confirm Peggy Reeves Sanday's category of

> rape free societies (which) are characterized by sexual equality and the notion that the sexes are complementary. . . As might be expected, and as will be demonstrated below, interpersonal violence is uncommon in rape free societies. It is not that men are necessarily prone to rape; rather, where interpersonal violence is a way of life, violence frequently achieves sexual expression (1981:18).

Reference to the variables listed in Table 3 (p. 23) of Sanday's article—sexual repression, intergroup and interpersonal violence, childrearing, and the ideology of male dominance--raises questions about the correlations, certainly their applicability to the diverse Bornean societies. For example, Sanday concludes from the correlations presented in the table

> that intergroup and interpersonal violence is enacted in sexual violence against females. . . The intensity of interpersonal

violence in a society is also positively correlated with the incidence of rape, as is the presence of an ideology which encourages men to be tough and aggressive. Finally, when warfare is reported as being frequent or endemic (as opposed to absent or occasional) rape is more likely to be present. (Ibid.)

One can imagine few societies which have instituted interpersonal violence more completely than the Iban. Yet, while Iban certainly know of "rape", the act is portrayed as inconceivable and unthinkable. Though encouraged "to be tough and aggressive", Iban men have been constrained by a code of etiquette and scores of taboos to behave non-aggressively within the society.

How commonly has abortion been practiced?

The Appells report that Bulusu' women have aborted their fetuses, and Sutlive knows that Iban women have as well. But there is little more information about abortions in other societies, or the underlying reasons and the incidence.

What are the effects of foreign influences of sex roles, "gender meaning and gender representation" (Sanday and Goodenough, op. cit., p. 5).

Movies from India and the West, and television, which often titillate the imagination by presenting a full range of previously suppressed emotions and restricted displays of affection, have introduced new attitudes and behavior. Such attitudes and behavior are sources of conflict between traditional parents and acculturating youth.

From Bias to Balance

To end this introduction where we began it, we know little about human sexuality in Borneo, and what we do know is often fragmentary and nonsystemic. Sandra Morgen's publication (op. cit.) is important, as much for its omissions as for its inclusions, and because it illustrates the unevenness of our knowledge about human sexuality in Borneo and elsewhere.

In her "Introductory Essay", Morgen correctly criticizes

the pervasiveness of both androcentric (male bias) and Eurocentric assumptions and representations of women in anthropology (op. cit., p. 1),

and notes that over the past two decades there has occurred a "dramatic development of anthropological research on women and on gender." (Ibid.)

Gender, together with the impressive contributions of feminist anthropologists, has helped tell the other side of this story. The inescapable impression the reader forms, however, from the introduction and the essays is that "gender studies" are synonymous with "women studies", and that androcentric assumptions have been replaced with gynocentric assertions.

George Appell (personal communication) makes the important point that

> there is (an) ethical failure with "gender studies". Is it fair, is it right, does it represent justice, for those in western societies to go out and solve their intellectual and social problems on the cultural backs of indigenous peoples? In other words, aren't we being unethical in attempting to resolve our own societal problems through the study of them in other societies? This is not to argue that we should not do research; but it is to argue that when it is driven by our concerns and leaves the needs of the indigenous people out of focus, it is unethical. We should do total ethnography, the study of the whole society first, and then if it contributes to solving our own problems, well and good. But first, we must provide the local people with a full statement of their traditional ways, their customary ways, which they can use either now or later for their own benefit. They have to be able to see their social system and cultural system as an "object" to use, to modify, just as those who are in power and prey on the local peoples do. And to have it captured in ethnography enables them to deal with the modern world more successfully if they have to give it up, for then they have not lost it. In other words, in the west we have historical societies and associations to preserve the record of our progress. Why should not these also be made available for indigenous peoples who do not have the resources to do so themselves? We as anthropologists have an obligation to provide the materials for these through our research, and this will help fulfil the functions that historical societies and other types of cultural societies provide to others, functions which are critical for enabling the members of any society to adapt successfully to the stresses of social change.

Fundamental to gender studies must be an honesty about the complementary and competitive relations of women and men,[32] a balanced, bifocal approach which describes the ambiguities and ambivalences of their lives of both, apart and together.

The treatment of either men or women out of context and the neglect of one or the other is unacceptable. What is required is a total ethnography for each of the societies of Borneo.[33] These societies have produced symbolic and behavioral systems which are rich as well as diverse in their treatment of sex roles.

By the end of this century most of the indigenous societies of Borneo will lose their cultural heritage. There is an urgency, therefore, for research to record as much information as possible about these systems, their diverse and creative treatments of what it means to be human, before they are gone and lost forever.

BIBLIOGRAPHY

Appell, G. N.
　　1966　　　　Residence and Ties of Kinship in a Cognatic Society: The Rungus Dusun of Sabah, Malaysia. Southwestern Journal of Anthropology 22:280-301.

　　1969　　　　Social Anthropological Census for Cognatic Societies and Its application to the Rungus of Northern Borneo. Bijdragen tot de Taal-, Land- en Volkenkunde 125:80-93.

Appell, Laura W. R.
　　1988　　　　Menstruation among the Rungus: An Unmarked Category. In Thomas Buckley and Alma Gottleib, eds.,Blood Magic: New Perspectives in the Anthropology of Menstruation. Berkeley, University of California Press.

Beavitt, Paul
　　1967　　　　Ngayap (Changes in the Pattern of Premarital Relations of the Iban). Sarawak Museum Journal, Vol. XV, Nos. 30-31, pp. 407-413.

Brown, Donald E., James W. Edwards, and Ruth Moore
    1988   The Penis Inserts of Southeast Asia: An Annotated Bibliography with an Overview and Comparative Perspectives. Occasional Paper No. 15, Center for South and Southeast Asian Studies, University of California, Berkeley.

Colfer, Carol J. Pierce
    1981   Women, Men, and Time in the Forests of East Kalimantan. Borneo Research Bulletin 13(2):75-85.

Ellis, Lee
    1989   Evolutionary and Neurochemical Cases of Sex Differences in Victimizing Behavior: Toward A Unified Theory of Criminal Behavior and Social Stratification. Biology and Social Life, pp. 605-636.

Food and Agriculture Organization of the United Nations
    1989   Household Food Security and Forestry, Rome.

    1990   Community Forestry: Rapid Appraisal of Tree and Land Tenure, Rome.

Freeman, Derek
    1955   Iban Agriculture, London, Her Majesty's Stationery Office.

    1968   Shaman and Incubus. In Warner Muensterberger and Sidney Axelrad, eds., The Psychoanalytic Study of Society. New York, International Universities Press, Inc., Volume IV, pp. 315-343.

    1970   Report on the Iban. London, Athlone Press.

    1979   Severed Heads that Germinate. In R.H. Hook, ed. Fantasy and Symbol. London, Academic Press.

    1991   Franz Boas and the Samoan Researches of Margaret Mead. Current Anthropology. June 1991.

Geertz, Clifford
    1973   The Interpretation of Culture, New York, Harper and Row.

Gilmore, David D.
1990   Manhood in the Making: Cultural Concepts of Masculinity. New Haven, CT: Yale University Press.

Graham, Penelope
1987   Iban Shamanism, An Occasional Paper of the Department of Anthropology, Australian National University, Canberra ACT, Australia.

Hays, Terence E.
1990   Visiting Husbands, Amazons, and Perambulating Penises in Northern Irian Jaya. Paper presented in Migration and Transformations. Association for Social Anthropology in Oceania.

Heimans, Frank, Producer
1988   Margaret Mead and Samoa. Brighton Video.

Heppell, Michael
1975   Iban Social Control: The Infant and the Adult. Ph.D. Dissertation, Australian National University.

Leach, Edmund R.
1984   Glimpses of the Unmentionable in the History of British Social Anthropology. Annual Review of Anthropology 13:1-23.

Leaf, Murray.
1979   Man, Mind, and Science: A History of Anthropology. New York, Columbia University Press.

Mead, Margaret
1928   Coming of Age in Samoa. New York. William Morrow.

Morgen, Sandra, editor
1989   Gender and Anthropology: Critical Reviews for Research and Teaching. Washington, D.C., American Anthropological Association.

Munn, Nancy
1973   The Effectiveness of Symbols in Murngin Myth and Ritual. Washington. American Ethnological Society.

O'Meara, J. Tim
    1989   Anthropology as Empirical Science. American Anthropologist, 91(2):354-369.

Ong, Aihwa
    1989   Center, Periphery, and Hierarchy: Gender in Southeast Asia. In Sandra Morgen, ed., Gender and Anthropology: Critical Reviews for Research and Teaching. Washington, D.C., American Anthropological Association.

Sanday, Peggy Reeves
    1981   The Socio-Cultural Context of Rape: A Cross-Cultural Study. Journal of Social Issues. Volume 37, Number 4, 1981, pp. 5-27.

Sanday, Peggy Reeves, and Ruth Gallagher Goodenough
    1990   Beyond the Second Sex: New Directions in the Anthropology of Gender. Philadelphia, University of Pennsylvania Press.

Sather, Clifford
    1978   The Malevolent *koklir*: Iban Concepts of Sexual Peril and the Dangers of Childbirth. Bijdragen tot de Taal-, Land- en Volkenkunde. 134:310-355.

    1980   Symbolic Elements in Saribas Iban Rites of *padi* Storage. Journal of the Malay/Malaysian Branch of the Royal Asiatic Society. L no. 2:150-170.

Sellato, Bernard J. L.
    1989   Hornbill and Dragon, Jakarta, Elf Aquitaine Indonesie.

Solheim, Wilhelm.
    1972   Early Agricultural Revolution. Scientific American 226:10, 34-41. April.

Sutlive, Vinson H., Jr.
    1976   The Iban *Manang*: An Alternate Route to Normality. In G. N. Appell, Editor,Studies in Borneo Societies: Social Process and Anthropological Explanation. DeKalb, IL. Northern Illinois University, Center for Southeast Asian Studies. Special Report Number 12, pp. 64-71.

Sutlive, Vinson H., Jr.
    1977   The Many Faces of Kumang: Iban Women in Fiction and
                    Fact. Kuching. Sarawak Museum Journal, Vol. XXV, No.
                    46 (New Series), pp. 157-164.

    1988   The Iban of Sarawak (Second Edition). Prospect Heights,
                    IL, Waveland Press.

Tsing, Anna Lowenhaupt
    1990   Gender and Performance in Meratus Dispute Settlement.
                    In J. Atkinson and S. Errington, eds., Power and Differ-
                    ence. Stanford, Stanford University Press.

Tyler, Stephen A.
    1986   Post-Modern Ethnography: From Document of the Occult
                    to Occult Document. In James Clifford and George E.
                    Marcuse, eds. The Poetics and Politics of Ethnography.
                    Berkeley, University of California Press, pp. 122-140.

Uchibori, Motomitsu
    1978   The Leaving of this Transient World: A Study of Iban
                    Eschatology and Mortuary Practices.   Ph.D. Thesis,
                    Australian National University.

Van Hasselt, Vincent B., Randall L. Morrison and Alan S. Bellack, and Michel
Hersen
    1988   Handbook of Family Violence. New York, Plenum Press.

All endnotes are by and the responsibility of Vinson Sutlive.

NOTES

1.   The term "gender" is used despite its loading and popularization in recent
        studies and publications. By strictest definition, however, gender means
        "any of two or more subclasses within a grammatical class or a language
        . . . that are partly arbitrary but also partly based on distinguishable
        characteristics such as shape, social rank, manner of existence . . . or sex
        . ." (*Webster's Third New International Dictionary*, Springfield, Massachu-
        setts, G. & C. Merriam Company, 1969, p. 944).

2.	My observations and experiences corroborate Derek Freeman's comment to me in 1957 that the Iban were among the most open and honest of people about their sexuality. Before exploitation by photographers and public outcry for banning semi-nude photographs in the late 1960s, women were topless and on one occasion, I heard older women exhorting younger ones to expose their breasts for the cameras. On one occasion, I heard a young child exclaim, "Grandfather's 'eggs' have spilt," when an elderly man's scrotum had slipped out of his loincloth. I abandoned efforts to collect responses to Rorshach cards in the late 1950s when **every** respondent identified the inkblots as "female genitalia" (*utai orang indu'*).

3.	Some of the papers are shorter, others, longer. Some are essentially those papers presented during the organized session in Chicago, others have been completely rewritten and expanded.

4.	This is in stark contrast to reports from other regions of Asia, for example, India, where there is such a strong preference for boys that amniocentesis is used to determine the fetus' sex and unwanted girls are aborted (cf. "Getting Rid of Girls" (*Asiaweek*, August 2, 1987, pp. 25-29).

5.	I can identify several businessmen and state ministers who have succeeded in their careers in large part because of the drive and counsel of their wives.

6.	Cf. Carol J. Pierce Colfer, "Change and Indigenous Agroforestry in East Kalimantan," *Borneo Research Bulletin*, April, 1983, 15(1)3-21. See also Mary Rojas, *Women in Community Forestry: A Field Guide for Project Design and Implementation*, 1989, Rome, Food and Agriculture Organization of the United Nations.

7.	A partial explanation of the relatively equal positions of men and women in indigenous Bornean societies may be offered on the basis of the contributions women make to production and subsistence activities. Among all of the societies of Borneo for whom ethnographic accounts exist, women are fully as important as, if not more important than, their husbands or other male relatives in provisioning their families. The daily food collecting activities of Penan women contributes a steady diet of fruits, roots, and shoots, which are complemented by the hunting of Penan men. Among swidden farmers such as the Iban, men fell trees and perform the heaviest tasks, but women sow, weed (if any is done), harvest, and store the harvest.

An alternate explanation of the relatively equal positions of women and men lies, at least for the Iban, in an emphasis upon conflict avoidance within one's community. Michael Heppell's description of this strategy among the Iban may fairly be extended to other, but not all, societies of Borneo:

> A cardinal value of the Iban is that within the group and the society, quarrels and all forms of violence should be avoided. . . In the case of adult behaviour, the Iban clearly recognize that, though the immediate danger of a fight between adults is that one might get killed, the principal danger is that the fight might spread and engulf the whole group or society (1975:79, 91).

8. For those indigenous societies of Borneo for whom the concept and language of forced sex do exist, there is no evidence for the perpetration of rape in traditional indigenous communities. From the least to the most aggressive, there is no solid evidence that rape occurs. Abduction for sex is not done by human beings, but alleged to animals, such as the *orang utan*. We know that notions of "sex on the sly" perpetrated by "perambulating penises" (cf. Hays 1990; G. N. Appell, this volume), occur among the people of Borneo. But we cannot document any incident of rape among the indigenous people of Borneo in traditional, non-urban communities.

9. Menstruation, pregnancy and childbearing "are considered to be polluting, or ritually dangerous situations (Gana 1988:15seq.) . . . " (Davison and Sutlive, p. 163).

10. For an evolutionary and genetic theory of victimization, see Ellis 1989.

11. This seems unlikely to me as an explanation of the individuation of the drives of sex and aggression, for the traditionally aggressive Iban--who at least in language and metaphor have linked the drives--have carried their infants in the same way.

12. Marginal women do exist among the Iban, in contrast with Doolittle's description of their absence among the Rungus. One of the behaviors of such marginal women is to draw attention to themselves. This is illustrated in an incident which occurred in a longhouse community on the Rejang below Sibu. A "marginal" woman, physically marginal because she lived apart from the longhouse community in a single-family dwelling, and socially marginal because she was described by members

of the community as *Antu Uging* ("evil-spirited"), joined a group of Iban who had received instruction for baptism. To the astonishment of the group, the woman claimed to have received three visions of Christ. The community listened to her with rapt attention until a small ten-year old boy asked, with feigned innocence, "Auntie, did you bring a gourd?" After a moment of complete silence, the crowd erupted in laughter for having been caught in a lie. The boy used "piglatin", with "gourd" (*labu'*) for "lie" (*bula'*).

13.   This generalization requires some qualification, because there are great differences in degree of exposure and of change. Some remote Iban communities are probably little changed, while city-dwelling Iban have assimilated to the values and behaviors of other ethnic groups.

14.   This myth and the imagery connect men inseparably to the sphere of nature, providing yet another ethnographic challenge to the man-woman/culture-nature opposition of Simone de Beauvoir and Claude Lévi-Strauss. For a discussion of the provincialism and non-universality of the nature-culture opposition, see Peggy Reeves Sanday's "Introduction" in Sanday and Goodenough (1990).

15.   Gilmore explains the nurturant role of males in these words: "This 'manly' nurturing is different from the female. It is less direct, more obscure; the 'other' involved may be society in general rather than specific persons. Yet real men do nurture. They do this by shedding their blood, their sweat, their semen; by bringing home food, producing children, or dying if necessary in far away places to provide security for their families. But this masculine nurturing is paradoxical. To be supportive, a man must first be tough in order to ward off enemies; to be generous, he must first be selfish in order to amass goods; to be tender, he must be aggressive enough to court, seduce, 'win' a wife" (Ibid.).

16.   This anger on the part of women and the guilt (which we infer) borne by men gave birth long ago to a universal belief among Iban in "the malevolent *koklir*" (cf. Sather 1978), a vengeful spirit of a woman who died in childbirth and who returns to eat men's privates. To protect themselves, Iban men have hung a cluster of leaves (*daun pinggan*) over their sleeping places. As recently as the late 1960s, some men who had converted to Christianity protected themselves with a cross on the door, and leaves over their sleeping place.

17. In Nancy Munn's analysis of "The Effectiveness of Symbols in Murngin Rite and Myth," she describes the deaths of two women who have had to flee their clan after committing incest with clan brothers, and fall victim to a python which represents "the unbridled masculine principle" (cf. Munn 1973). The inference I draw from Munn's analysis is that the Wawilak share the concern expressed by Bornean societies about the socially-destructive potential of uncontrolled sexuality.

18. Among the Iban, couples caught in the act of incest, or known to have committed it, were placed on the ground in the man-above/woman beneath position, and killed by driving a sharpened bamboo through them. This ritual act averted natural disasters of all sorts. A bamboo grove at the mouth of the Poi River, a tributary of the Rejang, is a visible reminder of the horrors of incest and its consequences.

19. Tattooing has been a widespread, though by no means universal, technique for providing a corporeal code of the accomplishments of Borneo men and women. Backs of fingers and hands, forearms, upper arms, shoulders, necks, torsos, thighs and calves have signified deeds of derring-do, or at the very least, have attested to the individual's capacity to endure pain. Among the island's interior peoples, women as well as men wear magnificent tattooes.

There is no evidence of subincision, and it seems likely that the practice of circumcision followed the introduction of Islam and later, Christianity. Among Muslims, circumcision is performed by a ritual specialist, without use of anaesthesia. Among non-Muslims, it is performed by a knowledgeable adult, after the "initiate" has stood for an hour or more in water to numb his penis.

20. In Iban the *palang* is both "penis pin" and "crosspiece". The temptation arises to suggest that the penis pin is both a confirmation of a man's masculinity and of his basic position in the community. The *palang* provides stability for the supporting timbers of the longhouse and prevents their sinking into the surface beneath the house. It is the man who both supports and protects his family and community. The temptation to make the association becomes even stronger when it is recognized that the area beneath the house is part of the masculine domain where men are deposited without ceremony during the Iban *Gawai Ngelumbong*.

21. Reece's study is reminiscent of George Orwell's *Burmese Days* in its portrayal of the expatriate community determined by maintain itself distinct from the locals, and the threat and ultimate destruction of Flory for taking a Burmese mistress and letting down the side.

22. With few exceptions, a major deficiency in the studies of human sexuality in Borneo is the lack of details of the processes by which children become either men or women (or, in the case of some shaman—the subject of the next volume in this series—both or neither). These processes are either described superficially or not at all.

23. Until the late 1950s, high infant mortality rates were common. In a survey of 1,051 Iban families in the Sibu District over a ten-year period (cf. Sutlive 1988:39), I calculated that one infant in two died before the second year of life.

24. In my observations, confirmed by M. Stanley Bain (personal communication, January 8, 1990), men rubbed the vulva of an infant girl or stimulated the penis of an infant boy, uttering softly the terms of endearment, "My slave, my servant" (*Ulun aku, jaum aku*). Under any other circumstance, for example with an older child, such behavior would be unacceptable, and punishable by a fine.

25. It is at about age three or four that Iban, and possibly others, make use of the socially constructed and individually internalized project system of belief in evil spirits (*antu*) as a means of social control. Insofar as I have observed and am aware, only women don the tattered clothes and terrifying masks of the *Indai Guru* ("*Guru* Mother [Heppell op. cit.]) or *Antu Muam* ("Mimed Spirit") to impress upon small children the awful punishments they will suffer if they do not show respect for their elders.

26. M. Stanley Bain notes "7-8 by my observations" (personal communication, January 8, 1990).

27. My observations of such contests among the Iban are confirmed by Maxwell's statement that among the Kadayan,

> the exchanges were, reportedly, often quite risqué, but any suggestiveness was so deeply embedded in metaphor as to make it impossible to grasp, unless one were very adept at comprehending the rich inventory of complex symbols and allusions present in the poetry (p. 379).

28. Unlike the ovoid-shaped eggplant, with which many readers may be familiar, the Bornean eggplant is shaped like a phallus, and the youth's offer was unambiguous.

29. I suspect that the latter exchange was inspired by an episode from the delightful story, *Dayang Ridu enggau Bujang Kerimpak Labu'* ("The Princess Ridu and Junior 'Gourd-sherd'"), in which the two favorite animals of Bornean folklore, the tortoise and mousedeer, offer to harvest the princess' "fruit" only to be dismissed with a similar retort that his "pruning hook" was too short.

30. My comments are based upon my observations of Iban shaman whom I knew in the Sibu District, between 1957 and 1972. I do not generalize to other parts of Borneo, for there is considerable variation in shamanism, "the world's oldest profession," throughout the island. Elsewhere I have analyzed the making of an Iban shaman and have stated that shamanism represents "an alternate route to normality" for latent homosexuals (Sutlive 1976; see also Stephen O. Murray, 1991, editor, *Pacific Homosexualities*, San Francisco, CA, Garland Press). Derek Freeman identifies the Iban shaman as homosexual (1979). For a review of the subject, see Penelope Graham, 1988, *Iban Shamanism*, Canberra, Australia, Australian National University Occasional Papers.

31. Freeman's description of female-male relationships (1968:387-389) indicates an envy of men and mockery of their genitals by women. It is my opinion that the psychodynamics are much more complex than simple penis envy, and are filled with latent hostilities in both sexes. While women gang up on men during the festival *Ngelumbong* and physically deposit the latter in the muck beneath the longhouse, men also put women down by mocking their genitals. I was standing on a new jetty at Bawang Assan one evening as a woman paddled her canoe back from the farm. A man from Rumah Salleh was cutting a hole in which he would drive a metal eye for mooring boats. "What are you doing?" the woman called. "Making your vulva," was the man's reply.

Teasing is part of Iban childhood experiences, and often is brutal in its expression and excesses. Asking a young Iban woman why she was ragging on a smaller boy until the latter cried, I was told, "There's no fun if we don't tease" (*Enda' nyamai enti' enda' betundi'*). Such teasing programs children for self-defense and aggression.

32. See Virginia Woolf, *A Room of One's Own*, 1929, New York, Harcourt, Brace, Jovanovich, pp. 98ff.

33.   We urge researchers to follow the example of Sanday and Goodenough (op. cit.) who provide a model of balance which should be the goal for future research.

SEX ROLE SYMMETRY AMONG THE RUNGUS OF SABAH[1]

LAURA W. R. APPELL

INTRODUCTION

In any discussion of the equality or inequality of sex roles, problems of measurement and terminology need to be addressed. The literature is unclear on these points. Spiro made the important distinction between identity and equivalence in analyzing his data from his long-term study of sex roles in an Israeli kibbutz:

> Equality, it is obvious upon slight reflection, has at least two meanings, both in popular as well as in technical usage. According to one view, people are said to be equal if, but only if, they are similar if not identical with respect to one or more criterial attributes. This might be characterized as the "identity" meaning of equality. According to a second view, people are said to be equal (even if they are dissimilar with respect to the criterial attributes) as long as their differences are held to be of equivalent value. This view, which might be characterized as the "equivalence" meaning of equality, is based on a pluralistic system of values, one in which the different forms assumed by the criterial attributes are viewed as having (more or less) the same worth. Applying these two meanings of equality to the

1

problem of sexual equality, then according to its "identity" meaning, men and women are not equal if, with respect to the attribute of occupation, for example they are dissimilar. According to the "equivalence" meaning, however, the sexes may be said to be equal so long as their differences with respect to this attribute are held to be equally valuable [see Spiro 1980:7].

It is clear that Spiro believes a society's cultural values are a critical component in reaching any conclusion on the valence of sex roles.

Karen Endicott in describing male-female relationships among the foraging Batek Dé of Malaysia also stresses the importance of cultural values in determining the relationship between sex roles:

> ... I use the two terms equality and egalitarianism interchangeably to refer to individual control over one's own labour, decision-making, course of action, social contacts and sexuality; and to all individuals coming under the same cultural evaluations [Endicott 1981:1].

Endicott also goes on to stress the equivalence aspect of equality:

> ... my use of the words equality and egalitarianism do [sic] not presuppose that all activities of men and women must be identical. There can be many differences in what men and women do in an egalitarian society. What makes it egalitarian is how the activities are controlled and culturally evaluated [Endicott 1981:2].

But Endicott in referring to individual control over one's own labor, decision making, sexuality, etc., introduces the importance of extrinsic valuations of behavior in determining the relations of sex roles. For example, she also writes:.

> ... This [egalitarianism] is in large part due to the fact that both women and men in these societies procure and share food. While the daily food-getting responsibilities of the sexes differ--women normally gather vegetable foods and men concentrate on hunting--the contributions of each sex to the food supply are considered equally important by the Batek.... [Endicott 1984:45].

Furthermore, she writes:

I do not distinguish whether the societies actually talk about equality or simply live in an egalitarian way [Endicott 1981:1].

This view raises the problem in any discussion of sex roles of the relationship of cultural values to behavior. Is it necessary to have congruence between statements of cultural values and behavior in order to have role equality?

There are four possible variants to the question of congruence of ideology and behavior, as follows:

1. Ideology of equality; behavior of equality
2. Ideology of equality; behavior of inequality
3. Ideology of inequality; behavior of inequality
4. Ideology of inequality; behavior of equality

When there is a lack of congruence between behavior and cultural values one might expect to find some level of conflict between the sexes. However, among the Rungus, the society we are concerned with here, there is both the ideology of equality and behavioral equality in terms of female and male interaction, and conflict between the sexes is minimal.

Before proceeding I want to make two comments on terminology. First, the term "egalitarianism" is primarily associated with a political doctrine (see *American Heritage Dictionary of the English Language* and Scruton 1980), and it also tends to subtly infuse investigations of sex roles with issues of social philosophy which, in my opinion, distort the analyses by emphasizing the concept of identity in role relationships. Thus, I find it more useful to use the term "symmetry" in those situations where roles and status of both sexes are given the same social valuation. In other words, the ideology and behavior of the sex roles are of an equal value.

Second, in analyzing male-female roles among the Rungus I previously called their roles "complementary", and concluded that they exhibited what I term "sexual symmetry" (see L. W. R. Appell 1988). I have since discarded the term complementary, as it does not necessarily denote equivalence. Rather, complementary consists of two parts that may be of unequal proportions to make up a whole. I now prefer to use the concept of "equivalence", following Spiro (1980), or "sexual symmetry". Symmetry as I use it is "a relationship of characteristic correspondence, equivalence, or identity among constituents of a system...." (see *The American Heritage Dictionary of the English Language*). And the important point about the male and female roles in Rungus society is that they are interlinked forming a whole. It is very difficult for an adult man or woman to operate a household without a spouse. While the sex roles are not identical, they are equivalent and both behaviorally and ideologically they are of equal importance for societal functioning.

This is illustrated by the Rungus concept of balance between male and female roles. These roles are in fact balanced in all spheres of life with the one exception that men are expected to initiate sexual and marital relationships.

THE RUNGUS DUSUN OF SABAH[2]

The Rungus are an ethnic group inhabiting the Kudat District of Sabah, Malaysia. They speak an isoglot of the Dusunic language family (G. N. Appell 1968; see also G. N. Appell in this volume, footnote 12). Their social organization is cognatic, and the major social groupings are the domestic family, the longhouse (see Ills. 1, 2 & 3 at the end of this paper), and the village. The domestic family is the major unit of production, consumption, and asset accumulation in Rungus society (G. N. Appell 1976a, 1976b). The Rungus are swidden agriculturalists planting rice, maize, cassava, and a variety of vegetables. They raise chickens, pigs, and water buffalo (see Ills. 4, 5, 6, 7, 8 & 9 on agricultural activities).

Residence following marriage is traditionally with the bride's family until the next agricultural year. At this time a separate family apartment is built by the bridegroom onto the longhouse of the bride's family (G. N. Appell 1966, 1967, 1976a, 1978).

A typical household consists of a married couple (the founders) and their children. There are some households which include additional adults such as a widowed or divorced sister of one of the founders, a widowed or divorced daughter, or the aged parents of one of the founders. Though rarely practiced, polygamy is permitted. The preferred method is to establish a separate longhouse apartment for each wife. More frequently than not, when a husband attempts to marry a second woman this will result in the first wife divorcing her husband because of sexual jealousy. She is said to *mongivogu turoi*, "to be jealous of [the other woman's] vagina".

Kinship terminology is primarily of the Eskimo type.

The agricultural surpluses of the domestic family are converted into durable property consisting of brassware, gongs, and various types of ceramic ware, principally old jars. This property also forms the major portion of the bride-price that is required for each marriage.

The men wear headcloths which they obtain by trade from various Coastal Muslim groups. In addition they wear trousers of blue cotton and cotton shirts bought from the Chinese shops which are patterned on the traditional handwoven clothes of the Rungus. The women wear an underskirt which they weave from cotton grown in the swiddens and dyed with a variety of natural materials. In addition to this underskirt, the women wear a sarong made of black cotton cloth bought from Chinese shops which they embroider elaborately along the seams.

Female ornamentation consists of heavy gauge brass wire coiled around lower arms and legs, as well as necklaces of trade beads, many varieties of which are inherited. Above the arm brass wide bracelets made from the giant clam shell are worn. Traditionally women also wore a "collar" fashioned from brass wire coiled around the neck (see Ill. 10).

Each domestic family has its own apartment in the longhouse consisting of a closed compartment, *ongkob* (see Ill. 3), and an open gallery, *apad* (see Figure 1 and Ill. 2). The enclosed compartment is divided into a raised sleeping area, the *tingkang*, the eating and cooking area, the *lansang*, the hearth, *ropuhan*, and a small entryway, *salow*.

The gallery is composed of three sections. Immediately outside the compartment is an aisleway, *lansang*, which is used by all members of the longhouse to pass from the entry ladders, located at either end of the longhouse, to the various apartments. The pounding of rice also takes place along this aisleway. Though communally used, this aisleway consists of sections built and owned by each domestic family. There is a narrow section of the gallery, *salow*, which is used for storage of rice pounding blocks when not in use. The largest area of the gallery is the *tingkang* where all the daily activities take place. Here the women prepare food, weave, tend their babies, etc., during the day. In the evenings it is the gathering place for social intercourse. Men make baskets, sharpen knives, tell myths and stories; women rock children to sleep before putting them into the *ongkob* for the night; and young boys and girls play their musical instruments and flirt. This is where all young unmarried boys and visiting males sleep.

6

FIGURE 1
Floor Plan of Apartment of Domestic Family

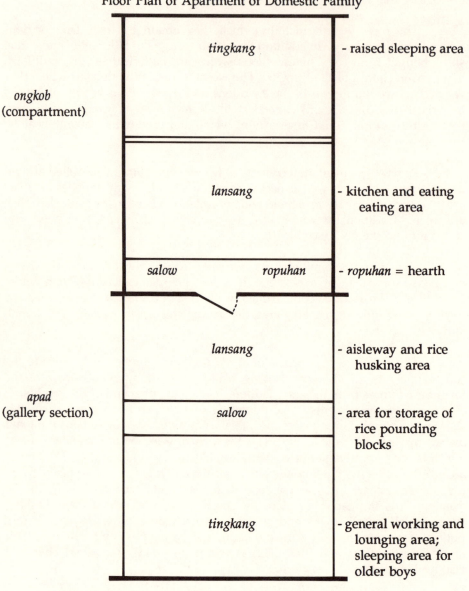

ongkob
(compartment)

tingkang - raised sleeping area

lansang - kitchen and eating eating area

salow   *ropuhan* - *ropuhan* = hearth

apad
(gallery section)

lansang - aisleway and rice husking area

salow - area for storage of rice pounding blocks

tingkang - general working and lounging area; sleeping area for older boys

Scale: 1/4" = 1'

━━━━━ wall
───── floor divisions

The Rungus believe in a variety of gods and spirits. There are household spirits that protect members of the domestic family, spirits of the rice, and localized spirits that are easily angered when cultural rules are violated. If angered these localized spirits can cause illness and bad fortune in human activities. The threat of harm from these potentially malevolent spirits is used by parents to control child behavior. A child when being admonished for bad behavior is told that his actions will anger the spirits. Thus, Rungus parents seldom use force or punishment in teaching a child proper behavior, but instead they place sanctions for behavior on the spirit world.

Illness is explained by the capture of one or more souls of an individual by any of the spirits that have become angered. These spirits request sacrifices of pigs and chickens in exchange for which they return the souls of the person upon whom they have inflicted illness. Various spirits also receive offerings to promote human fertility and the productivity of swiddens and domestic animals, and to provide success in the accumulation of property. Communication with these potentially malevolent spirits is managed by female spirit mediums who enter into trance and, with the help of their spirit familiars, determine the source of the offense. Sacrifices to the rice spirits in the swiddens, however, are generally handled by men.

All Rungus females are potential spirit mediums (*bobolizan*), and as such hold a position which commands much respect in the society. At the age of about eight to nine years old girls begin going off to the swidden houses with their mothers, grandmothers or aunts to learn the elaborate ritual texts that are recited at ceremonies for illness (see Ill. 10). It takes many years to learn all these texts, and a woman is not considered capable of performing a cure until she not only controls the texts but can also enter a trance state and communicate through her spirit familiar with the spirit world.

All members of Rungus society are born with a guardian spirit called *luma'ag*. The *luma'ag* of a *bobolizan* becomes her spirit familiar, and it is through this *luma'ag* that she has access to the members of the spirit world with whom she can converse during ceremonies to ascertain the cause of illness. She may communicate as well with the *luma'ag* of some of her deceased ancestors, who also help her deal with the spirit world. By the time a *bobolizan* attains such proficiency she is usually married and has begun bearing children.

In a sample of 60 households in the village where we resided, 23% had spirit mediums living in them. This represented 19% of the total of 73 adult women who were married, widowed or divorced living in the 60 households.

For her mediation with the spirit world and her curing of illness a spirit medium receives a ritual payment consisting of plates, bowls, yarn, knives, and a part of the animals sacrificed, etc. This, in addition to ritual payments she receives for tutoring prospective spirit mediums, brings in considerable income for the family. At death a spirit medium is afforded honor in receiving more respect and in being given more material goods at her grave.

Historical Changes in Male and Female Roles

The two major roles in Rungus society are that of spirit medium and for men that of political leader. Prior to *Pax Britannica* and the cessation of warfare, a particularly eminent spirit medium was not supposed to do any work, but had a room of her own, situated above the family quarters in the longhouse apartment. Here she would sit all day and weave the ritual clothes of the spirit medium, the elaborate skirts and shirts worn by women on special ceremonial occasions, as well as the ceremonial jackets worn by men (see Ill. 11 on weaving). Food prepared by others was brought to her here.

There was a role for men during that period which paralleled that of such an eminent spirit medium. This was the role of village champion, which may or may not have been identical with that of village political leader.

Although the Rungus were never headhunters themselves, historically they did engage in warfare to protect the village against raiding groups, or to plunder valuable property from other groups. Champions would attempt to kill and take the heads of other village champions outside Rungus territory. They would carry these heads with them on returning to the longhouse. In our recent field session in 1990 we found out that before the arrival of the British there was a ritual to welcome home a champion with his captured head. These heads were stored above the *ongkob*, but there was no subsequent ritual centered on the heads as occurs in true headhunting societies such as the Iban of Sarawak. Such leaders in warfare sought to obtain through private ordeal the protection of a forest spirit who made them invincible against the spears and swords of their enemies. Such men were called *kabalan* and obtained a position of great prestige.

With the abolition of warfare after British rule began, men no longer sought the position of *kabalan* and the role of specially exalted spirit medium similarly disappeared.

Although certain aspects of male and female roles have changed, their relationship has not. There is a strong mutual respect between the sexes, and their relationship can be described best by the use of the term "sexual symmetry".

SEXUAL SYMMETRY AND THE BALANCE IN MALE AND FEMALE ROLE RELATIONSHIPS

Basic Value Premise on Relations Between the Sexes

There is a major value premise in Rungus society on which all behavior between the sexes is predicated. This premise is that:

> ... all sexual relations are potentially deleterious for the partici-
> pants, as well as the rest of the society, the domestic animals, the
> crops, and the land itself, unless properly entered into through
> marriage [G. N. Appell 1976a:71].

Any illicit sexual relationship causes "heat" (*alasu*) to radiate outward from the offending couple. This heat angers the spirits who then cause illness and crop failure. Thus, an act of fornication or adultery will affect the health of the offending couple, their families, the longhouse members, the village, and the world at large. Not only is the health of humans involved, the productivity of the swiddens, success in raising livestock, and accumulating assets are all affected as well.

In order "to cool" (*monogit*) this heat, chickens and pigs must be offered to the offended spirits. And those affected by the act are marked with blood, but the offending couple is not so marked. A feather is dipped into the blood of the sacrifice and smeared on the ankles of those in the longhouse. The feathers are also wiped on the ritual plot in the swiddens and on family property.

This value premise on the potential deleteriousness of sexual relations finds expression in the relations between male and female roles, the developmental cycle of the Rungus family, and, as we shall see later on, in the management of menstruation.

Roles of Male and Female Founders of the Domestic Family

One of the basic tenets of a good marriage is that the husband and wife should *mitimbang*--"balance each other". The term *timbang*, which may be translated as "that which balances", is used to refer to an unmarried person's future spouse. A person has a *timbang* whether or not he or she is spoken for in marriage. Thus, if an unmarried person engages in any act that a recently widowed person might have to perform ritually, such as facing downstream while bathing, he or she is cautioned not to do that as it will cause his or her *timbang* to die. The symmetry of roles and their balance is also symbolized in there being only one term to refer to both husband and wife, *savo'*; and only one term to refer to both mother-in-law and father-in-law, *ivanon*. Similarly widows and widowers are both referred to by the same term, *bituanon*.

Upon marriage a bride-price is required, which is an expression of the cultural value of the female role.[3] The size of a maiden's bride-price is dependent first on the wealth of the suitor's family and the wealth of her family. But it is also dependent on the qualities of the maiden. If she is accomplished in the study of ritual, comely, and a hard worker, her parents can expect a larger price for her hand. Uxorilocal residence, bride-price, and the prohibition against premarital sexual relations are all indicators of the high value of the female role.

A further example of sexual symmetry among the Rungus is found in the role of *tandon do nongkob*. Upon the dissolution of the household of aging parents, they, or the surviving parent, will move in with one of their married children. This child is called the *tandon do nongkob*--"the one who sticks with his family". It is incumbent on children, both male and female, to take care of their aged parents. Which child they move in with is dependent on a number of factors. Ideally, it is the youngest child, regardless of sex, who is the *tandon*. However, if the youngest child is married before an older sibling, it may be the sibling who is married last who becomes the *tandon*. A father, if widowed, may be reluctant to move in with a daughter because during his terminal illness he will be uncomfortable being bathed and cared for by a daughter. Therefore, he will most likely move in with his youngest son. A mother feels her youngest child still needs her help in maturing and usually moves in with that child regardless of whether it is male or female.

Male and female roles are primarily balanced in the household economy. For each skill exhibited by a male, there is an equally important one possessed by the female (see Table 1). This applies to household tasks, agricultural activities, hunting and gathering techniques child rearing, etc.

RUNGUS MALE AND FEMALE ACTIVITIES

Male Activities	Female Activities

Agricultural

Male Activities	Female Activities
- clearing and burning swiddens	- help in clearing up small debris prior to planting
- planting swiddens	- planting swiddens
- weeding swiddens	- weeding swiddens
- harvesting swiddens	- harvesting swiddens

Care and Raising of Domestic Animals

Male Activities	Female Activities
- dogs	- pigs
- water buffalo	- chickens

Hunting and Gathering

Male Activities	Female Activities
- hunting with spears large game	- gathering snails and shellfish
- fishing with traps and nets for large fish	- fishing with scoops for small fish and prawn
- gathering honey and orchard fruits	- gathering wild roots, nuts, berries, and vegetables

Domestic

Male Activities	Female Activities
- collecting firewood	- husking the family's rice supplies
	- carrying water
- tending children	- tending children
- making knives, rope, fish traps, carrying baskets	- weaving, dying, sewing, making rice winnowing baskets, carrying baskets and a variety of baskets for general household use

TABLE ONE
(Continued)

Property Accumulation

- marketing of agricultural
  surpluses
- bargaining for purchase
  of brassware and gongs

- selling her weaving of
  valuable ceremonial clothes
- payments to spirit mediums
  for curing illness and
  righting ritual imbalance

Birthing and Child Rearing

- midwifery
- secondary role in child
  rearing and nurture

- ritual aspects of birth
- primary role in child rearing
  and nurture

Ritual

- ceremonies for swiddens

- ceremonies for property

- communication with spirit
  world through spirit
  familiars
- ceremonies for health and
  illness of domestic family
- ceremonies for village

Political Activities

- participation in village moot

- headmanship

- advise husbands in village
  moot

While equal importance is placed on the roles of husband and wife within a marriage this is not to say that all the tasks are identical. And while husband and wife are said to balance each other, *mitimbang*, it is also said that the man is heavier, *avagot*, than his wife with regard to legal matters and the trading of agricultural surpluses. While a wife will bow to the leadership of her husband in these matters, during village moots she sits alongside him and will advise and consent on matters concerning their family. In turn a husband will follow his wife's advice on religious matters which affect the health and fertility of the family and its domestic economy.

The interdependence of husband and wife is exemplified in Rungus myths and legends. The creation story is a prime example. The Creator God, *Minamangun*, when he set off to create the world (*manangun*; literally "to make the fate of the world and all living things in it") he had first to be prepared for the task by his wife. Before he embarked on creation she had to weave for him a ceremonial shirt and a headcloth. The woven designs in the shirt included a man, a crocodile and other animals, while the designs of the headcloth included lightning, thunder, floods, wind, etc. Until he put on the shirt and headcloth he could not create the world and all living things, which he did with a flick of his headcloth.

Another myth tells of a man who goes into the jungle to collect the elusive camphor. As he departs he leaves instructions for the ritual behavior of his wife, who remains in the longhouse. If his instructions are not carried out, his search for camphor will be fruitless. This myth forms the charter for the ritual followed in camphor collecting expeditions.

Thus, the equal responsibility shared by man and wife for all aspects of daily life is exemplified in their oral literature.

Child rearing is primarily the domain of the mother, as the father spends most of his time in the swiddens during the growing-up years of small children. However, when he does stay at home for the day or during the evening hours in the longhouse, while his wife busies herself with the tasks of husking and winnowing rice for the next day (see Ills. 12 & 13), a father will carry a young child around in a sarong against his body, rocking it and quieting it in preparation to retiring for the night. He does this as he carries on social intercourse with other members of the longhouse.

Another major area of child rearing performed by the father is that of taking over from the mother when a new baby has been born. A child is allowed to nurse from its mother until a subsequent child is born, when it is abruptly weaned. It is at this point that a father takes over care of that child, giving it affection and diverting it when it wants to nurse (see Ill. 14). This takes him away from his work in the swiddens for as long as it takes for the child to become accustomed to the fact that it can no longer nurse. During this time the father elicits help in the fields from his brothers or friends. He also relies on other female members of the family to help with the child for brief periods. However, he is the primary care giver during this time.

The father is also involved in the delivery of his children. A baby is delivered into the hands of its father. It is the father who also cuts the cord, puts wood ash on the stump and then hands the baby to its mother. Mothers in childbirth are also assisted by a male midwife (see Table 1). I use the term midwife here for lack of better terminology. Among the Rungus the male midwife is only an attendant, pushing with a contraction and helping the mother to relax between contractions.

While the accumulation of family property through trading and the settlement of disputes in the village moot lie in the hands of men, the women are concerned with the health and ritual welfare of the family. If she is not herself a *bobolizan*, a woman will make the decision to seek consultation with one and, if necessary, arrange for a ceremony to cure illness. It is only the *bobolizan*--the female spirit medium--who has spirit familiars (see Ills. 15 & 16). During trance she can pose questions through these familiars to members of the spirit world on the cause of illness or infertility, and receive answers from them. Thus, the health and spiritual well-being of the domestic family, as well of as the whole Rungus community, lies in the hands of women.

As a result of her pre-eminence in the fields of health, religion, child rearing, and domestic activities, including work in the swiddens, a woman more than fulfills her side of the "balance" in the male-female relationship. And she enjoys considerable prestige because of these roles. For her services in performing a ceremony a spirit medium will receive a knife, several pieces of ceramic ware and some brassware. For tutoring a young girl in the various chants necessary to become a spirit medium, she will receive payments of native spun cotton yarn, which is used in weaving skirts; knives, ceramic ware and brassware. All of these ritual payments are added to the family accumulation of wealth. In addition, a family with a spirit medium does not need to meet these expenditures for illness and other ceremonies, as she performs them without charge for her own family members.

Men usually perform the various rituals dealing with the swidden. They handle most of the ceremonies for the rice spirits which involve prayers and exhortations, and every few years the sacrifice of chickens. But they do not go into trance; they do not have spirit familiars or converse with the spirit world (see Ills. 17 & 18). There are also a few women who are equally as skilled as men at performing the agricultural rituals that involve sacrifice of chickens.

Tensions Between the Roles of the Sexes

With regard to relations between the sexes, there appear to be few of the tensions that are reported to exist in male dominated societies. And there appear to be few ambiguities over expectations of role fulfillment (see G. N. Appell in this volume). There are, however, two sources of conflict between the interests of men and women that arise from time to time.

The major one of these conflicts arises from the proscribed form of uxorilocal residence in cases of intervillage marriage, which occur in less than 30% of all marriages. The reason for uxorilocal marriage is that the bride will have the support of her kin as she becomes used to being married. After she begins producing children she also needs help from kin in caring for the children, doing household tasks, and at times of family illness, etc. Because he is far from his village, a man may miss his natal family, and will spend considerable time visiting during the first years of marriage. Tensions can arise over this desire to spend more time visiting them, and he may wish to move to his natal village. If the marriage is well established with children, the couple may move for a time to the husband's village. If the woman does not want to leave her kin, tensions may become irreconcilable and divorce may result. In our censuses we recorded only one such case that ended in divorce. However, both males and females have equal access to divorce should any irresolvable conflict arise.

Another conflict between men and women is over the use of domestic animals raised by the family (see Ill. 19). Men want to use these to exchange for brassware, gongs, and jars in order to build up the assets of the family. Women may want to retain them for sacrifice if there is threat of illness in the family. Again, this conflict is not frequent and is only episodic, so it does not constitute a major source of tension in defining male-female roles in Rungus society.

An indication of the mutual respect between Rungus males and females is the absence of sexual violence or rape. Women are seldom physically abused, and if this does happen, a woman's father, or brother, will bring suit for compensation. Furthermore, a woman is never taken against her will (see G. N. Appell in this volume).

An example of a society with a different outlook between the sexes is found among the Iban of Sarawak, who also have a cognatic social organization. It is reported that there is considerable antagonism between males and females. For example, V. Sutlive recounts an interview in which a man states: "For us Iban, females are the enemy--is it the same for you white people? Are women your enemies?" (see Sutlive ms.).

In sum, Rungus behavior is by and large congruent to its ideology of balance between men and women.

DEVELOPMENTAL CYCLE OF RUNGUS MALES AND FEMALES IN LIGHT OF THE BASIC VALUE PREMISE

Growth Stages of Rungus Children

The growth and maturation of males and females are divided into labeled stages (see Appell-Warren 1987). For example, after birth the first stage is "smiling", followed by "rolling over", "crawling", and "walking". These stages cover the period from birth to approximately one year or eighteen months of age. While not yet self-conscious about running around naked, boys and girls are still referred to with one term, *amupo ilo ikum*--"do not yet know enough to be ashamed". As soon as they start to wear clothes (about three or four years old for girls, a bit older for boys) a girl is referred to as *manintapi*--"wearing a skirt"--and a boy as *maninsuval*--"wearing trousers". By about the age of ten, before her breasts begin to enlarge, a girl starts wearing a sarong over her skirt. This period is referred to as *maninsukalab*--"wearing a sarong". When breast development is apparent, a girl is called *sumuni*--which can be translated as "maiden". She is referred to as a *sumuni* until she becomes contracted for marriage. It is important to note that menarche does not constitute a labeled stage in a girl's development.

There are no institutionalized rites of passage for either males or females upon reaching puberty or sexual maturity. However, in an effort to make themselves attractive to the opposite sex both males and females at the age of approximately 12-15 years will have their teeth filed and blackened. This is an individual act with no community ritual accompanying it. And it illustrates again the emphasis on sexual symmetry among the Rungus. A minor custom practiced by only a few unmarried young males to show their hardiness and, it is explained, to prevent them from becoming lost in the forest, is to burn bamboo dust on their forearms, leaving scars. For this custom there appears to be no female counterpart.

The change in social status on becoming a parent for the first time is marked for both males and females. Up until he enters the status of fatherhood a man wears his hair long, knotted at the back of his head. When his first child is born, a man shaves his head to indicate his new role. Upon first becoming a mother, a woman no longer covers her breasts while working in the longhouse, but keeps her sarong around her waist to facilitate nursing children. This continues even after all her children have reached adulthood.

Early Childhood

Young girls at a very early age start imitating their mothers in almost every aspect of daily life. As soon as a young girl is able--at the age of about three years--she has her own miniature pounding pole for husking rice and miniature trays for winnowing. She will sit beside her mother, at first practicing with chaff only. When she is accomplished enough, she is entrusted with a small amount of rice to pound and winnow. Her father will also make her a small water carrying tube of one joint of bamboo, and she will go to the river to fill it, carrying it on her shoulder in imitation of the older girls.

By the age of about five years she will feed chickens and pigs, calling them to her and chasing away those that do not belong to her family. Also at about five she has her own weeding knife and accompanies her mother and older sisters to the swidden. If there is a younger sibling, a girl of this age is also capable of staying in the longhouse to baby sit in the presence of other women so that her mother is free to go unencumbered to the swiddens for short spells. This imitation of her elders is carried over into the ritual realm as well. One of my informants told me that when she was a child, if she and other girls found a dead baby chick, they would build a small platform of sticks and hold a make-believe ceremony to cure illness.

In short, a young girl is brought up to imitate her elders in almost all aspects of Rungus life. And as she gets older she is entrusted with more and more responsibility. When a young girl starts to wear a skirt, she is perceived as old enough to take care of her younger siblings and run the household while her mother accompanies her husband to the fields. At the age of only eleven or twelve years she is an accomplished housekeeper and can be considered a suitable wife. In one instance a man, when his wife died in childbirth, was left with the motherless infant. He turned over his newborn to his eldest child, a girl of about seven, to feed and tend. The baby thrived and grew to adulthood.

Young boys, on the other hand, engage in play of various sorts which is mainly nonconstructive and not specifically in preparation for adult activities. They do not incorporate the imitation of adult tasks into their play. Although capable of collecting small faggots for starting fires on the hearth, young boys will resist strongly when asked to do so. Instead, young boys spend endless amounts of time playing in the water or running around on the ground near the longhouse. While a girl can demonstrate a high degree of competency and responsibility in female tasks at the age of about twelve, a boy at this age is just beginning to learn how to help in the swiddens. By the time he is in his midteens, however, he will be fully competent in the swiddens and other male tasks such as house building, etc., and is equal with a girl in his ability to start a family.

This difference in male and female socialization is partially a function of the adult tasks and their locations. Men work in the swiddens all day, unaccompanied by their wives and families while there are small children to be reared. Young boys are left to play around the longhouse with other boys because the swiddens are potentially hazardous. This is because the cutting of the jungle can anger the localized spirits of place that cause illness. The young girls, however, are with their mothers and start helping with the household tasks in the longhouse. As a result of this exposure to adult female tasks and the expectation that the young girls will help, they become active in learning adult tasks at an earlier age than do boys whose fathers are largely absent from the longhouse during the day in the early years of socialization of their sons.

Onset of Sexual Maturity

Where the social environment might facilitate sexual contact, Rungus males and females are required to remain apart. Children, male and female, under the age of nine or ten years, sleep with their parents in the enclosed family living area of the longhouse apartment. However, boys beyond this age must sleep in the gallery, the open area of the longhouse, while unmarried girls continue to sleep with their parents. Male visitors also sleep in the gallery, while their wives sleep in the compartment.

Young men and young women must not be found paired off together unless in the presence of a number of adults, and intentional physical contact with a girl on the part of a boy will be cause for litigation. The father of the girl who has been fondled by a boy can sue for compensation from the father of the boy.

While a young girl will find herself fully prepared for marriage insofar as she has all the skills to keep house, raise children, and work in the swiddens, she has been given no instruction from her mother about sexual matters. All she knows is that if she were to engage in sex prior to marriage it would have disastrous consequences. A Rungus mother, furthermore, does not inform her daughter about menstruation. I will discuss this more fully later on in this paper.

Prelude to Marriage

Although young Rungus males and females are enjoined from any activities that could lead to sexual contact, there are accepted forms of flirtation and courtship. Mixed work groups are formed whenever there is a sizable job to be done. When a ceremony is held or there are major agricultural tasks to be performed, groups of young boys and girls gather to help. The males and females are not paired off, but perform separate tasks. During rest breaks in such group work and also in the evenings while longhouse members relax and engage in light work, unmarried boys and girls engage in verbal games of riddles and poetry with disguised meanings and special vocabularies. And there are times in the evenings when boys play a stringed guitar-like instrument and the girls answer with their nose flutes. A boy may also indicate his interest in a girl by asking her to string some beads for him, or to comb his hair and rid him of lice and nits. Through these formalized patterns of interaction as well as through verbal and musical communication a young man can let a young woman know he is interested in her, and she can very indirectly encourage or discourage him. However, that is as far as any pairing off is permitted prior to marriage.

When a young man decides upon a certain maiden as the one he wants to marry, he says nothing explicitly to her about it. Before bride-price negotiations can begin, he must make his intentions known to her parents. This he does by arriving one evening on the gallery of their longhouse apartment and offering first to her father and then her mother his brass box containing betel chewing supplies which have been specially prepared. No words are exchanged. But if they accept his proffered box, it is an indication that they are willing to have his parents open bride-price negotiations. He then walks the length of the longhouse inserting betel chewing supplies into the boxes of each household. After this he returns to his family's apartment. Although she is most likely aware of what has transpired, the girl he intends to negotiate for must display no recognition of it; she must not show any interest in marriage. For a girl to express any interest in marriage is tantamount to saying she actually desires sexual relations, which is considered to be improper.

Bride-Price Negotiations and Function of Bride-Price

A maiden is not supposed to indicate her desires to marry a certain young man, either before or during the bride-price negotiations, but her parents usually have a pretty good idea whether or not their daughter will accept the young man. There are certain cases in which a maiden has not yet formed any definite decision about her desire or lack of desire for the young man who is negotiating for her hand, and will follow the decision of her parents.

Most parents will break negotiations off if they feel that if their daughter strongly objects to the young man. But, they will try to bring negotiations to a mutually satisfactory conclusion if they know their daughter is attracted to the boy. And there are times when parents reach a conclusion as to whom their daughter should marry and try to impose their decision on her. However, if she is truly unhappy about the man chosen for her husband, she can always refuse to accept her husband's advances after the wedding, which if protracted, can lead to divorce (see *amu tumutun* behavior in the section on *Marital Relations*).

Also, in unusual situations of mutual attraction, in which the parents of the maiden will not accept the courtship of the young man, a maiden may *muli*--"go home to" a man's village and move in with him. Negotiations are then opened to formalize the relationship, though a formal wedding ceremony is not held for the couple. If this action fails and the family of the maiden will not accept the young man as a son-in-law, he may try to force the marriage by getting her pregnant.

A bride-price consists of gongs, brassware, valuable jars and various pieces of ceramic ware. A very high value is placed on the services of a young Rungus maiden as a wife, and elaborate negotiations take place between her parents and the parents of the prospective bridegroom to arrive at the size of her bride-price (see Ill. 20). The stated function of the bride-price is to obtain the sexual, reproductive, and domestic services of the female. However, the size of the bride-price varies according to what the groom's family can afford, the wealth of the bride's family, and the bride's personal attributes, domestic talents and ritual accomplishments.

Thus, during the negotiations the father of the bride-to-be will tally all the attributes of his daughter in order to increase the value of the bride-price as much as possible. These attributes include her virtue, beauty, comeliness, and skills in household tasks, including sewing and weaving, as well as her diligence in swidden work. A diligent, hard-working wife is especially desirable. And a significantly higher bride-price will be asked for a maiden who is learning weaving and the ritual chants necessary to become a spirit medium.

Bride-price among the Rungus also contributes to insuring stable relations between husband and wife. If a woman is abused by her husband, she can divorce him. If this occurs early in the marriage, much of the bride-price is retained by the bride's family. The bride-price thus serves as protection of the female. A man, on the other hand, can ask for dissolution of his marriage and the return of part of the bride-price if no children result from the union. The same is true if his wife leaves without cause, unless there are children. If the marriage is not consummated because of refusal on the part of the bride to engage in coitus, all but a few basic pieces of the bride-price will be returned.

The Wedding

A girl is not supposed to acknowledge that she knows anything about the bride-price negotiations, even if they have been successfully completed. As elaborate preparations for the wedding festivities are begun, she is given devious answers by her friends and family if she should ask what is going on. Many people must be fed, as friends and relatives arrive from distant villages. Rice is winnowed and rice wine prepared, all of which takes several weeks. The bride observes all of these preparations and even participates, but still must not give any indication that she knows it is for her own nuptials. Of course, she most likely knows, but it would be indecorous of her to let on or to discuss it with anyone. All references to her as the bride are surreptitious. The longhouse members, out of her hearing, will refer to her as the *noponga'an*--"the one whose (betrothal) has been completed".

When the date of the wedding has arrived, the bride is referred to as the *valangan*--"the one to be told a secret" (see Ill. 21). At about sunset on the first day of the wedding the groom, his family and his attendants arrive at the longhouse of the bride. Some time before their arrival, the bride is approached by a number of the young married women in the longhouse who "catch" (*manabpo'*) her, pulling a ceremonial sleeping robe over her head, and at the same time telling her she is to be married. This is the first notification a girl receives from anybody that she is to be wed. She immediately tries to fight off her captors, falling to the floor, kicking and screaming or crying while they restrain her and carry her bodily to a neighboring apartment. Here she will be guarded by these young married women until daybreak the next morning, at which time she will be prepared for the marriage ceremony.

All night she may carry on a ritualized wailing about her desire to run away into the jungle to escape her fate. She must struggle and object enough so that she does not appear to desire marriage and the concomitant sexual relationship, but not so much that she will embarrass her groom and her family. This period of struggle can last from a few minutes to several hours. In extreme cases, when a girl is genuinely frightened of going through the marriage ceremony or not certain she wants to marry her suitor, she will carry on all night, and girls have actually been known to break free and run into the jungle to hide. But this is considered bad form, just as it is considered bad form for a bride not to show a struggle but to giggle and appear to be enjoying her fate. Even up to this point the mother of the bride has not herself communicated anything to her about her impending marriage.

While she struggles, wails, and declares her humiliation and embarrassment at the thought of being married, the bride is admonished by her companions. The following is my recording of some of the statements of the bride and the married women who have captured her during such a display.

B [bride]: I will kill my mother.

W [various women attendants]: Don't talk, just cry and thrash about.

W: Don't thrash about too much, you will tear your clothes, break your beads, break your shell bracelets, and hurt someone.

B: I won't [go through with it]. My mother's crazy. Let's run away.

W: You are hot and perspiring now. It is not good to act like that. Think about your parents. [Her mother was a widow with two adolescent girls and two pre-adolescent boys.] It is good to get married. Would you rather get pregnant in the jungle?

W: You are getting hotter.

B: Oh Mother, Mother! [Calls her mother.]

W: Your mother has gone away [although she is in the next apartment]. Be careful, Mogun [the groom] and his family will hear. It will make them ashamed; it will shame them. That is enough.

B: My mother, she is crazy, she doesn't feel sorry for me.[4]

W: She feels sorry, but you think about Mogun. Don't you want to get married ever until you are an old woman? If you go down to the ground and run away it will be the boys that will hunt for you, not just us girls.

W: The string is off your skirt and your sarong is off. If you stand up and go out of the apartment you will lose your clothes.

W: We will have to get the headman to arbitrate this. You knew about the *manamong* [gifts of betel chewing supplies to her whole longhouse by the groom] and about the bride-price negotiations and you could tell about the outcome from the behavior of your mother. Your father would not think much of this behavior. Lie down! This is not your apartment and people have work to do and there are little children. Think about your mother! There has been no one to help with the fields, the making of field houses, ... She has had to ask her sister's husband and his brother and her uncle to help her and now you will be bringing a boy into the family to help her.

B: [She stops screaming for her mother and starts calling for her older sister.]

W: All your family and the siblings of your parents have thought a lot about your husband, and it will be shame on them as well as on the family of Mogun if you do not stop. You are allowed to cry a bit, but not this long and you cannot talk like this. It is the fate of boys and girls all over the world, every race, to get married. And it is ridiculous to talk like this. Would you rather have a baby in the jungle, a bastard? Then no one would want to marry you. Look at all the girls you know who have been married and what fun they have with their children. My daughter had bad luck. [She was divorced.] I let her leave my house when she was not grown and she had a bad husband. But you have known Mogun for a long time, since he and you were small; you know his ways and his heart and you have known for a month that you were going to marry him. Now you have cried enough.

B: Why didn't any of you tell me I was engaged when we got together?

W: Yutog was a week in the jungle [having run away] and she got married just the same. [It was actually a day and a night.] Most girls just cry for a while and say "I won't."

On the morning of the second day the bride is led to her own family's apartment with her head still covered and still objecting to the proceedings. Here she is readied for the actual ceremony by her attendants. She sits completely passive while being dressed and adorned, not actively resisting but not cooperating with her attendants.

This passive resistance is sustained through every phase of the wedding--when bride and groom must feed each other cooked rice, address their in-laws by the proper term of address for the first time, and so on. Although the bride knows what is expected of her, because she herself has witnessed many previous weddings, she "plays dumb" so that her attendants must physically take her hands and move them in the correct direction for her. All of this resistance is to indicate her reluctance to being married because a virtuous woman should not be desirous of sexual relations (See Ill. 22 of a wedding party).

Marital Relations

When at last the formal wedding ceremony is concluded with a visit to the longhouse of the groom, the newly married couple returns to the apartment of the bride's family where they will reside until at least the next swidden harvest. Having been enjoined against all sexual relations for her entire life, and knowing of the dire consequences that will ensue if she should stray, the young bride is now expected to submit to the advances of her new husband. Moreover she is expected to do so while sleeping next to her parents and younger siblings. For some brides this could be a significant psychological discontinuity. And it appears to be so in a minority of women in that they refuse to accept their husbands' attention. However, a large proportion of maidens have little if any difficulty over this.

A bride's refusal to accept her husband is referred to as *amu tumutun*. Such a girl will not acknowledge or accept her husband, i.e. she shuns the sexual advances of her spouse. In addition to refusing coitus with her husband, a bride who exhibits *amu tumutun* behavior ignores him when in the presence of other people; she acts as though he does not exist. She does not talk to him, does not offer him food or betel, and she will not follow him to the swidden.

In a sample of 80 marriages 63 brides or 78.8% accepted the sexual attentions of the groom, while 17 or 21.2% at first did not (see G. N. Appell, 1965:71). These statistics indicate that *amu tumutun* is not a predominant phenomenon, though it does occur with some frequency.

Amu tumutun behavior is construed by people that the couple are not sleeping together, not engaging in coitus. In fact it may not represent private behavior but only the public embarrassment of the bride, because exhibiting a close relationship with her husband would lead people to surmise that they were also engaging in sexual relations. In one extreme case a wife did not publicly display *tumutun* behavior, i.e. "acceptance" of her husband, until after her first child was born.

Thus, a maiden is enjoined against contact with men prior to marriage so that now she is reluctant to show that she enjoys someone of the opposite sex. Whereas, in some cases these institutionalized behavior patterns may represent deeply felt emotional traumas, in a vast majority of cases the bride is fulfilling an expected role without deep emotional involvement.

A continuing refusal to consummate the marriage brings shame on the groom and embarrasses the family of the bride. A family, because of their embarrassment over having a daughter who rejects her husband, will take measures to ensure consummation of the marriage. At first they will start by vacating the apartment for a night or two, taking the younger children out onto the gallery to sleep, leaving the young couple alone. If this fails, they will move to their swidden house for a week or so, hoping their absence will encourage the girl to shed her self-consciousness.

While it is predominantly a female behavior, there are also cases when a groom will *amu tumutun*. In such cases it is said that he did not desire the spouse that his elders had chosen for him. However, the most frequent reason given for such behavior, exhibited by either the bride or the groom, is that the young people are not used to each other and are embarrassed to engage in coitus in the sleeping area of their elders. In these cases it is only a short while before they settle down to cohabitation.

Statistical analysis of the phenomenon of *amu tumutun* shows a tendency for a bride to be less apt to reject the overtures of her husband if her mother died before they were married, as opposed to those brides who have mothers still living. Another factor affecting this phenomenon is that of placement of the bride in her sibling set. Brides who are the eldest child in the sibling set accept the attentions of their husbands significantly more frequently than brides who are not eldest children (see G. N. Appell 1965).

Although force is not used to bring a bride around from this behavior, a man will divorce his bride if she is particularly obdurate. We were told of one extreme case of *amu tumutun* in which a man committed suicide because his wife continued shunning him for a long period of time.

The roles of fiancé and affianced, and the relationship of newly married husband and wife, may not appear equivalent and consistent with the marked symmetry displayed in Rungus male and female roles in other arenas. For example, there is the concern whether a new husband might physically abuse his wife, or not care for her. But the refusal to *tumutun* is also a means whereby a bride is able to take control and reject a husband who may have been forced upon her by her parents. (See also G. N. Appell in this volume for further discussion of *amu tumutun*.)

Bride-price also might be construed as indicating sexual asymmetry. But it actually emphasizes the value of the female role the bride brings to the family, that she may not be taken freely, and she may not be abused by her husband. For if the female is abused, she may divorce and the bride-price is not returned. Divorce is as accessible to the female as it is to the male.

Post Nuptial Residence

Residence among the Rungus is uxorilocal, whether the marriage is inter-village or intra-village. One of the stated reasons for uxorilocal residence is that it is the young man who chooses the bride, she does not seek him out. In the rare cases in which it is the maiden who seeks out a man she cannot expect him to live in her village, and he has the right to expect her to move to his village. The strong kinship ties between a bride and her natal family is another reason given for uxorilocal residence. When the wife starts having children, she will also be much more secure in her own longhouse in the company of her own kin than she would be in a longhouse of strangers. She is more comfortable eliciting help from her mother and other female relatives when the children are ill, or if she has to leave the longhouse to wash clothes or collect food from the swiddens. Another function served by uxorilocal residence is that it assures a young bride will be well treated by her husband as her parents are close by and will intervene if he abuses her.

During the first agricultural season after the wedding there is insufficient time for the husband to collect materials for house building. Therefore, the young married couple joins the household of the bride's family where they reside until the next harvest. It is during this time that they are getting used to being married. They do not cut their own garden due to insufficient time, and therefore the groom is expected to help his in-laws in the agricultural work.

Despite the fact that a mother observes her daughter going through a time of trauma in adjusting to her husband during the period after her marriage, she will not offer her any advice, nor give her any verbal guidance. These topics are simply not discussed. The same holds for the topic of menstruation.

THE MANAGEMENT OF MENSTRUATION AMONG THE RUNGUS

Because of Rungus attitudes toward sexual matters, even I as a female had difficulty eliciting information on menstrual customs. It was not a topic one discussed with young girls around the swimming hole in the river, nor could one sit on the gallery of the longhouse, always within earshot of others, and interview on such a subject. There are no explicit proscriptions against discussing menstruation. But, it simply is not considered a matter for discussion. It is embarrassing.

After several months working on collecting and translating religions texts, when I was sufficiently comfortable in the language, I asked my close friend and principal informant whether she would be willing to tell me a bit about *adat ondu*--"women's customs". She not only consented, but showed none of the traditional embarrassment and answered all of my questions openly.

She gave the following account to me of her own experiences which represent the norm.

Itulina was married at the age of about twelve. Her periods had not started and did not start until she had been married almost two years. When this happened, she was very frightened. Fearing she had contracted some dread disease, she ran to her mother only to be brushed off and told not to worry about it as it is perfectly normal for girls to have this happen to them. In a similar fashion she was unusually worried when her periods ceased upon conceiving her first child. She bore ten children, and after the first two or three she deduced the pattern and realized the connection between conception and cessation of her periods. She added that she rarely experienced more than one or two periods between pregnancies.

In another case, when an inexperienced young bride was confronted with the onset of her first period, she had no idea what to do since she had no knowledge of menstruation. And she became very distressed. She asked her husband what to do. But her husband became upset because he thought her parents had not informed him that she had an affliction at the time of negotiations for her hand. Had he known about it he would not have wanted to marry her, he said. She finally went to her mother who gave her the same reply as Itulina was given by her mother.

Traditionally neither males nor females were informed about menstruation or how to handle it. A Rungus woman observes no taboos when menstruating. She is not prohibited from working in the gardens, at the hearth, or in any other household tasks. She does not observe any special method of hygiene, except perhaps to bathe more frequently, and she employs no napkins or tampons. During the time of heaviest flow a woman chooses less strenuous tasks which can be performed while sitting on the longhouse gallery. She sits with her skirt discreetly pulled up and her legs covered with a cloth. In outward appearance, this is not different from the position frequently taken by women while tending babies or working at their daily tasks in the longhouse. If she gets up to move about she simply flushes the floor of bamboo slats with water from a bamboo tube which is kept handy to clean up after all messes, including piddling babies and spills.

A menstruating woman is not considered unclean or polluting by any member of the society. This is evidenced by the fact that a menstruating spirit medium can effectively communicate with her spirit familiar. Spirit familiars become angered and will not communicate with a spirit medium if she is unclean. A spirit medium can become unclean by going under the longhouse where she may come into contact with human or animal feces. Even mud is considered filth by spirit familiars. For example, a spirit familiar of my informant suddenly ceased "talking" with her while she was attempting to cure a sick grandchild. The next day when she was able to contact her familiar again and asked why he stopped talking so suddenly, she learned that he was angry because she was *asakau*–"filthy"––she had touched cat vomitus. And he told her what she must do to purify herself. It is all the more striking, then, that menstrual blood does not pollute spirit mediums.

Another illustration of the nonexistence of menstrual taboos can be seen when one examines Rungus sanctions regarding blood and bleeding. Human blood is believed to attract or summon spirits who will cause illness. If a man cuts himself with his machete while working in the jungle or swidden, he may not cross a stream or river until the bleeding stops. If he does cross and the blood is carried on the water, the indwelling spirits of the water will be angered. A menstruating woman is not enjoined from bathing in the river, however.

Menstruation among the Rungus is thus an unmarked category, both socially and culturally. There is no term specifically to refer to menstruation. It is covered by the term *adat ondu*, meaning, simply, "women's customs", a euphemism for menstruation. Neither women nor men are familiar with this term or its meaning until after marriage. A menstruating woman is neither polluting nor purifying, propitious nor dangerous. There are also no restraints, no forms of social separation regarding menstruating women. There are also no Rungus myths or rituals connected with menstruation. Even where other body by-products such as feces and vomitus are considered ritually filthy, menstrual discharge is not.

Various explanations have been advanced to account for menstruation in other societies being a marked category with heavy symbolic loading. Lawrence (1988) argues that this is associated with female solidarity. This does not seem borne out by the Rungus data. Female solidarity among the Rungus arises through uxorilocal residence and the association that arises as young women go about their work together. Yet there is no focus on menstruation.

Douglas (1966) finds that differences in power relations and contradictory gender norms in a society result in fear of pollution from contact with menstruating women; and Friedl (1975) holds that the separate and conflicting economic activities of male and female are responsible for such taboos. The arguments of Douglas and Friedl present some interesting hypotheses. They found an emphasis on menstrual taboos associated with certain sociological characteristics which are absent among the Rungus. Therefore, we might expect to find a lack of a cultural focus on menstruation among the Rungus, which we in fact do.

Thus, as we have shown, the Rungus exhibit sexual symmetry and there is no significant social dominance by males. There is also no conflict between roles in the economic sphere. Males may perform female tasks, except the ritual ones, and females may perform male tasks except for political arbitration, the cutting of swiddens, and hunting. The Rungus lack of focus on menstruation might, therefore, be said to be associated with their sexual symmetry, and the absence of conflicting economic roles.

However, a coordinate explanation for menstruation as an unmarked category among the Rungus, in addition to those of sexual symmetry and the lack of separate economic spheres, may be the basic value premise of Rungus society, which states that sexual relations, if entered into illicitly, are dangerous and deleterious to the whole society. And as a result sexual matters, particularly among unmarried females, are seldom discussed (see G. N. Appell 1965).

SUMMARY AND CONCLUSION

The Rungus have sexual symmetry. In my earlier article (1988) I referred to this as indicating equality. However, as I pointed out in the introduction to this paper, equality has two senses: identity and equivalence. Rungus sex roles are not identical, but are balanced and of equal value. Therefore, it might be better to say they are equivalent. There is but one term of reference, *savo'*, for both husband and wife, and one of the prime requisites for a couple to be considered suitable for marriage is that they *mitimbang*--"balance each other". Though their tasks are not always the same, equal value is placed on the contributions made by both sexes. The division of labor that occurs is critically interdependent, and on it rests the prosperity of the domestic family. While the major focus of the female work is in the home, and that of the male is in the swidden, males and females help each other considerably in both areas. The longhouse and swiddens are closely interrelated entities, and the activities of both husband and wife may occur in both places. The work done by males and females makes up an interdependent whole, their contributions are equivalent, and though they may be different, equal importance is put on the roles of each.

The payment of bride-price, which is for the female's sexual, reproductive, and domestic services, indicates the high value of the female role. The reluctance of the bride, in some cases, to engage in coitus immediately after marriage appears to suggest an imbalance. This is an understandable response to the basic value premise of the Rungus which constrains both men and women to avoid any sexual contact until married.

NOTES

1.   This paper is a revised and expanded version of my chapter, "Menstruation Among the Rungus of Borneo: An Unmarked Category," in *Blood Magic: The Anthropology of Menstruation*, edited by Thomas Buckley and Alma Gottlieb, 1988, Berkeley: University of California Press.

2.   This description and analysis of Rungus society is written on the basis of our original field work in 1959-1960 and 1961-1963 when the Rungus still lived a traditional life.

    At that time I carried out research among the Rungus on religion, language, material culture and women's activities. My husband, George N. Appell, was conducting research among the Rungus during this period under the auspices of the Department of Anthropology, Research School of Pacific Studies, the Australian National University. The brief description of Rungus social organization is derived from the works of G. N. Appell (1965, 1966, 1967, 1968, 1967a, 1967b, 1978).

    In the summer of 1986, twenty-three years after our original field work was completed, we returned to visit the village where we lived. Much social change had taken place, and most of the inhabitants of the village under the age of about 35 had abandoned much of their tradition in exchange for a more modern, but not better, way of life.

    I am indebted to my husband for his patience in reading all previous drafts of this chapter and offering innumerable valuable comments, but mostly for giving me the opportunity to accompany him in the extended fieldwork that resulted in our making many lasting friendships.

    I owe a tremendous debt of gratitude to my unfailing informant and dear friend the late Itulina binte Mago'ui, who had the courage to tell me about matters religious and sexual not often imparted to outsiders. She died during the period we were not allowed to continue our research, and I was able to visit her briefly for only for one-half hour just a week before she died.

Finally, I want to thank my daughter, Laura P. Appell-Warren, who at the age of five months accompanied her parents to the field and, as a beguiling baby, elicited much information on child rearing. Thanks also go to my daughters, Amity A. Doolittle and Charity R. Appell who assisted us immeasurably during our brief restudy in 1986.

3. I use the term "bride-price" here, rather than "bride wealth", which some prefer, as the Rungus themselves use the Malay word *harga*--"price"--in explaining its purpose.

4. A frequent statement by young girls about a bride-to-be is that they feel sorry for her.

5. In a previously published paper (L. W. R. Appell 1988) I mistakenly translated the term, *amu tumutun*, as "does not turn toward" a spouse. The best translation for *amu tumutun* would be "does not acknowledge", "does not accept", or "shuns" his or her spouse. A hunting dog is said to *amu tumutun* if he does not recognize (*otutunan*) his master, if he does not follow him closely when hunting. In the case of a dog, *tumutun* behavior is contrasted with *osizau*, "wild" and "unmanageable".

REFERENCES

Appell, G. N.

1965   The Nature of Social Groupings Among the Rungus of Sabah, Malaysia. Ph.D. Dissertation, The Australian National University.

1966   Residence and Ties of Kinship in a Cognatic Society: The Rungus Dusun of Sabah, Malaysia. Southwestern Journal of Anthropology 22:280-301.

1967   Observational Procedures for Identifying Kindreds: Social Isolates Among the Rungus of Borneo. Southwestern Journal of Anthropology 23:192-207.

1968   The Dusun Languages of Northern Borneo: Rungus Dusun and Related Problems. Oceanic Linguistics 7:1-15.

1976a   The Rungus: Social Structure in a Cognatic Society and Its Symbolization. In The Societies of Borneo: Explorations in the Theory of Cognatic Social Structure, edited by G. N. Appell. Special Publication 6. Washington: American Anthropological Association.

1976b   The Cognitive Structure of Anthropological Inquiry: Comments on King's Approach to the Concept of the Kindred. In The Societies of Borneo: Explorations in the Theory of Cognatic Social Structure, edited by G. N. Appell. Special Publication 6. Washington: American Anthropological Association.

1978   The Rungus of Sabah, Malaysia. In Essays on Borneo Societies, edited by Victor T. King. Hull Monographs on South-East Asia 7. Oxford: Oxford University Press.

Appell, Laura W. R.

1988   Menstruation among the Rungus of Borneo: An Unmarked Category. In Blood Magic: The Anthropology of Menstruation, edited by Thomas Buckley and Alma Gottlieb. Berkeley: University of California Press.

Appell-Warren, Laura P.
1987   Play, the Development of *Kakada'*, and Social Change Among the Bulusu' of East Kalimantan. In Meaningful Play, Playful Meaning, edited by Gary Alan Fine. Champaign, Illinois: Human Kinetics Publishers.

Douglas, Mary
1966   Purity and Danger: An Analysis of Concepts of Pollution and Taboo. London: Routledge & Kegan Paul.

Endicott, Karen Lampell
1981   The Conditions of Egalitarian Male-Female Relationships in Foraging Societies. Canberra Anthropology 4, 2:1-10.

1984   The Batek Dé of Malaysia: Development and Egalitarian Sex Roles. Cultural Survival Quarterly 8, 2:6-8.

Friedl, Ernestine
1975   Women and Men: An Anthropologist's View. New York: Holt, Rinehart and Winston.

Lawrence, Denise L.
1988   Menstrual Politics: Women and Pigs in Rural Portugal. In Blood Magic: The Anthropology of Menstruation, edited by Thomas Buckley and Alma Gottlieb. Berkeley: University of California Press.

Scruton, Roger
1980   A Dictionary of Political Thought. New York: Hill and Wang.

Spiro, Melford E.
1980   Gender and Culture: Kibbutz Women Revisited. New York: Schocken Books.

Sutlive, Vinson H., Jr.
1991   Apai: The Life and TImes of Tun Jugah of Sarawak, Kuala Lumpur, Penerbit Fajar Bakti.

Ill.1   Rungus longhouse.   The small structures to the left of the longhouse are built for a variety of purposes: for housing pigs, for storing rice, laying areas for hens, etc.   The family compartments are to the right of the entry ladder.

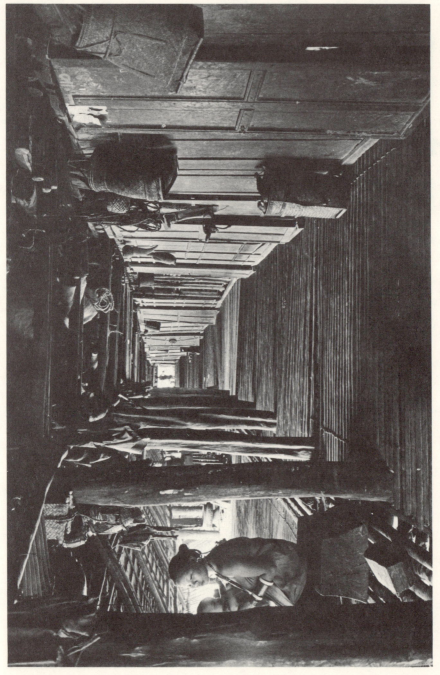

Ill.2   Interior of longhouse.   The compartment area is to the right and the gallery section is to the left of the compartment area.

Ill.3   Interior of a longhouse compartment (*ongkob*).   There are three spirit mediums performing a ceremony for the domestic family.   They are sitting and chanting on the sleeping platform (*tingkang*) of the compartment.   The second woman from the left exhibited latah behavior in trance only when she spoke to the gods and spirits, but not when they spoke through her.

I11.4

Cutting a swidden

I11.5   Firing a swidden

Ill.6   Planting Maize. In maize planting the husband makes the holes and members of his family go along behind him sowing the maize.

I11.7 Planting rice after the maize has started to grow. Young men and married men in a work exchange group move from family field to family field and make holes with dibble sticks to plant the rice.

Il1.8

Sowing Rice. The women and young boys and girls, also in a work exchange group, follow along behind the men tossing rice seeds into the holes.

Il1.9   A man and wife beginning to harvest their rice.

Il1.10   A grandmother teaching her two granddaughters the ritual chants in a swidden field house.

Ill.11   Weaving the ceremonial skirts worn by spirit mediums and female members of a wedding party.

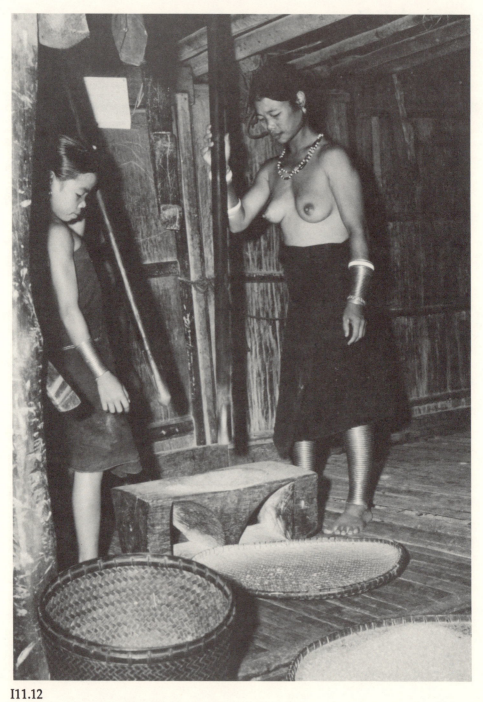

I11.12

A mother and daughter husking rice

Ill.13   A married woman with child winnowing rice.

I11.14

A man and his wife caring for their children together inside the longhouse

I11.15

A spirit medium (*bobolizan*) chanting over sacrificial pig on the ground outside the longhouse apartment

I11.16

A spirit medium (*bobolizan*) in dance trance

I11.17

Ceremony in the garden after the rice has been planted. In garden ceremonies the men perform the ritual prayers to the rice spirits that are accompanied by a sacrifice of chickens. This occurs in front of the ritual plot of the garden that has been prepared for the spirits of the rice.

I11.18

Ceremony after rice threshing is completed. A chicken is sacrificed to ensure that the rice will not diminish during the year, either by theft or vermin.

Ill.19 A married woman feeding the pigs and chickens of her domestic family outside the longhouse.

Ill.20   The gongs and brassware portion of a bride ... price for a wealthy woman. In addition jars will be transacted.

I11.21

The *valangan*, is under the sleeping robe, the bride-to-be has just been told that she is to be married. She has tried to escape but has been caught by the young women of the longhouse, and put into a special sleeping robe, where she hides from the marriage and cries that she wants no part of it.

I11.22

A bridal party for a formal wedding. The second male from the right, smoking a long cigarette, is the groom. His bride is to his right. Note that in these weddings men wear the neck brass of the women. Also note the waist brass of the women.

INDIVIDUATION OF THE DRIVES OF SEX AND AGGRESSION IN THE LINGUISTIC AND BEHAVIORAL REPERTOIRE OF THE RUNGUS

G. N. APPELL
Brandeis University

INTRODUCTION

To understand the relations between men and women in any society it is crucial to determine the degree to which the drives of sex and aggression are linked or individuated. Are these drives shaped and directed by the sociocultural system so that they overlap, with the result that the expression of sexual behavior has an aggressive component and aggression in turn has sexual content? Or are they so individuated that sex and violence seldom if ever are part of the same behavioral environment?

Among the Rungus the drives of sex and aggression are highly individuated.

In the literature on sex and aggression the focus usually falls on rape. Is rape a universal feature of all human societies? Is it the product of the biological constitution of humans, or is it a product of sociocultural factors? This narrow focus on rape behavior limits our understanding of the social construction of the drives of sex and aggression.

In some societies rape behavior may not be the only expression of sexual aggression; and in others it may not occur while other forms of sexual aggression may. Therefore, focusing on rape opens only a window on part of the universe of the interlinkage or individuation of the sex and aggression drives.

Furthermore, how do we define rape? Is rape a universal category applicable to the study of all societies? Or is it a category of the observer and therefore contaminated by the assumptions of his society so that it does not map adequately behavior in another society and may even distort the empirical evidence? Among the Rungus using the term rape to label certain behaviors seems inappropriate since violence and assault are lacking in instances of induced intercourse. In the final result it comes down to the Rungus woman either acceding to the man's pressures or refusing to. And if she refuses, it is stated, then the man proceeds no further.

In our analysis we must also distinguish rape, that is sexual assault which is unlawful in the society studied, from various forms of intercourse which are against the wishes of the female or male but which are not considered illegal, as in marital relations.

Finally, it is important to distinguish both linguistic behavior and projective behavior from social behavior. If we make these distinctions we can then scale societies more finely than has been previously done (see Table One).

HISTORY OF THE INQUIRY

The Rungus are a people of Sabah, Malaysia. It is useful to divide Rungus history into three periods: the pre-British period; the period of British colonialism; and the period of post-colonialism. The pre-British period lasted up until the end of the 19th century. In the second period there were two phases of British colonialism. In the first phase the British North Borneo Company governed the area, and this lasted up until World War II. Following the occupation of the Japanese during the war, North Borneo was again governed by the British, but this time as a colony under the jurisdiction of the colonial office. This lasted up until the formation of Malaysia in 1963, when the Colony of North Borneo was incorporated into Malaysia as the State of Sabah, and the post-colonial period began.

TABLE ONE

DEGREE OF INTERLINKAGE OF DRIVES OF SEX
AND AGGRESSION IN A SOCIETY

Linguistic Behavior
       Aggressive language involves threats to genitalia
       Terms for coitus involve metaphors of war and violence
       Term for rape exists
       Acts of aggression described by metaphors of coitus
       Verbal aggression expressed by metaphors of coitus

Projective Systems
       Do the items in the following category of social behavior appear in dreams, jokes, myths and legends, and the religious domain? Are they attributed to animal behavior? To other ethnic groups?

Social Behavior
       Female refusal to engage in coitus respected by males
       Pressure by verbal persuasion to achieve coitus with wife or other woman
       Threats of physical harm to achieve coitus with wife or other woman
       Forced coitus not jurally recognized
       Sexual act used as a means of expressing dominance over wife or other woman
       Violence is an integral aspect of coitus with wife or other woman
       Sadistic coitus with wife or other woman in which aggression is itself eroticized
       Forced coitus is illegal

Accounts we collected of the pre-British period indicate that among the Rungus there was considerable fear of attack and looting of villages by other ethnic groups.[1] Each Rungus village had a champion, who fought attackers and in turn went to villages of distant ethnic groups to kill their champions. Headhunting was based on obtaining the head of the opposing champion and was not a prominent feature of Rungus society or its religion. This type of warfare appears to have ceased by the time of the British arrival. However, the sacrifice of human captives purchased from coastal Muslim groups for the purpose of obtaining village fertility was still practiced up until World War I or shortly afterwards. Also during the Pre-British period the accounts we have collected indicate that there was always the fear that the customary law would be upset by aggressive, powerful men who would take the law into their own hands.

Our first period of research among the Rungus in 1959-60 and 1961-63 took place during the second phase of British colonialism. At that time the Rungus modal personality can be characterized as being intropunitive, which is frequently found with peoples under colonial rule where the fear of the strong external sanctions of the colonial power inhibits the expression of aggressive acts.

We were not permitted by the Sabah government to continue our research until the summer of 1986, which was well into the post-colonial period. Then in 1987 we worked with two informants brought to the United States. In the summer of 1990 we again returned to the field.

By the time we were able to continue our research in 1986 the internal controls of Rungus culture had broken down. Most of the Rungus had become Christian by then, and their fear of supernatural sanctions from localized spirits, wandering spirits, and other deities no longer existed. As L. W. R. Appell in this volume has pointed out, the fear of illicit sexual behavior was originally founded on a variety of religious sanctions. However, during the period of post-colonialism these religious sanctions were generally superseded by Christian beliefs. Christianity, it is believed, protects the individual from malevolent or angered spirits and deities. Also during the British colonial period there were supernatural sanctions against aggressive behavior within the village. Again these have been eroded by Christianity.

It is important to note that some of our data on sexual behavior and aggression come from this period of post-colonialism where both the drives of sex and aggression are under less traditional control than previously. Thus, during our original field work in the British colonial period it was exceedingly difficult to get data on sexual behavior because of religious sanctions and what was considered to be proper behavior. Rungus at that time were very reserved about talking about sexual matters (see L. R. W. Appell in this volume). And it wasn't until our field work in the post-colonial period that we began to get data in depth. While the Rungus still are reserved about discussing sexual matters, with the erosion of traditional sanctions the etiquette of talking about such matters has also loosened.

Consequently, in the analysis of our data we have had to be constantly alert to the possibility that some of our data reflect assessments colored by social change.

However, by the end of 1987, after almost four years of working with a variety of Rungus informants, we were certain enough of our data to conclude in an earlier version of this manuscript that the Rungus both conceptually and behaviorally did not have forced intercourse and that sex and aggression were highly individuated in Rungus society. In 1987 we elicited a story that indicated some sexual violence, but we thought it was a myth or legend. Nevertheless, this sowed a seed of doubt so that when we returned to the field in 1990 we interviewed explicitly on the theme of sex and aggression, and as a result I have had to radically revise the preliminary manuscript. The Rungus do have the concept of forced intercourse, although we were unable to collect any clear-cut jural case material of this. And women deny that it ever could happen, as they always maintain the right to refuse any attempts at intercourse.

I include this cautionary tale to illustrate that ethnography is a difficult profession, full of many pitfalls, but most importantly, significant and reliable conclusions on many topics cannot be reached on the basis of a year or two in the field.

THE RUNGUS LEXICON OF SEXUAL BEHAVIOR

One measure of the degree to which the drives of sex and aggression are commingled is the use of metaphors of aggression to map the domain of sexual relations. For example, among the Trukese the term for one form of intercourse is derived from the lexeme used to tell a child that "I will hit you", and is reduplicated to indicate repetition and duration (Swartz 1958:481). Swartz translates this form of intercourse as the "man is 'striking' the woman". Therefore, the question to be addressed in examining the Rungus lexicon is whether there are any such metaphors of aggression used in the semantic mapping of the sexual act or in the relationship between men and women.

Terms for Sexual Activities

Among the Rungus there are various terms that refer to sexual activities, but in no case are metaphors of aggression used. Thus, unlike the Iban of Sarawak, the sexual domain is not mapped by concepts taken from fighting, raiding, or warfare.[2]

The Rungus distinguish unmarried women from married women by the term *modsuni*, alternately *sumuni*, either of which I gloss as "maiden". This most closely approaches their concept. Men not yet married are called *anak vagu*, literally "a new child", and I shall gloss this as "young man", or "bachelor". The following lexemes to be discussed generally refer to actions that are jural delicts when they involve unmarried individuals or those not married to each other. And it is interesting to note that the sex of the individual, i.e. natural gender, is not indicated in pronouns, in verbs, or in verbal clauses for the actor or the recipient of action. There is one exception to this. Certain morphemes indicating that the subject is taking action with respect to sexual behavior are considered inappropriate if they are used to refer to female behavior. Such assertive behavior on the part of the female is considered improper, although there are rare instances when females do in fact engage in such behavior.

Mongogobu' means "to embrace someone". The root is *-gobu'-*.[3] The stem formative is *-ngo-*. The morpheme {mV} with the allomorphs /-a ~ -o ~ -u/, here *mo-*, indicates an actor causing something to happen or is using something to achieve the action. In the context of sexual action, *mongogobu'* is what males do to females. The prefix *moki-* indicates that an action is asked for. When added to the root *-gobu'-*, it produces *mokigobu'* which may be translated as "to ask for an embrace", "to invite an embrace". The action of *mokigobu'* is that of females to males, but it represents an action that is not considered proper behavior.

Mongoliduk means "to peek at", "to watch secretly" in a sexual context. For example, it refers to a person taking a furtive look at someone's genitals or secretly watching sexual relations, for which the offender can be sued. The only jural case we have been able to collect is one involving a woman peeking at a man, which resulted in his going to the end of the longhouse one evening and fondling her breasts (*momosol*). This later action is also a delict, but in this instance no action was available since the two offenses canceled each other out.

Some men will hide and watch women swimming, hoping to catch sight of their genitalia. This behavior is reported to be very rare for women. However, women are alleged to watch secretly to see if their husbands are having an assignation, and in the longhouse it is alleged that they may also watch secretly others having intercourse.

Grabbing at someone's genitalia is called *monoholuk*.[4] This is a rare act undertaken by men to women. This is not done to maidens, it is reported. Maidens may have their breasts taken hold of, but again this is a rare act. The offense of *monoholuk* requires that the offender pay the victim a piece of brassware, the same as for embracing a woman or taking hold of her breasts. There are no cases of women grabbing the genitalia of men.

If a husband in public takes a hold of his wife's breasts or grabs her genitalia, this is also considered to be improper, and if he does not stop he will be sued by the headman or his father-in-law for a piece of brassware.

The vulgar term for coitus, whether legal or illegal, is *mizut*. The root is *-izut-* indicating the conjunction of sexual organs, and the prefix *mi-* indicates that it is reciprocal action, that both are doing it. For example, in *mitalib* the root *-talib-* means "to pass by"; *mitalib* therefore means "to pass by each other". *Mizut* can be roughly translated as "to fuck each other". It is considered impolite to use this term in front of women, children, or older persons.

Miagai refers to a relationship between a man and a woman that will lead to illicit intercourse. This term can be translated as "having an affair". It focuses on the growing interest of a couple in each other. It is constructed with the prefix *mi-*, indicating reciprocal action. *Miagai*, however, is predominantly used as a euphemism for intercourse, both adultery and fornication, and is the preferred term. It includes sexual relations between a married person and an unmarried person, or between married individuals who are not spouses, or between unmarried individuals.

Mangagai is constructed of the affix *ma-*, the stem formative *-ng-*, and the root *-agai-*. It literally means "to cause an affair", but it perhaps is better translated as "to bring about an affair". The morpheme {*mV-*}, refers to an act of using something or causing an action. For example, *salampad* is a "comb". The prefix *ma-* added to this lexeme, with /-n- <- (s-)/, produces *manalampad*, "to comb", "to use a comb", "to make use of a comb". In the lexeme *mangahaba'*, the root is *-haba'-*, "to fall over", for example, with regard to a housing structure. The affix *ma-* with the stem formative *-ng-* indicates the action of causing a housing structure to fall over or making it fall over.

Mangagai is also used as a euphemism for sexual intercourse. In this latter sense it covers a behavioral field all the way from seduction to induced intercourse. As the morpheme {*mV*} also has the sense of "making" something, *mangagai* may best be rendered as "to make a woman". I use this term from American slang, meaning "to persuade to have sexual intercourse" (*The American Heritage Dictionary of the English Language*), as there is no other standard word in the English language that adequately maps the sense of this term. However, as we shall discuss, in the various projective systems it may also include forced intercourse.

The use of the term *mangagai* in contrast to *miagai* also has jural consequences. The prefix *mi-* indicates that the woman has gotten together with the man and agreed to have intercourse, has participated in this from the beginning, and therefore she also is culpable and also has to pay a fine. The use of the prefix *ma-* indicates that the woman was approached and seduced or otherwise induced to agree to intercourse. As a result, she has committed no jural delict as it was the man's fault.

In all contexts of sexual relations the prefix {*mV-*} with the stem formative *-ng-* is used to refer to actions initiated and brought about only by men.

Kumiagai also refers to intercourse, but it involves specifically the action of a female towards a male. The prefix *ku-* is a rare prefix and can be translated as "to come to" something, "to get together" on something. In this environment I believe the best translation of *kumiagai* is "to encourage an affair". Rather than using the verbal prefix *ma-* which focuses on the action of doing or accomplishing something, the *ku-* verbal prefix reflects the cultural role of the female, in which it is expected that she will not be taking an active role in matters pertaining to sex (see L. W. R. Appell in this volume and A. A. Doolittle in this volume). If a woman is accused of encouraging a man to have illicit sexual relations but denies doing it, the man is blamed and is the focus of the dispute.

The root *-tampak-* refers to coitus, most usually in the context of married sexual relations. The lexeme *manampak* is constructed of the morpheme {*mV-*}, with /n <- (t-)/, indicating the action of the man. Its underlying sense is "to mount", as the normal form of intercourse is the man on top of the woman. One informant mentioned, as alternative forms, facing side by side or the woman on top of the man, but there are no special terms to refer to these forms.

Tampakan is formed of *-tampak-* with the suffix *-an* indicating the receiver of an action, "to be mounted". It is used to refer to the female who is being mounted.

We next come to the various lexemes derived from the root *-tabpo-'*, i.e. *manabpo'*, *tabpa'an*, and *tinabpo'* (past tense of *tabpa'an*). They all involve the concept of catching or taking hold of something. These are the most difficult lexemes in the Rungus language to render in English because of their wide range of meanings and their use as euphemisms for coitus in which the female is verbally pressured into it after having been taken hold of. Even Rungus are at times not sure of what is meant in a specific context and have to enquire further.

Manabpo' is the active focus of the root *-tabpo'-* with the prefix {mV-} and /n <- (t-)/. It refers to the act of catching something that might escape, such as a pig. *Tabpa'an* in this context is the pig that is going to be caught, and *tinabpo'*, formed of the root *-tabpo'-* with the infix *-in-* indicating narrative past, refers to the pig caught in the past. *Tabpa'an* can be translated as "to be grabbed hold of", "to be caught", "to be seized or constrained".

Tabpa'an is used to refer to a child to be caught. It is also used in another very interesting context. When "unbeknownst" to a maiden her fiancé is about to arrive on the day of the wedding, some of the married women go and "catch" her, put her into a sleeping sarong, and seclude her so that she will not run away when she hears that it is her wedding day. ("Unbeknownst" must be read as representing public behavior and may not reflect the private knowledge of the maiden; see L. W. R. Appell in this volume.)

The term *tabpa'an* is also used in jural cases, in stories dealing with men laying hands on women, in reference to fornication or adultery, and in the context of inducing a woman to agree to intercourse. In the first sense, if a man grabs hold of a woman, puts his hands on her to restrain her, catches her arm, this is referred to as *tabpa'an*, "to be grabbed hold of", "to be caught hold of", "to be seized", "to be constrained". This is a finable offense if the woman reports it to the village headman. A recent case of *monoholuk*, grabbing the genitalia of a married woman, was also referred to as *tabpa'an*.

In another sense *tabpa'an* is used euphemistically for induced coitus. In one of the stories discussed below the term is used both for the act of constraining a maiden to proposition her and for constraining to induce coitus. Finally, it is stated by men that *tabpa'an* could also imply that a struggle had taken place, but we have no jural cases of this. Women state that physical force would never happen as the man would respect the wishes of the woman. Thus, the use of the lexeme *tabpa'an*, or its various forms, marks the fact that the woman has had no part in initiating the fornication or adultery that took place and therefore is not to blame. And the fine of the man is larger in this latter sense than if he had just grabbed hold of the woman.

To return to the root *-izut-*, used in reference to "fucking", the lexeme *mongizut* is constructed of the prefix {*mV-*} and stem formative *-ng-* to indicate that the action was brought about, caused by a man. Its use also has certain ambiguities similar to *tabpa'an*. It refers to actively seducing a woman, i.e. to talking her into coitus. And it also refers to the use of pressure to induce the woman to copulate. Literally it means "to make use of fucking", "to bring about fucking", "to get a woman to fuck". In some instances this can best be translated either as "to make a woman" or "to lay a woman". In polite company the term *mangagai* is used as a substitute for *mongizut*, which is considered a vulgarism.

Is there a term for rape in the Rungus language? There is no term dedicated specifically to indicate this act. The Rungus distinguish between illicit intercourse in which the man and woman participate equally and illicit intercourse in which the woman is "made". And what happens in these instances is hard to determine. The situation is ambiguous because of the cultural imperatives that a woman must publicly show no interest in sexual relations and it is improper to talk explicitly about sexual matters. Thus, it is almost impossible to determine in cases where these words are used whether the woman was seduced, was pressured into intercourse by various verbal stratagems, or agreed to coitus from fear or constraint. Women deny that this latter aspect is ever an issue because they say that they maintain control over their own volition in matters of coitus, as we shall discuss.

Furthermore, while there are many jural cases of grabbing hold of a woman and while there are cases of seduction, actual cases of physically forced intercourse do not exist, as we shall discuss. This does not mean that the concept of physically forcing intercourse is absent, for it comes up in various cultural projective systems, particularly those of men. And the possibility of being accosted and propositioned is always present in a woman's cognitive world. But for women the idea that violence would be used to overcome their refusal to engage in intercourse is completely lacking, which makes it difficult to translate the Rungus lexemes *tabpa'an*, *mongizut*, and *mangagai* as "rape". This would distort the logic of the Rungus cognitive world. Women uniformly stated that they could always say no, and a man would respect their wishes.

The complexity of this matter is illustrated by an interview I had with the village headman in 1986. And this again suggests that there is an absence of sexual violence among the Rungus. By that time most of the Rungus had become either Christian or Moslem, and much of their old culture was gone. Young men and women who had gone to school in the late 1960s were bilingual, speaking both Rungus and Malay, which is the official language of the government. Thus, when I asked the village headman about rape among the Rungus, I used the

Malay term for rape, *rogol*, as I was not sure if a Rungus word existed for it. He said that there was no term for rape in the Rungus language and that rape did not occur among the Rungus.

However, in 1990 when I began to understand that *tabpa'an* was a euphemism for being induced to have coitus, I questioned him further. He agreed that *tabpa'an* in certain senses was equivalent to the Malay term for rape, as it lacked the aspect of an assignation. Then he indicated that the Malay term included force, and he used the Malay term for this, *paksa*. In reply to my question as to why he denied that there was a term for rape in 1986, he said that he was not skilled in Malay at that time. This was hard to believe given the fact that he had children who had gone to a Malay school and he had worked for years with the government in which Malay was the official language. He added further that rape was common among the coastal Muslim populations in contrast to the Rungus.[5]

Another informant said that the meaning of *rogol* was to *mongizut*, "to lay a girl" who had not reached sufficient age. Age of consent is a new concept introduced by the government.

An interesting point is that induced intercourse, that is *mangagai*, *mongizut*, or *tabpa'an*, does not result in a threat to one's soul. Various acts of aggression, as we shall discuss, can frighten one's soul with the result that the offender has to give a chicken to the person who was the target of the aggression to bring the person's soul back. This is primarily when blood is drawn by accident, a threat is made with a knife, or one's clothes hung out to dry are cut up, and so forth. On the other hand, just hitting someone, or beating them with a stick also does not cause this ritual delict, as long as blood is not drawn.

In any case, the acts of *mangagai*, *mongizut*, and *tabpa'an* are not considered in Rungus society as a hostile intrusion of one's ritual state, nor are they considered physically damaging.

Terms for Sexual Arousal

It is important now to analyze the terms for sexual arousal, for it might be concluded that one term for penile erection involves the use of a metaphor of aggression. The first term for penile erection is *kumodow*, "to become hard". This is derived from the word *okudow*, "hard", with the infix *-um-* indicating "becoming". But the other lexeme for penile erection presents on the surface certain problems. It is *humungot*, which also is used to refer to someone "becoming angry". Yet the concept *humungot* is not isomorphic with our concept of anger. A blowfish when it inflates is said to be *humungot*. Also, there is a type of frog that puffs up, and it is said to be *humungot*. A cock's comb when erect is said to be *humungot*. A chameleon when it changes color from green to brown and/or its crest becomes erect is said to be *humungot*. When the dorsal spine of a fish rises, it is *humungot*. Thus, this term appears to map the spectrum of "becoming aroused", including "becoming angry". In the instance of sexual relations its focus is on arousal not anger.

Semen is called *gotut* or *ilob*. *Ilob* is the more common term, and it also means vomitus. To ejaculate is called *mongilub*, which also means "to vomit". Lubricating secretions of the female are also referred to as *ilob*.

One informant said that female arousal is referred to as *pagkatalan*, "to have become itchy", or *pagkarahan*, "to have become tickling". No female informant knew of any terms for female arousal.

There are no terms for male orgasm or female orgasm.

Rungus men may opine with regard to the sexual organs of a particular female that her mons veneris is large. Women will mention that a penis is long or large in circumference. One woman who had difficulty conceiving gave as the reason for this that her husband's penis was too short.

Terms for Wiving, Marriage, and the Evolving Relationship of Spouses

When a young man begins to visit villages to search out an attractive woman to marry, it is referred to as *monodung*. Maidens are known to flirt (*osigat*). Flirting with the eyes only is referred to as *pinokosidatsidat*.

The term *manansavo'* is used to refer to the courting that a young man may do. It also refers to the early part of the wedding ceremony when the groom arrives at the longhouse of the bride. The root of this is the substantive *savo'*, the term used for spouse of either sex. There is no specific term to indicate the sex of a spouse, such as "husband" or "wife". *Manansavo'* is constructed from the morpheme {*mV-*}, with an infix *-nan-*. This infix is also used to indicate the putting on or wearing of clothing, the taking up of a pack basket to put on one's back, etc. *Manansavo'* thus might best be translated, "to wive", "to take a wife". It has the sense of taking deliberate action, which reflects the active part the man plays in marrying and the reluctance of the woman to indicate interest in becoming a wife (see L. W. R. Appell in this volume and below). This cultural pattern of female behavior in which she publicly expresses no interest in sexual matters and a resistance to anything related to marriage I shall call the "reluctant bride" behavioral pattern. This only occurs with a first marriage, not when a woman marries again after being widowed or divorced.

A betrothed maiden is referred to by the term *savo'on*, which is constructed from *savo'* with the passive affix *on*. When used with a substantive, it indicates a future state, "to become"; in this instance "to become a wife".

The concept of the man taking the initiative in marrying has its expression in arguments between spouses in which a wife will say to make her point, "You married me [using the term *manansavo'*]; I didn't marry you!"

An extreme expression of the reluctant bride behavior is when the bride refuses to accept the attentions of her husband or provide any domestic services for him. This is called *"amu tumutun"*. *Amu* is the negative used with verbs. *Tumutun* has the root *-tutun-*, which indicates "recognition". Thus, the lexeme *otutunan*, *-tutun-* with the *-an* suffix forming a passive focus, can be translated as "to be recognized".

In the environment of marriage, *tumutun* means "to accept", "to recognize", and/or "become accustomed to" someone of the opposite sex. It is constructed from *-tutun-* with the infix *-um-* indicating the subject is "becoming" or is in the process of being transformed. It refers to the critical stage in marital relations when just after the wedding, sometimes a bride and very rarely a groom will not acknowledge a spouse (see L. W. R. Appell in this volume). Thus it is said of the bride that she *amu tumutun*. This can be translated as "does not accept", "is not accustomed to", or "is not attracted to" her spouse, and in its strongest behavioral manifestations it could be translated as "shuns" her spouse.

-tutun- with the suffix *mo-*, indicating focus on causing an action, then becomes *monutun*, an action only of a man to a woman, which may be roughly translated as "to woo", "to make (the woman) accustomed (to him)", "to bring about (her) acceptance (of him)". This is done by being attentive to her, engaging her in conversation, finding her betel chewing supplies, waiting for her to go to the fields with him, etc.

After marriage residence is uxorilocal, unless an extra payment in the bride-price is given. A woman who is taken to the husband's village is referred to as *natazangan*, "that which is snatched and run away with", a term also used to refer to a bone or something to eat that a dog takes and runs away with.

The level of emotional involvement of a bachelor and a maiden or a husband and wife is described by using various forms of the word *ginavo'*. *Ginavo'* refers to the animating force in living things, and as such it can be translated as "spirit", although in many contexts it is equivalent to the metaphorical sense in which "heart" is used in English. *Ginavo'* is located somewhere within the chest cavity but in fact has no physical embodiment. It is the seat of emotions and is used in many contexts to describe the emotional state of an individual. If someone is sad, he is described as having an *oru'ol ginavo*. *Oru'ol* may be translated as "sore" in most contexts. Therefore, this phrase can be roughly translated as "sick at heart". In relations between a bachelor and a maiden, if they enjoy each other and have the same interests, they are said to be *miginavo'*, "to have the same feelings", "to feel the same about each other". After marriage if there is no rankling about anything, if husband and wife enjoy each other's company, are glad to see the other when they have been separated, laugh together, they are said to be *koginava'an*. The root is *ginavo'*. The prefix *ko-* indicates a completed action and with the suffix *-an* produces a substantive. We would say that they are of one mind, they are in accord with each other, they have mutual understanding.

The verb *mana'od* refers to "taking care" of someone. This means feeding him or her, looking after him or her. It is used for taking care of babies. But it is also a critical aspect of married life and a bone of contention. A spouse is supposed to take care of the other spouse, particularly when ill or indisposed. And there are not infrequent arguments between spouses as to whether one or the other has fulfilled this aspect of the spouse role satisfactorily. And of course fulfilling it is a sign of affection.

Mana'od is also the term used for the second or subsequent marriage of an individual to another person who has also been widowed or divorced. He or she "takes care of the other" (*mana'od*), i.e. marries her/him. A spouse so married is referred to as *tina'od*. This is constructed from the root *-ta'od-* of *mana'od* with an infix *-in-* indicating past tense.

Finally, when two spouses really care for each other, love each other, do not fight, they are said to *misamod*. The focus here is on the emotions felt for each other, and it is the product of a long relationship.

Thus, there is no Rungus term that adequately covers the English concept of love, with perhaps the exception of *misamod*. The various forms of the term *ginavo'*, which are used to indicate that two people have the same feelings for each other, seem to represent emotions more of "liking" than "loving".

For couples who do not get along with each other, divorce is fairly simple. This requires a village moot in which cause or fault is determined and the division of family assets agreed upon with the spouse having been at greater fault getting a smaller share.

The term *mirutut* refers to a couple that stays married even though they have a hard time getting along with each other and have arguments.

SEXUAL METAPHOR IN VERBAL AGGRESSION

One indicator of the degree to which the sexual and aggressive drives are interlinked in any sociocultural system is the extent to which sexual metaphors are used in verbal aggression.

In American usage metaphors of intercourse are constantly used in expressing aggression, so that you can conclude that one of the fundamental metaphors of American society is that SEXUAL INTERCOURSE IS AGGRESSION. This is illustrated in the phrases "screw you", "up yours", "fuck you" (see G. N. Appell 1987; Beneke 1982). But aggression is often mapped in turn by sexual terms, such as "I have been screwed!", "I feel like I have been raped!", etc. (see G. N. Appell 1987). Thus, there is a related metaphor in American society: AN AGGRESSIVE ACT MAY BE SEXUAL.

That these metaphors are not human universals is demonstrated by the use of abusive language among the Rungus. The concept of sexual intercourse is not used as a metaphor for aggression.

Rungus Forms of Verbal Abuse

Verbal expressions of aggression among the Rungus involve the mention of genitalia or the implication of death (see Table Two). These fall under the general rubric of *monginsasana*, "to anger", "to provoke".

In mentioning genitalia some forms of verbal abuse can be very aggressive. But these aggressive insults do not involve the concept of sexual intercourse as an aggressive act.[6]

In addition to mentioning genitalia, there is the very rare gesture in which a person extends his index finger downward and spits on it. This is a reference to one's penis being short. This is also a genitalia insult. There are no gestures which indicate sexual intercourse as an aggressive act.

Reference to another's genitalia uttered in anger, intentionally to insult, or to show disrespect are grounds for jural action. The person insulted can bring the matter to the village moot, and compensation for the insult is a piece of brassware. If the person so vilified returns the insult, this obviates jural action. This form of insult is classed as *komolu'an*, "to be shamed". It does not impute any physical impairment as does the next form of insult.

In the case of death insult, there is the fear that it may come to pass. To prevent this the person insulted can ask for a chicken in payment. The chicken is then sacrificed with prayer to remove the possibility of harm and the blood of the chicken is wiped on the ankle of the person affected.

In both instances of death implication and genitalia insult the abuse can be compounded and made more serious by including reference to a wounding (see Table 2; see *kotiguras* below). Also, rather than a statement of wounding or a threatened wounding, an individual can symbolically act out the wounding. For example, an individual may refer to a man's penis in anger while cutting a stick with a bush knife. This commingling of threat and insult requires a larger fine, involving both a chicken and brassware.

Terms for sexual intercourse occur in abusive language only in one instance, *mongizut do ondu*, "(you) get women to fuck!", "(you) induce women to fuck!" The sense of this phrase might also be indicated by translating it with American slang terms: "(you) lay women!", or "(you) make women!" There are no other terms in American English to indicate sufficiently the nature of this insult in which a man is imputed to be actively engaged in seeking out women for fornication.

TABLE TWO

RUNGUS FORMS OF VERBAL ABUSE

1. *Mongimbuhal* : "To insult by reference to genitalia"

Toli nu!	: "Your penis!"[a]
Ontolu nu!	: "Your testicles!"
Turoi nu!	: "Your vagina!"
Ondila nu!	: "Your clitoris!"
Mongizut do ondu!	: "(You) get women to fuck!"
Kinisan turoi nu!	: "(I will) tear your vagina!"[b]
Govilon turoi nu!	: "(I will) rip out your vagina!"[b]

2. *Mongolupu'* : "To curse someone by saying or implying he is going to die"

Matai ko!	: "You are going to die!"
Akanon do rogon!	: "You will be eaten by the spirits!"
Mindakud do kazu om aratu!	: "Climb a tree and fall!" (All the various forms of death may be used.)

3. *Mongimbuhal om Moniguras* : "To insult by reference to genitalia and cause the ritual delict of a threatened wound"

Tibason toli nu!	: "Your penis will be slashed!"
Tibason ku toli nu!	: "Your penis will be slashed by me!"

(All variations of genitalia and methods of cutting can be substituted.)

TABLE TWO
(Continued)

4. *Mongolupu' om Moniguras* : "To curse by mentioning death and to cause the ritual delict of threatening to wound..,"

    Matai ko, tibason dikau! : "You are going to die, you will be slashed!"

---

[a]I have translated the Rungus terms for genitalia with the standard American English terms, not slang terms, as the same Rungus terms are used in standard Rungus as well as in environments of [verbal abuse, with but the exception of *mongizut* (see text).

[b]We never heard of these two expletives during our original field work but only discovered them in 1990. I was told that these were old types of expletives and not recently devised. The term *govilon* is hard to translate. It also refers to the action of putting one's finger in another person's mouth and tearing away at the corner of it when fighting or wrestling.

Flynn in his analysis of insults cross-culturally remarks (1976:4): "In most cultures it is considered very insulting to accuse someone of engaging in unacceptable or deviant sexual behavior. The severity of the insult is usually related to the seriousness of the norms against the particular kind of sexual behavior that the insulted person is accused of." Thus, "You get women to fuck!" is indeed a powerful insult, the furthest that Rungus go in using intercourse as a form of insult. I shall be exploring the context of this most deviant of sexual behaviors and its implications to Rungus society in the rest of this study.

In conclusion, there is no form of insult involving the use of sexual intercourse as a metaphor for physical aggression towards another. This form of verbal aggression does not appear in the Rungus cognitive world. Nor are terms of sexual intercourse used to devalue another, with the one exception of "You get women to fuck!" Finally, aggressive acts are not described using any metaphors of sexual intercourse.

HOMOSEXUALITY AND BESTIALITY

Are there forms of sexual acts that involve aggression? In discussing homosexuality in this context I must make it clear that I am not claiming that homosexual behavior necessarily entails aggression only that it sometimes may. Thus, it is a form of sexual relations that has relevance for our discussion here. Homosexuality is not found among the Rungus to the best of our knowledge. Furthermore, there is no term for homosexual behavior. During our field research in 1986 and 1990 I explicitly inquired about this. Not only is there no knowledge of homosexuality ever having occurred, but also one of my informants, the village headman, asked what was involved. He was incredulous when I explained.

I have only one case of bestiality. In a distant village sometime ago a man killed a deer and had intercourse with the body. The headman of the village took a stick to his buttocks, and he ran off.

Furthermore, verbal insults involving the implication of sexual relations with animals do not occur.

LOVE SICKNESS[7]

The term for what is referred to in the English language as love sickness is *upos*. This can be glossed as "grieving", as it is also used to refer to the emotional state felt by someone who has lost a parent, spouse, or child. The behavior associated with *upos* is refusing to eat or drink and sometimes running away into the forest. The behavior is stated to be equivalent to that of someone starving. It can lead to suicide attempts. Both men and women can experience this emotion and display such behavior.

People behaving like this are also referred to as being *mulau*--"crazy", no longer able to think clearly.

This state can occur over an unmarried love object, or over a love object who is marrying someone else. There are no statements that the love object could be a spouse of someone else.

Love sickness can only occur if there has been the application of love magic, called *pugai*. This is derived from the root *-agai*, which refers to having an affair. The prefix {*pV*}, used to form a substantive, indicates in this context that brought into being as the result of an action. Love magic can be used to cause another to desire you, to want you. It can also be used by a third person against two other people whom he wants to involve in an affair with each other.

It is important to note that love sickness does not involve aggressive behavior against a love object who does not reciprocate affections.

ANIMAL MODELS

Another approach to determine the degree of interlinkage of sex and aggression is the cultural use of animal models in discussions of sex or in theatrical or ritual performances. In certain species aggression leads to access to the female, so that there is a conjunction between sex and aggression. To what degree have the Rungus taken up animal examples of aggressive sexuality to serve as models for human behavior?

In the discussions of sexual relations or in Rungus joking, no animal models are used with the exception of the dog, the mouse deer, and the orang-utan. In discussing this material we are now in a transition in our argument. Animals not only can serve as models. They also can serve as projective subjects in that humans may attribute to animals the ideas and impulses that are unacceptable for them to admit as originating in themselves.

There is a myth about the dog. In the beginning the Creator God gave men the penises of dogs. This caused all sorts of trouble as when a man and woman were surprised in intercourse, the man could not withdraw to protect himself or to run away. So a lot of people were killed as a result of the fighting between the cuckolded and the adulterer. And even the adulteress was subject to being wounded and killed by the angry husband. When the Creator God saw what he had wrought, he exchanged the penises of the dogs and humans.[8]

There are cautionary accounts that females may be sexually attacked by male orang-utan if they go alone into swiddens situated near the primary jungle. The term used for this is *tampakan*, "to be mounted", which is also used for the female in sexual relations between spouses. The orang-utan will not try to attack a man as he is afraid of his bush knife, said one informant. But another, older informant stated that there were no such tales of a woman being mounted by an orang-utan, as the orang-utan would bite if a woman got near.

However, it is reported that about two generations ago a man had a captive male orang-utan, who would attempt to "mount" (*manampak*) human females. This is a fairly widespread account, and it is used to illustrate why one should not keep a captive orang-utan.

In general women have not heard any stories about orang-utan sexually attacking human females. When one female informant was told about such stories her response was how could it be done, "Humans and animals can't fuck."

EVIDENCE FROM THE RUNGUS SOCIOCULTURAL PROJECTIVE SYSTEMS

To discover further evidence on the degree to which the drives of sex and aggression are individuated or interlinked, it is useful to consider the various cultural projective systems (see Spiro 1965; Spiro and D'Andrade 1958; Whiting and Child 1953; Whiting 1959, 1961; Whiting and Whiting 1978).

The lack of sexual aggression in Rungus projective systems, with the exception of the material on the orang-utan discussed above, is in marked contrast to the Iban. In Iban society sexual conflict becomes overt in female mockery of men's genitalia and in the projection of sexual aggression in the religious system (Freeman 1968; Sather 1978). There are sexually aggressive incubi, primarily forest and river spirits, who seduce married women and, as a result of sexual intercourse with them, "spoil" their wombs so that they are unable to bear living offspring, or if they do, the child lives only a short time (Freeman 1967; Sather 1978). And there are malevolent ghosts of women having died in childbirth who attack and destroy men's sexual organs (Sather 1978).

Dreams

Dreams are an important source of material. But it is hard to get information on Rungus dreams as they indicate the wandering of one of the seven souls of the dreamer and usually involve its encounters with spirits that cause illness. Talking about such spirits is equivalent to summoning them and inviting sickness. Thus, if a male or female dreams of intercourse it means that sickness may, but not necessarily, follow as the dreamer has had an encounter with one of these spirits. However, this is not a sexually aggressive encounter as may happen in encounters with spirits among the Iban.

If a Rungus maiden dreams of a handsome man who wants to marry her, it means that her guardian spirit wants to be in communication with her. If a man dreams of marrying a beautiful woman, it means that he will accumulate a lot of brassware, gongs, and jars, as the woman in the dream is the soul of this property.

Joking and Teasing

The Rungus do not have formal jokes, but they are fond of making joking remarks and teasing. In none of these with sexual content did we find any evidence of sexual aggression.

Religion

In the religion, as far as we have been able to ascertain, there is no mention of any action of sexual aggression among the various spirits and gods in the long ritual chants that accompany sacrifices to them. And there are no public performances in which sexual acts are alluded to. Nor are women subject to sexual assault by spirits or gods such as occurs among the Iban.

Myths, Folktales, and Legends

In the various myths and folktales there are sexual themes. But aggression is not an integral aspect of them, at least in the ones that we were able to collect, with two exceptions, one in which antagonism is directed in a minor way towards the penis and one in which a female orang-utan forces a man to have intercourse with her.

First, there are folktales about the mouse deer similar to those found throughout Borneo. The Rungus versions only include what one might call sly sex. That is the mouse deer tricks a female into having sexual relations with him; he does not force her to do so. For example, in one story the mouse deer tricks a woman into chasing him through a hollow log, where she gets stuck with her bottom up in the air accessible to the mouse deer.

Then there are two myths I collected in which there is a symbolic linkage between the penis and a snake.

In the first myth a man is particularly good at seducing women. The term used for this in the story is *mangangkam*. *Mangangkam* refers to illicit intercourse that occurs when a person slips into the bed of a member of the opposite sex after everyone in the longhouse has gone asleep, usually with the connivance of the other. In this story the man saw a beautiful woman in the forest, and she agreed to have intercourse but only if he promised to tell her when he was finished. He agreed. They had coitus, and he told her that he was finished. As he withdrew, she cast a spell that resulted in his penis being drawn out to an extraordinary length, similar to a snake. All coiled up it would fill up one of the largest rice carrying baskets. After that whenever he wanted to sleep with a woman, he didn't have to go himself, he could send his penis. And thus he had intercourse with women before they understood what had happened, as his penis could sneak unheralded into their longhouse apartment. Women would have a feeling (of it), but since they did not see a man they were not sure what was happening. Finally, they realized that they could tell when it was approaching from the noise it made as it slipped along the floor boards. One woman poured boiling water on the penis as it was leaving. It then lost its outer skin from the scalding, and out came seven children. From then on it was a normal penis.

This is the only folktale in which there is any indication of sexual antagonism or aggression, and it arises as the result of the illicit sexual behavior of the man. It is the product of the misuse of male sexuality. And it is a female who expresses this antagonism towards the penis, first in coitus and then when it bothers women. And it is a woman which brings the penis back to its socially sanctioned use, the production of children. This is very interesting in the context of the expected behavior of virgins, who are supposed to be disinterested in sexual matters and reject sexual advances. And it shows what can happen to a man if he engages in fornication. But it must be analyzed in the context of another story about a snake.

In this story a snake appears and curls up around an infant girl's sleeping hammock. He announces that he wants to marry her but he is told he must wait till she is older, which he does. After the marriage his wife's parents try to get rid of him as he can do no work. But then he turns into a handsome young man who is a god.

These two stories may indicate the conflicted behavior of some maidens in their first marriages (see below). But they do not include strong antagonism or aggression. There does not appear to be any pattern of sexual antagonism or aggression in the Rungus projective systems.

There is a legend of forced intercourse in which violence is involved. It is the story of a form of marriage that occurred long before the British arrived, called *monundikut*. The father and brothers of the young man wanting to marry dress up for a wedding ceremony and carry all the bride-price and expenses for the wedding for both the groom's family and the bride's family to the longhouse of the maiden. They also bring the bride's sleeping robe. When they arrive, they grab the maiden and put her in the sleeping robe. Then the young man copulates with her in front of the wedding party. Beforehand they have notified the headman of the village, so that he is ready to placate the father and relatives of the girl and prevent a fight breaking out with weapons. The parents of the bride accept the marriage, as it could be attempted only by a wealthy father with a good-looking and hard-working son. The male offspring of such a marriage are alleged to be particularly brave and become village champions.

There are no names of historical figures or ancestors associated with this story, and it cannot be ascertained whether or not this is an account of an actual happening. And it is said that women don't really know this story, but there are some men who do. This story appears contradictory to Rungus cultural values as sexual intercourse is a very private act and must not be observed, particularly by close relatives for it puts them in ritual jeopardy.

The retired headman of the village when asked about this form of marriage gave a different story in which the maiden was not touched but instead the young man went into the apartment of the maiden and immediately addressed her parents as "in-laws", thereby forcing the issue. However, he had another story of a form of wiving to force the issue. In this account the bachelor goes to the apartment of the girl with a bridal sleeping robe. He quickly puts it over her. She struggles, and he holds her till she stops. Then the parents start the negotiations over bride-price. If the maiden's parents do not accept the young man, then he brings action for compensation for the bodily hurt that he has received from the maiden. Again, no actual cases of this could be elicited.

Finally, there is a myth about sexual relations between a human and an orang-utan related by a male informant. A man was working in his swidden and an orang-utan grabbed him and took him up into the canopy. She asked him to have sexual relations with her. He refused. She then took him by the leg and dangled him from the tree, threatening to drop him. He again refused. She did this three times until he finally agreed. They had a child. The story becomes involved at this point, but the relevance for our discussion is that at the end the orang-utan turned into a beautiful spirit who had been banished to earth because she had not yet married.

We obtained this story from a major and well-respected male informant, but we do not know how widespread it is within the Rungus community. Nevertheless, it is interesting that while we have stories in which human females are sexually attacked by male orang-utans told mostly by men, and that while we have stories of forms of marriage that indicate forced intercourse, again by men, there is also a myth about a female orang-utan, as a disguised spirit, forcing intercourse with a male.

SEXUAL ASSAULT: ACTUAL CASES OR LEGENDS?

In our field notes from our original research (1959-60, 1961-63) I found no reference to any behavior that could be classed as rape or intercourse achieved by physical force. In the summer of 1986 we returned to the Rungus and found that major sociocultural changes had taken place. One informant reported an instance of sexual assault that occurred during our absence in which a Bugis man, notable for their aggression, killed a Rungus woman. My informant surmised that the Bugis tried to have intercourse with her, but she did not want to, and therefore he killed her. This story is labeled in my fields notes under the Rungus term *manabpo'*, which means "to seize", "to catch", or "to constrain". It is the active focus of the stem *-tabpo-'*.

Thus the Rungus are aware that sexual assault can occur, the men more so than the women. There are the stories told about the orang-utan. And there are stories told by men about *Pinonguvakan*, the name of a bathing pool in a stream.

The Bathing Pool Called *Pinonguvakan*

We first discovered this story in 1987 from an informant who had been my assistant in 1959-60 and 1961-63. At that time I worked for two years with two village headmen on Rungus customary law, and my assistant had sat in on all these sessions during which I collected numerous cases on marriage, fornication and adultery, assault, and verbal aggression. In no instance did I elicit any cases involving sexual aggression. However, in 1987 he told me the story of *Pinonguvakan*, in fact two versions of it.

In the first version a woman is killed at a bathing pool called *Pinonguvakan*, allegedly named after an aspect of this event. All bathing pools in rivers are named, usually after a natural feature. The name of the pool called

Pinonguvakan can be translated as "the place where (her legs) were pulled apart", as one would pull apart a forked stick. This lexeme focuses on the action of pulling something apart, and does not specify what is being subjected to this. In the case of the bathing pool my informant stated that a man had done this to a woman because she did not agree to have intercourse, and she died. Both were Rungus, but my informant did not know their names or the name of the village where this happened.

In the second version, given by my informant seven months later, the woman survives, and she and the young man are put to marriage by the headman. The man wanted the woman, wanted to have intercourse, but the woman did not agree. He apparently violently spread her legs apart, dislocating her hips. She could not walk. And he was afraid she would die. So he carried her back to the longhouse on his back and got someone to put the joints back into place. They were then put to marriage.

In the first version this account was referred to as a *tuturan* or "story", that is an account of an actual happening. In the second version it was referred to both as a *tangon*, a "myth", and a *tuturan*, "story". And the act was referred to as *mangagai*, "to bring about sexual intercourse", "to make a woman". These terms are used in everyday language with no connotation of violence. My informant later on remembered the name of the village where the bathing pool is located, near to the village in which we did our research.

During field work in 1990 we systematically followed up on this story and tried to determine its distribution and the variation in themes. All subsequent versions of the story, with but one exception, refer to a bathing hole located not in a distant village but in the village where we resided for field work.

The exception involves a *Pinonguvakan* in a neighboring village where a head was discovered floating in the river with its jaw pulled open so that its mouth was split. My informant for this story also opined that there must be *Pinonguvakan* water holes in almost every village, as it can refer to a split branch of a tree, a common occurrence along rivers, as well as other similar happenings.

To return to variations on this story of forced sexual intercourse, several male informants have never heard of the story or the water hole. But another informant said he had heard the story from his father, an elderly man in 1959. The story is essentially the same, but they were not made to marry. This informant used the term *mizut* for the sexual attack, which means "to fuck each other", although in the story he told it was clear that it was against the wishes of the female. A term such as *mongizut*, "to lay the woman", "to get the woman to fuck", would have more been more appropriate, even though the violence indicated in this story goes beyond the usual sense of the term.

Another version told by one of the old and knowledgeable informants in the village involved two young men who were suitors for the same maiden. They each grabbed a leg to take her away and as a result split her apart so that she died. The two young men then killed each other. This occurred by a bathing pool in our village but far upstream... However, he did not know the names of any of the participants...

A former headman gave roughly the same story as the second version I had elicited from my first informant, except that the water hole was in our village of research. A young man wanted to have intercourse with a maiden at the water hole. She refused. He tried to argue her into it. She still refused. He grabbed her legs; she held them together. They were dislocated at the hips. The young man then carried her back to the longhouse. The headman put them to marriage, as no one else would marry a maiden who could not walk. Some medicine was applied, which alleviated the dislocation enough for her to walk about but with a limp. The young man's family had to give a water buffalo to the maiden's family, and provide a large bride-price as well.

This informant, younger than my elderly informant whose version of the story involved two young men, also maintained that he did not know the names of the participants in this story, but he did know their descendants. However, he could not give us their names. They had moved to another part of the Rungus territory. But a headman in another village, now long dead, had lived in that longhouse with the girl, he stated.

It is important to note here that the explanation advanced for the events in the Bugis case and in the various versions of the Rungus case is that the woman refused to have coitus. As we shall discuss shortly, Rungus cultural expectations are that women have the right to refuse intercourse at any time, extramaritally or within marriage. Thus, there are several questions that remain unanswered in the accounts recorded. Why was the woman alone at a bathing pool? To avoid charges of being improper, Rungus women do not generally go unaccompanied to bathing pools. Was she encouraging the man? Was the dislocated hip the result of a passionate mating, or was it the result of forced intercourse? We are not clear on this as there were no witnesses to this event. If there are no witnesses to illicit sexual intercourse but the couple are found out, it is expected that the woman will claim that she was induced to have coitus, that she was not actively inviting sexual relations, and this claim will be accepted. So we do not know whether the reportage of the event is accurate or not. What is more, we don't even know whether this story reflects an actual event or whether it is constructed to justify the unusual name of a bathing pool so that it is only a projection of feelings of sexual aggression. What we do know is that after almost four years of research we have only one verbal report of a possible case of physically forced intercourse, not a pattern of sexual aggression.

While this case illustrates that it is possible to talk about physically forced intercourse, although there is no word to differentiate it specifically as such, discussions of it are in fact extraordinarily rare. And women are not familiar with stories about the *Pinonguvakan*, not even the wives of the men who related the story to me.

Two Accounts of Maidens Having Hands Laid On Them

There is a line between being grabbed hold of by a man, being constrained by a man, and being induced to have intercourse, although at times when women are accustomed to following the wishes of men this may be a fine line. And the Rungus use the same term to refer to both actions. This is based on the root *-tabpo'-* and appears in various forms, *manabpo'*, *tabpa'an*, etc. In 1990 I recorded the following two accounts.

In the first account it is questionable whether it is an account of an actual happening or a cautionary tale told by a father to his son, my informant. In attempting to ascertain whether it represented an actual legal case, I found that my informant referred to it at different times as both being a myth or legend (*tangon*) and a story (*tuturan*).

There was a young man who had been catching hold of girls to get them to have intercourse with him. (In the story the verb *manabpo'* is used for what he did.) The maidens told the headman, but the young man maintained he was being falsely accused. This happened three times. Then the headman told the maidens not to admonish the offender when he grabbed them, but to take his headcloth and run. There was a maiden who decided to entice the young man to catch her (*mokitabpo'*). When they had had intercourse and she was leaving the scene, she said that she would not tell the people in the longhouse, and maybe they could meet again. Then she asked where he got his headcloth from. He replied it was his own. She asked to see it, and then asked the young man if she could take it home so that she could learn the weaving pattern. He agreed.

On returning to the longhouse she went immediately and told the headman. And he recognized who the young man was by the headcloth. There was a village moot and the young man had to give as compensation a large gong to the parents of the maiden. The other girls who had been taken earlier (*tinabpo'*) received nothing. (This seems anomalous, given the following story.)

I asked my informant why the maiden didn't just take the headcloth and run. He replied that she was afraid that the young man would outrun her and perhaps kill her to prevent her reporting the incident to the headman.

The second account deals with an alleged actual case that occurred before the British arrived. There was a young man who chased maidens when they went to get water at the river and caught hold of them (*manabpo'*). Some maidens agreed to have intercourse. But some didn't and were left alone. These latter maidens reported to the headman what had happened. But the youth denied the accusations.

The headman suggested to the maidens that they get together and beat the young man. A strong maiden said, "Wait I minute. I will go for water by myself."

So she went, and as she bent over to fill her bamboo water tubes, she was caught hold of (*tabpa'an*) by the man. She told him to wait until she was finished filling her water tubes to have intercourse. In the meantime she told him to hold on tight to her back. When she finished filling the tubes she took hold of the youth around his legs. She then took him piggyback to the longhouse. The youth did not want to go, and his trousers fell off as she carried him up.

Then the headman said that the reports really were true. The maidens who told the headman about being accosted were not lying as the youth had claimed. The youth could no longer deny what he had been doing. The headman at the moot said that the big strong maiden should get a large gong from the youth. And the others who reported his behavior to the headman got two small gongs each. The youth stopped this behavior as he was afraid of being caught again.

One informant present while this story was collected said that among the Rungus if a man tried to force a woman into intercourse and she refused, he would stop. And if a woman is propositioned, she can tell the headman and ask for a fine. It is notable that in these two stories women got their own back at the men who had taken advantage of them.

Finally, it is important to note that the root -*tabpo'*- is used in two senses in these stories: "to grab hold of a woman" and euphemistically "to make a woman".

THE ABSENCE OF SEXUAL ANTAGONISM AND AGGRESSION
IN RELATIONS BETWEEN THE SEXES

Freeman (1968) reports that Iban women are envious of Iban men and the mockery of males, particularly male genitalia, is one of their favorite pastimes. And he points out the aggressive nature of mockery. Swartz (1958) argues that on Truk the expression of aggression is not permitted in marital relations. However, in adulterous relations, "sweetheart relations", aggression is permitted, and it is directed not only toward one's sweetheart but also to the kin of the sweetheart by the very act of this illicit intercourse. Swartz writes (1958:482), "The refusal consciously to characterize acts as aggressive allows the sweethearts to inflict considerable bodily harm on each other. ... The pain inflicted on each other by sweethearts is now mostly limited to cigarette burns on the arm, but formerly included cutting with a knife and knocking out teeth with stones." And among the Trobriand Islanders, Malinowski reports (1932:217, orig. 1929) that "It is a general rule in all districts ... when a boy and girl are strongly attracted to each other, and especially before their passion is satisfied, the girl is allowed to inflict considerable bodily pain on her lover by scratching, beating, thrashing, and even wounding with a sharp instrument."[9]

Among the Rungus there is no evidence that females envy males, or vice versa, and there is no evidence of an underlying layer of aggression or antagonism with respect to the opposite sex as represented in mockery, jokes, overt statements, or the play of children. Boys do not tease girls or belittle female roles, and girls in their play do not tease boys or ridicule any of the male roles. Nor is there any association of aggression in coitus in terms of bodily injury either in cases of fornication, adultery, or marital intercourse. There is no evidence or discussion of marks rendered on a partner's body during passionate intercourse. Aggression in coitus was never a matter of discussion among the Rungus, and we have no observational data to suggest that it occurs.[10]

There is also no evidence of sexual antagonism or aggression in the myths we have collected, with two exceptions. These are the myth of illicit sex that results in an elongated penis, subsequently scalded when it continues to misbehave, and the ambiguous report of a woman hurt in the act of intercourse, which may or may not have been forced.

This is not to be read that spouses do not have arguments, and that these sometimes result in the woman or man being hit, although this latter case occurs less frequently. But sexual antagonism and aggression is not part of the fabric of everyday relations between the sexes.

SEXUAL JEALOUSY AND ASSAULT

While there is little or no sexual antagonism in Rungus society, sexual jealously (*mongivogw*) is prevalent. There is the story of a girl who was being courted by two youths. And one day, as she passed them on the way to the river, she made up a short, highly metaphorical poem. The underlying meaning of the poem was that she liked them equally and could not make up her mind between the two of them. Then each said that as long he was not going to marry her, the other wouldn't either. And they stabbed her and then killed each other. The event is supposed to have happened before the arrival of the British. But the story along with the poem is repeated frequently. No one now knows who was involved in the incident. But it is a clear cautionary tale of the potential danger of sexual jealousy.

There is also the myth of what happened when men had penises of dogs. Violence lies just below the surface of sexual infidelities. And sexual jealousy over one's spouse is a very prevalent and strong emotion.

Either just before the British arrived or just after, about four generations ago, a man in our research village killed his wife in a jealous rage. Her brother then killed him. In a neighboring village before the British came, a man enraged with sexual jealousy over his wife killed her, it is alleged, by pulling her legs apart.

It was our observation at the time of our original research that sexual jealously was more common among wives than husbands. By 1990 cases of jealousy predominately involved wives. While some informants maintain that it is not any more frequent at present after sociocultural change than during our original research, others say it is more prevalent because men move about more and take work in distant areas. It is certainly talked about much more frequently, and this gossip primarily involves jealous wives. Another explanation may be the change in marital residence. Previously when the Rungus economy was based on the swidden cultivation of rice, uxorilocal residence in cases of intervillage marriage resulted in men being the strangers among the kin of their wives. Now that residence is virilocal as a result of ownership of land by men and the development of coconut and rubber plantations, wives are the strangers. There are now many more women than before without kinship ties within their spouses' village.

But assault as the result of sexual jealousy is not sexual assault. It is the response to a violation of the rights and duties of a wife.

FORCED COITUS IN MARRIAGE

To determine the degree of association of sex and aggression in Rungus society, we will now explore the questions as to whether or not forced coitus exists in marriage and whether or not it is recognized as such in the Rungus conceptual system. Does a husband force his wife to have coitus against her will, or does he give her the choice to refuse coitus? If forced intercourse occurs, is it recognized as having happened or is it an unmarked event? And if it is recognized as having happened, at what level is the response? Is it handled at the level of interpersonal relations or at the level of community sanctions? That is, does the jural system recognize the right of a spouse to refuse to have coitus?

It is stated that a wife may refuse intercourse at any time, and her wishes will be accepted. It is expected that women will want to refrain from intercourse during their menstrual period, if they are sick, or after giving birth. However, a husband will get angry if he is frequently refused by his wife, and this will be the cause of disputes and divorce. Specifically, one informant stated that if a man's wife no longer wants intercourse, the man just gets up and leaves.

A man may also show no interest in intercourse. But if lack of interest in intercourse on the part of either spouse continues, it is suspected by the other that he or she is having an affair.

However, it is known that there are men who will *tabpa'an*, "hold on to", "grab hold of" their wives to induce intercourse, but this is a rare occurrence. It is important to note that *tabpa'an* is also used in jural cases where a woman is grabbed hold of by a man, a fineable offense, or is induced to have intercourse, again a finable offense. But in the case of a wife, there are no jural sanctions against such behavior. That is, a wife induced to have intercourse against her will, if it occurs, does not bring it up before the village moot. I say if it occurs, for we have no cases of intercourse in such instances being consummated. In time, one informant said, this kind of behavior would be a source of arguments between the man and his wife, and, if she hadn't already, she would return to her parents' household (*lumaping*). And she will stay there until the matter is resolved satisfactorily. And a husband to get her to come back would have to give a small piece of brassware to his father-in-law.

There was a case of this about 1972 in a neighboring village. Two weeks after his wife gave birth, the husband wanted to have intercourse. The term used in the narration of this case was *mongizut*, "to induce intercourse", "to get her to fuck", a term that may be substituted for *tabpa'an*. The usual waiting period is about three months, which is the time when the child begins to smile, or until the wife is no longer is sore. However, this husband tried to pressure his wife into it, so she left for her father's house. She wouldn't come back until her father made her husband promise not to try this again, and if he did, the father said he would bring about a divorce.

Is There Forced Coitus in Those Cases Where the Bride Does Not Accept Her Husband?

Under certain conditions a bride will engage in behavior that is termed *amu tumutun* and which I have referred to as "the reluctant bride" pattern of behavior. The bride may refuse to acknowledge her husband's existence in her family's longhouse apartment. She may refuse to feed him, sleep near him, or go to the fields with him alone. If the husband makes advances, she may hit at him with her arm brass. Not only does she refuse to have intercourse with him, she also refuses to engage in the usual domestic tasks of a housewife. In other words she in essence shuns him (see L. W. R. Appell in this volume for a fuller description of this behavior).

The explanations given for this are: the spouse selected by the bride's parents is not acceptable; the bride is "ashamed", "embarrassed" at publicly performing the role of wife, which implies coitus, before her parents and other members of the longhouse; she may be afraid of engaging in coitus, particularly if she is very young; and finally if she does not show a certain amount of reticence it would indicate that she lacked character and wanted to have intercourse. At these times, does her husband use force to engage in coitus?

This is a difficult question to get reliable data on. In some instances a husband who is shunned will finally divorce his wife. In rare instances, a husband will threaten or attempt suicide. Frequently, the relatives of the bride will engage in activities to bring about a marital union, to pressure the bride into accepting the sexual advances of her husband.[11] For instance, one bride during the daytime would sew up the bottom of her sleeping robe to prevent her husband from intercourse, while her sisters undid it when her back was turned.

From one informant we learned that even though she was engaging in coitus with her husband shortly after marriage, she nevertheless displayed *amu tumutun* behavior in front of her parents because she was "ashamed" of having her parents think she was engaging in sexual activities. In another instance, a woman who displayed this behavior for six months nevertheless had become pregnant.

So we have to deal with the unresolvable problem of disentangling public from private behavior.

Sometimes the shunned spouse will resort to love magic to bring about coitus with the reluctant spouse. However, there are no forms of magic, as there are among the Gusii of Africa (LeVine 1959:968), that a bride might use to hinder or bring about the failure of her husband's sexual competence.

It is not entirely clear in each case of rejection of the husband whether these behaviors of the bride represent deep-seated feelings or whether they are only a presentation of the social self to the longhouse community, a public display of how a proper young woman should feel about the possibility of sexual relations. Whatever the case, we have no evidence that a woman in any instance was forced to have intercourse. She was always able to refuse her husband's advances.

However, in one unusual, ambiguous case of a bride rejecting her husband, her husband complained that he had only been able to have coitus with his wife by deceit or cunning. When he would try otherwise, she would be angry with him. So he would wait till she was asleep. Then he would quickly pull up her skirt and have coitus. One wonders if this could have occurred without some acquiescence on the part of the bride. And in this particular case her shunning her husband may have been brought about more by his past behavior rather than any ambivalent feelings towards fulfilling the role of wife. Prior to initiating bride-price negotiations for her, he had been involved in a case of alleged fornication with another woman, and it was said that his wife was still angry about this. Also, she may have had a certain reluctance to get involved physically with him because of this. He would have been ritually "hot", if he actually had engaged in fornication. Only the public sacrifice of a pig could nullify the ritual consequences of his act. And if he were hot, this disability would have endangered the health of his wife and any children (see L. W. R. Appell in this volume for a discussion of the consequences of the ritual heat arising from illicit intercourse). Their marriage occurred in 1962, and the shunning of her husband went on for a couple of months. But by 1986 they had nine children.

It is important to note that if a husband mistreats his wife, causes bruises or hurts her, she has recourse to her father who will sue his son-in-law. A husband is not allowed to beat, hurt, or injure his wife.

Finally, the reluctant bride behavior only occurs with women on a first marriage. Remarriages as a result of being widowed or divorced do not involve any such behavior on the part of women.

TABPA'AN, MANGAGAI, AND *MONGIZUT*: FEMALE ATTITUDES ON THE POSSIBILITY OF INDUCED AND FORCED INTERCOURSE

We have pointed out that *tabpa'an* is used as a euphemism for inducing a woman to have intercourse, the only physical forcing being used is to constrain the woman until she agrees or refuses. The terms *mongizut* and *mangagai* I have translated respectively as "to get a woman to fuck" and "to make a woman", since the initial morpheme {*mV-*} in each case carries the sense of causing something to happen, to use something, to make something, which in these two cases is sexual relations. They cover the same semantic field except that the latter term is considered more acceptable, more proper. And the behavior indicated in all three lexemes covers the field from seduction to persuasive argument.

However, in the projective systems the use of these three terms sometimes also includes the application of physical force, which can include the tearing of a woman's blouse and causing her to thrash about in an effort to escape.

But in terms of actual behavior we have no jural cases involving this type of force. And there is much ambiguity in using these terms. For example, in eliciting the story about the water hole *Pinonguvakan*, a retired headman said this was a case of *mangagai*. The only case, he said. A few days later I asked him for other cases of *mangagai*, and he said that there were a lot of them. And he gave me an example of one that occurred during our original field session, which we knew was in fact *miagai*. *Miagai* indicates that both were engaged in "having an affair", and it was not the instigation only of the man. In this case a man and a married woman had mutually been involved in this and had carried on for some time before being caught.

Also in discussing the problem of forced intercourse I have statements from most of my male informants that this never happens among the Rungus. For example, an informant in discussing the death of a married woman who had been raped and killed on an oil palm plantation at some distance from the village of our research opined that she must have resisted the attack and so she had been killed. He furthermore thought it must have been a Filipino who had done it, as he said: "Our ethnic group does not kill; we only wait for the desire (on the part of the woman)." The same informant said that if a man puts his arms around a maiden (*mongogobu'*) when she is alone, and she says no to the advance, he will go away as he is afraid of having the case brought before the village moot and being fined. At another interview he said that if a woman was accosted and did not want to have coitus, she would pick up a stick or a bush knife and attack the man.

Another male informant in discussing physically forced intercourse by the various ethnic groups and races in the district stated that it was common in the various Islamic groups, but that it did not occur often among the Chinese, the Europeans, and the Japanese. As for the Rungus, he said they never did it. The woman can say that she does not agree to it, and the man will stop; this is the *adat* (customary law) of the Rungus.

Another informant said that if a woman is accosted and does not want the man's attentions, all that she has to do is call for help. But he added that if a woman was by herself and no one could hear if she screamed, she could be forced into intercourse.

Our discussion of forced intercourse deals with the period when Rungus culture was in full flower and before it had been eroded by modernization. By 1990 a married Rungus woman was actually raped in a nearby village by another Rungus. The explanation by the headman of our village for this event was that now houses are scattered, since people have moved out of the longhouse, and this makes the woman vulnerable. Also, which he did not add, is the fact that all the cultural controls of traditional Rungus life have been lost. But this points out the fact that in traditional society it was not only the cultural controls that inhibited rape but also the social organization militated against a woman being sexually attacked because of the lack of opportunity of a woman being found alone.

Male-Female Dominance

To return to the ethnographic present of our first period of field work, women are perceived as not being as strong as men. "How could a woman get away if a man held on to her, as he is bigger and stronger!", one man said. Women are also not perceived as being able to run as fast. They are not as brave as men. They are more afraid of the potentially evil spirits called *rogon* than are men. They are more afraid of headhunters. They won't go to the swiddens alone, nor wait to come back after dark when there are *rogon* about.

There are instances of a husband hitting his wife, referred to as *momobog*, "to hit with fist or a stick". If a wife complains to her relatives about this, there will be a moot. If the woman is beaten without cause, the husband will have to give a piece of brassware to her father, or her closest living relative. There are times when a female hits her husband. However, one headman stated that there would not be a village moot over this as she is not strong enough to hurt him, to make him sore or bruised. But later the same informant and other men said that there are cases of women hitting men, and this has led to her giving a piece of brassware to her husband's father.

This relationship of dominance is mirrored in the linguistic forms used to indicate sexual relations. The man takes the initiative; he is the actor. The woman is the recipient of the action.

Does *Mangagai* Ruin a Woman's Name?

If a maiden is induced to engage in intercourse (*mangagai*), or if it were to happen that a maiden was actually forced to have intercourse, this does not ruin her reputation. It does not lessen the amount of her bride-price, and her wedding ceremony is the same as if she were a virgin.

However, if a maiden has agreed to an assignation, then when she is married, the wedding ceremony held for her is abbreviated, comparable to that for previously married people. And she will not get the one special item in the bride-price, a piece of brassware, that is designated for her and given to her after the wedding. The other items in the bride-price, as usual, are used to make up bride-prices for her brothers or may be consumed by her natal family in hard times for buying rice.

Jural Rules for *Miagai* and *Mangagai*

If a maiden and a bachelor are caught in intercourse, whether or not it was the result of a previously arranged assignation, they are made to marry. If it were the result of an assignation, as I have discussed, the bride-price is smaller and the wedding abbreviated.

However, if a maiden is induced to have intercourse (*mangagai*) by a bachelor, the bride-price and the wedding ceremony are the same as if she were a virgin, except that the young man must give to the bride's father a small piece of brassware on top of the bride-price.

In both instances, the pig given for the marriage ceremony has to be larger than usual, and the spirit medium receives a higher payment for her work over the sacrificed pig because of the ritual heat that must be dissipated in the ceremony.

If the parents of the maiden, in the instance of *mangagai*, do not accept the young man, he must pay a fine of a gong to them. However, we were not able to obtain any cases of this.

If the individuals engaged in illicit intercourse have spouses, in addition to providing a larger pig for sacrifice to dissipate the ritual heat, ritual payments must be made to their spouses as well as compensation in the form of a piece of brassware.

The fine for forcing a married woman to have intercourse is two gongs. However, again there are no cases of this that I could elicit. It was the opinion of the headman that, nevertheless, there must have been cases of forced intercourse in the past, or there would not be the knowledge of the appropriate fine.

If a married man only accosts a woman (*tabpa'an*), he must also give a piece of brassware to his father-in-law in addition to the compensation he has to pay the woman's husband or the maiden's father.

Female Accounts of and Attitudes Toward Forced Intercourse

None of our female informants knew of a case of forced intercourse. A woman can always refuse, it was maintained, and a man would always obey the woman's wishes. It is not possible for a man to force a woman to do anything she does not want to, it was stated. However, it is the "behavior", the "make up" (*buatan*) of men to want to try to get women to engage in intercourse. Furthermore, if forced intercourse were attempted, the woman would scream, and the man would be ashamed, would be afraid of suffering a fine, and would stop, it is stated.

In marriage, if a man wants intercourse, and his wife doesn't, he would not force it, unless he did not have bahazan. Bahazan can be translated as "character", "honor", "integrity". One could never say that a man forces intercourse after the married couple have become *miobas*, "accustomed to each other". One informant said that women never tell their husbands that they don't want to have coitus, unless they are sick or menstruating. Women always want children, and they know that coitus makes children.

Evidence of Induced Intercourse

After eliciting the story given previously of the headman needing evidence from women who alleged that they were accosted, I asked one middle-aged woman what could be used as evidence of *mangagai*, induced intercourse. She replied but used the term *miagai*, which indicates that both were equally involved rather than the term *mangagai*, which marks that it was the action only of the man. She listed the following types of evidence: a headcloth, a shirt, and the wide belt worn by men. Also a woman can mark a man on his back with the lime used in betel chewing.

With women denying that forced intercourse can happen, and maintaining that if they say no their wishes will be respected, it is somewhat contradictory that some women know of ways to identify men who attempt forced intercourse or succeed in such. There are, of course, several sources and interpretations for this. Woman may have learned of these methods from the cautionary tales that are narrated. These techniques for identifying any man forcing intercourse may themselves be informal sanctions to prevent this, since the man can be identified. And the discussion of these techniques may also represent a projection of their unvoiced fears of having to submit.

POPULATION BASE AND PREVALENCE

When discussing behavioral phenomena such as forcible sexual relations, fornication, adultery, and homosexuality, it is critical to have some evidence on the size of the population base and the prevalence and incidence of such behavior in order to reach a sound judgement on the claims presented.

The time period we are primarily dealing with is that of our original field work, 1959-60, 1961-63. The Rungus are found on two peninsulas in the Kudat District of Sabah: the Kudat Peninsula and the Melabong Peninsula. As we were not able to visit the Rungus villages on the Melabong Peninsula at that time, we have excluded these from our analysis. They represent roughly 21% of the total Rungus population.

To determine the number of Rungus on the Kudat Peninsula we multiplied the number of men on the head tax rolls by a multiplier derived from our own sociological census of several villages. This produced a population of

4,545 Rungus in villages of pure Rungus ethnic identity and 4,063 in mixed villages.

The mixed villages lie on the boundaries of the Rungus territory and include members of the Nulu and Gonsomon ethnic groups who have moved in or married in. We do not know how many individuals in these mixed villages were at that time Rungus in their ethnic identity or belonged to these other two Dusunic groups. While the Gonsomon and Nulu have a distinct ethnic identity, their isoglots are completely mutually intelligible with each other and with the Rungus isoglot.[12] Even so the accents of both Nulu and Gonsomon speakers are sufficiently different so that one can identify the ethnic group of an individual by his speech. Their customary laws, however, are almost identical with the customary law of the Rungus. Furthermore, Gonsomon and Nulu individuals identify themselves to outsiders as being Rungus. As a result, we feel confident that the results of our inquiries on the jural system and behavior from the headmen and other knowledgeable people in our village also applies to the mixed villages as well. This is substantiated by the fact my informants would also refer to cases that had occurred in these mixed villages. We are dealing with a small area in which gossip and news is readily exchanged, and members of our village had kin in many of the mixed villages. The Kudat Peninsula is roughly 32 miles long and has a width varying from 11 to 16 miles. The Rungus from both fully Rungus and mixed villages also met at the two weekly markets.

Therefore, we conclude that our data refers to a population base of approximately 8,500 individuals.

However, it is impossible to develop any prevalence or incidence rates of illicit sexual behaviors. These behaviors appear in village moots only when jural actions are taken. They are not recorded by the government. They form an oral corpus, which we drew upon and found no cases of forced intercourse. But this does not mean that the lack of cases of sexual aggression is because of the small size of the population involved. For we are dealing here with an accumulated cultural memory of events and jural caes, which at a minimum includes 50 to 75 years of group experience.

EXPLANATIONS FOR THE INDIVIDUATION OF
THE DRIVES OF SEX AND AGGRESSION

In the context of inquiries such as this anthropologists tend to use two major modes of explaining behavior. Behavior is the result of child-rearing patterns, or it is explained as the project of sociocultural models for and of behavior and their sanctions.[13]

The Repression, Inhibition, and Channeling of The Sexual Drive

Sociocultural Sanctions. In Rungus society the sexual drive is channelled into marriage. Its expression other than in marriage is highly prohibited by a number of sanctions both formal and informal. When cases of illicit intercourse are discovered, a village moot is held to determine who is the guilty party or parties and how to resolve the issue. This may take several meetings, and extended discussions are held concerning the degree of responsibility, when to put the two to marriage if they are unmarried, or the amount of compensation that must be paid to aggrieved spouses, the size of the pig that must be sacrificed to nullify the ritual heat, and what ritual payments must be given to the headman, witnesses, and the spirit medium who performs the ceremony to nullify the ritual jeopardy. Thus, illicit intercourse brings into play a wide variety of sanctions and involves the whole community in the resolution of this.

While fornication and adultery do occur, it is our impression that these behaviors are not a frequent feature of Rungus society. But when they do occur, they are subject to intense scrutiny and interest by the community. However, it is impossible to determine their prevalence since not all instances become public knowledge.

Thus, to channel the sexual behavior of the individual into the institution of marriage, a child as he or she matures is subjected to a number of sociocultural conditionings, models for and of behavior, and the possibility of jural sanctions that direct his behavior to this end. Women are subjected to a stricter code of behavior than men in expressing publicly any interest in sex or awareness of it. And it is difficult to judge to what degree the sexual drive of women, and perhaps men, is subject to repression or is only inhibited from expression prior to marriage as a result of these sociocultural sanctions. We will return to this issue shortly.

Location of Sexual Intercourse. The locations where sexual intercourse may take place further elucidate the nature of the relationship between males and females.

Sexual relations normally take place quietly at night in the sleeping area of the longhouse compartment after the children are asleep. If the children wake up, the parents stop intercourse as it would put the children in ritual jeopardy if they observed it. Coitus also takes place in the couple's field house during the day. At no time did we ever see or hear coitus taking place. A wife will sleep between her husband and their children.

Illicit sexual relations, when they occur, take place in the forest during the day, as women do not go out from the longhouse at night. A child born out of wedlock is called a *lapau* and is also referred to as having been conceived in the forest. Seldom if ever is a child born out of wedlock, however, as an unmarried couple are put to marriage immediately when discovered. No *lapau* appeared in any of our several censuses (see G. N. Appell 1969). No social stigma or disability is associated with being a *lapau*. The fault lies with the mother and father and does not accrue to the offspring.

Separation of Unmarried Females From Young Men. A young girl refrains from being seen alone in the company of a male even before she begins to wear a sarong to cover her breasts. This starts a year or so before she becomes pubescent. Girls even before this age move about in a group of several girls or with their families (see L. W. R. Appell in this volume). Maidens group in this fashion for several reasons.

First, they are afraid of being caught or constrained by men (*tabpa'an*), and propositioned or induced into intercourse. Second, they are afraid of the jungle, particularly the primary forest, because of it being inhabited by potentially malevolent spirits. They are also concerned that if they go about by themselves they will be gossiped about as encouraging sexual attentions from men or engaging in illicit sexual relations (*miagai*). A maiden who does this is scolded by her parents as they are afraid that she might meet up with a man bent on no good or that she will become loose. Women going alone are also afraid of the possibility of meeting up with headhunters, although there has been no case of this since the early days of British administration in the early 1900s when it is alleged some of the North Borneo Company native police force did engage in this.

Married women are expected to behave in a similar fashion as maidens for the same reasons.

<u>Relations between Married Persons and Others</u>. It is believed unseemly for a married woman to spend too much time in the longhouse away from her apartment, to go for any length of time into the forest alone, or go to the fields alone. It is because women might be accused of engaging in illicit sexual relations or soliciting attentions, which would arouse their husbands' sexual jealousies (*mongivoguw*). A husband who also spends too much time visiting another longhouse apartment may likely arouse jealousy in his wife and will be accused of philandering.

<u>Are There Child-Rearing Behaviors to Ensure the Segregation of the Drives of Sex and Aggression?</u> Can we explain the lack of Rungus sexual aggression by the patterns of child rearing? Children are wanted and cared for. They are nursed for four to six years if there is no subsequent sibling. And they are closely held in sarongs to the mother's or father's body while the parent goes on with his or her daily tasks. Children are frequently carried in these sarongs even while they are asleep but particularly when they are fussing and the parent is trying to put them to sleep. This goes on until they are two and a half to three years old and want to run about the longhouse. But even older children, if sick, are put in carrying sarongs to comfort them.

Toilet training is not focused on. Mothers generally ignore urinating babies, with the exception of rinsing themselves off, and respond to a defecating child by opening up a floor board and sitting him over it. Children are never admonished or scolded in this, nor are they specifically toilet trained.

The only behaviors that might be significant in segregating the drives of sex and aggression, other than the overall patterns of expected social behavior, are the prolonged physical contact between parent and child and the permissive toilet training. However, we have no evidence that these facilitate the individuation of these drives. Nor do we have any hypotheses as to how these behaviors might account for this.

Looking at the problem from another perspective, are there any child-rearing behaviors that specifically focus on the problem of keeping the drives of sex and aggression segregated? Is it perceived that the drives of sex and aggression are being commingled as they emerge in the development of Rungus children and young adults so that specific child-training methods have to be undertaken to segregate these? We saw no evidence of the drives of sex and aggression being commingled nor any concern on the part of Rungus parents to ensure that these drives were segregated.

<u>Are There Any Child-Rearing Behaviors That Might Foster the Conjunction of Sex and Aggression</u>? Are there any stages in the development of a child that are handled in such a manner that male aggression toward females or female aggression towards males are fostered which later on have to be individuated?

Parents may at times play affectionately with their children's genitalia while they are still toddlers rubbing them, kissing them, mouthing them, and shaking them. Occasionally older siblings do this to their younger siblings. Sometimes young boys have their genitalia tweaked by a male or female sibling, although by the time they are four or five they get rather irritated by this attention. Thus, during the early stages of child-rearing genitalia are not given an emotional loading of being potentially dangerous.

However, the genitalia become a source of shame later on. The terms for genitalia are relevant here. *Toli* refers to the penis; *turoi* refers to female genitalia. But there is a general term to refer to both male and female genitalia, *kikuman*. The root of this word is *ikum*, which means to be ashamed, so that *kikuman* literally means "that which can be shameful".

The only point in child rearing where a major crisis arises that has relevance for the question of developing male aggression toward females is when another child is born. At that point, the elder child is taken from the breast and given to the father to care for. Then for a period of several weeks the child may cry for his mother's attention and breast, and may exhibit temper tantrums when she or he is unsuccessful. While this is a major rejection, we found no evidence of any specific consequences from it in later life in the relations of men with women.

L. W. R. Appell (personal communication) argues that the social life of the longhouse may account for the apparent lack of a significant psychological insult from this deprivation. A longhouse is composed of many closely interrelated families who are in continual interaction. And the children are constantly playing together and participating in the activities of these other families. Thus, a young infant deprived of the breast and maternal care as the result of the birth of a subsequent sibling sees other children treated the same way, all through his or her life; and he or she also has other care-givers to turn to for solace. It thus becomes a fact of social life and not the psychological insult that might occur if this were experienced by a child in an isolated nuclear family.

Discontinuity in Sociocultural Conditioning.[14] In addition to the discontinuity that occurs at weaning, there is another discontinuity in the developing personhood of a woman that occurs at marriage. She is expected to reverse her previous behavior of disinterest in sexual matters and now engage in sexual relations.

Prior to marriage, she is to express no interest in or knowledge of sexual matters, although in reality this is hard to achieve in a small longhouse community where marital relations are going on around her, where breeding dogs run in and out of the longhouse, and where success in pig and chicken raising, in which young females are closely involved, lies in the fecundity of sows and hens and the sexual arousal of boars and cocks. Whatever the extent of her knowledge, her public persona must be that of propriety itself prior to marriage. But immediately after marriage she is supposed to engage in close and intimate relations with a man, in which she has had no practice at any level. Since childhood she has been expected to avoid any close contact with males, except when groups of boys and girls go weeding together, sit around the longhouse and gossip, or help out in preparing and serving food and drink during religious occasions. Furthermore, Rungus etiquette demands that a married woman in public continue to behave circumspectly after marriage and not engage in public discussions of sex, joke about it, or display any behavior to encourage sexual advances. If men are discussing sexual matters or joking about them, women ignore the conversation, pretending not to hear what is being said. Instead they continue to pursue their own conversations and activities.

Marriage is also a period of discontinuity for men. And a few will refuse to engage in sexual relations with their wives for a time. But it is more usual for the bride to express that she is not attracted to, does not accept or desire her spouse (*amu tumutun*; see L. W. R. Appell in this volume). Does this behavior represent a major psychological cost of the discontinuity in cultural conditioning? Some repression must surely be at work in the cases of those brides who refuse their husbands' sexual advances. But it is difficult to separate those situations where the problem represents repression of the sexual drive from those where it is only a public display of what a young bride is supposed to do, or from those where the bride genuinely dislikes her husband and is intent in her shunning of him to obtain a divorce.

For most women we judged the repression of the sexual drive not to be severe. Their behavior is primarily the product of the inhibition of public displays of sexual interest, which is rewarded by positive sanctions for proper behavior and shaped by the threat of major, community-wide negative sanctions for illicit behavior. An indication of the validity of this conclusion is the ease with which sexual topics arise in the language of even young, unmarried Rungus females when startled (see A. A. Doolittle in this volume on latah among the Rungus). Furthermore, we never heard any complaints from wives over too many demands for coitus from their husbands.[15] And we were rarely asked about medicine to prevent conception. When we were, it was by women who had six, seven, or eight children.

However, the question of psychogenetic dyspareunia and infertility is raised by the enculturation of the female, the expected behavior of the bride at the wedding in which she is to show no interest in any of the proceedings, the lack of instruction for the bride on sexual matters prior to marriage, and the resultant discontinuity in cultural conditioning that occurs when the bride is supposed to respond to sexual advances. We have no evidence of dyspareunia, which may not be significant due to the inhibition on talking about sexual matters. Nevertheless, we never heard any complaints from men about female frigidity. This concept just did not appear in their lexicon.

Moreover, in a sample of 57 females 77.2% produced children prior to or within the second year of marriage, and a further 12% had produced children within the third year of their marriage. These numbers are high, considering the fact that not all women have begun to menstruate at the time of marriage. And they indicate that inhibitions with respect to coitus are not deeply seated and that there appears to be an absence of psychogenic infertility or even dyspareunia as a result of the cultural imperatives with regard to fornication, adultery, and public displays of sexual interest.

Moreover, children are wanted and appreciated. Abortion does not occur. There is no term for it, nor does the concept arise in any discussion of pregnancies. And husbands and wives closely depend on each other for support and affection. In fact, sexual jealousy is very prevalent and is a major feature of the relations between men and women. Both sexes frequently display emotions of jealousy, and accusations of infidelity arising from ungrounded suspicions or even just from the fear of infidelity are common. Brides are known to engage in these even during the period when they are publicly rejecting their husbands and refusing to accept the role of wife.

Inhibition of Aggression

Aggression, even the symbolic expression of aggression, is highly inhibited by various jural and supernatural sanctions which support each other. First there is the concept of *komomoli*. *Komomoli* is a ritual delict that occurs when the action of an individual implies that someone has died. For example, a corpse can not be removed for burial by way of the entry ladders at either end of the longhouse, as it takes the corpse past other apartments implicating them in a death. It can only be removed from its apartment out the side of the working area where a special opening is made. Thus, if an individual on leaving the longhouse exits through this working area in the front of an apartment rather than by the end ladders, this is similar to the removal of a corpse, and it is *komomoli* to the members of that apartment. If a spouse starts repairing that side of the apartment or the roofing over it while his spouse is asleep, this suggests that she is dead and is considered *komomoli*. If a spouse gets up and leaves while the other is still sleeping without waking him or her, this is an implication of death, and causes *komomoli*.

Thus, there are various ritual acts and statements that occur only when someone has died, and for a widowed spouse these are highly elaborate. And if an individual engages in any of these ritual acts when there has been no death, the offender must give a chicken to the members of the domestic family that has been implicated. This is so they can kill the chicken and put blood on their ankles along with the proper prayers to remove the threat of an actual death occurring.

Thus, there is the possibility of expressing aggression to one's spouse by engaging in any of these various acts and thereby implying she or he is dead. And if this is done in anger and intentionally, it is viewed as a very serious delict, and ritual compensation must be paid.

Kotiguras (a form of *moniguras*--see Table Two) involves an act of cutting the personal possessions of an individual or those of a domestic family. It can be roughly translated as "has been threatened". If an individual finds his clothes cut, if fences of the family's swiddens are cut by someone else, particularly in anger, then the offender must give a chicken to blood the family. If this is not done, the action of using a bush knife on the property of another is considered a threat to the soul of the owner or owners so that they will fall ill. If there is no way to identify the offender, the family or the individual threatened will take one of the family's chickens for the ritual cleansing.

Thus, there is an extensive cultural pattern of inhibiting any acts of aggression. Acts of *kotiguras* and *komomoli* seldom occur both because of the fine and the ritual implications.

In addition to the inhibition of expressing aggression to another Rungus, there is an extensive cultural pattern of inhibiting illegal sexual acts. Sex and aggression are highly segregated in Rungus society, as we have also shown in linguistic behavior. The behaviors of sex and aggression do not appear in the same environment. And when there is the possibility that they might come together, there are jural sanctions to inhibit such behavior. For example, where the concepts of sex and aggression do begin to conflate as in the mentioning of genitalia to give insult or to express anger toward someone, the offended individual may sue the offender for a piece of brassware (see above). Finally, there is an attitude towards women whereby they are highly respected, which results in their volition in matters of sex remaining unimpaired.

SEXUAL ASSAULT: CULTURALLY CONSTRUCTED OR BIOLOGICALLY DRIVEN?

Is sexual aggression primarily the product of sociocultural factors? Sanday (1981, 1986) takes this position. She divides societies into what she terms rape-free and rape-prone societies, and she lists the sociocultural characteristics she maintains accompany each type.

However, a number of scholars have taken the position that sexual aggression is largely biologically determined (see Thornhill, *et al.* 1986 and Eibl-Eibesfeldt 1989; see Palmer 1989 and Sanday 1981 for a review of this literature).

Parker (1976) in reviewing a variety of evidence concludes that there is a close functional association of the sexual and agonistic responses. Some of the evidence comes from experimental psychology where the subjects show increased aggressive arousal when their sexual arousal is heightened experimentally and vice versa. But these were American subjects who were culturally conditioned to link sex and aggression, as demonstrated by the prevalence of rape behavior in American society and the use of sexual metaphors in abusive language (see G. N. Appell 1987). Would the same results have occurred in those societies where the drives of sex and aggression are socioculturally highly individuated?

Parker also brings in evidence from research on the brain to show that the loci for sexual arousal and aggressive arousal are closely interconnected. However, Restak (1984:142) concludes that aggression is not a unitary entity with a concrete existence. Instead, "the brain is like a mosaic in which only the complete aggregate of seemingly unrelated parts suggest the whole picture" of drives such as aggression (1984:133).

Furthermore, as the brain has some plasticity in its organization, and as the final wiring of it occurs after birth as a result of early experience (see Aoki and Siekevitz 1988; Annis and Frost 1973), the close wiring of sexual and aggressive arousals claimed by Parker may in some way be a cultural artifact.

However, if those who claim that sexual aggression has a strong biological component are correct, then we would expect some cost for the redirection of this biological impulse in Rungus society, some evidence in the biosocial energetics of the cultural control of these biological factors (see Appell 1984, 1986). Yet there is little evidence of psychological, physiological, or behavioral impairments as a result. There is the fear and anxiety over the consequences of illicit sexual intercourse. It is believed illicit intercourse can cause illness and death of children, the loss of crops, loss of fecundity of domestic animals, and the withering of swiddens. And these consequences are believed to touch everyone, not just those who have been engaged in illicit intercourse. So Rungus individuals have to cope with the anxiety over the proper behavior of their village mates, and even those in neighboring villages. And this anxiety may produce dreams in which sexual intercourse can indicate that one's soul is in jeopardy from malevolent spirits, and illness may follow. However, the anxiety created can be relieved by the sacrifice of a pig or chicken, which also provides a source of protein unusual in the regular diet.

There is also the cost from the discontinuity in cultural conditioning of young men and women in that some are anxious over performing the role of spouse and reject for a brief time their spouses' sexual attentions. But this does not appear to be a significant psychosocial cost, as for those who experience it the anxiety quickly dissipates into the typically close, mutually dependent relations with their spouses.

Furthermore, all societies regulate sexual relations. But if there are strong biological roots to sexual aggression, those societies that do not inhibit illicit sexual intercourse to the degree the Rungus do must experience other costs. There is the cost of the fear of sexual aggression; the cost of the fear of rape. And there are the psychic and physical costs to the victims of sexual aggression.

The inhibition of aggression in Rungus society does have the consequence of producing an intropunitive modal personality (see Appell 1966). And this is manifested in threats of suicide when an individual finds himself frustrated in achieving his goals or believes that he or she has not been given sufficient consideration or respect. And actual suicides do occur. But the prevalence of the threats and actual suicides do not appear any greater than the fighting, assaults, and murders that accompany an extropunitive modal personality.

Thus, up to this point I have been unable to discover any significant costs to Rungus society from the individuation of the drives of sex and aggression. This suggests that claims for the biological basis of rape need to be reassessed.

However, this does not eliminate the possibility of any biological component to sexual assault. Rungus males do phantasize about this, do talk about it, do have examples of it in their projective systems. The fact that there are few if any behavioral manifestations of sexual assault and that, furthermore, there are few if any biosocial costs of redirecting this impulse suggests that if there is a biological component in sexual aggression, it is a weak one, the control of which requires little investment.

SOCIOCULTURAL EXPLANATIONS FOR SEXUAL ASSAULT

Sanday (1986) has argued that societies which are rape free have certain sociocultural characteristics. In such societies women are respected and are influential members of the community, and the relationship between the sexes is characterized by equality and complementarity. The evidence presented by L. W. R. Appell in this volume and the analysis here tend to support these hypotheses.[16]

Sanday (1986:85) goes on to argue that rape is a form of silencing or concealing male vulnerability and maternal dependency. Rape is part of a sociocultural script in which the expression of personhood for males is directed by interpersonal violence and an ideology of toughness. Thus, she writes (1986:90):

> The various cultural transformations of the theme of male vulnerability and fear of the feminine so far discussed suggest that a logical question to ask of both rape-prone and rape-free societies concerns the cultural mechanisms for resolving male vulnerability and alleviating what may be a generically human potentiality for fearing entrapment by the maternal.

Let us examine Rungus male behavior in the light of these propositions. The personhood of the Rungus male is not constructed on the capacity for interpersonal violence and an ideology of toughness. Headhunting was never a major part of Rungus society. And raiding for property ceased even before the arrival of the British in the late 1880s. The personhood of the Rungus male is constructed on the skills of farming, trading property, and oral argument at the village moots.[17]

Furthermore, we have not been able to find any evidence to suggest that Rungus males are threatened in any noticeable degree by vulnerability and attributes of the feminine, nor is there any evidence to indicate that they have a fear of maternal dependency. Rungus men are deeply involved in child rearing and the family. It is also believed that to "make" a child intercourse must progress for up to five months before the child is "completed". So they participate more intimately in the act of maternity than in many other societies. Furthermore, at birth the husband receives the child and cuts its umbilical cord. The issue of male personhood being threatened by participating in female activities does not exist.

How do the Rungus resolve the conflict over male toughness and female vulnerability and maternal dependency? They don't. It is not an issue, it is not a cultural construct, as far as we have been able to ascertain.

SUMMARY

The female role and the male role in Rungus society are considered equivalent, of equal value, symmetrical (see L. W. R. Appell in this volume). Men are considered more dominant in political affairs, trading, and village moots, and women more dominant in the knowledge of rituals for health and fertility. Men are considered to be physically more dominant than women, and women are considered to be less brave. The value of the female role is represented in the bride-price that must be paid. And she is protected by this from mistreatment by her husband as all of it or the major part of it will have to be returned if a wife leaves her husband before the birth of children. None is returned, however, if she has children.

The male role is to initiate relations that lead to marriage. And the role of the female in Rungus society is that publicly she is to exhibit no knowledge of sexual matters before marriage, no matter what her private knowledge may be, and that after marriage she must continue to be publicly uninterested in sexual matters. But private knowledge may be intimated by the behavior of females who exhibit latah behavior (see A. A. Doolittle in this volume). And there are ways by which a maiden can encourage attention. Women are expected to be sexually attractive so that maidens do put considerable effort into making themselves attractive. And it is expected of men to try to make advances to women.

Sexual intercourse between individuals unmarried to each other is highly prohibited, and this prohibition is supported by major ritual sanctions. Violation can put the whole community into danger and require both ritual fines and significant material compensation. Furthermore, the structure of community relations and the behavior of females inhibits such illicit intercourse. But it does occur, and if the couple are unmarried they are put to marriage immediately.

Natural sex is not marked linguistically. But morphemes implying that the subject of the verb is taking action when affixed to roots referring to sexual intercourse are inappropriate to use with reference to female behavior. This mirrors the cultural imperatives that the female publicly does not put herself forward in matters of sexual relations. Linguistically, there is also little evidence of sexual aggression. Terms are not used that link sex and aggression or aggression and sex.

There is also no term that specifically refers to forced coitus in which violence is used. The term that is used in such situations is the same term that is used to refer to attempts at seduction or to indicate that verbal pressure was applied to persuade a woman into coitus.

This does not mean that the concept of violence in sexual intercourse does not exist. But it is primarily in the phantasies of men and in projective systems of men. And while men may have such phantasies and stories of rape, both men and women agree that if a woman refuses a proposition of intercourse her wishes will be respected. Woman, however, try to avoid situations where they might be propositioned by a man, and are concerned that they might be accosted by a man.

Women in general exhibit little knowledge of forced intercourse or stories about this. However, there is the knowledge of what compensation is expected if there were a case of intercourse being forced without the woman's permission. And women know of ways to secure evidence that they have been taken advantage of. But there were no actual jural cases of this.

In the domain of social behavior, some of the illicit acts such as touching a woman's breast, holding on to her (*tabpa'an*), grabbing a woman's genitalia, do exhibit a certain amount of aggression, particularly the latter. These are rare events. And there is little evidence of sexual antagonism or aggression between men and women either behaviorally, linguistically, or in the projective systems.

There is the story of forced intercourse at the water hole in which the woman was either killed or had her hips dislocated. If this represents a true historical account and not a legend, it is the only instance of violence in coitus we have been able to collect.

There is also the story of a woman acceding to intercourse in order to get evidence, by means of the man's headcloth, that he had been accosting women. Again it is not clear if this is an actual case or not. These stories may be cautionary tales only.

The one actual case we have is of a man accosting women when they went to the water hole, catching hold of them to talk them into intercourse. In this his intentions were eventually thwarted by a strong maiden who carried him back to the longhouse. Thus, as in the previous story, men were caught and fined. And in both these stories there is no evidence that force was used to obtain coitus.

There are also instances in the projective system of animal behavior in which the orang-utan is reputed to sexually attack women. But then there is the myth of the female orang-utan who threatens to drop a man out of her tree until he agrees to coitus.

It is reported that husbands may try to force intercourse with their wives. But the wife can always return to the household of her parents or other male relative. And there is no evidence that violence is associated with such coitus.

In sum, women recognize the superior physical power of men. But they do not perceive that their volition in matters of sexual intercourse is ever taken away from them by force. Thus, it would appear that the drives of sex and aggression are highly individuated in Rungus society.

CONCLUSIONS: QUESTIONS OF INTERACTIONISM AND BIOSOCIAL ENERGETICS

The Rungus individuate the drives of sex and aggression to such a degree that any interlinkage is minimal. As a result sexual aggression, including rape, does not occur behaviorally.

In the analysis of this I have addressed the problem of how sociocultural factors have shaped biological drives. There is another side to this interactionism that I briefly touched on earlier.[18] Has this shaping had in turn any attendant biological consequences? I will now return to this problem with the caution that the contrasting concepts of environment and hereditary or culture and biology are not natural categories but are constructed ones that may only partially map the reality that we are attempting to discover.

In analyzing the biological consequences of sociocultural behavior two distinctions have to be made. There is the interactionism in which the environment has a critical influence on developmental processes during sensitive phases. This may result in the developmental sequence being interrupted; or being facilitated so that development proceeds onto the next phase; or being transformed so that a new sequence of development follows. I shall refer to this as developmental interactionism.

There is also the interactionism in which all sociocultural processes require the expenditure of physical and psychological energy. This I have termed "biosocial energetics" (G. N. Appell 1984). A human population uses its sociocultural system as a means of adaptation to its environment. Physical and psychological energies are expended in responding to the energetic requirements that arise from adaptation demands. And these responses are molded by each sociocultural system, so that the expenditure of energies is channeled through its own unique organization. But the very organization of the sociocultural system also has its own built-in requirements for energy expenditure to maintain it, and these also have adaptational consequences. A measure of the effectiveness of any sociocultural system in meeting both these external and internal demands for adaptation is the degree to which health impairments or enhancements result, as these are in part the product of the overload or the efficient management of adaptation demands (see G. N. Appell 1984, 1986).[19]

To return to the problems posed by the Rungus data, does the segregation of the drives of sex and aggression have any explanation in terms of developmental interactionism? Are there any child-rearing behaviors that might interact with a particularly sensitive period for the individuation of these drives and thus facilitate this individuation? There is not enough evidence as yet to determine if there exists such a sensitive period in child development. And as we have noted, there appear to be no major child-rearing techniques that have relevance here, unless it is the permissive toilet training, which is not particularly unique, the process of weaning that occurs with the arrival of a subsequent sibling in which the father substitutes as the primary care-giver for this period, or the long-term physical contact between child and parent that arises from regularly carrying the child in a sarong close to the parent's body during the child's first two to four years. I am speculating here to stimulate research.

I have also examined the biosocial energetics of this drive differentiation to determine what consequences there might be to various behavioral domains and the biology of the population. That is, what are the biosocial costs of this segregation of drives? And can we measure the demands for adaptation that this requires? To further this inquiry and deal with the issue of the biological roots for sexual aggression, I made the distinction between strong and weak biological factors. This distinction is analytically a blunt instrument. But it permits us to pose certain questions. We would expect that the sociocultural modification of behavior with a strong biological component would involve greater psychological, social, and physical costs. That is, there would be greater demands for adaptation requiring greater biosocial energies to be expended. And the greater the modification, the greater the costs. These costs of adaptation by the society can again be measured by the level of health impairments, psychological, physical, and behavioral.

On the other hand, we would expect that the sociocultural shaping of behavior which has a weak biological component would not involve the same level of energetic costs, and these may not even be significant enough to measure.

Thus, if there are strong biological roots for the interlinkage of sex and aggression, as many have argued, there should be some biosocial energetic costs to the Rungus population as a result of the separation of these drives, some distinctive level of impairment. But we have not yet discovered any. Biologically, the Rungus population does not express any obvious stresses from the energetics involved in segregating these drives either in reproductive capacity or in other physical, behavioral, or psychological impairments. Nor do the cultural projective systems indicate that there are any significant costs in the development of defensive mechanisms as a result of this. This lends considerable substance to the claim that sexual aggression is primarily a product of sociocultural factors. But our conclusions may be an artifact of our ethnographic methods, and further field investigation of this issue would be welcome.

Thus, the only explanation that we have been able to advance to date for ensuring this segregation of the drives of sex and aggression is the overall pattern of jural sanctions, rules of etiquette, and the background belief system. That is, models for and of behavior. Obviously, child rearing must play a large part in this, but we have found nothing particularly distinctive in Rungus child rearing to indicate what this might be.

These conclusions thus suggest several things. First, the enculturative costs of ensuring the segregation of the drives of sex and aggression may not be high. And the biosocial costs of maintaining the segregation of these drives may also not be high. On the other hand, the enculturative costs in creating the interlinkage of the drives of sex and aggression may be high, and certainly the biosocial costs from the consequences of this interlinkage appear to be high in other societies.

To get a better grasp on these problems we need detailed studies of child rearing among the Rungus and other societies of Borneo. For there are other

Bornean societies, such as the Iban (see Sutlive in the Introduction), in which rape appears to be unknown but which vary significantly in terms of the expression of the aggressive drive. And there are societies with a different cultural ecology, such as the foraging Penan, who also exhibit no sexual aggression (Peter Brosius, personal communication). Thus, research on the societies of Borneo offers a unique opportunity to cleanse many of the anthropological generalizations about society and human nature that are culturally contaminated from the presuppositions of our own cultural system and from cross-cultural research that is not yet truly cross-cultural.

ACKNOWLEDGEMENTS

Our original field work among the Rungus in 1959-60 and 1961-63 was conducted under the auspices of the Department of Anthropology and Sociology, Research School of Pacific Studies, the Australian National University. I would like to express my thanks to the Australian National University for support of this research and the preliminary analysis of my data. I owe a very special debt of gratitude to my supervisor and friend, Professor Derek Freeman, who guided my field research. It is difficult to fully express my appreciation to my wife, Laura W. R. Appell, who has always participated fully in my research and the analysis and writing up of our data. Religion among the Rungus, with the exception of certain agricultural ceremonies, lies in the hands of Rungus females. Without Laura's help it would have been impossible to gather data in this realm, for which she was primarily responsible. Nor would it have been possible without her help to collect data on the female view towards sex and marriage, as these subjects are not accessible to a male researcher. I also want to express my thanks to the National Science Foundation and the ACLS-SSRC, which have supported portions of the analysis and the writing up of my field data and further research; and in particular the Halcyon Fund which has been very generous in its support of my research over the years. I would like to express my gratitude to the Wenner-Gren Foundation for their grant in 1989 to support our recent collection of the oral literature, its translation, and the revision of our Rungus dictionary.

I want to thank Cornelia Ann Kammerer and Clifford Sather for very helpful criticisms of the original version of this manuscript. I particularly want to express my appreciation to Benson Saler for his very fruitful and insightful comments on previous versions of this paper, which have been extraordinarily useful. And to Vinson H. Sutlive, Jr., I owe a deep debt of gratitude for his encouragement and support for the writing of this article.

NOTES

1. When I use the plural personal pronoun "we", I am referring to observations made and data collected by both my wife and myself.

2. Among the Iban sexual intercourse is conceptualized as armed combat, the penis as a "sword", and ejaculation as the loosening of a spear or the firing of a gun (Sather 1978:343).

3. Glottal stops are rendered by an apostrophe.

4. We did not discover this form of sexual aggression until field work in 1990 when we collected our first case.

5. There is no term for rape in the dictionary by a missionary (Forschner 1978) that is labeled as Rungus. However, it in fact contains lexemes from the neighboring Nulu isoglot (see footnote 12 for a definition of isoglot). This is a rather short dictionary and contains many errors. There is a dictionary of Kadazan, another isoglot of the Dusunic language group (Antonissen 1958). Kadazan is spoken in Penampang about 71 miles on a direct line south of the Rungus. Kadazan and Rungus are not mutually intelligible. This dictionary was made by a missionary with long experience in the country. There is no term for rape in it. The lexeme *manabpo'* appears, which is cognate with the Rungus *manabpo'*. It is translated as "to catch, to grab, to grasp, to snatch, to lay hold of". There is no indication of any implication of rape in this word.

6. Flynn in a cross-cultural study of insult behavior found that in every culture examined "direct or indirect references to genitals were a common, often the most common, content of insulting remarks or gestures" (1976:3).

7. I am indebted to Donald E. Brown for his useful comments on my research and in particular suggesting the importance of inquiring into the nature of love sickness.

8. The distribution among the Rungus population of myths and other projective materials is of course of critical importance to determine the degree to which they are idiosyncratic or represent the projections of the majority of the population. For example in this instance of the myth of the dog's penis, I recorded this from a major informant, but two other informants never heard about it. Unfortunately, we were unable to

investigate the distribution of most such projective items except superficially.

9. It is important to emphasize in this context of sexual aggression that it is not males in Truk and the Trobriand Islands but females who exhibit aggression in coitus. Spiro (1982) provides a psychoanalytic explanation of this behavior among the Trobriand Islanders.

10. This contrasts markedly with what LeVine discovered among the Gusii of Kenya. He writes: "Legitimate heterosexual encounters ... are aggressive contests, involving force and pain-inflicting behavior which under circumstances that are not legitimate could be termed 'rape'" (LeVine 1959:971).

11. In my dissertation (Appell 1965), I used the term "force" to refer to the actions of the bride's family to get her to accept her husband. In reviewing my notes and rereading what I wrote I find this an inappropriate term as it carries the connotation of physical force when I actually meant social pressure.

12. By the term "isoglot" I indicate a self-conscious speech community. That is, it refers to the speech of an ethnic group, the members of which consider their language or dialect to be significantly different from that of neighboring communities and thus have an indigenous name by which to identify it. I coined this term to avoid the problems involved in the terms "language" or "dialect", which imply a certain status in linguistic analysis. The term "isoglot" is neutral in this regard. But as it reflects the indigenous organization of their linguistic and ethnic environment, it has greater ethnographic validity (see G. N. Appell 1968).

13. The weakness of both approaches is that they do not include procedures for explaining social change. They do not view organization of society as emergent (see G. N. Appell 1988). While this is an important issue, we shall not consider its implications further here. There are, of course, other modes of anthropological explanation: historical particularism, environmental determinism, sociological determinism, economic determinism, functionalism, etc. None of these seem particularly applicable to the purposes of this inquiry.

14. Benedict (1954, orig.1938) first drew attention to the psychological consequences of discontinuities in cultural conditioning.

15. This is in marked contrast to the Gusii of Kenya where some wives do express a distaste for coitus, and those that do refuse to have coitus for up to a week at a time may be beaten by their husbands (LeVine 1959:970).

16. However, the characteristics claimed by Sanday to produce low rape societies may only be sufficient conditions rather than necessary conditions if the preliminary data on the Japanese prove accurate. It is reported in the *Japanese Statistical Yearbook* (Statistical Bureau 1989) that the occurrence of rape is relatively low. Yet among the Japanese there appears to be a marked differential in male and female roles.

17. It is interesting to note, however, in contradiction to Sanday (1986) the Iban male does construct his personhood on being tough and aggressive, but this still does not result in producing a rape-prone society, as Sutlive in the introduction to this volume has pointed out.

18. It might be useful to use the term "biocultural interactionism" to distinguish this from the usage of interactionism in reference to the mind-body problem. See Freeman 1990 for his most recent statement on the interactionism of culture and biology.

19. In developing a theory of population adaptation in which physiological, psychological, and behavioral impairments are one measure of the efficiency of the populations's ongoing adaptation processes, I have referred to this as General Adaptation Theory (see Appell 1986). This theory must be distinguished from Selye's concept of the General Adaptation Syndrome (see Selye 1980). Selye's concept does not include a population and its social assets. General Adaptation Theory, which also integrates the General Adaptation Syndrome into it, does focus on a population and its cultural assets that are used in the processes of coping and adaptation. The resultant health impairments or enhancements from these processes of coping are the precursors of phylogenetic adaptation.

BIBLIOGRAPHY

Annis, Robert C. and Barrie Frost
  1973   Human Visual Ecology and Orientation Anisotropies in
                Acuity. Science 182:729-31.

Aoki, Chiye and Philip Siekevitz
  1988   Plasticity in Brain Development. Scientific American
                December:56-64.

Appell, G. N.
  1965   The Nature of Social Groupings Among the Rungus
                Dusun of Sabah, Malaysia. Dissertation submitted for
                the degree of Ph.D., The Australian National University.

  1966   The Structure of District Administration, Anti-administra-
                tion Activity and Political Instability. Human Organiza-
                tion 25:312-20.

  1968   The Dusun Languages of Northern Borneo: Rungus
                Dusun and Related Problems. Oceanic Linguistics 7:1-15.

  1969   Social Anthropological Census for Cognatic Societies and
                Its Application to the Rungus of Northern Borneo.
                Bijdragen tot de Taal-, Land- en Volkenkunde 125:80-93.

  1984   Freeman's Refutation of Mead's Coming of Age in
                Samoa: The Implications for Anthropological Inquiry.
                The Eastern Anthropologist 37:183-214.

  1986   The Health Consequences of Development. Sarawak
                Museum Journal 36:43-74.

  1987   Sexual Metaphors in Verbal Aggression: Rungus and
                American Cultural Patterns. Paper presented at sympo-
                sium Male and Female in Borneo, Vinson H. Sutlive, Jr.,
                Chair, 86th Annual Meeting of the American Anthropo-
                logical Association, Chicago, November 22, 1987.

Appell, G. N.
1988   Emergent Structuralism: The Design of an Inquiry
                        System to Delineate the Production and Reduction of
                        Social Forms. In Choice and Morality in Anthropological
                        Perspective: Essays in Honor of Professor Derek Free-
                        man, edited by G. N. Appell and T. N. Madan. Buffalo:
                        State University of New York Press.

Antonissen, The Rev. A.
1958   Kadazan-English   and   English-Kadazan   Dictionary.
                        Canberra: Government Printing Office.

Benedict, Ruth
1954 (orig. 1938) Continuities and Discontinuities in Cultural Condition-
                        ing. In Personality in Nature, Society, and Culture,
                        edited by Clyde Kluckhohn and Henry A. Murray.
                        Second Revised Edition. New York: Alfred A. Knopf.
                        (Reprinted from Psychiatry 1:161-67, 1938).

Beneke, Timothy
1982   Rape Language. In Men on Rape, by Timothy Beneke.
                        New York: St. Martin's Press. Pp. 11-22.

Eibl-Eibesfeldt, Irenäus
1989   Human Ethology. New York: Aldine de Gruyter.

Flynn, Charles P.
1976   Sexuality and Insult Behavior. Journal of Sex Research
                        12:1-13.

Forschner, T.
1978   English-Rungus Dictionary. Second Edition. Mimeo-
                        graphed. Kudat.

Freeman, Derek
1967   Shaman and Incubus. Psychoanalytic Study of Society
                        4:9-33.

1968   Thunder, Blood and the Nicknaming of God's Creatures.
                        The Psychoanalytic Quarterly 37:353-99.

118

Freeman, Derek
    1990   After Margaret Mead: An Antipodean Rethinking of Anthropology. Lecture delivered at Institute for the Humanities, Simon Fraser University, March, 1990.

Groth, A. Nicholas and Martha A. Field
    1983   Rape. In Encyclopedia of Crime and Justice, Volume 4, edited by Sanford H. Kadish. New York: The Free Press.

LeVine, Robert A.
    1959   Gusii Sex Offenses: A Study in Social Control. American Anthropologist 61:965-90.

Malinowski, Bronislaw
    1932 (orig. 1929) The Sexual Life of Savages in North-Melanesia. Third Edition. London: Routledge & Kegan Paul.

Palmer, Craig
    1989   Is Rape a Cultural Universal? A Re-examination of the Ethnographic Data. Ethnology 28:1-16.

Parker, Seymour
    1976   The Precultural Basis of the Incest Taboo: Toward a Biosocial Theory. American Anthropologist 78:285-305.

Restak, Richard
    1984   The Brain. New York: Bantam Books.

Sanday, Peggy Reeves
    1981   The Socio-Cultural Context of Rape: A Cross-Cultural Study. Journal of Social Issues 37:5-27.

    1986   Rape and the Silencing of the Feminine. In Rape, edited by Sylvana Tomaselli and Roy Porter. Oxford: Basil Blackwell.

Sather, Clifford
    1978   The Malevolent *Koklir*: Iban Concepts of Sexual Peril and the Dangers of Childbirth. Bijdragen tot de Taal, Land- en Volkenkunde 134:310-55.

Selye, Hans
    1980   Preface. In Selye's Guide to Stress Research, edited by
                    Hans Selye. Volume 1. New York: Van Nostrand
                    Reinhold.

Spiro, Melford E.
    1965   Religious Systems as Culturally Constituted Defense
                    Mechanisms. In Context and Meaning in Cultural
                    Anthropology, edited by Melford E. Spiro. New York:
                    The Free Press.

    1982   Oedipus in the Trobriands. Chicago: Chicago University
                    Press.

Spiro, Melford E. and Roy G. D'Andrade
    1958   A Cross-Cultural Study of Some Supernatural Beliefs.
                    American Anthropologist 60:456-66.

Statistics Bureau, Management and Coordination Agency
    1989   Japan Statistical Yearbook 1989. Japan: Statistics Bureau,
                    Management and Coordination Agency.

Swartz, Marc J.
    1958   Sexuality and Aggression on Romonum, Truk. American
                    Anthropologist 60:467-86.

Thornhill, Randy, Nancy Thornhill and Gerard A. Dizinno
    1986   The Biology of Rape. In Rape, edited by Sylvana
                    Tomaselli and Roy Porter. Oxford: Basil Blackwell.

Whiting, John and Beatrice Whiting
    1978   A Strategy for Psychocultural Research. In The Making
                    of Psychological Anthropology, edited by George D.
                    Spindler. Berkeley: University of California Press.

Whiting, John W. M.
    1959   Sorcery, Sin, and the Superego: A Cross-Cultural Study
                    of Some Mechanisms of Social Control. In Symposium
                    on Motivation, edited by M. R. Jones. Lincoln: Universi-
                    ty of Nebraska Press.

Whiting, John W. M.
    1961   Socialization Process and Personality. In Psychological Anthropology: Approaches to Culture and Personality, edited by Francis L. K. Hsu. Homewood, IL: Dorsey Press.

Whiting, John W. M. and Irvin L. Child
    1953   Child Training and Personality: A Cross-cultural Study. New Haven: Yale University Press.

LATAH BEHAVIOR BY FEMALES AMONG THE RUNGUS OF SABAH[1]

AMITY APPELL DOOLITTLE

INTRODUCTION

Over a century ago European observers began to document a malady known as latah which was peculiar to Malay society (see Ellis 1897 and O'Brien 1880). When frightened or startled an individual with latah would shout an obscene word (coprolalia), imitate words or phrases of others (echolalia), imitate actions of others (echopraxia), or even obey commands of others (command automatism). H. O'Brien's report of latah is one of the most comprehensive of the earlier accounts. O'Brien wrote:

> I ... met a young Malay who was of ... assistance to our party in pulling our boat across a narrow watershed... . His comrades told me that the man was *latah*, but I could see nothing in his conduct or conversation which was not perfectly rational.

... one night we let off a signalling rocket for the amusement of those who had given us assistance ... I was preparing to fire a second rocket myself, when the *latah* pushed me violently aside, snatched the torch from my hand, fired the rocket, and fell down on his face making an unintelligible noise, to all appearances the expression of fear.

... When I sought an explanation from the by-standers, I was informed laconically "*latah tuan*" [it is *latah*, sir].

I saw him alone on the bank as we put off down-stream, and I waved my hand to him. To my surprise he began waving his hand frantically in return.... . I had began to whistle an air. He also began whistling... [O'Brien 1880:149].

Europeans could not understand latah. It was not comparable to any type of behavior found in Western cultures and, therefore, did not fit in with either their common-sense frameworks or their psychiatric categories used to define human behavior. The closest that Europeans could come to finding a comparable behavior in the Western culture to latah was Tourette's syndrome, characterized by involuntary spasms and the blurting out of obscenities (Garelik 1986), or various forms of schizophrenia, also characterized by echolalia and echopraxia. As one group of psychiatrists said, "echolalia and echopraxia have been recognized as symptoms expressive of seriously disturbed behavior in adults for over a century" (Carluccio et al. 1964:623). Thus, it appeared to the Western mind that latah must be a pathology, as were these similar Western disorders. As a result, latah was classified as a mental disturbance which was found only among Malays and Indonesians. The *Dictionary of Malay Medicine* gives the following description of latah:

latah ... A paroxysmal mental disturbance endemic in the Malay peninsula and East Indian archipelago.

Latah is a specific psychosis in Malaya, practically confined to adults.... . The psychosis persists throughout life, but in other respects the *latah* subject appears to enjoy normal health...

All cases of *latah* are characterized by great increase of susceptibility to stimulus from without, especially when the subject is in a fit of absent-mindedness. The paroxysm is induced by sudden mechanical shocks and visual and auditory surprises, such as direct commands and startling appeals, which disturb the balance of an unstable nervous system. The *latah*-stricken person then behaves according to the type of *latah* from which he or she suffers... .

... echokinesis, or involuntary imitation of movements seen, and echolalia, repetition of words heard, are the chief features... .

A common and milder form of *latah* ... is known as *latah mulut (mulut,* the mouth). In this type there is no mimicry, the paroxysm is confined to an involuntary torrent of abusive language, in which the same obscene words are used over and over again... .

Some writers consider *latah* to be a serious sexual neurosis. The word is used metaphorically by the Malays for love-madness. Malays do not look upon *latah* as an illness ... [Gilmette 1939:141-42].

In the 1960's P. M. Yap, a transcultural psychiatrist, developed a theory to explain behaviors found in non-Western cultures which could not be explained by existing Western nosology. He categorized these behaviors as "culture-bound syndromes". Yap included latah in his category of the "culture-bound syndromes".

In recent years there has been a revival of the attention that latah received when it was first discovered by Westerners. Researchers are no longer certain that latah is a pathological condition, as it was labeled in the past. They are now realizing that the means by which non-Western behaviors had been classified in the past are extremely ethnocentric, often based on Western behaviors as the implicit norms. This realization has led researchers to challenge the notion of "culture-bound syndromes". A few of the questions raised are: How can researchers determine what behaviors are normal or abnormal in different cultures? Can a behavior be abnormal regardless of the cultural milieu? Even more importantly it led researchers to examine the applicability of any diagnostic system. They questioned whether any diagnostic system could be culture-free.

In this paper I focus primarily on the ethnographic description of latah among the Rungus and how they label, define, and explain this behavior. Later I will compare the Rungus explanations to the existing models on latah.

THE RUNGUS

The Rungus are a people of northern Sabah. A general sociocultural description of the Rungus is provided in the introductory sections of L. W. R. Appell (in this volume), and so I will not repeat this here (also see G. N. Appell 1976a, 1976b, 1978; and L. W. R. Appell 1988). There are two aspects of particular interest that should be mentioned here in terms of the content of latah performances, particularly with regard to coprolalia, the use of obscene language, and the utterance of words prohibited in respect behavior.

One of the basic value premises of Rungus society is that all sexual intercourse is potentially dangerous if entered into other than through marriage. Illicit sexual intercourse brings ritual heat to the village and can cause illness of the participants, comembers of the village, illness and death to children, the failure of domestic animals to reproduce, the failure of crops and lack of fertility of the village. As a consequence of this, females are expected not to publicly express any interest in sexual matters.

The second aspect is the respect behavior that is shown parents, grandparents, and in-laws. Respect behavior is most fully developed with regard to one's in-laws, which includes both parents-in-law and all grandparents, aunts, and uncles of one's spouse. For example, it is prohibited to walk on the floorboards of the longhouse so that they jiggle the area where an in-law is sitting. It is also prohibited to utter the name of any in-law or say any word that is similar in sound pattern to an in-law's name. One must use substitute words for even the most common everyday words, if there is any similarity to the name of an in-law, no matter how distant.[2]

OBINGSALA BEHAVIOR AMONG THE RUNGUS

Obingsala is the Rungus term for latah. Literally, *obingsala* means "often in error", "often mistaken", or "frequently in fault". *Obingsala* behavior can be considered a latah form of behavior as it is characterized by echolalia, coprolalia, echopraxia, and command automatism. It also involves repeated paradigmatic errors in speech and the utterance of words ritually forbidden in respect behavior, features which are not usually discussed in the literature dealing with latah.

Throughout the literature the use of the term latah shifts from referring to the behaviors themselves to indicating the person who exhibits the behaviors. *Obingsala*, in Rungus language, forms an adjective group indicating the type of behavior. Although it is awkward to be continuously saying "a woman who exhibits *obingsala* behavior", I feel that it is important to keep with Rungus terminology. This terminology demonstrates how the Rungus perceive *obingsala* behavior--they emphasize it as a personality trait as opposed to a type of person--a point which is central to my thesis.

Obingsala behavior is exhibited only by Rungus women. My Rungus informants, however, stated they have heard there are some men who exhibit *obingsala* behavior, but in the community where I was living no one had ever seen such an individual. It is also generally considered that these men who exhibit *obingsala* behavior do it on purpose, whereas the women have no control over their behavior. Usually the women who exhibit *obingsala* behavior do not begin to do so until they are married and have one or more children, although there are some women who have been known to start while they are still young girls (see Case 3).

SELECTION OF SUBJECTS

At the onset of the investigation, I spent about three weeks getting to know the Rungus, and in particular determining which women exhibited *obingsala* behavior and which did not. This was done mostly through interviewing people. These interviews were conducted on a very informal basis. If people came to visit, I would ask them if they knew of anyone in the village who exhibited *obingsala* behavior. At other times my mother, Laura W. R. Appell, and I would visit people in their houses and question them about *obingsala* behavior. I had no difficulty in finding women who exhibited *obingsala* behavior. These interviews also enabled me to get a general cultural definition of *obingsala* behavior.

In a sample of women, (N=55 women out of the community total of 680 men, women, and children), 53 percent of this sample exhibited *obingsala* behavior. From this sample I selected six women who exhibited *obingsala* behavior frequently and six women who did not exhibit *obingsala* behavior at all. These women I chose on the basis of their accessibility and their willingness to talk about themselves. These twelve women I interviewed extensively concerning their family histories, medical histories, and their *obingsala* behavior--or lack of such behavior. In addition, I conducted spot observations for three non-consecutive hours for each of the women. These spot observations consisted of observing the individual woman for an hour. Each minute, on the minute, I recorded her behavior. These twelve women were my major informants.

SELECTED CASE STUDIES

Below are several case studies illustrating the form and content of *obingsala* behavior among the Rungus. These cases are designed to illustrate the range of *obingsala* behavior from extreme to mild examples. At this point I will not analyze these cases. Later in the paper I will refer to them in order to determine their function in Rungus society.

Case One

Rubaian is a married woman in her forties. She has four children, the oldest being about twenty years old and the youngest being about twelve. She is one of ten children. Her mother very often exhibited *obingsala* behavior, and so does Rubaian. One afternoon Rubaian was sitting in our house. She was carrying on a conversation with my father and mother, her brother and another adult male, named Mindahing. I brought out a very large wind-up toy spider and put it on the floor in front of Rubaian. (This spider was not chosen for any particular reason other than that I knew, as a foreign object, it might startle Rubaian.) She became immediately frightened. She began to shake and move away from the spider. Mindahing became amused by Rubaian's fright and decided to use the opportunity to tease her. He said things like, "It's alive! It's going to eat me," and Rubaian would mimic everything that he said. Rubaian became more and more frightened. She started to talk uncontrollably, and I tape recorded her performance. She said, "What is it? It's a *luma'ag* ["guardian spirit"]. It's mother's *luma'ag*. It is the *luma'ag* of a pig. Sooooi [a sound used to comfort babies]. I won't eat pig ... chicken, I don't feel like eating. I don't want to eat a dog. Oh, testicles of a — [indistinguishable word]. It is walking up my leg brass [she was not wearing any leg brass at that point]. It's going to stick to my finger. It's going to stick to my skirt. Its teeth are long. Testicles of a hornbill. It is a butterfly. I have no character."

After a while it was clear that Rubaian was very frightened so I removed the spider. Then a piece of paper began to blow in the wind. It caught Rubaian's eye and she became frightened all over again. Mindahing told her that the paper was alive and that it was breathing. He also told her that the paper would bite her. Rubaian became even more frightened. She said, "Help, the world is moving! Help, it is going to fall down. It's flying. Its opening its mouth. It's slippery. It has wings. Its mouth is so wide."

Rubaian had entered a semi-hypnotic state. She could not control what she was saying and had become hypersensitive. She was intensely monitoring her surroundings so that every movement startled her. When we finally calmed her down completely, she said that she could not stop shaking and that she was *ohuzan*, "exhausted".

Case Two

Yomizan is in her fifties. She has five children and comes from a family of fourteen children. Her mother did not often exhibit *obingsala* behavior, but Yomizan does. One afternoon Yomizan came to visit us accompanied by Mindamau, another woman who also exhibited *obingsala* behavior. Mindamau said to me, "This is the woman you want to talk to. She often exhibits *obingsala* behavior." Mindamau and Yomizan sat down on our porch and proceeded to make a chew of tobacco, betel nut, and sirih leaf. Mindamau began to try to make Yomizan imitate everything that Mindamau said. Mindamau repeatedly poked Yomizan in the ribs while Mindamau was speaking. Soon Yomizan began to repeat everything that Mindamau said. Mindamau began to sing and Yomizan sang each line after Mindamau.

Case Three

Lamonut is in her late thirties. She comes from a family of seven children. She has herself had eight children of which two died at birth. Lamonut is an extremely excitable and energetic person. She is always moving about and laughing. Ever since Lamonut was a little over ten years old she has exhibited *obingsala* behavior frequently. Although Lamonut has exhibited verbal *obingsala* behavior for so long, she has never followed peoples' actions or obeyed commands. (Usually this behavior is considered as a more extreme form of *obingsala* behavior.) Instead Lamonut constantly repeats sentences and phrases or substitutes incorrect words for correct ones. She refers to people's genitals often. Once when there was a mosquito on my arm Lamonut said, "There are horns on your head, I mean your legs, I mean your arms." This kind of sentence involving paradigmatic errors is common for Lamonut, and she makes such mistakes frequently.

Lamonut said that the first (and last) time that she ever rode in a car she was so frightened that she babbled nonsense the entire way.

Case Four

Dorimon is a woman in her late fifties. She has had ten children, of which only five are still alive. She often exhibits *obingsala* behavior. When Dorimon talks she usually repeats phrases or entire sentences that she, herself, said. When other people are talking she will also repeat words that they say. She says that she just can't get the right word, that her tongue is just "too soft". Of all the women who exhibit *obingsala* behavior Dorimon was the only one that considered her condition as an affliction and wished that there was some way that she could stop. She said that she sounded like a fool and could never say what she wanted to. Dorimon believed that the reason that *obingsala* behaviors are not as common among the younger generation as it was in the old days is because the young are learning how to read. She says that if they can see the words then it is easier for them to think of them when they are talking.

Case Five

Malatung is in her fifties. She has had eight children of which seven are still alive. She is a very talented spirit medium and weaver and a shrewd trader. She often exhibited *obingsala* behavior and says she has even done so in trance. One day Malatung was talking with a friend in our house. Malatung's friend was trying to make Malatung say her father-in-law's name. (A ritual offense in normal Rungus life, but it is excusable if a woman does it when in an *obingsala* state.) Malatung's friend was singing a song with a word that sounds just like Malatung's father-in-law's name--*Kalawut* (also meaning gibbon). Malatung's friend poked Malatung in the ribs and said Kalawut repeatedly. Finally Malatung began to sing and said Kalawut herself. Malatung told me that, "My tongue is bad, I try to say things and it just comes out all wrong."

THE RUNGUS DISTINCTION OF DEGREES OF *OBINGSALA* BEHAVIOR

The Rungus themselves make a distinction in the degree of frequency of *obingsala* behavior exhibited: *obingsala* ("often in error") and *obingsala oholian* ("very often in error"). The Rungus say that <u>all</u> women exhibit *obingsala* behavior every now and then. Thus, some women occasionally exhibit *obingsala* behavior, but they are not labeled by the Rungus as *obingsala* women. An example of this was demonstrated to me by a woman named Mondoloput. Her friends, her husband and Mondoloput herself all told me that she did not exhibit *obingsala* behavior. Yet one day when the truck in which we were all riding to the market hit a large bump unexpectedly, Mondoloput shouted "*Kikuman do rogon!*" ("Genitals of a spirit!"). What the Rungus meant when they said that Mondoloput did not exhibit *obingsala* behavior is that she rarely exhibited such outbursts of coprolalia or rarely made errors in speaking in which nonsense words were substituted for the right word.

This distinction between an occasional error and continuous (and labeled) *obingsala* behavior is important. It shows how *obingsala* behavior is part of the normative structure of everyday Rungus life, but is not considered as a character trait until a woman exhibits such behaviors frequently enough and so becomes labeled.

Women who exhibit *obingsala* behavior and are labeled by the Rungus as *obingsala* make such errors daily. The women who the Rungus consider as being *obingsala oholian* have difficulties saying a sentence without committing a verbal error.

I adopted the Rungus *obingsala* categories, excluding those women who only occasionally made slips of the tongue. However, the reason the Rungus included certain females in these emic categories was not always clearly evident to me. The Rungus differentiated the categories of *obingsala* and *obingsala oholian* by degree of frequency, although in actual discourse people disagreed on which individuals belonged in which of these two categories, and the boundaries of the categories themselves appeared to overlap.

In addition to these Rungus categories, I imposed some distinctions that the Rungus themselves did not make. In this etic category system, I divide *obingsala* behavior into two forms, each of which may be seen in women who exhibit *obingsala* or *obingsala oholian* behavior. The first category includes verbal *obingsala* behaviors, and the second one includes in addition the more extreme but less frequent forms of echopraxia and command automatism (see following section on "Content" for definitions of these behaviors). The milder, verbal *obingsala* behavior includes coprolalia, echolalia, auto-echolalia, paradigmatic errors and the saying of prohibited words. The distinction thus is between those who only made verbal errors and those individuals who exhibit kinesthetic errors as well as verbal displays.

It is difficult to try to arrange these different behaviors in any hierarchical form. While we, as Westerners, may want to find some clear delineation between the occurrence and the extremity of these behaviors, the Rungus do not make such distinctions (see Diagram I).

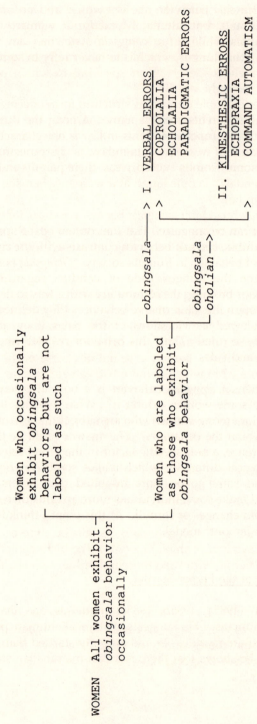

EMIC LABELS

ETIC LABELS

MEN   Never exhibit
       obingsala behavior

WOMEN All women exhibit
       obingsala behavior
       occasionally

Women who occasionally
exhibit *obingsala*
behaviors but are not
labeled as such

Women who are labeled
as those who exhibit
obingsala behavior

obingsala ——> I. VERBAL ERRORS
                    COPROLALIA
                    ECHOLALIA
                    PARADIGMATIC ERRORS

obingsala
oholian ——> II. KINESTHESIC ERRORS
                    ECHOPRAXIA
                    COMMAND AUTOMATISM

DIAGRAM I

Organization of Emic and Etic Categories of *Obingsala* Behavior

CONTENT OF *OBINGSALA*

Coprolalia is the use of obscenities in normal discourse. Among the Rungus such obscenities usually refer to another person's genitals and are often embellished upon or embedded in a silly phrase. This use of obscenities would under normal circumstances be considered as *mongimbuhal*, which means to insult someone or show disrespect by referring to their genitals. For example, if someone says, "*Kikuman do Yolimban!*", literally meaning "Yolimban's genitals!", it is usually done out of anger, and the victim may sue for a fine from the person who insulted him. When a woman in an *obingsala* state mentions someone's genitals, however, a delict is not considered to have occurred. This is because the Rungus do not believe that it was the woman's fault. They feel that the woman did not mean what she said; that she did not have control over her tongue.

The following are examples of incidents when Rungus women used coprolalia as *obingsala* behavior.

One afternoon Lamonut was walking toward my father. She slipped in the mud and exclaimed, "*Toli do aki ku ki amas!*", or "My grandfather's penis is golden!" The relationship between a granddaughter and grandfather is usually characterized by respect behavior. For a granddaughter to mention her grandfather's genitals is not only violating the respect codes associated with mentioning another person's genitals, but it also violates the respect that one should afford to an older kinsman.

Lina'an was talking to my mother when a frog jumped out of the grass and hit her in the forehead. She exclaimed, "*Ontolu do Saronkit mapit-kapit sed rabas ku!*", or "Saronkit's testicles are stuck onto my forehead!" Saronkit, her son, was there at the time and was extremely embarrassed. Although the respect relation of mother toward son is not as rigidly defined as is child to parent, it is nonetheless disrespectful to <u>anyone</u> to mention their genitals.

Malatung was in a field house with my mother performing a ceremony to ensure the safety of the rice harvest. She was praying over a tethered chicken when the chicken tried to fly away and landed near her outstretched legs. Malatung exclaimed, "*Kankaput minduk-tinduk turoi ku!*", literally "*Kankaput*, the Sacred Chicken, is pecking at my vagina!"

Another example of coprolalia among the Rungus, in which, however, genitals were not mentioned, occurred when a woman knocked over a glass of water. She exclaimed, "*Sobu do keribau!*", or "Water buffalo's urine!"

In general, these obscenities are not random; they reflect the context of the particular situation, as in the previous examples. This fact can be used to argue that *obingsala* behavior is not an unconscious behavior, but rather one that is learned and practiced and adapted as needed to the appropriate situation. I bring out this point in juxtaposition to diseases like Tourette's syndrome, a known pathology. Tourette's syndrome is also characterized by spasms and bursts of obscenities. The obscenities, however, rarely reflect the current situation. They reflect the subconscious, and it appears that their occurrence is controlled by various neurochemical imbalances (Garelik 1986). *Obingsala* behavior differs from this pathology in that it appears that the content of the words is dependent on the context of the situation. This evidence I believe confirms the hypothesis that *obingsala* behavior is not a pathology. In the remainder of this paper I shall draw on other information that demonstrates that the Rungus also do not believe that *obingsala* behavior is a pathological or abnormal behavior.

Echolalia is the repetition of a word, phrase or sentence that someone else has spoken. Echolalia appears to be as common as coprolalia among the Rungus women who exhibit *obingsala* behavior. An example of echolalia is seen in Case Two where Yomizan would sing each line of a song after Mindamau sang it.

Another related type of behavior which is found among Rungus women who exhibit *obingsala* behavior I refer to as auto-echolalia. This term refers to behaviors in which women repeat what they themselves say. In the literature on latah, echolalia and echopraxia are the terms used for the repetition of words or actions. The implicit understanding is that this is the repetition of words or actions of someone else. For example:

> *echolalia* The repetition by imitation of the speech of another...
> *echopraxia* ... the repetition by imitation of the movements of another ... [Hinsie and Campbell 1960:242-43].

Most of the authors do not explain whether or not their use of the terms echolalia and echopraxia include auto-echolalia or auto-echopraxia. Among the Rungus, however, they often repeat the sentence or phrase that they themselves last said, and occasionally the action that they last did. Chiu *et al.* (1972) are the only authors that I have read who explicitly say that latah behaviors include the repetition of words and actions that an individual said or did him or herself.

Another form of *obingsala* behavior I refer to as "paradigmatic errors". Saussure distinguishes paradigmatic from syntagmatic relations of linguistic units (see Lyons 1977:240). Syntagmatic relations exist between units of the same level.

> For example, the lexeme "old" is syntagmatically related to the definite article "the" and the noun "man" in the expression "the old man"... [In contrast,] the paradigmatic relations contracted by units are those which hold between a particular unit in a given syntagm and other units which are substitutable for it in the syntagm. For example, "old" is paradigmatically related with "young," "tall," etc. in expressions like "the old man," "the young man," "the tall man," etc., as "man" is paradigmatically related with "woman," "dog," etc. in expressions like "the old man," "the old dog," "the old woman," etc. [Lyons 1977:240-41].

An example of a paradigmatic error occurred one day while I was talking to Lamonut. We were talking about the different types of deer found in Borneo. Her six month old baby was crawling all over the place when he fell down and hit his head. Lamonut exclaimed, "This deer is going to fall and hit its head." She continued to refer to the child as a deer for several minutes as she continued to babble about him falling and hurting himself.

Another example of paradigmatic error occurred one day as I was leaving Lamonut's house, which illustrates how paradigmatic errors can be repetitive. My shoes, which were outside on the ground, had been moved about by the domestic animals. Lamonut cried out, "Oh, the pigs ... the chickens ... the cats ... the dogs are eating your shoes!"

The women who exhibit paradigmatic errors in their speech often have a variety of patterned phrases that they repeat or insert into sentences. These patterned phrases vary from woman to woman. One woman, when she became confused or flustered would use the words *kolibambang*, "butterfly", or *manuk*, "chicken", whenever she was trying to refer to something.

The worst of the verbal errors committed during *obingsala* behavior is to say one's parents-in-law's name, which is highly prohibited in Rungus culture. In usual conversation if a person says his or her parents-in-law's name it is believed that the person's stomach will blow up and burst when he or she dies. However, a woman exhibiting *obingsala* behavior may not only say her parents-in-law's name, but might also mention the genitals of her in-law, a particularly offensive act. Yet it is not believed that an offense has occurred since it is beyond the power of the woman to control what she says.

The second etic category of *obingsala* behavior, kinesthetic errors, which occur less frequently than the verbal errors, includes *echopraxia* and command automatism. An example of echopraxia followed by command automatism was witnessed one day when two women were sitting on our porch talking to us and chewing betel nut. First one woman began to prod and tickle the other one. At the same time the aggressing woman was singing. Soon the other woman began to sing, repeating each line after the first woman said them. Then her friend told her to throw away her betel nut and she did. The woman who threw away the betel nut then told her tormentor to stop or we would be angry with her for wasting our betel nut supply.

There was one woman in the village who was more prone to echopraxia behaviors than anyone else. Her name was Sinapinding. The entire village would tell stories of the time Sinapinding saw a television show. She was so surprised that she mimicked everything that she saw. If people were boxing, she punched at the air. If people were dancing, she danced also.

HOW AN EPISODE OF *OBINGSALA* BEHAVIOR IS BROUGHT ABOUT

An episode of *obingsala* behavior can be brought on by several different types of stimuli ranging from an unexpected sound or gesture, a slight but unexpected touch, being ticked or poked (even when it is expected), fright, thunder, dropping an object, tripping, or confusion due to a large crowd of people or an ambiguous social situation.

An ambiguous social situation may occur when a woman does not understand the context of a question. She may think that someone has asked her an embarrassing question. Rather than answering the question the woman will become flustered and engage in *obingsala* behavior. Another example is if a woman thinks that people are laughing behind her back, but she really does not know what is going on. This will also cause her to exhibit *obingsala* behavior. An example of this is seen in Lamonut's reaction to my father simply calling her name. My father was well-known as a prankster among the Rungus. Lamonut was a favorite of my father's to tease because she was so good-humored and because her reactions were so colorful. One day when Lamonut was sitting in our house, my father stopped what he was talking about and said, "Oh Lamonut," several times but nothing else. Lamonut kept replying, "What, what," and acted as though she thought that there was some joke going on. Pretty soon she became very flustered. Every time she tried to say a sentence she would make many paradigmatic errors. She simply could not say what she wanted to.

The Rungus enjoy teasing the women who are particularly susceptible to such behaviors. Usually the female companions of the women who frequently exhibit *obingsala* behavior teased them the most. Occasionally young children would join in the fun. According to Rungus custom, men should never tease a woman by touching her or tickling her. As a result the men do not tease the women who exhibit *obingsala* behavior as much as do the women and children. The men do, however, like to verbally frighten or surprise women in order to elicit a reaction.

Women who exhibit *obingsala* behavior frequently claim that they also do it when they are alone if they drop something, trip, or if they are surprised by a sudden noise (i.e. thunder) or an unexpected object (i.e. a snake or insect). Chiu *et al.* (1972:155) claim that latah never occurs when the individual is alone, but all Rungus women who exhibit *obingsala* behaviors told me that they had and could exhibit *obingsala* behavior if they were alone. They did say, however, that the more people present the worse the *obingsala* behavior became and the harder it was for them to stop. But nevertheless they had exhibited *obingsala* behaviors when alone.

The majority of the stimuli which cause a woman to exhibit *obingsala* behavior are very mild or benign. Often the stimuli will be as slight as a woman being poked in the ribs, tripping on a root, or dropping something. Although sudden or severe shock, like hearing a loud noise or being surprised by someone will bring on *obingsala* behavior, such stimuli are not always necessary.

ORIGINAL ONSET

Generally, Rungus women do not know what made them initially start to exhibit *obingsala* behavior. Not one woman suggested that a dream brought on the first episode, although this point has been mentioned in the literature on latah (Chiu *et al.* 1972). Only a few women can remember the first time they actually did it; and although these women do remember a time when they did not exhibit *obingsala* behavior (usually while they were young girls), none of the women claimed to have had a particularly traumatic experience or a sexual dream that initiated their *obingsala* behavior.

One woman did tell me about the first time she exhibited *obingsala* behavior. She said that it was at her brother's wedding. She picked up a plate that was covered with pig grease and it slipped out of her hand. She exclaimed, "*Kikuman do opinai ku!*", meaning "My brother's genitals!" Perhaps she was unsettled by her brother getting married. In general, a situation in which the individual feels uneasy is a common stimulus for *obingsala* behavior in many Rungus women.

That the Rungus women rarely remember the first time they exhibit *obingsala* behavior and say that they did not experience a traumatic event which initiated the behavior is in keeping with the Rungus perception that *obingsala* behavior is not a dysfunctional syndrome or abnormality. They do not ask themselves "When did it start?" as though it were a disease. They do not see *obingsala* behavior as <u>caused</u> by something, as an illness or pathology is, nor do they treat it or try to cure it, as they would treat or cure an illness or pathology.

TRANCE AND *OBINGSALA* BEHAVIOR

Some authors have suggested that latah is associated with shamans, their marginal position in society and their ability to enter trance (Kenny 1978, Shirokogoroff 1935). The Rungus do not see any relationship between the trance behaviors of their *bobolizan* (spirit mediums) and *obingsala* behavior. Women do say, however, that one can exhibit *obingsala* behavior while in a trance. One spirit medium said that when she herself spoke during trance she would make errors. But when her spirit familiars or other spirits spoke through her mouth they were not subject to *obingsala* behavior (see Ill. 3). In fact several told me that they often do. The distribution of *obingsala* behavior among women who are *bobolizan* is not significantly different from those who are not. This fact leads me to conclude that *obingsala* behavior is neither related to the ability to go into trance, nor to any status attributed to the spirit mediums. I do, however, see a relationship between the underlying structure of trance behaviors and *obingsala* behavior. They both occur in an altered state of consciousness; they are found only in women; and neither behavior is negatively valued. I submit that both these behaviors serve to define specific core Rungus values, which indicate not <u>marginality</u>, but <u>centrality</u>. While *obingsala* behavior in its breaking of cultural norms does define respect and sexual values, trance behaviors also define religious values. There is, however, one important difference in these. Trance behaviors cannot be considered as anti-structural behaviors (as I suggest *obingsala* behavior is) for trance behaviors do not violate any cultural norm. Nevertheless, I feel that both behaviors are powerful ways in which the Rungus women assert and define values which are paramount in Rungus society.

RUNGUS EXPLANATORY MODELS OF *OBINGSALA* BEHAVIOR

The Rungus do not view *obingsala* behavior as a noteworthy trait. The Rungus will more often talk about a person who *mumudut* ("lies"), or *akabang* ("talks too much"), or someone who is *inumpaladan* ("jealous"), than a woman who exhibits *obingsala* behavior. This distinction may occur because the Rungus see *mumudut, akabang,* and *inumpaladan* as distasteful traits and ones that are in the individual's control to stop or avoid doing. They do not see *obingsala* behavior as something one can control.

When asked the question why some women exhibit *obingsala* behavior and others do not, they commonly reply that it is their *vangun*, their "fate". Other events, such as the ability to bear children, one's life span, or accidental deaths are also considered as *vangun*, or "fate". In addition they believe that it is part of the woman's *buatan*, her "personality", her "make-up", to exhibit *obingsala* behavior. The Rungus believe that some people laugh a lot, some are often angry, and some are "often in error". All these traits are aspects of the individual's given personality. In short, they see *obingsala* behavior as a natural aspect of a woman's personality and as normal as someone who laughs a lot or talks a lot.

But a few Rungus also discuss *obingsala* behavior as though it was a learned habit. They say that one starts as a child. Children hear their mothers doing it, and they play games at surprising each other and practicing what to say. Occasionally I observed a mother overhear her child mimicking her when she has said an offensive phrase when in an *obingsala* state and the mother would scold the child.

The Rungus women say that you just start doing it once or twice and then pretty soon you cannot stop doing it any more. Before you realize it you cannot control your tongue from saying what it wants to say. All Rungus told me that *obingsala* behavior got worse as they got older. In fact, when I once asked a girl if she ever exhibited *obingsala* behavior, she replied, "No, not yet." Clearly she thought that she might start as she got older.

The Rungus also say that once you start exhibiting *obingsala* behavior you can never stop until you die. The only time that you might stop is if you were very sick. Then, because no one would bother you and you would not be moving about or talking much there would be no reason or stimulus to make you exhibit *obingsala* behavior. It is clear that the Rungus do not see *obingsala* behavior as a thing which is under the individual's control (once the behavior has started), but rather as an integral aspect of women's normal personality.

All Rungus deny that *obingsala* behavior is any sort of *sakit*, or "sickness". They insist that it is a normal behavior.

The Rungus do have labels for psychological and behavioral abnormalities. A few of these labels bear some resemblance to what Westerners mean by mental illness. In particular the Rungus term *norginoi utok*, or "ruined brains", and *mulau*, or "crazy", refer to any abnormal behavior which serves no social purpose, cannot be rationally explained and which is seen in an individual over an extended period of time. The Rungus have curing ceremonies through which they try to heal a person who is considered *norginoi utok* or *mulau*. But if they fail, they accept the person's state of mind as it is. In addition, the Rungus conceptualize a difference between mind and body, adding even another aspect to this dichotomy--the *hatod*, or "soul". The soul is closely related to the function of the body. Illnesses of the body are caused by the wandering of one or more of one's souls or the torturing of one's soul by a *rogon* ("spirit"). Such illnesses the Rungus try to treat with religious ceremonies in which a *bobolizan* ("spirit medium") tries to communicate through her guardian spirit to the *rogon* who has captured the ill person's soul.

Obingsala behavior, however, does not fall into either of the Rungus categories of mental or physical illnesses. As they regard *obingsala* behavior as a normal behavior, they treat the individuals who display *obingsala* behavior no differently from other individuals. And while the Rungus believe that *obingsala* behavior is not under the control of the individual, they do not negatively value this lack of control, as many Western societies and some other societies in Southeast Asia do. Instead, they believe that *obingsala* behavior is simply an aspect of the individual's personality: a character trait, but not a pathology or a syndrome. Time after time women told me that women who exhibit *obingsala* behavior are neither *sakit* ("sick") nor *mulau* ("crazy"), but that it was just their *vangun* ("fate") and *buatan* ("personality").

Therefore, as a normal behavior, *obingsala* behavior must serve a purpose in Rungus society. Drawing on the works of Victor Turner (1969), McKim Marriott (1971), and Raymond Lee (1981), I suggest that *obingsala* behavior can be seen as an example of anti-structural behaviors. These anti-structural behaviors are used as a means for the Rungus to define and structure their special codes of conduct in their cultural reality.

LATAH AMONG THE RUNGUS: DO THE PREVIOUS THEORIES APPLY?

Obingsala behavior, considered as an example of the various behaviors most often referred to as latah, does not fit into the theories put forth by other researchers. I shall now address each of the most noted models and their relationship to *obingsala* behavior.

The first two theories, Hildred Geertz's and Michael Kenny's, draw on specific aspects of Malayo-Indonesian cultures to explain the role of latah. While I agree generally with this approach to understanding latah, I feel that the specifics of both these authors' arguments are weak. In addition I feel that they have neglected any consideration of a possible biological aspect of latah.

Hildred Geertz's Theory

Hildred Geertz (1968) argues that latah is a pathology. The expression of this pathology is congruent with four core themes in Javanese culture: the value of elegant and polite speech, concerns of social status, sexual prudery and the fear of being startled.

The Javanese value elegant and polite speech. Thus, the standardized behavioral patterns and the standardized use of obscenities associated with latah is a means to communicate severe psychological distress within the rigid boundaries of Javanese society. While I cannot argue whether or not this theory is appropriate in respect to Javanese society, it certainly does not apply to the Rungus.

It could be argued that the use of sexual words could be a means to express a psychological pathology within a society, but only if that society perceives it as such. The Rungus do not see *obingsala* behavior as an abnormal behavior, nor do they interpret it as a means to express any psychological disorder. Therefore, it is not valid to argue that the use of sexual words by the women who exhibit *obingsala* behavior is a way of expressing a pathology. If this were the case, we would expect that Rungus would respond to the use of sexual words during exhibitions of *obingsala* behavior differently than they do. If *obingsala* behavior was indicative of a psychological disorder, instead of laughing, encouraging and accepting the behavior, we might expect the Rungus to censure, punish or ostracize the woman who exhibited *obingsala* behavior. It becomes difficult, therefore, to apply Geertz's argument that this form of latah is a means to express deviancy in behavior in a culture that values a highly structured manner of discourse.

Geertz then argues that since the Javanese are highly concerned with social status, latah becomes the only means by which a person can parody the relationship between a person of lower status and a person of higher status. Through repeating and mocking the behavior of a superior, a person of lower status has a temporary advantage over a person of higher status--an advantage that he or she could not gain in everyday situations. However, among the Rungus, the social structure is not characterized by such pronounced hierarchies of status. Thus Rungus social structure is egalitarian with no hereditary class system. The class system is a permeable one, comprised of three levels: *lumundu* ("wealthy"), *osokop akanon* (middle class, or literally, "enough to eat"), and *musikim* ("poor"). People of different wealth, however, consider each other as equals, in other frames of behavior. Examples of this are seen in how people respect a good farmer, regardless of his material wealth, or how they will listen to an individual who is considered as particularly intelligent, again regardless of his material wealth. In addition, men and women are considered as equal. Their roles in the family are often shared, and when different tasks are divided between the males and females, one task is not considered more prestigious than the other. While only men hunt and concern themselves with trading and the accumulation of wealth, only women can be spirit mediums and are able to heal the sick. Thus, the role of *obingsala* behavior cannot be seen as a parody of the relationship between a person of inferior status and one of superior status, since the Rungus social organization is not constructed in such a way.

Second, while *obingsala* behavior does involve language that is prohibited in respect relations between cognates and affines, the Rungus do not perceive this as a parody, only an unfortunate slip of the tongue.

Geertz then makes the argument that latah breaks down the barriers of the sexual tension that exists between the men and women in Java, again in a formalized manner. The Rungus, like the Javanese, do have a very strict sexual morality. They do not sanction premarital sex or adultery and these offenses have serious repercussions in the village. If sexual rules are violated, it is believed the *rogon* ("spirits") will get angry, and people will become sick, droughts will kill crops or floods may occur. Not until a ritual sacrifice occurs to *monogit* ("to cool") the village which has become *alasu* ("hot") due to the loose sexual morals will people become healthy again and the natural world return to a productive state. In addition, the Rungus do not talk about sexual matters in front of people they respect. Thus, it could be argued that *obingsala* behavior is a means through which the Rungus symbolically break down the barriers of etiquette and release sexual tension, as Geertz argues. I do not, however, view that this breaking down of sexual barriers through latah is a way to express a pathology or abnormality, as Geertz argued. If it were a way to express a pathology, the cultures involved would then label latah or *obingsala* behavior as an abnormal behavior. Neither the Javanese nor the Rungus perceive these behaviors as pathological, nor does Geertz convince us that they are.

It is, however, important to consider the sexual content of *obingsala* behavior, since such behaviors are integrally connected to the culture. However, the sexual content of *obingsala* behavior should <u>not</u> be regarded as a symbol of pathology. Later I will discuss how it is possible to consider the sexual content of this behavior as anti-structural behavior.

Finally, Geertz makes the point that the Javanese are extremely afraid of being startled. This fear stems from the belief that one's soul can be lost when one is startled. Latah helps the startled individual overcome the fright and regain possession of her soul. The Rungus, however, do not believe in the notion of losing one's soul through being startled. While they do have a strong belief that the soul can be separated from the body and cause illness, this is a result of (1) one's soul wandering during a dream and being captured by a *rogon* ("spirit"); (2) the capture of a soul by a spirit angered as the result of the perpetration of a religious offense; or (3) or a person being threatened so that his soul is frightened away. This loss of one's soul will cause a severe illness, but not the onset of *obingsala* behavior. Therefore, *obingsala* behavior cannot be related to a fear of soul loss through startle in the Rungus culture.

It is apparent that the explanation that Geertz puts forth for the existence of latah among the Javanese does not apply to *obingsala* behavior among the Rungus. While Geertz's explanation of the role of latah may be congruent with Javanese culture, it is not a useful explanation of latah for two reasons. First, it cannot be applied to other cultures in the Malayo-Indonesian archipelago to explain other latah-like behaviors. Second, and more importantly, I argue that Geertz's conclusion that latah is a symbolic representation of a psychological disorder is incorrect.

Kenny's Theory

Kenny (1978, 1985), like Geertz, argues that the latah behavior has an intimate relationship to the core themes in Malayo-Indonesian culture. Unlike Geertz, who believes that latah is a pathology, Kenny sees latah as a means to symbolize marginality. He draws on different examples of Malay culture and folklore to demonstrate this point. As is the case with Geertz, this explanation does not fit the Rungus situation.

Kenny's main thesis is that all latah-like behaviors are a performance through which the individual can communicate to the rest of the society that he or she is occupying a role of marginality. First, women per se do not occupy marginal roles in Rungus society (see L. W. R. Appell in this volume). They are as valued as men. Second, women who exhibit *obingsala* behavior are not found significantly distributed in any one of the three socioeconomic classes and, therefore, cannot be considered economically marginal. Finally the Rungus do not negatively value *obingsala* behavior, nor do they treat an individual who exhibits *obingsala* behavior in any manner that would indicate that they are marginal individuals.

From the data I have concerning the social distribution of wealth, and the manner in which the rest of the community treats the women who exhibit *obingsala* behavior, it is clear that there is a fairly even distribution of wealthy and poor, highly respected and less respected women throughout the group of women who exhibit *obingsala* behavior. In fact one old Rungus man when I asked what kind of women exhibit *obingsala* behavior told me that: "The good as well as the bad, and the rich as well as the poor. All exhibit *obingsala* behavior. There is no difference."

Furthermore, as the Rungus do not negatively value *obingsala* behavior, women who exhibit *obingsala* behavior are <u>not</u> ostracized by the rest of the community or perceived as inferior. When I was constructing my sample, I was faced with the difficulty of women claiming that they did exhibit *obingsala* behavior when other people in the community said that they did not. On the other hand, not one woman who actually did exhibit *obingsala* behavior ever attempted to deny that she did. It became clear to me that women were actually somewhat proud, not embarrassed of their ability to exhibit *obingsala* behavior. The rest of the community also did not believe that the women had anything to be embarrassed about. They believed that it is not in their powers to control these behaviors. And in addition, these behaviors were generally considered amusing and in good humor. In fact, there was a great entertainment value attributed to a display of *obingsala* behavior. As a result, I do not believe, that anyone considers women who exhibit *obingsala* behavior as socially marginal in the community or treats them as marginal as a result of their *obingsala* behavior. Thus, Kenny's notion that latah-like behaviors function in order to express social marginality does not hold with the Rungus.

Kenny draws on several specific aspects of Malay culture to demonstrate how latah can be considered as a symbol of marginality. These aspects are: witchcraft, midwifery, and shamanism (particularly the idea of gaining religious insight and power through loss of self). These particular aspects of Malay culture, however, are not relevant in Rungus life. The Rungus do not engage in witchcraft or employ it as a mode of explanation for behavior. They believe that the *rogon*, "spirits", are capable of doing injury to a person if angered, but they do not believe that an individual has the power to do harm to another individual through the use of supernatural powers. Secondly, the relationship between midwifery and *obingsala* behavior cannot be drawn as only the men in Rungus society are midwives, and none of the men exhibit *obingsala* behavior.

The final point of gaining religious insight through loss of self is an interesting one. Among the Rungus only the women are the spirit mediums or priestesses (*bobolizan*). During religious ceremonies the women do go into trance (*rundukan*). But the Rungus themselves do not believe that this experience constitutes "loss of self", nor that the spirit is inhabiting the spirit medium's body. Rather the Rungus believe that the spirit medium is communicating through her spirit familiars to the rest of the spirit world. As mentioned before, the Rungus do not have a fear of losing one's soul through fright and do not believe in soul loss during religious trance. As a result, it is difficult to draw a causal relationship between religious insight and loss of self and *obingsala* behavior.

One final aspect of latah which Kenny places heavy emphasis on to support his theory of marginality is that latah is found more often in older, menopausal women. Among the Rungus, however, the onset of *obingsala* behavior is predominantly seen in women who are still capable of conception.

In summary, I can only conclude that Kenny's theory of latah as a means through which an individual can communicate marginality is clearly not substantiated by the case of *obingsala* behavior among the Rungus.

A New Theory: *Obingsala* as the Intersect of Biology and Culture

I suggest a new theory to explain *obingsala* behavior which views the content as representing an anti-structural component and the recruitment of women to this role as a result of biological propensities. This theory draws partly on Lee's (1981) theory of anti-structure, partly on Simons' (1985a, 1985b, 1985c) theory of latah in terms of there being a biological basis, and partly on Tart's (1983) theory of levels of consciousness and transitional states. Thus, I believe that *obingsala* behavior is an example of the use of anti-structural behaviors to define the codes of respect which serve as a core aspect of Rungus culture. I also believe that there is concomitantly a biological correlate which makes some women more prone to exhibit *obingsala* behavior than others. I will discuss this theory in more detail after I present Lee and Simons' argument in relation to its relevance to behavior among the Rungus.

Lee's Theory of Anti-structure

While Geertz and Kenny develop the argument that latah is <u>congruent</u> with core themes in Malay and Indonesian culture, Lee (1981) suggests that latah behavior expresses the <u>opposite</u> of the cultural norm. Lee (1981), drawing on Victor Turner, suggests that latah can be regarded as a form of anti-structural behavior. Anti-structural behaviors are those which represent the opposite of cultural norms. Latah, as a form of an anti-structure, allows the individual to display behaviors which are the opposite of the norm, thereby defining the norm. Thus, Lee does not see latah as an abnormal behavior, since abnormal behavior, by definition, would be censured by the society. Rather he sees latah as a means to define structure and thereby maintain cultural reality.

I believe that there are several problems with the specifics of Lee's theory. In particular, he does not develop any biological argument to complement his cultural argument. Moreover, his cultural argument is specific to sections of Malay culture while latah behavior occurs in other sections as well. However, I do not want to dwell on these issues because I feel that the framework of Lee's theory is a valuable new way to look at *obingsala* behaviors. This theory of anti-structure fits closely with the role of certain *obingsala* behaviors among the Rungus, although it does not explain all types of *obingsala* behavior. The most common form of *obingsala* behavior is a form of coprolalia, in which an individual's genitals are referred to. Among the Rungus this is considered a disrespectful insult when occurring in normal conversation, and the offended person is allowed to ask for a fine. However, when a woman does it during an exhibition of *obingsala* behavior, she is excused and no one is offended. Thus, when people laugh, but ultimately excuse a woman who has referred to someone's genitals while in an *obingsala* state, they are defining the normal behavior among the Rungus, which is to never refer to someone's genitals out of anger.

Another example of the anti-structure form of *obingsala* behavior is when a woman says her parents-in-law's name. Among the Rungus this relationship between an individual and his parents-in-law is one characterized by respect. To say the real name of your parents-in-law is disrespectful. Yet, while in an *obingsala* state some women not only say their parents-in-law's names but also refer to their genitals. People laugh at a woman when she does this, but, again, do not condemn her.

Thus, it can be suggested that the content of the speech characteristics of women who exhibit *obingsala* behavior contrasts with the rules of conduct which structure respect behavior in Rungus society. *Obingsala* behavior can be seen as a way to define the Rungus code of conduct regarding respect behavior. *Obingsala* behavior provides the community with a way to demonstrate alternative behaviors. Through these alternative behaviors they delineate the rules; yet since they are not viewed as violations of the rules, they are not in danger of undermining these rules. Thus, this behavior re-establishes and revitalizes the cultural norms and rules.

Why then, if *obingsala* behavior is a normal behavior defining societal norms, do only some women exhibit it? What explains the non-occurrence of *obingsala* behavior among women who are subject to the same conditions as those women who exhibit the behaviors? The answer could be that there exists some biological difference, a non-specific factor in the broad sense of the term, just as there is a biological difference which makes some Americans more aggressive than others and some to be more inhibited than others. Such a biological difference could make some individuals more anxious than others, or less able to incorporate rapid changes of stimuli. At this point I think it is important to take a closer look at Simons' model.

Simons' Model of the Hyper-Startler

Simons' (1985a, 1985b, 1985c) model is one that stresses biological universals in humans. He suggests that in all human populations there are individuals who are more easily and strongly startled than others. Drawing on animal studies he shows that there is a pan-mammalian startle response which involves characteristic behaviors like the eye blink and the facial grimace. Simons suggests that latah behaviors are a specific cultural elaboration of this startle response. Thus, Simons' model differs significantly from the ones discussed thus far in that he considers the biological correlates to latah. Unfortunately, because he does not use a great deal of cultural data to relate latah to the cultures of Malaysia and Indonesia, I cannot argue that his model may not be relevant to Rungus culture. I do, however, question Simons' hypothesis that latah can be seen merely as a cultural elaboration of a universal startle response, particularly in the Rungus situation. Is *obingsala* simply a startle response?

Tart's (1983) Concept of Levels of Consciousness and Transitional States

Startle is a very subjective term that cannot be applied to all the stimuli that elicit the *obingsala* behavior. For example, why is a large crowd of people considered a startling situation? When a woman sees that someone is about to tickle her and exhibits *obingsala* behavior, has she really been startled?

I propose that a more broad term of reference should be applied to the group of stimuli that elicit the *obingsala* behavior than the term startle. From there it may be more easy to develop a theory which can be applied to the *obingsala* behaviors. This new term of reference should encompass the notion that there are several different levels of consciousness which humans normally operate at (Tart 1983:63-69). For example, there is the state of day-dreaming, the state of sleeping, the wake (or day) state, or the state of hyper-monitoring (or extreme awareness) of the internal environment of the body or the external environment. Each one of these levels of consciousness requires a certain amount of tension in order for that specific attitude to be maintained. Once that tension is unexpectedly broken the person experiences a state of shock (Schutz 1962:230-32). When a person experiences this kind of shock, he often adopts a particular stabilizing behavior (like the use of patterned phrases) to help him return to normal, wake-state consciousness. Thus, what Simons calls the startle response can be better understood as a response to the breaking of the tension of one's state of consciousness in a disruptive manner. This new term of reference would help explain why exhibitions of *obingsala* behavior among the Rungus are often the result of a very mild stimulus. This stimulus is not necessarily startling, but rather a disruption of one's current state of consciousness in an abrupt manner. The individual who is susceptible to *obingsala* behavior can be regarded as an individual with a dysfunctional mode or manner in processing the state of transition from different levels of consciousness.

This new frame of reference for startle should be explained in relation to an actual episode of *obingsala* behavior. An example was seen when a woman was sitting quietly in her house. Several people were there talking in their wake-state consciousness, but this women was not involved in the conversation. She was staring off into the distance, clearly thinking about other matters. Tart would refer to this state of consciousness as a state of hyper-monitoring one's internal environment. Suddenly a dog fight began to take place nearby. While the other women were somewhat startled, they were not startled enough to make any comment and none of them exhibited *obingsala* behavior. This woman who was hyper-monitoring her internal environment was brought to normal (or wake-state) consciousness extremely rapidly. She physically startled and then explained, "*Kikuman do rogon!*", or "The genitals of a spirit!" This example shows how the tension of her current state of consciousness was abruptly disrupted by an external stimulus. When this happened the woman indicated her inability to rapidly process the stimulus by exclaiming in a patterned manner that involved the release of inhibited behavior. This behavior helped her return to wake-state consciousness.

CONCLUSION

I have argued that *obingsala* behavior, as an example of latah-like behaviors, is not a pathology or an abnormal behavior, statistically or normatively, as many researchers have suggested. Furthermore, the distinction must be made between the <u>content</u> of the behavior (which is influenced by cultural values) and the biological structure or <u>form</u> of the behavior. Based on the evidence that the Rungus regard *obingsala* behavior as a normal behavioral trait, and based on the ethnographic evidence, I conclude that *obingsala* behavior can best be described as anti-structural behavior. The Rungus consider *obingsala* behavior as a normal personality trait that is not noteworthy. Yet they use these behaviors to help maintain their cultural boundaries of normality, particularly in the areas of respect for another individual's personhood. This theory helps to explain the particular content of *obingsala* behavior. It does not, however, explain why one person has more difficulty than another in moving from levels of consciousness, thereby being susceptible to *obingsala* behavior. I submit that there are normal variances in the biological makeup of an individual which makes them more susceptible to stimuli, and thus more liable to move from one level of consciousness to another with a transitional states in which inhibitions are uncontrolled.

While among the Rungus I attempted to investigate one possible normal variable in biological makeup. I made a study of the different level of salivary cortisol between women who exhibited *obingsala* and those who did not. Cortisol has been shown to be related to excitation and the startle response. This investigation, however, did not provide any conclusive results. This may lend support to that aspect of my hypothesis that *obingsala* behavior among the Rungus is related to abrupt changes in state of consciousness, which may or may not involve the startle reactions.

NOTES

1.   This paper is based upon my undergraduate honors dissertation for the Department of Anthropology, Harvard University, entitled *The Study of a "Normal" Culture-Bound Syndrome: Latah Among the Rungus of Borneo,* 1987. This research is based on two months of field work during the summer of 1986 in the Rungus village where my mother and father originally did field work during the years 1959-60, 1961-63. Before leaving for the field I had developed an interest in latah behavior and had decided to do research on this among the Rungus. On the way to the field, I had a fortuitous meeting with Professor Robert Winzeler in Kuching, Sarawak. Winzeler, who has been studying latah in Malaysia for several years, kindly briefed me on his findings and gave me a copy of his interview schedule. I based much of my research on Winzeler's advice on how to direct my questions and his interview schedule.

    The research situation proved to be extremely harmonious as the Rungus were very welcoming and pleased that my parents had been able to return for further research. My father's previous three years of research and his subsequent writings offered me a tremendous base of knowledge. During the early aspects of this research, my mother, who had previously done research on the language and religion of the Rungus, acted as interpreter for me. Although I had learned to speak Indonesian when I was involved in research among the Bulusu' of Kalimantan, the particular dialect of Indonesian that I knew, which was influenced by Tidong languages, was different from the dialect of Malay that the Rungus spoke, which was influenced by Dusunic languages.

I would also like to thank my dissertation advisor at Harvard, Paul Brodwin, and also Dr. Peter Ellison and Dr. Robert Barrett who both gave me unstintingly of their time and gave me much incentive and help.

2.   See L. W. R. Appell in this volume for a discussion in greater detail of the value premise on sexual behavior and the respect behavior among cognates and affines.

BIBLIOGRAPHY

Appell, G. N.
   1976a   The Rungus: Social Structure in a Cognatic Society and Its Symbolism. In The Societies of Borneo: Explorations in the Theory of Cognatic Social Structure, edited by G. N. Appell. Special Publication 6. Washington: American Anthropological Association.

   1976b   The Rungus Dusun and Other Dusunic Groups. In Insular Southeast Asia: Ethnographic Studies. Section 3: Borneo and Moluccas. HRAFLEX Books AL1-003, Ethnographic Series. New Haven: Human Relations Area Files.

   1978   The Rungus of Sabah, Malaysia. In Essays on Borneo Societies, edited by Victor T. King. Hull Monograph on South-East Asia 7. Oxford: Oxford University Press.

Appell, Laura W. R.
   1988   Menstruation Among the Rungus: An Unmarked Category. In Blood Magic: New Perspectives in the Anthropology of Menstruation, edited by Thomas Buckley and Alma Gottleib. Berkeley: University of California Press.

Carluccio, C., J. Sours, and L. Kolb
    1964   Psychodynamics of Echo-Reaction. Archives of General Psychiatry 10:623-29.

Chiu, T. L., E. J. Tong, and K. E. Schmidt
    1972   A Clinical and Survey Study of Latah in Sarawak, Malaysia. Psychological Medicine 2, 2:155-65.

Ellis, W. G.
    1897   Latah. A Mental Madady (sic.) of the Malays. Journal of Nervous and Mental Disease 43:32-40.

Garelik, G.
    1986   Exorcising a Damnable Disease. Discover pp. 74-84.

Geertz, H.
    1968   Latah in Java: A Theoretical Paradox. Indonesia 3:93-104.

Gimlette, J.
    1939   A Dictionary of Malay Medicine. New York: Oxford University Press.

Hinsie, L. and R. Campbell (eds.)
    1960   Psychiatric Dictionary. New York: Oxford University Press.

Kenny, M. G.
    1978   Latah: The Symbolism of a Punitive Mental Disorder. Culture, Medicine, and Psychiatry 2:209-31.

    1985   Paradox Lost: The Latah Problem Revisited. In The Culture-Bound Syndromes, edited by R. Simmons and C. Hughes. Boston: D. Reidel. Pp. 63-76.

Lee, R.
    1981   Structure and Anti-structure in the Culture-Bound Syndromes: The Malay Case. Culture, Medicine, and Psychiatry 5, 3:233-48.

Lyons, J.
    1977   Semantics (Volume I). Cambridge: Cambridge University Press.

Marriott, M.
1971   The Feast of Love. In Krishna: Myths, Rites, and Attitudes, edited by M. Singer. Chicago: University of Chicago Press. Pp. 200-12.

O'Brien, H. A.
1883   Latah. Journal of the Straits Branch of the Royal Asiatic Society 11:141-53.

Schutz, A.
1962   On Multiple Realities. In Collected Papers. Boston: Martinus Nihoff. Pp. 207-59.

Shirokogoroff, S.
1935   The Psychomental Complex of the Tungus. London: Paul, Trench, and Trubner.

Simons, R. C.
1985a   Introduction: The Startle Matching Taxon. In The Culture Bound Syndromes, edited by R. Simons and C. Hughes. Boston: D. Reidel. Pp. 41-42.

1985b   The Resolution of the Latah Paradox. In The Culture Bound Syndromes, edited by R. Simons and C. Hughes. Boston: D. Reidel.

1985c   Latah II - Problems with a Purely Symbolic Interpretation. In The Culture Bound Syndromes, edited by R. Simons and C. Hughes. Boston: D. Reidel.

Tart, C.
1983   States of Consciousness. El Cerrito, CA: Psychological Processes, Inc.

Turner, V.
1969   Ritual Process. Chicago: University of Chicago Press.

Yap, P. M.
1951   Mental Disease Peculiar to Certain Societies: A Survey of Comparative Psychiatry. Journal of Mental Sciences 97:313-27.

Yap, P. M.

1962 Words and Things in Comparative Psychiatry, with Special Reference to the Exotic Psychoses. Acts Psychiatrica Scandinavica 38:163-69.

1966 Unusual Forms of Mental Disorder in Different Cultures. East-West Center Today 6, 4:8-10.

1967 Classification of the Culture-Bound Reactive Syndromes. Australian and New Zealand Journal of Psychiatry 1:172-79.

1969 The Culture-Bound Reactive Syndromes. In Mental Health Research in Asia and Pacific, edited by W. Caudill and T. Lin. Honolulu: East-West Center Press. Pp. 33-53.

1974 Nosological Aspects of the Culture-Bound Syndrome. In Comparative Psychiatry: A Theoretical Framework, edited by M. P. Lau and A. B. Stokes. Toronto: University of Toronto Press. Pp. 84-104.

1977 The Culture-Bound Reactive Syndrome. In Culture, Disease and Healing, edited by D. Landy. New York: Macmillan. Pp. 340-48.

THE CHILDREN OF *NISING*:
IMAGES OF HEADHUNTING AND MALE SEXUALITY
IN IBAN RITUAL AND ORAL LITERATURE

Julian Davison
and
Vinson H. Sutlive, Jr.*

Introduction

Until the middle of this century, headhunting, as a cultural institution, was practiced widely by numerous tribal societies in Southeast Asia. From the upland regions of Taiwan, as far west as Assam, and extending southwards to Sulawesi and the outer islands of the Indonesian archipelago, the purposeful taking of heads was a dominant feature amongst peoples such as the Bunun, Kalinga, Naga, Ifugao, Iban and Toraja. Above all, headhunting was identified with the island of Borneo, the stealthy Dayak with his blowpipe and *parang* being compounded in the Victorian imagination with the "wild man of the woods" to provide an archetypal image of the Other.

Early commentators tended to concentrate upon the more sensational aspects of headhunting, which were linked to associated reports of cannibalism

---

*We would like to thank Traude Gavin for the use of unpublished material from the field, and also for her comments and advice in relation to our discussion of the ritual significance of weaving. We also thank the members of Iban communities in the Rejang and Baleh regions, in particular Tuai Rumah Janggu of Nanga Sempili for his hospitality and assistance to Dr. Davison.

and human sacrifice. The desire for heads was seen as proof indeed of the bloodthirsty nature of "primitives" when encountered in the savage state. Thus an anonymous account in the *Sarawak Gazette* of 1909 reads as follows:

> [T]he women take possession of the fresh head and start at once their horrible dance with it. I have seen them myself with the heads, dripping with blood, and exhaling an awful stench; with devilish joy they were taken by the dancing women, who in their rage - for they get enraged over it - bit the head and licked it, whilst they were dancing through the house like mad women. Horrible! (Anonymous 1901:208).

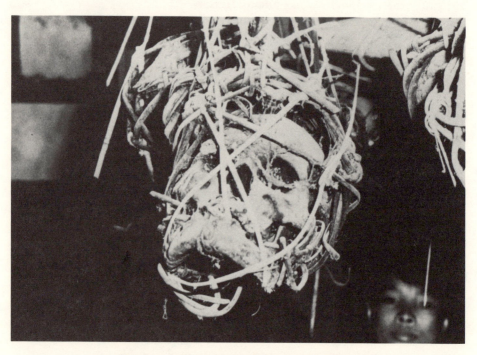

Trophy skull suspended in cane bindings

But headhunting was more than simply an institutionalized channel for native aggression and bloodlust. It was an important ritual activity that had to do with the promotion of fertility, particularly the fertility of crops and women. The situation is typically described by St. John, who writes that

> of all the feasts and ceremonies, the most beneficial in its influence is the 'Head Feast'. The object of them all is to make their rice grow well, to cause the forest to abound with wild animals, to enable their dogs and snares to be successful in securing game, to have the streams swarm with fish, to give health and activity to the people themselves, and to ensure fertility to their women. All these blessings, the possessing and feasting of a fresh head are supposed to be the most efficient means of securing. The very ground itself is believed to be benefitted and rendered fertile ... (1862 I;47).

In this instance, St. John is referring to the Land Dayak, or Bidayuh, of Sarawak, but their neighbors and enemies, the Iban, or Sea Dayak, were no different in making this connection. Thus Freeman writes:

> trophy heads and the rice seed (*benih padi*), on the fertility of which the welfare of the Iban principally rests, are directly equated. Indeed, the trophy head .. [is] .. a veritable fount of fertility - a most potent object which not only confers undying prestige on the warrior who has procured it, but becomes, for his community, a source from which their sacred *padi* may draw an ever-continuing fecundity (Freeman 1979:243).[1]

This connection between the taking of heads, on the one hand, and fertility, on the other, has provided a central problem for anthropological interpretations of headhunting as a cultural phenomenon. Various theories have been put forward at different times. Some of these have argued for the existence of a quasi-physical fertilizing agent located in the head; others have appealed to cosmic cycles of life and death; a structural opposition between the giving of life and the taking of it; the desire to integrate alien peoples into one's own society; and - in the Iban case - a cult of phallic symbolism. All of these attempts are unsatisfactory in different ways, but chiefly because they fail to provide an adequate account of the symbolic aspects of headhunting as portrayed through the collective representations of the peoples concerned.

Part of the problem, it would seem stems from ethnocentric preconceptions operating within anthropology, especially when it comes to ideas of cause and effect. As Needham has shown, there is often a marked divergence between the statements about headhunting made by Western observers, and those of their native informants (1976). This discrepancy, Needham argues, arises out of certain theoretical biases, or preconceptions, on the part of anthropologists and ethnographers - most notably a rigid adherence to mechanistic ideas of causation. The result has been that not only have previous investigators sought to provide answers to the wrong questions, but in doing so they also have tended to obscure the possible existence of alternative models of cause and effect. In this respect, one finds that the views expressed in the ethnographic literature can often be more readily linked to a prevailing theoretical climate within anthropology than they can to indigenous explanations of headhunting and fertility.

There has also been a tendency to marginalize headhunting as a cultural phenomenon - to see it as a self-contained activity, an historical practice not directly related to the understanding of society and culture as a whole. For example, Jensen dismisses headhunting altogether from his account of Iban religious beliefs due to the fact that "[s]ince its successful suppression in the 1920s, headhunting has not played an active role in Iban behavior" (1974:6). But if headhunting has not been actively pursued for several decades now, it nevertheless remains a central feature of Iban ritual practices, as Freeman has pointed out (1975:288). In this respect, Jensen's omission is a serious one if his intention is to provide a full account of Iban religious life.[2]

The Shorter Oxford English Dictionary defines headhunting as "the practice ... of making incursions for the purpose of procuring human heads as trophies." The taking of heads dominated Iban society in the not-so-distant past and it remains a key element in contemporary Iban perceptions of themselves and their cultural heritage. This is particularly seen in the celebration of *gawai amat* - lavish and spectacular ritual performances which center around the invitation of the gods to a feast held in their honor. Traditionally, these could only be sponsored by leading warriors, the highest honors and status in Iban society being accorded to those who had taken heads. Today Iban aspirations have a different focus - the acquisition of material worth, political influence and higher education. Nevertheless, those who are successful in life still choose to identify themselves with their illustrious predecessors by celebrating the rituals and festivals formerly associated with headhunting and warfare. In this respect, the cult of headhunting, in its ritual aspect, is not only kept alive, but remains at the center of Iban values. The thesis proposed here, then, is that any attempt to understand Iban society and culture - be it past or present - must take into account this singular importance of headhunting as a social institution.

Recognition, as a successful warrior, was the ideal that Iban men aspired to, a cultural achievement that was endorsed in the myths and legends of headhunting heroes and gods. Great war leaders went by the title of *tau serang* (lit. "those who know how to make war"), and such men were accorded the highest status and honor among their fellows. In this respect, headhunting provided the means for male social mobility and ascendancy in what was an essentially egalitarian society (see below). Freeman comments:

> Among the Iban certainly the head of an enemy was, beyond all compare, the most highly valued of trophies, being regarded as a *tanda berani*, or sign of fighting prowess. It was by taking a head, above all else, that a man acquired prestige among his fellows. As the Iban phrase it: *'Sapa enda' berani, enda' bulih antu pala', enda' berita.'* 'Those who are not daring, who do not take heads lack renown' (1979:238).

He adds that

> [w]hen he had taken a head, and only then, was an Iban male entitled to have the back of his hands tatooed. With this achieved his prowess was on constant display. On formal occasions he could bask in the adulation of the women who, sitting before him on the public gallery of the longhouse, would ply him with rice wine (*tuak*), chant his praise for all to hear, and incite him to further deeds of derring-do (Freeman 1979:238).

What is more,

> [a] successful young headhunter ... could have his pick of the most desirable young women, and was much sought after as a husband. In contrast, a man who had never taken a head, or who was known to be reluctant in battle, would be told by the women he courted: *Dulu niki tiang; dulu belabong isang.* (First scale the posts of an enemy longhouse; first bedeck your hair as does he who has taken a head) (Freeman 1979:238).

The taking of enemy heads then, was the prescriptive act for Iban males - an act through which an individual could win for himself prestige and status within the longhouse community, while at the same time enhancing his desirability as a potential suitor and husband in the eyes of the opposite sex. But, as we have indicated, headhunting also had a ritual dimension which was of the utmost significance. It is the latter aspect which chiefly concerns us here, being to do with Iban conceptions of male and female gender roles and relations of production and reproduction within Iban society.

Background

Space does not permit anything other than the briefest outline of those features of Iban society most directly relevant to the discussion that follows. For obvious reasons, the situation described relates more to the traditional aspects of Iban society -i.e. as extant at a time when headhunting was still a flourishing institution - than to the present-day circumstances of contemporary Iban. Nevertheless, in the essentials there is much that remains the same, particularly in up-river areas, such as the Baleh, where geographical remoteness has tended to preserve and sustain the traditional way of life of the Iban and its attendant value system.[3]

The Iban are a riverine people, whose main areas of settlement in Sarawak are along the Saribas, Batang Lupar and Rejang river systems of the Second, Third, Sixth and Seventh Divisions.[4] The 1985 census for Sarawak gives the Iban population at some 439,000 individuals which represents almost 30 percent of the total state population.

Iban society is characterized by the longhouse community. This is made up from a number of autonomous, though interrelated, family units, living side-by-side within the longhouse. Each family occupies a separate apartment (*bilik*) with independent domestic arrangements, but these are joined together under one roof so that the community consists of a single physical structure.

A notable feature of the longhouse is the covered gallery, or *ruai*, which runs the full length of the building. This provides an important public space for social activities and ritual performances. There is also an open-air verandah (*tanju'*) which extends along the outer wall of the *ruai*. This provides a drying area for wet clothes and rice. The longhouse as a whole is raised on piles some ten to twenty feet above the ground with a notched log, or *tangga'*, providing access at either end, or at some other suitable point. In the past, perhaps the most obvious advantage of longhouse living was protection from attack. Being raised on piles, however, also removes the risk of flooding, increases ventilation, and allows for disposal of waste (which is simply thrown below the building to either rot or else be consumed by free-ranging domestic pigs).

Iban society represents a classic example of cognatic social organization, based upon an ego-focused system of bilateral kinship terms.[5] In the absence of any form of unilateral descent group such as clans or lineages, it is the family which provides the key element in Iban society, the idea of "family" in this instance being primarily defined by co-residence within the *bilik* apartment.

Members of the "*bilik*-family" (Freeman 1970:9) are almost always intimately related by ties of consanguinity and affinity, although the adoption of children is commonplace, and the incorporation of individuals without families not unknown. No distinction is made between natal, affinal, adoptive or incorporated members, in that they all have equal rights within the *bilik*-family. Nor are family members distinguished on the basis of their age or sex, although the most senior member by virtue of his or her descent from the previous owners of the *bilik* is recognized as the "foundation of the *bilik*" (*pun bilik*), and is acknowledged as the person from whom the rights of ownership and inheritance of all the other family members ultimately stem.

Typically the ownership of the *bilik* apartment passes from parents to children. It is rare, however, for married siblings to share the same *bilik*, and so the apartment usually goes to just one child and his or her spouse. The remaining brothers and sisters will then marry into other *bilik*-families, or else establish a new *bilik* on their own. As will be evident from this last statement, residence patterns following marriage may be either virilocal or uxorilocal,[6] with no particular preference being given for either one form of the other. Nor is there any formal principle - such as a rule of primogeniture - to decide which individual in a group of siblings gets to inherit the *bilik* in which they were born.

The Iban are shifting agriculturalists, whose subsistence economy has traditionally been based upon the cultivation of hill rice, or *padi*. Each *bilik*-family is an economically independent land-owning unit, whose individual members hold joint and equal rights in the family estate. Land ownership is established by the felling of primary forest, with usufructory rights maintained for as long as the *bilik*-family continues to exist, or at least remains resident within the longhouse community. Most *bilik* will also own sago and cocoa plantations, wild or semi-wild fruit trees, rubber small holdings, pepper gardens, pigs and poultry. In addition, each family will also possess its own farming equipment, tools, weapons, shotguns, canoes and other essential items needed in everyday life. In more recent times, those who are better-off will have long-boats, outboard engines and luxury items such as videos, bedding, furniture and other modern conveniences.

The economic self-sufficiency of the *bilik*-family is reflected in other areas of Iban social life. Unlike the Kayan, Kenyah, pagan Melanau and several other Bornean peoples, the Iban are not divided into social classes.[7] Nor is there any form of institutionalized leadership based upon hereditary succession, or some other socially divisive principle. Instead Iban society is characterized by a strongly egalitarian ethos. In this respect, each *bilik*-family jurally constitutes a discrete and autonomous social unit, which manages its own affairs and recognizes no higher authority than that of its own household head.

An egalitarian ethos does not, however, preclude the existence of leaders and status distinctions. But in the Iban case, those who rise to positions of power and influence within the community, do so by virtue of their personal qualities and achievements as individuals, rather than as a result of inherited privilege or rank. In the past such men would have included warrior "chiefs" (*pun ngayau*)[8] and the leaders of migrations (*pun pindah*); in the present day they are represented by longhouse headmen (*tuai rumah*), local leaders (*penghulu*), and regional "chiefs" (*temenggong*). Other influential positions within the longhouse community include bards (*lemambang*), shamans (*manang*), omen specialists (*tuai burong*), and "elders" (*tuai*), the latter acting as informal consultants and adjudicators on matters of Iban customary law, or *adat*.

Status and prestige can be achieved in a number of ways, but in the past was primarily identified with agricultural success and the taking of heads. The two went hand-in-hand in that surplus rice supplies allowed those who had taken heads to sponsor a festival, or *gawai*, and thereby publicly proclaim their status within the community. In more recent times, prestige and merit have been attached to those individuals who venture forth on expeditions (*bejalai*) to other parts of Borneo and Southeast Asia in search of wealth and adventure. Such men find employment in the timber camps and oil fields of the region, returning home, often after years of absence, with money, goods and luxury items which are then shared with other *bilik*-family members. It is because of this that successful men are known as *raja berani* - lit. "both rich and brave" - in that the two qualities are seen as going together.

Politics, business ventures, and education, provide alternative routes to positions of influence in modern Iban life. And in each instance, inherited wealth provides an obvious advantage for the achievement of desired gains. The traditional value system nevertheless remains, in that personal acclaim comes only to those who have succeeded in life, rather than as the consequence of a privileged birth. In this respect, Iban society may be properly described as a meritocracy, where status and prestige must be achieved, rather than inherited.

We have mentioned that the Iban are swidden agriculturalists, and the importance of rice farming in traditional Iban society cannot be over-emphasized. Catch crops may be planted to supplement the daily fare, while hunting and fishing play an important role as a source of protein, but it is rice which, for generations, has provided the Iban with their staple diet.

Rice is also a source of disposable income - at least in those years when harvest yields exceed the annual rate of consumption. This "capital" may be exchanged for essential goods, such as salt and iron, or can alternatively be used to purchase luxury items - traditionally Chinese ceramics and local brasswares, but more recently, videos, cassette-players and other Western consumer products. Surplus rice supplies may also be put towards the sponsorship of a festival, or *gawai*, bringing prestige and social status to the families who do so.

For the Iban, however, rice farming is more than simply an economic activity; rather it is an integral feature of their whole existence, embracing the very idea of what it means to be Iban. As Sutlive has remarked, in Iban eyes "rice cultivation is not merely a technique for acquiring food but a total way of life that is supported by and in turn reinforces Iban theology, cosmology, and eschatology" (1978:63).

In the first place, rice farming is held by the Iban to be a definitive feature of their way of life: *Bumai padi nya jalai idup* (Sather 1980:67; see also Jensen 1974:152). It is the cultural hallmark of their society, so to speak, an activity which on the one hand separates them from their remote ancestors, who were ignorant of rice cultivation,[9] and on the other, distinguishes them from those peoples who farm rice according to different cultural prescriptions and agricultural methods (Jensen 1974:151).

Secondly, Iban rice farming is as much a ritual activity as it is one of agricultural technique. Central to this is the idea that rice is animated by a "soul" or "spirit". Freeman writes: "It is the fervent conviction of the Iban that their *padi* is a spirit, that it possesses a soul, a personality of its own, and it is this belief that permeates the whole of their agricultural practice" (1970:153). This rice soul, or *semengat padi*, is particularly associated with the idea of sacred rice, or *padi pun*. The latter is a special strain of rice--often with mythical origins--which every *bilik*-family has in its possession. It is never sold or given away, but instead is planted every season to act as a focal point for the annual rites of the agricultural calendar. In this respect, Freeman describes the *padi pun* as "the sanctum sanctorum of the soul or spirit of the *padi* plant, . . . the plinth, as it were, upon which the elaborate fertility cult of Iban agriculture is based " (1970:188).

The special importance of rice farming, for the Iban, is also linked to the idea that rice, and the knowledge of its cultivation were first introduced to them by the gods. Iban myths of ethnogenesis tell of how the legendary culture hero

Surong Gunting - half-man, half-god himself - spent a year in the company of Lang Sengalang Burong and other Iban divinities, in order to learn the different stages of the annual rice cycle. During this period, he was instructed in the correct ritual observances that should accompany these events. Surong Gunting then returned to the realm of mankind to spread his knowledge of these matters amongst his mortal followers, thereby giving rise to the Iban way of life and its earliest cultural traditions. In this respect, rice farming is, for the Iban, a kind of divine patrimony passed on to them by benevolent deities.

An important component in this scheme of things is the observance of auguries. The Iban, like many Bornean peoples, believe that their gods communicate with them via the calls and flight patterns of certain species of bird (Freeman 1961; Richards 1972; Sandin 1980; Sather 1985).[10] These birds are gods in their own right, and their auspices are sought whenever the Iban are about to embark on an important undertaking. Freeman writes: "The augural birds, it is important to realize, are benign creatures, favorably disposed towards man (*nadai jai' ati enggau Iban*); their *raison d'etre* is to help and not to hinder, to conform men in enterprises that are likely to succeed, to forewarn them of action and intentions likely to end hurtfully in failure or disaster" (1961:147).[11] Divine insight such as this is particularly looked for in connection with rice farming, each stage in the rice cycle being carefully monitored by the observance of auguries. In this respect, agricultural successes are understood to proceed directly from the correct observance of augural signs, a bountiful harvest reflecting the beneficence of the gods and confirming the Iban in their traditional way of life.

For the Iban, then, rice is a god-given thing, and its cultivation, an activity over which the gods themselves preside.[12] This, in itself, places a special significance on rice and all activities associated with its cultivation. There is, however, another level of meaning, or significance, associated with the cultivation of rice which has to do with Iban ideas of human destiny and the ultimate fate of the soul. We refer here to the notion that the souls, or *semengat*, of the ancient dead return to the world of the living as dew (*ambun*), which is then absorbed into the rice crop, thereby contributing to its fertility and increase. In this instance, the Iban see their connection with rice in existential terms, whereby rice and man participate in a single cycle of being. Indeed, they even refer to rice as their ancestor (*aki' ini'*), and give this as the reason why it must always be treated with respect and handled reverentially. There is, however, no specific notion of a re-cycling, or transmigration, of the soul. Nevertheless, it should be noted that when the Iban say that rice is "life itself" (*pengidup*) (Jensen 1974:152), far more is being implied than simply that it is their staple diet.

These, then, are the main features of Iban society and culture as are relevant to the discussion below. If we have dwelt at some length on Iban agriculture it is because it is important to understand the traditional significance of rice farming, which in Iban eyes has been seen as an activity that is central to their whole existence. In this respect, the collective representation of headhunting as an agency of agricultural fertility placed a special emphasis on the role of Iban warriors vis-à-vis the continued existence and well being of Iban society. Quite simply, if men did not go headhunting, then it was supposed that the rice harvest would fail, or at least be severely diminished, and that the future livelihood and prosperity of the longhouse community would thus be placed under serious threat.

Men and Women in Iban Society

Before opening our discussion of Iban headhunting, some mention must be made of the relationship between men and women in Iban society. This is not simply to provide a balanced account of the sexes in a volume dedicated to the study of male and female in Borneo; rather it is because our analysis of this ritual significance of Iban headhunting owes as much to the perceived role of women in society as it does to our conception of masculinity and male gender.

The first point to be made is one of sexual equality and mutual respect. This principle is evident in a number of different areas of Iban life. We have already mentioned the bilateral kinship system and the "utrolateral" (Freeman 1970:14) patterns of residence following marriage. It can also be seen in the sharing of economic responsibilities and the even distribution of jural rights and obligations. Similarly, in terms of decision-making, due consideration is given to the views of women as well as those of men. Furthermore, although menstruation, pregnancy and childbearing are considered to be polluting, or ritually dangerous situations (Gana 1988:15 seq.), the "otherness" of women in this respect is not something that is unduly emphasized (see below). In short, Iban society is characterized by a remarkable equity between the sexes.

The egalitarian nature of male and female relationships in Iban society has often been remarked upon in the past (Gomes 1911:86). There is (or was), however, one important area of traditional Iban society which was denied to Iban women, and this was the cult of headhunting. Certainly Iban women played an important ritual role in connection with headhunting - particularly with regard to the ceremonial reception of newly-taken heads into the longhouse (see below). But as non-combatants, they were automatically disqualified from participating in this system of prestige and status acquisition.

Sather comments: "From their display of skill and leadership in warfare, men alone derived the highest honours and achieved positions of status and power in Iban society, further symbolized by praise-names and ritual distinctions, from which women, as a sex, were totally excluded" (1978:343). He adds that "[w]arfare as an institution and its attendant glorification of male aggressiveness thus directly conflicted with the principles of sexual equality and egalitarianism otherwise inherent in traditional Iban society structure" (1978:343).

But if women were unable to compete with men in the arena of headhunting, this does not mean that the acquisition of prestige and status was altogether denied them. On the contrary, women were able to claim honor and positions of influence in Iban society through their skill at weaving and their ritual mastery of the art of dyeing cloth. These activities were traditionally identified as the female equivalent of headhunting (see below, and also Mashman in this volume). In this respect Iban women were compensated - at least in part - for their exclusion from the exclusively male domain of headhunting. In the end, however, it was to those who had taken heads that the highest honors in Iban society went, and in this respect Iban women were socially disadvantaged.

The result of this, it has been suggested, was a conflict of interests between Iban men and women. Certainly there is evidence for this in the explicit sexual mockery of men, by women, which occurs at specified points during major Iban headhunting rituals. On such occasions, Iban women dress up as men - in the past sporting grotesquely carved wooden penises - to ridicule the pretentious posturings of their menfolk as warriors (Freeman 1968:388-90). Freeman reports that Iban men frequently become incensed by this mockery, retaliating in kind with crude jests at the expense of women which leave little to the imagination.

No doubt tensions and antagonisms do exist between Iban men and women, just as in any society. To see this, however, as evidence for a collective envy of men, on the part of Iban women, is perhaps to go a little too far (Freeman 1968:388). Contemporary Iban describe the sexual banter at headhunting festivals as "play" (*main-main*), and men themselves willingly participate n the role reversal farce, collecting firewood and forest vegetables, which they then cook, in imitation of the domestic duties of Iban women. Furthermore, one finds that many Iban women express little interest in the status-seeking self-aggrandizement of their menfolk, preferring instead to concentrate on achieving recognition in their own domain as expert weavers and ritual specialists in the art of dyeing cloth (Gavin; private communication). The latter attitude can, of course, be interpreted as symptomatic of a suppressed rivalry between men and women, whereby thwarted women reject a dominant male ideology and replace it with a value system of their own. It is quite possible that this may be true in

individual instances; to argue, however, that Iban society as a whole is characterized by sexual rivalry and conflict would be to overstate the case. At the same
time, it should also be pointed out that if the institution of headhunting can be
identified as a major source of conflict between the sexes, nevertheless both men
and women alike had an interest in the taking of heads which were ritually
portrayed as a source of fertility for the longhouse community. In this respect if
should be noted that women actively encouraged their menfolk to go on the
warpath and scorned those who were not able to live up to the warrior ideal (see
below).

On Iban Headhunting

The taking of heads was a common feature of many Bornean societies, the
Kayan, Kenyah, Bidayuh (Land Dayak) and pagan Melanau among them. Of all
these headhunting peoples, the Iban were the most notorious. They were the
scourge of Sarawak and beyond, with some groups, such as the Saribas-Skrang
Iban, taking to the sea to carry out Viking-like raids along the coast as far south
as Pontianak in West Kalimantan.[14]

Hose and McDougall, in an account of Iban raiding, write that

An attack upon a house or village by Ibans is usually made in
very large force the party is more of the nature of a rabble than
of an army; each man acts independently. They seek above all
things to take heads, to which they attach an extravagant value,
unlike the Kayans and Kenyahs who seek heads primarily for the
service of their funeral rites; and they not infrequently attack a
house and kill a large number of its inmates in a perfectly
wanton manner, and for no other motive than the desire to
obtain heads (1912 i:185).

Hose and McDougall add: "So strong is this morbid desire of the Ibans to obtain
human heads, that a war-party will sometimes rob the tombs of the villages of
other tribes and, after smoking the stolen heads of the corpses, will bring them
home in triumph with glowing accounts of the stout resistance offered by the
victims" (1912 I:185).

It seems likely that the extraordinary Iban demand for heads had its
origins in the fiercely competitive nature of Iban society, where status is achieved,
rather than inherited. That is to say, unlike the socially stratified Kayan and
Kenyah peoples, Iban society is, as we have indicated, distinguished by its
egalitarian ethos and spirited individualism. And whereas among the Kayan and

Kenyah, rank is primarily defined by birth, for the Iban prestige and influence were traditionally linked to the taking of heads. In this respect, a man's status was commensurate with the number of heads he had taken. Thus Morgan, in describing Iban headhunting in the second half of the nineteenth century, writes of an "inflationary spiral to be stopped only be force" (1968:143).

But if the Iban desire for heads was largely fueled by the desire to gain prestige and status, one should also note that headhunting went hand-in-hand with territorial expansion. The Iban "conquest" of Sarawak has been one of the most remarkable features of Bornean history.[15] Originally, the Iban came from the headwaters of the Kapuas river, West Kalimantan, where a number of related peoples continue to live today. However, from the sixteenth century onwards, groups of Iban began to cross the Kalimantan-Sarawak watershed to the Batang Ai river, in the First Division. Since then, they have continued to expand through the region, generally in an easterly direction, so that today there are Iban in every division of Sarawak, and in Brunei and Sabah as well.[16]

The causes of Iban territorial expansion can be readily linked to the nature of Iban rice farming which makes periodic migration desirable. In the Bornean rain forest, several millennia of organic decay and decomposing vegetable matter have created a thick top soil, or humus, which is rich in nutrients. Consequently, swiddens prepared in areas cleared of primary jungle tend to produce exceptionally good harvest. What is more, the virgin soil, previously untouched by man, is so rich that the same rice fields can be cultivated two years running, thereby greatly relieving the work involved in preparation of farm lands in the second year.[17] In addition, weed growth is very much less in swiddens cleared from primary forest, which again represents a considerable saving in labour. All of these factors have contributed to an Iban preference for farming virgin lands. As Freeman comments: "The main incentive behind the remarkable migrations of the Iban has been a desire to exploit new tracts of primeval forest, and the tendency has been for communities to abandon their land as soon as a few lucrative harvests have been reaped, and move on to new precincts" (1970:76).

Typically, a longhouse community would march for four or five days, then settle for a couple of years, before moving on again, until they had reached a suitable location (Brooke 1866 I:327). For much of the time the Iban were able to spread into areas of virgin forest unopposed. In many instances, however, they met a fierce resistance from other peoples already living in the region, or on its borders. Sometimes the people that lay in their advance were hunters and gatherers, such as the Ukit and the Bukitan (Freeman 1970:130). More often than not, they too were swidden agriculturalists such as the Kayan, Kenyah, Melanau, Kanowit, Sian, Tanjong and Lugat peoples (Sandin 1967a: passim; Freeman

1970:130). In the latter instance, there was direct competition for possession of the land, and in this respect, Iban headhunting operated alongside territorial conquest. Thus Freeman, in describing the Iban entry into the Rejang basin, writes:

> It may be noted that Iban head-hunting raids on the Kayans, Kenyahs, Punans, Ukits, and other tribes of the Rejang basin, had more than mere ritual significance. The Iban ... were invaders, and in a very real sense they were fighting for the possession of new territory (1970:150 n.).

He adds:

> Significantly, the Iban took not only heads. Whenever possible, they burnt down the enemy long-houses, and cast all the iron implements they could find into a near-by river. In this way they hoped to discourage farming and compel their enemies to withdraw (Freeman 1970:150 n.).

The history of Iban migration, therefore, is also one of confrontation and dispute over land, and in this respect, headhunting raids were a natural adjunct to territorial conquest.

It should, perhaps, be pointed out here, that while traditional Iban farming methods favor periodic migration, migration is not, in itself, a necessary pre-condition of slash-and-burn agriculture. That is to say, it is quite possible for a stable population to support itself by a cyclical use of resources in a cropping-fallow system of land rotation. The Bidayuh, or Land Dayak, are perhaps the best known exponents of this in Sarawak (Geddes 1954), but the Iban, too, manage such a system in areas where they have long been settled. For example, in the Second Division, where the Iban have been established since at least the seventeenth century, and perhaps even earlier, a wide variety of different field types have been employed, including the cultivation of swamp rice, or *padi paya'* (Padoch 1982). This intensification of land usage belies the Iban reputation as prodigal *mangeurs du bois*). This is not to deny that Iban prodigality exists. It does. However, it seems that it is more likely to occur in pioneering communities, where an apparently limitless availability of virgin forest encourages wasteful, but high-yielding farming methods. Elsewhere, when faced with diminishing resources, the Iban have turned to a broader-based economy built upon a diversification of agricultural strategies and a rotation of land. The point to be made here is that the migration and territorial expansion are not essential accompaniments to the Iban way of life, but rather are contingent upon specific sets of circumstances. In the past, the circumstances were right for an almost continuous expansion into new areas of virgin forest. It should be noted here, however, that the impetus for migration came from cultural preferences - chiefly a desire to farm in areas of primary forest - rather than conditions imposed ecological constraints.

Generally speaking, headhunting raids were directed against distant peoples living well beyond the local area of the longhouse and its immediate environs.[18] Typically, the enemy would be situated some days', if not weeks', journey away, along the reaches of another river system. This is reflected in Freeman's definition of an Iban "tribe", which he describes as "a diffuse territorial grouping dispersed along the banks of a major river and its diverging tributaries ... whose members did not take one another's heads" (1970:126). And while personal animosities may have led to an occasional killing within the community, these were treated as homicide and the victim's head was never taken (McKinley 1976:108).

Obviously, directing violence away from the longhouse community, and not waging war on one's neighbors, makes sense in purely strategic terms. There were, however, certain cosmological implications which legitimized, or sanctified, the taking of heads from geographically distant peoples. That is to say, traditional Bornean cosmologies are typically socio-centric, being polarized between the longhouse community and its immediate environs, on the one hand, and on the other, the realm of the gods, spirits and legendary heroes. The farther one proceeds away from the locality of the longhouse, the more one enters into a quasi-mythical realm inhabited by supernatural beings and deities. In this respect, in cosmological terms, distant peoples occupy a position somewhere between the realm of mankind (*menoa mensia*) and the domain of the gods (*menoa petara*). This intermediate zone - a hostile region of unknown forests and mountain ranges - is identified in Iban collective representations as the realm of capricious, and for the most part malevolent, spirits, or *antu*, who prey upon the lives and well being of man.[19]

That the enemy are conceptually identified with malevolent supernatural forces can be seen in their portrayal in Iban oral literature as *antu gerasi* - demoniac huntsmen who roam the forest with their hounds (*pasun*), attacking the unwary and feasting off their flesh. It is also evident in the fact that trophy heads are themselves classified as *antu - antu pala'* - and must be treated with care and respect, lest they wreak vengeance on those who have been responsible for their fate.[20] In this respect, in symbolic terms, the enemy and *antu* are as one,[21] providing the Iban with a supernatural legitimacy for the taking of human life.

The Persistence of Headhunting as a Cultural Institution

The coming of Western influence in the nineteenth century, and the cession of Sarawak to James Brooke and his successors, heralded the beginning of the end for headhunting in the region. An interesting point to note in this connection, however, is that the Brooke regime may itself, for a while, have been responsible for an intensification of Iban headhunting (Pringle 1970:322; Wagner 1972:passim). That is to say, it was government policy to exploit traditional tribal animosities as a means of extending their dominion over the interior. So-called "friendly tribes" - for example, the Lingga, Undup and Sebayau Iban - were deployed against up-river "rebels" who were resistant to Brooke rule. And in return for their participation in "punitive expeditions", those who had sided with the White Raj were allowed to take heads. In this way the Brooke government managed to actively sustain, and even encourage, headhunting, while ostensibly being dedicated to its suppression.[22]

Illegal headhunting continued in many Iban areas up until the 1920s and 1930s. There was also a brief resurgence at the end of the Second World War, when heads were taken in mopping up operations against the Japanese.[23] Again, one or two isolated occurrences were reported during the period of confrontation with Indonesia (1963-1966).

The persistence of headhunting as a living tradition, up until at least the Second World War, and even beyond (albeit in a drastically curtailed form), has meant that many of the details connected with the taking of heads are well documented. Moreover, the ritual significance of headhunting, and its attendant ceremonies, continue to play an important role in contemporary Iban society. We have already spoken of headhunting festivals (*gawai amat*) held as celebrations of male prestige and achievement, but the traditional role of the Iban warrior continues to survive elsewhere in Iban culture, most notably in connection with mortuary rites. A visit to a Saribas Iban festival for the dead (*Gawai Antu*), for instance, reveals a more than sufficient number of candidates to drink the sacred wine (*ai' garong*) dedicated to those who have passed away. Previously, only those who had distinguished themselves as headhunters could partake in this sacred symposium with the dead; today the taking of a life - usually when on active service in the Sarawak Field Force - suffices. In this instance, and others of a similar nature, the warrior tradition of Iban society is maintained, and the ritual significance of headhunting preserved, as a major component in the Iban value system.

Elderly warrior preparing to drink *ai' garong*

Iban Explanations of Headhunting

When asked about headhunting, contemporary Iban say that it was the custom of their ancestors (*adat aki' -ini'* [c.f. Low 1848:188-89]) - a part of their traditional way of life (*adat lama'*). They may add that heads were taken in order to end mourning for the dead - *ngetas ulit*.

The need for a new head to end mourning is well documented in the ethnographic literature (St. John 1863 I;63; Perham 1884:299; Brooke Low, in Ling Roth 1896 I;155; Howell 1977:78, 126-27; Gomes 1911:139, 186; Uchibori 144, passim). For example, St. John writes that

> [a]fter the death of relative, they [the Iban] seek for the heads of enemies, and until one is brought in they consider themselves to be in mourning, wearing no fine clothes, striking no gongs, nor is laughing or merry-making in the house allowed; but they have a steady desire to grieve for the one lost to them, and seek a head as a means of consoling themselves for the death of the departed (1863:63).

The idea that mourning (*ulit*) could only be properly ended by procuring an enemy head is established in Iban mythology. The story of Serapoh tells of a time when the ancestors of the Iban were ignorant of the correct way to deal with the head; they did not know how to "look after" (*ngintu*) their deceased (Uchibori 1978:216). Consequently, they were continually plagued by a high incidence of mortality and threatened with social extinction. Eventually, however, the proper mortuary rituals were revealed to Serapoh by the spirit Putang Raga. Among his stipulations was the requirement that heads should be taken: *Ulit orang ke mati enda' tau enda' diketas enggau pala' munsoh* ("Mourning for the dead must be cut away with an enemy's head" (Sandin 1962:12). Since that time, heads have been sought in connection with the termination of mourning and Iban society has flourished.

Perham mentions that the newly taken head trophies are said to be conveyed by the wind spirit (*antu ribut*) to the Land of the Dead, where they are received with joy and gladness by the deceased, who feels that his own death has been avenged upon others (1885:295). In some instances, the Iban say that the soul of the victim will become the slave (*ulun*) of the deceased in the Afterworld, just as those who are taken captive in war become the slaves of the living. But as to why heads should have been taken for this purpose or as a sign of vengeance having been fulfilled, there is no mention.

Clearly, the taking of heads was once a key element in Iban mortuary rites, and indeed remains very much in evidence to this day (Morgan and Beavitt 1971:303, 309-11; Uchibori 1978:110, 112ff). But what of the connection between headhunting and fertility that Freeman speaks of? The idea that trophy heads avenged a loss of life in the community, or provided the dead with slaves for the Afterlife, seems only part of the explanation of Iban headhunting, for as Freeman points out, in Iban eyes the trophy head is also regarded as "a veritable fount of fertility - a most potent object ... from which their sacred *padi* may draw an ever-continuing fecundity" (1979:243; see also above). If contemporary Iban cannot themselves supply us with an answer, then we must turn to the anthropological record, and examine what previous investigators have had to say on this matter.

Anthropological Interpretations of Headhunting

The fact that headhunting and territorial expansion can be linked together has encouraged some authors to seek an ecological base for Iban headhunting (Vayda 1961, 1968, 1969, 1976; Wagner 1972). At the risk of oversimplification, the general thesis proposed is a functionalist one, whereby cultural institutions are evaluated in terms of their supposed contribution to the survival of the social group. In the case of the Iban material, warfare is identified as an adaptive response to competition for natural resources, namely land, with headhunting as a kind of terror-tactic - a secondary elaboration, so to speak - aimed at driving out the opposition.

That headhunting had this effect, there can be no doubt; that its existence, as a cultural institution, can be explained in this way, is at best, questionable. In the first place, there is the problem of evidence. Quite simply there is not enough of it, and what there is, is often inconsistent with the ecologist's position. King. who has examined the ecological argument for Iban headhunting at some length, writes: "My main quarrel with ecological theorists is not that an ecological analysis is out of place but that the necessary data are inadequate, and the processes underlying migration often grossly oversimplified and sometimes misinterpreted" (1976:312).

Space prevents a detailed review of the material, but the main point can be made quite simply. If it is the case that Iban headhunting and territorial expansion frequently operated together (c.f. Freeman 1970:150 n.; cited above), then equally they were found independently of each other; that is to say, headhunting without territorial conquest, and territorial expansion without headhunting. The maritime headhunting and coastal raiding of the Saribas-Skrang Iban provides a striking example of the former instance,[24] but it should be mentioned that the long-settled groups of the Second Division, some of whom had been established since the seventeenth century, also persisted in headhunting, even though territorial gain was clearly not their intention. On the other side of the coin, it should be noted that for much of their time in Sarawak, the Iban were able to move into uninhabited areas of virgin forest unopposed. If, then, in some instances the Iban came into contact with other groups who were competing for the same lands, this was more a matter of historical circumstance rather than conditions imposed by ecological factors.

In the end, perhaps the most serious objection to the ecologist's model of warfare, and by extension, headhunting, is that like many functionalist accounts of society it tends to overlook the motivations and intentions of individual actors in favor of group responses, and their supposed benefits to society. Again space does not allow a proper consideration of the arguments - instead, we refer the reader to Hallpike's critique of functionalist interpretations of warfare (1973). However, the crux of the matter, as we see it, lies in the translation of biological models of behavioral adaptation - borrowed from the field of ethology - into social theories. Quite simply, social groups cannot be treated in the same way as animal populations, in that while the behavior of animals is, to a greater or lesser extent, governed by instinct and the immediate demands of the environment, man is able to stand back, as it were, and take stock of the situation - his actions are guided by ideas, assumptions, and beliefs about the world. King makes this point when he writes that while "analyses of migration and warfare must give due recognition to the values and beliefs of the society in question ... [t]he tendency of ecological analysis is to relegate them to a secondary position or largely ignore them" (1976:319). In this respect, the ecological account of Iban migration and headhunting owes more to the rationalizations of Western academics, who have judged human behavior in terms of its adaptive value as a survival strategy, than it does to the groundswell of Iban aspirations that gave rise to both phenomena.

In summary then, to dismiss the ecological argument as an explanatory factor of Iban headhunting is not to deny that the Iban competed for land; nor that headhunting was good business for territorial expansion. The desire to beat off rival claims to virgin tracts of land was an obvious factor in Iban headhunting raids. But as to whether one can go beyond this simple statement of fact to establish some intrinsic relationship between Iban warfare and ecological factors is doubtful. In the end, it must be said that the Iban went headhunting because they wanted to. That is to say, they took to the warpath in order to win renown and status for themselves; because it would enhance their appeal in the eyes of the opposite sex; because it was ritually prescribed for the termination of mourning; in order to seek vengeance in a tribal feud; and last, but not least, because they wanted to gain possession over new tracts of virgin forest which were already being claimed by rival groups. To pass over, or ignore, all but the last of these considerations, is to overlook the fact that human actions are motivated by individual desires and goals. Motivations, in their turn, are contingent upon cultural beliefs and values. The latter find their expression through collective representations, and it is with these that we should be chiefly concerned if we are to understand the practice of headhunting in traditional Iban society.

For anthropologists, the relationship between headhunting and fertility has been a key issue in anthropological explanations of this practice. An influential and widely accepted account from the early years of this century favored the idea that trophy heads contained "soul-substance", or "life-force" - a kind of propagating agent which enhanced the fertility of anything brought into contact with it, be it crops, women, livestock, or whatever (Kruyt 1906; Elshout 1926; Hutton 1928, 1938). Attempts to understand the precise nature of this mystical agency have met, however, with a singular lack of success. Indeed, the most consistent response to enquiries into this matter has been one of bafflement on the part of native informants (Needham 1976:78).

For Needham, this is because the very suggestion of "soul-substance" in the first place, arises out of specifically Western notions of causation, which require a contiguity between causes and their effects. In this respect, he argues, past interpretations of headhunting have often tended to bear a closer resemblance to the investigator's own preconceptions about the nature of cause and effect, than to the statements of the peoples he has been studying (1976:84). That is to say, that while indigenous explanations state quite simply that the taking of heads procured the fertility of crops, women and so forth, the mechanistic nature of Western ideas of causation demands that the ethnographer should find some quasi-physical medium, or agency, by which the beneficial consequences of headhunting are transmitted to their recipients. It is this inherent ethnocentricism in approaches to headhunting, which, Needham argues, has led to the assumption that there must be some kind of fertilizing "substance" contained inside the victim's head. As Needham points out, however, "[i]f the Toradja or the Kenyah or the Naga say something equivalent to a --> b [i.e. that taking heads (a) procures fertility (b)], and nothing more, than there are no logical grounds to interpolate a third term [soul-substance], and to do so is to multiply the entities beyond necessity" (1976:79-80; parentheses added).

As an alternative to the soul-substance theory, there was the idea that headhunting should be seen as a form of "ritual combat", symbolizing a conflict between two antagonistic halves of a divided universe (Downs 1955). This interpretation derives from the structuralist tradition at Leiden, and rests upon the notion of a pan-Indonesian dualism. In this scheme of things, everything in the universe is seen as coming in pairs of symbolic oppositions: male and female; sun and moon; life and death; and so on. Against this background, headhunting is interpreted as a ritual re-enactment of a cosmic struggle between Life and Death. In particular, the fact that headhunting is frequently linked to the termination of mourning, is identified by the author as a symbolic assertion of a cosmic principle of Life in ascendance over one of Death.[25]

The objection to this argument, at least in the Iban case, is that while it is certainly true that Iban death rituals do require the procurance of a freshly taken head (see above), there is no real evidence to suggest that the Iban subscribe to a dyadic cosmological principle in the manner, say, of the Ngaju of central Kalimantan (Schärer 1963).[26] Furthermore, this argument fails to make a great deal of sense in relation to much of the imagery and symbolism that surrounds Iban headhunting rituals.

A more recent structural analysis of headhunting sees the marginal location of the enemy, in cosmological terms, as posing a "phenomenological threat" to Iban existence (McKinley 1976). That is to say, the presence of human beings in an ostensibly non-human zone (see above), is seen as generating a cosmological paradox which threatens to undermine the Iban world view. This is "resolved" by going headhunting.

In this instance, trophy heads are represented as symbols of humanity - the concept of social personhood being identified with the fact[27] - while the special treatment of newly taken heads upon their arrival at the longhouse is interpreted as a form of ritual socialization. In this respect, the taking of heads provides the *modus operandum* by which an alien enemy - "matter out of place" (Douglas 1966) - can be ritually incorporated into the longhouse community, thereby neutralizing the cosmological threat that their existence poses.

That the Iban regard their enemy as not quite human - at least in symbolic terms - is clear from their portrayal as *antu gerasi*. That they should wish to incorporate them into Iban society by cutting off their heads is not quite so self-evident. In the first place, the identification of the head with social personhood remains unqualified by the ethnographic evidence. Secondly, the argument loses something by the fact that the Iban were quite ready to absorb other peoples who did not oppose them - through allegiances and inter-marriage - which is surely a far more satisfactory means of social integration than cutting off their heads.[28] Thirdly, as with the previous analyses, this account shows little understanding of the symbolic nature of Iban headhunting rituals, which are interpreted here as rites of socialization.

The Rite of *Ngelampang*: A Symbolic Account of Iban Headhunting

Any understanding of headhunting must make sense of the symbolic elements associated with this practice. Previous attempts, as we have seen, have been singularly unsuccessful in matching a theoretical account with that of native informants. Freeman, however, in his analysis of Iban headhunting goes straight to the heart of the matter (Freeman 1979). He begins with an ethnographic problem, namely that trophy heads (*antu pala'*) are, on occasion, ritually depicted as containing seed, and in particular, *padi pun*, or sacred rice (Freeman 1979).

This "culturally accepted fantasy" (Freeman 1979:237), occurs in the rite of *ngelampang*, which forms a part of the ritual sequence at major headhunting festivals, or *gawai amat*. The term *ngelampang* means "to cut into pieces", and at this point in the festival, the accompanying chants (*timang*) describe "the ritual splitting of a trophy head, or *antu pala'*, by Lang Sengalang Burong, the Iban god of war" (Freeman 1979:234). Freeman writes:

> Lang achieves this feat (which symbolizes the actual beheading of an enemy) with one swift blow of his sword, and from the head which he has split open there pours forth seed which when sown grows into a human crops - as did the dragon's teeth strewn by Cadmus on the plain of Boeotia (1979:234).

And as the words of the *timang* describe this event, it is acted out in real life by aspiring headhunters, the only difference being that a coconut is used in placed of the severed head described in the chants.

For Freeman, then, the "crucial question ... for anyone wishing to understand the Iban cult of headhunting, is, 'Why should a trophy head (of all things) contain seed?'" (1979:234). Freeman's own informants were unable to supply an answer to this ethnographic puzzle, and having dismissed - quite rightly - existing theories of headhunting for "failing totally to detect any breath of the symbolism integral to the [Iban] cult of headhunting" (Freeman 1979:233-34), Freeman turns to a general consideration of the symbolic significance of the head among various other peoples from around the globe. A perusal of De Vries' *Dictionary of Symbols* (1974), informs him that "the human head has been given a multiplicity of meanings from wisdom and authority, to virility and fertility" (Freeman 1979:236). Given the Iban representation of the trophy head as containing seed, Freeman argues that "[i]n the present case it is obviously with the head as a symbol of virility and fertility that we are mainly concerned" (1979:236).

Participant in *Gawai Antu* carrying coconut instead of skull

With this in mind, Freeman turns his attention to suitable ethnographic examples of this theme. In particular, he draws attention to the ancient Greek belief that the psyche was present in the seed or semen, which in turn was supposed to be enclosed in the skull and spine in the form of a "generative marrow" (Freeman 1979:236). Freeman writes: "The head and the male genitalia were regarded as the principal repositories of this generative power, and so were identified, the one with the other" (1979:236). In this respect, the head was attributed with phallic properties, and Freeman cites a number of other examples from the ancient world to support this equation at a more general level: the Roman conception of genius, the mitre of Osiris, the Phrygian cap of Mithras, and the phallic head of Siva (1979:236).

Freeman supplements this material with selected extracts from the literature of psychoanalysis. In particular, he points out that Freud once recorded a dream in which a hat was accorded a phallic significance (Freud 1900:360); also that Freud himself remarked that "in phantasies and in numerous symptoms the head too appears as a symbol of the male genitalia, or, if one prefers to put it so, as something standing for them" (Freud 1916:339; cited in Freeman 1979:236).

According to Freeman, this "symbolic equation Head = Phallus has since been confirmed in the writings of very many other psychoanalysts" (1979:236), which allows him to suggest that this equation "may be accepted as one of the basic symbolic identifications of many human cultures" (1979:236). And this in turn permits him to "consider the interpretation that the trophy heads by which the Iban set such store have a phallic significance as symbols of the generative power of nature" (Freeman 1979:237). Freeman adds that in this respect, "a trophy head, in terms of unconscious symbolism, is another kind of 'golden bough'" (1979:237).

For Freeman, then, "[t]he primary evidence ... for a trophy head having phallic significance is the culturally accepted fantasy that such a head contains seed" (1979:237). There are, however, a number of other factors that can also be taken into consideration. Freeman writes:

> Further evidence for the symbolic significance of trophy heads is contained in the metaphors uses to describe them in the *timang* which is chanted during a headhunting *gawai*. These metaphors, for the most part, refer to fertility and abundance as when trophy heads are equated with a cluster of betel nuts (*sit pinang kuncit*) or a mass of durian fruit (*tambong rian melujong*); or are implicitly phallic as when a trophy head is referred to as a pointed red pepper, a quick river fish, or a scalded pendant cucumber (*langgu rampo betu*) (1979:237).

Freeman also points out that mythical serpents (*nabau*) are particularly associated with Iban headhunting (1979:240), and that there are a number of references in *timang* chants to creatures such as the cobra or crocodile which, according to Freeman, "have a significance both phallic and aggressive" (1979:240).[29]

It is this assortment of supposedly "phallic" images - snakes, serpents, pointed red peppers and pendant cucumbers - that confirm, for Freeman, his suspicions that Iban trophy heads are endowed with a significance that is at one "phallic and procreative" (1979:243). It should be noted, however, that nowhere does he mention that the Iban themselves explicitly identify their trophy heads with penises. Nor can we find any evidence to suggest that in terms of Iban collective representations, snakes, serpents, crocodiles and spears are similarly ascribed a phallic status.

What then are we to make of Freeman's account of Iban headhunting? Do the Iban really conceptualize their trophy heads in phallic terms? And if so, why is this association never made explicit? A slight shift of perspective is useful here. What concerns us most is not so much whether Iban trophy heads have a phallic significance - almost anything can be seen as a phallic symbol, from a clock tower to a fountain pen; rather it is Freeman's implicit suggestion that trophy heads were taken *because* they were phallic symbols. If this seems rather obtuse, the point we are making here is this: Did the Iban take heads because of their phallic significance? Or do Iban trophy heads acquire a phallic significance because of the nature of Iban headhunting?

What is clear is that in Iban headhunting rituals, trophy heads are depicted as containing seed, and that this seed, when planted, matures into a human crop. What remains unclear, however, is Freeman's assertion that these collective representations are evidence of an Iban association of trophy heads and phalluses. As we have seen, Freeman supports his argument with material drawn from the literature of psychoanalysis and the ethnography of the ancient world. But whereas the Greeks and others may well have identified the head with male genitalia, there is nothing to suggest that the Iban subscribe to a similar set of ideas. In our opinion, then, Freeman's initial problem, namely "Why should a trophy head (of all things) contain seed?", remains unanswered.

Trophy Heads as 'Fruit'

A recurrent image in Iban headhunting symbolism is the portrayal of trophy heads as "fruit". This theme appears repeatedly in Iban collective representations: in the chants that accompany headhunting rituals (*timang gawai amat*), in myths (*ensera*) and stories of the legendary heroes (*jerita orang Panggau*), in dirges for the dead (*sabak*), and even in love songs (*ramban*). Typically, trophy heads are referred to as a cluster of betel nuts (*sit pinang*); the fruits of the *nibong, mudur*, and other species of wild palm; jack-fruit (*nangka*); durian (*rian*); coconuts (*piur*) and other seed-bearing fruit of the forest (c.f. Freeman above). The most recurrent image, however, is that of *igi' ranyai* - "the seed of the *ranyai* palm".

The *ranyai* palm does not actually exist - at least not in the world of everyday experience - but is a mythical *nibong* palm (Oncosperma tigillaria), which is said to grow in Sebayan - the Iban land of the dead. In the Iban *sabak*, or funeral dirge, the party of the dead, who escort the newly deceased to the Afterworld, is described as coming to a beautiful grove - Madang Ranyai - where this wonderful tree grows in great profusion (Sandin 1966:64 ff.). Here the party halts, whereupon the women members urge their menfolk to drive away the wasps that swarm around the trunks of these trees and to cut down their fruit - the *buah ranyai*. This request has an immediate effect on the men who leap up ...

> ... *manjong munyi burong pangkas encai,*
> *Lalu nangkin berangin pedang penguji,*
> *Tak kebu kebu ulu ke bekambu ka bulu elabubu buok nyadi;*
> *Lalu nyimpong ujong nibong beranyi,*
> *Dinga rak balat nyawa ricah rami,*
> *Munyi nengeri pasar melintang.*

> ... shouting excitedly like the pangkas omen-bird,
> with sword girded on their waists;
> Whose hilts are quickly decorated with human hair,
> And handsomely blowing in the wind.
> They slash off the tops of the *nibong* palms,
> And cut away the fruits of the *ranyai*;
> Which sounded loudly like the noise of a busy bazaar.[30]

These fruit fall to the ground and as they do so they metamorphose into human heads, which are then gathered up by the women (Sandin 1966:68).

The sequence is, of course, an allegorical account of headhunting, in which the slashing of the *ranyai* palm, and the cutting down of its fruit, describes the mortal wounding of an enemy and his decapitation. In this context, the images of swarming wasps and the cries of a noisy bazaar are metaphors for flying bullets and the tumult of battle. The mention of the omen-bird Pangkas is also significant here, for the cry of this bird - the Maroon Woodpecker (Blythipicus rubignosis) - is said to be "like a man shouting in triumph"; because of this his call is always welcome in that it signals the cries of victory that traditionally accompanied the return of a successful war-party (Freeman 1961:152).

The portrayal of combat and decapitation as the slashing of the *ranyai* palm, and the gathering of its fruit, appears again and again in Iban oral literature. Its significance, however, is more than simply that of a literary device; rather it provides us with a key image, or root metaphor, for understanding Iban ideas of headhunting. This is most clearly seen in the context of major headhunting ceremonies, or *gawai amat*.

Gawai Amat

The *gawai*, or festival, stands at the center of Iban religious life. They are spectacular occasions that often continue for several days on end with no expenses spared. Their principal concern is to invite the gods to a feast held in their honor. In return, it is hoped that the gods will bring magical charms (*pengaroh* or *ubat*) for their hosts, and provide them with assistance in their future undertakings.

There are many different types of *gawai*, some of which are distributed on a regional basis. Broadly speaking, however, there are four main categories: agriculture *gawai*; *gawai* for gaining good fortune and material wealth; *gawai* for the dead; and those *gawai* that have to do with warfare and the taking of heads. It is the latter class of *gawai* that are distinguished by the title of *gawai amat*, or "true festivals".

Gawai amat are themselves differentiated into a number of specific ritual performances. Together they form a recognized sequence, or cycle, which is organized in a series of ascending stages, each step reflecting the age and relative status of the festival sponsor. A man will begin, in his youth, at the lowest level, or grade, of festival, and gradually work his way up the scale according to his lifetime's achievements. The lowest ranking *gawai* last only for one night, but the highest may continue for a week or more and involve considerable expenditure on the part of the *bilik*-families of the sponsors.

Often the decision to hold a festival will be endorsed by dreams in which the legendary heroes of *Panggau Libau* appear. They give instructions as to what type of festival should be held (Masing 1981:477, 479). Those who choose to disregard this supernatural command, for whatever reason, do so at their peril, in that they are likely to incur the displeasure of the gods by so doing. Conversely, should a man presume to hold a festival which is incommensurate with his level of achievement, then it is felt that this may endanger his health and might even shorten his life. For this reason, in the past, only those who had regularly taken heads could hold the highest ranking ceremonies such as the *gawai kenyalang*, or "hornbill festival".[31] Outstanding war leaders, on the other hand, having completed one *gawai* series, might start the cycle again for a second or even third time.

The principal deity involved in *gawai amat* is, of course, Lang Sengalang Burong, the Iban god of war (usually known as Lang for short). Freeman describes Lang as "an amalgam of Jupiter and Mars, with a touch of Bacchus" (1979:239). He adds that

> [i]n his human form he is an imposing man of heroic propor-
> tions, who, despite his mature age, is in full command of his
> great physical powers. His animal form is the Brahminy Kite:
> a predatory bird of great strength and beauty. Above all else
> Lang is the god of headhunting: custodian of severed heads
> from the beginning of time (Freeman 1979:239).

Lang lives in the sky realm of Langit, together with his wife and daughters, and his seven sons-in-law: Ketupong, Beragai, Bejampong, Embuas, Papau, Pangkas and Nendak. The latter, in their avian manifestation, are omen-birds of Iban augury.[32]

The main purpose of *gawai amat* is, as we have indicated, to invite Lang and his extended family to a feast held in their honor. Festival proceedings are structured by the performance of an invocation, or *timang* (in some areas *pengap*), which summons the gods to the *gawai*, and describes their journey from their celestial home to the longhouse of men. The *timang* is performed by professional bards - *lemambang* - who carry out their duties between dusk and dawn. Often the invocation lasts for several nights in succession, its length being determined by the type of *gawai* being celebrated.

As we have mentioned, the *ranyai* palm, and its curious fruit, provide a central image, or ritual focal point, at *gawai amat*. On such occasions, this mythical tree is physically represented by a specially constructed "shrine", which is erected in the *ruai*, or longhouse gallery, for the duration of the festival. The shrine is itself referred to by the term *ranyai*, and ideally should be assembled by someone who has taken a head, or who is renowned for his bravery in warfare. It consists of a framework of bamboo and rattan, reaching from the floor of the *ruai* to the rafters, wrapped around with a mat to create a vertical column some six or seven feet in circumference. Concealed in the center of this construction is a plate of offerings (*piring*) and a basket of charms and other items that are to be "blessed by the visit of the gods. Woven fabrics - *pua' kumbu'* - whose patterns and designs are related to headhunting themes, are draped around the outside, which is then adorned with weapons and the accoutrement of war: swords, spears, rifles and so forth.[33] The shrine is also hung with coconuts, representing the fruit of the *ranyai - buah ranyai -* and sometimes old head trophies are added.[34] Bunches of betel nut (*pinang*), again representing head trophies, may also be attached, while the ruddy coloured leaves of a species of croton (*sabang api* - Dracaena sp.) are placed at its foot. In the past these were subsequently planted along the path leading up to a longhouse as a sign for the return of a successful war-party. The leaves of another species of plant are also included in the construction of the *ranyai*. These are referred to as *daun sukong ranyai* - "leaves that support the *ranyai*" - but their significance remains unclear.

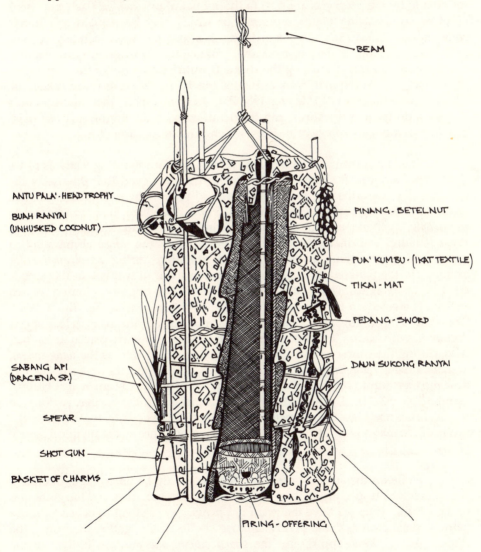

Figure 1. Sketch of *Ranyai* Shrine

The *ranyai* shrine is said to be the abode of the gods for the duration of the festival, and is circumambulated by the bards, or *lemambang*, in the course of their performance of the *timang* invocation. In this respect it provides a focal point for ritual activities during the *gawai*. More importantly, the *ranyai* shrine is identified as the physical representation of a fruit bearing tree. Thus Masing, in his account of this ritual assembly, comments that "[t]he shrine itself is often referred to by the *timang* as a *nibong* (a thorny palm) or a *nangka* (jack-fruit tree), or other seed-bearing plants the seeds of which may be planted for human consumption" (1981:73). In some instances, a *nibong* palm may actually be used in the construction of the *ranyai* shrine, making this association quite explicit. Furthermore, the act of erecting the shrine is called *nanam ranyai* (lit. - "planting the shrine"), while the man responsible for this is addressed as *orang nanam* (lit. "the person who plants") (Masing 1981:73). In this respect, then, there is little reason to doubt that the shrine can be identified with the mythical *ranyai* palm growing in the Iban Afterworld, from which it takes its name.[35]

The *ranyai* shrine plays a crucial role in Iban headhunting festivals as we shall presently see. It should be mentioned here, however, that the use of the term *ranyai* to describe this ritual edifice would seem to be restricted to the Ulu Ai and Ulu Rejang regions (Richards 1981:299). Elsewhere they are referred to as *pandong*, a generic term for all ritual structures of this kind (Richards 1981:248). What is more, one finds that, in some areas at least, the *ranyai* shrine may be supplanted as the principal focus of ritual attention during *gawai amat*. For example, in the Saribas *gawai burong*, or "bird festival", it seems that its place is taken by the *tiang kelingkang* - a tall pole decorated with brightly coloured cottons - which is erected on the verandah, or *tanju'*, of the longhouse (Sandin 1977:53). One should note however, that like the *ranyai* shrine, the *tiang kelingkang* is decorated with *sabang* (croton) leaves, while head trophies are placed at its foot. Also, during the course of the festival, this post is referred to as the *tiang ranyai*, or *ranyai tiang kelingkang* (Sandin 1977:48, 68, 70), while the festival itself is described as *gawai ranyai ensebam* - the "festival of the luxuriant *ranyai* (palm)" (Sandin 1977:53-54). In short, it would seem that, if, in the Saribas region, the *ranyai* shrine itself has been superseded by the *tiang kelingkang*, nevertheless the image of the *ranyai* palm still retains its central importance as the mythical source of trophy heads.

While on the subject of festival titles, it should be noted here, that there are several which specifically refer to the slashing or palm trees and the gathering of their fruit. Thus we have the *gawai ijok pumpong* - "festival to behead the *ijok* palm (Arenga pinnata)"; the *gawai mudur ruroh* - "festival to gather the fruit of the *mudur* palm (Salacca spp.)"; and the *gawai mulong merangau* - "festival of the weeping sago palm". The latter is especially interesting in that Sandin describes the "sacred pole" [c.f. *tiang kelingkang*] erected on such occasions as being "cleverly carved like an old sago palm when all its fruit are fallen to the ground" (1980:350). There is also mention of a *gawai gajah meram*, or "broody elephant festival", where "the pole is made of strong wood with branches decorated with skulls and *isang* palm leaves" (Sandin 1980:42).[36] These accounts would seem to confirm the idea that for the Saribas Iban, the *tiang kelingkang* stands as a material representations of the mythical *ranyai* palm.

In the past, there was also a festival which was actually called the *gawai ranyai*. Howell describes this as "the greatest of all feasts" (1977:140), and tells us that on such occasions "all the heads are collected and placed in a winnowing basket or *capan* and spears hung round it by means of cords" (Howell 1977:140). Howell adds that the "spears are put in an upright position in imitation of this so-called *ranyai* [i.e. the mythical *nibong* palm] and the bravest warrior present is invited to fell them" (1900:137). Here, the cutting down of the spears can be recognized as a ritual enactment of the slashing of *ranyai* palms - an action which is simultaneously identified with combat and the taking of heads, as allegorically portrayed in Iban oral literature.

The *gawai ranyai* no longer seems to be held today, although Sandin does mention it as one of the stages in the Saribas *gawai burong* cycle (Sandin 1977:13; 1980:42). The *gawai ijok pumpong*, mentioned above, does, however, provide us with a contemporary equivalent. This festival, Masing writes, "deals directly with the rites of headhunting" (1981:64). He adds: "The depiction of beheading an enemy occurs at the conclusion of the rites when the [*ranyai*] shrine is dismantled by severing the rattan length that holds up the shrine with a single blow of the sword" (Masing 1981:64). Clearly, the ritual action here is very similar to that described by Howell in his account of the *gawai ranyai*.

In summary, then, the image of the *ranyai* palm and its variations must be seen as a central element in the Iban cult of headhunting. That this mythical tree is identified as the source of trophy heads, which are its "seed" (*igi*) or "fruit" (*buah*), there can be no doubt. However, in order to fully understand the significance of this device - the lietmotif of Iban headhunting rituals, so to speak - we must turn to the chants, or (*timang*), that accompany and structure the performance of Iban *gawai amat*.

Timang Gawai Amat

Sather has described the chants accompanying Iban headhunting rituals as being "rich in religious and historical allusion, symbolic metaphor, expressions of social values and shared assumptions regarding the relationship of man, nature and the spiritual world" (1977a:ix). We shall argue that it is through the text of the *timang gawai amat*, and its enactment in Iban ritual, that the significance of Iban headhunting is properly revealed.[37]

The ritual action at Iban *gawai*, or festivals, is based upon an oral narrative, or *timang (pengap* outside the Ulu Ai and Ulu Rejang). *Timang* are performed by professional bards, or *lemambang*, assisted by a two-or three-man chorus (*orang nyagu*). All *timang gawai amat* follow the same general pattern, or "path" (*jalai*), but their length varies according to the grade of festival being celebrated (see above). Each level takes the *timang* invocation a stage further in the narrative, with the highest grade of festival completing the cycle.

The main body of the *timang gawai amat*, that is to say the part which is always performed at every *gawai amat*, can be broken up into a number of key episodes, or narrative sequences. These are as follows: the opening sequence, in which Lang Sengalang Burong's absence is noticed; the sending of an invitation to the house of Lang (*ngambi' ngabang*); the headhunting expedition of the gods (*ngerampas*); Lang's journey to the longhouse of men; and the ceremonial welcome of Lang on his arrival there (*mansang ngabang*) (Masing 1989:61-62).

The most important of these episodes - at least in as far as appreciating the ritual significance of Iban headhunting is concerned - is the one in which the gods themselves are described as setting out on an headhunting raid. The attack is directed against a powerful and malevolent demon, or *antu*, known variously as Nising, Bengkong or Beduru. The war-party is made up of the sons-in-law of Lang (*menantu* Lang), who are, of course, the omen-birds of Iban augury. They must take to the war-path in order to satisfy the demands of Endu Dara Ticin Temaga - the youngest daughter of Lang - who refuses to go to the festival without having something to bring as a gift for their hosts. The gift she has in mind is nothing other than a freshly taken head:

Enti isang lama enggai kitai dia aku enggai mai,
Ke bereba di pala tiang,
Enti rangkah pala aku enggai mai,
Enggai enda mai ka baru agi ciang.

I do not want to bring with me old *isang* leaves,
Which uselessly crowd the top of the post,[38]
I do not want to bring the ancient skull,
I must bring a new one which is still dripping with blood

(Sandin 1977:69, 71).

This ultimatum dispatches the omen-birds on a journey to the ends of the earth. As they pass through different regions of a largely mythical universe, they enquire from those they meet if they have seen "the precious seed of the *ranyai*". Time and again the answer is "No", but eventually they encounter the spirit Rintong Langit Pengulor Bulan, who tells them that he has heard it "crying" (*nyabak*) in the house of Nising.

At this point there is a sudden change in the imagery of the *timang*. Up until this moment, trophy heads have consistently been represented as "fruit" (*buah*) or "seed" (*igi*) of one description or another. Here, however, they are portrayed as the "children" (*anak*) of Nising.

Nising is in fact an *antu gerasi*: a frightful ogre, with eyes as big as cups and ears as large as winnowing baskets. His breath is described as roaring like a blacksmith's hearth, while his teeth grind like the hammering of steel at an anvil (Sandin 1977:108, 111). His territory is situated at "the edge of the yellow and red sky" (*tisi langit kuning, tisi langit radu*) - i.e. on the horizon where the sun sets (and rises). In this respect, Nising is located, like so many real life enemies, at the very limits of the known world.

The omen-birds, having located their prize, decide to make a reconnaissance of the enemy longhouse. Hiding beneath its floor, they hear the "children" of Nising whimpering and crying out in their sleep. Their distress is caused by terrifying nightmares in which they have dreamt they were bitten through by snakes, or else carried off by crocodiles. This, their mother tells them, does not bode well, for they have seen their own deaths at the hands of enemies.[39]

That night, the omen-birds themselves are visited by strange dreams in which they see themselves cutting down great bunches of coconuts, or else being greeted by beautiful maidens with flowers in their hair. According to Lang, these images foretell their success in taking heads on the morrow.

The next day, the omen-birds stealthily enter the longhouse of Nising to take him unawares, so that he has no opportunity to resist them. They then proceed to flatter him with extravagant compliments and false praises. At the same time they ply him with vast quantities of palm wine (*arak*), which Nising gulps down with a great roaring noise, like the sound of a forest fire. In the end he collapses to the floor in a drunken stupor; whereupon the omen-birds leap forward to gather up their prize - the fabulous seed of the *ranyai* palm.[40]

As this point in the *timang* narrative is reached, those men who are sponsoring the festival cut down the coconuts that are attached to the *ranyai* shrine. They have previously dressed themselves as for the war-path, with fine jackets of woven cloth and coats of bearskin, or leopard cat. On their heads they wear plaited war bonnets adorned with hornbill feathers, and at their sides they carry swords ornamented with the hair of slain enemies. It is with the latter that they cut away the *igi' ranyai*, or "seed of the shrine", uttering as they do so, the war-cry that traditionally accompanied the return of a successful headhunting party. The entire sequence is, of course, a ritual re-enactment of beheading the enemy.

The *timang* narrative then goes on to describe the return of the omen-birds to the longhouse of Lang where they are welcomed by the women of the community. The newly taken heads are themselves ceremonially received by the wife of Lang - Indai Kecendai - who wraps them in the very best of her *pua kumbu'* blankets. With the demands of Ticin Temaga thus fulfilled, Lang and his household are then able to proceed to the festival.

All *timang gawai amat* reach this point in the cycle. That is to say, they all describe the headhunting expedition of the omen-birds, and the journey of Lang and his entourage to the festival of men. This takes one night, and the *timang* closes at dawn with the ceremonial welcome of Lang by the longhouse community. Subsequent stages in the narrative depend upon the type of festival being held: each ascending level taking the *timang* one step further towards completion.

The next episode in the *timang* cycle, after the arrival of Lang, is among the most dramatic in the narrative, for it describes the rite of *ngelampang* and the splitting open of the trophy head to release its seed (see above). It begins with Lang getting up to perform the dance of Iban warriors (*berayah*). This imitates the soaring flight of the Brahminy Kite (which is of course Lang's own avian manifestation). Lang has previously been well supplied with rice wine (*tuak*), and so he is a little intoxicated by now. As he dances, Lang lets fall, from the basket on his back, the head trophy that he has brought. The women are appalled by the horrible spectacle and complain that it is not the splendid thing talked about by their husbands - that "most precious ornament" about which they have heard so much - but something ugly and disgusting. On hearing these words, the head trophy bursts into tears and begins to wail, just like a small child or infant.

Various female deities are then summoned to "nurse" (*ngua*) the unhappy head, among them the wives of the legendary headhunting heroes of Panggau Libau. But even the best attempts of Kumang, Lulong, and the others are to no avail - the trophy head is inconsolable. In the end, in desperation, it is passed to the highest ranking shamans in the community - the *manang bali'*. The latter are individuals who have changed their sex from male to female in the pursuit of their vocation (*bali'* lit. = "changed"), their adopted status being reflected in their female attire. The position of *manang bali'* in society is a very special one in that they are able to slay malevolent demons (*antu*) in ritual combat. In this respect their role is comparable to that of Iban warriors, except that their deeds are performed in the supernatural realm against unseen foe, rather than on the ground against enemies of flesh and blood.[41]

Upon being handed to the *manang bali'*, the trophy head immediately ceases its crying and begins to laugh instead. Its humor, it seems, arises from "the droll appearance of the transvestite shamans, with their female attire all awry, their unformed breasts, and their broken and dangling penises" (Freeman 1979:241). Having successfully stopped its tears, the *manang bali'* announce that the reason for the trophy head's unhappiness is because "it has yet to find its beloved mother, ... it has yet to greet its father" (Masing 1981:323, 323b). At this point it is passed to the wife of the festival sponsor, who assumes the role of "mother" to the head (Masing 1981:323 n.). The *manang bali'* then announce that what the head would really like is to be planted (*nanam*) - "to be thrust into the earth like the sucker of a banana plant, or a taro shoot" (Freeman 1979:242).

Lang agrees to this, but only on condition that the head first be split in two (*ngelampang*). He then forges a brand new sword for this purpose, carefully tempering the steel and honing its blade. With this in hand he slices through the trophy head with a single stroke to release its content of seed and sacred rice (*padi pun*). And as the words of the *timang* describe this scene, it is simultaneously enacted by aspiring headhunters on the verandah (*tanju'*) of the longhouse. In this instance, however, the trophy head is substituted by a coconut, which had previously adorned the *ranyai* shrine.[42] The rite of *ngelampang* is explicitly identified with the act of decapitating the enemy (*pumpong*), and Freeman comments that "the success of the aspirant in performing this rite is taken as a measure of his future prowess as a headhunter" (1979:243).

A crucial feature of the rite of *ngelampang* is the idea that the trophy head, when split open, contains seed - most importantly that of the sacred rice, or *padi pun*. This seed, Lang says, must be planted. At this point the *timang* invocation enters into a remarkable allegory in which warfare and headhunting are portrayed through images of rice farming.

The main stages in the allegory are as follows: the forging of farming implements / the forging of weapons; the search for new farm lands / reconnoitring enemy territory; seeking propitious omens for farming / seeking propitious omens for going on the war-path; felling the forest for swiddens / hacking at the posts of the enemy longhouse; firing the swiddens / putting the enemy longhouse to the torch; sowing the rice seed / planting the eyeballs of the enemy; reaping the rice crop / beheading the enemy; storing away the harvest / receiving new head trophies.

In this light, Iban warfare is explicitly identified with the circumstances of rice farming. In particular, a symbolic parallel is drawn between the taking of heads and the reaping of rice. Freeman, in describing this episode in the *timang* invocation, writes: "It was the faith of the pagan Iban that by this prefiguration in symbolic form they would be certain to succeed in capturing further heads in minutely planned raids into alien territory, so ensuring the fertility of the *padi* they aspired eventually to plant there" (1979:244).

The final stages of the *timang* cycle have to do with the cultivation of cotton plants and the weaving of war-jackets for the festival sponsors. The Iban have traditionally grown their own cotton (*taya*), which they plant in subsidiary swiddens some time after the rice crop has been harvested. The cotton is used in the weaving of *pua'* textiles which play an important role in Iban ritual life and are particularly associated with the cult of headhunting (see below). As with the earlier agricultural allegory, the cultivation and harvesting of the cotton fields is identified with warfare and the taking of heads (Masing 1981:430, & n.). In particular, Lang cautions that if the cotton pods be broken, then the pieces should be placed in a gourd (*genok*) and covered with a hat made from plaited lily fiber (*uyok ketapu senggang*). This is precisely what is done if a trophy head has been accidently broken into pieces (Masing 1981:430, & n.). Once the cotton has been harvested, and the pods dried in the sun (this is allegorical of the smoking of trophy heads), it is spun into thread (*ubong*). This is then woven into war-jackets, or *baju*, which are to be worn by those men who are sponsoring the festival (Masing 1981:431-38). The ogresses Samambai and Panggit are summoned to perform this task, and as this point in the *timang* is reached, the festival sponsors themselves put on their woven war-jackets and again dress as if for a headhunting raid. This time they descend from the longhouse to slash at a head trophy mounted on a pole in front of the building. The head is then brought back to the longhouse and presented to their wives who are seated at the foot of the *ranyai* shrine (Masing 1981:441-42). And as in earlier instances, this sequence is explicitly identified with beheading the enemy.

The harvesting of the cotton fields and the weaving of war-jackets is reached on the seventh night of the *gawai amat* invocation and marks the end of the *timang* cycle. At this point, the gods "bless" (*nenjang*) their hosts and present them with magical charms (*pengaroh*). They then depart for their longhouse in the skies. And with the completion of the *timang*, so ends the *gawai amat*.

Only the highest ranking festivals in the *gawai amat* cycle see the *timang* performed all the way through. Lower level *gawai* pause at some earlier stage in the narrative - for example at the point describing the forging of farm imple- ments, or when Lang sets out in search of land for his swiddens. To have completed the cycle is the greatest achievement that an individual can aspire to within the traditional Iban prestige system. The only option left is to return to the beginning and celebrate the *gawai amat* cycle for a second time.

Discussion

What, then, are we to make of the symbolism of the *timang gawai amat*? The first thing that can be done is to distinguish the principal themes, or motifs, that emerge as the narrative unfolds. There are three: the portrayal of trophy heads as the fruit of the *ranyai* palm; the ritual treatment of trophy heads as infants; and the allegorical representation of headhunting as agriculture.

The first and last of these go together in a logical sequence: the omen- birds go on an expedition to gather the "fruit" of the mythical *ranyai* palm; they return home with their prize; this is brought to the *gawai*, where it is cut open to release its contents, namely seed; this seed is planted and grows into a human crop; the harvest is gathered-in and brought back to the longhouse; it is dried in the sun and stored away in the rice-loft. In this scheme of things, headhunting is consistently portrayed in terms of an extended metaphor modeled on Iban subsistence economics. Trophy heads are like the fruit of the forest: they are gathered, and their seed is planted to provide the Iban with sustenance.

As we have seen, Freeman, in his examination of Iban headhunting rituals, has argued for the phallic significance of trophy heads. His case rests on the collective representation of trophy heads as the containers of seed, and an equation of this seed with semen. For Freeman, "[t]he primary evidence in the

Iban case for a trophy head having phallic significance is the culturally accepted fantasy that such a head contains seed" (1979:237; see also above). He adds, however, that "[f]urther evidence for the symbolic significance of trophy heads is contained in the metaphors used to describe them in the *timang* which is chanted during a headhunting *gawai*" (Freeman 1979:237). According to Freeman, "[t]hese metaphors, for the most part, refer to fertility and abundance as when trophy heads are equated with a cluster of betel nuts (*sit pinang kuncit*) or a mass of durian fruit (*tambong rian melujong*)" (1979:237). In some instances, however, Freeman sees them as "implicitly phallic as when a trophy head is referred to as a pointed red pepper, a quick river fish, or a scalded pendant cucumber (*langgu rampo betu*)" (1979:237).

Whether or not pointed red peppers, quick river fish and scalded cucumbers can be seen as phallic symbols is perhaps a moot point. What is clear - and most emphatically so - is that trophy heads are identified as seed-bearing fruit, and in particular, the fruit of the mythical *ranyai* palm. As we have seen, the latter image plays a central role in Iban headhunting ceremonies, and it is, of course, this same "fruit" which is cut in two during the rite of *ngelampang* to release its contents of seed. Our suggestion here is that one need look no further than the imagery of the *timang* invocation for an explanation of the ritual significance of Iban headhunting. Quite simply, to take heads is to gather the fruit of the magical *ranyai* palm. The fabulous fruit of this tree, when cut open, is found to contain seed, most notably that of the sacred rice--*benih padi pun*. This seed is identified as the source of agricultural fertility, and when planted provides the longhouse community with sustenance and material well-being. With these representations before us, there seems little need to appeal to a cult of phallic symbolism, which is neither called for by the ethnography, nor necessary as a means of explanation.

Alongside these images, however, there is an alternative frame of reference in which trophy heads are represented as infants. In the *timang* invocation, it will be recalled, trophy heads are identified as the "children" of Nising, who whimper and wail in anticipation of their terrible deaths. Similarly, the head brought to the *gawai* by Lang is described as crying inconsolably, as if it were a small child. In this instance it is "nursed" (*ngua*) by a succession of female spirits, before finding comfort in the arms of its "mother"--the wife of the festival sponsor.

These remarkable sequences from the *timang gawai amat* find a close parallel in the rites of *encabau arong*, which marked the return of a successful headhunting expedition. On such occasions, the women of the community would parade the newly taken heads along the length of the longhouse, singing the valedictory "head-song" (*naku*) as they went. Nyuak tells us that

> in the chant the head is asked how it came by its fate? The head answers that it dreamed it had been bitten by a snake, or carried off by a crocodile. It is told, 'That was a lucky dream for it directed the spear that struck you, it rendered keen the edge of the sword that struck you from your body' (1977:203).

Clearly this is very like the *timang* sequence describing the dreams of Nising's children before they are taken by the omen-birds.

What is the significance of these images? And how do they relate to the representation of trophy heads as seed-bearing fruit? In the rite of *ngelampang*, it will be recalled, the head is much amused by the curious spectacle of the transvestite *manang bali'*, and their pathetic attempts to pass themselves off as women. Freeman comments that "[h]ere, I would suppose, we have a projection of the male ridicule of the transvestite homosexual" (1979:241). He adds: "it would seem the head stops crying because it feels more secure and happy in the care of the transvestite shaman, whose hands are without envy and only wish to possess and fondle" (Freeman 1979:241).

Quite what Freeman is trying to say here is not exactly clear, but he would seem to be suggesting that the *manang bali'*, by virtue of their transvestitism, are also homosexual, and that given the supposed phallic significance of trophy heads, this ritual has homosexual connotations. Furthermore, it seems that the previous distress of the trophy head is to be accounted for by the fact that it feels uncomfortable in the hands of penis-envying female spirits (c.f. Freeman 1968:388; cited above).

But what of the representation of heads as infants? In advancing his phallo-centric interpretation of Iban headhunting, Freeman chooses to ignore the fact that in the *timang*, trophy heads are explicitly identified as children. He also chooses to disregard the reason given for their unhappiness, namely that they have yet to find their father and mother. In the latter instance, the failure of the female spirits to comfort the weeping infant is due to the fact that they are not its proper mother. When, however, the trophy head is passed to the wife of the festival sponsor - who is identified as the "mother" of the head - the infant immediately halts its tears.

The significance of the imagery here seems to be perfectly straightforward. On the one hand, trophy heads are portrayed as "infants", while on the other, Iban warriors are identified as "fathers" to the heads they have taken, and their wives as "mothers". Clearly, in this particular context headhunting is equated,not with rice farming, but rather with human procreation. And if no direct correspondence can be drawn up as in the case of headhunting:rice farming allegory, the metaphorical representation of trophy heads as "infants" nevertheless makes this connection between the taking of heads and reproduction quite explicit. In short, in symbolic terms, Iban men go headhunting in order to procure children for their wives.[43]

As it happens, a number of structural correspondences can be found between headhunting and childbearing. Men risk their lives to take heads for the community, women risk their lives in giving birth. Men observe ritual prohibitions (*pemali*) during the time of their wives' pregnancy; women observe restrictions when their husbands are on the war-path. Those who are killed in battle, or are beheaded, proceed to a special location in the Iban Afterworld; so do women who die in childbirth.[44]

There are also a number of sexual metaphors in which coitus is portrayed in terms of warfare. For example, Sather reports that "[s]exual congress is commonly described metaphorically as 'combat', the penis as a 'sword' or other weapon, and ejaculation as the loosening of spear or the firing of a gun" (1978:343). In themselves these metaphors and similies may not, perhaps, seem especially significant - they are, after all, hardly unique to the Iban language. Nevertheless, they are consistent with a ritual association between headhunting and procreation.

The role of the transvestite *manang bali'*, on the other hand, probably does have a special significance in this scheme of things. That is to say, as longhouse champion against malevolent spirits and demoniac being (*antu*), the *manang bali'* can, in ritual terms, be identified with the male realm of headhunting and warfare.[45] At the same time, however, his (or her) female, or transvestite, status, also places the *manang bali'* within the society of women. In this respect the *manang bali'* crosses the divide between male and female in Iban culture, thereby providing an appropriate vehicle for the introduction of trophy heads from the masculine domain of headhunting into the feminine realm of childbearing and motherhood.

In summary then, it seems that Iban headhunting, as a ritual activity, is linked, not only to agricultural production, but also to sexual reproduction. This, in turn, suggests that the Iban may simultaneously draw a parallel between human fecundity, on the one hand, and the increase of rice on the other. Certainly this is implied in Freeman's analysis of trophy heads which, though supposedly phallic in their ritual significance, are found to contain, not semen (*cinit*), but seed (*benih*), the one, it is suggested, being identified with the other. It should be noted, however, that the equation of human reproduction with agricultural increase, though a common representation around the world, is everywhere a product of cultural associations, rather than one given by nature. That is to say, it is not something we should take for granted. For this reason we now turn to the Iban rice cycle in order to identify an indigenous model of agricultural fertility based on the lives and childbearing capacities of Iban women.

The Iban Rice Cycle

The annual rice cycle begins in June and ends in May the following year. Farming methods conform to much the same pattern as those of other swidden agriculturalists in South East Asia (Spencer 1966). The principal stages are as follows: clearing (*nebas*) and felling (*nebang*) the jungle; firing the fields (*nunu*); dibbling (*nugal*) and sowing (*menih*); weeding (*mantun*); reaping (*ngetau*); carrying in the harvest (*berangkut*); threshing (*nungku'*); winnowing (*muput*); and storage (*besimpan*) (Freeman 1970:228-29).

Iban rice farming is an extremely arduous occupation, requiring a great deal of effort on the part of every able-bodied person in the community. But although men and women are equally concerned in ensuring the success of the annual harvest, there is a clearly distinguished division of labour between the sexes. Freeman writes that "[i]n general, those tasks requiring great strength and energy fall to the men, while women are responsible for work that is more onerous and time devouring but well within their physical capacities" (1970:27). He adds that "the division of labour is so arranged that most of the essentially male jobs (e.g. slashing, felling and dibbling) fall within a span of about three or four months (i.e. June-September), leaving the rest of the year free for all those men not actually responsible for managing a farm" (Freeman 1970:227).

This male freedom has important economic and social implications. In the past, it allowed men to set off on extended journeys into the forest in search of jungle produce which could then be exchanged for essential requirements such as salt and iron. It was also the time for mounting headhunting raids - these usually required some preparation and often involved long absences from home as war-parties penetrated deep into enemy territory. More recently, it has allowed men to go off in search of wage labor in the logging camps and oil fields of the region.

The male enthusiasm for traveling away from home is a well recognized Iban institution, being defined by the term *bejalai*. Those who embark upon *bejalai* are expected to return to their longhouses with money and valuables: in the past, prestigious Chinese ceramics and brasswares; nowadays, outboard engines, chainsaws, videos and cassette-players. Thus, as Freeman points out, the custom of *bejalai*

> is generally approved of, and indeed encouraged, by those who stay at home .. [for] .. the property which a man does succeed in acquiring is put into the general pool of his *bilek*-family's possessions, and thus becomes part of the general family inheritance. In other words, the *bilek*-family as a whole benefits (1970:226).

With the men absent on *bejalai*, the principal responsibility for looking after the rice crop as it grows in the fields falls to the women of the community. Their main concern is to ensure that the fields are free from weeds. Weed growth can have seriously detrimental effect on the outcome of the harvest, and the Iban are well-aware of this.[46] Even so, Iban men prefer to leave the responsibility for this arduous task to their womenfolk. In doing so they actually place a physical constraint on the size of their farms, the area cleared each season being directly related to the area that can be weeded by the women of the *bilik*-family (Freeman 1970:195).

Iban men generally return to their longhouses towards the end of the agricultural year in order to assist with reaping and help carry in the harvest. Even at this time of year, however, it is women who lead the proceedings (see below), and who are responsible for such tasks as selecting next year's rice seed. Indeed, Iban women generally are far more knowledgeable about rice, its different varieties, and how long each strain takes to reach maturity, than are their menfolk.[47]

Iban agriculture, then, is characterized by a fairly well- defined division of labor between the sexes. We have presented, of course, what is very much an ideal model of the way things should be; the demography and personal circumstances of individual *bilik*-families frequently demand that Iban men should participate more fully in weeding and other essentially female farm duties. Nevertheless, there is a sense of propriety governing male and female agricultural labor which remains firmly embedded in Iban consciousness, regardless of exigencies. As Freeman remarks, "[t]his system of division of work between the sexes is supported by various social sanctions, and particularly by the strongly held traditional attitudes of young men" (1970:229). He adds:

Young men are perfectly willing to join in the manly tasks of felling, dibbling, and the carrying in of huge loads of *padi* for threshing, but nothing will persuade them to participate in the essentially feminine duties of sowing, weeding and reaping. To do so would excite the immediate ridicule of their fellows, and of shame, the Iban are extremely sensitive (Freeman 1970:229-30).

Women Cultivators and the Fertility of Rice

The division of agricultural labor in Iban society can, on the one hand, be seen quite simply as reflecting the different physical capacities of men and women. At the same time, it can also be seen as serving the interests of men, who wish to participate in the custom of *bejalai*. There is, however, another level of meaning involved which has to do with an idea of appropriate male and female gender roles. In this instance, the demarcation of duties is defined in terms of a conceptual distinction between the sexual identities of men and women.

The sowing season is one occasion when the sexual division of labor is dramatically emphasized. For example, Freeman tells us that "[t]he Iban method of planting *padi* is a simple, though onerous one" (1970:183), and adds that "[i]ts leading feature is the sharp division of labour between the sexes" (1970:183). The procedures are as follows: the men dibble (*nugal*), using a dibble-stick (*tugal*) some five to six feet in length, while the women follow behind dropping seed (*benih*) into the dibble-holes. Typically, a number of related families will join together to sow each other's fields in a system of reciprocal labor exchange (*bedurok*), the owners of the field being sown supplying food and drink in their turn.

The separate roles of men and women during planting is well-document-ed in the ethnographic literature, and is one that has often been remarked upon (Brooke-Low 1892:24; Sandin 1967b;252; 1980:16; Freeman 1970:183; Jensen 1974:177; Sutlive 1978:75). Furthermore, it seems that whenever possible, this division of labor is fairly strictly adhered to. Thus Freeman reports that although sowing usually takes about half as long again as dibbling, so that the men always finish much sooner than the women, "it is rare for men to assist in the work of sowing" (1970:186). Instead, they turn their attention to such tasks as clearing the fields of unburnt brush wood, erecting fences or hut-building. They might even "merely lounge in the shade to smoke, and chew betel" (Freeman 1970:186). What they are reluctant to do, however, is to join the women in their task of sowing.

Young Iban women carrying *anak padi* (Courtesy of Richard Schwenk)

Contemporary Iban, when asked about the reasons for this division of labor, simply say that men dibble because women are not strong enough (*indu' enda' ulih tan*). In the past, however, it seems that these separate male and female roles had a ritual significance which was couched in terms of human sexual relations. Thus one finds that in the *timang gawai amat* invocation, dibbling is explicitly identified with sexual intercourse (Freeman 1979:244), while Iban dibble sticks themselves are traditionally carved in phallic representation (Richards 1981:125, 397). What is more, the wife of Pulang Gana, the paramount god of Iban rice farming, is called Serentum Tanah Tumboh - "Serentum of the fertile soil" (*tanah* = soil; *tumboh* = to grow, or shoot up, as of plants), while their daughter is named "Seed Dissolving in Soil". These titles can be seen as reflecting an association between the fertility of women and that of the soil. That is to say, the earth is like the womb - a container for new life - and it is in this respect that men, with their phallic dibbles, must penetrate the (female) soil, while their wives sow the seed, which is the germ of life.

This association between the fecundity of women and the fertility of rice extends beyond the planting season to provide an underlying structure for successive stages in the development of the rice crop. To begin with, young rice plants are referred to as *anak padi* or rice "children".[48] Later in the season, rice is described as *dara biak* - a term for young girls; and then subsequently, as *dara tuai* - a slightly older, but still unmarried, maiden (Freeman 1970:196 n.1; Jensen 1974:185). Later still, as the panicles begin to swell with ripening grain, rice plants are said to be like a woman with child: *baka orang indu' ngandong* (Jensen 1974:185; see also Banks 1949:81; Freeman 1970:196 n.1; Richards 1981:137). Finally, Richards tells us that at the harvest rites of *matah padi*, women members of the *bilik* "must be present to act as midwife to the grains which is spoken of as *kandong* (pregnant)". In short, the development of the rice crop during the course of the agricultural season is metaphorically identified with different stages in the lives of the women who care for it. Moreover, this comparison equates the ripening of rice with a passage from childhood into sexual maturity, realized in pregnancy and childbirth.

This imagery, it seems, may be more explicit in some areas than in others. For instance, in the Saribas region, we are told that "the Iban take delight in the appearance of ripened grain and its 'comeliness' and 'beauty' are explicitly likened to that of a young woman" (Sather 1977b:161). Furthermore, during the harvest rites of *nancang padi*, one finds that ripened rice plants, which previously have been tied together with red thread, are "figuratively .. addressed as a 'maiden', or *dara*" (Sather 1977b:161). These bound rice plants - the *padi tancang* - provide a focal point for the rice soul, or *semengat padi*; a place where they can congregate prior to their transportation back to the longhouse for the interval between farming seasons. Sather writes:

> Having attained maturity, or 'maidenhood', the *padi tancang*, representing here the collective souls of the now ripened *padi*, is addressed as if it were a young woman about to be received in ceremonial welcome by the longhouse from which she has long been absent, having passed her 'childhood' in the *padi* field (1977b:161).

The imagery of maidenhood is important here, in that it can be linked to the idea of a future, or potential, fertility, as embodied in the ripened grain. That is to say, the *padi tancang* - in its role as a vehicle for the aggregate *semengat padi* of the family's rice field - can, for the duration of the harvest, be regarded as the principal locus of agricultural fertility. The agricultural cycle having been completed, this fertility is latent in the ripened grain, some of which will be selected for next year's rice seed. The latter notion is, of course, of crucial importance to the family concerned, for it is upon this store of latent, or potential, fertility that the outcome of future farming seasons depends. The suggestion here, then, is that it is this prospect of further agricultural successes that is highlighted, and anticipated, in the imagery of maidenhood which underwrites the Saribas harvest rites of *nancang padi*.

A similar set of ideas can also be discerned in the myth of Kumang's daughter. Kumang is the wife of the legendary hero Keling, and paragon of all female virtues. In one story she is described as giving birth to a daughter called Padi Mati Bejalai Lemi Pinggang, Benih Lalu Tugal Sa-Taun Mati Nawang, - "Ripe *padi* becomes young and gives life to new seed" (Brooke-Low, in Roth 1896 I:336; Sutlive's translation [1977:158]). This child is born a widow, but then miraculously grows progressively younger. According to Brooke-Low, comments that inversion of order is allegorical of the rice cycle where ripened rice plants provide not only this year's grain, but also next year's seed (Roth 1896 I;336).

The idea of future fertility is also present in the notion that the harvest should be led by women. The Iban term for this is *ngindu'* (Richard 1981:233), which derives from the root word *indu'*, meaning 'woman', 'mother', 'female', 'feminine' (Richards 1981:115). The use of the term *ngindu'* in this context reflects an intimate association between the fertility of rice and the women who cultivate it. As Sutlive has previously noted:

Harvesting has its ritual as well as its technical aspects and focuses on the dominant concern with fertility. The lead is taken by the senior active woman who sets the pace in cutting the grain in each family's field. It is she who 'fecundizes' or 'feminizes' - the Iban term for her pacesetting, *ngindu'*, being a verb form of the root *indu'* meaning 'woman' or 'source' (1978:80).[49]

The same theme is also apparent in Iban storage rituals (*besimpan*, at least in the lower Rejang, where it is the senior most female member of the *bilik*-family who is ultimately responsible for storing away the harvested grain in bark storage bins (*tibang*). According to Sutlive:

> The symbolism of fertility marks this climatic event in the rice year, just as it has every other aspect. ... Seed is handled by women in sowing. And it is woman who replaces seed in the family's womb of life (1978:83).

It is evident, then, that the Iban do draw some kind of parallel between the fertility of rice and the fecundity of women. To say that this association is particularly systematic, or paradigmatic, would be perhaps to overstate the case. Nevertheless, it seems clear that Iban women are consistently identified with their rice crop, and that this identification has ultimately to do with a supposed correspondence between female fertility and the natural increase of rice.

Women, Fertility, and the Taking of Heads

The association of women and crops is fairly widespread in Southeast Asia. Rosaldo and Atkinson, in a discussion of Ilongot gender relationships, comment that "[e]xplicit birth imagery in the context of agricultural rites is found throughout the area, suggesting that female fertility serves as a metaphor for associating the women cultivators with their crops" (1975:64). Perhaps the best known example of this is found in traditional Malay agriculture, where harvest rites are identified with childbirth (Endicott 1970:23, 146-53). In this respect, it is interesting to note that there is a close similarity between Malay harvest rituals and the Iban rites of *matah padi* (Freeman 1970:203; Jensen 1974:189-90, 190 n.).

Rosaldo and Atkinson relate this association of women, female fertility, and agriculture, to a "Male:Female :: Culture:Nature" model, in the manner of Ortner (1974). That is to say, child bearing and the growth of plants are conceived as natural processes, with pregnancy and childbirth providing a model for linking women cultivators to the crops that they care for. In this respect, women and agriculture are consigned to the realm of Nature or at least are more closely identified with Nature than are their menfolk. The latter go hunting and headhunting. These activities revolve around the premeditated taking of life, and can thus be seen as reflecting man's control over the natural world. In this respect hunting and headhunting are identified with the domain of Culture.[50] Thus we have a situation: Male:Female :: Life-taking:Life-giving :: Culture:Nature.

At one time the Nature : Culture dichotomy, as formulated by Levi-Strauss, has achieved an almost axiomatic status within anthropological theory. The whole world, it seemed, subscribed to the idea of a fundamental distinction between the realm of nature on the one hand, and that of Culture on the other. Problems arise, however, when we come to consider just what is meant by the terms Nature and Culture, both in our own society and in those we seek to study. In Western thought these categories bear a heavy semantic load, with a constantly shifting field of meanings and values, and there is no reason to suppose that other cultures and societies should share the same set of assumptions about Nature and Culture as ourselves. As MacCormack has pointed out:

> although Lévi-Strauss has attempted to cast the nature-culture contrast in a timeless, value-free model concerned with the working of the human mind, ideas about nature and culture are not value-free. The 'myth' of nature is a symbol of arbitrary signs which relies on a social consensus of meaning. Neither the concept of nature nor that of culture is 'given', and they cannot be free from the biases of the culture in which the concepts were constructed (1980:6).

In the Iban case, there is no evidence to suggest that male:female relationships can be aligned with a symbolic or conceptual contrast between Culture and Nature. As far as agriculture is concerned, the Iban see rice farming as central to their way of life - the definitive feature of the Iban cultural tradition or *adat* (see above). Thus the Iban say that their ancestors, before they started growing rice, lived in the jungle like wild beings, even like *antu* (Jensen 1974:151; Sutlive 1978:62). It was only through the acquisition of rice cultivation that these remote predecessors became fully Iban, and in this respect rice farming has a Promethean quality, representing an accession to a state of humanity. Furthermore, the cultivation of rice is regarded as a ritual undertaking and one that is sanctioned by the gods. In this light, if the Iban were to appeal to a Nature:Culture dichotomy, then the cultivation of rice might just as well be placed within the domain of Culture, as that of Nature.

But if an appeal to Nature and Culture seems unjustified in the absence of further ethnographic evidence, it is nevertheless clear that some kind of male:female divide does exist, with headhunting (and hunting) on one side, and rice farming and childbearing on the other. In other words, men go hunting and take heads, while women bear children and grow rice. One should note here, however, that if these separate male and female realms are clearly distinguishable, nonetheless they are but two halves of a single model of fertility and increase. That is to say, in terms of the "logic" of Iban collective representative, headhunting, human reproduction and agricultural productivity, are all brought into conjunction with one another through a series of allegorical and ritual associations. Thus, as we have seen, headhunting procures sacred rice seed and symbolic children, while the fecundity of women provides a metaphor for the increase of rice.

Freeman's account of Iban headhunting suggests that this indigenous model of fertility and increase can be interpreted as a cult of phallic symbolism. We have argued, instead, that it is a vegetative model of reproduction, based on the imagery of fruit and seed, which sustains the ritual significance of Iban headhunting. That is to say, while there may well be an equation of semen with seed - in the same way that young rice plants are identified with children, and the ripening grain with images of maidenhood and pregnancy - nowhere is it evident that the Iban see their trophy heads as phallic symbols. Indeed, even Freeman has to admit that pointed red peppers and so forth are only "implicitly phallic" in their reference. On the other hand, there is a constant emphasis on imagery of seed-bearing fruit of one description or another. In this respect, the suggestion here is that the ritual significance of Iban headhunting, as a cultural institution, is built upon an organic metaphor of frugiferous reproduction, rather than one of phallic procreation.

In many respects, this is hardly surprising. The Iban are the inhabitants of a vast equatorial rain forest, in which an unbroken cycle of vegetative growth, fructuation and decay, is continuously at work. Against this background, headhunting has come to be identified with the basic facts of life. In symbolic terms, to take heads is to gather the fruits of the forest: Iban warriors must go headhunting to bring back the fruit of the mythical *ranyai* palm and thereby supply their community with the means for their continued existence, namely rice seed and children. In this light, when the Iban identify their trophy heads with seed-bearing fruit, that quite simply is that, and there is no need to look elsewhere for phallic symbolism and the like. Indeed, to do so, would be, in Needham's words, "to multiply the entities beyond necessity" (1976:80).

So, Iban men go headhunting to gather the fruit of the *ranyai* palm. But what of the women who wait behind and who tend to the rice crop? In the first place, it is useful to recall that, traditionally, the taking of heads considerably advanced a man's marriage prospects. Those who had taken heads were known as *bujang berani*, or "brave bachelors", and were much sought after as future husbands. Indeed, the women actively encouraged headhunting in this respect. Thus, Hose and McDougall report that "Iban women urge on the men to the taking of heads; they make much of those that bring them home, and sometimes a girl will taunt her suitor by saying that he has not been brave enough to take a head" (1912 I:186-87; c.f. Freeman 1979:238, cited above). Similarly, James Brooke records in his journal that "[s]ome of the young Dayaks have plainly stated that they would give up headhunting were it not for the taunts and jibes of their wives" (Brooke, in Keppel 1853:123). Again, an anonymous correspondent in the *Sarawak Gazette* tells us that

> the women, in their cruelty and blood-thirstiness are the cause of this headhunting. At every festival the old skulls are taken from the fire-place, where they are preserved and smoked from generation to generation, and carried through the house by some women. A monotonous song is sung by the women in honour of the hero who cut off the head, and in derision of the poor victims whose skulls are carried round; and again and again the infernal chorus is heard: '*Agi ngambi, agi ngambi*'; (bring us more of them) (1908:208).

The same theme emerges in Iban oral literature, where women are again identified as the principal instigators of headhunting raids. For example in the *sabak* dirge quoted above, it is the female members in the party of the dead who urge their menfolk to cut down the fruit of the *ranyai* palm. Similarly in the *timang gawai amat* invocation, it is Endu Dara Ticin Temaga and the daughters of Lang who refuse to go to the festival without a freshly taken head. In short, it seems that Iban men went headhunting, not only to win renown and secure prestige for themselves, but also because their womenfolk insisted upon it.[51]

This female enthusiasm for headhunting stems directly from the idea that the taking of heads could positively influence the fertility of both rice and women. A direct parallel can be drawn here, between the biological circumstances of human reproduction, on the one hand, and the ritual significance of Iban headhunting, on the other. In the first instance, if women, in their childbearing capacity, are identified as the physical agents of reproduction, they nevertheless require men as progenitors to set their cycle of reproduction in motion. At the same time, however, at a symbolic level, they also need men to go headhunting in order to provide them with the raw materials of reproduction, namely the seed of the *ranyai* palm. In this context, the equation of seed and semen establishes a logical necessity between the taking of heads and its supposed effect - the fertility of women and the increase of rice. Accordingly one can argue that if in the past women were identified as the cause of men's headhunting it was because the taking of heads was ritually portrayed a necessary first step in bringing about, or enhancing, the fecundity of their bodies, and by extension, the fertility of rice.

The Representation of Male and Female

The Iban say that when a child is conceived, the as yet unsexed embryo, or proto-human being, is offered the choice of a spear or weaving implement to hold (Jensen 1967:167). Should it choose the former, then it is a boy who will be born; the latter, and it is a girl. The Iban add that neither choice is considered better, or more worthy, than the other, a view that is reflected in the essentially egalitarian relationship of men and women in Iban society.

A similar theme is expressed at the ritual first bathing of a new born infant (*meri' anak mandi*). This takes place a few days after the birth and serves to introduce the child to the river and the spirits and deities associated with water. On such occasions, the wing of a sacrificed fowl is cut off and placed with an offering (*piring*) on the river bank. If the child is a boy, the wing is transfixed on a spear; if it is a girl, then it is attached to a weaving heddle (Howell 1977:53; Gomes 1911:100; Jensen 1967:175-76; Sandin 1976:11; Gana 1988:30).

In Iban society, the spear (*sangkoh*) is identified with headhunting and warfare, while the weaving heddle (*letan*) stands for their female counterpart - the design and manufacture of woven fabrics (*pua'*). This equation of male headhunting on the one hand, with female weaving, on the other, is found throughout Iban culture. Thus in Iban oral literature, the headhunting heroes of Panggau Libau, marry the women weavers of Gellong, while in real life, women who are skilled in weaving are identified with men who have been on the warpath and who have taken heads. In particular, those women who are experienced in the ritual preparation of mordants used in the dyeing of cloth (*indu' tau' nakar, tau' ngar*) are said to be the female equivalent of great war-leaders (*orang tau' serang*). And just as young men were traditionally not considered eligible for marriage until they had taken their first head, or at least been on the war-path (Leach 1950:70), neither could Iban maidens be properly considered for marriage until they had demonstrated their accomplishments at weaving *pua'* (Howell 1912:64).

Time and again, and in a dozen different ways, one finds male headhunters and women weavers juxtaposed with one another in Iban collective representations (Mashman, this volume; Gavin 1992). The portrayal of women as mothers, or cultivators, on the other hand, receives almost no recognition whatsoever. Yet we have seen that the Iban do make a connection between female fertility and the increase of rice, and that this association does play a significant role in the organization of farming activities and agricultural rites. Given the obvious importance of rice farming and childbearing in traditional Iban society, it remains to be asked why it is that weaving should be singled out as the quintessential female activity, over and above childbearing and the cultivation of rice.

Part of the reason for this may lie in the male-oriented circumstances of Iban social life (cf. Mashman this volume). That is to say that although in most respects there is a parity between the sexes in Iban society, it is men who have traditionally claimed the center stage in Iban public life, most notably through their role as headhunters. This cultural orientation towards the achievements of men may have tended to obscure the presence of alternative, women-oriented views of the world, which have been marginalized, or else passed over in silence. In this respect, the relative weakness of female models of fertility and agricultural production may represent a form of "mutedness", in the Ardnerian sense (Ardner 1975), while weaving which is represented in terms of male headhunting and is thus contained within the world view of men, receives a relatively high profile in the ethnographic literature.

A more functionalist interpretation of this state of affairs is suggested by Rosaldo and Atkinson in describing a similar situation for the Ilongot of Northern Luzon (1975). In this instance, they see the relatively weak symbolic elaboration upon the themes of childbearing and female fertility as a reflection of sexual egalitarianism within Ilongot society. They write: "Strong statements linking agriculture and fertility would, we suggest, emphasize woman's 'otherness', and implicitly, her inferiority, and would therefore be incompatible with the egalitarian ethos which governs much of Ilongot life" (Rosaldo and Atkinson 1975:61).

Rosaldo and Atkinson's argument again rests on a Levi-Straussian dichotomy between Nature:Culture, and the assumption that women must inevitably be assigned an inferior status on the strength of their biological role as mothers (see above). In the Iban case whetehr or not an emphasis on the symbolic juxtaposition of female fertility and agricultural increase would actually undermine the status of Iban women vis à vis their menfolk is a moot point. What is clear, however, is that it is weaving, rather than childbearing and/or rice farming, which is identified as the quintessential activity of women. Furthermore, weaving constitutes an areas of Iban social life in which the role of women is both positively valued and from which men, as a sex, are entirely excluded. In this respect it provides Iban women with a prestige system through which they too can compete for status and influence in a way comparable to male headhunters.

Weaving

But what is so special about weaving? Why is it singled out as the quintessential female activity? And in what respects is it comparable to male headhunting?

In the first place, Iban textiles, or *pua'*, are endowed with mystical qualities that go right back to the very beginning of time. In Iban creation myths, the first couple are covered with a *pua'*, before being brought to life by the shouts of the creator deity Raja Entala (Jensen 1974:74-75). Here, *pua'* textiles are identified, not only with the first awakenings of human life, but also as an artifice of the gods. That is to say, they have divine origins that lie beyond the earliest moments in the history of mankind.

These supernatural qualities are reflected in everything that has to do with the manufacture of *pua'*. The inspiration for their design lies in the spirit world, and is communicated to women through dreams (Gavin 1992). Just as Iban men have spirit helpers - *antu nulong* - to assist and protect them on the war-path, so too do women weavers. These typically are the women of Gellong, who marry the legendary headhunting heroes of Panggau Libau. They call women weavers to their vocation, instruct them as to what patterns they should weave, introduce them to new designs, and provide them with charms to protect and assist them (Gavin 1992). We use the term "protect" here, because the actual process of weaving is considered to be a spiritually endangering exercise. That is to say, Iban textiles are ranked in a hierarchy of "potency": novice weavers begin with low grade patterns and gradually extend their repertoire to include more powerful designs (Richards 1981:144; Gavin 1992). Only women who are spiritually strong (*semengat tinggi'*), are able to weave the most potent patterns, but the most dangerous activity of all is the preparation of mordants (*nakar*). The latter is as much a question of ritual skill and knowledge, as it is one of preparing the ingredients, and very few women know how to carry out the correct procedures (*ngemban*). Those who do possess this knowledge (*indu' tau' nakar*), as mentioned earlier, are acknowledged as the female equivalent of great war-leaders, and receive comparable recognition in commemorative rites for the dead (Gavin 1992). Indeed, the actual task of preparing the mordants is specifically identified as *kayau indu'*, or the "war-path of women" (Howell 1912:64; Gavin 1992).

The second point to be made here, is that *pua'* serve in a ritual capacity - this is the essence of their supernatural qualities. New-born infants are wrapped in them the first time they are presented to their grandparents (*anak betemu*); *pua'* are placed over the shoulders of the sick in healing rites (*pelian*); shamans (*manang*), bards (*lemambang*), and others whose activities bring them into contact with supernatural dangers, may drape themselves with *pua'* to protect them-selves.[52] Iban corpses - which before burial are laid out in the gallery of the longhouse - are contained within an enclosure (*sapat*) constructed from *pua'* and offerings to the gods (*piring*) are always arranged on a *pua'* spread out on the floor of the longhouse gallery or verandah.

Pua' are particularly associated with the cult of headhunting, and many of the designs specifically relate to headhunting themes, for example, the *tangkai ranyai*, or "trunk of the *ranyai* (palm) design, and the *tiang sandong* pattern, which refers to the pole (*tiang*) raised on the longhouse verandah during Saribas headhunting rituals (Sandin 1980:86). At the same time, the woven jacket and waistband was an important part of the Iban warrior's ritual paraphernalia, safeguarding him from attack whilst on the war-path.[53] Most important of all, *pua'* were used to receive newly-taken heads on their first entry into the longhouse following the return of a successful headhunting expedition.

The designs used in the latter instance - the rites of *encabau arong* - belong to the highest grade of *pua'* and could only be woven by the most accomplished and highly qualified weavers in the community. Thus in the *timang* invocation, the daughters of Lang are told that they cannot receive the head trophies of the omen-birds because they are not sufficiently well-qualified in the art of weaving:

Lalu bejako Endu Dara Ticin Temaga,
Endu Cerebok Mangkok Cina,
Nama utai ke lunyong enda' lunyong nya indai,
Ngabong merakunyit?
Nama tak munyi panjong sida' Ketupong nya indai,
Ke ngelampong tucong bukit!
Sapa kitai dulu nerima' nya ila' indai,
Ngena pua bali tengkebang?
Kita' enda' tau nyambut iya anak,
Enti nyelaku kumbu,
Kita' agi betanya ari aku,
Ngambi gambar dagu baya butang!

Then speaks Endu Dara Ticin Temaga,
Endu Cerebok Mangkok Cina
What is that faint sound, mother.
Coming from the top of the *merakunyit* tree?
Why, it sounds like the shouts of Ketupong and the others, mother,
Coming from above the top of the ridge!
Who among us will be the first to receive it [the head trophy] later on,
        mother?
You cannot receive it, dear daughter,
Since you have yet to make a pattern in the woven blanket,
You still ask my advice,
On making a pattern in the form of the jaw of an adulterous crocodile!
        (Sandin 1977:113-14).

Instead, it is Indai Kecendai, the wife of Lang, who receives the newly-taken
head, wrapping it in her finest *pua'* blanket, before bringing it into Lang's celestial
longhouse:

> O lalu meh peruji ati ambai lalai,
> Ke aki Lang Menaul Nyakai,
> Lalu diketas iya laka begumba balang begundai,
> Ke lalu diterima indai dara nganta,
> Ngena pua' bali belulai,
> Au kitai peruji ati ambai lalai,
> Kita' anang telengga laun pulai,
> Enggai ka kita' kena tiup selulut ribut bebarai ngesai,
> Enggai ka kita' kena tinggang telian leka ujan,
> Ke nelian laboh beka-berai,
> Enggai ka kita' basah salampai mansau menyaang,
> Lalu bejalai sida' niti gentali rumah panjai,
> Nyangkah leka begumba niti ruai.

> O, come here, dear loving sweetheart,
> Says Aki Lang Menaul Nyakai,
> Then he cuts the string by which hangs the precious skull,
> Which the mother of the pretty daughter receives,
> In her woven bali belulai blanket.
> O my dear loving sweetheart,
> You must not delay returning home,
> So that you will not be blown by the whirlwind,
> Or be wet by the rain drops,
> Which fall very heavily,

So that your red scarf will not be wet.
Then they walk along the passage of the longhouse,
Singing the song for the reception of heads all along the verandahs
(Sandin 1977:115-16).

The rites of *encabau arong* are of special significance in the cult of Iban headhunting. Not only do they mark the entry of head trophies into the longhouse, they also signal their movement from the male realm of Iban warriors to a female domain of childbearing, fertility, and increase. That is to say, it is at this point that returning headhunters pass their newly claimed trophies - the fruit of the *ranyai* palm - to their womenfolk, who then sing to them and nurse them as they would a small child. This marks a moment of transformation, or transition, as trophy heads are removed, quite literally, from the hands of men, and are re-located - in their guise as "infants" - within the realm of motherhood and female fecundity. And it is at this point that Iban *pua'* have a special role to play in containing the ritually powerful and dangerous head trophy, transforming its threatening and disruptive influence,[54] into one of beneficence for the longhouse community (Gavin, personal communication).

There is, however, one further point of particular interest here. Gavin reports that the Iban say that the designs of certain *pua'* actually have the power to "incite" - *meransang* - men to go on the war-path (Gavin 1992). The title, or praise-name (*julok*) of one such blanket is given as follows:

> *Ginti besi rantong nyabak seremidak ransing rong rong, minta umpan pengkilong peruit Badang,*
> *Ginti besi lantai nyabak seremidak ransing rerangi, minta umpan kerigai rusok marang.*

> The pattern of the iron hook is crying, weeping and howling, proudly demanding the stomach of a Badang[55] for bait.
> The pattern of the iron hook is crying, weeping and softly pleading, proudly demanding the ribs and both flanks for bait (Gavin, personal communication).

It seems, then, that women, through their mastery of weaving, are able to encourage, even compel, Iban men to go headhunting. We have seen that women are frequently said to be the cause of men going on the war-path, and Gavin argues that here we have a ritual vehicle for bringing this about, in that women's weaving is represented as an instrumental factor in inciting men to go headhunting.

In summary, the mystical properties of *pua'* textiles, and the ritual significance of weaving as a female institution, can be seen as "compensating" Iban women for their exclusion from the male domain of headhunting and warfare. That is to say, if Iban must rely on Iban men to supply them with trophy heads in order to realize the fertility of their bodies, then they themselves are able to precipitate the taking of heads through the weaving of magical *pua'*. In this respect, a sense of balance is restored to Iban gender relations which might otherwise have been distorted by the high prestige and ritual significance attached to the role of men as warriors.

Concluding Remarks

In this study we have set out to re-examine the significance of headhunting, as a male institution, within the framework of traditional Iban society. In the past, the taking of heads was central to the Iban way of life, providing Iban men with a route to status and authority within the longhouse community. Those who had taken heads were able to celebrate their successes through the sponsorship of prestigious festivals, or *gawai*, thereby publicly proclaiming their social worth as warriors and leaders of the community. The fact that these festivals continue to be held in the present day is indicative of the once crucial significance of Iban headhunting, and its lasting importance as a cultural institution. In this respect, it may be said that the Iban warrior tradition still exerts a powerful influence over the lives of contemporary Iban males.

But headhunting, as we have seen, was more than simply a prestige system that provided an institutionalized outlet for male aggression. It was a also a ritual activity. We have shown how a close reading of Iban oral literature and ritual liturgy reveals a systematic identification of headhunting with the circumstances of reproduction, both human and agricultural. In the first instance, Iban trophy heads are ritually portrayed as 'infants' seeking their 'mothers', while in the second, they are identified as seed-bearing 'fruit' and the source of sacred rice (*padi pun*). These alternative representations are quite distinct within the framework of Iban headhunting rites. Nevertheless, they both participate in a single model of reproduction and increase whereby women cultivators are intimately associated with their rice crop through the notion of a shared, or common fertility. The fact that in the *timang* invocations accompanying Iban head-hunting festivals (*gawai amat*), warfare is allegorically equated with the annual rice cycle, while heads themselves are metaphorically portrayed as 'children', endorses the view that, for the Iban, the taking of heads was traditionally identified as promoting, or enhancing the fertility of both rice and women.

Freeman has linked these ideas and representations to a cult of phallic symbolism; we have argued, on the other hand, for a frugiferous model of reproduction and increases. In the latter instance, the equation of seed and semen still stands, but rather than see Iban trophy heads as phallic symbols - for which there is little evidence, if any at all - we prefer to see them as seed-bearing fruit - an identification which is repeatedly emphasized in Iban oral literature and ritual invocation. In particular, we have argued that trophy heads can be seen as the fruit of the mythical *ranyai* palm, which is said to grow at the very edge of the universe, or in the Iban Afterworld. Iban warriors take to the war-path to gather the fruit of this fabulous tree which when it is cut open on their return releases seed of every description, but most importantly, sacred rice of *paid pun*. The latter, when planted, provides a "home" to the rice soul, or *semengat padi* and is identified in Iban ritual as the ultimate source of agricultural fertility. In this respect the taking of heads is intimately liked to the success of the annual rice harvest and is thereby seen as making a vital contribution to the daily sustenance and wellbeing of the longhouse community.

But if headhunting is represented as harvesting the fruit of the *ranyai* palm, we have also seen that trophy heads are metaphorically equated with "children". The omen-birds are described in Iban oral literature as attacking the house of demon *Nising* to rob him of his 'offspring', while in the rites of *encabau arong* which marks the return of a successful headhunting expedition, Iban women are identified as 'mothers' to the newly acquired trophies.

In both instances, the activities of men as warriors are represented as introducing new life into the longhouse community. This theme can be readily linked to the traditional association of headhunting with the termination of mourning. That is to say, the taking of heads can be seen as a restorative measure in the face of social losses brought about by death: fresh heads = new seed = a new cycle of fertility and increase. In this instance, however, our appeal is not to the logical concatenations of structural analysis, where life and death are articulated in a system of binary oppositions, or else as a pair of cosmic principles forever enaged in an endless struggle for ascendancy, the one over the other. Rather, we turn to the idea of organic regeneration and vegetative growth which we suggest provides the underlying model, or metaphor, for Iban headhunting, and its special relationship with the termination of mourning. Quite simply: from the seed there comes forth new life.

These ideas have important implications for the relationship between men and women in Iban society. If women, through the fertility of their bodies and their identification with the soil which brings forth rice, can be seen as the physiological agents of reproduction, they nevertheless, require men to go headhunting in order to provide them with seed; only then may they realize the potential fecundity of their bodies. In this respect, headhunting is identified, not only as supplying the raw material of reproduction, but also as its logical precursor or antecedent. This sets up a fundamental asymmetry between the perceived role of men and women in Iban society, in that while both men and women alike may have an equal interest in seeing the success of the rice harvest and the birth of children, it is men, as headhunters, who are ritually identified as being ultimately responsible for setting this cycle of fertility in motion and who, accordingly, are granted the highest honors in Iban society. This potentially antagonistic situation--which may at times manifest itself in the mockery of men by women at headhunting ceremonies--is countered by the ritual significance of weaving. The latter is not only portrayed as the female equivalent of headhunting, but is in turn identified as a "cause" of men's headhunting. In this respect, women achieve control over their own fertility, while at the same time the essentially egalitarian ethos of Iban social values is seen to be upheld.

To conclude, the practice of taking enemy heads in warfare cannot be approached as something separate from the rest of Iban society and culture, but must instead be seen as central to the Iban way of life as it existed up until the early decades of this century. While on the one hand Iban men went headhunting to secure fame and fortune for themselves within the longhouse community, their actions were at the same time identified in myth and ritual as contributing to the fertility of rice and women. In this scheme of things, a parallel can clearly be drawn between the ritual significance of taking heads and male sexuality, whereby seed is equated with semen, and the role of men as headhunters implicitly is identified with their biological role as fathers, or progenitors. The point to be made here, however, is that the symbolic language of Iban headhunting is not one of phallic procreation, but rather that of fructuation and germination. Ultimately, it is the Bornean rain forest, with its endless cycle of vegetative growth, decay and regeneration, which underpins the Iban cult of headhunting and sustains its ritual significance as an agency of fertility. In this respect, the equation of trophy heads with seed-bearing fruit endows Iban headhunting with a "natural" imperative for the renewal of life.

NOTES

1.	For the sake of consistency, we have adopted Richards' (1981) spelling of Iban terms throughout.

2.	Jensen's fieldwork was carried out amongst the Lemanak Iban and their neighbors between 1959 and 1966. It may be that the ritual significance of headhunting had declined greatly in those areas at that time. (His monograph is also remarkable for its failure to discuss Iban festivals [*gawai*]). If this is the case, then it is unfortunate indeed that his study of Iban religion should have been carried out in such an area, when the cult of headhunting, in its ritual aspect, still flourishes elsewhere.

3.	The situation is, of course, rapidly changing as logging brings roads, services and money, to even the most remote corners of Sarawak.

4.	Sarawak is divided into seven administrative Divisions, which are further sub-divided into Districts and sub-Districts, each with an administrative officer in charge.

5.	The bilateral symmetry underlying Iban kinship is ritually expressed in the ceremony of *gawai tusok*, which has to do with the piercing of a child's ear lobes. Freeman tells us that "[t]his operation is an event of some moment in the life of an individual, for it is believed that on its proper performance will depend his (or her) subsequent health and welfare" (1960:79). The rites include an invocation to tutelary spirits and employ the use of charms and other magical materials. They culminate with the piercing of the ears with a small steel augur. The important point to note here, however, is that "[i]t is common practice to have the lobe of one ear pierced by a cognate of the father and that of the other by a cognate of the mother" (Freeman 1960:70). This, Freeman remarks, symbolizes "the child's equal dependence on both sides of his (or her) personal kindred" (1960:79).

6.	These are Freeman's terms: virilocal refers to residence with, the husband's family; uxorilocal, residence with the wife's (Freeman 1970:14). In this respect, the formation of the *bilik*-family is 'utrolateral' (Freeman 1970:14-15).

7.	For a discussion of Iban social stratification, apparent or otherwise, see Rousseau (1980) and Freeman (1981).

8.   The use of the term "chief" in this context should not be thought of as implying any form of hereditary leadership and is applied here only in the absence of a better alternative. Such men might have been able to command the following of several longhouse communities, through their exploitation of ties of kinship and personal loyalties. But as in other areas of Iban social life, the strength of their leadership rested entirely upon their ability to attract followers (*anembiak*), rather than on any institutionalized system of authority.

9.   The Iban say that their remote ancestors lived in the jungle like the Penan - nomadic hunter gatherers (Jensen 1974:151). They may sometimes even compare their cultural predecessors to *antu* - capricious spirits and malevolent supernaturals, who are associated with the depths of the forest, mountain tops and caves (Jensen 1974:151).

10.   The omen-birds of Iban augury are as follows:

Ketupong	Rufous Piculet	*Sasia abnormis*
Beragai	Scarlet-rumped Trogon	*Harpactes duyauceli*
Embuas	Banded Kingfisher	*Lacedo pulchella* Horsefield
Pangkas	Maroon Woodpecker	*Blythipicus rubiginosis*
Bejampong	Crested Jay	*Platylophus galericulatus*
Papau	Diard's Trogon	*Harpactes diardi*
Nendak	White-rumped Shama	*Copsychus malabaricus*

11.   It should be noted here that the omen-birds are not the only augural emissaries to be employed by the gods in their communications with man. Other omen creatures include snakes, lizards, bears, wild boar and different species of deer (Sather 1985:6-7; 9-12). Dreams and visions (*mimpi*) also play an important role in this scheme of things, as does hepatomancy, or divination (*beatau*), using the liver of a sacrificial pig.

12.   On occasion, the gods themselves may actively participate in agricultural affairs, as, for example, when there has been a succession of bad harvests, or the *padi* has been destroyed by disease. At such times, the Iban will hold a festival, or *gawai*, inviting the principal agricultural deities - Pulang Gana, Sigai, Anda Mara, and others - to attend a feast in their honor. In return it is hoped that they will bring new supplies of rice seed,

together with magical charms (*pengaroh*) to ensure the success of subsequent harvests.

13.   The importance of Iban rice farming as a repository of social values remains undiminished to this day, even in those areas where traditional agricultural practices have been displayed by more modern farming methods and the planting of cash crops such as rubber, pepper and cocoa. Thus Sather, in describing the situation extant along the Paku river (a tributary of the Saribas), writes that "[f]or the Iban who continue to live in the countryside, success in growing rice is still a crucial first step in gaining status and social prominence" (1980:70). He adds:

> the basic values that traditionally invested rice agricul-
> ture remain largely intact. Through the cultivation of
> rice ... a family demonstrates its social worth, and its
> fields continue to represent, not only a major form of
> heritable wealth and a source of economic security, but
> are a place of worship, sanctified by myth, and blessed
> by continuing ritual contact with the gods and spirits
> (Sather 1980:70).

14.   This is how the Iban first came to be christened "Sea Dayaks", despite the fact that they are traditionally a people of the interior and, for the most part, are not at all inclined towards seafaring.

15.   Our knowledge of Iban migration comes to us from a variety of sources: mythological narratives (*jerita tuai*), epics and ritual invocations (*timang*, or *pengap*), folktales (*ensurai*), genealogies (*tusut*), and other forms of oral literature, all of which are rich in their allusion to historical events (Sandin 1967a). From the latter half of the nineteenth century, they have also been documented in colonial records (Pringle 1970).

16.   Some Ibans groups have even returned to the Kapuas basin, settling first in the vicinity of the Kapuas lakes in the 1830s, and then spreading out towards the Leboyan and Embaloh rivers (King 1976:322).

17.   Freeman reports that while it does sometimes happen that a farm cleared from primary forest is replanted in its entirety for a second year - the so-called *krukoh* method - more usually only one-half to two-thirds of the acreage is replanted the second time around. The rest of the desired acreage is then made up by felling a further area of virgin forest, thereby

increasing the land holding of the *bilik*-family without imposing undue strain on its labor resources (1970:284).

18. It should be noted in passing that it was quite usual for the "enemy" to be another Iban group, there being many cases of *intra* Iban rivalries, particularly in the latter half of the nineteenth century (Sandin 1967a:65).

19. *Antu* are regarded as being a primary cause of sickness and misfortune. They are also associated with a fear of the dark, being lost in the jungle and attack by wild animals (Jensen 1974:95).

20. Trophy heads are periodically "fed", and offered cigarettes and chewing ingredients, in order to placate them and ensure that they will not turn against their "hosts". Howell writes: "Dayaks think it essential for the preservation of their own lives that the heads taken in battle should be given food at intervals, their idea being that should this fail to be done the heads are capable of "eating" them; that is to say, of bringing sickness and death amongst them" (1977:129).

21. Jensen mentions that in Iban hepatomancy by pig's liver, the lobe that is normally associated with the activities of *antu* may, on occasion, be alternatively identified with the enemy (1974:138 n.2).

22. Haddon, writing at the turn of the century, has the following to say:

> I cannot refrain from mentioning what strikes one as being, to say the least of it, an illogical action on the part of the Sarawak Government. Headhunting is rigorously put down, and rightly so; but when the Government organizes a punitive expedition, say to punish a recalcitrant headhunting chief, the natives (generally Iban) comprising the Government force, are always allowed to keep what heads they can secure. Surely it would be a more dignified position not to allow a single head to be taken away by any one in the Raj under any pretext whatever, and to remunerate the punitive force in some more direct manner (1901:396-97).

23. Harrisson records that in "the few weeks in 1945 when headhunting became again a semi-legalized activity in parts Sarawak - on the Brunei Bay coast gangs of Sea Dayaks from the Limbang followed Australian 9th Division patrols everywhere in a most peculiar symbiosis" (1947:177).

24. As Morgan remarks: "Land was available to the north and east; the pirates went southwest for heads" (1968:143).

25. Downs writes *apropos* headhunting: "the religious aspect .. [is] .. based on a conception of the division of the universe into two antagonistic halves, the struggle between the two corresponding to an alternance between life and death" (1955:70). He adds: "In real life the killing of a member of the opposing group means the death and temporary eclipse of that group and the rebirth and ascendancy of the other" (Downs 1955:70).

26. It is, of course, possible to draw up any number of binary oppositions for the Iban ethnography - for examples, see Richard (1972:68-69), Jensen (1974:109-10); King (1977:75 ff.) - but the question is: Are they meaningful? That is to say, does it reflect some abstract ordering principle that the Iban themselves would recognize? The answer here, in our opinion, is "Probably not"; even Jensen, who tries to draw up a table of binary oppositions, or "complementary pairs" (1974:110), has to admit that "Iban thought lacks the strong antithese elsewhere associated with right and left" (1974:109).

27. McKinley comments that "the concept of the social person is so linked with an appreciation of the face that the English word for person comes from the Latin *'persona'*, for 'mask'" (1976:119).

28. Freeman mentions "the special relationship ... which existed between the Iban and the Bukitans" (1970:134). In this instance the nomadic Bukitan of the Rejang basin, who initially acted as guides and allies to the Iban, eventually became completely absorbed into the Iban way of life adopting rice cultivation and longhouse residence (Freeman 1970:134).

29. The aggressive significance is because in Iban oral literature and ritual invocation, snakes frequently metamorphize into spears and vice versa (Freeman 1979:240); the phallic significance, on the other hand, would seem to come from Freudian psychoanalysis.

30. The translation is Sandin's, and is perhaps not the best that might be made.

31. Festivals may have a different status in different regions. For example, Masing reports and in the Baleh, the highest ranking *gawai amat* is the *gawai tangga ari*, or Notched Ladder of the Day festival (1981:65). In the Saribas, however, it would seem to be the *gawai gerasi papa*val which completes the *gawai burong*, or Bird Festival cycle (Sandin 1977:13).

32. It should be noted here that there is some controversy as to how many of the omen-birds really are the sons-in-law to Lang (King 1977:64-65). It seems that differences of opinion may be linked to regional variations. But in the end, as King observes, "for practical purposes these different familial ... arrangements dissolve in the more general belief that the seven main omen birds are in some sense Lang's family and in consequence are collectively known as Lang's sons-in-law (*menantu lang*)" (1977:65).

33. Freeman attributes a phallic significance to these adornments of the shrine (1979:239).

34. This is a contemporary description of the *ranyai* shrine; earlier accounts seem to suggest that trophy heads were a more regular, if not integral, feature in the past (Howell 1977:92, 140).

35. There are a number of accounts describing the erection of *ranyai* shrines in the ethnographic literature (Nyuak 1977:216; Freeman 1979:239), but only Howell specifically mentions that it is in fact a representation of the *ranyai* palm itself (Howell and Bailey 1900:137).

36. The *isang* is another species of forest palm (unidentified).

37. There are two main sources for the *timang gawai amat* in the ethnographic literature: Sandin's version from the Saribas region (1977) and Masing's from the Baleh (1981). Other accounts of the main sequences are provided by Perham (1878) and Freeman (1979).

38. The post referred to here is the *tiang kelingkang*. This extract comes from Sandin's transcription of a Saribas *gawai burong* invocation (1977:69/71).

39. n.b. Freeman's description of snakes and crocodiles possessing an aggressive significance (1979:240).

40. The trophy head is sometimes described at this point as a "precious jewel" in Nising's turban (Perham 1878:131; Sandin 1977:110/113).

41. For a more detailed account of the Iban shaman as warrior in the supernatural realm see Freeman (1967), Sutlive (1976).

42. This coconut, it will be recalled, had previously been hacked down at the point when the omen-birds make their attack on Nising and his "children".

43. Freeman, in arguing for the phallic significance of Iban trophy heads, mentions that among the Rungus Dusun of North Borneo, an infertile woman is treated by having a trophy head planted between her thighs (1979:237). If this is meant to suggest that we should see the head in this context as a phallus, one could just as well argue that this ritual is symbolic of childbirth, with the trophy head representing the child that it is hoped will subsequently be born.

44. In Iban eschatology, those who die unfortunate, or "bad", deaths--for example, the victims of drowning, suicide, fatal accidents, and other premature and unnatural ends--are said to be excluded from the Afterworld proper, and remain instead in limbo, in separate areas of their own, where they keep company with all those who have met a similar fate as themselves.

45. This is quite explicit in the symbolism of Iban healing rituals, particularly the *pelian bebunoh antu* in which a malevolent demon, or *antu*, is dispatched in mortal combat (see Freeman 1967; Sutlive 1976).

46. Freeman writes: "Time and again I overheard such as 'If the weeding is not thoroughly done there will not be a good crop' ('*Enti enda' mantun badabadas enda' bulih padi*'); 'Amid weeds *padi* refuses to thrive' ('*Alam babas enggai padi idup*'); and 'The grain of unweeded *padi* lacks substance' ('*Padi enda' di mantun nadai isi*') (1970:193). He adds: "On another occasion a group of men made the point that after a thorough weeding insect pest are fewer, and that this is greatly to the advantage of the growing *padi*" (Freeman 1970:193).

47. Freeman writes: "it is rare to find a man with an accurate knowledge of all the varieties of seed owned by his *bilek*-family" (1970:191). He adds: "This is essentially the woman's province, and whenever I began to record the names, and other details of *padi* seed, the man of the family, hopelessly out of his depth, would hurriedly summon his wife, or some other woman of the family to enlighten me" (1970:191).

48. The term *anak* may actually be used in a more general sense to denote the quality of youthfulness or immaturity, thus rendering *anak padi* simply as 'young rice'. Richards, however, specifically translates *anak padi* as "rice baby" (1981:242), and likens their role in transplanting rituals to that of a corn dolly (Richards 1981:242).

49. Sather has objected to this interpretation of the term *ngindu'*, pointing out that the term *indu'* also has "the meaning of 'source', "premier' or 'leading example', and the verb *ngindu'* is generally used with the sense of 'to take precedent', or 'to lead'" (1980:73 n.). The Iban, however, are quite explicit about the significance of *ngindu'* in this particular context. One should also note here that Richards derives *indu'* from Sanskrit origins where it means, among other things, "life-giving" (1981:115).

50. Rosaldo and Atkinson write that "[m]en's life-taking, because of its intentionality, becomes a means of transcending the biological; whereas childbearing, despite social values attached to it as the means of perpetuating the social group, remains grounded in the 'naturalness' of women's sexual constitution" (1975:70).

51. Perham, in referring to Ticin Temaga's demands for a freshly taken head, comments that "the story is a distinct assertion of that which has been often said, viz, that the women are at the bottom, the prime movers of head-taking in many instances" (1878:132). He adds: "and how should they not be with the example of this story before them?" (Perham 1878:132).

52. The women who prepare the mordants for dyeing also drape a *pua'* over themselves (Gavin 1992).

53. c.f. the final stages of the *timang* invocation.

54. c.f. the fact that trophy heads must be ritually placated with food and offerings of tobacco and chewing ingredients (see note 20).

55. The Badang are a Kenyah-related people who live in the upper reaches of the Rejang river. They were the traditional enemy of the Iban of the Baleh river where this particular design was created some time before 1950 (Gavin, personal communication).

ABBREVIATIONS

Bijdragen   *Bijdragen tot de Taal-, Land-, en Volkenkunde*

JMBRAS   *Journal of the Malay/Malaysian Branch of the Royal Asiatic Society*

JSBRAS   *Journal of the Straits Branch of the Royal Asiatic Society*

REFERENCES

Anonymous
          1901   Headhunting in Borneo. Sarawak Gazette p. 208, reprinted in Richards (1977).

Appell, G. N.
          1976   Studies in Borneo Societies: social process and anthropological explanation, (ed.), DeKalb, IL, Northern Illinois University Press.

Ardner, E.
          1975   Belief and the Problem of Women. In Perceiving Women, (ed.) Ardner, S. London: Malaby Press.

Brooke C.
          1866   Ten Years in Sarawak. 2 vols. London.

Brooke, Low
          1892   The Natives of Borneo. London: Harrison and Sons.

Douglas, M.
          1966   Purity and Danger. London: Routledge and Kegan Paul.

Downs, R. B.
1955   Headhunting in Indonesia. Bijdragen 111:40-70.

Elshout, J. M.
1926   De Kenja-Dayaks uit het Apo-Kajangebeid: bidragen tot
                       de Kennis van Centraal-Borneo. The Hague: Martinus
                       Nijhoff.

Endicott, K. M.
1970   An Analysis of Malay Magic. Oxford: Clarendon.

Freeman, J. D.
1960   The Iban of Western Borneo. In Social Structure in South
                       East Asia, (ed.) Murdock, G. P. Chicago: Quadrangle
                       Books.

1961   Iban Augury. Bijdragen 117:141-167.

1967   Shaman and Incubus. In Warner Muensterberger and
                       Sidney Axelrad, eds., The Psychoanalytic Study of
                       Society, 4:315-343.

1968   Thunder, Blood and the Nicknaming of God's Creatures.
                       The Psychoanalytic Quarterly 37:353-399.

1970   Report on the Iban. London: Athlone Press.

1975   The Iban of Sarawak and Their Religion - a review
                       article. Sarawak Museum Journal XXIII (n.s.) No. 44:275-
                       288.

1979   Severed Heads That Germinate. In Fantasy and Symbol,
                       (ed.) Hook, R. H. London: Academic Press.

1981   Some Reflections on the Nature of Iban Society. Occa-
                       sional Paper of the Department of Anthropology, The
                       Australian National University, Canberra.

Freud, S.
1900   The Interpretation of Dreams (2nd. part), Standard
                       Edition.

Freud, S.
    1916   A Connection Between Symbol and Symptom, Standard
                        Edition.

Gana, H.
    1988   Ritual Acts: A Description of Forms and Functions. M.A.
                        Thesis, University of Hull.

Gavin, T.
    1992   *Kayau Indu'*, The War-path of Women: A *ngar* ritual at
                        Entawau, Baleh in October 1988", forthcoming issue of
                        Sarawak Museum Journal.

Geddes, W. R.
    1954   The Land Dayaks of Sarawak. London, Her Majesty's
                        Stationery Office.

Gomes, E. H.
    1917   Seventeen Years Among the Sea Dayaks of Borneo.
                        London: Seeley and Co.

Goody, J.
    1977   The Domestication of the Savage Mind. Cambridge
                        University Press.

Haddon, A. C.
    1901   Headhunters: Black, White and Brown. London.

Hallpike, C. R.
    1973   Functionalist Interpretations of Primitive Warfare. Man
                        Vol. 8:451-470.

Harrisson, T.
    1947   Correspondence, Sarawak Gazette, September 1st:175-78.

Hose, C. and McDougall, W.
    1912   The Pagan Tribes of Borneo, 2 vols. London:
                        Macmillan and Co.

Howell, W.
    1912   The Sea Dayak Method of Making Thread from Their Home-Grown Cotton. Sarawak Museum Journal (old series) no. 2:62-66.

    1977   Contributions to the Sarawak Gazette, reprinted in Richards (1977).

Howell, W. and D. J. S. Bailey
    1900   A Sea Dayak Dictionary. Singapore: American Press.

Hutton, J. H.
    1928   The Significance of Headhunting in Assam. Journal of the Royal Anthropological Institute 58:399-408.

    1938   A Primitive Philosophy of Life (Frazer Lecture 1938), Oxford: Clarendon Press.

Jensen, E.
    1967   Iban Birth. Folk 8-9:165-78.

    1974   The Iban and Their Religion. Oxford: Clarendon Press.

King, V. T.
    1976   Migration, Warfare, and Culture Contact in Borneo: a critique of ecological analysis. Oceania No. 4:306-27.

    1977   Unity, Formalism and Structure: comments on Iban augury and related problems. Bijdragen 133:63-87.

Keppel, H.
    1853   A Visit to the Indian Archipelago in H. M. Ship Maeander with Portions of the Private Journal of Sir James Brooke, 2 vols. London.

Kruyt, A. C.
    1906   Het Animisme in den Indischen Archipel. The Hague: Martinus Nijhoff.

Leach, E. R.
    1950   Social Science Research in Sarawak. London: HMSO.

Ling Roth, H.
    1896   The Natives of Sarawak and British North Borneo. 2 vols. London: Truslove and Hanson.

Low, H.
    1846   Sarawak: Its Inhabitants and Productions. London.

MacCormack, C.
    1980   Nature, Culture and Gender: a critique. In Nature, Culture and Gender, (eds.) MacCormack, C. and Strathern, M. Cambridge University Press.

Mashman, V.
    1986   Warriors and Weavers: a study of gender relations among the Iban of Sarawak. M.A. thesis, University of Kent, Canterbury.

Masing, J.
    1981   The Coming of the Gods: a study of the invocatory change (*timang gawai amat*) of the Iban of the Baleh region of Sarawak, PhD thesis, Australian National University, Canberra.

    1989   Iban and Their Symbols (Language and Oral Tradition). Sarawak Museum Journal XL (n.s.) no. 61:59-67.

McKinley, R.
    1976   Human and Proud of It! A structural treatment of head-hunting rites and the social definition of enemies. In G. N. Appell, ed., Studies in Borneo Societies: Social Process and Anthropological Explanation, DeKalb, IL, Northern Illinois University Press.

Morgan, S.
    1968   Iban Aggressive Expansion: Some Background Factors. Sarawak Museum Journal XVI (n.s.) nos. 32-33:141-185.

Morgan S. and P. Beavitt
    1971   An Iban Funeral Near Saratok (1960). Sarawak Museum Journal XIX (n.s.) nos. 38-39:277-313.

Needham, R.
    1976   Skulls and Causality. Man 11:71-88.

Nyuak
    1977   Religious Rites of the Iban. In A.J.N. Richards, ed., The
                        Sea Dayaks and Other Races of Sarawak, 4th impression,
                        Kuching, Borneo Literature Bureau.

Ortner, S.
    1974   Is Female to Male as Nature is to Culture? In Women,
                        Culture and Society, (eds.) Rosaldo, M and Lamphere, L.,
                        California: Stanford University Press.

Padoch, C.
    1982   Land Use in New and Old Areas of Iban Settlement.
                        Borneo Research Bulletin 14 no. 1:3-14.

Perham,J.
    1878   *Mengap*, Song of the Dayak Head Feast. JSBRAS 6:123-
                        135.

    1884   Sea Dayak Religion (Continued). JSBRAS 14:287-304.

Pringle, R.
    1970   Rajahs and Rebels: The Ibans of Sarawak Under Brooke
                        Rule 1841-1941. Ithaca, NY, Cornell University Press.

Richards, A. J. N.
    1972   Iban Augury. Sarawak Museum Journal XX (n.s.) nos.
                        40-41:63-81.

    1977   The Sea Dayaks and Other Races of Sarawak, (ed.) 4th
                        impression, Kuching: Borneo Literature Bureau.

    1981   An Iban-English Dictionary. Oxford: Clarendon Press.

Rosaldo, M. Z. and J. M. Atkinson
    1975   Man the Hunter and Woman: Metaphors for the Sexes
                        in Ilongot Magical Spells. In The Interpretation of
                        Symbols, (ed.) Willis, R. London: Academic Press.

Rousseau, J.
    1980   Iban Inequality. Bijdragen 136:52-63.

St. John, S.
    1862   Life in the Forest of the Far East: Or Travels in North Borneo. 2 vols. London: Smith, Elder and Co.

Sandin, B.
    1962   Sengalang Burong. Kuching: Borneo Literature Bureau.

    1966   A Saribas Iban Death Dirge (*Sabak*). Sarawak Museum Journal XIV (n.s.) nos. 28-29:15-80.

    1967a   The Sea Dayaks of Borneo Before White Rajah Rule. London: Macmillan.

    1967b   Simpulang or Pulang Gana: The Founder of Dayak Agriculture. Sarawak Museum Journal XV (n.s.) nos. 30-32:245-406.

    1976   Iban Way of Life. Kuching: Borneo Literature Bureau.

    1977   Gawai Burong: The Chants and Celebrations of the Iban Bird Festival. Pulau Pinang: Universiti Sains Malaysia.

    1980   Iban Adat and Augury. Pulau Pinang: Universiti Sains Malaysia.

Sather, C.
    1977a   Introduction to Benedict Sandin, Gawai Burong: The Chants and Celebrations of the Iban Bird Festival. Pulau Pinang: Universiti Sains Malaysia.

    1977b   *Nanchang Padi*: Symbolism of Saribas Iban First Rites of Harvest. JMBRAS L no. 2:150-170.

    1980   Symbolic Elements in Saribas Iban Rites of *padi* Storage. JMBRAS LIII no. 2:67-95.

    1985   Iban Agricultural Augury. Sarawak Museum Journal XXXIV No. 55:1-35

Schärer, H.
1963   Ngaju Religion: The Conception of God Among a South
        Borneo People.   Trans. Needham, R.   The Hague:
        Martinus Nijhoff.

Spencer, J. E.
1966   Shifting Cultivation in Southeastern Asia.   Berkeley:
        University of California Press.

Sutlive, V. H.
1976   The Iban *Manang*: An Alternative Route to Normality.
        In G. N. Appell, ed., Studies in Borneo Societies: Social
        Process and Anthropological Explanation, DeKalb, IL,
        Northern Illinois University Press.

1977   The Many Faces of Kumang: Iban Women in Fact and
        Fiction. Sarawak Museum Journal XXV (n.s.) no. 46:157-
        164.

1978   The Iban of Sarawak. Arlington Heights: AHM Publish-
        ing Corporation - Worlds of Man Studies (2nd Edition
        1988, Waveland Press).

Uchibori, M.
1978   The Leaving of This Transient World: A Study of Iban
        Eschatology and Mortuary Practices.   Ph.D. thesis,
        Australian National University, Canberra.

Vayda, A.
1961   Expansion and Warfare Among Swidden Agriculturalists.
        American Anthropologist 63(2)1:346-58.

1969   The Study of the Causes of War with Special Reference
        to Headhunting Raids in Borneo. Ethnohistory Vol.
        16:211-24.

1976   War in Ecological Perspective. New York and London:
        Plenum Press.

Vries, A. De
1974   Dictionary of Symbols and Imagery.   Amsterdam:
        North-Holland Publishing Co.

Wagner, U.
1972   Colonialism and Iban Warfare. Ph.D. thesis, Stockholm
              University.

WARRIORS AND WEAVERS:
A STUDY OF GENDER RELATIONS AMONG
THE IBAN OF SARAWAK

VALERIE MASHMAN

A myth says that Selampandai offers the Iban an instrument to be used in weaving or a spear, and according to the choice, the child selects his or her sex before birth. Neither is felt to be significantly better than the other (Jensen 1967:167) (emphasis added).

The spear and the loom are symbols used in Iban society to evoke the differentiation of male and female gender roles. These complementary pairs, which represent headhunting and weaving, trophy heads and woven textiles, are significant as cultural constructs that elaborate Iban notions of maleness and femaleness. Iban society has been identified as egalitarian, both in terms of class and gender. Institutionalized subordination or superordination do not exist in Iban social structure. A newborn child can belong to either his mother's or father's bilik family, and married couples can reside with either the wife's or husband's kin group (Freeman 1970:15). A number of ethnographers (Freeman 1967:334; Kedit 1980:96; Sutlive 1977:158; Sather 1978:34), however, have suggested that in Iban society, with its cognatic kinship system, male values prevail:

Iban social life is dominated by male values...through the attainment of prestige in a series of exclusively male activities, the chief of these traditionally being in the cult of headhunting, which for the Iban, has long been a major cultural obsession. (Freeman 1968:334)

Iban longhouse viewed from the river.

To date, Iban history and ethnography have emphasized the dominance of the male prestige system and minimized the importance of women. Iban society has been presented in a male idiom because anthropologists have, for the most part, been men[1] and have been biased by their own cultural perceptions of gender. Male activities, values, and modes of expression have been taken as the norm.[2] This has led scholars and others to perceive women as excluded from what would seem to be significant in Iban society. According to this view, women are dominated by an exclusively male prestige system and merely "set the stage for the accomplishments of Iban men" (Sutlive 1977:158).

Despite the under-representation of women in Iban ethnography, it is possible to approach gender relations in Iban society from a different perspective. Women have their own system of prestige differentiation and do not derive their own status solely from the male value system. While male and female prestige systems operate parallel to each other, each sex projects its own perspective of reality, with distinctive priorities. At the same time, each gender belongs to a wider community and shares the same system of symbols. The meanings attributed to these symbols, however, vary according to the context of the social actors.

The male prestige system will be considered in the historical context of headhunting to determine whether it is "exclusively male" and to analyze women's relationship to this male prestige system, which, as Freeman suggests, constitutes the dominant values in Iban society. In addition, the significance of the loom will be examined to determine whether textiles function as a complementary index of prestige for women, and whether this index is subsumed by a more dominant male prestige system.

The construction of gender will then be considered from a different perspective, which is perhaps more appropriate to a contemporary context in relation to the heritage of the "traditional" value system mentioned above. Two complementary categories derived from the organization of space in the longhouse will be examined. The *ruai* or veranda, which extends the length of the longhouse as the public area, and the *bilik* or family room, are identified with the male and female gender respectively.

> When locust Selampandai is heard at night near the house the Iban say that a woman has conceived. If Selampandai is heard from the bilek, it is likely to be a girl, from the ruai, a boy..."
> (Jensen 1967:166)

The ruai represents an outward orientation formerly manifested through hunting and warfare and now revealed through "wandering," migration, politics, and public affairs in a state society. The bilik, a domestic sphere with indefinite boundaries, is the locus of production and reproduction for Iban women.

WARRIORS AND WEAVERS
Headhunters, Warfare, and the Iban

Western writers and scholars have subjected the Iban to severe stereotyping. The chroniclers of the Brooke regime probably exaggerated the "savagery" and barbarism of the Sea Dayak "pirates" in order to justify the massacres of the Brooke punitive expeditions (Wagner 1972:320), calling them "aggressive expanding shifting cultivators and warriors." McDonald (1985:17), furthermore, has labeled them the "wickedest headhunters in the whole wide world."

The debate on the reasons for headhunting, warfare, and expansion has never been satisfactorily resolved, probably because the relevant data are insufficient and open to misinterpretation. Nevertheless, there does appear to be a connection between headhunting, land, fertility, and rice cultivation in the Iban belief system. This connection is important because rice farming is women's work for the most part (Freeman 1955:78). It is thus possible to understand that men's interests as warriors overlap with those of women as farmers. Both men and women regard the trophy head as a significant symbol.

Generations of writers have perceived a link between headhunting and farming: St. John (1862:204) noted that the taking of heads promoted an abundant harvest and Kennedy (1942:113-114) wrote about the presence of a spiritual juice inside the trophy head that promoted rice growth and fertility in women. Sather (1980) establishes a convincing connection between headhunting, rice cultivation, and fertility. The Iban belief that *padi aki ini kami* ("rice is our ancestor"), he argues, is reinforced by the belief that the souls of the deceased turn to dew, fall to earth, and nourish the rice crop. The rice plant is mystically composed of the spirit of the Iban's human ancestors (Sather 1980:93). Sather links this to the Iban belief that a human head must be taken to terminate a period of mourning.[3] This enables the spirit of the deceased to enter the land of the dead (*sebayan*) and be changed into dew that will nourish the next rice crop.

Iban skulls hanging over a *ruai*, as bards chant during a festival, with *pua' kumbu'* on the inner wall to create the ritual center.

This connection between trophy heads, rice, and fertility can be more fully examined by focusing on symbolism in oral literature. In the *Timang Gawai Amat*, an oral narrative in honor of Lang, the god of war, the themes of headhunting and rice cultivation are closely tied. Lang arrives at a festival at the longhouse of the *orang panggau*, or culture heroes, bringing a trophy head with him. It is eventually decided that the head should be planted. In order to do this, Lang ceremoniously cuts the head open, causing different strains of rice seed, including the sacred *padi-pun*, to issue forth. Masing (1978) has demonstrated that at this point the timang becomes an allegory and that hill padi cultivation becomes symbolic of head-hunting and warfare. The longhouse decides to plant the padi seed, but the menfolk equip themselves for war rather than farming. Felling trees to clear land for farming symbolizes demolishing the enemy longhouse and killing the enemies. Burning the land symbolizes burning the enemy longhouse. When the padi is ready for harvest, human heads are gathered instead of rice. As the rice is laid out to dry in the sun, the narrator recalls the smoking of human heads in the longhouse.

This shows the close relationship between headhunting and rice cultivation. At a basic level, both are crucial to Iban survival. Ideologically, each is connected with the prestige system: the possession of fertile land means the possibility of rice surpluses and the acquisition of prestige items such as gongs and jars. Masing has summarized this circular connection: "A large surplus of padi could only be obtained if a constant supply of virgin forest was available for cultivation and the availability of virgin forest depended upon the Ibans' ability to conquer fresh territory" (1978:66). Trophy heads, then, represent the intertwined goals of the sexes: territorial control over primary forest that will result in an abundant supply of fertile land for good rice harvests. It is in women's interests to support the male value system, the cult of bravery, in order to ensure that these ends are reached.

The Iban Value System and the Cult of Bravery

The underlying values of bravery (*berani*), boldness (*kempang*), and strength (*kering*) are central to any explanation of Iban aggression, warfare, and headhunting. A man of bravery and strength will have tattoos on his throat, a sign of that he has endured pain, and a headhunter will have tattoos on his fingers (Freeman 1979:238). These values are reinforced through myth, ritual, and the daily division of labor. Bravery may be considered as a means of acquiring status in what Freeman has identified as an egalitarian society. The leader of a longhouse, the *tuai rumah*, is elected by both men and women of the longhouse for his skills in oratory, warfare, and farming, and his familiarity with *adat*, or customary law, in order to resolve disputes (Freeman 1970:111ff). Although usually a man, women tuai rumah are not unknown. The tuai rumah must inspire the confidence of his followers and exemplify the qualities of bravery, endurance, and determination that are essential for survival. Skill in farming and warfare is important in the pioneering context, in which the tuai rumah leads a group to establish a new settlement. The tuai rumah has no authority to command others, but is empowered to resolve disputes through influence and by reference to custom.

Bards chanting around a blanket-encased shrine.

Prior to the arrival of James Brooke in 1841, the highest positions of status in Iban society were the *raja berani* and the *tau serang*. The raja berani is a man recognized for his skill in pioneering, warfare, and leadership. The tau serang, whose status equals that of the rajah berani, is a man who has been guided by the spirits to mobilize and lead large war parties. This was a significant accomplishment in a society that had no institutionalized authority and where war parties consisted of hundreds or thousands of men. Iban war leaders led a "company of equal men, by consent" (Freeman 1961:211). These two positions disappeared with the rise of the state (Sutlive 1978:33) and today leadership is founded on allegiance to the ruling political parties. Women have clearly been denied the opportunity to achieve such positions. With this in mind, it will be important to determine the nature of women's status differentiation which operates outside the male prestige system.

It is also important to consider how the values of courage, strength, and boldness are consolidated in Iban society. From his earliest days, an Iban boy is taught to be brave and courageous:

> At birth the soles of the male infant were spanked "that he might know pain and have courage to withstand it." His lips were rubbed with chilli so that his speech might be strong (Sutlive 1976:65).

Childhood games such as top-spinning, wrestling, boxing, and tug-of-war reinforce the importance of courage, strength, and bravery. These values are further manifested in the young men. During festivals, the oral narratives sung by the bards recount the secrets of upward mobility through the deeds of the culture heroes. Keling in particular emulates the most desirable qualities in Iban manhood; he is described as "handsome, strong, brave, dauntless, resourceful and possesses powerful magic" (Sutlive 1976:66). The Iban are said to believe that the recitation of the narratives can actually thwart enemies and encourage bravery (Masing 1981:134). One could argue from this that the values of the male prestige system are taught and influence daily reality.

These values are further reinforced and made to appear "natural" through the sexual division of labor. In keeping with the male prestige system, the daily division of labor requires strong and courageous men. Men take control of the forest by clearing large tracts. They construct large scaffolds around enormous trees and fell the trees from rudimentary platforms. After this, men fire the farms and assist with the padi planting. At harvest time, their principal task involves carrying the heavy padi-baskets back home from the farm, a task young men take pride in (Freeman 1970:228).

Thus bravery, strength, and daring are important values for the community as a whole, not only in warfare, but also in farming and migration. It is in women's interest that their men are effective warriors, since they stand to gain both from the labor power gained from slaves acquired in battle and from adequate protection when they farm outlying swiddens (Wagner 1972:133, 150). Moreover, the ritual significance of the trophy head is important to women, as it promises successful harvests.

The cult of bravery does not represent an absolute value, as demonstrated by women's relationship to the values of bravery and daring and the *manang*. Women do not in any way compete with men for bravery. In a difficult situation, a man may not withdraw or submit, whereas a woman may if it will ultimately benefit the community. This is well illustrated by a dispute between the Batang Ai Iban and the Iban from the Kalimantan border (Heppell 1975:98). When the Batang Ai Iban began attacking the Kalimantan longhouse, the women in the longhouse prepared for an act of submission. They dressed in ceremonial clothing and made food and ritual offerings for the enemy and thus saved the longhouse.

It does not appear that women are less respected because they have no status in this prestige system based on courage, daring, and strength. A man who does not measure up to the value system and who spends too much time in the longhouse might be considered a coward. Women might accuse such a man of wearing "a woman's sarong" (Sandin 1976:15) or being a "a female-male" (*laki indu*) (Sutlive 1978:55). These figurative expressions do not necessarily imply that women are denigrated, since women stand outside the male prestige context. Masculinity and femininity are figurative idioms and women as people are detached from such negative valuations (cf. Strathern 1984).

The manang, or shaman, also seems to have uncertain status in the conventional value scheme. The notion of this ambiguous sexuality may provide further insight into the nature of the dichotomy between the sexes. The manang, quite a common figure, is apparently a person who does not conform to the male value system. Sutlive identifies the manang as one who is unable to compete for prestige as he lacks the appropriate qualities that define manliness; he may be blind or handicapped and unable "to respond to the cultural demands for bravery and achievement" (1976:66).[4] The highest grade of shaman, the *manang bali*, is a man who has adopted the role of a woman (Jensen 1974:145) and takes a "husband" whose main interest in life is to inherit his "wife's" property (Howell and Bailey in Richards 1963:159). He is often referred to as a transvestite or a hermaphrodite in 19th-century literature and would appear to be a phenomenon of the past.[5] Masing (1981:322) notes that the last manang bali in the Balleh died around 1870 or 1880. However, the figure remains significant in Iban culture and appears in the myths surrounding shamanism (Sather 1977; Sandin 1983).

Jensen (1974:145) states that the manang is clearly set apart from other people "in a society where the sexual roles are clearly if not dogmatically defined." From this ambiguous position outside the conventional order of gender, the manang has the spiritual power to deal with sickness in the longhouse that has resulted from a violation of the adat order. He is able to make courageous journeys into the spirit world, a realm which would normally fill most mortal Iban with fear and dread (Sutlive 1978:102; Jensen 1974:100). It could possibly be argued that the existence of the manang in Iban society demonstrates the arbitrary nature of definitions of gender. The manang has no gender and both genders at the same time. He apparently gains his position of superhuman power from this liminal position, outside the conventional notion of masculinity. The male value system does not remain the sole focus of strength and power, which suggests that the gender dichotomy is less polarized and asymmetrical than it first appears.

For example, Sather (1978:340-343) argues that inequality exists between the genders in Iban society, since women are excluded from the cult of war and the high honors achieved through success in war. The resulting tension is expressed though the ceremonial mockery of men by women during *gawai* celebrations. Women dress up as warriors, complete with wooden swords and enormous wooden phalli, behavior which Freeman has interpreted as penis envy (1968:388). One could argue that attempts to explain women's ritual mockery in terms of jealousy and subordination are indicative of male cultural perceptions that regard male activities and values of predominant importance. The presence of the manang, alternatively, supports the notion that the male prestige system is not conceived as an absolute value. It is possible that women perceive their own activities as more valuable than those of men. Through institutionalized mockery of the male values, Iban women articulate their distinctive perspective of the male prestige system and their perception of themselves as a separate entity.

Headhunting and Women

The values of bravery, strength and daring are taught to the baby Iban boy through lullabies (Sandin 1976:12) and through the words of the women who look after him:

> The child, unable to speak, scarcely able to walk is addressed by his grandmother in the following way: "We put all our confidence in you, for you have to avenge us. For the head of your grandfather or some other relative is hanging somewhere over the fireplace and you have to avenge us...." (Anonymous in Richards 1963:118).

Women subject Iban males to the values of warriors from birth onward. Females derive this power from the fact that males do not have access to them until they prove themselves by obtaining a trophy head (Sandin 1976:15, Pringle 1970:25). This provides women with the opportunity to manipulate a courtship; they may be selective and reject men who have not achieved status (Masing 1981:349, 381).

Women, then, actively encourage men to take heads. There is even evidence in Iban literature that women goaded men to headhunt (Masing 1981:238). Nineteenth-century observers seem to have little doubt that women are the power behind the headhunting cult: "Women in their cruelty and blood-thirstiness are the cause of this headhunting" (Richards 1963:119). Another writer, quick to apportion blame to "the evil disposition of the women," remarks that "some of the young Dayaks have plainly stated that they would give up headhunting were it not for the taunts and jibes of their wives" (Keppel 1853:123). Peer pressure is an important factor because men have to compete against one another: *enggai alah pangan diri* (Masing 1981:459). Thus heads are not only for important in themselves as signs of bravery, *tanda berani*, and as the guarantee of fertile land. They also render a man eligible for a wife, who not only produces children and ensures the continuity of the bilik, but also who produces rice, the staple means of survival. A head and a wife give a man the mark of adulthood in Iban society.

While the men are away at war, the women believe that their daily, routine actions can have an affect on the men's success. Rice, for example, is put out for them at meal times so they might not go hungry. The women will not go to sleep in the daytime, for fear that the men will become less alert, and they will not use perfumed flowers in case the smell gives away the men's position to the enemy (Hewitt 1908:599). By observing these restrictions, or *penti ngayau*, women have the power to affect men's performance in war.

Women also play a prominent part in the ceremonies surrounding the headhunting cult. They carry down the old skulls from the fireplace and, according to one witness, sing *Agi ngambi, agi ngambi* ("bring us more of them") (Anonymous in Richards 1963:118). The trophy heads are clearly for the women. Those of a special status, skilled in the style of receiving the heads (*naku antu pala*, [Masing 1981:224]), accept them on shoulder cloths woven from *ikat* fabric, singing in procession.

The women take possession of the fresh head and start at once their horrible dance with it. I have seen them myself with heads dripping with blood, and exhaling an awful stench; with devilish joy they were taken by the dancing women, who in their rage--they were enraged over it--bit the head and licked it whilst they were dancing through the house like mad women (Anonymous in Richards 1963:118).

Although this description may be somewhat exaggerated, it conveys the idea of the trophy head as a symbol of male sexuality, epitomizing the male values of strength and bravery. While the women might relish the trophy head as a sexual symbol in such ceremonies, their relationship to the trophy head differs according to the context. For example, in the *Timang Gawai Amat*, the women make fun of the head, calling it "as ugly as a bat" and "a red pepper." At this point in the narrative, the head cries and the women elect one of their number to nurse it as if it were a baby (Masing 1981:308-309). If the head is a symbol of male sexuality, then women clearly have an ambivalent attitude toward it. They mock it, relish it as they would their lovers, and nurture it as they would their children.

Women, then, have a distinct relationship with the male prestige system. They set the onus on the men to conform to and maintain its conventionally accepted standards, because it is in their interests to do so. Moreover, they can negotiate their position according to the situation, either to reinforce the values of the system, represent the alternatives of submission and withdrawal, or demolish the system through ritual mockery. Women can afford to do so because their locus of status is set in a different idiom, that of weaving, as discussed below. Men, however, are constrained to act within the male prestige system. The only alternative available to them is to become a manang.

The Weaving of Textiles

Throughout Southeast Asia, there is a correlation among femaleness, fertility, and textiles. The themes of weaving and gender recur not only in Iban myth but also in ritual as well:

After the baby has been bathed and if he is a boy, one of the wings of a slaughtered fowl is hung onto the shaft of a multi-pronged spear, tied with a red ribbon. If the baby is a girl, the wing is fastened by a heddle rod (Sandin 1976:11).

Sources on Iban ideology suggest that weaving is linked with the concept of female gender identity and that it is counterbalanced by the spear as a symbol of maleness, in opposition and interdependence. Weaving is a constant theme in myths and songs and in oral narratives in honor of Lang, the god of war (Masing 1981, Sandin 1977). In the *Timang Gawai Amat*, the last part is dedicated to the planting and harvesting of cotton. The motif of white ripe cotton balls, glistening eggs, recurs throughout the poem.

Although ostensibly about headhunting, war, and the epic deeds of the culture heroes abroad, the narrative contains sections on weaving that reflect the stability of life in the longhouse and the lyrical intimacy of courtship. The language of weaving is the language of love, and lines such as the following draw a connection between the creativity of women as weavers and as mothers. A man thus addresses his lover:

> In your mother's eyes, my darling
> You are the most beauteous of the threads
> By which her loom is graced (Masing 1981:1978).[6]

In this oral narrative, cotton balls are associated with eggs, thread with little fish, and the sound of the shuttle with bird song, all of which suggest the setting for courtship (Rubenstein 1973i; Masing 1981).

In the *Timang Gawai Amat*, Kumang, the Iban culture heroine, describes a meeting with an ex-lover who has fashioned a "weaving sword" (*belia*), carved with designs of "ravenous dogs eating their own heads waiting to slip indoors" (351).[7] This illustrates how male and female elements unite in the creation of a woven textile: the man provides a "weaving sword" and the woman provides cotton balls and her knowledge of design. The interdependence between the sexes extends further, since a woman needs a man to construct the weaving apparatus. In return he might be rewarded, like Kumang's ex-lover, with a waistband for his sword (Masing 1981:352). Men, in turn, rely on women to weave them cloths and jackets that will protect them in war. Courtship thus promotes sexual interaction that provides the basis for successful weaving.

An Iban woman spinning thread.

The weaving of a textile indicates maturity. According to Iban tradition, a girl must be skilled in weaving to become worthy of a husband, just as a man must take a head to become worthy of a wife. A really expert weaver will exhibit skill and control that is suggestive of sexual knowledge and power:

The stranger makes haste to start her weaving
She picks up a ball of cotton, like the eggs of a bird
Pulls out the white thread that leaps about like a fish
With care she presses against the backstrap of the loom,
She knows her shuttle like a fish darting though still waters
(Masing 1981:354).[8]

A girl learns to weave from her mother or grandmother. The secret of the designs are kept within the family. A skilled weaver may work in complete secrecy, hiding her work until it is completely finished. Each woman has her own exclusive repertoire that may include as many as a hundred different designs. A woman may sell her designs at a price, but in so doing forfeits her copyright (Gill 1968:153). Originality in design is a criterion of excellence and every woman seeks to develop new patterns. For example, Mene in the *Timang Gawai Amat* is praised for the uniqueness of the waistband she weaves for Lang, the god of war (Masing 1981:355).

Women weave not only to provide their menfolk with ceremonial jackets and waistbands, but also for their bilik family. The Iban family requires woven textiles for a number or ritual purposes, including various agricultural festivals, the Feast of the Whetstones, and festivals for warfare and the dead (Gittinger 1979:217; Sandin 1976:46). Large woven blankets (*pua*) are placed underneath offerings or used to delineate and protect a ritual area, to screen a corpse on the veranda, or to cover a newborn child on its first ritual meeting with its grandmother (Sandin 1976). Perhaps the most significant use of the pua in the context of this discussion is in the rituals attached to the headhunting cult, when a woman skilled in weaving receives the trophy head, the symbol of bravery, *tanda berani*, on a specially woven cloth (*pua kumbu muau* [Sather 1977:xv]).

Woven textiles have mystical qualities. The Iban use them as protection from evil spirits and physical enemies and as a means of communication with the spirit world: a shaman requires a *bidang* or woven skirt as a fee for transporting a soul to the world beyond and to ensure a safe return from the underworld (Howell 1911:7). The *Timang Gawai Amat* contains several references to the jacket of Lang, dexterously woven (Masing 1981:283) in a superb pattern with a frog motif (1981:283). This jacket will make Lang invincible (1981:178, 145). The spiritual qualities of woven textiles is also illustrated by a myth in which one of

Lang's daughters marries a mortal and weaves him and their son "jackets of birds" to enable them to fly and join her in heaven (Howell 1909:186-187).

The Iban believe that designs have a certain ritual power and may harm a woman who tries to weave them. To protect herself, a woman may use special charms and make an offering of betel nuts and eggs to Kumang before beginning to weave (Masing 1981:436). An apprentice weaver is particularly vulnerable and must rely on the assistance of an older woman to tie the dangerous part of the textiles (Vogelsanger 1980:117). A woman's repertoire of designs may be limited by ritual prescriptions, which only the spirits can lift. When Nangku anak Dingat was almost fifty years old, for example, Kumang told her that she could weave any design she wanted (*nadai pemali*). This initiated her career as a master weaver. Her pua were much sought in her longhouse and she wore a porcupine quill adorned with several warp threads in her hair (Edric Ong 1986:26).

Dyeing cotton thread is also a difficult ritual process, which perhaps only one out of fifty women master. Restrictions similar to those enforced during childbirth are imposed, and the process is said to take place covertly, away from the gaze of men.[9] Dyeing has been described as *kayau indu*, "the warfare of women." A woman who is skilled in dyeing is called *indu gaar* or *indu takar*, a status similar to that of a war chief (*tau serang*) (Sather 1977a:xv).

Unfortunately, not enough is known about the functioning and order of women's status differentiation in weaving. A skilled woman is paid handsomely for her services to other women who require dyed thread (Haddon and Start 1982:22). Through success in weaving, women achieve recognition of their maturity, some specific ritual honors in gawai festivals, such as receiving a skull or decorating the *kelingkang* pole (Sather 1977a:xv), and the distinction of having tattoos on their fingers (Komanyi 1972:102). It is also said that a husband can earn recognition and honor in certain rituals though his wife's status as a weaver.

In traditional Iban society, then, women are not subordinated by a male value system that emphasizes prestige in warfare. This is because they have the power to manipulate their position in relationship to the male system through their facility to endorse, challenge, or represent alternative values. It is in their interest to recreate the male value system through the indoctrination of male infants and boys, because trophy heads mean abundant rice harvests. Women are able to shift their position in relation to the male prestige system because their gender identity is located outside the system in their knowledge of weaving. As weavers, women play a vital part in protecting the life, health and fertility of the community, objectives shared by men as warriors.

The difficult and potentially dangerous task of dyeing thread for weaving.

The idiom of weaving articulates the cultural construct of femaleness in Iban society, in opposition to warfare and maleness. This is conveyed in myth, ritual, and oral literature through imagery of fertility, life, love, and sexuality, which are alternative ideals to bravery and warfare but still in the interests of the goals of the community. Knowledge of weaving and dyeing is held exclusively by mother and daughter. Each design is the original work of one woman, inspired by the spirits. Through their relationship with the spirit world, the textiles women weave mediate between heaven and earth. If a woman successfully establishes a relationship with the spirit world, she will be able to weave designs that will earn her adult status and, moreover, recognition as an expert weaver.

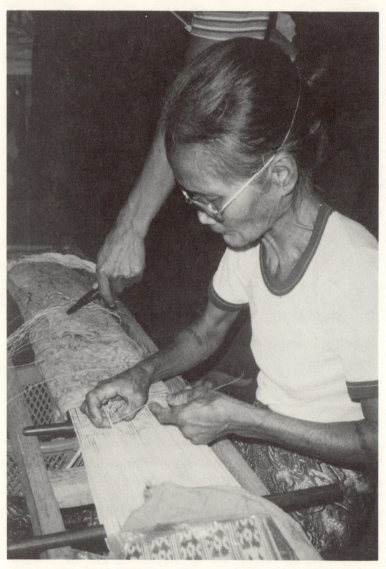

Master weaver at work.

Weaving with the back-strap loom.

Men, in contrast, lack women's flexibility in relation to the male prestige system. They have only two alternatives to complying with the values of male prestige and bravery: becoming a manang or facing the mockery of the label *laki indu* (female-male). Although this ideology of gender identity through warfare and weaving continues in the post headhunting era, through myth and ritual, not enough is known about how the decline of weaving has affected status differentiation between the sexes. The ways in which the male prestige system is recreated in the contemporary context also merits additional consideration.

SPACE, GENDER, AND THE LONGHOUSE

Another symbolic relationship, that between the *ruai* (male) and the *bilik* (female), exists in Iban society. This relationship is discussed below in terms of both the ideology of male mobility through *bejalai* and women's association with bejalai-related values, based on their position in the household, which is unseen and unstated in both ideology and ethnography.

The outer orientation of the longhouse is historically rooted in warfare and headhunting and is recreated in the present-day though bejalai or male migration. This ideology is further reflected by the organization of ritual space in the longhouse. The part that extends outward from the *tangga* (the notched log used to climb onto the tanju or porch) to the ruai, or verandah, has been identified with maleness, while the inner part, the bilik, or family room, has been associated with femaleness (Sutlive 1978:53). These associations are encoded through myth (Jensen 1967:166), augury (Jensen 1974:131), ritual (Sutlive 1978:53), and, most importantly, through the practice of social actors (Freeman 1955:8).

While considerable emphasis is placed on male mobility and bejalai as the dominant values in both the ethnography and the oral literature, little mention has been made of women's role in sustaining the household through the production of rice and the reproduction of children. This issue will be explored more fully through an analysis of women's role in the maintenance of the bilik and the way male mobility affects that role.

The study of living space has been identified as central to cosmology and symbolic systems of Southeast Asian societies. The house has stood as a microcosm for the world-view of a people, a "comprehensive presentation of orderly universal forms and relations." For Ellen (1986), the house as "microcosm" raises certain theoretical issues. First, he considers whether such an exegesis is constructed for the convenience of the anthropologist and whether the social actors themselves perceive the same order as the anthropologist. He then observes that local people create their own functions and meanings of spatial order.

In my experience, what is most interesting about houses is that they not merely express order (as they may certainly do), but that the orders may be of different kinds, understood in different ways by different people on different occasions (1986:4). Space, then, is experienced differently, according to the age and sex of the social actors. An interpretation of space that considers these factors will inevitably evoke ideas of contradiction, conflict, and power rather than systemness and coherence (Moore 1986:74). An approach to space that follows the trend of the male value system is examined below, followed by a consideration of how such a reading may mask the reality of longhouse life.

Male/Female Orientations

The longhouse is reached by climbing the tangga, "a kind of portal connecting the longhouse with the outside world; by this route good and evil may come to its inhabitants" (Freeman 1970:107). Not surprisingly, the tangga is given male attributes and is sometimes carved with a head and face at the top of the pole and male genitals at the bottom (Richards 1981:315; Sutlive 1978:55).

From the tangga, the visitor moves onto the tanju, or porch, which consists of an open platform that extends the length of the longhouse. Firewood, rice, and clothing are often left out to dry on the tanju. It is considered the "highest" part of the longhouse in ritual, open to the dangerous and beneficent forces of the outside world (Sutlive 1978:52). Furthermore, it is the terminal point for a series of rituals that are conducted at different stages of a boy's development, beginning with his birth in the innermost corner of the bilik. A boy's entry into the adult world is symbolized by the staging of the ceremony on the tanju, the most perilous part of the longhouse as it is closest to the outside world (Masing 1981:60-61).

The tanju leads to the ruai, a long covered corridor that also extends the length of the longhouse. It presents the visitor with the communal side of Iban life: here small groups of men or women may sit for company while completing tasks such as splitting rotan or weaving mats. The ruai is also a convenient place for an elderly relative to keep an eye on a group of playing children. More importantly, it is where the community shares all major life-crises and honors the spirits at every major festival. Ownership of the ruai, however, is not communal. Each section is built and maintained by the bilik family that also owns the antu pala, or trophy head, that hangs from the ceiling of the ruai.

The male association with the ruai is found in myth and augury (Jensen 1967:166; 1974: 131) and in practice. It is where bachelors and male visitors sleep. Sutlive suggests that the division between the ruai and the bilik represents the division between male and female, public and private (1978:55). He notes that the most prestigious place in the longhouse is along the outer wall of the veranda, where men sit on ceremonial occasions and elders sit to discuss disputes to be settled under adat law.

Further to this, Iban men have pride of place in the context of the discussion of public affairs; Heppell (1975:228) notes that the most experienced men sit along the outside wall of the ruai to discuss disputes to be settled under adat law. Women and younger men sit in separate circles outside this group. Men obtain standing to discuss these matters through their experiences of bejalai. Women participate only in a consultative role (Heyzer 1986:31). They are, however, influential in public space and are exposed to discussions of longhouse affairs through their everyday presence on the ruai. It is not unusual for young women of fourteen or fifteen to contribute actively in such conferences (Komanyi 1972:81). There is some indication that Iban women speak and are listened to in the public area:

> Iban women are more outspoken than most, and timidity among
> women in this and other respects is not considered a virtue
> (Rubenstein 1973i:44).

Despite this, it is possible that a greater dichotomy between the public and private spheres has resulted from changes in the nature of public life, which have occurred as the longhouse community participates in state bureaucracy. Women most likely have less power in the public sphere as authority over natural resources, law, and personal rights has moved from the longhouse to the administrators of the state bureaucracy (Sutlive 1978:52). Unfortunately, there is insufficient information in Sutlive's work to explore the implications of these changes.

The bilik is located off the ruai. Traditionally, it consists of one room "used as a kitchen, as well as a mess room, as a nursery as well as bed chamber" (Ling Roth 1968:10). More recently, it has been partitioned into separate areas for sleeping, cooking, and receiving guests. The central part of the bilik is the hearth, where women prepare and cook food. There is less indication that the bilik is ideologically defined as a female sphere, except in myth (see Jensen 1967:166) and in opposition to the ruai, as implied by the public/private association that Sutlive suggests (1978:53). Notably, women's role in the bilik is not considered of great symbolic significance. Still, there is little doubt that through the daily division of labor the bilik can be identified as female space. Sutlive has recognized the material, as opposed to cultural, significance of the women in the bilik in the widest possible sense, that is, as a productive household unit:

The identification of the bilik as the female domain is indicative of the importance of Iban women. It is here that the basic tasks are performed, where the bilik family unites, and whence their life derives (Sutlive 1977: 198).

A longhouse decorated for festival.

Above the bilik, and extending out over the ruai, is the sadau, or loft. There rice is stored in bark rice bins, the sacred strain of rice padi pun is kept, and unmarried girls may sleep (Sutlive 1978:55). As the highest physical point of the longhouse, it has special spiritual importance. In certain rituals it is a point of entry to the spirit world through a specially constructed dream house (Freeman 1975:284). It is also the place where the manang undergoes his initiation with the assumption of female dress. Through the association of use, it is possible to suggest that the sadau is an area of "feminine" space.

One can detect a major horizontal orientation in the longhouse, extending outward from the ruai, that represents the male practice of bejalai. This is counterposed by the female, based in the bilik. Rather than concentrating on the rather tenuous data regarding the way these associations are made through myth, augury, and ritual, the sections below consider the implication of these spatial orientations for the division of labor and the household. The practice of bejalai is considered first, followed by an analysis of the significance of rice cultivation and women's role as producers in the bilik economy.

Contradictions in Space

So far, then, we have considered the major horizontal orientation in space, from the male association with the ruai and the female with the bilik. Male mobility facilitates male control over the public sphere, while women assume control of the domestic realm of production and reproduction.

Although it is possible to interpret gender relations based on a horizontal reading of the social actors use of space from the bilik to the ruai, it is important to bear in mind that spatial order can be interpreted in different ways by the social actors according to the context (cf. Ellen 1986:4).

The major horizontal orientation in space, from the male association with the ruai to the female with the bilik, has received considerable scholarly attention. Male mobility facilitates control over the public sphere, while women assume control of the domestic realm of production and reproduction. However, it is important to remember that oppositions are muted and that the ruai is not exclusively male space nor indicative of male control of longhouse affairs. Sutlive (1978:53) describes the wall that separates the bilik as "dividing the public and the private, male and female domains," and emphasizes the importance of the "high front" of the ruai in comparison with the "lower rear" of the bilik, valuations of space he identifies in ceremony and ritual (1978:67)

Despite men's apparent control of public affairs, men's outward orientation suggests that they are peripheral to the longhouse and that women retain power in the bilik. Women are central to the survival of the longhouse, as has been demonstrated above. On the basis of a horizontal reading of space, Sutlive (1978:53-54) suggests that the tanju, or open porch, is spiritually the highest point and the bilik the lowest point of the longhouse. One could argue instead that the bilik is central on two planes, the horizontal, as discussed by Sutlive, and the vertical. The vertical plane extends upwards through the loft, which serves as a sanctuary for the sacred rice, the rice bins, and area of feminine influence, to the roof and the spirit world beyond. Thus the bilik can be seen as central to two major orientations of the Iban cosmic view: outward to the river and upwards to the sky. In addition, women have the power in the invisible territory of the spirit world through their role in the rituals of rice cultivation and by weaving potent designs.

It has been argued, then, that the major orientations of the longhouse, the male aligned outwards to the world beyond the female aligned inwards to the household, need not necessarily be interpreted in the context of the dominant male prestige system, but can also be reconsidered in terms of the economic, ritual, and structural centrality of the household.

BEJALAI

The Dayak is fond of travel, and like other people loves to visit foreign countries and to return and relate his adventures to his stay-at-home friends (Gomes 1911:231).

Although the values of headhunting are still in currency in Iban culture through myth, legend and ritual, the practice of headhunting has been replaced by bejalai, or extended journeys from the longhouse. Such journeys were also common in the 19th century when Iban went to the coast, into Dutch Borneo, or even farther afield to Brunei and North Borneo, to trade jungle produce and rice for prestige items such as gongs, Chinese jars, silver jewelry, and brassware (Pringle 1970:197). It has been suggested that the Brookes actively encouraged bejalai within Sarawak in the interests of self-sufficiency (Heppell 1974:76). As headhunting has died out, bejalai has replaced it; for young men, "going on journeys is the greatest and most consuming interest life has to offer" (Freeman 1970:224).

Most men now go on journeys to find wage labor on plantations, in timber camps, or on the oil rigs of Miri and Brunei. Such journeys vary in length, some lasting from one harvest to the next, others continuing for one to four years. Jensen (1974:52) reports that one man was away in Sandakan for twelve years, yet was still considered a member of an Iban bilik family. In practice, it is not unusual for men to be away for extended periods. Freeman records that 20 percent of the labor force was away throughout the farming year in the Balleh in 1955. Jensen notes that 50 percent of the men were away for between one and five years in the Lemanak (1966:51).

The main motivation behind bejalai is social prestige. Bejalai has supplanted headhunting as the major component of the male value system (Freeman 1970:233; Wagner 1972:161; Jensen 1966:51). A man who has made successful journeys is considered eligible to marry (Freeman 1970:223) and, as he becomes older, to perform a series of rituals that confer status. Men who have travelled are distinguished by tattoos on their bodies, souvenirs of their experiences in far-off places.

To the Iban community as a whole, bejalai bestows certain advantages. Contact with Iban from other river systems reinforces ethnic solidarity, while contact with other groups facilitates openness to change. An Iban story, for example, states that the first rubber seeds were introduced to Paku by Iban who brought them back from Sumatra (Kedit 1980:227). In a riverine society where settlements are isolated, news of the outside world is much sought after; items brought back from bejalai symbolize knowledge of the world beyond, of trade and travel. Men often time their return from bejalai to coincide with the major festivals. Their exploits are celebrated by the longhouse as a whole, with abundant supplies of rice cakes and locally brewed rice wine. In some longhouses, however, the status of delicacies produced by women is declining in favor of imported beer and biscuits.

Freeman (1970:226) and Kedit (1980:88) suggest that women accept bejalai because as members of the bilik they enjoy the benefits of the prestige items brought back by the menfolk. It is common to hear a mother speak proudly of the powers and enterprise of her son or to hear a wife describe the valued possessions that her husband has brought back from his travels (Freeman 1970:226). In addition to these benefits, Padoch (1982:114) notes that bejalai helps maintain the longhouse population in difficult times, since absent men sent back cash remittances and do not consume the fruits of the land.[10] However, government reports are highly critical of bejalai because it reduces manpower in an area and thus has a profound effect on agricultural production.[11] In settled areas where there is little heavy tree-felling to be done, women manage to cultivate rice alone, in addition to caring for their children and managing the household. Women are unable, though, to keep the longhouse in good repair, maintain boats, or do blacksmith work. As a result, families become much more impoverished (Kedit 1980:88).

Men view bejalai as a way to escape the drudgery of farm work: "It is easier than staying at home because one is not involved with work" (Kedit 1980:222). This attitude appears to be quite common; Jensen (1974:52) explains that bejalai takes priority over the demands of domestic work. Freeman has neatly summarized this perception: "While young men gad off on their journeys, their sisters stay at home to sow, weed and reap" (1970:227). Kedit (1980:88) notes that women in the downriver areas are not enthusiastic about bejalai and that they resent having to bear the double burden of child-care and farm work without help. Additionally, women often have to cope with separation and desertion. Court records from the 19th century document cases of abandoned Iban women, whose husbands remarried into groups of Tagals, Muruts, and Dusun in North Borneo (Pringle 1970:197). In contemporary Iban society, the plight of deserted women is more acute as rural communities are no longer self-sustaining and depend on cash remittances.

Another negative effect of bejalai has been its impact on the value system of the community. One might argue that cash is the motivating factor behind bejalai. Padoch (1981:113) and Kedit (1980:141) indicate a lower incidence of bejalai in areas where income is readily available through employment in timber camps or the cultivation of cash crops. Jensen (1966:81) notes that since the introduction of a cash economy, property formerly shared by the bilik is owned by individuals. Items such as gongs and Chinese jars are investments for the bilik as a whole. They can be used as collateral for loans or sold in difficult times (Wagner 1972:89).

With economic change, however, the nature of this property has diversified. Major items purchased on bejalai, such as guns, outboard engines, chain saws, furniture, radios, sewing machines, and bedding (Jensen 1966:63, Kedit 1980: 89) enhance the productive resources of the bilik. While they last, such items are not only useful but a source of status for both men and women of the bilik. Men, however, tend to select goods that will be of maximum benefit to themselves. Unlike traditional prestige property, consumer goods offer no security for the bilik because they lose value over time, particularly given the lack of maintenance facilities in rural areas. Such changes indicate that men have greater control over cash resources in the context of a changing economy.

Men may also have more control over the disposal of surplus money, as suggested by the popularity of gambling as a pastime (Kedit 1980:88). Because men are perceived as in control of the cash economy, it is not uncommon for them to be awarded land titles for rubber in their own name, in accordance with western notions of heads of households (cf. Harris 1981). This goes against the code of customary bilik law, which prescribes usufructuary land rights to the bilik rather than the individual. In the case of divorce, a woman may not receive recognition for her hours of labor in the rubber garden (Jensen 1966:80).

Bejalai also has associations with education. Masing (1981:480) states that "education and other **masculine-oriented activities**" (emphasis added) are means for men to achieve renown. There is some evidence that education in rural areas takes place in boarding schools, often at some distance from the longhouse. Education is considered a priority for boys in accordance with the values of the male prestige system. Iban girls are more likely to be kept at home than boys to help with the farm and look after their younger siblings (Kedit 1980:910).

Overall, women stand ambiguously in relation to bejalai, depending on their specific circumstances. They may enjoy the material benefits and share vicariously their men's prestige and knowledge of the outside world. It must be remembered that formerly men and women culturally shared a common goal, the acquisition of trophy heads. Today, consumer goods have replaced trophy heads, which are important to women not only because they signify knowledge but because they contribute to the resources of the household. However, in the contemporary context, the goals of prestige, wealth, and abundant rice harvests are at odds with one another as male migration limits the availability of farm labor. While male migration through bejalai is celebrated in myth and ritual, the fact that women's presence in the longhouse, maintaining the family and looking after the next generation, enables men to go away and see the world is unrecognized and unstated.

Rice Cultivation and Iban Society

For the Iban, rice cultivation is a religion and a way of life fundamental to existence (*pengidup*) (Jensen 1974:172). *Adat kami bumai*: "We farm hill rice and live according to the order revealed by the spirits" (Jensen 1974:5). Iban myth teaches that rice cultivation distinguishes the Iban from their primitive ancestors, who according to indigenous belief, were *baka antu*, or "wild beings," and from other neighboring groups who do not cultivate rice in the same manner. Furthermore, it confirms the "spirit pedigree" of the Iban, since their knowledge of rice cultivation has been revealed to them by the spirits (Jensen 1974:172). The Iban always treat rice with the utmost reverence because it has certain mystical qualities. They believe that rice contains the spirit of their ancestors, which is taken into the grains of the plant in the form of dew (Sather 1980:70). Rice cultivation is deeply engrained in the Iban belief system, to the extent that families continue to cultivate a little hill rice, even in areas where it no longer has economic importance, to fulfill a need to maintain its ritual significance (Sather 1977b: 152, 171).

Rice is also linked to the prestige system. An abundant harvest commands the opportunity to be generous, to give loans, to celebrate by brewing rice wine and making rice cakes, and possibly to convert surplus into prestige property.[12] Rice is clearly the most important possession of the bilik family; a family that is successful in rice cultivation is recognized as knowing the adat and honoring the ritual. The whole bilik-family shares the goal of *bulih padi*, a good yield that will ensure ample resources and good health. Despite this, it would seem that men absent on bejalai contribute little to that goal. Instead, mainly women achieve the goal through their untiring labor. Although a woman might be "judged by her ability to feed and otherwise care for family, and the hospitality she extends to guests" (Sutlive 1977:162), there is little recognition ideologically for women's labor in rice cultivation. While at one level women are praised and celebrated as weavers, there appears to be little reference in oral literature to women's role as rice farmers. The male prestige system that celebrates men's exploits in the outside world overlooks the material importance of women's work in rice production for the household.

Rice is associated with women as "custodians of fertility" (Sather 1980:77) through language and rituals. Jensen describes how the growing rice is likened to the different stages of a woman's development (1974:185). For example, it is referred to at one point in its growth as *dara tuai*, or "unmarried maiden," and later as *kandong indu, batang iya besai endang baka orang indu ngandong*, meaning, "female with child, with a swollen stem like a pregnant woman." Moreover, women seem to have a particularly intimate relationship with the growing rice, as mothers have with their children. They take pity on rice grains (Freeman 1955:53), and nurture rice as they would babies (see photograph, Davison and Sutlive, p. 200). Women also take the predominant role in private family ceremonies surrounding different stages of rice cultivation, from the pre-pubescent girl who initiates the *minta panas* ritual, in which the spirits are requested to provide fine dry weather for burning the fields (Jensen 1974:173), to the senior woman of the bilik who leads the reaping ceremonies that precede the harvest of the new rice (Jensen 1974:183, 192; Freeman 970:112; Sather 1977b:158). In his study of the Iban in the lower Rejang area, Sutlive notes associations between women, fertility, and rice:[13]

> Seed is handled by women in sowing...and it is (a) woman who places seed in the family's womb of life....To obviate the possibility of any untoward sexual play either natural or incestuous, male members of the storer's family are not permitted to pass rice up to the woman (1978:83).

The female symbolism in language and ritual reflects the wider knowledge and control of women in rice cultivation. It is clearly evident in the ethnography that women have greater ritual and technical expertise (Freemen 1955:78, 1970:191), and make the major decisions about planting and harvesting (Sather 1977b:168). Komanyi (1972:125) observes that women are in firm control of all aspects of household management, whether their husbands are absent or not. One could argue further that the cohesion of Iban society lies in the efficient control women exercise in the household:

> Moreover, because of the utrolateral structure of the Iban bilek family, women exercise considerable influence, and this is undoubtedly a factor of considerable importance, in producing the marked stability of culture and social custom which characterizes the Iban tribes of the interior (Freeman 1970:227).

Thus, although women bear a double workload of rice cultivation and household management as a consequence of a cultural ideology that gives priority to male migration, they assume material control over this sphere through their command of ritual and skill in rice cultivation.

Women as Rice Cultivators

> A Dayak woman generally spends the whole day in the field. Every night she carries home a load of vegetables and firewood, often for several miles, over tough and hilly paths. Not infrequently, she has to climb up a rocky mountain by ladders and slippery stones to an elevation of a thousand feet. Once she arrives at home, she spends an hour pounding the rice with a heavy wooden stamper, which violently strains every part of her body (Ling Roth 1968:106).

This observation was made in the 19th century, but contemporary evidence suggests that the lot of Iban women has not changed. It is not unusual for women to be completely responsible for farming because of the extended absence or sickness of their menfolk (Freeman 1955:75). It is suggested that women bear a heavier work load than men who remain in the community. "A woman's day is more equal than a man's day" (1955:89). If the experience of women in other parts of the world can be projected, this asymmetry results from women's dual role in agricultural production and child care and food preparation:

> The most characteristic feature of rural women is their long and arduous working day. Many case studies of South-East Asian societies show that housework, the fetching of water and fuel, the caring of animals combined with their direct participation in production, occupy the rural women fully (Heyzer 1986:12).

Freeman clearly states that women bear the responsibility for agricultural production in addition to their roles in the domestic sphere. As noted above, the male prestige system is reinforced by the division of labor; it therefore appears "natural" that men should have the opportunity to display their daring and strength by felling giant hardwood trees and carrying heavy loads at harvest time. Most of the male tasks in rice cultivation, such as felling, burning, dibbling, take place within a four-month period, leaving men free to travel. It is generally accepted that bejalai takes priority over the requirements of farm work (Jensen 1974:52), even though the availability of labor power for weeding can affect the size and success of a yield (Freeman 1970:195). Young men are particularly disdainful of weeding, "uninviting, unremitting work calling for diligence and disciplined effort" (Freeman 1970:193), and consider the task an affront to their manliness (Freeman 1970:195). Young women, on the contrary, are "remarkably versatile" and in the absence of men perform all the male tasks except the felling of the primary forest (Freeman 1970:231). The values of male mobility clearly work in men's favor.

"Farm Work is Not Real Work"

It has been argued above that rice cultivation has major significance for the Iban value system and that although rice production is women's responsibility, they receive little ideological recognition. This argument does not take into consideration the changing value system of the Iban, which has been affected by the dynamic influence of bejalai. The remark "farm work is not real work," made by an Iban male, indicates the low status of subsistence farming in a changing economy.

The inevitable consequence of such attitudes is the complete disregard for women as farmers on the part of planners and development agents. The invisibility of women has already been discussed with regard to land titles. If the experience of women in other parts of the world can serve as an indication, it is unlikely that Iban women will have access to credit and loan schemes in their own right (cf. Boserup 1970; Rogers 1980).

The effects of the penetration of a cash economy on the longhouse are complex and little documented and can only be briefly outlined here. The Ibans' dependence on the credit extended by Chinese merchants has had a major impact on the household. This dependency has arisen out of the instability of market prices and the need for consumer goods and farm inputs to ensure successful returns on cash crops. The strain on land caused by the introduction of cash crops has contributed to the underproduction of rice and other food crops (Jensen 1966:71). More research is needed to explore the effects of possible food shortages on individual households. In a predominantly subsistence economy, such as Freeman describes in the Balleh, the entire community used to cope with shortages through a system of reciprocity based on the exchange of labor or food stuffs.

It is possible to make a number of inferences from these circumstances. The introduction of cash crops meant the commercialization of the relations of production and exchange and the inability of indigenous survival strategies to adapt to capitalist penetration of the local economy. As a result the Iban became bound through debt to the Chinese merchants and the international market. One may hypothesize that relations between households under such circumstances may change from co-operation and interdependence to competition. In the face of a changing economy, Iban women are probably losing control over the resources available to maintain their households. Their control over decision-making and their technical expertise may be undermined as the male-oriented values of a cash economy affect rural agriculture. As their material and cultural position shifts from interdependence to dependence, women have no grounds for negotiating with the values of the male value system as they did in the past.

CONCLUSION

The first part of this study focused on the cult of bravery and warfare as the male prestige system in a "traditional" Iban society. Women have the power to determine their relationship to this ideology because their gender identity is culturally located in weaving, outside the dominant system. Nonetheless, women share the symbolic significance of the trophy head because it is the prerequisite for successful harvests. While men and women have separate prestige systems and control separate resources, they depend on each other to achieve commonly shared goals. Thus, in the context of gender differentiation articulated through weaving and warfare, the sexes do not relate hierarchically but dialectically.

Neither sex is dominant, but each is dependent on and in opposition to the other (cf. Rogers 1978:158).

In the post-headhunting era, weaving continues. Little is known, however, about the operation of the female prestige system in a wide sphere or about the effect of the introduction of synthetic dyes on the status of the indu gaar. The categories of weaving and headhunting, as opposed to bejalai and the bilik, are not part of an ordered temporal sequence but rather shifting perspectives of different articulations of gender relationships. Clearly, the trophy head has now been replaced with consumer goods and material wealth as a symbol of prestige and status, as expressed by anthropologists and the social actors themselves (Masing 1981:478).

These goods are valued by both sexes as status items and for their material advantages. However, it is likely men control cash resources and primarily select items that directly serve their own specific tasks in the division of labor. Men are responsible for the transmission of the values of a cash economy to the longhouse through bejalai. Women depend on the values of the male prestige system and have no space to negotiate their position. Furthermore, there is no ideological recognition for their work in the household, as women's labor in subsistence agriculture is not cash remunerative. There is little evidence that rice cultivation provides women with a separate arena of prestige and a position outside the male value system. However, if we examine the material world of social relations it might be argued that while men assume dominance in formal power and public life, gained through knowledge of the outside world, and through the prestige system based on bejalai, they are on the margins of longhouse life. Women are central to the longhouse because of their ritual expertise and specialist knowledge of rice cultivation, which are essential for the survival of the next generation. They provide a point of stability in Iban consciousness, so that as the male migrant on bejalai faces the insecurity of casual labor during a world recession, he can return home to enjoy the fruits of his wife's labor.

NOTES

1. With the exception of Komanyi (1972) and Padoch (1982).

2. Cf. Reiter (1975) and Ardener (1977).

3. St. John (1883i:195) also notes the requirement of a fresh head to end a period of mourning.

4. Freeman's account of the confident masculinity of Manang Bungai (1967) would appear to contradict Sutlive and Jensen, who focus on the ambiguous sexuality of the *manang*.

5. Low (1848:176) and St. John (1863i:73) both suggest that the *manang bali* was uncommon.

6. Kena lagu pengempu baju penyumat
   Kumbai indai senirang ubong sikat
   Lama laun bakenayat di punggai lampong pengani. (Masing 1981:178b)

7. Ukir aso begempuro betegam iko bejangkam pala
   Ngena ukir belia di gaga emparaja pala
   Bengkeramaba udok rangka enda meda
   pintu telenga lawang tatukang. (Masing 1981:351b)

8. Anak temuai beguai belaboh betenun.
   Jengkau iya tabo jengo jengo baka telo barong ketupong
   Batak lilak benang burak bakejengkak baka juak ikan adong,
   Achi ka iyi lida dua betuntong.
   Paut tempaut ngedut punggai papan punggong,
   Nya baru tikam ka jengkuan ada danjan
   baka ikan nanjak lepong. (Masing 1981:354b)

9. Such restrictions appear to have been less in evidence on the Rejang River in 1985 (see photograph).

10. In the Engkari area, the consumer population is 10 percent lower than the census figures indicate (Padoch 1982:114)

11. *Sarawak Gazette* 67:42 (1/2/37), 76:310 (11/12/50); Lee Long Yeng (1970:87); Kedit (1980:87).

12. Many of these data are based on Jensen (1974). It is likely that the economic significance of rice to the prestige system has changed since Jensen did his fieldwork in 1966.

13. Sather (1980:77) notes the absence of such connections in the Paku area.

REFERENCES

Ardener, E.
    1977   Belief and the Problem of Women. In S. Ardener (ed.) Perceiving Women. Oxford University Press.

Boserup, E.
    1970   Woman's Role in Economic Development. London, Griffin Press.

Ellen, R. F.
    1986   Microcosm, Macrocosm and the Nualu House: Concerning the Reductionist Fallacy as Applied to Metaphorical Levels. Bijdragen tot de Taal-, Land- en Volkenkunde 144.

Freeman, J. D.
    1955   Iban Agriculture, London, H.M.S.O.

    1967   Shaman and Incubus. In Walter Muensterberger and Sydney Axelrad, eds., The Psychoanalytic Study of Society. New York International University, pp. 313-343.

    1968   Thunder, Blood and the Nicknaming of God's Creatures. Psychoanalytic Quarterly 37.

    1970   Report on the Iban. London, Athlone.

Freeman, J. D.
  1975   The Iban of Sarawak and their Religion. Book Review of Jensen (1974) in Sarawak Museum Journal, No. 44.

  1979   Severed Heads that Germinate. In R. H. Hook, ed., Fantasy and Symbol, London, Academic Press, pp. 233-246, .

Gill, S. H. S.
  1968   Selected Aspects of Sarawak Art. Ph.D. Thesis, Columbia University, New York.

Gittinger, M.
  1979   Splendid Symbols: Textiles and Tradition in Indonesia. Washington Museum.

  1980   Indonesian Textiles. Washington Textile Museum.

Gomes, E. H.
  1911   Seventeen Years Among the Sea Dayaks of Borneo. London, Seely and Co.

Haddon, A. C. and Start, L.
  1902   Sea Dayak Fabrics and Their Patterns. Bedford, Ruth Bean (New Edition).

Harris, O.
  1981   Household as Natural Units. In Of Marriage and the Market, K. Young, C. Wolkowitz, R. McCullagh, ed. London, Routledge and Kegan Paul, pp. 136-156.

Heppell, M.
  1975   Iban Social Control: The Infant and the Adult. Unpublished Ph.D. Thesis, Australian National University, Canberra.

Hewitt, F. E.
  1908   Dayak Pemali. In A.J.N. Richards, The Sea Dayaks and Other Races of Sarawak, Borneo Literature Bureau, 1963.

Heyzer, N.
  1986   Working Women in South-East Asia. Open University Press.

Howell, W.
1909   The Hornbill or Kenyalang. Sarawak Gazette 39:124-5.

Howell, W.
1911   A Sea Dayak Dirge. Sarawak Museum Journal 1(2):5-73.

Jensen, E.
1966   Money For Rice. Danish Board for Technical Cooperation.

1967   Iban Birth. Folk, 8-9:165-78.

1974   The Iban and Their Religion. Oxford University Press.

Kedit, P. M.
1980   Modernization Among the Iban of Sarawak. Kuala Lumpur, Dewan Bahasa dan Pustaka.

Kennedy, R.
1942   The Ageless Indies. New York, John Day.

Keppell, H.
1853   A Visit to the Indian Archipelago. In H. M. ship Meaender with portions of the private Journal of Sir James Brooke,London, K. C. B.Bentley.

King, V. T.
1976   Migration, Warfare and Culture Contact in Borneo: A Critique of Ecological Analysis. Oceania 40:306-309.

Komanyi, M.
1972   The Real and Ideal Participation in Decision Maiking of Iban Women. Ph.D. Thesis, New York University.

Low, H.
1848   Sarawak. London, Bentley.

MacDonald, M.
1985   Borneo People (originally published in 1956) Singapore, Oxford University Press.

Masing, J. J.
   1978   Timang and the Cult of Headhunting. Canberra Anthropology
           1(2):59-67.

Masing, J. J.
   1981   The Coming of the Gods. Unpublished Ph.D. Thesis, Australian
           National University, Canberra.

Moore, H.
   1986   Space, Text and Gender. Cambridge University Press.

Ong, Edric
   1986   Pua Iban Weavings of Sarawak, Kuching, Society Atelier
           Sarawak.

Padoch, C.
   1982   Migration and its Causes Among the Iban. The Hague, Nijhoff.

Pringle, R.
   1970   Rajahs and Rebels. London, Macmillan.

Reiter, R.
   1975   Men and Women in the South of France: Public and pRivate
           Domains. In R. Reiter ed., Toward an Anthropology of Women.
           New York Monthly Review Press.

Richards, A.J.N.
   1963   The Sea Dayaks and Other Races of Sarawak. Kuching, Borneo
           Literature Bureau.

   1972   Iban Augury. Sarawak Museum Journal 20:63-81.

   1981   An Iban-English Dictionary. Oxford, the Clarendon Press.

Rogers, B.
   1978   A Woman's Place; A Critical Review of Anthropology Theory.
           Journal of Comparative Studies in History and Society, pp. 123-
           162.

   1980   The Domestication of Women.

Roth, Henry Ling
  1968 The Natives of Sarawak and British North Borneo (originally published in 1896), Kuala Lumpur, University of Malaya.

Rubenstein, Carol
  1973 Poems of the Indigenous Peoples of Sarawak: Some of the Songs and Chants. Sarawak Museum Journal Special Issue. Two Volumes.

Sandin, Benedict
  1967 The Sea Dayaks of Borneo Before White Rajah Role. East Lansing, Michigan University Press.

  1977 Gawai Burong. Penang, University Sains Malaysia.

  1983 The Mythological Origins of Iban Shamanism. Sarawak Museum Journal 53:235-250.

Sather, Clifford
  1977a Introduction to Sandin (1977).

  1977b Nanchang Padi. Journal of the Malaysian Branch of the Royal Asiatic Society, 50:150-70.

  1978 The Malevolent Koklir. Bijdragen tot de Taal - Land - en Volkenkunde 134.

  1980 Symbolic Elements in Saribas Iban Rites of Padi Storage. Journal of the Malaysian Branch of the Royal Asiatic Society, 58:67-95.

St. John Spenser
  1862 Life in the Forests of the Far East (2 volumes). London, Smith and Elder and Co.

Strathern, M.
  1984 Domesticity and the Denigration of Women. In D. O'Brien and S. W. Tiffany, eds., Rethinking Women's Roles: Perspectives from the Pacific, University of California Press.

Sutlive, V. H.
    1976   The Iban Manang: An Alternative Route to Normality. In G. N. Appell, ed., 1976, Studies in Borneo Societies, DeKalb, IL, Northern Illinois University Press.

    1977   The Many Faces of Kumang. Sarawak Museum Journal 46.

    1988   The Iban of Sarawak. Prospect Heights, IL, Waveland Press.

Van Esterik, P.
    1984   Continuities and Transformations in South-East Asian Symbolism: A Case Study from Thailand. Bijdragen tot de Taal - Land - en Volkenkunde 140:77-91.

Vayda, A.
    1961   Expansion and Warfare Among Swidden Agriculturists. American Anthropologist 63:346-358.

Vogelsanger, C.
    1980   A Sight for the Gods. Notes on the Social and Religious Meaning of Iban Ritual Fabrics. In M. Gittinger, ed., Indonesian Textiles, Washington Textile Museum.

Wagner, U.
    1972   Colonialism and Iban Warfare. Stockholm, Obe-Tryck.

Whitehead, H.
    1981   The Bow and Burden Strap: A New Look at Institutionalized Homosexuality in Native North America. In Sherry Ortner and H. Whitehead 1981, pp. 80-115.

THE CULTURAL LOGIC OF TEXTILE WEAVING PRACTICES AMONG THE IBANIC PEOPLES

RICHARD ALLEN DRAKE
Department of Anthropology
Michigan State University

Government officials, missionaries, anthropologists and travelers have long admired the textiles of the Ibanic peoples and many have collected them as worthy specimens of the art of primitive textile weaving. The women of these societies weave these attractive textiles with the tie-dyed designs from home-spun cotton thread. The designs are achieved by dyeing the threads in vegetable dyes and mordants and weaving them on a simple back-strap loom. The recent and most satisfying understanding of these practices is that they constitute a female prestige system parallel to the male prestige system based on headhunting. Several earlier commentators had noted that one of the phases of the weaving process was referred to as *kayau indu'* (women's war). This paper examines this idea and will attempt to demonstrate how it fits so comfortably with the cultural logic of the Ibanic peoples as we know it.

There have been various treatments of weaving in the Iban literature over the years. Although most of them were either tangential or fragmentary, there was among them enough to begin to construct an understanding of weaving as having considerable religious significance. While Eric Jensen's *Iban Religion* (1974) did not, regrettably, make this case, the recent work of Cornelia Vogelsanger (1980) is an important advance in this regard. Based on fieldwork and access to the fieldwork materials of Derek and Monica Freeman, Vogelsanger has given us an understanding of textile weaving among the Iban in terms of religious practices and as a mechanism of social prestige. My own research among the Mualang, one of the Ibanic peoples living in the middle Kapuas region of Kalimantan Barat, generally confirms her analysis.[1] Accordingly, I shall supplement Vogelsanger's understanding with Mualang data. The Mualang data provokes interesting questions about the relationship of weaving practices to gender roles in Ibanic society. The recent development in anthropology of

Mualang woman weaving at her backstrap loom, late 1930s. The first missionaries in the area, the Reverend J. Arthur Mouw and his wife, Edna, encouraged the Mualang to continue weaving when they perceived it to be declining. They attributed this decline to the increasing availability of inexpensive cloth and cotton thread obtained through downriver trade. (Photo courtesy of Edna Mouw)

attempting to specify more thoroughly the place of women in the societies studied has given the parallel prestige proposition a new emphasis that will be profitable to consider.

Alfred C. Haddon and Laura Start made the first attempt to analyze Iban textiles, working necessarily from rather thin ethnographic sources (1936). Their analysis of specimens from both museums and private collections depended heavily upon the labels of motifs Charles Hose had provided from Iban informants many years before. Haddon and Start collected the motifs into categories such as anthropomorphs, zoomorphs, phyllomorphs, etc. on the basis of these labels. Undaunted by the fact that certain anthropomorphs looked just like certain zoomorphs, they pushed on to an explication of these "representations," reasoning that their real-life characteristics or their cultural characterizations pointed to behavioral aspects that could be of imitative magical benefit to the user. Having concluded that what was involved was religious expression in decorative art, in particular the weaving of charms, they concluded:

> They may be regarded in some cases as being protective, to ward off dangers of various kinds, in others as being a means to obtain blessings and good fortune. Thus they express a constant reliance upon supernormal power, and it is probably no exaggeration to say that these attractive people are literally clothed in prayers (1936:146).

Sarah Gill had much better ethnographic material to work from when she made her study of "Selected Aspects of Sarawak Art" (1971) which devoted some space to the consideration of weaving among the Iban. She attempted to refute Haddon and Start's analysis, offering instead a different set of formal categories of the motifs. By limiting the argument to the motifs and the circumstances in which the various textiles were worn, she erroneously concludes that this weaving is secular and erotic.

The religious character of this textile art had been attested to earlier in a very useful article that has stood the test of time by the Reverend W. Howell (1912), and also by tangential references to weaving in the articles by the Reverend Dunn (1906:21-2, 1912:136-8) and Freeman (1957:173). Subsequent treatments in the publications of Benedict Sandin (1976, 1980) and A. J. N. Richards (1981) have provided further details and confirmation of this religious character of weaving as art technics.

Mualang women spinning cotton thread and weaving in the shade near the longhouse. The warp beam is secured to the saplings and the breat beam tension is altered by the pressure on the backstrap. (Photo courtesy of Edna Mouw)

From present understandings there is no single satisfactory account of the ethnographic details of Iban women's textile weaving, so I offer a brief synthetic account emphasizing those features essential to the arguments to be made about the social prestige and religious aspects of these practices.

Apparently little religious significance attaches to the cultivation and harvesting of cotton and its ginning and spinning into cotton thread. It is with dyeing the threads to effect the desired patterns that we encounter the first enchantment practices; particularly the preparation of the red dye from the skin of the root of the *engkudu* tree. The process is led by a specialist. Perhaps one in fifty can do this according to the Reverend Howell (1912:64). Freeman has characterized this as the most crucial stage in the entire process (1957:173). Although there are variations in the order of the steps from one area to another, the accounts of Howell, Sandin (1980) and Richards illustrate that the character of the steps are consistent. I quote Richards's description because of its completeness:

> Only warps are dyed: [the] weft does not show after weaving. Special care is taken over warps to be died red or red and black. [The] mixture is prepared by (burning and?) pounding together (*nipah*) salt, *kepayang* (or coconut) oil, various fruit (*kemuntin, kelampai, engkeringan*), bark 'soap' (*pau*) and the dye (*selup*) required. Hot water is added in a large trough (*dulang*) and all the warps plunged in as a batch (*renggat*): when cool enough, each woman involved treads the warps in the mixture. After some hours' soaking, the warps are lifted out and sorted. The process (*nge-renggat*) is repeated on several days after which the warps are stretched on frames (*tangga' ubong*) and left on the open veranda (*tanju'*) for seven or more days and nights (*ngembun*, to take the dew) but they must not be left in rain. After fresh tying for the next colour the whole process is repeated for that colour...The work is done away from the house and the gaze of men, and is referred to as 'women's war' (*kayau indu'*). The women dress as for a *gawai* and are led by the expert among them who is paid a fee, including pottery, beads and iron (*kering semengat*). She knows the rites and possesses amulets to assist her, including porcupine quills (*bulu landak*) against madness. A fowl or pig is sacrificed and an offering (*piring*) set in a bamboo holder (*teresang*). Prayer (*sampi*) is said to invoke the aid of *Meni* and other water deities from whom the art was obtained, and also probably *Kumang* and others (snake deities) of the *Gelong*. A woman able to use the most significant designs without suffering evil, and skilled in the whole art, including dyeing, 'knows *takar*' and is entitled to have her hand tattooed (like a man who has taken a head trophy): the tattoo is usually small at [the] base of [the] thumb or on one or two finger-joints" (1981:361).

The designs tie-dyed into these fabrics have been the predominant interest of analysts since the attempt by Haddon and Start to understand them from this perspective. But it has turned out that it is not the designs themselves that are decisive with respect to meaning, so much as it is the origin of those designs. The Reverend Dunn's translation of an Iban informant's account of "Religious Rites and Customs of the Iban" (1906) emphasizes that the origin of weaving designs is in dreams. He relates how certain goddesses such as *Kumang* and *Sulong Indai Abong*:

> help women to weave and to work the ornamental patterns on the native cloth...Without being empowered in a dream by these spirits, how could women attempt to work these patterns? Should they make the attempt they would certainly go mad. That a woman may weave good blankets and fine dresses, she must be endowed by the spirits in a dream with a charmed porcupine's quill. Without this charm women can never weave the curious patterns of their cloth" (1906:22).

Dreaming is, of course, a salient feature of Ibanic culture. Dreams are thought to be communication with the spirit world, and, when interpreted correctly, a most valuable source of guidance for even ordinary affairs. People are thought to vary in their capacity to use dreams and "leadership is commonly associated with a flair for constructive dreaming" (Jensen 1974:119).

It should be obvious that the processes for preparing the threads for weaving are numerous and complex, requiring considerable skill which a women can master only over time with the accumulation of experience. Thus there are levels of designs appropriate for particular stages of skill mastery (Richards 1981:144). Michael Dove has reported a similar set of customs concerning the weaving of mats among the *Kantu'*, an Ibanic people of Kalimantan Barat:

> It is prohibited for any woman to attempt to weave a mat of a given stage without having first learned how to weave the mats of all lower stages (in order). Further, if a woman had a bad dream (*mimpi jai*) while in the midst of weaving a particular mat type for the first time, she must pull apart what she has woven and never again attempt to weave that type of mat. The basis for these pros[cr]iptions is an association of personal danger to the weaver and perhaps the weaver's household as well, with the more complex and difficult weaving techniques (1981:898).

Mualang skirt with the very common "lozenge" design hand-somely executed. This design would put the weaver at no risk of irritating the spirits.

Mualang skirt with a pattern employing a dream-envisioned creature within the basic lozenge motif. Typically, colored threads are used to decorate the borders. These are imported machine-spun threads and have long been available through trade with the coast.

The relationship between the origin of the designs and skill levels is an important matter that the authorities have not been clear about. I take Vogelsanger's treatment as the latest word on the matter. Most women copy the designs they weave from previous works woven by family members. To copy a design from a known originator of the design, a small fee is paid. Designs differ in degree with respect to supernatural potency and so any potent parts of the design inappropriate for the novice can be tied by an older woman. Copying designs does not put the weaver at the same level of supernatural risk as that born by the originator of a design and helps explain the high frequency of copying. The origination of textile designs is a major source of respect for women. This is so because it involves an encounter with the spirit world that can be dangerous. All who have contributed to this topic agree that the designs occur to the originator in dreams, although the possibility of non-dream sources is also held out by all of them. Vogelsanger describes this creation of a pattern from a dream:

> If a woman has seen a pattern in a dream, she will start working on a pua [or other *ikat* textile]. She will not talk about the pattern until the weaving is finished, which usually takes one to two years. During this whole process she is in an endangered state and takes ritual precautions (*pemali*) not to irritate the spirit represented in the pattern. If the spirit gets irritated, he may attack the weaver, make her ill, or even kill her...a weaver who creates her own designs, (*tengkabang*) needs not only creative imagination, but considerable psychic strength and a gift for communication with the spirit world. Some women protect themselves by charms (*pengaroh*), medicines (*obat*), and other magical precautions; others maintain that they do not need charms being strong "from the heart" (*ari ati*). Above all, a weaver must have reached a certain stage in skill and experience before starting a potent design (1980:118).

The uses to which these attractive textiles are put are many. Prominent among them are the marking off of sacred space in a ritual, to decorate a shrine, or to place beneath an offering to the spirits. The first eleven stanzas of the Iban "*Mengap Bungai Taun*," the "'Chant of the Flowers of the Year,' a sacred chant used...on the occasion of a sacrificial feast to invoke a blessing on the fruits of the field" as collected and translated by Reverend Dunn, acknowledge the contributions of *pua* by eleven named women used "to decorate the *pagar api* containing the charms" (1912:135). The *pua* may be "suspended from the ceiling as a cover for a newly born baby, to cover a child during the first ritual meeting with the grandmother...(and) to cover a child during a name changing or adoption ceremony...or to wrap the dead body for the journey to the cemetery" (Vogelsanger 1980:119). According to Sandin they

> were used in ancient times by wives to receive ceremoniously the heads of the slain enemy from the hands of their husbands on the latter's return from the warpath...(and) for making a roof of boats used for taking the bride to the groom's house on her wedding day or for making a *sapat* partition within which is placed the body of the dead during the three days and nights of vigil before it is buried in the cemetery (1980:86).

Richards mentions how they can be "used for waving to drive away *Antu Rau*, [demons] (during eclipses) or heavy rain clouds, when dry weather for burning off a farm is threatened by them" (1981:144). Finally, Freeman mentions they are a sign of wealth (1970:3) and Jensen says they can be paid as a fee to a *manang* (a curer) (1974:150). In all these examples, except perhaps for the last, they can be considered as "charms." They are anticipated to have the beneficial effects of charms.

Vogelsanger understands the meaning of the Iban *ikat* textiles to lie in communication with the goddesses and gods. She cites the testimony of Derek and Monica Freeman that they are pleasing to the gods and so the gods will intervene in human affairs on their behalf:

> Pua [and other weavings] have not only a beneficial quality when used in rituals, but are, through their designs, a means of communication with the spiritual world. Freeman calls them 'icons' in this context (personal communication, June 1978). The individual Iban communicates frequently with his gods, often outside of formalized rituals, and for this may use a pua (Vogelsanger 1980:120).

Several questions about the potency of the designs seem to me to be raised by Vogelsanger's study. What exactly is potency related to? Does potency relate to the beauty of the design or to the matter of representation of the spirit within the design? If the designs are communication with the spirit world are all the potent designs communicated in dreams? To what extent can copied designs afford potency to the textile? If an initiate copies a potent pattern by having an older woman assist with the potent parts of the design, does that product enjoy the appropriate potency or is diminished potency anticipated?

The Mualang data I was able to collect on these matters of art magic suggest directions for further inquiry in Iban contexts. Mualang women formerly wove several kinds of cotton cloth and decorated them by several methods, but only the red-colored, tie-dyed textiles, the *kain amat* (real, true cloth), is relevant to the discussion at hand. Of these there were the *kain kebang* entailing the weaver originating the design by recourse to dreaming, and those decorated by rather conventionalized motifs uninspired by dreaming. This latter kind of cloth involved no danger to the weaver and involved the highly geometrical designs shared with the Iban (Haddon and Start 1936: plates I-XXV). While it is forbidden to copy a design in its presence, it is permissible to copy from memory. As among the Iban, to produce an original, dream-inspired design is to put the weaver at some risk should she fail to get the design exactly right. These designs involve "animals," not animals of the real world but dream-envisioned creatures that are representations of the inspiring spirits. A pig will be sacrificed to the spirit to implore its cooperation in the endeavor. Not only is the form of the creature discovered in a dream, but also the food (*umpan*) it will require to eat must be precisely determined and included in the pattern. Such a creature unmollified can change into an evil spirit and injure the weaver by blindness, madness, illness or even death.

The most common spirit-representation motif among the examples I saw was the double *nabau* pattern, a pair of snakes stretched out facing each other, head-to-tail, and supplied liberally with fanciful creatures to eat. This motif is potentially the most potent of them all, and the most dangerous to attempt. Any motif involving animal figures is so risky that only women beyond the childbearing years will risk it. You must have made several textiles without animal designs before attempting one with animals and you must allow at least a three year period to lapse before attempting another pattern involving animals. As has been emphasized for the Iban, originating a design has a high value and the originator enjoys prestige according to her accomplishments in this regard.

The generalization from the Mualang case can be made that the potency of the designs, the levels of skill involved, and the prestige attained by weaving vary directly with age. As females move through the stages of the life cycle certain customarily specified expectations are appropriate for them with respect to weaving. Young maidens with an eye to marriage begin to acquire the fundamental skills of weaving by joining in on the preparatory processes being led by a weaving expert. This is evidence that she would be a worthy wife. The patterns woven are simple, traditional, geometrical, and decorative; hopefully pleasing to the gods and beneficent in charm capacity. Through adult married life the weaving products form her loom become increasingly more sophisticated in pattern. These are combinations of traditional motifs copied from memory.

Mualang skirt with the double *nabau* (mythical sperpent) motif. The *nabau*, the "king of the serpents," is the most dangerous of all motifs to attempt to weave. Formerly, spirit helpers of famous headhunters often took the form of *nabau*.

Their capacity to please the gods is enhanced by greater sophistication and, correspondingly, charm capacity is strengthened. By this stage, certain women have begun to distinguish themselves as extraordinarily adept and more highly motivated in this respect. However, because these are the childbearing years the risks of originating patterns are prohibitive. Robert Mckinley explains that this avoids bringing a pregnancy to the attention of the spirits (personal communication). Competing evil spirits fighting over the unborn baby's soul is much feared and a common explanation of miscarriage and infant mortality (Freeman 1967, Sather 1978). Beyond the childbearing years those women who have enjoyed particular success in weaving begin to seek out personal relationships with the spirit world in dreams that, like all spirit encounters, are fraught with danger, but, if successful, promise magical potency. It is in the post-menopausal stage of the life cycle that women achieve prestige for originating the dream-inspired, potent weavings that play such a prominent place in many Ibanic rituals. Post-menopausal relaxation of role restrictions is a "well-nigh universal pattern" (Hammond and Jablow 1976:93-4). Clifford Sather mentions it for the Saribas Iban (1978:320-3) and it is pronounced in Mualang society. This highest level of weaving achievement appears to have some of the features of *nampok*, the spirit encounter to boldly confront the spirits to grant their favor "to secure courage, strength...or invulnerability...but sometimes as a last resort for illness" (Richards 1981:226).

Vogelsanger follows Freeman in asserting that "head-hunting and pua weaving are two parallel prestige systems" (1980:121). Robert Pringle has also made this point in his study of the history of the Brooke Raj's struggle with the Iban tribes (1970:24-5). Both weaving-based distinction for women and headhunting-based distinction for men appear to be a graded series of competitions for prestige, validated by demonstration of favor with the gods, as evidenced by prosperity. Freeman has characterized headhunting as a male fertility cult (1979:243ff) and weaving can be characterized as a female charm cult. The double meaning of charm is applicable here. The charming textile skirt of an Ibanic maiden worn at important ceremonies symbolizes beauty and prosperity, and will hopefully be irresistible to the young lad of her attentions. The charming textile blanket will hopefully be irresistible to the gods who can assist in beneficent and protective ways.

Beauty is a high ideal for the Ibanic female as courage is for the male. The courageous, ideal Ibanic male takes heads allegorized in the headhunting *gawai* ritual as the "reaping of Lang's *padi*" (Freeman 1979:244); that is, the gathering of sacred rice seed. The head of the slain enemy symbolically contains the sacred rice seed upon which the fertility of rice and the prosperity of the Iban depend. To quote Freeman again, "the trophy head, phallic and procreative, becomes a veritable fount of fertility" (Ibid:243). The beautiful, ideal Ibanic female weaves the charming cloth of protection and prosperity from threads incorporating the dew, a process earlier noted to be highly fetishized.

Dew is a very important substance in Ibanic cosmology. Dew is an essential link between conceptions of rice and human souls. The souls of people (*samengat*) upon death have a cyclic course described by Eric Jensen:

> The *samengat* remains an *antu* spirit in *Sebayan* [the land of the dead] for an indefinite period until eventually dissolving into dew. The dew is taken up into the ears of rice which are eaten by living men who in their turn die" (1974:108).

The *sampi* (invocation) recited at a *gawai nunu lilin*, which is conducted to promote the ripening of the *padi* for an abundant harvest illustrates the point:

> And may the dew of those who harvest rice in plenty,/abundant sweet rice/ (who have success, fame and wealth)/Enter into my rice (Ibid:189).

Dew, rice seed germination, the spirits of ancestors and the living are phases of a cycle of regeneration (cf. Sather 1978:329) that men invigorate by head taking to capture seed and women enhance by weaving charm textiles that capture the dew, the celestial essence. No better illustration of the conjunction of the symbolic of the male and female contributions to this cycle of regeneration can be found than the female receiving the head of the slain enemy from her husband at the top of the longhouse steps, wrapping it in her charm blanket, and, thereby welcoming its power to promote prosperity and fertility into the community (cf. Dunselman 1955:photo "a" following p. 284). The phallic symbolism of headhunting is united with feminine nurturing. The creative/procreative character of the feminine is a necessary complement to this symbolic system, encompassing both life and death in a convincing theory of the ritual regeneration of fecund nature.

There is another aspect of these weaving practices which should be understood in the context of the "total social fact" of the Ibanic headhunting cult. That is the double *nabau* motif described above for the Mualang as the most potent and the most dangerous to attempt. Its significance as a spirit representation seems straightforward. As Freeman has said:

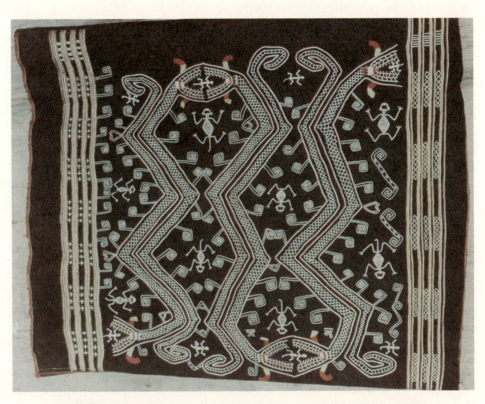

Mualang skirt made of embroidered cloth, the *kain sulam*. Although Mualang women no longer weave, they still enjoy wearing the old-style short tube shirt on ceremonial occasions. These are made from trade cloth that they embroider with traditional motifs. Here a more typical version of the *nabau* motif is used.

Mythical serpents are particularly associated with the Iban cult of head-hunting. Almost every renown head-hunter of former days was aided by a dream-inspired spirit helper. The most wished for of all of these spirit helpers was the *nabau*, a mythical serpent, or water dragon, which was believed to accompany the head-hunter, aiding him in his gruesomely heroic task (1979:240).

Considering weaving as a prestige system parallel to the male prestige system gives rise to a clear difficulty. It is obviously a weak parallel to the male prestige system. Vogelsanger makes this point:

there is a marked difference between women and men regarding social importance and power. There can be no doubt that a headhunting ritual is a much more important ceremony for the whole longhouse than a gawai ngar. The women's prestige system expressed in weaving seems to be an imitation of the men's prestige system (1980:121).

The idealized Ibanic female sits at home devoting herself in spare moments to the very complex, tedious, time-consuming domestic task of weaving in pursuit of supernatural favor and the associated social prestige. However enchanted these processes might be by Ibanic cultural constructs, in reality they are hardly the formula for social prominence. As Vogelsanger asserts, in reality the social prestige system is heavily dominated by the male-focused institutions. Freeman has characterized these male-focused, *gawai*-sponsorship institutions as follows:

Among pagan Iban the consuming life interest of all adult males of substance and ambition was gradually to work their way up an ascending sequence of *gawai amat* (that is, the real *gawai*), gathering the approval and acclaim of their peers and gods as they achieved this spiritual and temporal progression (1975:280).

The way clear of this difficulty has been to consider the weaving practices to be enhanced ideologically to better reflect the otherwise high standing of female gender roles in the organization of Ibanic society. According to Pringle:

Since the position of women is extremely high in Iban society, it is not surprising that there was a female equivalent of headhunting in the traditional value system (1970:24).

This assertion is echoed by Vogelsanger (1980:122), and also in the study of Iban gender relations by Valerie Mashman (1986). In Sandin's *Iban Way of Life* (1976), which is an overt ideology of Iban social roles, weaving is depicted as the predominant activity of adult women. By associating weaving, the preeminent, self-defining adult female interest with the "total social fact" of headhunting, the preeminent adult male interest, male and female gender roles are placed on par, befitting their places in the actual arrangements of social life.

The Mualang case illustrates this ideology of the compatibility of gender roles in Ibanic society. For the Mualang this ideology of gender roles is celebrated in the *Kana Sera* as collected and translated by Father Donatus Dunselman while serving among the Mualang Hilir of the Sungai Ayak area. The *Kana Sera* is the most sacred hymn of the Mualang Hilir, so sacred that no mistakes are permitted in its recitation even though the perfect memory of its 3,065 lines is a near-Herculean feat. This "song of pregnancy" is sung at the wedding *gawai* and depicts the ideal female and male qualities that bode well for the successful life of the newly wed couple as the Mualang define it. The song traces the life of a young woman from her birth through childhood and adolescence to her marriage with a courageous headhunter. This pair turns out to be the famous culture heroes *Kumang* and *Keling*, major characters in all the *Kana Tangi* of the Mualang, and prominent figures in Iban oral literature as well. Clearly the ideology is one of gender cooperation. The young maiden of the song is, according to Father Dunselman:

> educated by the famous 'nymph' *Pupu' Perua*...who teaches her the arts of weaving and plaiting. Here the girl obtains also magic stones and learns magical formulae. In this way she becomes the ideal woman: beautiful, skilled in the important arts of weaving and plaiting, and filled with magical powers to protect the men during their wanderings and their head-hunting expeditions (1955:280).

This song also reveals, however, all the possibilities of a hierarchic structuring of gender conceptions. The song is a journey through the cosmos, and how that cosmos is organized suggests a very widespread set of cultural constructs contrasting male and female commonly put to hierarchic ends. The journey through the cosmos is a journey from earth to the underworld, where feminine weaving takes place, to the upperworld, where masculine headhunting takes place, and back to earth again. This can be recognized as a very wide-spread mapping of the cosmos on gender attributes. The lower regressive domain is a watery underworld (often a primal ocean) symbolized by water, snakes, lunar rhythms, and the erotic, presocialized self; the realm of more

Mualang woman models her just completed *kain sulam*. An heirloom bead belt from which Dutch coins are suspended holds up the folded-over skirt.

"natural" women. This is contrasted with the higher domain of the heavens, of cultural man, fully socialized and repressed; symbolized by the sun with its annual agricultural cycle. These characterizations are not inconsistent with the ideal-typical cosmological model for tribal Southeast Asia constructed by Robert McKinley (1976:103-7). However, as has been generally appreciated, the Southeast Asian societies have not instituted the model to the same hierarchical purposes as is found in the South and East Asian societies. The fact that the female prestige system is a weak parallel to the male prestige system must be placed in the social context in which prestige articulates only weakly with political manipulation. Instead, prestige articulates strongly with the religious domain. Hosting the gods to maneuver their favor bestows prestige, and provisioning these feasts requires material success which validates this favor with the gods.

The Mualang share not only Iban cultural constructs, but also the Iban social organizational principles for which the ideology is relevant. The jural equality of women with respect to property and use rights is well-documented. In this society structured fundamentally on principles of egalitarianism--unproblematic access to productive resources and the jural equality of individuals--wealth is produced and accumulated by the cooperative efforts of a family corporation. Men's and women's contributions to material success are both highly valued, an extensive division of labor notwithstanding. The self-understanding is one of necessary cooperation.

Perhaps, for the sake of argument, there are some women for whom the "reflected" prestige of the male members of their family is not sufficient. In such an event the excelling in art magic for prestige could be a clever mechanism of psychodynamic compensation. This ego defense mechanism, often ascribed to those industrious in arts and crafts, was shown above to coincide admirably with the cultural logic of headhunting as facilitating the cycle of regeneration; their particular "theory of prosperity" (Hocart in Becker 1975:16).

From the psychological perspective several other aspects of these weaving practices can be more fully informed as well. The place of dreams in this quest after supernatural power by art magic is not only highly consistent with Ibanic cultural logic, but is also consistent with the contemporary psychology of cognition. Freeman has argued for the necessity of appreciating the prominence of dreaming for the Iban in understanding the nature of Iban society (1975:287). Dreaming as a discourse with the unconscious processes is, for psychoanalysis, wish fulfillment--the projection of a "lack." For cognitive psychology dreaming is a regression into primary process cognition where wish and reality are not differentiable. Such is essentially the characterization of magic Freud offered in

Totem and Taboo. The principle of magic, Freud said, is the "principle of the 'omnipotence of thought'" (1950:85). The questing for supernatural power by a cognitive foray into primary process cognition by means of "dream work" is a consistent extension of Ibanic cultural logic to this art magic of female textile weaving.

"But is it art?" The intent has been to demonstrate that the self-understanding of the Ibanic peoples is that it is art magic; that is, art created for religious ends. It has been noted how Westerners have valued these textiles as fine specimens of decorative weaving. The missionaries who worked among the Mualang have assured me that they made a special effort to encourage them to preserve their textile weaving and missionary wives can be seen in old photos proudly wearing *kain kebats* to this end. Presumably the missionaries viewed it as decorative art rather than as religious expression in the form of pagan image magic.

Is it really decoration instead of art? While admittedly this would appear to be an unjustifiable imposition of modern Western concerns onto an alien sociocultural milieu, in fact, once again Western concepts and categories fit surprisingly well the native concepts and categories in this regard. The distinction alluded to here is the commonplace one of decoration, meaning merely form in the service of beauty, while art in the restricted sense is a creative, aesthetic expression that communicates a unique "vitality," to use Lewis Mumford's term, or to have an "affecting presence," as Robert Plant Armstrong speaks of it (1975). It seems to me the Ibanic peoples make use of this distinction in their according different virtues to the copied motif and the dream-inspired creation. Recall that Vogelsanger's understanding emphasized the pleasing of the gods by attractively decorating the cloth. How is this to be reconciled with the understanding that by this art magic the supernatural beings are being danger-ously confronted to attempt to manipulate them to favor the creative weaver with metaphysical potency? I have shown from Mualang data (cf. Vogelsanger 1980:118) that there is a special category of cloth, the *kain kebang*, that consists of the dream-inspired productions, marking off these creative, communicative, aesthetic products from the merely decorative. There are high stakes in this creative work. These charmed cloths are, by Ibanic cultural logic, an integral mechanism of Ibanic society's theory of prosperity based on the axiom of regenerative natural fecundity.

NOTE

1.   This research was funded in part by a grant from the National Science
      Foundation and sponsored in Indonesia by the Lembaga Ilmu
      Pengetahuan Indonesia to which I am most grateful.

REFERENCES

Armstrong, Robert Plant
      1975   Wellspring: On the Myth and Source of Culture. Berkeley:
              University of California Press.

Becker, Ernest
      1975   Escape From Evil. New York: The Free Press.

Dove, Michael
      1981   Subsistence Strategies in Rain Forest Swidden Agriculture.
              Unpublished Ph.D. dissertation, Stanford University.

Dunn, Reverend E.
      1906   Translation of Religious Rites and Customs of the Iban or Dyaks
              of Sarawak. By Leo Nyuak. *Anthropos.* I:11-24, 165-85, 403-25.

      1912   The Mengap Bungai Taun, the 'Chant of the Flowers of the Year,'
              a Sacred Chant Used by the Sea-Dyaks on the Occasion of a
              Sacrificial Feast to Invoke a Blessing on the Fruits of the Field.
              Anthropos, VIII:135-54.

Dunselman, Donatus
      1955   Kana Sera, Zang der Zwangerschap. Verhandelingen van het
              Koninklijk Instituut voor Taal-, Land-en Volkenkunde, No. 17,
              Leiden: Martinus Nijhoff.

Freeman, Derek
>   1957   Iban Pottery. The Sarawak Museum Journal. Vol. VIII, No. 10 (New Series):153-76.

>   1967   Shaman and Incubus. The Psychoanalytic Study of Society. Vol. 4:315-343.

>   1970   Report on the Iban. London: Athlone Press.

>   1975   Review of The Iban of Sarawak and Their Religion by Erik Jensen. The Sarawak Museum Journal. Vol. XXIII, No. 44 (New Series):275-88.

>   1979   Severed Heads that Germinate. In R. H. Hook. (ed.) Fantasy and Symbol. London: Academic Press. pp. 233-46.

Freud, Sigmund
>   1950   Totem and Taboo. Authorized Translation by James Strachey. New York: W. W. Norton and Co.

Gill, Sarah Hall Sharples
>   1971   Selected Aspects of Sarawak Art. Unpublished Ph.D. dissertation, Columbia University.

Haddon, Alfred C. and Laura E. Start
>   1936 (1982)
>   Iban or Sea Dayak Fabrics and their Patterns. Cambridge: Cambridge University Press.

Hammond, Dorothy and Alta Jablow
>   1976   Women in Cultures of the World. Menlo Park, CA: Cummings Publishing Co.

Howell, Reverend W.
>   1912   The Sea-Dayak Method of Making and Dyeing Thread from their Home-Grown Cotton. The Sarawak Museum Journal. Vol. I, No. 2:62-6.

Jensen, Erik
>   1974   The Iban and Their Religion. Oxford: Clarendon Press.

Mashman, Valerie
    1986   Warriors and Weavers: A Study of Gender Relations Among the Iban of Sarawak. Unpublished M.A. Thesis, University of Kent.

McKinley, Robert
    1976   Human and Proud of it! A Structural Treatment of Headhunting Rites and the Social Definition of Enemies. In G. N. Appell. (ed.) Studies in Borneo Societies: Social Process and Anthropological Explanation. Special Report No. 12. Northern Illinois University Center for Southeast Asian Studies.

Pringle, Robert
    1970   Rajahs and Rebels. London: MacMillan.

Richards, Anthony
    1981   An Iban-English Dictionary. Oxford: Clarendon Press.

Sandin, Benedict
    1976   Iban Way of Life. Kuching: Borneo Literature Bureau.

    1980   Iban Adat and Augury. Penang: Penerbit Universiti Sains Malaysia for School of Comparative Social Sciences.

Sather, Clifford
    1978   The Malevolent Koklir: Iban Concepts of Sexual Peril and the Dangers of Childbirth. Bijdragen tot de Taal-, Land- en Volkenkunde van Nederlandsch-Indie. Vol. 134:310-55.

Vogelsanger, Cornelia
    1980   A Sight for the Gods: Notes on the Social and Religious Meaning of Iban Ritual Fabrics. In Mattiebelle Gittinger. (ed.) Indonesian Textiles: Irene Emery Roundtable on Museum Textiles. 1979 Proceedings. Washington, D.C.: Textile Museum.

"MEANWHILE, BACK HOME...":
BEJALAI AND THEIR EFFECTS ON IBAN MEN AND WOMEN

PETER M. KEDIT
Sarawak Museum, Kuching, Sarawak

INTRODUCTION

The Ibans' custom of *bejalai* clearly shows that they consider journeying an important part of their cultural heritage.   Such journeys outside their longhouses must have a significant impact on Iban social structure and behavior. Indeed, government reports from the Second Division of Sarawak dating from the 1950s indicate that colonial administrators regarded bejalai as a primary concern because it resulted in the absence of many able-bodied men who left their longhouses to work in other districts or countries.   Administrators estimated that at least one-third of Iban men left their villages in the Batang Ai district.

The present study shows that this process continues not only in the Batang Ai District but in other regions of Iban settlement as well.[1] For example, a 1968 survey of 162 Skrang Iban demonstrated that 57 percent of the men had been on bejalai at one time or another. A 1972 interview with 227 people in Batang Ai showed that approximately 30 percent of the male population was absent on bejalai. Other studies likewise indicate that about one-third of the male population was on bejalai at any given time of the year and that about 80 percent of the males in Batang Ai have taken at least one bejalai in their lifetime.

295

Two young Iban leaving their long-house, at Nanga Mepi, Batang
Ai, on their way to *bejalai* to Miri. They were sent off by
members of their family by the beat of gongs. (Sarawak Museum
Photograph)

Iban tradition and values have assigned meaning to bejalai as a cultural institution. The Iban pantheon, concepts of souls and dreams, ritual festivals, cults, mythologies, and traditional values are connected with the custom. Iban values of equality, valor, and individualism have supported bejalai and made it a viable institution throughout Iban history. The cultural heroes in Iban mythology perform triumphant bejalai, undertaking feats that both inspire and guide bejalai aspirants. The rewards of a successful bejalai are not only material gains but also the right to perform esoteric rituals which enhance the performers' social status.

In general, only men participate in bejalai. This results in part from the socialization of male and female children in the longhouse. Socialization steers men toward bejalai while directing women toward a passive, supportive role that primarily involves maintaining the family economy at home. This corresponds with the longhouse economy, in which a marked sexual division of labor frees men at some seasons, while an emphasis on the household assures women that the bilik family ultimately benefits when men go on bejalai.

The lengthy absence of males on bejalai clearly affects their home communities, particularly their wives and children. Although most children apparently miss their fathers, they support bejalai as a means of earning money for the family. Batang Ai women approve the institution and yet complain about their husbands' absences. In some cases, absences due to bejalai result in adultery, separation, and/or broken marriages.

VIEWS ON BEJALAI

When asked about bejalai, virtually everyone claims that it is not for women. According to Iban women, only women of low repute go on bejalai. A self-respecting woman would not leave her home to "seek adventure" outside the longhouse territory. Women contend that while men on bejalai can find jobs anywhere, they have few employment opportunities beyond the longhouse environment. Single women going on bejalai would be suspected of prostitution or, more charitably, searching for a husband. Although some girls go on bejalai and end up in the red light districts of Sibu, Kuching, and other main centers of Sarawak, the men especially ignore this and maintain that women do not go on bejalai. One woman admitted that some women do go, adding, "but not from our longhouse." Married women who join their husbands and young women who accompany their families on bejalai are not stigmatized.

Conversely, everyone questioned invariably expected Iban male to go on bejalai. Indeed, an Iban male risks his self-esteem if he does not go at least once. Adult men who were interviewed all expressed the belief that bejalai is good and commented that they expect Iban men to maintain the custom. They perceive bejalai not only as a way to find employment, which is difficult to find at home, but also to gain respect and experience, acquiring new skills and learning about the various local and foreign people with whom they work.

A group of Iban on bejalai in a transit house of a shipping agent in Kuching, on their way to Miri and abroad.

Iban women long have been reconciled to the fact that men have the prerogative to hunt heads or to collect food and hunt in the jungle by virtue of their ability to defend themselves in the often hostile environment outside the longhouse territory. This attitude has apparently been carried over to the present day, for women accept the fact that men, not women, go on bejalai. As one elderly Iban woman said: "If they [men] want to go there is no way we can stop them. After all, it is the former way of life [*sigi gaya*]."

Attitudes toward bejalai seem to be changing among school boys and girls, however. Significant numbers stated that bejalai is not for them. They would rather do well at school and secure a good job in the future. Some said they would rather work in cash cropping, which would provide the same if not better income than bejalai. Some girls said that they would prefer to marry someone who has not gone on bejalai, because those who have been usually earn a bad reputation as gamblers and womanizers. In their minds, a "stay-at-home" man is more likely to be a good husband and much less likely to abandon them.

MALES ON BEJALAI

Twenty percent of the male population of the communities surveyed have been on bejalai (see Table I). These men were all adult males (i.e., older than ten years) and in most cases unmarried when they undertook the journey.

TABLE I
Males on Bejalai

	Frequency	Percentage
Have been on bejalai	106	16.3
Have never been on bejalai	348	53.6
Currently on bejalai	64	9.9
On bejalai as salaried workers	11	1.7
DNA	120	18.5
TOTAL	649	100.0

Since the populations under study have roughly equal numbers of each sex, these figures show that virtually all adult males have been on bejalai at least once in their lives. When the survey was carried out in 1981, 11 percent were away from their longhouses on bejalai or permanent employment with government agencies and private firms. Only 21 percent were known to be returning on specific dates within the next two years. Some men had left approximately 30 years ago and still not returned; in most cases no one knew when they would return.

Sarawak Shell Bhd. Photograph showing a Miring Ceremony being conducted by Iban on bejalai, at the opening of a new oil-drilling site of land at Miri, Sarawak.

Fifty percent of those interviewed took their first journey between the ages of 16 and 27. Approximately five percent were between the ages of 10 and 15 years. Only two said that they were married when they began their initial journeys. Progressively fewer men left on their first bejalai as they grew older and none began bejalai above the age of forty.

The average man took 2.93 trips, usually between the ages of 16 and 40. Between 1900 and 1980, 97 men went on bejalai 285 times for a total of 695 years. On average, each man went on three bejalai, each trip lasting an average 2.43 years. Men were absent for an average of seven years. Men infrequently spend more than ten years way from home. Most of those who said they were away for more than 13 years at a time had permanent employment, in the military, for example, and served until retirement.

An Iban 'Oil-man' working at Miri Oil-fields, with a 'piring' ritual sacrifice at a Miring Ceremony to propitiate any malevolent spirits found at a new site in Miri.   (Sarawak Shell Berhad Photograph)

The number of journeys is inversely related to the length of each journey. Some men were away for more than ten years on the initial journey, but none stayed away that long on their fifth bejalai. This may be a function of the participants' increasing age, but it also indicates that bejalai is not economically viable for a person who is approaching middle age, married, and increasingly responsible for his family. Half of the married men on bejalai were gone between one and two years; a quarter were away for less than a year. Only three were away for three years and only one was away for eight years.

Iban men on bejalai are a common feature on board oil derricks, off the coast of Borneo, working with multi-national oil-companies.

REWARDS OF BEJALAI

One of the intangible rewards of bejalai must be the attention and even admiration given to a returned bejalai man when he relates his adventures to kinsmen and friends gathered on the ruai in welcome. He tells stories about working in foreign lands, different peoples and customs, and leisure activities to listeners in the ruai, peer groups at social gatherings, and lovers in tete-a-tete sessions.

Men on bejalai have seven common pastimes: cock-fighting, sight-seeing, social drinking, hunting and fishing, attending movies, and staying at home (*diau diri*). Cock-fighting, which is an integral part of Iban culture, is one of the most popular pastimes. Half of the men surveyed participated in this activity. Those who claim that they did not participate in cock-fighting gave two main reasons. First, they went to places with no cock-fighting and second, they disliked the idea of gambling away their money at cock-fighting sessions.

For travellers within Borneo, a cock-fight is synonymous with the presence of Iban men on bejalai. Fighting-cocks are not only companions and topics of conversation; they are an investment which can be sold in times of need. During field work, observations were made of cock-fighting sessions in Miri and Brunei. These sessions were similar to those in the Batang Ai area, although they involved more people. Besides fulfilling its obvious function, a cock-fighting pit serves the Iban as a market and meeting place, where they encounter old friends and make new ones, discuss jobs and settle contracts. Such occasions imbue Iban away from home with nostalgia and community spirit. For example, Iban women who accompanied their men on bejalai in Brunei and Miri were seen selling food at the outskirts of the cock-fighting pit, just as they did at their home base in Batang Ai.

Another favorite pastime is taking an evening stroll after work. Almost half (46.5 percent) of those questioned said they participated in this free activity. The Iban are generally very conscious of saving while they are away. One young man told me that while on his first bejalai he was reprimanded by an older kinsman for eating an orange. The kinsman told him that foreign fruit was expensive and that he should not develop a taste for luxurious food lest he spend all his money on it while away.

Fishing and hunting are also popular. Iban men love to fish and hunt whether at home or away. Men going on bejalai often include a fishing net in their luggage. Hunting and fishing in new and strange places seem to give the Iban the sensation of "pioneering" new areas; certainly they relate such episodes as if they had explored new land.

Sixty-nine percent indicated that they indulged in "social drinking" while on bejalai. Drinking home-brewed rice wine is both a social custom and ritual requirement for the Iban. Since the introduction of other alcoholic beverages, such as the Chinese *arak* and Western beer, some Iban have consumed non-rice drinks outside the context of gawai festivities. They are usually introduced to them at coffee shops at the bazaar, where they meet friends for social drinking. This does not suggest that serious problems are caused by alcoholism. Drinking beer, stout, and sometimes more potent drinks like brandy and arak in the bazaar is related more to socializing and sharing feelings of bravado than alcoholic addiction. Understandably, people have greater need to socialize with their friends and kinsmen when away from home.

The Iban would find it inconceivable not to drink in town, just as they would find it inconceivable not to drink with friends at the coffee shop on occasional visits to the bazaar. Social drinking is customary especially after getting paid at the end of the month or returning from a two-week stint on an off-shore platform, where alcohol is normally prohibited. Even in the early morning, it is quite common to see a group of young Iban sitting around a table covered with empty beer bottles at the open market in the oil-rich town of Miri. They are usually men who have arrived from the off-shore platforms and are celebrating their one-week leave after two weeks of hard work. The Iban in Miri and Brunei frequent certain coffee-shops, which are easy to spot by the loud and out-going sociablilty of their Iban patrons.

Iban do not spend much time going to "modern" forms of entertainment, such as movies (29 percent) and night life (5 percent), given the accessibility of such facilities. Younger Iban are most likely to frequent movie theaters and, one would think, night clubs or brothels. One of the main criticisms of young men who go on bejalai is that they tend to acquire "bad habits" such as womanizing and modern dancing ("go-go" in the words of the Iban at Batang Ai). Generally, however, Iban men do not spend their time and hard-earned money on such indulgences. They eschew these activities as a waste of money and as contrary to Iban moral values regarding marital fidelity and maintaining an untarnished reputation for "clean living." Furthermore, the Iban work ethic mandates that they dedicate themselves fully to their work, which would conflict with late nights on the town.

Iban on bejalai tend to congregate in various centers, which suggests that a network exists among Iban communities. Job vacancies in these centers are announced by word of mouth or correspondence between bejalai men and their kin. Employers, especially small concerns such as Chinese building contractors, prefer continuity in their labor force and often replace departing Iban with their kinsmen or friends from home.

Strong friendships usually develop among those who go on bejalai or work together. Iban on bejalai seem to keep to themselves and forge friendships with other Iban rather than with work-mates who belong to other ethnic groups. They interact and make friends with the Chinese more than with any other group (4 percent). This is because they work with the Chinese more than others. Iban also befriend groups such as Europeans, whom they meet while working at multinational companies, and natives such as Kayan, Malays, and Kadazan.

THE RETURN AND THE RESULT

As mentioned above, most bejalai last for a period of six months to two years. Figures culled from a survey on why men decide to return home help explain the emergence of this pattern. Most people returned after six months to two years because they had a clear conception of the appropriate length of absence. Some, mostly men who had been away for several years, decided to return because they felt that they had been absent for too long. Others returned because they wanted to start a new project such as planting rubber or pepper, because of family obligations, or because their job contract expired. Most men seemed to make a conscious decision to return rather than drifting back, as indicated by evidence that most return during the harvesting and clearing periods when their labor is most needed.

The desire for material goods is one of the most important reasons for going on bejalai. Iban commonly return by bus from bejalai in Kuching or Sri Aman burdened with goods such as mattresses, suitcases, and other household items. The scene is similar at Lubok Antu, where returning men load their longboats with goods purchased at the bazaar shops. Only a third of those surveyed, however, said that they had succeeded in obtaining material goods, primarily because they take home money instead. More than 60 percent returned with between $250 and $1000, while nearly 20 percent accumulated more than $1000. These figures suggest that it is becoming easier to bring back cash and purchase goods at places nearer to home.

TABLE II

Sources of Material in Eight Bilik-families, Ng. Mepi Batang Ai, 1981

	Heirloom	Bejalai	Cash Crop	Rice	Illipenut	Ritual	Others
Chinese jars & ceramics	17	29	6	21	3	5	11
Brassware	9	70	2	14	1	5	5
Traditional weapons	3	4	-	-	-	-	2
Blankets, costumes & jewelry	9	19	4	3	2	1	19
Musical instrument	-	2	-	-	-	-	-
Shotgun	-	3	1	-	-	-	1
Elec. goods	-	5	-	1	-	-	5
Furniture	-	24	-	-	3	-	11
Sewing Machine	-	2	-	-	-	-	2

TABLE II
Cont'd.

	Heirloom	Bejalai	Cash Crop	Rice	Illipenut	Ritual	Others
Outboard motor	-	2	-	-	-	-	-
Tools	-	-	-	-	-	-	1
Total	38	159	17	39	9	11	57
Percent	11.5	48	5	11.8	2.7	3	17

A detailed survey of valuable properties of eight families at Nanga Mepi, taken in 1981, revealed that 48 percent of material wealth in the bilik-families was acquired through bejalai activities. This indicates that bejalai contribute substantially to the material wealth of the Iban. The main goods brought back are clothes, wristwatches, and other items for personal use; heirlooms for the bilik, including gongs, antique Chinese jars, and jewelry; household goods to furnish the bilik; and tools or machines, especially outboard engines, chain saws, radio and television sets. Most of those surveyed spent less than $500, but a few bought large chain saws and outboard motors costing thousands of dollars. Iban men suggested that they had a tendency to buy tools and machines rather than "traditional" items such as jars and gongs.

MEANWHILE AT HOME

Bejalai affects not only the men who leave but also the children and wives they leave behind. The impact of bejalai on families must therefore be considered, as well as the community's response to the unfulfilled roles of absent men. Finally, it must be determined whether men's absence created villages of women, children, and old people and, if so, how those people coped.

Demographic Effects

If bejalai is the provenance of young and single males, it follows therefore that "the absence of many young men from the village increases the proportion of the groups—women, children, or the old...." According to a January, 1981, survey of four longhouses at Batang Ai, 25 percent of 140 males over the age of 12 were away from their longhouses on bejalai (26 males) or attending boarding schools (see Table III). Significantly, figures show that proportionately more younger people than older people and many more males than females were absent from their longhouses. Most people who were away were younger than 31 years. About two-thirds of males were away, compared with only 16.4 percent of females.

TABLE III
Males (12 Years and Older) on Bejalai or Absent from
Four Longhouse Communities in the Batang Ai
as of January 1981

Longhouse	Away on Bejalai including working permanently in town	Schooling away from home	Total Male pop. 12 yrs. +
Ng. Mepi	14	4	47
Mepi Pasir	5	3	39
Menyang Taih	3	1	25
Menyang Sedeh	4	1	29
Total	26	9	140

These figures support the assertion that longhouses effectively become "villages of women, children, and old people" because of the virtual absence of young men. It should be noted, however, that this phenomenon does not occur throughout the year. At times, the longhouses have nearly all their occupants. On weekends, public holidays, and school holidays, children return home from school. From April to June, men on bejalai and kinsmen from other longhouses come to the village to help with the harvest and attend the various *gawai* festivals usually celebrated at this time. During planting season from July to December, however, when the women and any young people at home are away in the rice fields and the men are either helping in the fields or away on bejalai, the longhouses are indeed desolate during the day. Only a few old people and women who are either disabled, baby-sitting, or taking a "day off" because of dreams or sickness remain at home.

Another demographic consequence of bejalai is the preponderance of widows over widowers. According to the 1981 survey, widows outnumbered widowers 22 to 2. This finding apparently supports Freeman's (1970:24) argument that the the relatively later age of marriage of Iban men and their choice of wives younger than themselves leads to more widows than widowers. Generally, Iban men marry between the ages of 21 and 30, by which time they would typically have gone on bejalai at least once or twice. Getting married does not stop men from going on bejalai, however; 21 went at least twice after they married.

Effects on Children

It would seem that children of bejalai men are affected by the absence of their fathers. To investigate this question, 45 boys and girls between the ages of 14 and 17 who attended Form III at the Lubok Antu Junior Secondary School in 1981 were interviewed about the primary effects of their fathers' absences. Most of the children said they missed their fathers while doing house or farm chores, such as fetching firewood, that required the strength and skill of their fathers. They also felt their fathers' absence during the fishing and hunting seasons, when other children enjoyed fresh fish and meat. The children also mentioned that they missed their fathers at seemingly insignificant moments, such as sitting on the ruai, because they felt deprived of their father's companionship while observing others. Some expressed concern at the risks their fathers took in occupations such as construction work. The children sympathized with their mothers, who had to assume their fathers' responsibilities and do farm work, such as harvesting, without the men's help.

A few felt that their schooling was affected by having to go without pocket money, uniforms, and books. Their fathers' absence may have had a more serious impact. In the Malaysian educational system, school children have to pass an examination at the Form III level before they can proceed to a senior secondary school. It is common knowledge that few children from rural schools obtain good results and reach the secondary senior level. One of the main complaints of teachers serving in rural areas, and especially in Iban areas, is the high rate of truancy. Children often miss school during periods of clearing, dibbling, and harvesting. Teachers say that parents take their children away from school to provide farm labor. One of the main reasons for this labor shortage is the absence of men on bejalai. This creates a pernicious cycle of missing school, failing examinations, lacking skills, and having to go on bejalai to obtain well-paid work.

Despite their negative comments, however, school children generally approved of their fathers going on bejalai, deeming it the only way for their families to earn necessary money. They claimed that no jobs were available in the district and that the money their fathers earned was used for their schooling.

Women's View of the Effects on Children

When Batang Ai women were asked about the effects of their husbands' absence on their children, most agreed they were significant. A common response was that the children shamelessly covet the food of children whose fathers provided them with side-dishes. "*Nadai orang ngiga lauk*," was the usual response, meaning that there is no one to look for relishes to eat with the rice at meals. One woman whispered that the children next-door usually visited her bilik at mealtimes when their father was away on bejalai. She then had to share her family's food with them out of pity.

Women also stated that the children of bejalai men were deprived of authority figures. Boys especially tended to be more mischievous (*manchal*), quarrelsome (*selalu belaya*), silly (*tatau*), and lazy (*ngelusu'*). *Nadai apai ke ditakut'*, the women said, meaning that the children have no father to fear or respect. The women also claimed that children who were young when their fathers left pined for the men and cried more than other children. Such children had no toys, pocket-money, or paternal support. The effects of fathers' absence on their children is summed up in the saying: "*Nadai apai nupi semua utai ngining orang magang*," which means that without a father to fend and provide for them, the children can only covet everything belonging to others.

There were also advantages for children whose fathers were on bejalai, however. These children were often independent (*ngering ka diri*), whereas those whose fathers are present became spoiled (*sida ke bisi, nya neraya amat sida*). They learned to do things more quickly because they were used to working alone without elders to depend on and lead them (*sida ke ditinggal ka apai deka lebih tumu nemu gawa kediri, nadai orang ke tuai ngulu ka gawa*). They also tended to compete with those whose fathers were home (*sida ia kira enggau ka bepekekit orang ke bisi apai*). One woman commented that some children had extra pocket money because their absent fathers sent money home.

Some women noted that even when their husbands were away on bejalai, their mothers, uncles, and aunts were there to guide and teach them. In addition, children received support and care from people in the next bilik, and the next, and so on. The women also observed that the effects of the absence of the men were mitigated by the mothers' ability to carry out the fathers' tasks (*indai ia nyau megai pengawa apai ia*). "After all," they said, "the mother is much closer to the child than the father..." (*indai endang rapit agi enggau anak*), "...therefore without the father it is all right" (*nya alai nadai apai, nadai ga gawa*).

On the whole, Iban apparently see few differences between "father-less" and "fathered" children. As one woman summarized, "There is not much difference, because we who live in longhouses treat all children equally. Not only the father of the child can discipline the child--uncle, aunty, grandfather and all others can teach the child."

Effects on Women

Women seem ambivalent about bejalai. While they complained of men's absences and of their irresponsibility, women seemed to approve of their husbands' bejalai activities. A Lubok Antu District Officer reported:

> The women of the Ulu Ai and Engkari are prepared to accept the
> extra work involved in return for the promised cloth and finery
> and the prestige which travelling gives to their men-folk and
> indirectly to them. (M.M. McSporran, SG. Dec. 11, 1950:110)

More than half the women questioned said that they approved of bejalai. They cited the household's need for cash and the difficulty in earning it any other way, especially for uneducated or unskilled workers, as the main reasons for their approval. Some needed cash to start their own bilik-family or support their children at school, but the majority wanted to purchase goods for the bilik and supplement their subsistence income. A few women mentioned that they wanted their husbands to earn large sums of money like other men so that they would receive the attendant social approval.

Nevertheless, the woman drew a distinction between "approving" and "encouraging," saying that they "allowed, encouraged him not" (*ngasoh, ngeransang ia enda*). A few women said that they had resigned themselves to the fact that the men made their own decision. They thought the men went on bejalai to see foreign places, earn cash to support the family, or because it was accepted that they should go. One woman complained that her husband had left in 1978, claiming that he would be absent briefly to earn some money, and still had not returned. Another said that there was no way to keep her husband at home; even before their marriage he had been a person who often went on bejalai. A few others also bemoaned the difficulty of changing men's decisions (*penemu ia empu. Enti utai dikedeka ka orang, mar kitai nan*).

About half of the women interviewed (n=66) said they farmed mainly on their own, but joined in *bedurok*, the Iban labor-exchange system, when necessary. They usually sought help with the sowing and weeding, both of which are labor-intensive. One woman said she sometimes paid people to help her. Others commented that they usually worked independently and only joined *bedurok* when frightened. Women living in their natal bileks could seek aid from their affines, but those without assistance from immediate kin had to resort to *bedurok* with non-kinsmen (*Bedurok enggau orang belama, laban ti nadai tuboh....*).

These women indicated strongly that they "suffered" (*merinsa'*) from the men's absence. Farm work was particularly difficult in that they had to do the men's share (felling and clearing) as well as their own, in addition to looking after the children. One woman explained that she had to work on the farm until late in the evening, return home, cook, do housework, and care for the children. Four women said they fell sick because of overwork. A third of the women saw sickness as the main problem during their husbands' absence. The double burden of nursing their children and tending the family's rice farms was a main problem faced by the wives of men on bejalai. Mainly, their children fell ill, which hindered farm work. If children became ill during crucial stages of the farming cycle, their mothers felt the men's absence more acutely than usual.

In addition to the problems of sickness and farm work, women mentioned the loss of companionship with their spouse. About one-third of those interviewed emphasized their loneliness while their husbands were on bejalai. In some extreme instances, the lack of companionship led to adultery and separation. Cases of divorce or separation because of bejalai were often brought to court. The Simanggang Court Case Books record proceedings of hearings to request or contest divorce as early as 1879. Women interviewed knew of 11 cases of adultery in the study area that resulted from bejalai.

There are also reports of husbands who remarried while on bejalai and were fined according to Iban custom by the District Officer. One Iban, originally from a longhouse in the Lubok Antu District, went on bejalai to the Mukah District of Sarawak and there married another Iban woman, thus deserting his first wife and two children. His wife reported him to the District Officer at Lubok Antu, who in turn contacted the District Officer in Mukah. The errant husband was called to the District Office and fined according to Iban customary law of "*berangkat*" as follows:

> for discarding his wife, he was fined 30 mungkuls (which was equivalent to $302)

> for deserting his two children, the man had to pay $301 "pemali" (share of his property for the children) each for his children

the woman who married him was also fined $331 (or 33 mungkul)

one third of the fines was paid to Government and the rest given to his wife

The Community's Response

Bejalai is not only men's prerogative; it is considered part of the ideal male role. Conversely, farming padi is women's work, with which men are obliged to assist. There seems to be mutual understanding between Iban men and women regarding bejalai and *umai*, each of which is a sex-linked role. In the past, the male's main preoccupations were to defend the community and seek fresh lands for padi cultivation. The female's role was to provide the staple food for the family and attend to the bilek. Today, however, there is no strict division in farm work and the Iban themselves insist that farm-work is the task of both men and women.

Although the community accepts that men go on bejalai, it does not give men license to go anywhere or stay away as long as they like. Social pressures in the longhouse confine men to an accepted notion of proper bejalai activities. These norms are comprised of six pairs of positive and negative responses by the community toward bejalai activities. The degree to which a particular bejalai journey approaches the principles listed on the left column of the table is a measure of the extent of community approval (see Table V).

An ideal bejalai is a man who is young, unmarried, and either leaves for a short duration or sends money home frequently. He returns with goods for the bilek and without adverse reports which could disgrace the family. A man of mature age who still goes on bejalai meets with neither approval nor respect. He is seen as too immature to accept the responsibilities of managing his house and farm. The longhouse community is also intolerant of married men who leave and neglect their families. The only bejalai approved for married men are short or involve regular remittances. There are exceptional cases in which the longhouse will accept the absence of an older man. For example, a man may be away from his house because of the nature of his work or family problems.

TABLE V
Norms of Bejalai

Acceptable Degree of Bejalai		Non-Acceptable Degree	
1.	Young--expected to go on bejalai	1.	Old--neglect longhouse responsibilities; a no-hoper, non-worker
2.	Unmarried	2.	Married--neglect family
3.	Short Duration	3.	Long Period--forget kin/country
4.	Send remittance	4.	No remittance neglect dependents
5.	Return with material goods or cash and achieved intended goal	5.	Return empty-handed, wasted time and became spend-thrift
6.	Achieve good name/reputation	6.	Disgrace bilek-family's name

As noted above, bejalai is supported in part because it enables a bilek family to acquire goods which demonstrate their prosperity and provide some insurance in times of financial need. An unexpressed but nevertheless very important motive for bejalai is to gain social prestige. A man who succeeds in his endeavor enhances the standing of the bilek family, not only in the eyes of his longhouse community but throughout the river system. This prestige is expressed by the Iban phrase *bisi ambi berita*, meaning one who is acclaimed by others for his achievement. Nothing pleases Iban parents more than to hear that their son is *bisi ambi berita* for his achievement "tau dipuji" (that can be praised).

Nothing thrills the son more than to be surrounded by kinsmen and friends on the ruai listening to news and stories of his bejalai. It is customary for a man to meet his household on his ruai and celebrate his return by distributing drinks. A common sight is the bejalai-returnee seated on the important section of the ruai, facing his admiring audience and describing the risks he took on the oil-rigs, the times he had in drinking sessions with his mates, the thrills and delights the towns offered. But should the bejalai man fail in his endeavor, get himself in trouble with the authorities, and disgrace himself and his longhouse, it is most unlikely that he will return. This leads to a extended period of bejalai or, more accurately, *belelang,* for he is *malu* (feels ashamed) to face his own people at home.

NOTE

1.   Data for this study were collected over the years since 1968, during numerous field trips to the Batang Ai, Skrang, and Saribas Iban. In 1979 and from 1980 to 1981, special attention was given to bejalai activites among the Batang Ai Iban.

LATAH IN SARAWAK, WITH SPECIAL REFERENCE TO THE IBAN

ROBERT L. WINZELER

Introduction

Malayan *latah* is a rather dramatic and exotic behavioral pattern, especially in some of its stronger manifestations. Upon being startled or otherwise provoked, persons who are slightly *latah* will typically exclaim an obscenity, strike out or throw an object. Those who are more strongly latah will enter a state of altered consciousness and mimic words or sounds, imitate gestures or patterns of movement and follow orders. Not all such *latah* behavior is necessarily "genuine" in the above sense, and much of both what is and what is not occurs within a customary social framework of teasing or joking. Therefore, not all *latah* is necessarily pathological in either a social or a psychological sense as, having been labelled a "culture bound reactive syndrome," it has generally been interpreted to be.[1] *Latah* is linked to age. It occurs among adults rather than children and it is more prevalent in older age groups. Adolescence is the earliest that true *latah* appears and its occurrence at this age is uncommon.

Two facts have special significance for what follows. The first (which makes the topic appropriate for a volume on male and female) is that *latah* is strongly related to gender. In some areas of the Malayan world *latah* occurs among both men and women but is apparently always much more common among the latter. In Kelantan, West Malaysia, where I also gathered extensive information on *latah* I encountered a number of *latah* men, including five in one village--though many more *latah* women. In Sarawak, however, I found no *latah* men in the course of the household or village surveys I conducted, or during any of the other inquiries I made. Here my questions about *latah* men sometimes produced the amused reply that "men are not *latah*". When I noted that I knew of men in Kelantan who were *latah*, the general reaction was that such men would be *pondan*, that is transvestites. While a few persons in Sarawak mentioned *latah* men I was never able to locate any of them or to determine whether or not this was so. Several reports of *latah* in Malaya note *latah* men who were transvestites and in Kelantan there is also some tendency to associate *latah* among males with transvestism. However, none of the many *latah* men I met and interviewed were overtly transvestite.

The second fact is that while *latah* occurs commonly and widely among some ethnic groups or in some regions it is absent and unknown in others. Much of the paper will be concerned with documenting and explaining this distribution but, in brief, *latah* is common in the coastal and down-river areas and absent in the interior. Beyond this, however, I found that *latah* was more common among one group of Iban--the Sebuyau--than among any of the other ethnic populations in the region.[2]

In this paper I shall first note the significance of Borneo regarding *latah*, then discuss the occurrence of *latah* in Sarawak and then focus in particular on the Iban.

The Study of *Latah*

Malayan *latah* apparently first came to the attention of Western observers around the middle of the nineteenth century. Since this time a substantial body of descriptive and interpretive literature has accumulated (Winzeler 1984). In recent years discussion about the nature and development of *latah* and other hyperstartle patterns has been revived by scholars representing both anthropology and transcultural psychiatry. H. B. M. Murphy (1972, 1976), Michael Kenny (1978) and Ronald Simons (1980) have all offered initial, sharply differing interpretations followed by a further exchange (Kenny 1983, Murphy 1983, Simons 1983a, 1983b). The issues that have been especially important have concerned: a) whether or not *latah* is a reflection of very specific "Malay-Indonesian" cultural patterns or of more basic and widespread human behavioral tendencies; b) whether *latah* has undergone distinct historical development from the mid-nineteenth century to the present, or whether it is more simply "traditional;" and c) whether or not *latah* is a form of mental illness (malady, syndrome, psychosis, neurosis, affliction, and so forth) or whether it is a more normal and culturally appropriate mode of behavior.

Generally longer on argument than on new information, this discussion has turned especially upon assumptions about which ethnic groups in Southeast Asia and elsewhere do and do not have *latah*. Yet data on the occurrence of *latah* in the Malayan world outside of Malaya and Java—and more especially among ethnic groups other than the Malays and Javanese--is meager. It was because of this that I was led to do research in Sarawak in the first place. There are two previous reports of *latah* in Borneo that are well known in the literature on Malayan *latah*. The first of these is an early one by the Dutch colonial psychiatrist F. H. van Loon (1924). It discussed the results of an effort to establish the occurrence or frequency of *latah* in various areas of the Netherlands Indies and to collect information on the characteristics of *latah* persons. Van Loon circularized physicians serving throughout the region, asking if *latah* had ever been observed and, if so, about the race (ethnic status), age, sex and occupation of the *latah* persons observed. The results showed *latah* to be heavily concentrated in Java. However, the survey also showed that it was known in Borneo. Specifically, van Loon reported that *latah* occurred among Malays, but not among Dayaks, Buginese or "people from Batjan." Except that the survey was limited to Kalimantan, that is the three quarters of Borneo controlled by the Dutch, the location of the areas in which instances of *latah* were noted was not indicated. Van Loon did report that *latah* in Borneo was called "*gigiren*" but did not discuss the ethnic origin or meaning of this term.

The second report is more recent and concerns Sarawak in particular. In this report Karl Schmidt and two other investigators report the results of a psychiatric survey carried out in the late 1960s (Chiu, Tong and Schmidt 1972). It showed that *latah* occurred among Iban and Malays, and provided information on the characteristics of *latah* among the two groups. However, it provided little or nothing in the way of contextual ethnographic information about the particular regions or sub-groups involved. It did note that Iban *latah* was limited to areas in close proximity to Malay villages, but did not elaborate. And nothing was mentioned about other groups.

The present situation in both Sarawak in particular and Borneo in general is much more complicated than either of these two reports indicate. In Sarawak *latah* does occur among some Iban groups and not among others, but it also occurs among some Bidayuh (Land Dayak) and Melanau populations but, again, not among others. For other areas of Borneo recent reports of "*latah*" concern the

Rungus Dusun of Sabah (A. Appell, this volume) and the Kadayan of Brunei (Maxwell n.d.) have been or are in the process of being published. Further inquiries would doubtless produce other instances.

The Distribution of *Latah*

Latah is well known and relatively common in all of the Malay areas where I was able to make inquiries, including those in the vicinity of Lundu, Kuching and Betong. In the case of the non-Malay groups the distribution of *latah* in central and southwestern Sarawak is, in brief, as follows. Overall, the occurrence of *latah* varies greatly among different sub-groups or regions from being common (that is well known and occurring in every or nearly every particular village) to being unknown. Among the Selako Bidayuh in the Lundu region *latah* is relatively common though it tends to be clustered, with some villages having several or more *latah* women and others none. Even the coastal village of Pueh, perhaps the most traditional Selako community in Lundu District, has several *latah* women. On the other hand, several Indonesian Selako informants, who had come to Lundu in search of work and whom I questioned about *latah*, said that it did not exist in their own communities, or in others in Kalimantan with which they were familiar, all of which were in remote, roadless areas. Nor did I find *latah* in the Bukar Sadong Bidayuh villages in the Mongkos area of Hulu Sadong, which are located in the deep interior of the First Division near the Indonesian Border. Several of the older inhabitants of one longhouse in this area knew what *latah* was, and said that in the past a *latah* person had lived there, but went on to say that person had come from Kalimantan. Otherwise, my inquiries drew a blank.

In the case of the Melanau the occurrence of *latah* also varies significantly. In this instance, however, the variation is mainly between the Muslims, on the one hand, and the non-Muslims (some of whom are Christians and some of whom are followers of traditional practices) on the other. Overall *latah* is not common among Muslim Melanau but it is generally known and does occur. I interviewed a total of eight Muslim Melanau women and learned of several others. On the other hand, during my inquiries in all of the Melanau villages of Batang Oya, Sungai Kut, and Batang Igan above the juncture of Sungai Kut, I did not turn up any cases or any knowledge of *latah* among either Christian or traditional Melanau. This seemed unlikely at first since Muslim Melanau generally knew about *latah* and since they are not isolated from the non Muslims, some of whom are neighbors, at least in the Dalat area. It became more understandable as it became apparent that while *latah* is fairly common in the coastal Muslim communities, it is much rarer, at least on the Oya, in the interior ones; and further, that the proportion of Muslims drops quickly in relation to distance from the coast to the interior.

Here two questions seem pertinent. The first is the extent to which *latah* among these various groups in Sarawak is really the same phenomenon. While Chiu, Tong and Schmidt (1972: 159) seem to have no doubt that the *latah* they found among the Iban was "*latah*," they argue that it is not entirely the same as "*latah*" among the Malays. For one thing, they report that, while among both groups recurring dreams are typically associated with both the onset of *latah* and with its continuing occurrence, the dreams are different in each case. While the Malay dreams were predominantly sexual, those of the Iban were more varied, but with ghosts and dead persons being predominant themes. In addition, they concluded that the total configuration of psychiatric symptoms characteristic of Iban and Malay *latah* individuals were not the same; that among Iban it was clearly associated with a mild depressive syndrome while among Malays this was not so.

Since I was not in a position to attempt a psychiatric evaluation of any of the *latah* persons of any group, I can neither confirm nor deny the latter difference. I did find that the eight Selako women whom I interviewed in detail (most of whom were non-Christian) generally had more extravagant, supernaturally oriented, accounts of how they had first become *latah* than did either the Christian Iban, the Muslim Melanau or the Muslim Malays. One woman told of becoming *latah* after dying and coming back to life the next day. But these and other culturally mediated differences that could be mentioned, while interesting and worthy of further analysis, seem secondary from the perspective of the current inquiry. The basic features of *latah* in Sarawak are the same among all the groups in which it occurs, though these features may vary in frequency or in the manner in which they are developed. What appears to vary in a significant way is the extent to which *latah* occurs. This is apparent in all of the different kinds of data I collected, and in a general way at least, in the views of both the Malays and the non-Malays in Sarawak who are familiar with *latah*. For all such people *latah* is simply *latah*.

The second question that needs to be raised concerns an opposite sort of possibility. This is whether "*latah*" may exist under another name or names in areas or among groups where I did not find it referred to as such. This was a possibility in which I took considerable interest, for outside of the Malayan world in Southeast Asia "*latah*" definitely does occur by a variety of other names. Further, as noted earlier, van Loon (1924: 11) reported that in Kalimantan the term for *latah* was "*gigiren*", and I have also been informed that "*latah*" occurs among the Ngaju of Central Kalimantan where it is known as "*giren*" or "*gagiren*"--

obvious reflexives of *gigiren*--(Schiller 1987), as it does also among the Kadayan of Brunei (also as *gigiren*) (Maxwell n.d), and among the Rungus of Kudat District, Sabah, as *obingsalah* ("often mistaken") (A. Appell, this volume). It seems likely that further inquiries in other regions of Borneo would yield other examples. As for Sarawak, it remains possible that such instances may also be found, but this seems unlikely for the central and southwestern regions. The very limited inquiries I was able to make among and regarding the various *Orang Ulu* (Kenyah, Kayan, and Kajang) groups in the upper Rajang and lower Balui region of Belaga produced negative results.

How then is this distribution of *latah* in Sarawak to be explained? It was once suggested to me by a Melanau informant that since most people who have *latah* are found near the coast there might be something in the environment--such as the effect of the tides or the climate--which caused *latah*. This seems unlikely. It is obvious that *latah* is not associated exclusively with a set of ethnic groups defined in terms of language. For example, it is highly unlikely that there are significant differences in dialect between those Melanau or Selako which have *latah* and those which do not. Nor for similar reasons can religion be a decisive factor. It is true that here we have the interesting fact that Muslim Melanau as well as Malays (all of whom are Muslim) have *latah* while Christian and traditional Melanau apparently do not. This suggests a possible link between Islam and *latah*, in this region at least. But in the case of the Selako *latah* is found among Christians and traditionals. Therefore, while it is possible that certain aspects of Islam relating to the status of women might favor *latah*, this is at most a secondary factor. The link with Islam in the case of the Melanau probably has little to do with Islamic culture in itself. It is rather simply that the Muslim Melanau have had the closer contact with Malays than have the non-Muslim Melanau.

Contact with Malays in fact appears to be a part of the explanation in all instances in central and southwestern Sarawak. In this region all of the groups which have *latah*, that is, which recognize a hyperstartle pattern among themselves and so label individuals, refer to it as "*latah*." Further, with the exception of Melanau country, *latah* exists in areas in which Malays are present in substantial numbers and in fairly close proximity to non-Malays. Elsewhere in Borneo the occurrence of *latah* may or may not have Malay origins. The apparently widespread "gigiren" and its reflexives also suggests a common Malay or Javanese source, though local terms such as the Rungus Dusun "obingsalah" (the only such instance I am aware of) do not.

On the other hand, there is almost certainly more to the distribution of *latah* in Sarawak than simple diffusion. The areas in which *latah* occurs are not only ones in which extensive contact and interaction between Malays and Dayaks have taken place over a relatively long period of time. They are also regions which have experienced the greatest social, cultural, economic, and ecological change. It seems likely that such changes have had a direct affect on women in ways likely to promote *latah*. Here the evidence is clearest and most abundant in the case of the Iban.

Latah and the Iban

The Iban (see e.g., Freeman 1955, 1981; Jensen 1974; Pringle 1970: 247-282; Sutlive 1988; Uchibori 1984) are the largest and most widely spread of the indigenous non-Malay Bornean populations of Sarawak. Significant differences have by now come to exist and to define Iban populations in some areas. These, however, appear to be a matter of relatively recent local adaptive and accultura- tive changes that is ones which derive from varying histories of migration and contact with Malays and other non-Iban peoples, especially over the past century and a half. At the one extreme are the interior or "upriver" Iban of the middle Rajang and various other rivers. These are the more "traditional" or, perhaps more accurately, "pioneering" shifting cultivators of Derek Freeman's (1955) account of the Baleh River dwellers.

At the other are the Sebuyau Iban of Lundu (see e.g., Low 1848: 165-168; Pringle 1970: 46) and the Kuching area, which together comprise most of the Iban of the First Division. These Iban migrated from the Sebuyau River, near the lower Batang Lupar, around the beginning of the nineteenth century either before (according to Sandin 1967: 6-7) or after (according to Low 1848: 166-168) wars with the Skrang River Iban. Today they recognize themselves as a distinct group of Iban. The men are no longer tattooed, and all are at least nominally Christian. Many Sebuyau are educated urban dwellers. Some of those in Lundu are government employees, but most are farmers.

The occurrence of *latah* among the several different Iban areas where I conducted surveys or made systematic inquiries also varies considerably and in much the same way that it does among the Bidayuh and the Melanau. Among the Sebuyau of Lundu *latah* is well known and occurs frequently. There were, for example, a total of eighteen *latah* women in the two Sebuyau villages in Lundu (which total slightly more than one hundred households) in which I did a complete survey. And *latah* appears to be equally common in the Sebuyau villages to the south of Kuching town where I made limited inquiries. In the Betong area of Saribas *latah* among Iban is also common, though more sporadic in occurrence. Here, for example, one large longhouse of over 40 doors had four *latah* women, another had three, while several others had none. In the Sibu area *latah* occurs among both the longhouse dwellers and among the urban Iban of the town fringes, though in both cases again sporadically. Finally, and in contrast, my extensive inquiries at longhouses along the middle Rajang from Song to Nanga Baleh, in the lower Baleh up to the Mujong, and well up the lower Mujong, turned up neither any instance nor any real knowledge of *latah*.

The question is why this is so. Again, it is partly a matter of simple diffusion. In his survey of Sarawak, Edmund Leach (1950: 34) labelled the Sebuyau "para Malays" because of the extensive acculturative change they had undergone. Evidence of this influence can be readily seen in the Sebuyau villages in Lundu. In one instance a village is divided into halves, separated by a narrow open area, one Malay and Sebuyau. The other villages are located close to Malay areas, and all are commonly oriented to the bazaar at the center of town. Except for an occasional mosque or prayer house there are no differences to be noted between in the external appearance of Malay and Sebuyau neighborhoods, for the houses are identical. The Saribas Iban of the Betong area, among whom *latah* is also well known, have also undergone much acculturative change and are therefore similar in some respects to the Sebuyau, though unlike the latter they continue to live in long houses.

Thus while the Iban would seem to have learned *latah* from the Malays as they learned other things, there is also reason to suppose that they were disposed to do so both as a result of certain facets of traditional social organization and culture and by some of the changes that the downriver and coastal groups have undergone.

Here my particular point of departure is the assertion by Derek Freeman (1968: 388) that relations between male and female in traditional Iban society are marked by considerable tension, and this tension had an explicitly sexual focus. *Latah* does not occur among the traditional interior Iban of the Baleh or, so far as I have been able to determine, of other such interior regions. It seems to occur only among those Iban that have undergone acculturative influence in downriver and coastal areas. If, however, *latah* also has much to do with cultural tensions between male and female, an understanding of the situation of the traditional Iban may help explain why *latah* has become particularly common among the Sebuyau.

The literature on the traditional Iban is extensive, as is the literature on the patterns of change they have undergone over the past century and a half. The relationship between men and women in Iban society has occasioned comment over a long period of time. The conventional view is that Iban women had high, more or less equal, status--that they inherited equal shares of property, chose their own husbands, and that men and women shared the tasks of food production, though with men doing the heavy work of clearing and women doing the much of the routine work of cultivation. It was also observed that men sought prestige through headhunting and then through travel to work and trade while women participated extensively in the ceremonial side of the head cult and sought prestige through weaving, the "woman's warpath."

As a result of his extensive fieldwork in the Baleh in 1949-51, Freeman added further ethnographic validity and depth to this general picture. In particular he demonstrated absolute male-female symmetry in certain basic areas of Iban social organization such as postmarital residence. However, in some of his subsequent publications dealing specifically with headhunting, shamanism and symbolism he presented a more complex picture. In these (Freeman 1967, 1968) he asserted that male and female (and also parent and child) relationships were marked by tension and conflict, and he noted a strong double standard in postmarital sexual morality and custom. Michael Heppell (1975), Freeman's student, provided further documentation of Iban domestic tension and conflict and noted the role of sexual transgressions as sources of fights, killings and feuds.

In an explicitly psychoanalytical interpretation of the ethos of male-female relationships Freeman (1968: 387-389) argued that Iban women are intensively jealous of the men and that their jealousy takes the form of penis envy:

> It is a not uncommon to see an Iban mother fondling, in an admiring way, the penis of her infant son. This is erotically stimulating to the child but also, I would suggest, threatening, for to look on an object not one's own with intense longing is also, in most cases, to envy its possessor. This is also seen when a mother and young son quarrel, as they often do. Then the boy, enraged, will shout at his mother (as in a case I observed): 'Your vulva! Your vulva'. And the mother, also angry but partly in mockery, will retort: 'Your stiff penis! Your testicles'...

> Adult women in Iban society are, virtually without exception, envious of males and mockery of males, and particularly the male genital, is one of their favorite pastimes...

> Again, during head-hunting rituals which are occasions for the celebration of the preoccupations and narcissism of men, bands of women as comically dressed transvestites complete with grotesquely ornamented phalli, for hours on end will chant songs

in which they mock male pretensions and denigrate the male genital.

What is notable about the examples which Freeman provides is that whatever they show about classic Freudian penis envy, it takes a highly explicit rather than a "symbolic" or repressed form. If traditional Iban women felt envious toward Iban men they also had the means of directly expressing such feelings. Freeman does not tell us whether such open displays of sexual joking and clowning served to alleviate the feelings they expressed. Presumably they provided some satisfaction for he notes that they angered the men who could, however, only weakly retaliate with inept taunts of their own.

The extensive social and cultural changes which the Iban have (very differentially in various areas of Sarawak) undergone over the past century and a half have likely had important psychological correlates. These, however, have been so far little described. Material of the sort provided by Freeman and Heppell concerning the more traditional Iban of the Baleh and the Batang Ai regions have generally not been provided by those scholars who have studied the more modern Iban of downriver, coastal and urban areas. It may be assumed that some of the facets of traditional Iban life which gave rise to female animosity at male privilege and pride diminished as the Iban were brought under European and post-European domination, especially as active head-hunting and warfare were suppressed.

But the accounts of modern developments also suggest that not all bases of tension between Iban men and women have been eliminated or even reduced as a result of modern developments. I am speaking here especially of those relating to the practice of *bejalai* as described by Peter Kedit (1987 [and Freeman 1955 for the earlier period]). *Bejalai* refers to lengthy journeys or expeditions by men to distant places to collect jungle produce, engage in trade, or wage labor or to serve in the military but which, in any case, have as a primary purpose the achievement or validation of male status. Apparently *bejalai* was always important. But it has generally been argued that as headhunting was suppressed it became more important. Men returned with goods and tales of adventure and distant places as they had formerly returned with trophy heads. In the modern period *bejalai* is undertaken above all for wage labor in logging camps, oil fields and on cargo ships. Hence the practice merges with the circular labor migration activities of men of most Dayak groups in Sarawak and in much of the Third World in general.

Women, however, have no culturally sanctioned means of going on journeys and thus escaping the routines of long house life and the work of cultivation. Women who leave the long houses and migrate to towns are presumed to be engaged in prostitution rather than in worthwhile, status enhancing activities (Sutlive 1988: 163-165). While *bejalai* for wage labor has economic and other benefits it also has drawbacks for women. These include being left behind, being required to perform the agricultural labor normally performed by men as well as that done by themselves, being uncertain when men will return or whether they will return at all. For married women with absent husbands the drawbacks include loneliness and the temptation to engage in adultery.

But if the sources of tension between men and women in Iban society have not necessarily diminished as a result of modern developments, it would appear that opportunities for women to express these tensions seem to have lessened. As the Iban are drawn closer to the more modern sectors of Malaysian society the possibilities for women to express deviance and rebelliousness within the general framework of social acceptability have diminished. In particular, the opportunities for sexual clowning and ridiculing men that were of the traditional head-hunting ceremonies described by Freeman have disappeared among the Sebuyau Iban. It is therefore not surprising that *latah* has become popular and widespread among the women of this group. *Latah* interaction has certain parallels with the sexual joking behavior of traditional Iban women noted by Freeman (1968: 388):

One of the forms which this mockery [of men] is for two women to share a nickname (*emprian*) which they regularly use in addressing one and other in a bantering tone of voice. It is always a nickname directed at males, and usually at the male genital.

The parallels with *latah* interaction become apparent when it is noted how the provocation works. I asked all of the *latah* persons I interviewed who usually startled them and was frequently told--somewhat to my initial surprise--that it was their own friends. I also asked if they startled other persons who were *latah* and many said that they did, in spite of the fact that they almost inevitably say that they do not like to be provoked themselves. Being *latah* is said to involve being made *malu* (shame, embarrassment) but when it happens to others it is regarded as amusing. Some women who are *latah* have friends who are also *latah* and such women not uncommonly startle one another when the opportunity arises. What is said and done on such occasions, which are frequently public, generally has a strong sexual content and sometimes involves mockery. *Latah* episodes among the Sebuyau Iban, as among other groups, are regarded as very funny, but for men at least the humor is tinged with embarrassment. In some instances men become the butt of what occurs. Here is an example from my own experience.

During the course of a household survey in one of the Sebuyau communities in Lundu we (my assistant and I) called upon an older women in an area near the far end of the village. Someone else in the village had told us to watch out in that area, though I had not known what had been meant by this remark. It turned out that there were several women in the that area who were *latah*. During the course of the interview of which I am speaking, the woman whom I had previously interviewed in the next house arrived to watch. Since the house had no western style furniture we sat on mats on the floor. When I stood up at the conclusion of the meeting I bumped my head on the pressurized oil lantern that was hanging above me. Immediately the women blurted out something in Iban and every one burst into laughter. I quickly asked my assistant what she had said and he told me in Malay that it was that "you bumped your penis." However, as quickly as he responded the neighbor lady, who was also *latah*, repeated this and then blurted out "have intercourse," provoking even more riotous laughter.

Among the Sebuyau Iban, as among other groups which have *latah*, such behavior is regarded as naughty or deviant but only slightly so. To openly express the sexual obscenities which are blurted out in the course of *latah*, or to follow orders to engage in behaviors which are foolish or obscene is to violate standards of proper, dignified behavior. But the violations are not usually that serious and in any case they are excused by the accepted view that *latah* persons are not responsible for what they say and do. Men especially may harbour suspicions that women are not necessarily really or always unaware of and unable to control their actions, but this does not seem to make a great deal of difference. As is generally the case, the Sebuyau women who are *latah* are mainly from the poorer economic strata. Such women are perhaps both especially in need of a little attention and somewhat less concerned about the possibilities of a loss of prestige in the community. However, women may also be pillars of respectability and be *latah*.

Among the Iban and the other groups in which it occurs, *latah* is often best regarded not as a form of "psychopathology" but as a means by which women--who lack many other means of doing so--may call attention to themselves and express aggression in socially acceptable or excusable ways, especially, if not only, regarding men. In particular, in Iban villages such as those in Lundu in which there are large numbers of women who are *latah* it would seem appropriate to regard the pattern as a mode of social interaction.[3] In such situations much, though perhaps not all, *latah* is closely related to (or represents a form of) the sort of sexual joking behavior that has been extensively analyzed by anthropologists. But *latah* also appears to be related to another pattern of behavior which has often been shown to be a means by which women are able to draw attention to their problems, express otherwise unacceptable wishes, behave aggressively toward men and so forth--spirit possession (Lewis 1971, 1986: 23-50). *Latah* combines elements of classic sexual joking with culturally recognized states of altered consciousness. It is the latter which makes the former permissible or excusable when it would not otherwise be.

NOTES

1. See Kenny 1978 for a discussion of this point. My position here is similar in certain respects to his. Kenny, however, believes that *latah* is bound up with "Malay-Indonesian" metaphysical and supernatural notions while I have found little evidence that this is so. Also, Kenny asserts that *latah* is restricted to the Malayan world and can therefore be explained only in terms of local cultural notions. This is also an assumption with which I disagree.

2. The present report is based upon information gathered by myself in the First, Second, Third and Seventh Divisions between December 1985 and June 1986 and in July and August 1987. For the Iban, systematic inquiries were made at thirty nine scattered long houses located mainly on the Saribas, the Rajang, the Oya, the Igan, the lower Baleh and Mujong Rivers. Among the Sebuyau Iban detailed information was collected in two villages in Lundu while more limited inquiries were made in several villages around Kuching. For Land Dayak detailed information was gathered among Selako in Lundu District, specifically in four rural villages situated from five to eight miles to the west of Lundu town. More general information was gathered concerning Selako in Pueh, Lara in Lundu District, and on Bukar Sadong in the Mongkos area of Hulu Sadong. For Malays, general information was obtained in the Lundu

area, and in the main interior Rajang River towns of Kanowit, Song, Kapit and Belaga, while detailed information was collected in Betong, Saribas District, in the Second Division. Information on Melanau was gathered especially in the Dalat area on the Oya River as well as in the towns of Mukah and Oya and in all of the eighteen villages on the Oya and Kut Rivers.

My investigation was supported by research grants from the National Science Foundation and the Fulbright Program and sponsored by the Sarawak Museum, to all of which I am grateful. I also wish to thank Lucas Chin and Peter Kedit for the great help that they and the Museum have provided.

3.   In an interpretation of *latah* based in part upon fieldwork among Malays in Melaka, Simons (1980) argues that there are three forms of *latah*, one of which is "role *latah*." By this he means *latah* in which neither the provocation nor the reaction are genuinely felt by the person, and which is performed for the amusement of others and as a means of gaining attention. Simons is both more confident at being able to distinguish between role *latah* from real *latah* than I am and more certain of the value of doing so. Anthropologists at least are probably better off supposing that all *latah* is role *latah*, that it is a mode of cultural and social interaction. The problem is somewhat similar to that of studying shamanism and spirit posession with the purpose of learning whether the shaman is really in a state of altered consciousness and so forth, which has turned out to be relatively fruitless.

REFERENCES

Aberle, David F.
    1952   Arctic Hysteria and *Latah* in Mongolia. The New York Academy of Sciences 13(7):291-297.

Chiu, T. L., J. E. Tong and K. E. Schmidt.
    1972   A Clinical Survey of *Latah* in Sarawak, Malaysia. Psychological Medicine 2:155-165.

Freeman, Derek.
    1955   Report on the Iban. Kuching: Government Printing Office.

    1967   Shaman and Incubus. Psychoanalytic Study of Society 4:315-344.

    1968   Thunder, Blood and the Nicknaming of God's Creatures. The Psychoanalytical Quarterly 37:353-399.

    1981   Some Reflections on Iban Society. (An Occasional Paper of the Department of Anthropology, Research School of Pacific Studies). Canberra: The Australian National University.

Geertz, Hildred.
    1968   *Latah* in Java: A Theoretical Paradox. Indonesia 3:93-104.

Heppel, Michael.
    1975   Iban Social Control: The Infant and the Adult. Ph.D. thesis, Australian National University.

Hughs, Charles C.
    1985   Culture-Bound or Construct-Bound? The Syndromes and DSM-111. Pp. 3-24. In R. Simons and C. Hughs, eds., The Culture Bound Syndromes. Boston: D. Reidel.

Jensen, E.
    1974   The Iban and Their Religion. Oxford: Clarendon Press.

Kedit, Peter.
    1987   Iban Bejalai. Ph.D. thesis, Australian National University.

Kenny, Michael G.
    1978   *Latah*: The Symbolism of a Putative Mental Disorder. Culture,
            Medicine and Psychiatry 2:209-231.

    1983   Paradox Lost: The *Latah* Problem Revisited. Journal of Nervous
            and Mental Disorder 171 (No. 3), 159-167.

Leach, Edmund.
    1950   Social Science Research in Sarawak. London: His Majesty's
            Stationary Office.

Lewis, I. M.
    1971   Ecstatic Religion. Harmondsworth: Penguin Books.

    1986   Religion in Context. Cambridge: Cambridge University Press.

van Loon, F. H. G.
    1924   *Latah*, A Psycho-Neurosis of the Malay Races. Mededeelingen
            van den Burgerlijken Geneeskundigen Dienst in Nederlandsch-
            Indie 3, 305-20.

Low, Hugh.
    1848   Sarawak: Its Inhabitants and Productions. London: Bentley.

Maxwell, Allen.
    n.d.   *Gigiren*: The Kedayan Hyperstartle Reaction. Sarawak Museum
            Journal. (forthcoming)

Murphy, H. B. M.
    1972   History and the Evolution of Syndromes. In Psychopathology:
            contributions from the Social Behavioral and Biological Sciences.
            Edited by M. Hammer, K. Salzinger, and S. Sutton, 33-55. New
            York: John Wiley and Sons.

    1976   Notes for a Theory of '*Latah*'. In Culture-Bound Syndromes,
            Ethnopsychiatry and Alternate Therapies, edited by William P.
            Lebra, 3-21. Honolulu: The University Press of Hawaii.

Pringle, Robert.
    1970   Rajahs and Rebels: The Ibans of Sarawak under Brooke Rule,
            1841-1941. Ithaca: Cornell University Press.

Sandin, Benedict.
 1967 The Sea Dayaks of Borneo. East Lansing: Michigan State University Press.

Simons, Ronald C.
 1980 The Resolution of the *Latah* Paradox. Journal of Nervous and Mental Disease 168:195-206.

 1983 *Latah* II - Problems with a Purely Symbolic Interpretation. Journal of Nervous and Mental Disease 171:168-175.

Sutlive, V.
 1988 The Iban of Sarawak. Arlington Heights: AHM Publishing Corporation.

Uchibori, M.
 1984 Transformations of Iban Social Consciousness. In History of Peasant Consciousness in Southeast Asia (eds) A. Turton and S. Tanabe. National Museum of Ethnology. Senri Ethnological Studies No. 13. pp. 211-234.

Yap, P. M.
 1957 The *Latah* Reaction. Journal of Mental Disease XCVIII (413):515-564.

Winzeler, Robert L.
 1984 The Study of Malayan *Latah*. Indonesia 37: 77-104.

THE ANGER WITHIN THE FLESH OF THE HOUSE: MENGALONG LUN COSMOLOGY AS ARGUMENT ABOUT BABIES AND BIRDS[1]

JAY B. CRAIN
Center for Pacific Asian Studies
California State University, Sacramento

Mengalong Lun Dayeh notions of a dualistic cosmos are embodied in arguments about development, sexuality, and the dangers of birds. By associating the dangers of separation, fornication, and nature, the Lun Dayeh both affirm and experience their unique ideology. This cosmology may be approached as persuasion or argument, just as people use ideology concerning what "must be" to justify their decisions and actions to themselves and others. (Douglas 1982) A description of the form of such arguments illustrates the linkage between ideology and experience.

This is shown by the way in which specific dangers in the universe provide both coherence and emotional commitment among the Lun Dayeh. They are part of a larger, as yet undefined linguistic and cultural homogeneity found in the interior valleys and tablelands of northern Borneo, where the borders of the Malaysian states meet the province of East Kalimantan, Indonesia. Numbering approximately 40,000, the Lun Dayeh practice subsistence agriculture and live in small villages surrounded by tropical rain forest. The ideas and arguments described below were those of the Lun Dayeh of the middle Mengalong River area recorded in 1968-1969. In at least one village, Ranau, they had remarkably altered by 1980 (see Crain 1985). The cosmology presented, however, is most likely still intact in those areas where swidden remains the central agricultural strategy.

Lun Dayeh ideas may be expressed as themes (Opler 1945). First, the world, including human nature is made up of two opposing and interdependent forces--natural and cultural. The relation between these forces is complementary; the influence of one is inversely proportional to the influence of the other. While natural forces are often destructive, they are necessary; cultural forces are never destructive, but not necessary.

Second, illness is a natural condition of humanity; health is the cultural consequence of social solidarity. The maintenance of health is interdependent with the existence of the proper relations between persons. Working, living and playing together in large groups promotes health; being alone damages health or causes disease.

Third, females and males are complementary and interdependent. Females are naturally sexual; males learn about intercourse from females. Society involves distinctions between women and men to control the necessary but potentially destructive consequences of sexuality.

Finally, proper relations between individuals are expressed through continuing, reciprocal exchanges between persons as representatives of corporate domestic family groups. Physical proximity and social solidarity are identical. The proper relations between families are those found in the physical and social intimacy of the long-house. Persons should give whatever is asked (be generous); they should never ask for what cannot be given (not cause embarrassment).

Lun Dayeh marriage and social exchange (Crain 1970a), residential models (Crain 1970b, 1970c), agricultural organization (Crain 1973), agricultural ritual (Crain 1976), social structure (Crain 1978), and engagement negotiations (Crain 1982) have already been described. Those discussions focus on patterns of behavior as abstracted from field notes and recollection. This paper is intended to illustrate the ways in which the Lun Dayeh bring their cosmology to bear upon their daily lives and thus bring it to life.

The social and intellectual life of the Lun Dayeh centers around the longhouse. The *ruma' kadang* consists of individual, attached apartments belonging to each domestic family (*uang ruma'*, "flesh of the house"). The family room of each apartment is called *takap*, a term which connotes village life as opposed to the forest and, by extension, culture as opposed to nature. The takap is the place where one is born, learns to walk, marries, procreates, rears children, and dies. The arrangement of apartments in the longhouse represents the proper arrangement between families, that is, side-by-side and moving forward together.

The opposite of this egalitarian mode of cultural and residential custom is the condition known as *rarag*, which literally means "one behind the other" as in a line or file. Rarag describes the mode of traveling along jungle trails, clearing fields, and being physically alone. By extension it represents the dangerous natural world beyond the longhouse.

Takap and rarag are also opposed in a sexual context. Takap is the preferred and apparently side-by-side position of marital intercourse. Rarag is the "animal-like" rear-entry position said to occur during illicit, extra-marital intercourse. At night, the Lun Dayeh longhouse is filled with the sounds of love-making as married couples experience the natural sexuality of women in the appropriate setting and manner of takap. Mixed with the sounds of passion are the rhythmic sounds of *dui, dui, dui,* meaning "mine, mine, mine," as mothers rock their children and respond to the movements of their husbands.

During my fieldwork among the Lun Dayeh, I witnessed first-hand the embodiment of their ideology. After spending a few nights in the longhouse, I realized that my plan to build a new takap at one end would not work. The Lun Dayeh did not leave me alone to work at night, but expressed their concern and hospitality, which I mistook for curiosity. Moreover, I anticipated difficulty in sustaining my own marriage when my wife and infant son arrived in a few months. I therefore asked for, and received, a separate residence. Within a month, I was comfortably established in my own house, built in an old *ladang*. I spent my days in the fields and longhouse and retired at night to type field notes. I usually awoke to visitors, most of whom pulled a few weeds growing alongside the house as they left.

The next month, my wife and 11-month-old son arrived and became very popular with the villagers. Their arrival proved that I was really married with a child and not the unattached bachelor they had perhaps imagined. Instead of a second honeymoon under tropical stars, we experienced an extended second wedding reception as the villagers redoubled their efforts to visit almost continually. The villagers were especially fascinated with my son Andy, but not for the reasons I assumed. Andy's attempts to explore his new home were constantly interrupted as he was passed from arm to waiting arm (Figure 1). The Lun Dayeh disregarded his blond hair, blue eyes, and fair skin and instead discussed his lack of language and ambulatory skills. After they discovered that Andy's baby sounds were not English words, the Lun Dayeh assured me that he would walk and talk soon. They continued to weed the area around our house until it was bare.

FIGURE 1
Andy held by young Lun Dayeh girl.

While I assumed that the Lun Dayeh, in their polite way, were bringing my yard and son up to village standards, they were actually expressing genuine concern. At this time I began a sociological census and learned the Lun Dayeh terms for age categories. I then discovered that the villagers assumed that Andy was at least two years old because of his size. They therefore thought that his development was retarded.

Our approach to child-rearing differed markedly from that of the Lun Dayeh and heightened their anxiety. Lun Dayeh infants rarely cry and when they do it signifies serious illness or danger. Crying, *tenge*, is equated with the calls of birds and, like crawling, is an human action that shows the influence of nature, or rarag. The Lun Dayeh hold their infants until they are ready to walk, sometime in their second year. Andy was the only crawling child that the villagers had ever seen. Furthermore, when Andy cried his parents often merely reassured him with words and when he asked we did not always give.

Children are never supposed to be alone. One day I encountered a young boy playing in the remains of a fallen sago palm. He had found a rhinoceros beetle and was imitating the sounds and motions of playing with a toy car, a form of play he obviously learned from Andy (Figure 2). A few minutes later, I met his parents, who were anxiously looking for their son. I directed them to the sago palm and followed to learn the source of their concern. When they reached the boy, his mother picked him up, held him, and told him that they were concerned for his health. To be alone, she reminded him, would cause him to become ill. His father said that even when men hunt, they do so in the company of others. The boy, visibly anxious at this point, did not tell them about the beetle-car. I also remained silent on the subject.

FIGURE 2
Boy with beetle playing alone.

Children should play in the longhouse or in the space in front of the longhouse where nothing is allowed to grow (Figure 3). This patch of soil, in the midst of green vegetation, is constantly weeded. Its size and clarity are seen as a reflection of the cooperative togetherness of the families inside. It would seem the closest the Lun Dayeh come to having corporate enterprise. This "anti-garden," which has no name among the Lun Dayeh, is a boundary between takap and rarag. It is a transitional space for children who are between infancy and adulthood. The Lun Dayeh believe that if infants are constantly held, fed, and loved, they may overcome the separateness that is the meaning of death and a consequence of rarag. The villagers of Ranau did their best to protect Andy from the invariable consequence of his un-takap-like parents. By filling our house with people, holding our child, and maintaining our anti-garden, the villagers tried to save Andy's life and promote the well-being of his unworthy parents.

FIGURE 3
Children playing in cleared area in front of longhouse.

Later in our stay, we were adopted into the kinship structure of the village and my "father" encouraged me to visit relatives in the Ulu Trusan of Sarawak. In one of these villages, I met a boy who would never become takap. Exhibiting behavior which we would interpret as a severe neurological-developmental deficit, this boy of six or seven wandered the village in much the same manner as a domesticated animal (Figure 4). He was naked and covered with his own filth, had no capacity for speech, and often moved around the longhouse veranda on all fours.

FIGURE 4
ana' rarag.

The villagers traced his defects to a breach in the decorum and togetherness of his longhouse. As the result of an argument, by then too distant or painful to relate, one of the families in the center of the longhouse moved away. They took their portion of the longhouse with them, making what was once one longhouse two and what was takap rarag (Figure 5). The boy was born some months later. He bit his mother's breasts and soon wriggled and crawled

FIGURE 5
Longhouse with missing apartment in center.

from the arms of his exhausted family. On my return to Ranau, I was asked if I had seen the *ana' rarag*, the "wild child." Andy soon had a classificatory "aunt" in daily attendance.

Andy eventually learned to walk and talk, because of nature, according to my perspective, and in spite of it, according to the villagers' perspective. The Lun Dayeh, however, never seemed quite sure. When I returned to Ranau eleven years later, most of their questions concerned Andy. He is now a a young adult, physically affectionate with his parents and nurturing to his younger brothers and sisters. He likes being with people and is unhappy being alone. While Andy remembers nothing of his Borneo days, he remains the embodiment of a once-experienced Bornean philosophy.

NOTE

1.   Research among the Lun Dayeh in Sabah and Sarawak, East Malaysia, was conducted in 1968-69 with a brief revisit in 1980. The research was supported by the U.S. Public Health Service, Cornell University, The National Institute of Mental Health, and a Fulbright-Hays Senior Research Fellowship (U.S. Embassy, Singapore). Funding and support for analysis and publication was provided by the Department of Anthropology, University Foundation and Center for Pacific Asian Studies, California State University, Sacramento, the Department of Psychiatry, School of Medicine, University of California-Davis, and the Institute for Southeast Asian Studies, Singapore.

REFERENCES CITED

Crain, Jay B.
   1970a   The Lun Dayeh of Sabah, East Malaysia: Aspects of Marriage and Social Exchange. Ph.D. Dissertation, Cornell University.

   1970b   The domestic family and long-house among the Mengalong Lun Dayeh. Sarawak Museum Journal 18:186-192.

   1970c   The Mengalong Lun Dayeh long-house. Sarawak Museum Journal 18:169-185.

   1973   Mengalong Lun Dayeh agricultural organization. Brunei Museum Journal 3:1-25.

   1976   Ngerufan: Ritual process in a Bornean rice harvest. In George N. Appell (ed.), Studies in Bornean Societies: Social Process and Anthropological Explanation, DeKalb, IL, Center for Southeast Asian Studies, Northern Illinois University. Pp. 51-63.

Crain, Jay B.
    1978   The Lun Dayeh. In Victor T. King (ed.), Essays on
                    Borneo Societies, Hull, Hull University and Oxford
                    University Press. Pp. 123-142.

    1982   A Lun Dayeh engagement negotiation. Contributions to
                    Southeast Asian Ethnography I(1):142-187.

    1985   A Borneo revisited: reflections on culture change in a
                    Sabah kampong 1969-1980. Borneo Research Council
                    Organized Session, Nation States and Tribal Societies,
                    Annual Meeting of the American Anthropological
                    Association, Washington, D.C.

Douglas, Mary
    1982   Introduction. In Mary Douglas (ed.), Essays in The
                    Sociology of Perception, London, Routledge and Kegan
                    Paul. Pp. 108.

Opler, Morris
    1945   Themes as dynamic forces in culture. American Journal
                    of Sociology 51:198-206.

MALE/FEMALE DISTINCTION AMONG THE SELAKO

WILLIAM M. AND MARY JO SCHNEIDER
University of Arkansas

Selako culture and behavior sharply distinguish male from female.[1] The distinction is the primary organizing principle of Selako society and is important in Selako thought and activity. This paper explores and describes the function of this important binary opposition in Selako life.

Selako gender relations highlight several interesting theoretical issues. Selako, like other Bornean cultures such as the Iban (Freeman 1958, 1960) and the Land Dayak (Geddes 1957), are rather egalitarian in terms of the social relations between the sexes. In light of their intermediate position in terms of the hierarchical/non-hierarchical dimension, women's rank among Selako should illuminate theory on the determinants of female rank in human societies. Moreover, their use of several important symbols in ritual and social life leads one to question the received wisdom on the relative rank of male and female and their relation to other fundamental binary pairs such as nature/culture (Levi-Strauss 1969a, 1969b; Ortner 1974).

Understanding the issue of gender in human cultures requires attention to both the symbolic and the social domains (cf. Ortner and Whitehead 1981:2). Our concern with the meaning of the male/female distinction leads us to unpack the binary opposition itself, as opposition, and to relate it to other symbolic formulations of the nature of the world. Sociological concerns lead us to inquire into how this distinction effects and affects actual social relations. The two approaches are, of course, closely related. The male/female distinction is not only a cognitive opposition but also as a primary biological fact generates one of the two fundamental social interdependencies (parent/child being the other) that orders all society.

Levi-Strauss (1963, 1966) and Leach (1976), Goodenough (1956) and Lounsbury (1956, 1964) have taught us that meaning lies in the relations of terms and systems of terms to each other. The terms 'male' and 'female' obtain meaning as an opposing pair each with its heavy freight of associated meanings, some of which themselves form binary opposites (e.g. active/passive, hard/soft). But the binary opposition, male/female, as a unit, itself enters into relations, paradigmatic and syntagmatic (or metaphoric and metonymic as Leach would have it), with other such binary opposites as nature/culture, raw/cooked, vegetable/meat, sky/earth, etc. (cf. MacCormack 1980).

Selako, like all people, deal with the world by constructing models of society and their environment and then acting to some degree in terms of the models they have constructed. Selako models are many and varied. Most are recorded in the system of ritual symbolism. The traditional longhouse, as we shall see, is also a fundamental text.

Selako models are explicitly binary. Like many Southeast Asian groups they live in a cognitive structuralist intellectual universe, and they themselves are aware that they construe the world in this fashion, although they might not see all of the oppositions or their transformations that are presented here. The most important and widely used binary model among Selako is the male/female opposition, usually put in Selako as *ambini/angaki*. Other primary oppositions are land/sea, *daya'/laut*, and spirits/humans, *antu/manusia*. There are many other subsidiary oppositions that are transformations of these such as rice/blood, wild pig/domesticated pig, mountain/beach, gods/demons, public room/family room. Between these are mediating elements, depending on the context, that may relate the triangular duality to like mental constructs in other domains. Thus, a sacred clearing in the forest, *kiramat*, connects men to spirits; distant ancestors who are between men and spirits created the wild/tame distinction embodied in rice/other foods and the longhouse/forest. Many of these subsidiary and primary distinctions can be recast in terms of the male/female.

The traditional Selako house serves as a text which details fundamental Selako structural contrasts (see Schneider 1975 for a more detailed description and analysis of the Selako house). Selako conceptualize the house as both a unity, *biik*, (in its most inclusive sense and highest level of contrast) and a duality, *saami'*, the gallery, and *biik*, the family room. This conceptualization parallels their notion of the household, also *biik*, as a unity created by the marriage of a man and a woman (*samiikatn*, husband and wife together before there are children; *sabiikatn*, after there are children).

The *saami'* is the male public portion of the house, open in a main street sort of fashion in a longhouse. The *biik* is the female, private part of the house, enclosed by four walls and usually restricted to family. There are other architectural sections of the house, the *pante*, the unroofed drying platform off the *saami'*, the *pangaro'ng* between the *saami'* and the *biik*, and the *tanga'*, the ladder up to the house door, but these are subsidiary to the *saami'* and *biik* although not physically parts of these. It is worthy of note that while in English it is usually the male term in a male/female pair that serves as the more general term as in the use of 'he' as a general pronoun where either sex is meant, here it is the female member, *biik*, that is used.

Major features of the house are duplicated in the saami' and biik. Each has its own hearth, *dapur*, and skylight, *tinga'atn*. This reflects an activity duplication as well as a cognitive duality. Ordinarily males only use the hearth on the saami' and females only the hearth in the biik. Male indoor ritual cooking is confined to the hearth on the saami'. Sacrificial offerings and prayers are made by male elders at both skylights. Some rituals require oblations to be duplicated at each skylight.

There is a strict sense in which the saami' is the male indoor activity area and the biik is the female indoor activity area. Females spend the great bulk of their indoor time in the biik and very little time on the saami'. Young women in particular work on the pangaro'ng, the passageway down the center of the longhouse between saami' and biik, because this is where rice is processed by pounding on a mortar, *nutuk*, exclusively a woman's task. Except for this task the pangaro'ng serves only as a transitional space between saami' and biik, between indoors and outdoors. In ceremonial contexts women may come out onto the saami', but when they do they almost invariably confine themselves to the biik side of the saami', close to the hearth on the saami'. They may also cross the saami' to go to the unroofed drying platform if they have work there. If there are no men around, women, particularly older women, will come out and use the saami' as a work area on which to weave large mats or husk rice. At festival times, if there is insufficient room at the hearth in the biik, an older woman may come out and cook *tumpi'* (see below) in a wok at the hearth on the saami'. Ordinary family meals are cooked and eaten in the biik. Husked rice, *baras*, is stored in a large jar, *kabarasatn*, in the biik. Women sleep only in the biik. Awang Hasmadi (1978) notes how the saami'/biik opposition is used to symbolize the birth of a male or female newborn.

Men spend most of their indoor time on the saami'. This is their indoor work area. It is where they sit and talk with other men. It is where public religious and political activities take place. Guests who are not family members or close friends are entertained here. Animals are killed on the saami' by men. Bachelor males and male guests always sleep here on the *nangkat*, a raised platform on the opposite side of the saami' from the biik. Married males sometimes sleep here and sometimes in the biik. Awang Hasmadi 1978:9) notes how the saami'/biik opposition is used to symbolize a male or female newborn in the house.

An opposition between high, *tinggi*, status and low, *babah*, status is also associated with the house plan. There seems to be a status gradient from high to low as one moves from the periphery of the house toward the center under the roof. This appears to emphasize the equal rank of male and female. The most male portion of the house, i.e., at the male extremity of the roofed house, is of highest rank as is the most female, i.e., at the female extremity of the house. In a earlier paper (Schneider 1975) I misinterpreted this phenomenon and related it to the positioning of the skylights as avenues to the spirit world.

The primary Sekako subsistence activities are conceived in terms of what is basically a culture/nature opposition. Farming occurs on cleared fields and primarily involves rice (*padi*) which provides the great bulk of calories in the Selako diet and also symbolizes food (and femaleness) for Selako. Hunting occurs primarily in the forest and today involves mostly wild pigs (*babi*). Hunting is exclusively a male activity. Killing animals, wild or domesticated, is a male task. Thus farming is female and hunting is male.

There is a clearly demarcated sexual duality in Selako farming activities. Clearing (*bauma*) is an exclusively male activity. It is sometimes done by a group of men who are clearing contiguous fields, or by a group simply working according to traditional principles of cooperative labor (*baae'*). It may be done by the men of one biik working alone.

After burning, men and women work together to plant (*nuga*) dry fields. Men wield long, heavy, pointed poles (*tuga*), to make holes in the ground into which women drop seed (*banih*). Men work upright, frequently with shirts open or off. Women work stooped over dropping seed, covered from head to foot in turbans, badju and sarong. The complementarity of tasks, tools, posture and dress could hardly be more apparent.[2]

Wet rice planting of seedlings is exclusively a female task. It is usually done by women working singly.

Weeding (*ngarumput*) is usually done by women working alone or in a group. It is supposed to be done a couple of times during the growing season.

The first three days of the harvest (*bahanyi*) are done exclusively by women working on their family's plots. After this the harvest is done by both men and women working in groups according to traditional cooperative labor exchange principles or by families working on their own plots.

Hunting is an exclusively male task carried out singly or in groups, with or without dogs. Wild pig is the usual prey although deer are sometimes brought down and, rarely, bear, monkey, gibbon or various birds. Hunting is like war for Selako. They hunt with spear (*tambak*) and parang (*isot*) as well as shotgun. Hunting and war both require great physical effort, strength, speed, agility and endurance. I hunted with Selako and I took part in a mock war party. They were much the same.

Most food is processed and consumed indoors at the traditional house. Women do the cooking in these circumstances except for special male ritual dishes and ritual occasions. Rice in particular is husked and cooked only by women, at the longhouse, except for the ritual dishes (discussed below). On the other hand, outdoor cooking, away from the house, is invariably done by men, even when women are present as at the planting of a new swidden field by cooperative labor. One or two men will build the fire and cook a soup that does not include rice, for lunch.

Meat cooked indoors in a traditional house is boiled by women. Men roast meat cooked outdoors. This boiling/roasting contrast holds generally for ritual cooking. Men roast. Women boil.

Men work metal, iron in particular, at an open fire with a bellows. One of the village officers, the *Tukang Tampa'*, has this as his only task. Selako say that in the past they mined and smelted iron and made steel, but today they just work preformed metal blanks bought from Chinese merchants.

Baskets and mats are an important traditional industry. Women only do the basketry and mat-weaving, sometimes with decorative patterns (*nyero'*). Men, however, mount the basketwork in wood and rattan frames to complete the basket.

Selako say that only men traditionally painted designs on boards (*oker*) but I saw no examples of this.

Only men do house construction and repairs. They fell trees, make poles and boards, and manufacture atap roofing.

Selako are quite aware of sexuality and concerned with its control. People do not casually expose their genitals even to members of their own sex. Men and women from different families routinely bathe together at the few customary bathing spots in the village, but even when bathing naked as men frequently do, do not expose their genitals.

Married women frequently expose their breasts, sometimes working for hours with a sarong tied at the waist. Breasts do, however, possess some erotic symbolic value because unmarried girls are never supposed to expose their breasts to members of the opposite sex. Young girls begin to cover their chests long before puberty.

Young girls typically wear western-style dresses. Older unmarried girls and married women usually wear sarongs, except on special occasions when they will don Malay-style dress, badju and sarong. The ordinary women's sarong is black.

Men wear western-style shorts sometimes with tee shirts. After bathing in the evening they will frequently wear a plaid sarong. Young children of both sexes up to four or five may run around without any clothes.

Parents are concerned that their young children adopt the appropriate dress style as they get older. I saw a father on the saami' send his four-year old son back to the biik in tears because the boy came out wearing his sister's dress.

Social relations between unmarried Selako of the opposite sex are difficult. Parents monitor their children closely. The cultural ideal is for parents to choose spouses for their children. Girls should marry in their middle to late teens and men not until their middle to late twenties. Girls are expected to be virgins when they marry. Severe penalties are imposed for pregnancy out of wedlock. The family of an unmarried girl who became pregnant paid substantial ritual fines and their house was torn up and symbolically destroyed by other villagers. They were required to sacrifice a pig in expiation for their daughter's wrongdoing. Under normal circumstances, a sacrificed animal would be eaten, but in this case the carcass was thrown away untouched. Broken engagements are serious matters, too, and public opinion weights heavily against the individual who backs out of a planned marriage.

Boys and girls are able to see each other most easily at public occasions such as festivals, national holidays, or rituals where a number of people gather. These frequently go on into the night and give a courting couple some opportunity for privacy. On at least one ritual occasion where people sleep down on the beach, unmarried couples may sleep together. In the ordinary routine of day-to-day life, boys and girls do not get much chance to be together.

There are two principal kinds of marriage for Selako, marriage proper (*nangket* or *nika*) and elopement (*batangkap*). The primary formal difference between the two is that marriage proper involves use of a go-between, *picara*, and thus avoids the potential conflicts inherent in refusal.

Both forms of marriage are initiated with three days of residence at the wife's parents' house followed by three days at the husband's parents'. Thus elopement involves the girl's showing up at home with prospective husband in hand. This severely limits the parents' options. They may accept the young man or risk creating bad feeling between the families. The husband's family visited after three days effectively is unable to prevent the marriage among the uxorilocal Selako and can only accept it or create much bad blood between the families.

There is a sense in which the marriage is not complete until after there have been children born to it. Ritual is minimal until then. Frequently the marriage is recognized by an extensive ritual and feast only after two or three years and one or more children (see Schneider 1985 for an example). It is also not at all unusual for a couple to take up residence at the girl's house and then never sexually consummate the marriage. After a week or so the young man will just slink back to his parents' house.

Selako insist that marital residence is uxorilocal. They go to great lengths to explain away virilocal residence, but about 25 percent of marriages are virilocal. They conceptualize marriage as uxorilocal, but there are clearly discernible rules and patterns that override the strong uxorilocal preference. Among these are the even stronger reluctance to allow a biik to become extinct for lack of heirs and the desire to maximize the younger generation's opportunities by allowing couples to attach themselves to the parental family in the best position to help them (see Schneider 1977 for a discussion of these factors).

Biik have a ritual and economic continuity through time. They are matrilineages. Certain household patterns of ritual, primarily relating to rice, certain rice strains, and rice storage and processing paraphernalia are passed down from the woman of the older generation to the woman of her successor generation, whether her daughter or daughter-in-law. Land belonging to the biik is divided among all the children born in the biik who reside long-term with the biik after marriage.

In conflicts over the use of jointly held land that arise after biik partition, sons always win out over daughters, grandsons over granddaughters, and so on. At least Selako say this should be the case.[3] Controversies appear to seldom get pushed to the point of formal hearings so my data are limited to hypothetical cases.

Marriage creates or regenerates the primary social unit of Selako society, the biik, by joining binary opposite categories, male and female. Once a couple are joined in marriage they become a social unit. They address each other's kin by kin terms and other address terms appropriate to the kin status of their spouse. Any conflicts in kin status are resolved ritually in favor of the closer relationship. They may involve considerable expenditure for a feast and ritual fine.

The household is a unit ritually and economically. Ritual distributions are to the biik as a unit, although the biik's entitlement is through the kinship connections of either husband or wife. Farm land is cultivated by the family as a unit, although husband and wife each have their complementary tasks assigned according to sex as noted above. Husband and wife need each other in order to get along economically according to the Selako traditional division of labor.

Selako kin terms deal with the sex distinction in an unusual way, considering the emphasis they place on it in other areas of culture and behavior. Gender is simply ignored as a dimension of contrast in every generation except for parents' generation, in the traditional Selako kin term system used by Selako who grew up before World War II. In the modern system Selako have adopted the Malay pattern of distinguishing sex among older siblings but not younger.

Selako cosmology strongly reflects the male/female distinction. Above all other deities and spirits are two, a couple, Ne' Panita (male) and Ne' Pangingu (female). These are the most senior and ancient *jubata*. All other creatures, natural and supernatural are descended from these two: *manusia*, humans; *binatang*, animals; and *antu*, supernaturals. But, jubata, who are good and helpful to humans, are in some sense the children of Ne Panita (male) only. Other antu, some of which may be good and some evil, and some equipotential, are the children of both Ne' Panita and Ne' Pangingu. Ne' Panita is also clearly the most senior of all the deities. Humans may not ask anything of Ne' Panita. We have here a clear association of seniority and goodness with a male deity who is opposed to a junior and chaotic (both good and evil mixed) female deity. But, like the husband and wife who together make up the unity of the basic social entity, the biik, these two together make the living world.

Supernaturals are called *antu*, but there are at least two and perhaps three subsidiary categories: *antu* in the sense of spirits who may disturb men (*ngacow ia*) and include the ghosts of the dead; *jubata*, 'deities'; *samangat*, soul substance in the sense of being the powerful but incorporeal essence of some animate or powerful entity. When people or animals die or when people fall sick their *samangat* separates from their bodies and becomes itself a free-standing entity.

The Afterworld, where go the souls of the dead and sick, is made up of several stages. The souls of the sick and the dead for whom there has been no *baiatn* ritual (see below) go to an initial station where they come under the authority of jubata according to their marital status and sex: SiDarada' for bachelor males; SiPuti for unmarried girls; Mundu for married males; and Andara Binse for married females.

Small houses are built for the souls of the most dead adults. The *samangat* resides there until the baiatn ritual can be held to usher them off to *Pulo Pandan Barani*. Such a house for a male is termed *panca* and for a female *padu'ng* (see Ingai [1968]). The male panca is erected on the ground off the pante side of the house, the side closest to the saami', the male portion of the house. The female padu'ng is erected on the *uatn*, the plot of ground next to the biik or female side of the house. The soul houses also differ somewhat in decoration.

Ritual performance is almost completely a male function. In practice only men are priests, the primary performers and directors of ritual acts who come by their roles through years of apprenticeship. Selako suggest the possibility of women's occupying the highest priestly office, but there have been none since the early part of this century. Where women perform ritually, they do so under the direction of men. Sometimes women are, however, the central focus of ritual, either as members of their sex as in the *batinek* and *babuis* rituals discussed below (as well as in the birth rituals described by Awang Hasmadi Awang Mois (1978) or as individuals who simply happen to be women.

Baiatn is the most important Selako household ritual. It may be employed in a number of circumstances, but its central focus and intent is a journey to the

Afterworld by the *Tuha Baiatn* to either retrieve lost souls or escort souls of the dead on the initial phases of their long journey to *Sabayatn*. The baiatn ritual and office originates mythically with a female jubata. But, since early in this century the Tuha Baiatn has always been a man among the Selako with which I am most familiar. Earlier, from the founding of Kampong Pueh in 1875 until late in the next decade the only Tuha Baiatn at Pueh was a woman. She continued to share this office with two men, one her elder brother, until the early part of this century. Note however that there have only been four Tuha Baiatn in this village since it was founded.

Ngoncong is an exotic, foreign ritual that has become popular among Selako. It is a shamanistic performance supposedly borrowed from the almost extinct Lundu Dayaks who were the aboriginal inhabitants of the area. Its sole performer during the period of my research is a nearly blind, half-Lundu, half-Selako shaman from a distant village. It too involves journeys to the spirit world to reclaim the souls of the sick, but I am not sure it is the same spirit world as in baiatn. The principal spirit that plays a part in the ritual by actually possessing the shaman is a snake.

A popular and attention-grabbing feature of ngoncong is the dancing girls, *koncong*, that accompany the tukang koncong. They do not appear to play a central role in the ritual. They are a sort of sideshow in which they entertain patrons from the audience who pay for the privilege of sitting on kain-draped benches up front and having the girls dance to them, light their cigarettes, etc. This all takes place during periods of rest for the shaman whose performance is an exhausting one requiring frequent breaks. In spite of the subsidiary nature of the girls' performance in the ostensible purpose of the whole ritual, Selako think of the ritual in terms of the girls' performance. This may not be so for the family who sponsors the ritual and are attempting to achieve a cure.

Basunat is the Selako male-initiation ritual. It involves ritual activities lasting over four days with its central focus the superincision of the initiate's penis at dawn on the first day. I was told that in past times the boy would go out and seek a head immediately after the end of a period of seclusion and rest (Awang Hasmadi Awang Mois [1981] gives a detailed description of the Basunat ritual).

Batinek is the ritual piercing of a girl's ears that usually occurs sometime before puberty. It is the closest female analog to the male basunat ritual, but it is far from being nearly as important. Only some Selako girls have the ritual and often a number of girls, in one case as many as five, have the ritual together. The tukang tinek is an older woman just as the knife wielder in the basunat ritual is a male elder. But the male elder is a village officer specifically charged with this duty, the Tukang Sunat, whereas the tukang tinek is simply an older woman. The ritual elements in the batinek are handled by male priests; the tukang tinek simply wields the needle.

Baransa is a symbolic tooth filing that is performed for a very few girls of high rank. The only time I saw this performed it was held at the same time as a batinek, but in this case the stone file was wielded by a man. Evidently the intent is to reduce the points of the girls teeth so she is less animalistic.

Basangsam is a ritual closing of the village that occurs at the very end of the hungry season and involves the people closing up their houses for two nights and a day while the antu from the forests and surrounding countryside roam the village.

Ngarantika is the festival that initiates the harvest season a week or two after basangsam. Women from each household, led by the wife of the *Tuha Binua*, the ritually premier village officer, go out to harvest the first of the dry rice for three consecutive days. Each day they prepare the ritual rice dishes. Ngarantika is the principal village feast of the year. The first night there is dancing and carrying on all night long. People visit from other villages and even other ethnic groups.

There are two *babuis* rituals held each year at the *pabuisatn*, an altar in the village. The first of these, *babuis minta' pakama'ng*, comes after ngarantika but before the bulk of the harvest and involves the sacrifice of chickens and presentation of offerings of ritual rice dishes in order to persuade the jubata to cause the padi in the fields and the storehouses to increase. The second is *babuis padingan banih* several months later when people are beginning to plan the clearing of new fields for next year and involves sacrifices and offerings to do with the potency of the seed for next year. In both of these ceremonies women, again led by the wife of the Tuha Binua, carry their offerings from each household out to the altar and sit separately from the men in a group behind the Tuha Binua who addresses the jubata from the altar. The men sit in front of the altar. The spirit ladder up to the altar is situated opposite from its position on the guna altar in the forest at the start of basangsam. It is toward the rising sun.

The rituals described above illustrate, delineate and perform the male/female opposition among Selako. Basunat, the male initiation, is unequivocally male in a number of very obvious ways. Basangsam, the closing of the village, appears also to be male, although the reasons this should be so are not as apparent. Ngarantika and babuis highlight the distinctive female association with rice. The other rituals described all call attention to the male/female difference.

Males are the priests, the principal performers in all the rituals described. Where women take part, they are only passive participants or they act under the direction of the priests. It is always a male who actually mediates between spirits and humans. The only exception here is the oral history and myth of the female Tuha Baiatn.

Women are associated with the rice rituals: ngarantika, the initial harvest, and the babuis rituals. Note however that there are other rice rituals not discussed here where women do not play as prominent a role.

Men always kill sacrificial animals, catch their blood, butcher their flesh. More on rice and blood below.

Men seem to be more closely associated with the tempat guna, the altar in the forest used at the beginning of basangsam, the ritual closing of the village; women with the pabuisatn altar in the village used for babuis. The first has a tanga' toward the setting sun and seems to be dedicated to unfriendly antu; the pabuisatn altar has its spirit ladder toward the rising sun and invites friendly jubata.

Rice is the ideal Selako food. It supplies most of the calories in the Selako diet, it is the object of most Selako rituals, and plays a material part in all Selako rituals of which we are aware. Rice is unambiguously female. Particularly in its processed and cooked forms it is extremely female, if we can imagine a continuum from the merely female to the extremely female. The household rice strains are under the guardianship of the senior female household head, inherited in the household line of descent. Rice is planted by females, and the initial harvest is by females only. Females do all the rice processing except for the initial threshing which separates the rice grains from the debris of harvest (and even this is done only by women during the three ritual days of ngarantika). Only females may husk, pound and cook rice.

Cooking, of course, makes food and perhaps people as well, cultural (Levi-Strauss 1969). Much the same could be said for all food processing, and rice undergoes much processing. Boiling as opposed to roasting is a female process. Women boil foods on the hearth in the private, female portion of the house. Men roast on the hearth in the male, public portion of the house and out-of-doors. Women do not roast food (cf. Levi-Strauss 1978;479-495). Frying is like boiling in that it involves cooking in a metal pot by immersion in a liquid. It is therefore female cooking.

There are three ritual rice dishes that are prominent in all Selako rituals in the house and village. These are always presented on a brass pedestaled tray (*apar*) to guests and family at any in-door ritual. They are an important part of offerings at any blood sacrifice (chickens or pigs) to the antu where they are presented on either the brass, pedestaled tray in the house or the bamboo *moso'ng* outdoors. They are included in the distributions of rice and pork given out each time a pig is ritually killed.

Pue' is a sweet confection of rice and coconut milk boiled in long thin bamboo cylinders by roasting over a male hearth. It is a rice dish, and as such female, but is the most male of the rich dishes. It is prepared by unmarried males who pour the ingredients into the phallic tubes and roast them over the male hearth.

Tumpi' is a pancake made of rice flour fried in a wok on the female hearth. It is extremely female in that it is not only rice cooked by women using a female cooking technique, frying, but is processed into flour by women.

Bonto'ng are small leaf-wrapped packages of rice grains inserted with water into a large bamboo cylinder and roasted over the male hearth by the boys. The packages are prepared by married women.

The primarily female rice dishes thus present us with several nice contrasts. Natural, wild bamboo is opposed to cultural metal pots and woks. Phallic bamboo opposes womb-like metal containers. Male hearths and unmarried boys oppose married women at female hearths. Roasting opposes cooking by immersion in a hot liquid. What is suggested by all this is an association of male, unmarried status, roasting, and bamboo as opposed to an association of female, married status, boiling/frying and metal pots.

Meat/blood clearly symbolizes the male, not only because of its similarity to hunted wild pig, but because it seems to be handled only by men (except when it is boiled for a feast meal) prior to offering or distribution. The blood/meat of sacrificial animals complements the female rice. In the rice offering to the spirits scattered over the drying platform from the saami' the rice is mixed with blood and perhaps bits of liver. In the distributions of ritual packages, *epet*, the packages are made up of the three ritual rice dishes and pork. In sacrificial offerings, *buis*, presented to the spirits on apar or moso'ng, both meat and the ritual rice dishes are employed.

Selako use of rice and meat/blood in offerings suggests an interesting perception of the male/female binary opposition, one that is both binary and continuous. Rice and meat/blood are clearly in opposition representing female and male respectively. But the three ritual rice dishes while all female also embody a continuum with the poles males and female. Pue' is a long, phallic cylinder of sweet rice in bamboo roasted (a male method of cooking) at the male hearth on the saami' by bachelors. Tumpi' is a fat cake of sweetened rice flour fried (a female method of cooking) in a wok by married women at the female hearth in the biik. These represent the polar opposition of male and female on dimensions of shape, method of cooking, place of cooking, and sex of cook. Bonto'ng, on the other hand, is in between on all of these apparently binary dimensions. While like pue' the complete package is a bamboo cylinder, bonto'ng is a fat cylinder (four to six inches by two feet, approximately) unlike the thin stick of pue' (one-and-half of two inches by two feet, approximately) and the individual leaf-wrapped packages of bonto'ng are neither phallic nor womb-like. Bonto'ng is boiled (a female method of cooking) in water brought to the boiling point by roasting (a male method of cooking) inside a bamboo cylinder. The individually leaf-wrapped packages of bonto'ng are prepared by married women in the biik but are roasted in their fat bamboo cylinders by unmarried boys on the male hearth on the saami'. Thus the gender distinction as represented in the ritual rice dishes is not one of polar opposition but rather has two poles and an intermediate position. If these ritual rice dishes are as central to Selako thought as they are central to Selako ritual this suggests an approach to the conceptualization of sexuality among the Selako for which we have no behavioral reflexes in the field observations discussed above.

The male/female contrast is at the root of Selako ideas about office holding and political legitimacy. This in spite of the fact that males hold all the principal chiefly offices. As a binary opposition it is also one of several, perhaps the principal one, that structures the complex of village offices and formal models of Selako social organization.

Selako villages require eight offices, *lapan isarat*, in order to be full, independent villages. These are as follows in order of ritual primacy with loose glosses that are not all literal translations but are close to what I believe are accurate renderings in English:

Tuha Binua	Lord of the Land
Tuha Kampo'ng	Lord of the Village
Tuha Baiatn	Lord of the Spirits
Tuha Laut	Lord of the Sea
Bidan	Midwife
Tukang Sunat	Circumcisor

Tukang Tampa'   Blacksmith
Pangarah Uma   Priest of the Fields

While there are several dimensions of binary opposition present here, let us focus on the male/female dimension. Clearly Bidan represents a female pole. She is always a female and her sole duty is to attend women in childbirth. Equally clearly the circumcisor (actually the process is one of superincision) is male since he always is a male and his sole "function is to cut the foreskin of the penis in order to initiate boys." The circumcision ritual is clearly associated with headhunting, and this suggests that Selako represent in the bidan/tukang sunat opposition the same opposition of headhunting and childbirth proposed by Rosaldo and Atkinson (1975) for the Ilongot of Luzon. The Lord of the Spirits may be conceptually female. In the origin myth a female jubata gives the office to a female ancestor. A woman occupied this office for perhaps forty years of the hundred-year history of the village. The Priest of the Fields is a male, but there may be a sense in which the office is female. The Priest of the Fields conducts magic in the rice fields. He also shares ritual duties with the Lord of the Land at the pabuisatn during the two babuis rituals where women and rice are primary foci of the ritual. The Blacksmith office is probably conceptually male. He is always a male (as is the Priest of the Fields). He works on metal for male tools, manufacturing or at least tempering *isot* (parang) and *insaut* (a small blade with a long wooden handle). The Lord of the Land is always referred to as the leader of the men of the village.

I am most uncertain about the statuses of the Lord of the Sea and the Lord of the Village. *Rumah* ('house') is frequently opposed to *uma* ('field') (in spite of the fact that these are from the same Austronesian root) in terms of ritual sites with, for example, offerings being necessary at both if a pig is killed for *ngabayatn* (the household rice storage ritual). It is worthy of note that if there is no uma then sacrifice is offered in the biik (female) section of the house when a pig is killed. Thus the female section is a substitute for the uma suggesting that the uma is female and the rumah male. If this line of reasoning is correct then the Lord of the Village office is male. The Lord of the Sea is clearly opposed to the Lord of the Land in the Land/Sea opposition. Is it also opposed in a male/female opposition? The Lord of the Land is frequently described as the leader of the village men, and his wife explicitly represents the village women at the harvest (ngarantika) and babuis rituals. It may, of course, also be that the Lord of the Sea and the Lord of the Village simply don't discriminate on the male/female dimension.

Selako officeholders claim office on the basis of ability and katurunan or family line. An officeholder should be from a lineage of officeholders, particularly of the office he claims. Furthermore a family has great legitimacy and prestige if it can claim to possess *pusaka*, a sacred inheritance given to ancestors by jubata (cf. Errington 1987:406, 423). The only such sacred pusaka among the Sarawak Selako was held by the chiefly family that controlled Kampong Pueh at the time I was there. My fieldnotes read, "A woman guards and keeps pusaka but a man bakuasa ['controls it']." The man must observe certain food taboos in order to use the pusaka. At the beginning of every month ritual rice dishes are presented to the pusaka in the biik were it is kept. People ask pusaka for help as if it is an antu and sacrifice to it as well. During the period of field research the Lord of the Land controlled the pusaka and his sister who lived next door in the senior biik in the main longhouse kept it. Thus in order for pusaka to function to lend political legitimacy to a chiefly family male and female must combine to hold it just as male and female combine in blood and rice for the sacrificial offerings to the antu and as husband and wife in making a biik family, sabiikatn.

Gender roles and ideology among the Selako evidence a society where men are clearly awarded more prestige than women in subsistence, political, and religious spheres. Although premarital sexual activity is harshly condemned and punished, women may file for divorce. Their cases are heard before the village authorities. Typically, a divorced woman returns home to her parents but soon finds another husband. Extramarital sex is condemned for both men and women.

Ambilineal descent patterns, coupled with a preponderance of uxorilocal marriages helps a woman maintain close lifelong relationships with her parents and village friends. An absence of bride price and the rarity of extravillage virilocality contribute to a relatively positive picture of female status.

While men generally hold all political offices, the Selako deny that political offices are closed to women. In the 19th century a woman temporarily held the highest village office, Lord of the Land. Women can and do voice opposition to the decisions made by officials and have the power to strongly influence the selection of village officers. Shortly after I arrived in Kampong Pueh I was told that an election for Lord of the Village which I witnessed the week before had been overturned because the women (who did not vote) were displeased with the result. Men's ceremonies are more elaborate than women's, and religious positions are dominated by men. Parents view daughters as at least as desirable as sons, since daughters are more likely to ultimately live near them and support them in their old age. Selako do not freely discuss sexual matters, and it is difficult to assess the frequency of or their attitudes toward homosexuality or other sexual practices. There is, however, some evidence that women are thought of as polluted or ritually dangerous for men to be near during initiation rites.

The male/female binary contrast permeates all spheres of Selako activity. Gender symbolism is important in food, dress, funerals, rituals of the annual cycle, and longhouse architecture. A structuralist interpretation of Selako gender symbolism reveals an integrated Selako culture based on a cognitive and economic division by sex. A review of Selako subsistence and ritual activities demonstrates a congruence between symbolism and actual social relations.

NOTES

1. The field research on which this paper is based was conducted between October 1969 and July 1971. It was sponsored by the Sarawak Museum and funded by a National Science Foundation Dissertation Enrichment award.

2. I have seen men working on their own fields drop seed in the holes if there are not enough women workers.

3. My fieldnotes read as follows in this:

"Mina [the Lord of the Land] is very definite in saying that men only bakuasa tanah. Ambini ana' dapat balawan. Akie numpang kahe, jaji ana' dapat." Translation: 'men only control land. Women can't fight it. Their husbands are just guests, thus they can't do it.'

"The eldest male resident in the kampong bakuasa ('controls') because he knows where the ancestral land is, he helped clear some of it, he worked longest with his father thus his knowledge is superior to any other's.

A father doesn't teach his daughters about these things as he does his sons, thus even if a daughter is eldest she doesn't know as much about what land they own and where are the borders as does a son."

4. According to Awang Hasmadi Awang Mois (1981, endnote 14) the Bidan and Tukang Sunat are explicitly associated.

REFERENCES

Awang Hasmadi Awang Mois
   1978   Beliefs and Practices Concerning Births among the Selako of Sarawak. Sarawak Museum Journal 26:7-13.

   1981   Selako Circumcision. Sarawak Museum Journal 29:59-72.

Errington, Shelly
   1987   Incestuous Twins and the House Societies of Insular Southeast Asia. Cultural Anthropology: Journal of the Society for Cultural Anthropology 2:403-444.

Freeman, J. Derek
   1958   The Family System of the Iban of Borneo. In The Developmental Cycle in Domestic Groups. Jack Goody, ed. Pp. 15-52. Cambridge: Cambridge University Press.

   1970   Report on the Iban. London School of Economics Monographs on Social Anthropology No. 41. London: The Athlone Press.

Geddes, W. R.
   1957   Nine Dayak Nights. New York: Oxford University Press.

Goodenough, Ward H.
1956   Componential Analysis and the Study of Meaning.
                      Language 32:195-216.

Ingai, Joseph
1968   Pancha and Padong Origins. Sarawak Museum Journal
                      16:195-199.

Leach, Edmund R.
1976   Culture and Communication. New York: Cambridge
                      University Press.

Levi-Strauss, Claude
1963   Structural Anthropology. New York: Basic Books.

1969a   The Elementary Structures of Kinship. London: Eyre &
                      Spottiswoode.

Levi-Strauss, Claude
1969b   The Raw and the Cooked: Introduction to a Science of
                      Mythology 1. New York: Harper & Row.

1978   The Origin of Table Manners: Introduction to a Science
                      of Mythology 3. New York: Harper & Row.

Lounsbury, Floyd G.
1964   The Structural Analysis of Kinship Semantics. In Pro-
                      ceedings of the 9th International Congress of Linguistics.
                      H. G. Hunt, ed. Pp. 1073-1092. The Hague: Mouton & Co.

MacCormack, Carol P.
1980   Nature, Culture and Gender: a Critique. In Nature,
                      Culture and Gender. Carol P. MacCormack and Marilyn
                      Strathern, eds. New York: Cambridge University Press.

Ortner, Sherry B.
1974   Is Female to Male as Nature Is to Culture? In Woman,
                      Culture, and Society. Michelle Zimbalist Rosaldo and
                      Louise Lamphere, eds. Stanford: Stanford University
                      Press.

Ortner, Sherry B. and Harriet Whitehead
    1981   Introduction: Accounting for Sexual Meanings. In Sexual Meanings: The Cultural Construction of Gender and Sexuality. Sherry B. Ortner and Harriet Whitehead, eds. Pp. 1-27. New York: Cambridge University Press.

Rosaldo, M. Z. and Jane Atkinson.
    1975   Man the Hunter and Woman. In Roy Willis, ed., The Interpretation of Symbolism, London, Malaby, pp. 43-75.

Schneider, William M.
    1975   Aspects of the Architecture, Sociology and Symbolism of the Selako House. Sarawak Museum Journal 23:207-219.

    1977   The *Biik* Family of the Selako Dayak of Western Borneo. Studies in Third World Societies 3:139-166.

    1985   A Selako Household Festival. Sarawak Museum Journal 34:51-66.

KADAYAN MEN AND WOMEN

ALLEN R. MAXWELL
The University of Alabama

INTRODUCTION

Approximately thirty years ago in his thought-provoking study of Islamic societies of South Asia and the Middle East, *Islam in Modern History* (1957), Wilfred Cantwell Smith recognized one of the important differences between the Islamic societies of Southeast Asia and those of the historical core area of this great tradition. He noted that Indonesia, and particularly Java, possessed the only "strong and ancient indigenous liberalism" in the Muslim world. Smith, a life-long student of the Islamic religion, suggests that there is something quite distinctive about the Southeast Asian approach to Islam, and that this perspective has something vital to contribute to the rest of the Muslim world. He pointed to the position of women in Islamic society and wondered if indeed this was not the only Muslim area that had never known the veil (Smith 1957:296).[1] Why should there be such a marked difference in the relations of men and women between the Islamic cultures of the Middle East and those of Southeast Asia? As will be seen in the case of the Kadayan of Brunei, it is a complex set of economic factors, tempered by underlying cultural values, which fundamentally conditions how men and women interact in society.[2] Only by examining the contributions of both males and females to economic and social life can we achieve a balanced understanding of relations between men and women in a Southeast Asian Islamic society (cf. Nissim-Sabat 1987:937). My purpose here is to construct a realistic picture of the roles of men and women in Kadayan social life as an example of one such Southeast Asian Muslim society.

Social relationships between Kadayan men and women have been shaped by the nature of their traditional subsistence economy, and particularly the demands it makes on the organization and scheduling of human activities. Patterns of interpersonal interaction are influenced primarily by the labor requirements of the Kadayan swidden rice regime, and secondarily by the labor needs of the other sectors of their food-getting economy. Kadayan social organization can thus be viewed as an overall solution to the general problem of how they obtain adequate food resources by exploiting the surrounding environment. Interactions between men and women thus become an important focus for the understanding of Kadayan social organization because of the patterns of cooperation on which the operation of their subsistence economy is built. In recent times there has been a movement away from these traditional patterns of relationships, as the influences of modernization, Westernization, and the expansion and intensification of formal Islamic teachings are increasingly felt in Brunei.[3] These new developments will modify traditional modes of interaction by altering the roles which men and women have played in subsistence production. Thus a new set of patterns of relationships between men and women are likely to emerge in the future, the shape of which has not yet begun to emerge clearly.

THE DIVISION OF LABOR AND FOOD PRODUCTION

Both men and women make important contributions to the economic life of a household. It is the household, usually consisting of at least one conjugal pair, that is the basic unit of both production and consumption. Because of the Kadayan rule of uxorilocal postmarital residence, a household may contain more that one conjugal pair. This unit will eventually fission when the young couple sets up their own household and domestic economy, and establishes their own rice fields. Any family thus oscillates between a nuclear and an expanded structure. If a family contains a number of daughters, the household will experience a succession of expansions and fissionings over time. At the other extreme, the old widow living alone is pitied. For economic and social purposes, she is usually attached to another household (normally that of a primary kinsman) as a satellite.

The routine of subsistence activities takes up the major share of a normal day's time, with the amount and type of work varying with the seasons. While increasing numbers of men in recent years have been taking up wage labor on a part-time basis, they continue to maintain a more or less traditional pattern of subsistence activities.[4] This situation is likely to change in the near future as more members of the younger generation pursue educational training, with hopes of obtaining positions in Brunei's burgeoning civil service. If this trend continues, the proportion of Brunei's population living in rural villages will probably decrease, and a larger proportion will live in urban and suburban settings.

1.   Subsistence Agriculture

Traditionally the Kadayan cultivated rice by swidden or shifting field techniques.   Earlier in the the 20th century British advisors encouraged the adoption of permanent field rice agriculture in Brunei. These new techniques were taken up by some Kadayan, especially by those living around the capital in Brunei District, which has always been a more densely settled area than other parts of the country. The Kadayan living in Temburong District were practicing both shifting and permanent field rice agriculture during my stay in Brunei.

Kadayan women make important contributions to agricultural production in a number of ways. They do a great deal of the laborious but less arduous work involved in cultivation. Women carry out all of the transplantation of rice seedlings and weeding in permanent rice fields. A number of tasks are shared by both men and women. These include dibbling and sowing, final preparation of fields, preparing seedlings from the seed beds for transplantation, and guarding and harvesting the ripe rice. Men execute the more strenuous tasks, such as carrying the large baskets (*lasuk*) heavily laden with the newly harvested rice to the granary (*durung*), which may be located either near the home (*rumah*) or the permanent rice field hut (*junjung*). Men also are in charge of swidden site selection, the management of water in permanent fields, transporting the seedlings from seed beds to the permanent fields for transplanting, and drying the newly harvested crop as soon as it has been harvested. Some of their work, including the felling of large trees and the burning of dried vegetation on swidden plots, can involve considerable danger. The general Kadayan pattern of the division of labor in agriculture is thus very similar to that described for the Iban by Freeman (1955:77-80).

One of the greatest opportunities for young unmarried men and women to make new acquaintances occurs during the special kind of labor exchange known as *pucangan* which is called for a variety of agricultural activities requiring more labor than a single household can supply. Large cooperative work parties of men, women, and older children are often assembled for the transplantation (*tanam*) of rice seedlings in permanent fields, and especially for the harvest (*katam*) of both the swidden and permanent field crops. The larger exchanges can include representatives from the majority of households in a village, members of other villages, and village children returning home for a weekend or holiday, when they often bring along schoolmates from other parts of the country. Smaller labor exchanges may be called for felling trees (*tabang*) and brush (*tabas*), and for dibbling (*tugal*) swidden fields, as well as building new houses and replacing decayed roofs. These tasks, however, are usually carried out exclusively by men. Timing is one of the primary determinants in calling a *pucangan*. When there is a pressing need for a task to be completed expeditiously, and the labor available within the household is insufficient to do so, then a *pucangan* will be called. Calling one of these work parties encumbers both cost and obligation. A large midday meal must be prepared for all participants, and the caller is obligated to return the favor by joining similar parties whenever they may be called by any of the participants in the future. There is a great deal of interaction between all participants, both male and female, and the high levels of sociability and conviviality expressed are much savored and enjoyed by the Kadayan.

EXCLUSIVELY FEMALE ACTIVITIES	JOINT ACTIVITIES OF BOTH SEXES	EXCLUSIVELY MALE ACTIVITIES
		site selection
		felling (*tabang*)
	light slashing (*tabas*)	heavy slashing (*tabas*)
	plot soil preparation	burning (*tunu*)
transplanting (*tanam*)	dibbling (*tugali*)	seedling transportation
weeding (*rumputi*)	seedling preparation	inundation & drainage
	crop guarding (*jaga*)	crop drying (*jamur*)
	harvesting (*katam*)	crop transportation

TABLE 1
Division of Labor by Sex in the Rice Cultivation Cycle

After the rice has been stored in the granary the next steps in the conversion of the crop into food lie in the hands of women. Rice is taken from the granary, dried (*dijamur*) again on mats in the village, trampled (*dilumak*) to separate the grains from the tops of the panicles, and then husked (*ditutuk*) in a mortar and pestle (*lasung*) or by a gasoline-powered hulling machine (*inggin*). If the grain is husked in a mortar and pestle, the chaff is winnowed away in the wind by tossing it in a *ngiru*, a shallow, wide tray woven from split bamboo. Now the rice is ready for cooking. Women normally husk enough rice at one time for the needs of a few days' meals. This preparation process, which forms part of the rhythm of daily village life, is a never ending one for a woman and constitutes a critical form of the labor she contributes to the well-being of her household.

2.   Other Subsistence Tasks

Most of the Kadayan in Temburong District still have easy access to large stands of forest, and continue to obtain large amounts of their flesh foods by fishing, trapping, and hunting. The resources of the tropical rain forest also yield large amounts of wild fruits and vegetables, as well as a wide range of economic products used for traditional constructional and manufacturing purposes.

Women collect wild foods from the rain forest such as bamboo shoots (*rabung*), fresh mushrooms (*kulat*), and numerous kinds of fruit (*buah*), often in the company of female friends and children. Men often accompany them on longer trips to collect fruit in stands far from the village. The inflorescences (*umbut*) of wild palms are harvested by men, as the trees must be searched out and felled in the forest before the cabbage can be extracted. Little girls can often be seen late in the afternoon wandering through the village collecting arm loads of young wild fern fronds (*pakis, Nephrolepis*) which grow in the scrub and grass (*samak*) throughout the settlement. This fern, when stir fried with spices and other condiments and served with rice, makes a quick and very tasty evening meal, although not one highly valued by the Kadayan themselves. Women and girls also collect tender young fronds of ferns (*piay sungay*) growing along the banks of the river from a dugout canoe. These can be stir fried or cooked as a watery vegetable dish.

Women join men and older children in fishing expeditions that involve damming a small stream with a tubular fish trap (*bubu*) embedded in the center of a barricade (*sawar*) of poles, branches, and leaves. The fish are then driven downstream into the trap. Men also place fish traps in the drainage ditches separating permanent rice fields, or lining both sides of the main footpaths leading to the fields. These traps are submerged in the water and usually left unattended overnight. In another approach women will plant set-poles with lines and baited hooks (*pancing*) in the mud along the banks of a small stream from a dugout canoe (*gubang*). This technique is often utilized by a woman alone with the intention of selling her catch to other villagers as a way of making a small amount of extra cash.

Men will set gill nets (*pukat*) athwart the flow of streams, blocking them completely in headwaters which are impassable to boat traffic, or only partially so as not to impede traffic in the lower reaches of rivers. Men also jack (*suluh*) fish at night with a small brass reflector lamp (*lampung panah*) from dugout canoes, spearing the fish along the banks of a stream with a fish spear (*sangkap*) or small harpoon (*tampuling*).

Small groups of men, women, and older children will sometimes take a boat down stream from the village to search for molluscs (*malukan*). At low tide they scratch along the exposed muddy bank with the back of a blade (normally the all-purpose Malay knife, the parang). The molluscs are located by the sound of the back of the blade scraping against them under the mud, after which they can be dug out.

Women do not participate in most types of hunting and trapping. These activities occasionally take men many miles from the village, following the long lines of snares, and the barricades constructed to guide the game into them, often with their older sons. There is one form of deer hunting in which all villagers join together in pursuit of the quarry; indeed, this activity can only succeed if large numbers of people are involved. If a deer, or sambar (*payaw, Cervus unicolor*), is sighted, attempts are made to drive it into a line of connected sections of a heavy rattan noose snare (*jaring*) which is suspended from forked poles implanted into the ground. Men station themselves just behind the snare line, armed with spears and parangs. Women, children, and other men approach from the opposite side of the deer, shouting, yelling, and beating empty tins with sticks to try to force the deer into the snare so that the men can kill the animal.

Men do all of the routine hunting. The commonest and most popular approach is searching for the small mouse deer (*palanduk, Tragulus spp.*) at night with a jacklight. The light used is a small kerosine-powered brass reflector lamp (*lampung panah*), with the upper end of the glass chimney covered with a top fashioned out of a piece of a tin can. The top prevents the rain from extinguishing the lamp. In this form of hunting the Kadayan take advantage of their knowledge of the behavior of this animal. Hunting takes place only in the middle of the night during a heavy rainstorm. Mouse deer do not like to stand in the water which covers the flat surfaces of the ground in the forest during heavy rains. The animals therefore congregate on small hillocks the locations of which are well known to the men of the village. The small deer are transfixed by the light of the lamp which allows the men to spear them with *sangkuh* (blade mounted on side of shaft), *lambing* (long narrow blade mounted in the center of the shaft), or *bujak* (asymmetrical lanceolate blade mounted in the center of the shaft).

The barking deer (*kijang, Muntiacus muntjak*) is taken with the spring snare (*jarat*), along with a variety of birds (including the emerald dove, *punay tanah, Chalcophaps indica;* the crested fireback pheasant, *hayam hutan, Lophura ignita;* the crested green wood partridge, *surukan, Rollulus rouloul;* the great argus pheasant, male-*karuhay,* female-*tambakaw, Argusianus argus*), and occasionally the common porcupine (*landak,* probably *Hystrix brachyura*). Occasionally a small group of men will join a police officer with his shotgun to hunt the sambar but this form of deer hunting has more of the flavor of a recreational outing than a serious quest for food.

Being Muslim, of course, the Kadayan do not eat wild pigs (*bay, Sus barbata*), but they hunt them as pests when rice fields and vegetable gardens are threatened. Two men in the village kept small packs of dogs for this purpose which they lent out to visiting Iban who wished to secure some fresh wild pork. Because the small valley in which this particular community is located contains no non-Muslim villages, the wild pig population grew unchecked by regular human hunting for food, unlike many other areas of the country.

Most of these methods of food production have probably been in existence for a very long time among the Kadayan. Whether they will continue into the future will depend on a number of other factors, including the development of more extensive networks of land communication, increases in the amounts and types of imported goods, including food, and any expansions of industrial development. Traditional ways of exploiting land animals and birds for food have been possible in part because of the severe restrictions on the possession of firearms in Brunei (two single shot 12 gauge shotguns--held by policemen--per village),[5] and in part by the lack of extensive commercial and industrial activity in most rural areas inhabited by Kadayan. Any dramatic shifts in the relationships among these factors would certainly alter the social roles of men and women in economic activities.

3.   Household Activities

Males and females make different contributions to the maintenance of a Kadayan household. Men are charged with the planning and construction of a house, including the procurement of the materials. Traditionally, wood, rattan, bamboo, nipa palm fronds, and vines were collected from the surrounding forest. A house could be built with little or no need to resort to the purchase of specialized materials. Many houses are still constructed in this manner, with two exceptions. In recent years when building a new house many people have purchased boards from a nearby sawmill when they have the available cash. Probably the most important product of industrial technology which has been enthusiastically adopted is the nail (*paku*), which allows men to save a considerable mount of labor in numerous constructional tasks. In the past all the pieces of a house were joined by lashing them together with vines (*akar*) and split rattans (*rawtan*). Granaries (*durung*) are still primarily built with vine lashings rather than nails. Another modern item utilized by many is the corrugated tin roof. A tin roof (*hatap jing*) lasts for about a decade, approximately the life of three leaf shingle roofs (*hatap dawn*) made of nipa palm fronds. The choice of a leaf roof or a tin roof depends on whether there is sufficient cash on hand for the purchase of the material. Women are involved in the preparation of refreshments which always accompany any cooperative work party, but all of the construction is done by men.

Women perform a wide range of household activities such as making, washing, and mending clothes; and keeping the interior of the house swept and neat. They manage all of the material cultural paraphernalia used in daily household affairs, especially the elaborate arrays of eating utensils (plates--*pinggan, piring, cuik*; bowls--*mangkuk*; cups--*cawan*; glasses--*galas*; trays--*talam*; water bottles--*taranang, butul, kaca*; and spoons--*sinduk, sudu*), which usually accompany all but the most private family meals. Women are regularly assisted by their older daughters in these routine tasks which are so necessary to the efficient running of a household. Any repairs to the house or its contents are carried out by the men.

Females often collect the unexploded fronds of the nipa palm (*pucuk apung*) from dugout canoes for use as cigarette papers (*kiray*) or for weaving various types of baskets (*bahay, bayung*) and mats (*tikar*). Numerous other leaves, grasses, and other plant products are also collected for making mats, baskets (*takiding*), winnowing trays (*ngiru*), and occasionally sun hats (*sirawng*) to protect the head against the strong rays of the sun during the harvest. It is usually the older married women who manufacture these items, rather than younger unmarried girls. The larger pack baskets (*ambin, barangay, garanjang, lasuk*) which are used for carrying heavy loads are manufactured by men from bamboo, sago bark, and rattan.

4.   Eating and Cooking

To a Kadayan, a meal is not a meal unless it includes some form of cooked rice. This important feature of Kadayan thinking is expressed most clearly in the use of the two verbs *makan* and *minum*, whose lexical meanings are, respectively, 'eat' and 'drink'. The verb *makan* 'eat' is used only when one of the items to be consumed is rice (*nasi*). The verb minum 'drink' is used to describe the consumption of all other solid foods, other than rice and liquids. This distinction receives important symbolic expression when a girl's family accepts the request for her hand in marriage from a suitor's representatives (the *bajarum-jarum*). If the girl's family wishes to signal that they have accepted the request but are still uncertain of the boy's worth, they simply neglect to serve the sweet rice cakes (*kalupis*--see Maxwell 1985), and only offer coffee, crackers, cakes, peanuts, and other nonrice foods for refreshments. If the parents-in-law-to-be fully approve of their prospective son-in-law, then the sweet rice cakes will be served.

The preparation and consumption of food by the Kadayan have important behavioral and symbolic correlates. Depending on the purposes and the circumstances involved, the roles of men and women are quite different in each of these activities. The settings in which Kadayan routinely consume food can be analyzed into four types of situations: the private and intimate setting of daily meals, the family setting including invited or accidental guests, and two different types of ritual occasions which can involve a number of families, a whole village, or a multivillage gathering.

In the ordinary meals of everyday life, all the members of a household--men, women, children, and grandparents--eat the food cooked by the wife of the male household head in the kitchen. The kitchen (*surambi*, or *dapur*) is the least formal--and the most private and intimate--room in the house. It is usually smaller and lies a few inches lower than the main room (*indung rumah*). If there are guests for an evening meal, special eating mats are laid out on the floor of the main room of the house. Dishes are then ferried in by the females of the household--the wife, the grandmother, and the daughters--to be consumed by the male members of the household and their male guests. Women and children then eat together in the kitchen after the men have finished their meals.

Ritual meals can be commemorative, as in the case of the initial death feasts, or celebratory, as in the case of the main marriage feast or the final death feast. The initial death feasts are simple meals served after the two evening prayer sessions (*magrip*, at the setting of the sun, and *isa*, just after all the red afterglow of sunset has disappeared). A number of other weekly death feasts (*jumat-jumatan*) are held for several weeks following the death. The death feasts are somber, intimate, and composed of a smaller number of participants, usually only the members of the immediate family and a representative from a number of the other households in the village. These meals are primarily for male participants and are served in the main room of the house by females, much like the everyday meals in which guests are present. Women and girls from the other homes in the village, however, assist in the preparation and serving of the food. The final death feast (*makan ampat puluh hari*) includes a much larger number of participants and celebrates the ending of the period of mourning, 40 days after the death of a family member.

The celebratory feasts include a larger number of participants and represent one of the highlights of Kadayan life exemplifying those features of social life most highly valued by the Kadayan themselves: conviviality, sociality, and all-around good cheer. A large number of guests participate, and in the case of marriage feasts the number of celebrants may be so large as to necessitate eating in shifts in the special temporary structures (*taratak*) erected just for the occasion.

These large celebratory feasts are always cooked out of doors by men. Very large handleless woks (*kawah*) are set up on sets of three or four short stakes (*tungku*, or *tumang*) implanted in the ground to cook the rice and curry dishes. The large number of guests at these feasts usually eat in the temporary structures attached at the end of a house. Male children may eat in these structures in a group after the adult males have finished, or individually with their fathers in the case of very small boys. Women and female children usually eat together in the house after at least some of the men have finished eating.

The pattern of living just described existed at the time of my research in Brunei and represents a fairly traditional mode of life, in the judgments of both villagers as well as urban dwellers, who now pursue a less traditional style of life. In a traditional style of life the work of men and women is marked by a high degree of cooperation. The Kadayan do not elaborate a conceptual distinction between "men's work" and "women's work", although there clearly are some tasks which are carried out primarily by men and others by women.[6]

SYMBOLIC

		PRIVATE	PUBLIC
B			
E			
H			
A	FAMILIAL	private, intimate	family meals
V		family meals	with guests
I			
O		smaller, intimate	larger festive
R	SUPRA-FAMILIAL	death feasts	meals
A			
L			

TABLE 2
Types of Kadayan Meals

The relationships between men and women and the roles that they play in subsistence production are changing in modern Brunei. As increasing numbers of youngsters achieve higher levels of education, and are drawn into employment in Brunei's large state bureaucracy, traditional patterns of production will be increasingly supplanted by a greater dependence on the products imported from industrialized economies. The large and increasing urban population of Brunei has depended heavily on imported rice since the end of World War II. Most of the food obtained from individual efforts in agriculture, fishing, hunting, and foraging remains in the rural areas, and has been consumed primarily by its producers, for at least the last several decades.

The performance of routine tasks of house construction and maintenance, as well as the traditional types of cooking, by males and females in Kadayan society, are very much geared to a traditional way of life. Greater reliance on wage and salaried employment will result in even greater dependence on market-supplied goods and services, as people have less time and motivation to continue their traditional techniques of food production. As the Kadayan become increasingly dependent upon organized markets for these goods and services, it seems likely that the types of symbiotic-like sharing of labor tasks which have characterized their pattern of life in the past will be modified. It is difficult to predict how and to what extent such changes may alter the kind of "indigenous liberalism", which Smith identifies in Southeast Asian Islamic societies.

THE SOCIAL SYSTEM

Social relations in Kadayan society are firmly anchored in the ethics and morality of kinship rights, obligations, and duties. There are no kinship based groups other than the family and the village. Families may be either nuclear or extended in type. The difference between the two types is primarily an artifact of either the interaction of the uxorilocal postmarital residence rule and the ages of daughters at marriage, or the application of the ideal rule which specifies that aging parents should be accepted into the household of their youngest married child. Any particular family is likely to oscillate between these two types diachronically, depending on which of these particular conditions applies at any particular time.

1.   The Kinship System and Social Life

The Kadayan kinship terminological system is Hawaiian Type in Ego's own generation, in both reference and address, and Generational Type in the parental generation. Two of its most salient semantic characteristics concern the specification of sex of relative and the bifurcation of all kinsmen into categories of senior vs. junior.

The sex of a designated relative is obligatorily marked only in the parental generation by the classificatory terms *mama* 'mother' and *bapa* 'father'. All other terms (excepting *bini* 'wife' and *laki* 'husband') are neutral with regard to the sex of the designated relative. But even in the parental generation, the sex distinction in the terms for mother and father can be neutralized by the use of the classificatory term for parent, *indung*.[7]

All terms for kinsmen in generations other than Ego's express the obligatory semantic differentiation of seniority (the terms for kinsmen in ascending generations) and juniority (the terms for kinsmen in descending generations). In Ego's own generation the meaning of the single classificatory term *sudara* 'sibling' can be optionally differentiated by specifying a relative as belonging to one of its two constituent classificatory subclasses, *kaka* 'older sibling' or *adi* 'younger sibling', depending on whether the relative is older or younger than Ego. In ordinary conversation this option is commonly taken. Thus all relatives are structurally either senior or junior to Ego.

Behaviorally both of these distinctions, sex of designated relative, and relative age with respect to Ego, are very important in Kadayan social life. Same sex and intersex behavior will be discussed shortly. The seniority/juniority distinction has far reaching implications for interpersonal behavior, especially in conditioning the degrees of liberty or familiarity one should take with a relative. Juniors should be respectful of their seniors, and should not initiate joking behavior with them. Joking and horseplay--both physical and verbal--are common pastimes in Kadayan life. But a man, for example, should not initiate joking behavior with his elder brother; he should treat with him with respectful decorum. On the other hand it is perfectly acceptable for a man to initiate these behaviors with his juniors, or with other men outside of his own family who are approximately his own age.

2.   Public vs. Private Social Life

One of the most striking features of Kadayan social life is the difference which can be observed in the interactions of males and females in private and public settings. This discussion is based primarily on my own observations. Informants' ideas on this subject tend, I believe, to be colored by ideology, as will be made clear in a later part of this discussion.

When one visits friends in their own homes, social relations between the sexes tend to be quite open and relaxed. After I had gotten to know people fairly well I was free to talk to anyone--male or female, old or young--on just about any matter.[8] Often during interview sessions at night after the evening meal, even though I might be interviewing the male household head, anyone who felt like it could comment on or enter into the discussion. At this point I might end up conversing with the man's mother, wife, or older daughter for a while, before returning to my earlier conversation. Females would often correct male informants in this setting if they felt that incorrect information had been given.[9] On other occasions, especially in a family I was particularly close to, I might be asked on the spur of the moment to join them for an evening meal. In such cases we would all eat together in the kitchen, at the same time.

In situations which involved members of other households in the village, the social character of meals in a household becomes somewhat more formal. If guests are specially invited (as I often was), males all eat together on mats in the main room of the house and are served by the females of the household. The women and children eat together later in the kitchen. This type of social situation, namely one which is intermediate between the purely private and the purely public, can also overtake the ambiance of the kind of evening interview session which I described earlier. If several male friends of the male household head stopped by, it often became impossible to continue the interview session. Females would draw back somewhat from the conversation, and often would go to the kitchen, either at the direction of the male household head or on their own accord, to commence the preparation of coffee and snacks to be served later, as called for by Kadayan ideas of hospitality. I soon concluded that in these situations my best strategy was to postpone the continuation of the interview and to join in with whatever discussion arose.

In highly public social scenes, especially gatherings for weddings, final death feasts, school sports days, and other similar occasions, men and women tend to socially segregate themselves. The bulk of social interaction--conversation, joking, and bantering--takes place within groups comprised of one sex or the other, but not both commingled. This separation extends into the performance of religious activities in that only men (and then only a few of them) traveled on Friday to the nearest mosque located in a village a few miles downriver. On those few occasions that I saw women engaged in groups for prayer, it was always in someone's home, without the men being present.

In any consideration of Kadayan intersex behavior, reference must be made to the locally articulated ideas on this subject. These generalizations were always given to me in the form of statements about how to behave and how not to behave with members of the opposite sex, what to do and what not to do in particular circumstances. My information is primarily from male informants, concerning how males should behave with respect to females. I know little about what a woman might tell another woman about how females should behave with respect to males.

Kadayan ethics and morality, as mentioned earlier, are grounded in a matrix of kinship sentiments and relationships. Thus the rules about intersex behavior should be understood in this context. Perhaps the most salient of these rules, to the Kadayan themselves, concerns the situation in which a man might visit another house in the village expecting to see his male friend (who would be one of his real or classificatory relatives) and find only a nubile female--wife, sister, or daughter--at home. The stated rule is that the man, should he stay, should sit with at least one foot on the outside of the threshold after climbing up the stairs from the ground. In other words the man should not enter the house with the woman and disappear from the view of passers-by.[10] Even though I was told many times by my best friend that I was always welcome to come to his house anytime, even when his wife was there alone, I always felt uncomfortable about doing so. I was not alone. Another friend, a young Kadayan schoolteacher seconded to the village from another part of Brunei, once told me how happy he was after finding out that he was related to people in the village.[11] Before learning this he had always felt uncomfortable about visiting with his students' parents in their homes except on formal occasions.

Another rule, unstated but found widely throughout Southeast Asia, concerns physical contact between members of the opposite sex. Any public physical contact--other than purely accidental--between members of the opposite sex would be considered an egregious breach of decorum. In my experience with the Kadayan this stricture extends to publicly visible behavior between spouses; physical touching simply does not take place. The one exception which I observed occurred between young people, as yet unmarried and unbetrothed. In those contexts which involved joking, bantering, and horseplay (which is normally of the verbal type), I occasionally saw a young girl punch a young man squarely on the shoulder, following some remark he had made. This kind of competitive interaction between unmarried males and females is a common ritual event in two types of settings, cooperative harvesting parties (*pucangan*), and the singing and dancing celebrations (*bamukun*) which can go on all night following a wedding. On these occasions, young men and women compete with each other (*balas-mambalas*) by hurling the well-known Malay quatrains, or *pantun*, at each other.[12] The exchanges were, reportedly, often quite risqué, but any suggestiveness was so deeply embedded in metaphor as to make it impossible to grasp, unless one were very adept at comprehending the rich inventory of complex symbols and allusions present in the poetry.

The underlying belief of men, about women, seems to be that, other things being equal, it would be the woman who would initiate a sexual encounter if the two were alone. (The Kadayan, of course, fully understand that men will also initiate sexual encounters with women.) As some informants phrased it, *bini-bini yang gagal, bukan laki-laki*, 'It's the woman who is randy, not the man.' It would, however, be unwarranted to read too much into this aphorism. There is no way to determine whether the statement is a post hoc rationalization of the fact, or a cause of the behavior it seems to account for.

One cannot argue that the Kadayan view males and females as being equal in either the "identity" sense or the "equivalence" sense of equality (see Spiro 1979:7-10). The Kadayan certainly do not view males and females as being "equal" in any strict sense of the term. They view them as different, but lack a developed ideology of the differences, which could intrude into everyday life to complicate routine tasks, especially those involving the economic cooperation and organization necessary in obtaining food by traditional means. The patterns of social interaction of males and females in a wide range of economic activities has more to do with ways of solving problems anchored in a traditional subsistence strategy, than with the working out of an ideology about the proper places of men and women in Kadayan society. Even though the analysis above indicates that it is possible to speak about men's work vs. women's work from an analytical perspective, this distinction has low saliency. It is not one to which the Kadayan devote much attention, either conversationally or emotionally.

3.   Monogamy and Polygyny

Because they are Muslim, Kadayan men have the privilege of marrying up to four wives at a time, if they should chose to do so. No one in the village in which I lived and worked had done so. I knew no man willing to even consider this option. Kadayan believe that it is in the nature of things that cowives should fight. Thus, as one man told me, if he were thinking of marrying a second woman, the first thing he would do would be to obtain the permission of his wife before contracting the marriage. I asked why he would do that and he retorted rhetorically, "How would you like to eat burned food for the rest of your life?" Kadayan men think it unseemly for a man to want more than one wife.[13] If he wishes, however, a man is certainly within his rights and welcome to take another wife. Here one meets the thoroughgoing Kadayan egalitarianism in which each person must be allowed to pursue his owns ends, providing that he does not in any way infringe on others, or upset the very strong sense of *communitas* one finds in a Kadayan settlement. This particular Kadayan attitude, of "live and let live" in which no one should direct the behavior of others, completely permeates all Kadayan life.

Kadayan men believe that it is natural that cowives should not get on well with each other, and fight.[14] Thus, if a man were to take an additional wife, certain precautions must be taken to ensure domestic tranquility. Two options are available. A man should either be wealthy enough to be able to provide each wife with her own residence, preferably far apart from each other and in different settlements if possible, or he should be a competent enough practitioner of the type of magic which will prevent cowives from fighting, if they are to live together.

While polygyny is possible in principle for a Kadayan man, there is no evidence that that it has been much practiced in recent times.[15] I knew of only one case of a Kadayan man who had two wives. His own father had had many wives and was a famous practitioner of the type of magic intended to prevent conflict among cowives. It was presumed by my informants that he had taught his son some of this magic. Kadayan genealogies indicate that while in the past many individuals had several spouses, the polygyny was usually of the serial variety. Multiple marriages have sometimes resulted from the death of one of the partners (*caray mati*) after which the survivor remarried. In other cases these unions occurred after divorces (*caray hidup*).

The Islamic method of divorce by the utterance of the three *talak* (< Ar. *talaq*) '[triple and complete] divorce' is well-known, and probably was utilized in Brunei in the past (Hooker 1984:184-185). However, informants indicated that it has become extremely difficult to obtain a divorce in modern Brunei by this method. They claimed that in order to have a union officially dissolved it was necessary to register the divorce with a religious judge (*kadi*), but in recent years the religious judges have resisted ruling favorably on requests for divorce until they have become satisfied the marriages in question could not be salvaged. In Brunei these judges have reportedly taken on roles not unlike marriage counselors in their efforts to reduce what historically may have been a rather high divorce rate.[16] The recent phenomenon of a declining divorce rate among Malay-speaking peoples in Southeast Asia has also been noted for Sarawak (Harrisson 1970:193), among the Barunay (Brown 1970:37), and in Singapore (Djamour 1966:143ff.).

The Kadayan attach no particular stigma to divorce. The dissolution of a marriage union, of course, can be problematic for them, but this is primarily a result of the economic consequences of the breakup. Here the major concern is with the disposition of the bride-wealth. Kadayan claim that the matter can only be settled after fault is found. If the woman is held to be at fault, the bride-wealth, or a portion of it must be returned. If the man is at fault, then the bride-wealth stays with the woman. Informants indicated that in the past this issue caused considerable friction, as the parties and their relatives often disputed who in fact was at fault. They believe such a situation always has the potential to lead to violence. This fact is remarkable because individual Kadayan virtually never exhibit any outward manifestations of physical violence.[17] (During the Brunei Rebellion of 1962, numbers of Kadayan were involved in fighting, during which some of them were killed. This violence, however, was an expression of protest against the then current social and political order, and not of personal or familial animosities and disagreements.)

Kadayan show considerable concern about the likelihood of the success of a potential marriage union before it is established. They are concerned about the psychological suitability of the two partners, and if a parent feels that the two potential spouses are quite unsuited to each other, he or she will work to prevent the union from taking place. They take the view that certain individuals simply are not suited to each other, due to the characteristics of their individual personalities.

Individuals do not contract their own marriages. Parents and close relatives organize and arrange the series of rituals and activities which usually take at least six months leading up to the final ceremony. When her parents are considering her eventual marriage, a Kadayan girl can exert a considerable amount of influence on the final disposition of a particular request. On the one hand, a girl may wish to refuse a particular suitor. If her protests about the young man her parents wish her to marry are strong enough, they will often demure to her wishes and indicate to the boy's relatives that the marriage will not take place. On the other hand, if she has a strong desire to marry a boy whose relatives have broached the matter with her parents, but her parents have an aversion to the fellow as their future son-in-law, the daughter may yet prevail in having them accede to her wishes if her pleas continue unabated. The girl's mother and father are particularly concerned that their daughter not be married to a man who, in their view, is lazy, a ne'er-do-well, or altogether irresponsible. Informants indicated that a girl's parents and close relatives very often consider decisive the strength of the emotional feeling their daughter expresses rather than the particular choice she has made. On the other hand in the case of a young man, parents tend to regard their son's opinions and feelings as less important. According to informants, Kadayan parents are more likely to ignore their son's wishes than their daughter's when it comes to deciding whether to agree to a proposed match.[18]

It is significant that men will turn so quickly to a wife's likely response to a question of why they do not have more than one wife, rather than to some kind of rationalized explanation centered on themselves, as one might expect for a number of other societies. Again, I would pin this to the relatively low level of saliency of and interest in males vs. females in Kadayan culture, as evidenced by the relative inattention devoted to it in conversation. The attitudes of Kadayan men, as well as the behavior of men and women with respect to marriage unions, appear to illustrate Smith's suggestion of a "strong and ancient indigenous liberalism", as seen from a Pan-Islamic perspective, for Southeast Asian Islamic societies. Kadayan do not now engage in polygynous unions to any appreciable degree, nor is there evidence they did in the past, despite the possibility of doing so within Islamic law.

The Kadayan thus represent an example of a society in which it is permitted for a man to have more than one wife, but with men generally expressing little interest and desire to avail themselves of this option. The opposite extreme type of social arrangement would appear to be the situation in which polygyny of any sort is expressly forbidden by religious authority, but yet appears to be the norm. Such a case is described by Hansen and Bastarrachea for the Catholic Yucatecan city of Merida earlier in the 20th century (1984:219-221). This appears to have been primarily an urban phenomenon involving men of the upper class (*la clase alta*) and women of the lower (*la clase baja*) or middle class (*la clase media*). These de facto polygynous unions were extremely common, produced children (eight in one case), and constituted full families, although not ones sanctified by the Catholic Church.[19] The incidence of polygyny is thus not necessarily dependent on whether there are cultural and legal norms permitting or forbidding it in a particular cultural system.

TRADITION AND CHANGE

Social relationships between Kadayan men and women are grounded primarily in the norms and values of Kadayan culture. While the 20th century has witnessed a considerable amount of cultural and social change all around the world, which the Kadayan have not escaped, they nonetheless remain fairly conservative in preserving traditional social arrangements. Tradition, and explaining actions and behavior by reference to custom (*adat*), is especially strong in rural areas. These traditional relations between men and women have undergone a number of modifications in recent years. There are, I believe, two general reasons for the alterations in these male-female relationships. One, of course, is the well-known pattern of social change just mentioned. The other is the more recent phenomenon of the surge of interest in Islamic thought and teaching, which has affected not only Brunei, but to varying degrees probably all parts of Southeast Asia.

1.   Men's Ideas About Women

Kadayan men do not belittle or depreciate women generically in the ways that I associate with growing up in my own society (e.g., "Women drivers!", "Isn't that just like a woman!", "Ah, women!", etc.; this situation appears to be changing in American culture). Generally, in conversations amongst themselves, men do not appear to be especially interested in the topic of women as a subject for discussion. One exception is the case of small groups of young unmarried men, who are especially good friends, discussing their hopes and plans for their future marriages. Another exception is a type of joking in which the subject of women may feature as a part of the conversation among a small group of men. This form of verbal banter has the spirit of poking fun, in which men sometimes try to mildly embarrass each other. The butts of such remarks, however, are primarily the young unmarried men; such comments are very rarely directed at married men.

There is one aspect of Kadayan life in which women are ritually impure and inferior to males. Women are prohibited from entering the village graveyard (*panguburan*), which is located on the top of a small hill about three-quarters of a mile from the village. The reason stated for this prohibition is that women might be menstruating (*badarah*) and thus are to be prohibited (*ditagah; dipantang; or dilarah*) from entering the burial ground, for fear of contaminating it. Men themselves enter the graveyard on only two occasions; to bury a deceased villager, and to clean the graves of the debris of fallen leaves and branches on the first day of the new year (*Hari Raya Malayu*).

While illustrating a differential evaluation of women by men, these few examples can hardly constitute evidence of disparagement. The small number of such examples supports the thesis that the Kadayan men have only a very weakly developed concern with females as objects of ideological concern.

There is one further possible feature of Kadayan life which could illustrate a clear differential evaluation of males and females, namely Islamic inheritance law; but, because no divisions of property occurred during the research period it is difficult to do more than speculate on this matter. The Muslim legal stipulation that inherited property should be divided to give a male heir double the portion of a female heir (Harrisson 1970:536 n.), is well-known to the Kadayan. Historically the Kadayan have been swidden cultivators and had little wealth in the form of objects of material culture. In addition they lived in very sparsely settled areas so that complex patterns of ownership of agricultural land never developed. Today the majority of land owned by rural Kadayan is either in the form of house plot sites or rubber gardens (not producing during the period of this research), and even then not everyone owns land in either category. I had the impression from a number of conversations with informants that the two-to-one ratio of property division of Islamic law might not always be followed, but then there were no real examples to deal with, and these discussions always seemed somewhat vague, with informants showing little interest in the matter.

2.   The Future and the Changing World of Islam

During the period of field work I observed a significant difference in the attitudes of older versus younger of males with respect to females. Older males, who usually were not literate and had little formal education, exhibited attitudes toward females which indicated that they held a view that males and females have more or less equivalent worth. On the other hand, the outlook of younger more literate and educated males expressed a different attitude. As one of my friends who was a village religious teacher put it, "We--that is, men--lead, and they--that is, women--follow." I interpret statements such as this one to indicate a differential evaluation of the place of men and women in social life, in which males possess greater amounts of social power and authority than females. In this view men are the protectors and guardians of women. I suspect that this opinion represents a view which is more Middle Eastern than Southeast Asian, and which very likely reflects more of the much stronger pater-familial bias of Arabic-speaking cultures than than it does the Southeast Asian world in which men and women are valued more equivalently.

The reasons for this apparent difference in attitude between older and younger generations in Brunei are obscure. They are probably related to the social currents which swirled through the region earlier in the century. During the period leading up to the Japanese invasion of Southeast Asia in 1941, powerful forces were generated by the intellectual ferment in religious thinking known as the Muslim Modernist Movement (Noer 1973, Roff 1967). Two issues were widely debated. A conflict between traditional custom and practice, and religious teaching, was perceived as limiting progress and development (Roff 1967:58). Reformists took the position that women were the equals of men and should not be discriminated against (Noer 1973:96, 141). One outcome was the creation of separate educational institutions for females in Indonesia (e.g., Noer 1973:53). So one step was to emancipate women by increasing opportunities for their education and at the same time they were separated from men in all-female schools. (It can be noted that Brunei has separate government high schools for boys and girls.) The major impact of these ideas and intellectual currents probably did not reach Brunei until after the end of World War II, with the creation of a system of universal education and the beginnings of massive economic development through the increased exploitation of Brunei's oil reserves. Many of Brunei's first school teachers and religious teachers were trained in Malaya (now Malaysia) and would likely have been influenced by the thinking of the modernists, then more current in areas outside of Brunei (cf. Brown 1970:160, Ranjit 1984:118-119).[20]

CONCLUSION

It is now necessary to return to the thesis of Wilfred Cantwell Smith introduced at the outset and his suggestion that the position of women in Southeast Asian Muslim societies contrasts clearly with that of women in Muslim societies of the Middle East and South Asia. I suggested that the social relationships between Kadayan men and women are structured primarily by the nature of the roles that the two sexes occupy in the subsistence economy. I believe that it is the nature of the particular kind of rice agricultural regime of the Kadayan, and how this regime is integrated with the other tasks of food production that the key to this contrast is found.

The cultivation of rice makes special demands on human beings, if it is to be carried out be successfully. Both swidden and permanent field agriculture require that farmers pay attention to weather, local climatic and edaphic conditions, annual variations in rainfall, crop pests, and a number of other factors. Both the incidence and effects of these factors can vary significantly from year to year, but their consequences require that farmers calibrate their activities and labor inputs to the rice regimes very carefully. If Kadayan are to consistently achieve successful harvests from year to year, the work of women as well as men is required to ensure adequate labor in meeting the needs of crop production, while at the same time attending to all of their other social needs and activities.

The exigencies of cultivating rice has consequences in Kadayan social life which rule out the kind of pronounced segregation of females from males which can be found in Middle Eastern and South Asian societies. The labor needs of both swidden and permanent field agriculture ensure that males and females will participate together in a number of tasks working side by side.

The situation of intersex relations of the Kadayan can be highlighted by contrasting it with that of the nonagricultural Barunay. Among the more traditionally-minded and high-ranking Barunay (especially nobles) it was, reportedly, common practice--which some still maintain--for a marriage to be arranged for a boy and a girl who would not set eyes on each other until the actual day of their wedding ceremony. I recall one high ranking noble who was quite proud that he had been married in accordance with this traditional Barunay noble practice. In another case, a Barunay girl's father had supervised his daughter's teenage years by keeping her out of social situations in which she might encounter males of her own age. In the capital area I heard reports of the behavior of teenage Barunay girls who were in high school being monitored by close friends and collateral relatives of their parents. Periodic reports would then be made to the parents, if a girl's behavior was thought to reflect badly on the family's reputation and social standing.

This Barunay practice of segregating young women for a few years before they married could only have been possible in earlier times if they did not occupy key cooperative roles in subsistence production, which would have placed them in social situations where they could regularly interact with unmarried men of their own age. This is not to say that these women did not participate in subsistence production, although there is little published information available on the role of females in the traditional economic life of the Barunay. In this century, for example, the women of the Barunay villages of Lurung Sikuna and Sungai Kedayan are well-known throughout Brunei for the high quality of the handwoven cloth they produce (see, e.g., Anuar 1970), but this activity does not require interaction with young men. Given that the economic activities of the Barunay in the traditional water settlement at the capital were described in the 19th century as primarily craft specialties and specialized types of exploitations of foods from the sea (St John 1863 II:277-281), the generalization that the younger Barunay females were typically not interacting with unmarried young men on a regular basis seems warranted.[21]

Had a similar situation developed among the Kadayan, in which young unmarried women were sheltered and kept out of social intercourse with young men, the consequences for the labor requirements of agriculture would have been highly disfunctional. Females, both before and after they are married, supply crucial labor to the successful cultivation of a rice crop. The tasks of dibbling, sowing, and harvesting in swidden cultivation are shared by males and females. In permanent field cultivation it is the women who do all the transplanting and the weeding, without which there would be no crop. If young women were not allowed to participate in these efforts, severe burdens would be placed on the ability of males to complete all the necessary work, within the scheduling constraints of the agricultural cycle and all the other required activities of everyday life.

This analysis, while revealing, still leaves important questions unanswered. What is needed is a comparative study of the roles women play in the subsistence economies of other Southeast Asian societies, both non-Muslim as well as Muslim.[22] The patterns derived from such a study should then be compared with those found in Muslim societies outside Southeast Asia, especially in nonrice-growing economies. One important question which needs to be examined is the following. Is it the interaction of Islamic tradition with particular kinds of economies which produces different outcomes, or should we look to the nature of the cultural base, which existed before the beginnings of the Islamic religion in the 7th Christian century, in order to account for these differences in the patterns of interaction between men and women?

For the Kadayan, requirements for cooperation are placed on the basic units of production and consumption--families--and their members. It is only with the close cooperation of male and female, young and old, and the individual families of a village, that a crop can be brought in successfully. The web of social relationships, in which these economic activities take place, is anchored in the larger social system. This social system is maintained through time, in large part, by the system of traditional ideas, norms, and values which each generation learns anew from the previous one. This system of ideology, too, has a momentum of its own, and, as for any Southeast Asian Muslim people, is a complex amalgam of both local and exogenous features. It is within this matrix of sociological, cultural, and historical themes that the relations between Kadayan men and women can be clearly seen to exemplify Smith's thesis about Southeast Asian Islam.

NOTES

1. Smith does not describe the position of women in Islamic societies in any detail. C. Snouck Hurgronje visited Mecca in 1884 and 1885. His observations on life there, even when recognized as colored by ethnocentrism, vituperation, and an attitude of European superiority, still paint a grim picture of relations between the sexes.

> We have already shown how this almost absurdly pompous introduction of the young couple to married life has very little real significance as of a lifelong union. What is the good of the songs of praise which the girl for once in her life hears, now she is entering into a society which despises her and her whole sex? Moslim literature contains some isolated pieces of true appreciation of women, but the view which in later times came always more and more to prevail, finds its expression only in the sacred traditions which represent Hell as filled with women, and deny to woman, with some exceptions, understanding or religion; in poems which attribute all evil in the world to woman; in proverbs which condemn

as pure extravagance any careful education of girls. So to women is left only to give man by her sexual charms a fortaste of heavenly joys, and to bear him children.

The young man, brought up in these views, regards his intercourse with his wife as almost nothing but sport, and his taste, unripe at the time of marriage, soon develops itself in some new direction, which either brings about a speedy dissolution of the marriage, or, where family considerations prevent this, leads him if not into unnatural vice, into concubinage with a slave woman, when the free wife will be lucky if she has the consolation of children of her own (Snouck Hurgronje 1931:144).

These observations, of course, do not describe relations between the sexes in Muslim societies in Southeast Asia, in the 19th or any other century. To the extent that they are accurate they depict the much stronger paterfamilial bias characteristic of Muslim societies of the Middle East, but uncharacteristic of most of the cultures of Southeast Asia. Mernissi (1975) presents a more sophisticated treatment of Muslim theory about women, especially in Part I, 'The Traditional Muslim View of Women and Their Place in the Social Order'. The existence of such a bias is depicted, for example, in Munson's oral history of a Moroccan family (1984). I believe Smith would concur with this assessment.

2. My research in the Temburong District of Brunei, 1968-1971, was supported by the National Institutes of Health Research Grant 1 TOL-MH-11,231-01 and Wenner-Gren Foundation for Anthropological Research Pre-Doctoral Fellowship No. 2173, and sponsored locally by the Dewan Bahasa dan Pustaka, Brunei. I would like to thank Michael D. Murphy and Norman J. Singer or critical readings of an earlier version of this paper. Discussions with Richard A. Krause have also contributed a number of clarifications.

3. The specific effects of the usually interlinked processes of modernization and Westernization on traditional societies around the world are well-known, and will not be discussed here. (See, for example, the collection of papers edited by Bernard and Pelto [1972], which focus on the relationships between the adoption of nontraditional technology and social change in a wide range of societies.) The intensification of Islamic thought and teaching in Brunei, however, is another matter. (It should be pointed out that my research in Brunei occurred before the surge of

Islamic fundamentalism became widely known or felt throughout the world.)

There is an abundance of evidence demonstrating that the leaders of modern Brunei are in agreement that Islam is crucially important to the future development and modernization of the country (e.g., Pehin Haji Muhammad Jamil's highly commendatory account of Sultan Hasan [reigned 1605-1619 ?], indicating that he was responsible for revising the traditional Brunei legal code [kanun] to bring it into correspondence with Islamic teachings [1973:27-156]; and the speeches of the late Sultan Sir Omar Ali Saifuddin, from the period 1959-1967, in which religious content becomes increasingly prominent, especially following the Brunei Rebellion of late 1962 [1971]; to cite but two examples). The reasons for the intensification of Islamic themes and teachings in modern Brunei (a society composed of numerous ethnic groups, each with its own customs and institutions) are unclear, but may represent a search for a more uniform guiding philosophy of life, and code of ethical and moral behavior, in an increasingly uncertain modern world. In this respect Brunei is no different from many other nations of the world.

4.   In a remote settlement such as the one in which I worked, most of these men work within the village for various departments of the Brunei government. Those who do not have government jobs with permanency will often take on work with private contractors taking them away from the village, but only for short periods. None were interested, for example, in working in the oil complex at Seria, at the other end of the state, because they would be too long away from both their families and relatives as well as their rice fields.

5.   In neighboring Sarawak, by comparison, where restrictions on the possession of firearms have been less stringent than in Brunei, game in subcoastal areas comparable to those inhabited by the Kadayan in Brunei is quite scarce.

6.   While it is beyond the bounds of the present discussion, it can be noted that on the basis of comparison with the types of role specialization found in other Malay-speaking groups elsewhere in Southeast Asia, the Kadayan exhibit a markedly weaker development of specialized roles than might otherwise be expected (cf. Laderman, 1983, on medical practitioners; Swift, 1965, and Djamour, 1966, on religious specialists; Raymond Firth, 1966, on shamans; Raymond Firth, 1966, and Fraser, 1960, on fishing specialists). Among the Kadayan knowledge and ability is widely dispersed, rather than concentrated in the abilities of a few

individuals. The reasons for this situation are probably related to the very special social and historical circumstances in which the Kadayan have always lived, as part of the larger social system of the plural society of Brunei (see Maxwell 1984).

7.   The term indung is used in contexts in which it is quite clear that a kinship terminological and not a progenitorial usage is intended. In addition the term indung behaves syntactically exactly like all other kin terms in the production of composite kin term lexemes, in ways in which, for example, the English term <parent> does not.

8.   Any subject, that is, except sex. Sex is not a topic which can be easily discussed with Malays, nor do they discuss it much themselves in ordinary conversation. I was single during the time of my fieldwork. Had I been married the subject would, no doubt, have been easier to broach with the Kadayan, but even then would not have been one they would have felt comfortable discussing.

9.   I have encountered this same situation with other groups in Borneo, such as the Kayan and the Kelabit, and have heard it described for the Iban.

10.   Informants related a case of how this rule was transgressed in the past, by a powerful leader who had been dead for some time. He had considerable magical ability and was considered to be invulnerable (kabal). If he wanted to have sexual relations with another man's wife, he could practice a form of magic known as *ilmu pisah* (lit. 'knowledge of [how to cause] separation'). While the seducer ascended the front steps, the woman's husband, who was quite unaware of what was transpiring, would leave the house by the back stairs, to carry out the errand whose urgency had just overtaken his consciousness. The magician could then have sex with the woman, who was now alone. People were aware of the man's behavior, but because of his invulnerability, he was impervious to any form of bodily injury or physical sanction. Hence no one dared to challenge him. As he was their relative and a formidable person, his memory was revered by all. Historically, the Kadayan were reputed throughout northwest Borneo as having been very powerful magicians. Their reputation extended as far as the Kelabit highlands, deep in the interior of the island (Tom Harrisson, personal communication). Brunei government policies in the 20th century have apparently led to a marked reduction in the practice of many traditional forms of magic by the Kadayan.

11. A Kadayan's relatives include all persons to whom he or she is genealogically related, either consanguineously or affinally. Consanguineal or affinal distance (including multiple affinal links) is irrelevant to whether a person is considered a "relative". Thus, in principal, a Kadayan's personal kindred literally includes all individuals to whom a genealogical relationship can be traced.

12. The four lines of a pantun or quatrain often follow an a-b-a-b rhyme. The first two lines have only a surface semantic reading. The last two lines have both a surface semantic reading and an extended metaphorical reading. The surface semantic readings of the two pairs of lines are unrelated to each other. The most accomplished performer is able to best his or her competition by sustaining a long series of exchanges by constructing his first pair of lines out of elements (nouns and verbs) of his opponent's last pair of lines, and then go on to challenge the other party with ever more daring metaphorical readings in the final pair of lines. The acknowledged champion in the village in which I worked was a man, perhaps in his mid to late 20s, who was mentally retarded. He was unmarried and according to my friends would never be allowed to marry. He was considered unable, without advice and help, of successful farming, or even visiting the capital and getting about in the vehicular traffic without being a danger to himself. He had, however, no peer in the region in pantun and was probably a true idiot savant.

13. I recall one distinguished Kadayan man telling me quite pridefully of the late Sultan of Brunei, Sir Omar Ali Saifuddin III, who in middle age on being told by his wife of many years that he should now feel free to take a second, young wife, replied to her that he had no desire for another younger wife and that he was entirely happy with her and the many children she had borne him.

14. Beliefs about the nature of relations between cowives are not easily found in the ethnographic literature. Reports usually concern the relations between cowives, not about local beliefs about the nature of these relationships. Among the Siuai cowives quarrel and fight, and their relations are generally conflict ridden (Oliver 1955:223-225). Among the Gusii enmity pertains (LeVine 1964:76), and among the Nyakyusa, Lozi, and Ashanti, jealousy, which can lead to witchcraft among the Nyakyusa and Lozi (Wilson 1950:113, Gluckman 1950:180, Fortes 1950:281). Among the Suku, harmony between cowives is desirable and common, but not indispensable (Kopytoff 1964:105-106). Among the Yakö, "The relations between wives of one man may range from real companionship to a minimum of contact punctuated with outbursts of hostility", and "The

relations among co-wives range widely from companionable equality to hostility or considerable domination, but these depend on differences not of formal status but of personality and prestige" (Forde 1964:87, 128). Plateau Tonga "Men expect their [co]wives to be jealous of one another and to quarrel over the husband's favours" (Colson 1958:132).

15. It is my impression that the same situation--infrequent polygyny--is also the case for the Barunay, although I do not have the necessary details to support this statement. Brown reports that polygyny among Barunay has been infrequent in recent years but that it may have been more common in the past. He also notes that concubinage was reported to have been common among nobles in the past (1970:37). I have no information that suggests that the Kadayan kept concubines in the past.

16. It seems clear that Malay-speaking peoples have historically had a rather high rate of divorce. Swettenham speaks of divorce being "easy" in the late 19th century (1907:154). Swift speaks of divorce being "very common throughout Malay society" (1965:119). Smith notes higher frequencies of divorce among Malays in the Peninsula, especially in Kelantan and Trengganu, than among migrants from Indonesia (1952:52-53). For 1939-40 in Perupok, Kelantan, Rosemary Firth notes that "Divorce is a very common feature of village social life, much more common, in fact, than, polygyny" (1966:35). In speaking of Jelebu, Negri Sembilan, for 1954-56, Swift states that "Although I did not find the very high levels of divorce which characterize Malay society as a whole...divorce is still common" (1965:109). For 1967-68 in Sik, Kedah Banks reports completed divorces (i.e., excluding divorces which were revoked) ranged between 33% and 49% on an annual basis (1983:106). In the case of Singapore, "For several decades up to 1950, divorce had been so frequent that annually, for every hundred Malay marriages taking place in Singapore, there had been about fifty divorces (Djamour 1965:110). For all Muslims in Singapore (mostly Malays) from 1921 through 1949, completed divorces averaged 52% of marriages on an annual basis, ranging from a high of 67% to a low of 35% (Djamour 1965:117). Swift's figures from Jelebu for 1950 through 1960 show completed divorces averaging 49% on an annual basis, ranging from a high of 71% to a low of 39% (1965:119). A summary of statistics for the eleven states of Malaya and Singapore over periods ranging from 6 to 13 years between 1945 and 1958 show an average of completed divorces of 52% (Gordon n.d.:26).

17.　This statement must be qualified. In the Brunei Rebellion of 1962, numbers of Kadayan were involved in fighting, during which some were killed. This violence, however, was part of a social and political protest against the then current social order, and was not operating at an individual and personal level.

18.　The reasons for this pattern of fathers' sentimental weakness for their daughters' (but not sons') opinions are unclear. A similar pattern of parental acquiescence to the wishes of female children reportedly also occurs among the daughters of Brunei Sultans. Barunay princesses are said to lead unhappy lives due to the importance of their fathers' positions. These girls are thought to be overindulged as youngsters by their fathers because they are so subject to the dictates of political necessity in their marriages and future adult lives. This is an recurrent theme in Brunei traditional literature, especially in the (unpublished) Dang Pandan Larangan and Dang Rokam tales (cf. Harun and Ismail 1983:106-107).

19.　Hansen and Bastarrachea distinguish between primary or monogamous unions (uniones primarios) which are sanctioned by the Church (uniones matrimonios), and secondary sexual unions (uniones sexuales secundarias) which, when considered together with the former, define the de facto polygyny (poligamia de hecho). The ordinality of the types of marriage unions, however, is irrelevant to my point about the Kadayan and the Yucatecans of Merida illustrating diametrically opposite social arrangements involving the intersection of the factors of incidence and cultural acceptance of polygyny.

20.　Barunay ideas about the place of women in society, expressed through the educational system, may also be influencing the Kadayan. Residential high schools are located in the major urban areas, which are near the main concentrations of Barunay settlements; Kadayan villages are located in more rural settings (see Conclusion).

21.　St John also reports a number of other specialist roles fulfilled by Barunay females, including professional story tellers who plied their trade primarily in the harems of important Barunay nobles, spirit mediums, and curers (1863 II:284-285). None of these roles, however, would lead to young unmarried women routinely interacting with members of the opposite sex.

22.   At this point I can only suggest a number of comparative examples, some of which are similar to the Kadayan situation and others contrastive. Of the non-Muslim Ifugao Conklin says "In general, women cultivate field crops and weave fabrics; men handle edaphic resources, metals, and forest plants; and both, with the help of older children, share most domestic chores" (1980:37). For the non-Muslim Iban Freeman indicates that "All Iban women, with the exception of those incapacitated by old age or sickness, participate year by year in the arduous routine of farm work" (1955:78), and "The younger women are remarkably versatile, and able to cope with all male tasks with the exception of felling virgin jungle" (1955:80). Morris reports for the Melanau, only some of whom are Muslim, that unmarried boys and girls work sago palms together (1953:32). Regarding the Muslim Javanese, Geertz indicates that "In a great many cases--perhaps most--the first meeting of husband and wife-to-be occurs at the wedding ceremony" (1961:56), and Jay suggests that unmarried persons of opposite sex do not work together in agriculture unless they belong to the same family or are closely related. He continues, "Since the rural Javanese of Modjokuto are prudish, in public at least, much care is taken to keep the sexes apart" (Jay 1969:43). Kiefer reports a more marked segregation for the Muslim Tau Sug; "The separation of the sexes, especially the unmarried, is quite marked in Tau Sug society. ... It is reflected first of all in a well-defined division of labor and sense of the propriety of men's work and women's work" (1972:35).

BIBLIOGRAPHY

Anuar A. R.
    1970   Meninjau Sa-pintas Lalu Mengenai Perusahaan Bertenun di-Brunei. Bahana 5(12)686-695.

Banks, David J.
    1983   Malay Kinship. Philadelphia: Institute for the Study of Human Issues.

Brown, D. E.
1970   Brunei: The Structure and History of a Bornean Sultan-
                ate. Monograph of the Brunei Museum Journal. [Brunei
                Museum Journal] 2(2).

Colson, Elizabeth
1958   Marriage & the Family Among the Plateau Tonga of
                Northern Rhodesia. Manchester: Manchester University
                Press.

Conklin, Harold C.
1980   Ethnographic Atlas of Ifugao; A Study of Environment,
                Culture, and Society in Northern Luzon. New Haven:
                Yale University Press.

Djamour, Judith
1965   Malay Kinship and Marriage in Singapore. Corrected
                Reprint. London School of Economics Monographs on
                Social Anthropoology No. 21.

1966   The Muslim Matrimonial Court in Singapore. London
                School of Economics Monographs on Social Anthropolo-
                gy No. 31.

Dubisch, Jill, ed.
1986   Gender & Power in Rural Greece. Princeton: Princeton
                University Press.

Firth, Raymond
1966   Malay Fishermen, Their Peasant Economy. [2nd ed.]
                New Haven: Archon Books.

Firth, Rosemary
1966   Housekeeping Among Malay Peasants. 2nd ed. London
                School of Economics Monographs on Social Anthropolo-
                gy No. 7.

Forde, Daryll
1964   Double Descent and the Matrilineal System. In Yakö
                Studies, by Daryll Forde, pp. 85-134. London: Oxford
                University Press.

Fortes, Meyer
1950 Kinship and Marriage Among the Ashanti. In African Systems of Kinship and Marriage. A. R. Radcliffe-Brown and Daryll Forde, eds., pp. 252-284. London: Oxford University Press.

Fraser, Thomas M., Jr.
1960 Rusembilan: A Malay Fishing Village in Southern Thailand. Ithaca: Cornell University Press.

Freeman, J. Derek
1955 Iban Agriculture, A Report on the Shifting Cultivation of Hill Rice by the Iban of Sarawak. Colonial Research Studies No. 18. London: Her Majesty's Stationery Office.

Friedl, Ernestine
1975 Women and Men, An Anthropologist's View. New York: Holt, Rinehart and Winston.

Geertz, Hildred
1961 The Javanese Family, A Study of Kinship and Socialization. [Glencoe, IL]: The Free Press of Glencoe.

Gluckman, Max
1950 Kinship and Marriage Among the Lozi of Northern Rhodesia and the Zulu of Natal. In African Systems of Kinship and Marriage. A. R. Radcliffe Brown and Daryll Forde, eds., pp. 166-206. London: Oxford University Press.

Goldman, Irving
1970 Ancient Polynesian Society. Chicago: University of Chicago Press.

Gordon, Shirle
n.d. Marriage/Divorce in the Eleven States of Malaya and Singapore. Intisari 2(2)23-32.

Hansen, Asael T. and Juan R. Bastarrachea M.
1984 Merida, Su transformación de capital colonial a naciente metrópoli en 1935. Mexico City: Instituto Nacional de Antropologia e Historia.

Harrisson, Tom
1970   The Malays of South-West Sarawak Before Malaysia, A
               Socio-Ecological Survey. London: Macmillan.

Harun Mat Piah and Ismail Hamid
1983   Koleksi Manuskrip-Manuskrip Melayu di Brunei: Satu
               akhlumat Awal. Sari 1(2)103-124.

Hooker, M. B.
1984   Islamic Law in Southeast Asia. Singapore: Oxford
               University Press.

Jay, Robert R.
1969   Javanese Villagers, Social Relations in Modjokuto.
               Cambridge: The MIT Press.

Kiefer, Thomas M.
1972   The Tausug, Violence and Law in a Philippine Moslem
               Society. New York: Holt, Rienehart and Winston.

Kopytoff, Igor
1964   Family and Lineage Among the Suku of the Congo. In
               The Family Estate in Africa, Studies in the Role of
               Property in Family Structure and Lineage Continuity.
               [Boston]: Boston University Press.

Laderman, Carol
1983   Wives and Midwives, Childbirth and Nutrition in Rural
               Malaysia. Berkeley: University of California Press.

LeVine, Robert A.
1964   The Gusii Family. In The Family Estate in Africa,
               Studies in the Role of Property in Family Structure and
               Lineage Continuity. [Boston]: Boston University Press.

Levinson, David and Martin J. Malone
1980   Toward Explaining Human Culture: A Critical Review of
               the Findings of Worldwide Cross-Cultural Research.
               n.p.: HRAF Press.

Maxwell, Allen R.
1969   Kedayan Ethno-Ornithology--A Preliminary Report. Brunei Museum Journal 1(1)197-217.

1984   The Place of the Kadayan in Traditional Brunei Society. Paper presented at the 36th Annual Meeting of the Association of Asian Studies, Washington, DC, March, 1984.

1985   Kalupis: A Delicacy of Brunei. Brunei Museum Journal 6(1)75-88.

Mernissi, Fatima
1975   Beyond the Veil, Male-Female Dynamics in a Modern Society. New York: John Wiley and Sons.

Mohd. Jamil Al-Sufri, Pehin Orang Kaya Amar Diraja Dato Seri Utama Awang Haji
1973   Chatatan Sejarah Perwira2 dan Pembesar2 Brunei. Vol. II. [Bandar Seri Begawan], Brunei: Dewan Bahasa dan Pustaka.

Morris, H. S.
1953   Report on a Melanau Sago Producing Community in Sarawak. Colonial Research Studies No. 9. London: Her Majesty's Stationery Office.

Munson, Henry, Jr.
1984   The House of Si Abd Allah, The Oral History of a Moroccan Family. New Haven: Yale University Press.

Nissim-Sabat, Charles
1987   On Clifford Geertz and His "Anti Anti-Relativism". American Anthropologist 89(4)935-939.

Noer, Deliar
1973   The Modernist Muslim Movement in Indoesia 1900-1942. Singapore: Oxford University Press.

Oliver, Douglas L.
1955   A Solomon Island Society, Kinship and Leadership Among the Siuai of Bougainville. Boston: Beacon Press.

Omar Ali Saifuddin
1971   Titah 1959-67, Kebawah DYMM Paduka Seri Baginda Maulana Al-Sultan Sir Omar Ali Saifuddin Sa'adul Khairi Waddin. [Bandar Seri Begawan], Brunei: Dewan Bahasa dan Pustaka.

Ranjit Singh, D. S.
1984   Brunei 1839-1983, The Problems of Political Survival. Singapore: Oxford University Press.

Roff, William R.
1967   The Origins of Malay Nationalism. New Haven: Yale University Press.

St John, Spenser
1863   Life in the Forests of the Far East; Or Travels in Northern Borneo. 2nd ed. 2 vols. London: Smith, Elder.

Smith, T. E.
1952   Population Growth in Malaysia, An Analysis of Recent Trends. London: Royal Institute of International Affairs.

Smith, Wilfred Cantwell
1957   Islam in Modern History. New York: New American Library.

Snouck Hurgronje, C.
1931   Mekka in the Latter Part of the 19th Century; Daily Life, Customs and Learning; The Moslims of the East-Indian-Archipelago. J. H. Monahan, transl. Reprinted 1970. Leiden: E. J. Brill. (Original: Mekka, Den Haag, 1888-1889.)

Spiro, Melford E.
1979   Gender and Culture: Kibbutz Women Revisited. Durham, NC: Duke University Press.

Swettenham, Frank
1907   British Malaya; An Account of the Origin and Progress of British Influence in Malaya. London: John Lane.

Swift, M. G.
1965   Malay Peasant Society in Jelebu.   London School of
            Economics Monographs on Social Anthropology No. 29.

Wilson, Monica
1950   Nyakyusa Kinship.   In African Systems of Kinship and
            Marriage.   A. R. Radcliffe-Brown and Daryll Forde, eds.,
            pp. 111-139.   London: Oxford University Press.

GENDER AND CLASS IN CENTRAL BORNEO

Jérôme Rousseau
Department of Anthropology
McGill University

In central Borneo as in much of the island, there is relatively little sexual inequality and no segregation of the sexes (cf. Colfer 1981). Nonetheless, there is social differentiation by gender, and some degree of gender inequality exists; it is closely linked to the class system.

We can consider first the factors which limit gender inequality. As with the Lun Dayeh, in central Borneo, "individuals have jural status within the village only as members of constituent domestic families. Individuals join the community as members of domestic families and have rights as residents by virtue of domestic family membership" (Crain 1978: 127). Insofar as the domestic unit is conceptually more important than any of its members, this can contribute to a relative equality of sexes.

Patterns of daily interaction do not overemphasize gender differences. Virginity is not valued: it is acceptable for young people of both sexes to have romantic attachments and premarital sexual relations with partners other than their eventual spouse. In societies which value premarital virginity, the onus for maintaining it falls primarily on women. Its absence in central Borneo is a significant factor towards equality.[1] There are no formal constraints to social interaction between adolescents and adults of the opposite sex; they join freely in

403

all kinds of conversations and talk about the same subjects. Menstruations are not socially marked, and menstruating women are not segregated.

Except when land is scarce, uxorilocality is the usual post-marital residence in central Borneo. By strengthening the mother-daughter bond, this contributes to maintain a relatively high status of women. When there is land scarcity, utrolocal residence follows. Even then, all Kayan (including the Busang and Mahakam-Kayan) have a rule of initial uxorilocality (Nieuwenhuis 1904: 85, 100),[2] and, given a high proportion of village endogamy, women in virilocal arrangements are close to their relatives. The preference for uxorilocality finds an echo in other practices; in the past, adolescent boys were encouraged to sleep on the gallery, not in their parents' apartment; this may have been a first step in separating them from their parents. Young men visit girls in their room when courting or for sexual intercourse, not the reverse.

Warfare and headhunting are male activities, and if a society emphasizes them, this increases gender differentiation. This has been the case for such groups as the Iban (Freeman 1970: 227ff.), but it is not the rule in central Borneo. Central Borneo chiefs, especially the Kayan, spent much energy in curbing uncontrolled headhunting which would have endangered their power and prosperity; the political system favored negotiated settlements over open hostilities. Consequently, men could engage in agricultural tasks nearly as much as women, thus reducing a gender-based division of labor.

Gender Differentiation

Nonetheless, gender differentiation is underlined by transformations of the body, dress, rituals and other forms of behavior. Women are extensively tattooed on arms and legs according to specific, culturally established patterns which also indicate their stratum ascription. By contrast, men are tattooed lightly if at all, and there are no specific male tattoo patterns; indeed, they may take the opportunity of a visit to a foreign group to be tattooed with an unusual pattern (see also Nieuwenhuis 1904: 451). Women's lobes are considerably more elongated than men's, sometimes as much as 10 cm. Men have a hole punched in the shell of the ears in addition to holes in their lobes. If men wear earrings, which they often do not, these are much lighter than women's. The penis pin emphasizes further the contrast between men's and women's genitals. Dress and other decorations are markedly contrasted on the basis of gender.[3] Religion also differentiates between men and women in a number of ways; for instance, in the Kayan naming ceremony, a cock is killed for a male child, a hen for a girl. Some dances are performed by men, others by women; headhunting rituals are reserved for men. Among the Apau Kayan Kenyah, only men can sit under the head trophies in front of the chief's apartment (Habbema 1917: 308). The theory of conception also contrasts father and mother; bones comes from the father, the flesh from the mother.

Sexual differentiation can also be marked by residence patterns: separate cubicles in apartments used to be reserved for nubile girls, while unmarried men slept on the gallery from the time they were seven or eight years old (Nieuwenhuis 1904: 29). Among the Modang and some Kenyah, the separation of unmarried men was marked further by the presence of bachelors' houses which also served a political role: meetings took place there. It was strongly forbidden for women of all ages to enter (Spaan 1901: 25). Men's houses could be erected by the ruling family as well as by lesser aristocrats; they served as meeting places for their clients (Guerreiro 1984: 590), and as gathering places for men when they were not otherwise occupied. The segregation of young men on the gallery or in bachelors' houses also had a defensive purpose, as it allowed them to respond more rapidly to enemy attacks.

Tasks are distributed according to gender and age. Adult men clear the swiddens; they cut trees for timber, canoes and firewood and they erect buildings. They make all tools, including those used by women. They hunt, fish and cut up large game; they go on trips to gather jungle produce and trade with nomads. All designs and decorations are drawn by men. Adult women pound rice, they prepare and cook all meals (men do so only on jungle trips), they grow and process tobacco and collect in the secondary jungle foodstuff used as relish (aromatic leaves, bamboo shoots...) and small fish they catch with hand-nets in streams; they gather snails to make lime for betel plugs. They sew clothes and make beadwork decorations and tattoos, using designs drawn by men. Women wake up first in the morning around 6 A.M. and start cooking rice; men rise soon afterwards and catch some fish for breakfast if necessary. Except for rice cultivation, male tasks involve a higher degree of cooperation than female activities which are individual. Some tasks are performed in part by men, in part by women. Men pare rattan and make most baskets and all basket straps. Women weave mats, headbands and women's baskets with rattan prepared by their husbands. Dogs are always fed by men and chickens by women, and pigs mainly by women or old men.

Cultivation is the main activity. The felling of trees is a male task, but a few young women help cut the underbrush. The firing of the swiddens is strictly men's duty. At the time of sowing, men dibble holes in which women and adolescents of both sexes place seeds. Men and women participate in the weeding and harvest, with a slight preponderance of women in these activities. It is the women's task to select rice seeds. The first ceremonial harvest is also performed by women. Before the Bungan religious reform, men were not allowed to touch seeds. In the past, weeding was primarily a female activity; this was the time of year when men were busy building fences around the fields, while nowadays a few men take the opportunity to undertake other tasks such as building boats or going on trading trips to the Penan. The other cultivars require less attention; fruit and rubber trees are tended by men, cassava, tobacco, sugar cane and other plants of less importance -- such as chili and maize-- mostly by women. Because of the distance between fields and farmhouses, and between farm areas and longhouse, carriage of agricultural products is an important activity in which men play the major role.

Before they are ten years old, children are usually left free to play, one of their few duties being to take care of younger siblings and to run errands in the longhouse. At that age girls start to help their mothers and work occasionally in the fields, but boys start productive activities a few years later. Adolescents are not fully productive until they marry.

Gender and age are only two elements in the division of labor. There are also technical, religious and medical specializations. Among the Baluy Kayan, one can distinguish priests and shamans; priests are slightly more likely to be men (14 men to 8 women), while most shamans are women. The shaman's role is limited to the cure of illnesses, and they have limited religious knowledge. Their status is lower than priests', who are in charge of public rituals and the omnibus *dayong* ceremony.

Power Differentials Between Men and Women

In daily life there is no great discrepancy between men and women, and no overall control of women by men; economic decisions affecting the household are taken together by adult members of the domestic unit, and women control at least the sphere of female activities. For instance, some villages now use powered rice mills which free women from a major activity. Men did not object in any way when women decided to use this new device; more importantly, it was never assumed that they should have much of a say in the matter.[4]

On the other hand, women are minorized at strategic moments of their lives. There are curbs on their participation in decision-making; furthermore, there is differential control of daughters and sons. a. Elders are men, or rather, there are largely distinct spheres of control for male and female elders, the males dealing with most of the structurally important decisions. Young women are typically shy, but as they grow older they participate more openly in social life. Women play a secondary role in inter-community relationships, the contrast being more marked for commoners than aristocrats, among whom there are a number of politically active women. Women rarely used to travel. For instance, a 20-year old Mendalam Kayan woman had never been to Putussibau, three hours away; a wife of the Mahakam-Kayan chief Kwing Irang visited for the first time the neighboring village of U. Suling when she was 50 years old, and she was not fluent in the lingua franca (Busang) (Nieuwenhuis 1904: 284). b. Parents exercise tighter control over their daughters than their sons. Young girls are expected to start helping their parents at an earlier age than boys. Parents interfere more in their daughter's choice of a spouse. This is explainable on two counts: at marriage, the groom is older than the bride and not easily controlled; at least at the beginning, marriages are uxorilocal and parents are less concerned about the sons' marital choices which do not affect their household.

Among the Mahakam-Kayan, child betrothal significantly contributed to reduce women's freedom. "The Kayan may have borrowed the custom of marrying their daughters at a young age from their many slaves from the Barito groups, where this is generally practiced. A young man might marry a 6-year old girl and live with her parents; when the girl was of age, he became her husband without any further ceremony" (Nieuwenhuis 1907: 98). The practice of infant betrothal is also attested among the Murut of the Lawas, Limbang and Trusan, and is associated with an inflation in the value of bridewealth (Pollard 1933: 151).

Gender and Class

Societies of central Borneo are stratified, and this pervades all aspects of life. In many cases, stratum ascription is of greater importance than gender differences. For instance, aristocratic women participate freely in public discussions at ages when commoner women would remain silent. Where uxorilocality is the norm, an exception is made for the chief's heir to enable father-son succession.

In central Borneo, while chiefs were usually men, some women occupied that position.[5] Women chiefs are usually widows of a deceased chief and their position is considered to be temporary until an appropriate son or son-in-law can take over (Whittier 1973: 55-56). In principle, it would be possible for a chief's daughter to take up the office in her own right if there were no suitable male candidate, but there is no clear example of this. While only a minority of central Borneo chiefs are women, this is still a significant contrast with the rest of Borneo. This underdifferentiation of gender follows from the predominance of the domestic unit: chiefship is not an individual's prerogative, but the duty and the privilege of the chiefly household, of which the chief is only the foremost member; when he is absent, any household member, man or woman, may replace him. It also happens that the nominal chief is a man, while the real power is wielded by his wife or his sister (e.g. Nieuwenhuis 1936-37: 221-222; Douglas 1908: 236).

Variation in Women's Status in Central Borneo

Women's participation in decision-making is not a constant in central Borneo. Nieuwenhuis (1907: 97) contrasts the position of women in the Mendalam and the Mahakam: in the Mendalam they play a more important role than men in decision-making, while they have a subordinate role in the Mahakam. There, they are not consulted and they do not come into contact with outsiders. However, Nieuwenhuis notes the presence of powerful women in the Mahakam. He attributes the lower position of women in the Mahakam to polygyny and to the habit of the Mahakam-Kayan of betrothing girls soon after birth (ibid.: 98).

The groups who erected men's houses thereby emphasized and maintained a political differentiation of genders. Insofar as these houses were the locus of political decisions, they also excluded and minorized women. For the stratum of high aristocrats (*hepuy pwun*), the Modang also ranked sexes differentially: the descendants of a male *hepuy pwun* were superior (*du' jehoe*, 'the head of the post') to the descendants of a female *hepuy pwun* (who were *welguak jehoe*, 'the middle of the post') (Guerreiro 1984: 591-592).

Insofar as post-marital residence affects women's status, this factor varies in central Borneo. The Kayan and the Modang have a preference for uxorilocality which is realized whenever possible. On the other hand, while the Kajang practice uxorilocality as frequently as the Kayan, they claim that utrolocality is the rule (de Martinoir 1974: 269-270). While uxorilocality is preferred among some Kenyah groups (Ulok Laeng 1977: 77), it may not be the general ideal. Among the Kelabit, uxorilocality is the ideal, but there are numerous exceptions (Harrisson 1959). Among the Murut of the Trusan and Lawas residence depends on which side sponsors the marriage feast, with a tendency to virilocality (Pollard 1933: 151-154 in LeBar 1972: 161). Lun Dayeh couples usually establish a separate household after the birth of their first child and thus practice a kind of delayed neolocality; 56 percent of couples practice initial uxorilocality, 44 percent initial virilocality, while 10.5 percent practice permanent uxorilocality and 23.5 percent permanent virilocality (Crain 1978: 128, 140; for more on post-marital residence, see Rousseau 1990: 90-98).

Finally, while there are many instances of women chiefs among the Kayan and the Modang, this is not the case among other central Borneo groups. This appears to be a consequence of the class structure. The stratification system appears to have a greater antiquity among the Kayan and Modang, while the Kenyah adopted it when they took up agriculture. Also, there is evidence that the stratification system has grown into a fully-fledged system of exploitation, hence a real class system, among the Kayan and Modang, while the level of exploitation is more modest among other groups. This suggests that the relative equality of genders among the Kayan is a consequence of the class structure, which has reduced the significance of inequality based on gender and age.[6]

NOTES

1. By contrast, virginity was valued among the Melanau: when a girl was of marriageable age, she could not go out unless accompanied by another woman. "On no account was she permitted to have converse with bachelors other than near relations, including first cousins, or even with old men unless she had received her parents' permission first" (Buck 1935: 160). This might be the result of Malay influence.

2. While this remained a permanent arrangement in the Mendalam (Nieuwenhuis 1904: 73), the Mahakam-Kayan practiced utrolocality after a few years of marriage (ibid.: 100). In the Mahakam, even initial uxorilocality could be waived in specific circumstances (ibid.: 85, 100).

3. In the Apau Kayan, the Kayan used to make textiles for festive occasions for themselves and the Kenyah. They used three kinds of fibre: pineapple, locally grown cotton and bast. The first two were for the use of men, the last for women (Tillema 1933-34: 98-103).

4. In every village where they were present during my fieldwork (1970-72, 1974), rice mills were owned by a domestic unit which received a portion of the rice in payment for the service. The machine was operated by the man of the household, but proceeds were the property of the whole domestic unit.

5.   Walchren (1907: 826) knows of no examples among the Uma Alim, the Kenyah or the Segai. There are in fact several reports of women chiefs among the Segai (Dewall 1855: 449, Spaan 1901: 11). Beech (1910: 147) who visited the Segai in 1906 in Bulungan, notes that "formerly *Titan*, a female who had four husbands, appears to have been the recognized chief". At the turn of the century, two women chiefs were the regional leaders in the Segah (Spaan, Ms.: 7). There is a description of Si Ba, the chief of the Segai village of Muara Lasan (Tehupeiorij 1906: 23). Similarly, Modang women have a high status, more than among the Bahau and Busang of the Mahakam (Guerreiro 1984: 59).

6.   However, as we well know, the rise of inequality can also bring about an increasing gap between the status of men and women. Why --or indeed, whether-- the opposite is the case among the Kayan can only be understood in a comparative context based on an as yet to be developed theory of the origin of inequality. On social inequality in central Borneo, see Rousseau (1990: 163-215).

REFERENCES

Beech, Mervyn W. H.
    1910   Some customs of the Sagai of Borneo. Man 10(86): 146-147.

Buck, W. S. B.
    1935   Notes on the Oya Milanos. Sarawak Museum Journal 4: 157-174.

Colfer, Carol J. Pierce
    1981   Women, men, and time in the forests of East Kalimantan. Borneo Research Bulletin 13: 75-85.

Crain, Jay B.
1978   The Lun Dayeh. In V. T. King, ed., Essays on Borneo
                    Societies. Oxford: Oxford University Press, pp. 123-142.

Dewall, H. von
1855   Aanteekeningen omtrent de Noordoostkust van Borneo.
                    Tijdschrift voor Indische Taal-, Land- en Volkenkunde 4:
                    423-458.

Douglas, R. S.
1908   Baram [monthly report]. June. Sarawak Gazette 38: 236.

Freeman, J. Derek
1970   Report on the Iban. London: Athlone.

Guerreiro, Antonio J.
1984   Min. 'maison' et organisation sociale; Contribution à
                    l'ethnographie des sociétés Modang de Kalimantan-est,
                    Indonésie. Thèse de doctorat, Ecole des Hautes Etudes
                    en Sciences sociales, Paris.

Habbema, D.
1917   Een en ander over Apo Kajan. De Indische Gids 39(1):
                    300-315, 463-476.

Harrisson, Tom
1959   World within: A Borneo story. London: Cresset.

Hose, Charles and William McDougall
1912   The pagan tribes of Borneo: A description of their
                    physical, moral and intellectual condition with some
                    discussion of their ethnic relations. London: Macmillan.

LeBar, Frank M. (ed.)
1972   Ethnic groups of insular Southeast Asia. Vol. I: Indone-
                    sia, Andaman Islands and Madagascar. New Haven:
                    HRAF.

Martinoir, Brian L. de
1974   Notes on the Kajang. In J. Rousseau, ed., The peoples of
                    central Borneo. Kuching: Sarawak Museum, pp. 267-
                    273.

Nieuwenhuis, A. W.
1904-07   Quer durch Borneo: Ergebnisse seiner Reisen in den Jahren 1894, 1896-97 und 1898-1900. Leiden: Brill.

1936-37   Het dagelijksch bestaan van Dajakstammen in onafhankelijke streken. Tropisch Nederland 9: 125-128, 143-144, 157-160, 168-173, 189-192, 205-208, 221-224, 237-240, 251-256.

Pollard, Frank Hugh
1933   The Muruts of Sarawak. Sarawak Museum Journal 4: 139-155.

Rousseau, Jérôme
1990   Central Borneo: Ethnic identity and social life in a stratified society. Oxford: Clarendon Press.

Spaan, A. H.
1901   Een landreis van Berouw naar Samarinda. Tijdschrift van het Koninklijk Nederlandsch Aardrijkskundig Genootschap, (2nd. ser.) 18: 7-33, 199-224, 1012.

Ms.   Extract uit de nota van overgave van de onderafdeeling Berouw. 19 x 1901. 12 p. In the archives of the Ministry of Colonies, the Hague, no. 507/03.

Tehupeiorij, J. E.
1906   Onder de Dajaks in Centraal-Borneo; Een reisverhaal. Batavia: Kolff.

Tillema, H. F.
1933-34   Uit Apo-Kajan. Tropisch Nederland 6: 34-43, 50-57, 66-69, 98-103.

Ulok Laeng, Joachim
1977   Communal life in a Kenyah longhouse. Sarawak Gazette 103: 76-77.

Walchren, E. W. F. van
1907   Eene reis naar de bovenstreken van Boeloengan (Midden-
               Borneo), 12 Nov. 1905 - 11 April 1906. Tijdschrift van het
               Koninklijk Nederlandsch Aardrijkskundig Genootschap
               (2nd. ser.) 24: 755-844.

Whittier, Herbert L.
1973   Social organization and symbols of social differentiation:
               An ethnographic study of the Kenyah Dayak of East
               Kalimantan (Borneo). Ph.D dissertation, Michigan State
               University.

ON "THE WATERSNAKE WHICH IS ALSO A HORNBILL": MALE AND FEMALE IN NGAJU DAYAK MORTUARY SYMBOLOGY

ANNE SCHILLER

Where now lies the centre by which the whole of Dayak culture and religion is determined, by which their entire life and thought must be interpreted, and to which everything must be referred? We answer: in the conception of God (Schärer 1963:6).

In the opening chapters of *Ngaju Religion*, the classic ethnography of a "primordial" Bornean belief system, Hans Schärer invoked the powerful imagery of the Ngaju Dayak supreme being, a deity referred to as the "Watersnake which is also the Hornbill" (1963:18). Drawing from informants' accounts, Schärer characterized the deity as manifest in two distinct yet interrelated aspects: one male, the other female. These two aspects, known as Ranying Hatalla Langit and Jata Balawang Bulau, respectively, were also reflected in other "ambivalences": sun and moon, Upperworld and Underworld, sacred spear and sacred cloth, west and east, upstream and downstream (1963:18-19). In his analysis, cast in the interpretive style of the Leiden School, Schärer argued that the complementarity of Hatalla-Jata's dual male and female aspects served as a conceptual model which summarized the whole of Dayak culture. In other words, the duality denoted a totalized system of classification.[1] Among other ways in which the deity's twin aspects were lent discernible form was the supposed organization of the Ngaju community into hierarchically-ranked moieties (1963: 41-43; 157). Though vague as to how marriage rules articulated with tribal subdivisions, Schärer explicitly proposed that relations between these "male" and "female" moieties were tempered through the performance of death rituals (1963:156).

The mortuary practices of contemporary Ngaju villagers confirm Schärer's observations regarding the pervasiveness of dualist symbology among the indigenous peoples of this region. Even fifty years later, one cannot help but be impressed by the often baroque imagery which recalls the categories male and female. The conspicuousness of these images, coupled with the explicit opposition of the sexes in many phases of ritual, suggests that the relationship between these classificatory categories continues to have extensive cultural significance.[2] While Schärer's assertion that the notion of a total/ambivalent deity directly informed the primordial structure of Ngaju social organization is difficult to assess, his contention that dual classification may be investigated to reveal mechanisms which uphold social and cosmological order represents an approach to the study of contemporary Bornean religions that warrants further consideration.[3]

This paper explores selected aspects of Ngaju mortuary symbology. Following Turner, it suggests that male and female representations comprise important symbols within the context of Ngaju mortuary celebrations.[4] Entrenched in a system of dual classification, these images bestir allegiance to a set of ideas concerning the quality and organization of Ngaju life; in this, they operate as vehicles of orientation and discrimination.[5] The potency of these symbols lies in their juxtaposition, a compelling icon which recalls the cultural compromise effected between physiological drives and values which govern behavior.[6] One compromise communicated through the symbols is sexuality made manageable by marriage. By means of socially-approved unions, villagers transform procreative potential into structurally-acceptable alliances. It is significant in this regard that the apposition of male and female symbols within the context of mortuary celebrations, celebrators, which in itself is said to contribute to cosmic revigoration, is usually described by villagers in idioms of conjugality.

To the Ngaju, "male" and "female" are exhaustive discriminations. Yet it can be argued that this particular opposition comprises a "unity in duality." Death and marriage, ritual spheres in which this dualist motif finds most prominent symbolic expression, are likewise mutually completing and systematically interrelated. When circumstances such as unacceptable marriages or the incomplete processing of the dead disturb the equation, veiled dynamics which inform personal relations are disclosed through ritual; here, ritual symbols reveal confluences between cosmological beliefs and idealizations of society. This adds a further dimension to analyses of meanings encoded in Ngaju dualist symbology.

Concerning the analytical implications of dualism in social and religious spheres this paper, as an ethnographic contribution to the study of polarity in symbolic classification, refers to a theme explored at length by Robert Hertz in his essay "The Pre-eminence of the Right Hand: A Study in Religious Polarity." In that important work Hertz noted that, "Primitive thought attributes a sex to all beings in the universe and even to inanimate objects; all of them are divided into two immense classes according to whether they are considered as male or female" (1973:9). Hertz went on to elaborate how this cosmic distinction was ineluctably grounded in a religious antithesis: man is sacred, woman is profane (ibid.:9).

This and other potentially important hierarchical elements of dualism notwithstanding, in some contexts it may be analytically more useful to emphasize the complementarity of oppositions rather than their differential status, as Rodney Needham has pointed out in an analysis of symbolic classification among the Meru of Kenya (1973:117). Applying Needham's insight to the case at hand, we may be able to illuminate certain peculiar aspects of Ngaju mortuary symbology. In a preface to Needham's translation of *Ngaju Religion*, for example, P. E. De Josselin De Jong cited one reviewer's concern with what appeared to be an oversight in Schärer's explanation of how the male/female opposition is played out in the symbolism surrounding the ornamentation of coffins:

> Van Baal...points out a curious lacuna in Schärer's exposé: he baldly states that women are buried in coffins with hornbill ornamentation, and men in coffins shaped like a watersnake - while one of the themes of the book is just the reverse: the association of women with Djata, watersnake, downstream, and underworld, and of man with Mahatala, hornbill, upstream, and upperworld. One can agree with Van Baal that the association of the sexes with the two types of coffins is "strange" and "unexpected", and that here Schärer would have done well to explain this puzzling feature. What we cannot do is to state that Schärer must be wrong (1963: vi).

In fact, Schärer was not wrong. His apparent omission makes sense in terms of the logic of Ngaju dual classification as it figures in treatment of the dead. So great is the importance of establishing unity in duality that, at the level of mortuary symbology, items evoking one or the other of the terms of the male/female opposition are consociated. Thus it is that women may be given hornbill coffins, and men are given watersnake coffins, that certain ritual observances must be performed by the deceased's opposite-sex sibling or cousin, that the "souls" of opposite-sex slaves should be sent to serve the deceased in the afterlife, and that "female" animals must be sacrificed on behalf of deceased males and vice versa, as will be seen below.

DEATH RITUALS AND ASSOCIATED SYMBOLOGY

The term "Ngaju" generally refers to the indigenous swidden horti-culturalists living along the middle and lower reaches of the Barito, Kapuas, Kahayan, Katingan, and Mentaya Rivers and their tributaries, who speak a dialect of a language known generally as Ngaju, and who do not claim to be members of neighboring groups such as the Ma'anyan or Ot Danum. Most villagers identify themselves by reference to the river they live along (i.e. *uluh Kahayan*, or "Kahayan person"), or to an even more delimited feature of their environment, rather than by the term Ngaju which many feel is denigratory. In the local language "ngaju" means "upriver." In some contexts, referring to someone as an "upriver person" intimates that they are extremely lowbred. Whether one observes the mortuary celebrations of Kahayan or other Ngaju groups, the broad outlines are similar throughout the region. In some sense, then, differences in religious practices can be seen as variations on a theme. The importance of overall similarities, however, should not obscure the fact that deviations in ritual practices have traditionally served as boundary markers between peoples on different rivers. It is to preserve this sense of place as well as to accurately portray the source of the data here that the present paper refers almost exclusively to ritual symbology of the Kahayan River Ngaju.

Also concerning the indigenous religion it is important to note that in 1980 the Indonesian Ministry of Religion declared the belief system of the Ngaju a Hindu sect. "Ngaju Religion" now goes by the name of Hindu Kaharingan. Official recognition of Hindu Kaharingan has paved the way for a local campaign aimed at religious rationalization, including ritual standardization and the codification of belief. The standardization of ritual and its effect upon the meanings imbued to symbols is beyond the scope of the present paper, however.[7]

The most elaborate of Kahayan River Ngaju ritual practices concern treatment of the dead. To Kahayan villagers, the death of a kinsman has immense sociological and cosmological significance. According to adherents of the indigenous religion, the souls of deceased kinsmen reside in a region of the cosmological Upper World. Souls can ascend to this place only after a ritual cycle has been performed on their behalf.   Until souls and physical remains are processed completely, both the living and the dead are prey to dangers of supernatural origin. This ritual cycle culminates with a secondary mortuary celebration known as *tiwah*. *Tiwah* is explicitly intended to reunite the deceased's three souls and escort them, together with goods and animals sacrificed on their behalf, to join previously processed ancestors.[8] The proper performance of death ritual, with full attention to detail, is said to please the souls, to recreate and reinvigorate the cosmos, and to strengthen family solidarity. Mortuary celebrations also, however, simultaneously accentuate symbolically series of differentiations between and within groups of participants, as will be seen below.

During primary treatment and *tiwah* various ritual accommodations are made for the deceased, depending upon his or her sex. These adjustments recall the importance of the classificatory categories male and female. For example, odd numbers are associated with Ngaju ritual activities: as will be demonstrated shortly, the lesser of two odd numbers is associated with women or with femaleness.[9] When no trace of a pulse remains, a gong is struck to announce the death. Staccato bursts (*titih*) make the death known and bid all within hearing distance of the deceased's home. The tatoo chosen indicates the deceased's sex: gongs are repeatedly struck seven times in a row for men, five times for women. Meanwhile, in the center of the front room of the house, a bamboo plank supported by a row of gongs is readied for the display of the corpse. The deceased is arranged upon the plank with his or her face exposed. Beneath the platform, tools appropriate to the deceased's sex are set out.   Women are displayed with their feet pointed upriver, recollecting the association of women with "downstream," upstream recollecting the reverse. The arrangement is explained by the women's yearning to travel to the headwaters to search for gold, and by men's desire to wander the length of the river toward the coast.

On the morning of the second or third day following death a black pig or cow provided by the bereaved spouse or children is sacrificed by the deceased's opposite-sex sibling or first cousin. Blood from the beast is used to anoint men who spend the rest of the day constructing a coffin. The blood is said to cool the mens' souls and protect them in their work.

Traditional coffins from the region are elaborate works of great beauty. Three types of decorated coffins are found in the Kahayan area. The woman's coffin (*raung basangkuwai*) is in the shape of a particular type of bird and sometimes identified as a hornbill. The man's coffin (*raung banaga*) has the head and tail of a watersnake. The third traditional-style coffin, suitable for either sex, has the head of a watersnake and the tail of a bird (*raung ambon ingang*) (see Illustration 1).

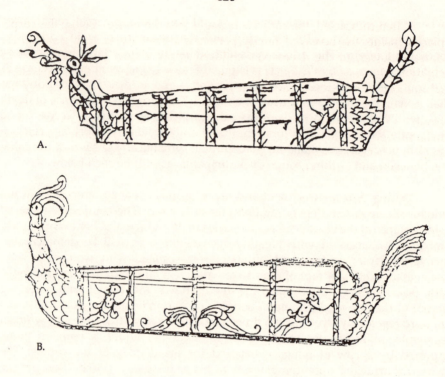

A.   Man's Coffin (*Raung Banaga*); note "watersnake motif."
B.   Woman's Coffin (*Raung Basangkuwai*); note "bird" motif.
C.   Coffin suitable for either sex (*Raung Ambun Ingang*).

Drawn by the late Damang J. Saililah.

When completed, the coffin is brought into the house. Before the corpse is placed inside, the bereaved family performs a brief ritual during which the widow, widower, or the deceased's children apply yellow juice, produced by crushing the leaves of a particular plant, to the hair and nails of the deceased, or touch the corpse's hair and nails with gold. Gold is "touched" (*manunding*) five times to women, seven times to men. Only then may the corpse be arranged in the coffin. Traditional coffins are narrow. The corpse is placed on its left side if female, its right if male. Finally, the coffin is secured with rattan bands (*saluang raung*). Five bands stretched over twenty-one wooden wedges secure a woman's coffin, seven bands over twenty-three wedges a man's.

During preparations for *tiwah*, men and women are assigned several complementary tasks. One is preparing cooked rice for the soul to carry on its journey to the Upper World. Women pound the rice and men oversee its cooking. Men and women not involved busy themselves with the erection of carved poles (*sapundu*), ideally made from ironwood, which stand about six to nine feet high. Sacrificial animals will be tethered here. First, men dig the post holes. Then, before they lower the poles into the earth, women scatter uncooked rice around the post holes and rub oil on the base of each pole. The animate essence of the pole is said to become the deceased's slave in the Upper World. If the deceased was male, the pole must resemble a woman (*sapundu bawi*) (see Plate 1). If the deceased was female, it must be carved in the shape of a man (*sapundu hatue*) (see Plate 2). Similarly, a male animal should be sacrificed on a woman's behalf, and a female animal on a man's.

Other participants not involved in cooking or in erecting sacrificial poles construct or refurbish ossuaries (*sandung*). These repositories are designed in the shape of the region's traditional houses. In *Ngaju Religion*, Schärer argued that houses are associated with femaleness (1963:70). His hypothesis appears to be borne out by the fact that these ossuaries are "paired" with wooden or cement representations of phalluses, ranging in height from about twelve inches in the Kahayan region to up to thirty feet or more along the Katingan River. These are erected alongside the repositories (see Plate 3).

PLATE 1 - *Sapundu Bawi*; Female *sapundu*.

Sacrificial pole carved to resemble a contemporary woman dressed in a tee-shirt and jeans. Suitable for a man's *tiwah*.

PLATE 2 - *Sapundu Hatue*; Male *Sapundu*.

In the foreground stands a sacrificial pole carved to resemble a man. Suitable for a woman's *tiwah*. In the background stands a post carved with two figures (*Sapundu Rahu Nyampang*), suitable for either a man or woman's *tiwah*.

PLATE 3 - *Pantar Panjang*, Katingan River Village.

Tall pole carved to represent a phallus. Placed alongside the bone repositories of renowned individuals.

As a final touch in the decoration of ossuaries, the repository's miniature doorways are decorated by a pair of figurines, a tiny man and woman. The "couple" is said to wed and produce children, who join them as guardians for the ossuary's inhabitants (see Plate 4).

PLATE 4 - *Sandung;* Bone Repository, Kahayan River Village

Of the *sandung munduk* type, this cement repository is built directly on the ground. Note male and female "guardians" and the phallus in the foreground.

Depending upon the specifics of particular *tiwah*, the celebration may be marked, before the animal sacrifices commence, by the arrival of one or more prestation ships (*kapal laluhan*) conveying contributions of foods and goods from families in neighboring villages. The arrival of such ships provides an opportunity for one of the most spectacular representations of male and female "complementarity" associated with *tiwah*. These prestation ships are festooned with flamboyant banners and waving fronds. The costumes of crew members are more striking still; their faces are disguised by horrific masks featuring long, curved noses, wild bulging eyes, and snarling lips. In addition to masks, these men and women bedeck themselves in raiment of banana leaves. Their frond robes but partially conceal the rest of their costume - enormous wooden phalluses or halved coconut husks representing female genitalia.[10] When the ships are in sight of the village, crew members commence an animated dance which mimics coitus. They call out, demanding that the sponsors of *tiwah* swim to the ship and join them. Villagers react to the invitation with horror, hilarity, and a barrage of blunted spears.

While an invitation to sexual congress with these raucous invaders threatens Ngaju notions of propriety at many levels, it does not, at least, intimate the potentiality of incest. The crew may not be related by blood or by marriage to the sponsors of death ritual. As non-kin, they may be metaphorically categorized as strangers. Their lack of recognized identity is further underscored by means of costumes which camouflage not only their faces, but their humanity. It is very significant that, although the arrival of a prestation ship is eminently desirable, its presence is optional. The presence of a ship specifically, and of non-kin generally, are not required to complete the processing of the dead.[11] As pointed out above, in *Ngaju Religion* Schärer suggested that "we may take it for granted that formerly the whole tribe gathered for [this] great religious/cosmic service" (1963:137-138). As that is not the case today, it is crucial to specify who is expected to participate in these rituals and what kinds of distinctions are made between the participants in order to explain how ritual practices are related to the dualist classifications under discussion.

OF HORNBILLS AND HUMANS

Regarding the duty to process the dead, it is instructive to note that ritual specialists liken treatment of the dead to the nesting habits of rhinoceros hornbills (*Buceros rhinoceros borneoensis*), extraordinary-looking birds that figure prominently in Kahayan mythology. When a female hornbill is ready to lay eggs, she prepares a nest in the trunk of a dead tree.[12] Her mate follows and entombs her behind an incrassate wall of resins and mud. The female hornbill would remain in the tiny chamber forever were she forgotten or abandoned. Each day, however, the male returns bringing food. On the thirty-third day of entombment the male liberates his trapped mate and hatchlings, using his massive beak to break open the entrance to the nest. Remarkably, if the male has died, other hornbills arrive to free the female. Like hornbills, the metaphoric alterselves of human beings, people depend upon others of their kind, ideally spouses, to breech their tombs. Only in this way can souls of the dead begin the final phase of their journey to immortality.

The analogy between hornbills and humans is most provocative. It conveys the value vested in the mutuality of the sexes which, as noted above, is epitomized in idioms of conjugality and procreation. The analogy also underscores the interrelatedness of marriage and the ritual processing of the dead. Villages aver that marriages should endure until one spouse cradles the other's bones. Couples about to wed are reminded of the legend of Nyai Endas Bulau, who requested of her immortal Upper World husband no marriage prestations save a hill for her grave site and a red cloth in which her bones would be wrapped. While Kahayan mortuary celebrations are usually completed jointly by the extended family, the proceedings are ideally initiated by the deceased's bereaved spouse. In time, it is said, husband and wife are reunited in the Upper World, just as their remains are destined to commingle in the ossuary.[13]

When questioned concerning their mortuary customs, Kahayan villagers are adamant that all their family members' remains would eventually come to repose in one ossuary if the circumstances of death so permitted. In actuality, however, this ideal is seldom, if ever, achieved. Certain kinsmen are in fact consciously excluded from the repository. The key to determining who has the right to be installed in a particular ossuary lies in Kahayan marriage preferences and conceptualizations of the parameters of kinship. Only the remains of individuals who are cognatic kin may be entombed together. And under ideal circumstances, one's spouse is one's cognatic kinsman: Kahayan villagers prefer that marriages be contracted between cousins. Although marriage with a nonkinsman offers the advantage of potentially enlarging the kin group, such a marriage simultaneously poses a risk: only one's cognatic kinsmen, whose genealogies are of course intimately known, are assuredly human. Other people may not be people at all; they may be supernatural beings, called *hantuen*, whom villagers particularly fear. *Hantuen* are soulless, sanguisugent creatures characterized by amoral dispositions and promiscuous sexuality. Villagers especially dread *hantuen* as these are reputed to have the potential to dwell both inside and outside human society. They can assume human guise and attempt to marry men or women whose families and fortunes they subsequently destroy. Many legends recount the unfortunate consequences of marriage to *hantuen*.

Among the Ngaju, attacks of *hantuen* are most feared within the context of two events. The first is parturition, the second is on the occasion of laying out the dead. That the risk of attack is said to increase exponentially at such times may well be due to the fact that at childbirth and at death, the unity of the family is most clearly juxtaposed against the presence of its social "other," strangers and nonkin. By virtue of marriage preferences, the birth of children should ideally be the outcome of a union between cousins. Similarly death constitutes kinsmen's final opportunity to place their loved ones' souls beyond the reach of anyone save the deceased's cognatic ancestors. That accounts for why, if the deceased's cognatic ancestor was an in-marrying spouse, a small repository built expressly for his or her remains must be constructed. In death, as in life, family members thus attempt to shelter one another from supernatural harassment. Here the intersection of idealizations of the family with popular cosmological beliefs is most clearly apparent. Dualist symbolism, particularly in its aspects associated with prestation ships *tiwah*, further illuminates the relationship between these spheres.

As noted above, the crews of prestation ships are unrelated to the sponsors of death ritual. Furthermore they are made to appear almost inhuman by means of startling costumery. Turner has suggested out that the distortion of human features may cause participants in a ritual to reflect upon the essence of their own humanity (1964). In the Ngaju case, the crews' grotesque appearance may conjure images of *hantuen*. Like those profligate entities, the crew members attempt to goad sponsors into wanton sexual relations. Such congress is unacceptable because it is not governed by social norms; rather than being procreative, as is marriage, the union is perilous. Mortuary celebrations, therefore, serve less to make villagers aware of their interdependence than to emphasize subconsciously the importance of maintaining boundaries between sponsors and outsiders. As villagers explain it, "death rituals tell us who we are."

CONCLUDING REMARKS

The complementarity of the classificatory categories male and female is clearly expressed in the mortuary symbology of the Kahayan River Ngaju. Symbols representing men and women, maleness and femaleness, are called into play and shape the dominant theme of the ritual processing of the dead. Treatment of the dead, in turn, is interrelated to Ngaju rituals of marriage. In this, both can be regarded as essentially generative. Juxtaposed in ritual, male and female symbols form compelling icons which communicate and inculcate cultural values. For their significance to be fully assessed, the representations must be viewed within the wider context of idealizations of the family and of contemporary cosmological beliefs. Within this broad perspective, the norms expressed through these dual symbols inform conceptualizations of the parameters of kinship, reverberate in cosmological beliefs concerning the perils of miscegenation, and govern relations between the sexes. To Kahayan villagers, the dualist representations discussed in this paper synchronously evoke ideas of both who they are, and who they are not. In light of contemporary ethnographic evidence presented here, then, we can return to a point made at the outset of this paper concerning speculations about primordial belief systems and their change over time. While Schärer's proposal concerning whether the complementary classificatory categories male and female directly informed Ngaju social organization remains dubious, the application of his general approach, i.e., the investigation of dualist symbols, may enable students of Bornean societies to educe social dynamics otherwise virtually unrecognizable. Schärer is correct, therefore, in stating that the extent of the importance of mechanisms which maintain order in social and cosmological spheres can only be known if we accord dualist representations full attention in analyses of indigenous ritual symbology.

ACKNOWLEDGEMENTS

Portions of this papers were presented at the annual meeting of the American Anthropological Association in Chicago (1987). I am grateful to Theresa Wilson for her comments on a later draft of the paper. The research upon which the paper is based was carried out in Indonesia from late 1982 through mid 1984. Support for the research was provided by a Fulbright-Hays Award for Doctoral Dissertation Research Abroad, a Wenner-Gren Foundation Grant-in-Aid of Research, an Alice Freeman Palmer Award granted by Wellesley College, and a Sigma-Xi Scientific Society Grant-in-Aid of Research.

I would like to acknowledge the assistance of the late Damang Johannes Saililah, who shared his expertise in matters of the details of ritual practice with three generations of ethnographers in Kalimantan, in helping me to appreciate some of the intricacies of Ngaju symbology.

NOTES

1. On the concept of totalized system see Fox 1980.

2. This relationship extends even to the sphere of language. Among the Ngaju a "ritual language," characterized by its use of semantic parallelism, is employed by ritual specialists on a number of religious occasions. Phrases in the ritual language are said to be either "male" or "female;" a male phrase is always followed by a female one. On Ngaju ritual language generally see Baier et al. 1987; Doko et al. 1982/3; Elbaar et al. 1981/2; and Fox 1971.

3. On the unusual abstractions employed in Schärer's prose note Needham 1963:ix-x.

4. On the concept of dominant symbols see Turner 1967:30-31 and Ortner 1973.

5. On the analysis of sacred symbols see Geertz 1973:129-131.

6. On the properties of ritual symbols see Turner 1977:52-53.

7. For an extended discussion of changes in the religious sphere and the implications of such change see Schiller 1987.

8. Although this paper follows Hertz in referring to *tiwah* as a form of secondary treatment (1960:30), it is actually the third stage of the Kahayan mortuary cycle. The first two stages are primary treatment, culminating with interment, and the performance of chants and requisite rituals intended to provide primary treatment for the deceased's souls.

9. Ritual specialists, known as *basir*, perform in odd-numbered groups. Depending upon the celebration at hand, three, five, nine, or eleven *basir* may be engaged. For a discussion of ritual specialists among the Kahayan River Ngaju see Schiller 1989.

10. Although the use of masks remains widespread, it is extremely rare for contemporary Ngaju to don the elaborate costumes described here.

11. A ship is sent as part of a single cycle of exchange; whatever is given by one family is reciprocated by those who receive the ship when the senders themselves perform *tiwah*.

12.   Support for this ethnoscientific account can be found in Smythies (1981:216-218). There is an inherent opposition between hornbill nest-making and human burial practices that should be pointed out. Hornbills lay eggs in the trunks of dead trees, whereas humans are buried in coffins made from the trunks of living trees.

13.   Reunion of the extended family in the afterlife is the crux of most villagers' comprehension of eschatology. Many ritual specialists assert a different view, however, namely that the deceased is transformed into an unmarried youth in the afterlife.

REFERENCES

Baier, M., with A. Hardeland and H. Schärer.
    1987   Wörterbuch Der Priestersprache Der Ngaju-Dayak. Dordrecht: Foris Publications. Verhandelingen van het Koninklijk Instituut Voor Taal-, Land- en Volkenkunde, no. 128.

De Josselin De Jong, P.E.
    1963   Preface. In Hans Schärer, Ngaju Religion. The Hague: Martinus Nijhoff, pp. v-viii.

Doko, D. et al.
    1982/83   Struktur Sastra Lisan Dayak Sangen. Palangka Raya: Departemen P dan K, Proyek Penelitian Bahasa Dan Sastra Indonesia dan Daerah Kalimantan Barat.

Elbaar, L. et al.
    1982/83   Struktur Bahasa Sangen. Palangka Raya: Departemen P dan K, Proyek Penelitian Bahasa dan Sastra Indonesia dan Daerah Kalimantan Barat.

Fox, J.

1971   Semantic Parallelism in Rotinese Ritual Language. In Bijdragen tot de Taal-, Land, en Volkenkunde 127:215-255.

1973   On Bad Death and the Left Hand. In Right and Left: Essays on Dual Symbolic Classification. Rodney Needham, ed. Chicago: University of Chicago Press, pp. 342-368.

1980   The Flow of Life. James Fox, ed. Cambridge: Harvard University Press.

Geertz, C.
1973   Religion as a Cultural System. In The Interpretation of Cultures. New York: Basic Books, pp. 87-125.

1973   Ethos, World View, and the Analysis of Sacred Symbols. In The Interpretation of Cultures, New York, Basic Books, pp. 126-141.

Hertz, R.
1960   Death and the Right Hand. (orig. 1907). Translated by Rodney and Claudia Needham. Introduction by E. E. Evans-Pritchard. New York, Free Press.

1973   The Pre-eminence of the Right Hand: A Study in Religious Polarity. Translated from the French by Rodney Needham. In Right and Left: Essays on Dual Symbolic Classification. Rodney Needham, ed. Chicago: University of Chicago Press, pp. 3-31.

Hocart, A.
1952   The Life-Giving Myth and Other Essays. London: Methuen.

Needham, R.
1963   Translator's Note. In Hans Schärer, Ngaju Religion. The Hague: Martinus Nijhoff, pp. ix-x.

1973   Introduction. In Right and Left: Essays on Dual Symbolic Classification. Chicago: University of Chicago Press, pp. xi-xxxix.

Needham, R.
1973   The Left Hand of the Mugwe. In Right and Left: Essays on Dual Symbolic Classification. Chicago: University of Chicago Press, pp. 109-127.

Ortner, S.
1973   On Key Symbols. In American Anthropologist 75(5):1338-1346.

Saililah, J.
            Unpublished manuscript.

Schärer, H.
1963   Ngaju Religion. (orig. 1946) Translated from the German by Rodney Needham. The Hague: Martinus Nijhoff (=Koninklijk Instituut Voor Taal-, Land, en Volkenkunde, Translation Series no. 6).

Schiller, A.
1987   Dynamics of Death: Ritual, Identity, and Religious Change Among the Kalimantan Ngaju. Ph.D. Dissertation, Cornell University.

1989   Shamans and Seminarians: Ngaju Dayak Ritual Specialists and Religious Change in Central Kalimantan. In Contributions to Southeast Asian Ethnography, 8:5-24.

Smythies, B.
1981   The Birds of Borneo. Third Edition. Kuala Lumpur: Sabah Society with the Malayan Nature Society.

Turner, V.
1964   Betwixt and Between: The Liminal Period in Rites de Passage. In The Proceedings of the American Ethnological Society-Symposium on New Approaches to the Study of Religion. Seattle: University of Washington Press, pp. 4-20.

1967   The Forest of Symbols. Ithaca: Cornell University Press.

1977   The Ritual Process. Ithaca: Chicago: Aldine Publishing Company

THE PENIS PIN: AN UNSOLVED PROBLEM
IN THE RELATIONS BETWEEN THE SEXES IN BORNEO

DONALD E. BROWN
University of California, Santa Barbara

Although little is known about human sexuality in Borneo, one aspect of Bornean sexuality has been the subject of scholarly writing in every decade since the 1830s: the use of the penis pin. In spite of this long period of scholarly attention, we still don't really know what the penis pin is all about; that is, we don't know what motivates the practice. Let us begin with a summary of what is known about Bornean penis pins.

The penis pin is part of a Southeast Asian cultural complex that in its commonest form involves surgery to the penis to install a device that allegedly enhances female sexual pleasure. This complex may have had its origin in India, and portions of the complex have diffused to peoples far outside Southeast Asia (Brown n.d., Brown et al. 1988; Vale and Juno 1989).

In Borneo the surgery involves piercing the penis--much as one might pierce an earlobe--so that a pin can be worn in it.[1] Sometimes the pins are

---

[1] There is a single report of an alternative form of surgery to the penis in Borneo: after presenting a conventional account of Bornean penis pins, Hansen (1988) also states that "Bahau River villagers" scarify the upper surface of the

435

simply straight rods with rounded ends. More typically, the pins have protuberances at each end, at least in part to keep the pins from falling out. In the simplest of these forms, the pins look like little barbells; in more complex variants, the protuberances have a considerable variety of shapes and textures. Sometimes a tube is inserted into the pierced hole in the penis to serve as a sleeve within which the pin can rotate (Friesen and Schuman 1964, Kleiweg de Zwaan 1920). One recent account (Macdonald 1982) says that the Berawan of Long Terawan use the various sizes of shear pins of outboard motor propellers as penis pins. (For published sketches or photos of penis pins see Appell 1968, Barclay 1980, Friesen and Schuman 1964, Harrisson 1964 and 1966, Kleiweg de Zwaan 1920, Miklucho-Maclay 1876a, Miller 1942, Moll 1912.)

Palang, which in Malay or Iban means cross or crossbar, is probably the commonest name for the penis pin in the literature. But the Kayan term, *uttang*, is also widely reported. Less frequent are the Kenyah term, *aja*, and a term used in southeast Borneo, *kaleng* or *kaling*. (For discussions of these terms and many of the terms for parts of the penis pin and the devices used to install them, see especially Barth 1910, De Waal 1855, Gaffron 1859, Mayer 1877).

The shafts of the penis pins are made from a variety of materials, including bone, bamboo, wood, and metal; brass is particularly common. The materials employed to construct the protuberances show even greater variation—including, for example, gemstone, glass, seeds, feathers, and pig's bristles (Bock 1887, Dalton 1837, Griffith 1955, Hardeland 1859, Harrisson 1959 and 1964, Hose and McDougal 1912, Mayer 1877, Miklucho-Maclay 1876b, Nieuwenhuis 1904-07, Richards 1981, St. John 1863, Veth 1854). The diameters of the pins vary from about 2 to 4 mm; lengths vary from 21 mm to more than 5 cm (Appell 1968, Burns 1849, De Waal 1855, Gaffron 1859, Juynboll 1909, Macdonald 1982, Richards 1981). One source (Richards 1981) says that the pin should be as long as the middle phalange of one's finger, while another source (De Waal 1855) says as long as the distance between the teeth (assuming that distance between the teeth means between the upper and lower incisors when the mouth is held wide open, these two measures are both about the same).

---

glans penis by making incisions into which ash is rubbed. As a modern variant, men go to a government dispensary, where the operation is performed with an anesthetic and the incisions are sutured so as to leave 3 to 5 parallel ridges.

The pins always or nearly always pierce the glans penis, and probably most commonly are placed in a horizontal position above the urethra (Bock 1887, Burns 1849, Dalton 1837, De Waal 1855, Griffith 1955, Hose and McDougal 1912, Kleiweg de Zwaan 1920, Kuhlewein 1930, Moll 1912, Nieuwenhuis 1900, Richards 1981, Tillema 1934-35). But sometimes the piercing deliberately transects the urethra (Griffith 1955, Kuhlewein 1930, Richards 1981), and sometimes the piercing is vertical or at an angle (Barclay 1980, De Waal 1855, Nieuwenhuis 1900). As many as five pins may be worn at once (Richards 1981), but a single pin is probably commonest. Most pins appear to be easily removable (Appell 1968, Friesen and Schuman 1964, Griffith 1955, Kuhlewein 1930, Mayer 1877, Nieuwenhuis 1900 and 1904-07, Veth 1854).

A clamp made of wood or bamboo is usually placed on the penis prior to the piercing operation in order to drive blood from the penis at the point where it will be pierced. This desensitizes the penis and reduces bleeding. The man who is about to be pierced may achieve further desensitizing by standing in water. A pointed shaft is then driven through the penis, guided by holes in the clamp. After the penis is pierced and the clamp has been removed, a temporary pin or wire may be employed to keep the piercing open during healing (Appell 1968, Harrisson 1959 and 1966, Juynboll 1909, Kleiweg de Zwaan 1920, Kuhlewein 1930, Low 1892, Miklucho-Maclay 1876b, Nieuwenhuis 1900 and 1904-07, Richards 1981).

There is little consensus on the extent of pain and the risk of medical complications that penis pins entail for either men or women (Bock 1887, Dalton 1837, Gaffron 1859, Griffith 1955, Low 1892, Mayer 1877, Nieuwenhuis 1900, St. John 1863). Kuhlewein (1930) looked into the matter most carefully--examining the genitals of 2500 Bornean men--and reports only that he found no evidence of lesser fertility among those native groups with the higher percentages of men who had penis pins. Friesen and Schuman (1964) give the only specific evidence of a medical problem: a penis pin that had been left inserted for a lengthy period acquired calcium deposits and thus had to be removed surgically.

Penis pins are normally installed at puberty or later (Burns 1849, Dalton 1837, Friesen and Schuman 1964, Kuhlewein 1930, Nieuwenhuis 1900 and 1904-07, Veth 1854). Sometimes specialists perform the operation (Dalton 1837, Hansen 1988, Harrisson 1959, Richards 1981). There appears to be little ritual or supernatural belief associated with the practice, though the piercing operation is conducted in secret among the Iban (Richards 1981). For some peoples there are reports of certain qualifications that must be met before one can wear the pin (De Waal 1855, Mayer 1877, Nieuwenhuis 1904-07). For example, a man may have to have been on a headhunt or have taken a head before he can wear the pin. Sometimes rank is indicated by the quality of the material of a man's penis pin

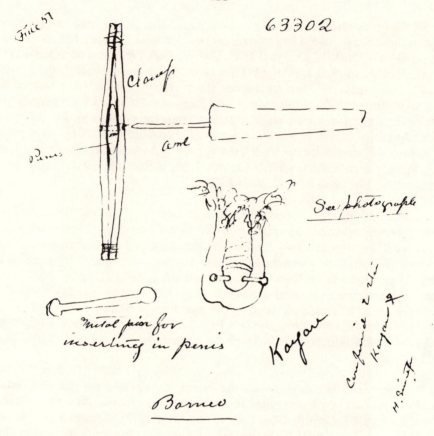

Fig. 57

63302

Clamp

Awl

Penis

See photograph

Metal pin for inserting in penis

Kayan

Confuse à the Kayan ?

H. Smith

Borneo

The clamp is placed vertically
over the glans penis with the aperture
at the point where the perforation
is to be made. The awl is then driven
through the aperture and pierces the
penis. A wood or metal pin is inserted after the clamp is removed
and allowed to remain permanently
The object is to increase sexual excitement
during coition. The woman it seems
encourages the practice to the extent of
boycotting those who have not adopted it.

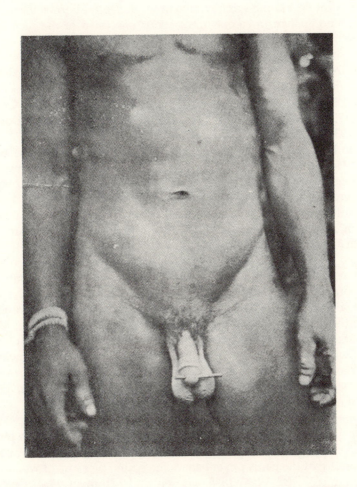

or by such ornamentation as accompanies it (Dalton 1837, Low 1892, Nieuwenhuis 1900, Veth 1854).

There is considerable variation in the proportion of men who wear penis pins. For example, among some groups in south central Borneo virtually all men had pins; among Iban in recent times about one third of the men wore them (Dalton 1837, Kuhlewein 1930, Richards 1981).

Although penis pins are either absent or rare among the coastal Malays of Borneo, the pins are widely reported among the pagans in all areas (Bock 1887, Burns 1849, De Waal 1855, Friesen and Schuman 1964, Gaffron 1859, Griffith 1955, Haddon 1936, Hardeland 1859, Harrisson 1959, Hose and McDougal 1912, Juynboll 1909, Kleiweg de Zwaan 1920, Kuhlewein 1930, Le Bar 1972, Low 1892, Macdonald 1982, Moll 1912, Nieuwenhuis 1900, Richards 1981, Schneebaum 1979, Tillema 1934-35, Walchren 1907) except north-central and northwest Borneo (Appell 1968, Walchren 1907). The most frequent reports seem to be from the south or southeast. The Kayan are the only group credited with the invention and dissemination of the practice within Borneo--allegedly having introduced it to the Iban, Kenyah, and some Punan groups (Burns 1849, Harrisson 1959, Low 1892, Veth 1854, Walchren 1907).

Among some peoples penis pins are very much a part of public culture. The Iban, for example, commonly depicted penis pins on fabrics (see, e.g., Haddon and Start 1936), and an Iban or Berawan man may tatoo himself in a way that advertises that he is equipped with a penis pin (Richards 1981, Macdonald 1982). Derek and Monica Freeman found the penis pin in a sketch by a young Iban boy, which implies that the use of the pins was common knowledge from an early age (D. Freeman, personal communication). In central Borneo, statues designed to ward off spirits are equipped with ostentatious penis pins (Nieuwenhuis 1904-07).

Finally, we know that one explanation for the use of penis pins is very widely reported, but that other explanations are given too. By far the commonest explanation is that the penis pin enhances the sexual pleasure of women (Barclay 1980, Dalton 1837, De Waal 1855, Friesen and Schuman 1964, Gaffron 1859, Griffith 1955, Harrisson 1959, Kleiweg de Zwaan 1920, Low 1892, Mayer 1877, Miklucho-Maclay 1876b, Richards 1981). This point is embroidered in a number of ways. For example, it is said that women may request their husbands to get pierced, or that women will divorce husbands who won't be pierced (Gaffron 1859), or that once habituated to it women cannot go without the pin (Miklucho-Maclay 1876). Women are alleged to say that the penis pin is to sex what salt is to rice (Gaffron 1859, Mayer 1877). On the other hand, it is also said that it is older women in particular (and so presumably not just women in general) who want their husbands to have the penis pin (De Waal 1855, Kleiweg de Zwaan 1920, Mayer 1877).

Among the alternative explanations, two that appear in the primary sources referring to Borneo require only brief comment. First, Miller (1942) says that the purpose of penis pins is to infibulate, i.e., to ensure celibacy. But there is little reason to trust his testimony—which runs counter to all other evidence—for he was merely a traveller in Borneo and he did not speak the local languages. Second, it is sometimes alleged—and the allegation may be indigenous to Borneo—that penis pins have been inspired by the *palang*-like protuberances on the penis of the Bornean rhinoceros (Harrisson 1956, Macdonald 1982, Richards 1981). However, even if this allegation is correct, it is not an alternative explanation of the purpose of the penis pin, of <u>why</u> the rhinoceros was imitated.

Three other explanations are found in the secondary or non-Bornean literature. One is that the penis pin is a precautionary measure against a folk illness, called *koro*, that is found in China and parts of Southeast Asia (Wulfften Palthe 1936). It is believed that the penis of a man afflicted with this disease shrinks into his body; when it shrinks all the way in, the man dies. The penis pin, according to this explanation, prevents the penis from shrinking all the way, or gives one something to hold on to should this fate seem imminent. There is no indication, however, that this explanation is known in Borneo. Another explanation from secondary sources is that the penis pin is an antidote or weapon against the vagina *dentata*, the vagina with teeth (Legman 1975). A belief that the vagina has teeth is widespread, and the penis pin might conceivably be a response to this male fear. Again, however, there is no evidence that this is a Bornean explanation. Yet another explanation is that penis piercing, like other forms of body piercing, results from the idea that such practices magically strengthen the body, or at least the part of the body that is pierced (Kleiweg de Zwaan 1920). Judging by published materials on penis inserts elsewhere in Southeast Asia (Brown <u>et al</u>. 1988), this explanation may have merit, but it is an idea that has not been pursued in the literature on Bornean penis pins. Since none of these three explanations has so far been put to the test by persons with experience in Borneo, their relevance to Bornean peoples is uncertain.

The only explanation of the penis pin that is found in the literature and that commands attention as a serious alternative to the woman-pleaser explanation is that the penis pin is a product of male machismo (bravado). This explanation is discussed in later sections of this paper.

....

The claim that the penis pin is a woman pleaser, even though it appears to be a widespread indigenous explanation, poses some real and very interesting problems--problems that lead away from what is known into areas of uncertainty. A few considerations about the woman-pleaser explanation are particularly important:

First, there is all too little evidence that it is <u>women</u> who say the penis pin gives them pleasure. Only a single published source gives unequivocal evidence that a woman was interviewed to obtain this explanation in Borneo, but what she is reported as actually saying is not a ringing endorsement of penis pins. When asked "how she enjoyed" her husband's three penis pins, she replied that "she preferred to make love when he only had one" (Barclay 1980:96). Moreover, this woman was interviewed by a man, in a bantering manner, in mixed company, and through two interpreters--so the result carries little weight anyway. While two anthropologists and a linguist (James Peter Brosius, B. J. L. Sellato, and Patricia Whittier, personal communications) report that at least one woman told each of them that the penis pin gave them pleasure, the questioning was not private and was not pursued in depth.

Second, the neurology, physiology, and anatomy of the female genitalia provide little or no clear evidence that the penis pin could bring pleasure to women. According to Kinsey and his associates (1953:580), the inner walls of the vagina are generally insensitive (a partial exception will be discussed below). This suggests that once intromission is achieved, the penis pin should give a woman neither pleasure nor pain (unless the pressure of the penis pin were transmitted through the insensitive vaginal walls to sensitive tissue that lies beyond).

Third, the subjective reports of women in the West provide little support for the woman-pleasing explanation of penis pins. Comfort (1972:174) reports that women in the West show little interest in "french ticklers," which are the nonsurgically-attached functional equivalents of penis pins. In the literature on piercers in the West, which is strongly oriented to a male--and particularly a male homosexual--audience, there are only a few statements by women who report enjoying sex with pierced men, along with a few who report not enjoying it, and a few noticing no difference (Brown n.d.; Buhrich 1983; Vale and Juno 1989).

Fourth, the shapes and sizes of some of the penis pins seem more likely to do damage in sexual intercourse than to give pleasure. Kuhlewein (1930:94) describes some of the penis pins as "monstrous" and "sharp;" Harrisson (1959) says some are elaborated with broken glass. Women that I have spoken to in the U.S. not only express skepticism that penis pins would enhance their sexual pleasure, they sometimes indicate that the very thought of some of the penis pins is painful and repugnant.

Thus there is no solid evidence from Bornean women that penis pins enhance their sexual pleasure, and there is little in the way of non-Bornean evidence to suggest that the pins really should or normally do give pleasure. What other evidence bears on the matter, and what are we to make of these reports that Bornean women find pleasure in the penis pin?

A potentially relevant piece of evidence is that traditional pagan Bornean societies were among the most sexually egalitarian societies known to ethnography (see, e.g., Freeman 1981; Ward 1963). Given the high level of female autonomy that this entails, perhaps it makes sense that Bornean men should go to unusual lengths to try to please Bornean women.

Another consideration is that under certain circumstances perhaps penis pins could give pleasure, or at least cause no harm. For example, if the pin had smooth ends and did not protrude too far it might cause no harm. If the pin caused no physical harm, the psychological effect of a man wearing a penis pin might be beneficial for a number of reasons (for example, Jerome Rousseau has suggested to me that a woman might derive an indirect pleasure from knowing how much her man was willing to endure in order to try to please her--the "thought" counting more than the actual "gift" to her). Or, since recent literature on what is called the "Grafenberg spot" (see, e.g., Jayne 1984) suggests that there may be a region in the vaginal wall that is pleasurably sensitive, perhaps the penis pin rubs this spot. In most cases, however, this does not seem likely: the Grafenberg spot--if indeed it exists--is on the upper surface of the vagina, while most penis pins protrude on the sides. Another possibility, mentioned above, is that the penis pin is felt through the vaginal walls, causing pleasurable sensations elsewhere (e.g., in the perineum, which, according to Kinsey et al. [1953:385; see also Masters and Johnson 1966], probably is pleasurably stimulated in some forms of deep vaginal penetration). Finally, since some individuals in the West find pleasure in pain, perhaps what is rare here might be commoner elsewhere (assuming that the penis pin could be felt at all).

But in contradistinction to these conditions that might make the woman-pleaser explanation plausible, consider the following questions:

If the idea is to give women greater sexual pleasure, why attach the device surgically? Why not just wrap something around the penis? Non-surgically attached penis augmentations for sexual intercourse (like the "French ticklers" mentioned above) are widely reported in Southeast Asia; among Bornean peoples they were already known in the nineteenth century, at least to the Iban (Low 1892). Surgical attachment must have some rationale that has no obvious connection with pleasing women (unless there are the indirect psychological benefits mentioned above).

If the penis pin is a woman-pleaser, why is it often associated with rank, prestige, or achievement? The association between rank and surgically installed penis augmentations of one sort or another is widespread in Southeast Asia (Brown, Edwards, and Moore 1988)--probably in part because rank-consciousness spills over into many facets of Southeast Asian societies (Brown 1976). Whatever the reason may be for this association, it suggests some factor or factors with no clear connection to providing sexual pleasure for women.

If the penis pin is a woman-pleaser, why is it associated with weapons? There are at least three indications in the literature that Bornean peoples saw the penis pin as a sort of sexual weapon:

One is that in an upland Kenyah account of the introduction of the penis pin the first woman on whom it was used died as a consequence; this would have ended the practice, according to Harrisson, "had counterbalancing impulses not been so strong" (1959:61). I take this to mean that although the Kenyah were willing to risk the danger of the penis pin for the pleasure that it allegedly afforded, they knew that the penis pin was lethally dangerous--and thus like a weapon.

Another indication is that the Mendalam Kayans erected large warrior-like figures to ward off disease-causing spirits. The figures had exposed outsize genitals with penis pins (Nieuwenhuis 1904-07). Since neither the Kayans nor other Borneans normally expose their genitals, and since such phallic displays are widely regarded as threats (Eibl-Eibesfeldt 1979:17), there is reason to think that the inclusion of the penis pin is part of the figures' threatening aspect. Surely it makes little sense to prominently place an object designed to give pleasure on a figure that is designed to frighten.

Yet another indication of the equation of the penis pin with weapons is found in the taunts from women that an Iban man is reported to endure if he does not wear a penis pin: that he is "unarmed" or is "with spear unsharpened" (Richards 1981:245). The latter taunt implies that the penis itself is seen as a weapon--as it sometimes is elsewhere.

In addition to the troubling questions I have just posed, there are a few indications of a skeptical attitude toward the woman-pleaser explanation from scholars well informed about Borneo. One of the most important is found in the report of an extensive medical study of men who wore penis pins (Kuhlewein 1930). As noted above, the medical personnel who conducted this study in 1929 examined the genitals of some 2500 adult males, representing several ethnic groups dwelling in the upper Mahakam region of Kalimantan. Kuhlewein thought that the "one sex will rather inculpate the other" for the perpetuation of the practice (1930:95). If I understand him correctly, Kuhlewein was suggesting that although men gave him the usual reason for wearing penis pins--that "the wives will it so" (1930:95)--he somehow formed the impression that women told a different story, i.e., that men wore the pins for their own (unstated) reasons.

Even Harrisson, who clearly accepts the woman-pleaser explanation (1959), notes that masculine ideals--the ability and willingness to endure the pain and danger of piercing--is part of the story (1966). Derek and Monica Freeman, who studied the Iban, concluded that male bravado was even more important than Harrisson thought (D. Freeman, personal communication).

The Freemans were able to discuss the penis pin with a few Iban women, who denied that it gave them pleasure and who viewed the penis pin as a "potentially, if not actually, injurious and injury-inflicting device." The women saw the use of penis pins as "a peculiar male conceit." The Freemans concluded that among the Iban the penis pin is an ornament that men wear for essentially male reasons: wearing the penis pin is a male "conceit or affectation," and the claim that it pleases women is "a male rationalization and projection" (D. Freeman, personal correspondence). If the Freemans are correct, the sexual pleasure of women may be a very small part of the explanation of penis pins.

....

What the evidence suggests, then, is a widespread Bornean folk conception that men wear penis pins in order to enhance the sexual pleasure of women--but with no clear evidence that this conception adequately captures the real reason(s) why Bornean men wear penis pins. The most glaring problem is that the validity of this conception is not supported by the most relevant kind of evidence: reliable female testimony to the effect that they do enjoy penis pins--or even that they allow their men to have intercourse with them while wearing the pins. Clearly we need a Bornean women's perspective on this matter, and those who are presently in a position to throw light on it--women's health care professionals, for example—could be of real assistance in providing this obviously important evidence (use of the "monstrous" and "sharp" penis pins would presumably leave telltale signs for the gynecologist or obstetrician, and surely even women from the more backward populations in Borneo occasionally see these specialists). If it should turn out that Bornean women do find pleasure in penis pins, it would then be of some interest to know why and how (in the anatomical or physiological sense).

But if it should turn out that Bornean women are not so pleased by penis pins as the reported folk belief would have it, the next question is: why is the practice nonetheless perpetuated? Two answers can be suggested, both having more to do with the male psyche than with female sexuality. One, already mentioned, is male machismo. Since machismo manifests itself in painful and dangerous mutilations of the male body among many peoples throughout the world, it is entirely reasonable to assume that penis piercing is a Bornean variant of the phenomenon, i.e., that machismo is at least a substantial component in the explanation of penis pins. Another component, I will argue, is the possibility of some Bornean cultural misconceptions.

One of the striking ways in which cultural conceptions and reality can and often do diverge is in each sex's conceptions of the other sex's sexuality (Symons 1979). Male conceptions of female sexuality in the West are heavily influenced not merely by ignorance but by wishful thinking and the projection of male attitudes onto females. Marcus (1966) coined the term "pornotopia" to refer to certain aspects of the fantasy world of pornography. The penis pin is perhaps an element in a Bornean pornotopia, a reflection less of Bornean female sexuality than of the Bornean male's image of female sexuality. Now, given the autonomy of Bornean women, as noted earlier, it is understandable that Bornean men might be particularly preoccupied with how to win and keep their women-- and so long as men imagined that penis pins would give them greater sexual access to women, the incentive to wear the pin might be substantial.

One of the few Bornean accounts of the origin of the penis pin clearly expresses this concern for men to please women and, in all probability, provides a glimpse of pornotopia. In a Kayan version of the invention of the penis pin, a woman who masturbates with a rolled up leaf tells her lover that he is no better than the leaf. So he invents and installs the penis pin, which she does find better (Harrisson 1964). There are some clear messages in this story--that the man wanted to please a woman, that he didn't think he could do it with nature's equipment alone, that the penis pin seemed like a reasonable solution to his problem, and that it worked.

But in spite of the concern for womanhood that this story expresses, there is reason to think that it isn't a woman's story: it assumes that vaginal penetration is a normal or even necessary part of female masturbation. This assumption, according to the findings of Kinsey et al. among American women, is another male "conceit" (1953:162; see also Masters and Johnson 1966). Few women in the West masturbate in a manner that involves anything more than superficial penetration of the vagina (since that is all that is required to stimulate the clitoris). Like so many origin stories, then, this one may be, as Freeman suggests, a rationalization rather than an explanation.

....

In sum, the most widely reported explanation of the penis pin in Borneo--an explanation that focuses on female sexuality and that derives from or is compatible with Bornean cultural conceptions--may have little or no validity. The true explanation may lie more with males than with females, more with male machismo and male fantasies than with female sexuality. At present we simply do not know which motives--conscious or unconscious--are the principal ones that lie behind the use of the penis pin.

The state of our ignorance is of course partly the result of the privacy or secrecy that surrounds the sexual act itself and often much else that relates to sexuality, in Borneo as everywhere else. But part of the problem is that many of those who have written about the penis pin probably did not realize that there even was a problem: the thought that Bornean women crave the stimulation of an augmented penis, even a dangerously augmented one, is a thought as much at home in Western pornotopia as it appears to be in Bornean. Until the pioneering research of Kinsey and his associates, and of Masters and Johnson--all of whom did get female perspectives on sexuality--most men simply lacked a reason for thinking that female sexuality might be other than what they imagined it to be. In readily accepting the woman-pleaser explanation of the penis pin, as many Western observers did, they may have been content to perpetuate a myth rather than identify it as such.

A careful attempt to find out what the penis pin is all about would not only give us a much better understanding of the traditional peculiarities of sexuality, of images of sexuality, and of the relations between the sexes in Borneo, but might well throw light on these topics nearly everywhere. For what may be fundamental components of the Bornean penis pin complex--male and female sexualities, machismo, and pornotopia--may also be fundamental components in the relations between the sexes among many if not all peoples, differing only in the local ways in which they are combined and expressed.

448

REFERENCES

Appell, G. N.
1968   The Penis Pin at Peabody Museum, Harvard University. Journal of the Malaysian Branch, Royal Asiatic Society 41:203-205.

Barclay, James
1980   A Stroll Through Borneo. London: Hodder and Stoughton. (See pp. 90, 94, 96, and photo.)

Barth, J. P. J.
1910   Boesangsch-Nederlandsch Woordenboek. Batavia: Landsdrukkerij. (See p. 174.)

Bock, Carl Alfred
1887   Reise in Oost-en Zuid-Borneo van Koetei naar Bandjarmassim...in 1879 en 1880. 's-Gravenhage: Martinus Nijhoff. (See p. 98.)

Brown, Donald E.
1976   Principles of Social Structure: Southeast Asia. London: Duckworth.

n.d.   Piercers in America. Unpublished typescript.

Brown, Donald E., James W. Edwards, and Ruth Moore
1988   The Penis Inserts of Southeast Asia: An Annotated Bibliography with an Overview and Comparative Perspectives. Occasional Paper No. 15, Center for South and Southeast Asian Studies, University of California, Berkeley.

Buhrich, Neil
1983   The Association of Erotic Piercing with Homosexuality, Sadomasochism, Bondage, Fetishism, and Tattoos. Archives of Sexual Behavior 12:167-71.

Burns, Robert
1849   The Kayans of the North-West of Borneo. Journal of the
                       Indian Archipelago and Eastern Asia 3:140-52. (Reprint-
                       ed in the Sarawak Museum Journal 3:477-489; see p. 486.)

Comfort, Alex, ed.
1972   The Joy of Sex: A Gourmet Guide to Love Making. New
                       York: Simon and Schuster.

Dalton, John
1837   [1831] Mr. Dalton's Essay on the Diaks of Borneo. In
                       Notices of the Indian Archipelago, and Adjacent Coun-
                       'tries. Ed. by J.H. Moor. Singapore. Pp.41-54. (See p.
                       53.)

De Wall, H. von
1855   Aanteekeningen omtrent de Nordoostkust van Borneo.
                       Tijdschrift voor Indische Taal-, Land- en Volkenkunde
                       4:423-458. (See pp. 457-58.)

Eibl-Eibesfeldt, Iranaus
1979   Human Ethology: Concepts and Implications for the
                       Sciences of Man. The Behavioral and Brain Sciences 2:1-
                       57.

Freeman, Derek
1981   Some Reflections on the Nature of Iban Society. An
                       Occasional Paper of the Department of Anthropology,
                       Research School of Pacific Studies, The Australian
                       National University, Canberra.

Friesen, Stanley R. and Norvid D. Schuman
1964   Medicine in Sarawak: The Medical Missionary Program
                       at Work. The Journal of the Kansas Medical Society
                       65:125-131. (See pp. 128, 129.)

Gaffron, von
1859   Over Menschen met Staarten op Borneo. Natuurkundig
                       Tijdschrift voor Nederlandsch-Indie 20:227-232. (See pp.
                       231-32.)

Galvin, A. D.
[1967]   [Kenyah Vocabulary]. Ms. [Miri, Sarawak]. (See p. 2.)

Griffith, G. T.
1955   Health and Disease in Young Sea Dayak Men. Sarawak Museum Journal 6:322-327. (See p. 327.)

Haddon, Alfred C. and Laura Start
1936   Iban or Sea Dayak Fabrics and Their Patterns. Cambridge: The University Press. (See pp. 42, 44.)

Hansen, Eric
1988   Stranger in the Forest: On Foot Across Borneo. London: Century. (See pp. 224-29.)

Hardeland, August
1859   Dajacksch-Deutsches Worterbuch. Amsterdam: Frederik Muller. (This source anomalously describes the *palang* as a ring worn on the male genitals. See p. 400.)

Harrisson, Tom
1956   Rhinoceros in Borneo: and Traded to China. Sarawak Museum Journal 7:263-74.

1959   World Within: A Borneo Story. London: The Cresset Press. (See pp. 59, 61-62.)

1964   The "Palang," Its History and Proto-History in West Borneo and the Philippines. Journal of the Malaysian Branch, Royal Asiatic Society 37:162-174. (Note that the Povedano MS 1578, which is quoted, has been shown to be a forgery by William Henry Scott.)

1966   The "Palang:" II. Three Further Notes. Journal of the Malaysian Branch, Royal Asiatic Society 39:172-74.

Hose, Charles and William McDougal
1912   The Pagan Tribes of Borneo: A Description of their Physical, Moral and Intellectual Condition with Some Discussion of their Ethnic Relations. Vol. II. London: Macmillan. (Reprinted 1966 by Barnes and Noble.) (See p. 170.)

Jayne, Cynthia
    1984   Freud, Grafenberg, and the Neglected Vagina: Thoughts Concerning an Historical Omission in Sexology. Journal of Sex Research 20:212-15.

Juynboll, H. H.
    1909   Katalog des Ethnographischen Reichsmuseums. Band I: Borneo. Leiden: E. J. Brill. (See p. 60.)

Kinsey, Alfred C. et al.
    1953   Sexual Behavior in the Human Female. Philadelphia: W. B. Saunders Company.

Kleiweg de Zwaan, J. P.
    1920   Over de Penis-staafjes der Inlanders van den Indischen Archipel. Nederlandsch Tijdschrift voor Genesskunde II (A):289-293.

Kuhlewein, M. von
    1930   Report of a Journey to Upper Mahakam (Borneo), February-May 1929. Mededeelingen van den Dienst der Volksgezondheid in Nederlandsche-Indie, Foreign-Edition 19:66-152. (See pp. 83, 92, 94-95, 112. This article appeared simultaneously in a Dutch-language version of the same journal.]

Le Bar, Frank M., ed.
    1972   Ethnic Groups of Insular Southeast Asia. Vol. I. New Haven: HRAF Press. (See p. 188.)

Legman, G.
    1975   No Laughing Matter: An Analysis of Sexual Humor. Bloomington: Indiana University Press. (See p. 431.)

Low, Brooke
    1892   The Natives of Borneo. Ed. from the Papers of the Late Brooke Low, Esq., by H. Ling Roth. Journal of the Anthropological Institute 22:22-64. (See p. 45.)

Macdonald, David
    1982   Expedition to Borneo: The Search for Proboscis Monkeys and Other Creatures. London: J. M. Dent & Sons. (See pp. 166-67.)

Marcus, Steven
1966   The Other Victorians: A Study of Sexuality and Pornog-
              raphy in Mid-Nineteenth-Century England. New York:
              Basic Books.

Masters, W. H. and V. E. Johnson
1966   Human Sexual Response. Boston: Little, Brown and
              Company.

Mayer, A. B.
1877   Ueber die Perforation des Penis bei den Malayan.
              Mittheilungen der Anthropologischen Gesellschaft in
              Wien 7:242-244.

Miklucho-Maclay, N. V.
1876a   Ueber die kunstlich Perforatio Penis bei den Dayaks auf
              Borneo. Verhandelingen der Berliner Gesellschaft fur
              Anthropologie, Ethnologie und Urgeschichte 22-24.

1876b   Perforatio glandis penis bei den Dajaks auf Borneo und
              analoge sitten auf Celebes und auf Java.
              Verhandelungen der Berliner Gesellschaft fur
              Anthropologie, Ethnologie und Urgeschichte 24-26 (and
              addendum).

Miller, Charles C.
1942   Black Borneo. New York: Modern Age Books. (See
              photo opp. p. 199.)

Moll, Albert
1912   Handbuch der Sexualwissenschaften, vol. I. Leipzig: F.
              C. W. Vogel. (See p. 240.)

Nieuwenhuis, A. W.
1900   In Centraal Borneo: Reis van Pontianak naar Samarinda.
              Leiden: E. J. Brill. (See pp. 68-69, 118.)

1904-07   Quer durch Borneo: Ergebnisse seiner Reisen in den
              Jahren 1894, 1896-97, und 1898-1900. Leiden: E. J. Brill.
              (See Vol. I, pp. 78-79, 223; Vol. II, p. 369 and plate opp.
              p. 390.)

O'Hanlon, Redmond
1984   Into the Heart of Borneo. New York: Random House. (See pp. 8-9, 17, 82-83.)

Perelaer, M.T.H.
1870   Ethnographische Beschrijving der Dajaks. Zalt-Bommel: Joh. Noman & Zoon. (See pp. 60-61 for the only doubts in a primary source that penis pins even exist.)

Richards, Anthony
1981   An Iban-English Dictionary. Oxford: Clarendon Press. (See pp. 245-46.)

Schneebaum, Tobias
1979   Wild Man. New York: The Viking Press. (See p. 124.)

Schwaner, C. A. L. M.
1853   Borneo, Beschrijving van het Stroomgebied van den Barito. Vol. I. Amsterdam: P. N. van Kampen. (See p. 127.)

St. John, Spenser
1863   Life in the Forests of the Far East; or Travels in Northern Borneo. Second ed., revised. Vol I. London: Smith, Elder and Company. (See pp. 122-23.)

Symons, Donald
1979   The Evolution of Human Sexuality. New York: Oxford University Press.

Tillema, H. F.
1934-35   Poenans (Apo-Kajan en Tidoengsche landen). Tropisch Nederland 7:2-11, 18-24, 43-48. (See p. 24.)

Vale, V. and Andrea Juno
1989   Modern Primitives: An Investigation of Contemporary Adornment and Ritual. Re/Search #12. San Francisco: Re/Search Publications.

Veth, P.J.
1854   Borneo's Wester-afdeeling, geographisch, statistisch, historisch, voorafgegaan door eene algemeene schets des ganschen eilands. Vol. I. Zaltbommel: Noman. (See p. 177-78.)

Walchren, E. W. F. van
1907   Eene reis naar de bovenstreken van Boeloengan (Midden-Borneo), 12 Nov. 1905 - 11 April 1906. Tijdschrift van het Nederlandsch Aardrijkundig Genootschap 24:755-844. (See pp. 822, 823.)

Ward, Barbara
1963   Men, Women and Change: An Essay in Understanding Social Roles in South and South-East Asia. In Women in the New Asia: The Changing Social Roles of Men and Women in South and South-East Asia. Ed. by B. E. Ward. UNESCO. Pp. 25-99.

Wulfften Palthe, P. M. von
1936   Psychiatry and Neurology in the Tropics. In A Clinical Textbook of Tropical Medicine, ed. by C. D. de Langen and A. Liechtenstein. Batavia: G. Kolff & Co. Pp. 525-47. (See pp. 536-38.)

EUROPEAN-INDIGENOUS MISCEGENATION
AND SOCIAL STATUS IN
NINETEENTH CENTURY BORNEO

ROBERT H. W. REECE

'Who's talking of <u>women</u>?' says Dravot, 'I said <u>wife</u> - a Queen to breed a King's son for the King. A Queen out of the strongest tribe, that'll make them your blood-brothers, and that'll lie by your side and tell you all the people thinks about you and their own affairs. That's what I want'.

'Do you remember that Bengali woman I kept at Mogul Serai where I was a plate layer?', says I. 'A fat lot of good she was to me. She ran away with the Station-master's servant and half my month's pay. Then she turned up at Dadur Junction in tow of a half caste, and had the impidence to say I was her <u>husband</u> - all among the drivers in the running shed, too!'

- Rudyard Kipling,
The Man Who Would Be King

-I-

Part of the folklore of colonial history is that it was 'the coming of the mems that spoilt everything': that it was European women who brought status and race-consciousness and a stratified colonial society in which Europeans emphasized their superiority over the indigenes by means of social distance. This was first put to me in the late 1960s in Negri Sembilan by an old planter who had come to Malaya as a cadet before World War One when few planters were married and most had Tamil or Malay 'keeps' or mistresses. Social historians such as John Butcher (whose history of the British in Malaya contains an excellent chapter on European men and Asian women)[1] dismiss the argument as simplistic. Feminist historians dismiss it as sexist in its undue apportioning of responsibility to women. Nevertheless, it is still worthy of closer examination.

The whole question of imperialism and sexual opportunity was opened up in a polemical way by Ronald Hyam in *Britain's Imperial Century*:

> There used to be a theory that territories came under the British
> flag as a result of the export of surplus capital. It would be
> much truer to say that the driving force behind empire-building
> was rather the export of surplus emotional, or sexual energy.
> The empire was a boon to the brokenhearted, the misogynist and
> to the promiscuous alike.[2]

Parodying the famous remark that the British Empire was acquired in a fit of absence of mind, Hyam quipped that it was acquired in an absence of wives. More seriously, he argued that greater heterosexual opportunity attracted Englishmen to the colonies where they were led by suppressed homosexuals who sublimated their sex-drive in empire-building. James Brooke's Sarawak is a nice example of this phenomenon.

Women, brown or white, had no place in the first Rajah's personal life. His first biographer, Gertrude Jacob, attributed this to a broken engagement with the daughter of a Bath clergyman who died shortly afterwards[3] and this story of tragic or unrequited love was fostered by James himself to explain his lack of interest in women. Another explanation offered by Owen Rutter and allegedly emanating from James was that his wound in the Burma wars had not been in the lungs, as asserted by Jacob, but in the genitals and that this had resulted in impotence.[4] In December 1857 James acknowledged a former servant, Reuben James Walker, as his natural son and there is a tradition that he was the product of a relationship with a housemaid after his return from Burma. However, the immediate members of his family were angered not only by the problems for the succession that were posed by what the Rajah called his 'dear little fellow' but also by what they evidently regarded as the unlikelihood of such a relationship ever having existed. Donald Brown has pointed to the report by the British Resident in Brunei in 1915 that Brooke had married a niece of the Brunei governor of Sarawak, Pengiran Muda Hashim, shortly after his arrival there in 1839[5] but it is odd that no corroborative evidence for this has come to light. Rutter suggested that Brooke's eccentric millionaire patron, Angela Burdett Coutts, 'fell madly in love with him'[6] but there is nothing in their extensive correspondence to support this. Indeed, Ronald Hyam has even suggested that one of the things which drew them together was their shared interest in young men and boys.[7] The stories of the broken engagement and the wound would have provided socially acceptable explanations for the Rajah turning his back on women.

The circumstantial evidence points to the possibility that Brooke was homosexual, at least latently so. All his close relationships seem to have been with young men and boys and his correspondence is full of affectionate letters to them. In Sarawak his little court consisted of young men like Charles ('Doddy') Grant whom he had recruited personally. Twenty years older than most of his subordinates, Brooke assumed the role of superior officer, confidant, adviser and Socratic teacher, if not of lover. He was a man of wide intellectual interests and the conversations he conducted during those long nights overlooking the Sarawak River were cosy gatherings of an all-male fraternity. There was a good deal of emotional bonding in this clubby, jolly, quarterdeck atmosphere and Brooke relied upon it very much for the cohesiveness and loyalty that his tiny and poverty-stricken government demanded. Although there are no explicit references in the Brooke family and other papers to any effeminacy in James' manner, Annie Brooke, the first wife of his elder nephew, Brooke Brooke, remarked to her sister-in-law, Annie Grant, on his informality: 'He helps himself to my perfume bottles not to say others also'.[8] It seems odd that in this age of greater sexual frankness, James Brooke's most recent biographer, Professor Nicholas Tarling, should have neglected to deal with the question of the Rajah's sexuality. Instead he reported, somewhat uncritically, Gertrude Jacob's story of the broken engagement. Apart from the possibility that James had a relationship with his young groom, Reuben George Walker, it seems very likely that he was involved with the lawyer John Templer who later edited a selection of the Rajah's letters to him and others. Significantly, when Brooke's former secretary, Spenser St. John, was writing his biography of James in 1878, he told Charles Grant that 'one judicious friend advised me to say nothing disagreeable about Templer and the young Rajah: I would carry out that wish as far as possible'.[9]

Spenser St. John in retirement in England c. 1900.
Courtesy Royal Geographical Society

On the question of Sino-Dayak miscegenation, James held positive views. During one of his first expeditions from Kuching in 1839 he visited Tungong (Setunggang) on the Lundu River and was greatly impressed with the people descended from the Chinese gold-miners of West Borneo who had settled there:

The mixed breed of the Chinese with the Malay or Dyak are a good-looking and industrious race, partaking much more of the Chinese character than that of the natives of this country. This mainly arises from education and early formed habits, which are altogether Chinese; and in religion and customs they likewise follow, in great measure, the paternal stock. <u>The race are worthy of attention, as the future possessors of Borneo.</u>[10]

Nor did James have any objection in principle to European-native miscegenation and indeed, as we shall see, his younger nephew Charles actually advocated it. This was no doubt due in part to the fact that James' father, Thomas Brooke, an East India Company official, had a son by his Indian *bibi* or mistress in September 1784 before marrying in 1793 Anna Maria Stuart who was herself illegitimate. Charles William Brooke was brought up in the same household with his half-brothers and sisters and while serving as a lieutenant in the 17th Native Infantry in 1803-4 maintained an affectionate correspondence with his father and half-sister, Sophia. When Thomas Brooke took his family back to England in 1817 the links were inevitably weakened but in later years James wrote that he 'had always loved our brother Charles' and he and his sisters assisted Charles' youngest son when he was in financial trouble in London.[11] Nevertheless, James was aware that in Sarawak miscegenation of more than a casual and transient kind might bring about political difficulties.

When the young botanical collector, Hugh Low, arrived in Kuching in January 1845, the tiny European population was entirely male and many of the Rajah's officers had liaisons with Sarawak women. One of these was Thomas Williamson, a Eurasian from Malacca whom Brooke used as Malay interpreter and envoy. So great were his linguistic and diplomatic skills that Captain Henry Keppel called him 'an excellent Prime Minister'.[12] However, Brooke had to admonish him in January 1846 for over-familiarity with local women. Williamson already had a child by a Sarawak Malay woman and the Rajah was obviously concerned that this might prejudice his standing:

> ...there is a point [he told Williamson] beyond which freedom in our intercourse with the natives ought not to be carried, viz., that point of familiarity, which, if it does not breed contempt, certainly acquires no respect.

I allude primarily to the habit of almost daily visiting native homes, and a degree of intimacy with the females of their families, which involves directly, or by implication, an official person in all the petty intrigues unceasingly being carried out by native women.[13]

Hugh Low, 1848. From a portrait in pastel by William Montaigne, R. A., formerly in the possession of Miss Eileen Low.

His concern, then, was not based on conventional European notions of sexual morality but on the loss of status (and hence authority) to be suffered by entering into anything more than casual relationships with native women. This principle was also implicit in his subsequent *Hints From the Rajah to Young Outstation Officers* which warned of the dangers of over-familiarity without specifying women.[14]

There are all too few personal records of how European men perceived and interacted with Borneo women but from the journal of Hugh Low in 1845 we have some indication of the way in which conventional notions of feminine beauty derived from the European experience underwent a subtle process of acclimatization:

> When I first came here I used to look upon the native women with disgust; now I can easily discriminate the degrees of beauty as one resident in a European country would there. Instead of saying degrees of beauty I ought perhaps to have said plainness or rather ugliness for certainly they are not a comely race, but as I said before my ideas from constantly seeing them have become so vitiated that what we call a pretty woman we look upon with as much pleasure or nearly so as we used at the divine forms at home.[15]

The young Charles Brooke also left this more specific description of Dayak women in his own memoir, *Ten Years in Sarawak* (1866):

> In youth and before marriage their figures are slight and graceful, with small waists, and not too largely developed to obliterate the sylph-like contour of a budding beauty.
>
> Their eyes in most cases, jet black, clear and bright, with quick intelligence and temper beaming through the orbs. The shape of the lid when open is very oval, the lashes are long and thick, forming an abundant fringe...The brow covering is often so perfectly arched and finely chiselled to lead people to think that the outline has been shaved...

Charles Brooke in 1864, four years before he became the second Rajah of Sarawak. (Courtesy, Bodleian Library, Oxford)

...The general expression of their countenances is attractive by the buoyancy and brightness emitted from the eye; this charm pleases and softens the remainder of their irregular features. The hair may be compared to a Shetland pony's tail, long, bright and coarse...

They seldom fail to shake their heads before a spectator, in order to toss their flowing tresses over their back and shoulders. The more favoured ones, too, when on a visit, are fond of the excessive heat requiring the jacket to be withdrawn, to expose a smooth, satiny, brown skin...[16]

A census of Europeans in Kuching taken in about 1858[17] indicates that the little society was marked by a strong representation of mixed relationships. Of the ten Europeans in government service in Kuching (including the Rajah and his elder nephew) three were married to native or Eurasian women and had children by them while at least one had a native mistress. From the large number of Sarawak Eurasians now bearing their names, it is also clear that most of the European employees of the Borneo Company formed relationships with native women. The only European women in Sarawak at this point were Harriette McDougall and Bertha Cruickshank (who had narrowly escaped death during the Chinese rebellion the previous year). Even in 1887 when Charles Brooke entertained the entire European community to a jubilee dinner, there were only five European women present, including his own wife Margaret.

It was the arrival of the first Anglican missionary, F. T. McDougall, and his wife Harriette in Kuching in 1848 that provided the first challenge to the practice of associating with native women. A central figure was the Rajah's also newly-arrived private secretary, Spenser St. John, who urged upon his younger colleagues the delights and advantages of such relationships and had no great respect for the forthright and often tactless missionary or for the faith he represented. McDougall clearly held St. John responsible for leading astray Harry Nicholetts, who was killed during the Chinese rebellion, and Charles Fox who had come out to Sarawak as a theological student from Bishop's College, Calcutta, in 1851 but resigned four years later to join the government service and was killed with William Steele at Kanowit in 1859. According to McDougall, who heard confession from both men at some time before their deaths, Fox had left the mission after being 'corrupted' by St. John. Four years after Fox's death, when St. John had published some trenchant criticisms of the Borneo mission in *Life in the Forests of the Far East*, McDougall told James Brooke's brother-in-law, the Rev. Edmund Evelyn:

Poor Fox last time I saw him...told me that not only had St. John excited his doubts about H[oly] S[cripture] and our Lord's Divinity, which made him leave the Mission, but that he afterwards never let him alone with his taunts and his sneers, until he followed his bad example and kept a native woman...[19]

F. T. McDougall

McDougall was certainly happy to marry European men to Sarawak women who became Christians, although he sometimes referred disparagingly to Eurasians as 'half castes' in his correspondence. In May 1849 he reported his success 'in persuading one of our Resident Gentlemen to marry the person with whom he has been living and by whom he has a family - his example will have a good effect as he...has deservedly a good deal of influence among us'.[20] However, when his Singalese Eurasian subordinate, William Gomes, wanted to marry the woman's sister, McDougall expressed his private disappointment. He

MAULL & C?   LONDON

Harriette McDougall

would have preferred Gomes to have married a Dayak woman, believing that this might advance the Mission's work amongst the Dayaks.[21] It is not clear if he ever made the explicit suggestion to his other catechists, but they would probably not have been very receptive to the idea because of the loss of status which they believed this would bring. William Chalmers, who had worked with Land Dayaks and knew their language, told Charles Brooke before his departure for Australia in 1861:

> I have no objection to native females, and believe I could live happily with them, but yet I do not think it desirable for a white man, who is so superior in intellect and understanding, to tie himself to one of dark skin and strange customs, obliging him to a certain extent, to lower himself in status.[22]

A year or so earlier, Spenser St. John, now British Consul in Brunei, paid a call to the Mission House during a visit to Kuching bringing with him his Malay mistress and their young daughter - a cholera epidemic had cost them their two other children some time before. He had always been on friendly terms with Harriette McDougall despite the Bishop's disapproval of him but she was mortally affronted by what she saw as the open parading of an illicit relationship, feeling 'nothing but disgust for him...he had not a particle of shame'.[22] From that time onward she refused to have anything to do with St. John, although the subsequent controversy arising from his remarks on the Borneo mission in *Life in the Forests of the Far East* no doubt strengthened her resolve. However, the Rev. A. Horsborough, who had been effectively dismissed by McDougall, revealed that the missionaries might well have concerned themselves with what had been happening at the Kuching Mission House itself where Dayak and Chinese adolescent students were living in dormitory conditions:

> ...I had told him that the Mission house at Sarawak was a nest of Sodomy and fornication giving him at the same time sufficient proofs of it and that Mrs. Stahl the matron though she denied it knew and wd. take no pains to prevent it...But I am not the first that told the Bishop of the Moral state of the School. Mr. Fox told him of the Sodomy and abominations before I ever set foot in Sarawak but he wd. not believe it, hushed it up and wrote home about the babes in Christ whom he was training up in the Lord.[23]

During the controversy which spilled over into missionary newspaper *Guardian* and a number of pamphlets, McDougall did not openly accuse St. John of keeping a native woman, contenting himself with the charge that he had 'corrupted' some of the young missionaries. However, his principal assistant (and subsequent successor) Walter Chambers and his wife were more explicit and it was this that caused Charles Brooke to write to his elder brother revealing his own involvement and attitudes:

> The mildest part of the business was that he [St. John] only kept one - he [Chambers] may bring to light some of my little affairs one of these days - but he [St. John] made allowance for many years and I believe thought that it was the right thing to do in a legitimate monogamy. These are the weak points a parson snatches at. It can't be helped - for society will excuse such natural indulgences. After all a Harem will be the proper thing when one gets richer.[26]

Harriette McDougall's drawing of the Mission House, Kuching, c. 1848.

In 1854, when he was only twenty-three, Charles had been posted to Skrang to replace Willie Brereton who had died of fever after fathering a child by a Dayak woman there. Charles studied the language and the customs of the Batang Lupar people and adopted their diet and dress. From his appreciative description of Dayak women quoted above, it is reasonable to suggest that he enjoyed their favors. He was also keenly aware of the political advantages to be obtained through association with them. Of the women of Lingga he wrote:

> I gradually made my friends among the people, particularly the
> female part of the community. I soon learnt that great power
> and influence attached to their opinions on matters in general,
> and that to stand well with them was more than half of any
> Dyak battle.[27]

In addition to his well-developed powers of natural observation, Charles was also intellectually curious and in his isolation during the following years happily devoured everything from popular novels to treatises on physical anthropology and tropical health. Notable amongst these was W. J. Moore's *Health in the Tropics*[28] which seemed to give scientific support to Charles' own belief that tropical climates were 'not adapted for the permanent residence of Anglo-Saxons'.[29] In Moore's words, 'An infusion of native blood is essential to the continuance of the race', and Charles believed that this was already happening in Sarawak through the widespread phenomenon of miscegenation. The 'half-caste children of Europeans', he wrote in *Ten Years in Sarawak*, would 'gradually merge into a more enlightened race, better qualified in every way for the duties required for them'.[30] Europeans, then, should take 'perhaps a worse half, instead of a better one',[31] and there is every indication that he acted on his own advice.

While this belief in the benefits of human inter-breeding went against all the conventional wisdom of contemporary European thinking, Charles went on to suggest what must have seemed absolute anathema, that Asian and Eurasian men should take European partners. There was nothing which suggested to him that Chinese men, for example, would not make as satisfactory spouses as European men and he believed that in time the latter would lose their 'fantastic notion' of race differences:

> Intermarriage, after the bitter prejudices are somewhat smoothed
> and broken, will effect this change, and Anglo-Chinese, Malays,
> and other coloured people, it is to be conjectured, will, at a future
> period, provide themselves with European helpmates.[32]

When Charles was posted to Simanggang in 1866 he had a series of *gundik* or mistresses, including a certain 'Tia', or Dayang Mastiah, by whom he had a son in August 1867. Named Isaka but known as Esca, the boy remained with his mother until 1873 when Ranee Margaret insisted that he should go to England with her and be fostered by the Rev. Daykin, a clergyman living near James Brooke's retirement home at Burrator in Devon. Esca was taken to Canada by Daykin and educated there and his claims to the succession as Charles' eldest son were a source of some subsequent embarrassment to Vyner Brooke, the Third Rajah. When the affair first blew up in the Canadian and British press in 1927, Ranee Margaret wrote to her nephew by marriage, Charles Willes Johnson, who then ran the Sarawak Government Office in London:

> I am sorry to say, that your uncle lived with several Simanggang women, one after the other, before he married me, only none of the others had children. I knew all about these antecedents because I often stayed at Simanggang alone, when your uncle went away on expeditions, and the Malay women thought such conduct rather fine on his part, as they said all men required lots of gundits [*gundik*] or mistresses, when they were really <u>men</u>.[33]

She then went on to describe how Charles reacted to the infidelity of one *gundik* whom, as she said, he 'evidently liked':

> During one of his absences from the Fort at Simanggang, she <u>fell</u> with a Fortman. He found out about it, he was furious. He had her head shaved, and tied the thick long tail of hair to the flag staff! Then she was put in a boat, shaven and shorn, and paddled to and fro in front of the campong, with a man who summoned all the people to the bank by a gong, and who informed the populace of her misdeeds. In a way, he was a queer fish![34]

If we follow through the European concern for status, there was nothing 'queer' about Charles' action. He was less concerned about the woman's sexual infidelity than with the fact that by going with a Malay fortman she was bringing him into ridicule and diminishing his status. When someone suggested that there had been a marriage between Charles and Tia, Ranee Margaret told Willes Johnson: 'Your uncle was monarch of all he surveyed, and certainly would not have married himself to a low Malay'.[35] As it happened, Tia was probably of aristocratic Melanau origin but an official relationship would have prejudiced Charles' position. Like Peachey Carnehan in Kipling's brilliant parable of imperialism, *The Man Who Would Be King*, he was well aware of the political

Esca Brooke, aged about six years, in Malay dress. The photograph was probably taken in Singapore in 1873 before he embarked for England with Charles and Margaret Brooke and their
three children. (Courtesy, Sarawak Museum)

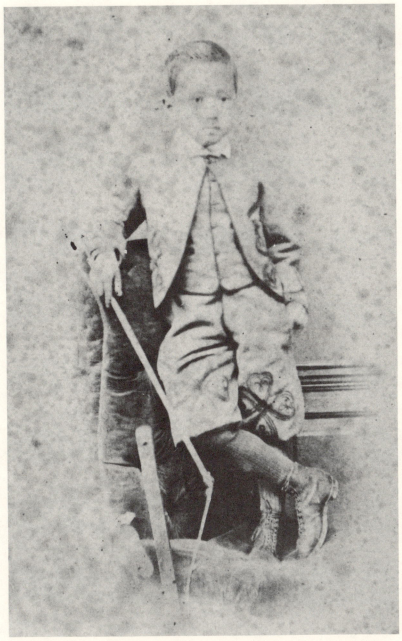

Esca Brooke, aged about seven years, taken at Bartmouth not long after his arrival in England. (Courtesy, Sarawak Museum)

Esca Brooke, taken in Canada in his 40s. By this time his Brooke
ancestry was very clearly marked. (Courtesy, Sarawak Museum)

dangers inherent in a formal liaison. Taking James' advice to find a rich heiress in Europe, Charles, who had become Rajah in 1868 after his uncle's death, went to England in 1869 where he initially courted his cousin, Mme de Windt, and then proposed marriage to her eighteen year old daughter Margaret.

It was left to Ranee Margaret to remove the embarrassment that Esca might have provided if he had remained in Sarawak. As she told Willes Johnson:

> When I came out, I met the child at Simanggang, and even then I had the nouse [sic] to see that he might be a bore in the country, besides I thought that illegitimate children should be looked after. I agreed that your uncle should take him to the Daykins, the Burrator parson, to be educated...[36]

By removing Esca, Margaret could be seen to perform a charitable act and at the same time protect her own sons and herself against any challenge to the succession and remove the evidence of her husband's past relationships with native women. In so doing she had safeguarded her own status and that of her children.

For all his talk about a Eurasian ruling caste, Charles had accepted the need for a European heir who would be beyond local rivalries and would also be acceptable to the Foreign Office in London. Nevertheless, he actively discouraged his consort from adopting the 'mem' lifestyle practiced in other colonies where European women expressed their superiority through social distance (and thus isolation) from the native population. In *Ten Years in Sarawak* he had observed:

> It is no easy matter for a European with a wife and family, while moving in the vortex of <u>his</u> civilization, to obtain any real knowledge of the native mind, or entertain any sympathy with them. My own personal experience and observation have told me how difficult it is to manage natives in active work, when one is placed among a largish assembly of Europeans. The interest of the latter subverts the capacity for embracing subjects that affect natives. There seems to arise, unavoidably, a separation - a one-sidedness; and no doubt it is natural to prefer the society of fellow-countrymen before that of people with strange habits.[37]

He persuaded Margaret to learn Malay, to dress Malay-style and to mix freely with the wives and daughters of the Kuching *datus* who formed the second echelon of Brooke government. All this the young Ranee did with great flair,[38] while her strange relationship with Charles was revealed to be the disaster that it was. Consequently, by the late 1880s she had ceased to make more than occasional brief visits to Sarawak while the Rajah presumably returned to his old habits. The failure of his marriage, and the more practical considerations of cost and the need to keep a finger on the native pulse, led him to discourage his officers from marrying until they returned to England at the end of their career and to accept their liaisons with native women as long as these were not paraded openly. In 1882, for example, he issued the following Order:

> Whereas it has come to my knowledge that certain European officers in the Service are in the habit of living openly with native women, I now issue this order for their information, that in future I forbid any of these women travelling or taking passage in Government steamers or boats and I strongly disapprove of any officer travelling in company or being seen publicly with such women.

> And hereafter any officer found acting contrary to this order will be liable to reduction of rank and pay or dismissal [from] the Service.[39]

-II-

In 1848 when Hugh Low took up the position of Colonial Secretary of the Crown Colony of Labuan, he was accompanied by his young wife Catherine whom he had met on board ship on his return with the Rajah from England. Catherine, as it happened, was the result of Labuan's new Lieutenant Governor William Napier's long-standing relationship with a Malacca woman before he took a European wife. After bearing a son, Hugh, and a daughter, Catherine (Kitty), Catherine died of fever in 1851 and the two young children were sent off to London to be looked after by Low's brother and father who ran a highly successful plant nursery at Clapton. A few years later, Low took up with a Malay woman, whom we only know as 'Nona Dayang Low' or 'Nona Tuan Low', and had a daughter by her whom they called Lucy. Accepting his responsibilities, he established her and the child, together with her mother and brothers, in a comfortable house at Sagumau on the Coal Point Road. Nona Dayang Low's family originally came from Kuching, where Low had no doubt known her earlier, and were probably of aristocratic Brunei origin. Nona Dayang Low's sister, Dayang Kamariah, had lived with Spenser St. John in Kuching and Brunei and bore him three children before he was appointed British charge d'affaires in Haiti. Kamariah subsequently went to Singapore to live with another European and returned to live with her family in Labuan.

In December 1866 Kitty Low returned from her Swiss school to live with her father in the house he had built in the early 1850s on a ridge overlooking the harbor. He told her about her half-sister Lucy but they did not have any contact with each other. At this time, Low was Officer Administering the Government (effectively Acting Governor) and had moved into the bungalow variously known as the Residency or Government House. Nona Dayang Low appears to have at least visited him because when the manager of the China Steamship and Labuan Coal Company and his wife came to the Residency unexpectedly, they found her there. According to the account subsequently sent back to the Colonial Office by Governor John Pope Hennessy who arrived a year later:

> Mr. Morel said he came one day with his wife to pay his respects to the Administrator, and finding the Malay mistress of the gentleman in the house, he thought it an act of such grave indelicacy to Mrs. Morel that he broke off all acquaintance with the temporary head of the Government.[40]

We know nothing of Mrs. Morel's background but it is probable that like so many other European men and women of modest social origins translated into a colonial environment, her sense of her own social status had become considerably inflated and the confrontation with Nona Dayang Low may have represented for her a dramatic challenge to or denial of that status. It was evidently a shocking experience, something like a slap on the face for someone who had assumed the position of a white colonial matron. The presence of Nona Dayang Low in the Residency also suggested the role of First Lady of the European colonial establishment, which the Morels would have found the most extraordinary affront. At the very least there was the suggestion that Nona Dayang Low and Mrs. Morel were of equal status, which of course meant a demotion for the European woman rather than a promotion for the Asian woman. Asian women, including those of aristocratic origin, were by definition of lower status and for European women to be treated as their equals was a mortal insult.

This was all the more important in Labuan where, as in Sarawak, conventional European standards of sexual morality were being honored in the breach rather than the observance. James St. John, the colony's surveyor and younger brother of Spenser St. John, had a number of children by a Malay woman before he was persuaded by the Colonial Chaplain to marry. Claude de Crespigny, the Harbour Master, and Dr. John Treacher, the Colonial Surgeon, also had native mistresses as did Morel's own European subordinates at the coal mines. Miscegenation was the rule rather than the exception and it is likely that Mrs. Morel felt morally besieged. Her husband's protest on her account reflected her insecurity rather than his, but the real reason for his antipathy towards Low was probably a dispute over the coal company.

476

Harriette McDougall's drawing of the first European settlement of Labuan, c. 1850. Her caption: "Labuan taken from 'Auckland Villa,'" Hugh Low's house is the third from the right.

Kitty Low in 1867

Government House ('The Residency'), c. 1867. This was occupied by Hugh Low on a number of occasions when he was administering the colony between governors. It was here that the Morels found Nona Dayang Loya one day in 1867.

Hugh Low, Labuan, 1868

Colonial officials, Labuan, 1869. Hugh Low is standing, center, and lying on the grass in front of him is John Pope-Hennessy, Dr. John Treacher is seated on the extreme right. Interestingly enough, a figure behind him has been erased. This may have been James St. John, brother of Spenser St. John.

Nevertheless, both Morels no doubt saw Low as 'letting down the side'. They would not necessarily have objected to his keeping a Malay mistress clandestinely, but to give her 'face' as his consort challenged the entire system which they were desperately endeavouring to uphold. They no doubt expected that as the senior European official he would set the rules of social distance for the entire community and enforce them.

As if Low had not been sufficiently injured by the appointment over him of Pope Hennessy, a young Irishman with not the remotest knowledge of Eastern affairs, fate ordained that the new Governor would fall in love with the ravishingly beautiful but bored Kitty within a few months of his arrival. They were married in February 1868 and it was not long before the Governor and his father-in-law were not on speaking terms. Pope Hennessy refused to increase his salary and Low published a strong attack on the Governor's tax policies in a Singapore newspaper. In his correspondence with the Colonial Office, whose volume was in absurd disproportion to the tiny and unimportant colony, Pope Hennessy made great play of Low's illicit relationship. He cited the experience of the new Colonial Secretary's wife, Mrs. Frances Slade, who was 'unable to walk up to the Coal Point Road because she found there were high officials who did not scruple to salute her when in the company of their Malay mistresses'.[41] The house where Low maintained Nona Dayang Low, her mother and their daughter (for what he properly described as reasons of 'honour and justice and duty')[42] was at Sagumau on the Coal Point Road. The fact that Pope Hennessy himself had two illegitimate daughters in England, one of whom was an actress, does not seem to have affected the high moral tone that he adopted on the northern coast of Borneo. The man described by one contemporary as a 'penniless, eloquent and horribly troublesome member for some remote Irish constituency'[43] was also a perfect hypocrite.

One evening in September 1870 when Low was riding out with Kitty, he received a message that his other daughter was ill. He immediately rode with Kitty to the Sagumau house and spoke to Lucy on the verandah. Kitty did not dismount from her pony but was within the house's compound and this grave breach of protocol was immediately reported to the Governor's sister, Mary, by the Colonial Apothecary, James McClosky, who chanced to be passing by at the time. Some months later, Pope Hennessy told the Colonial Office that the incident had given rise to 'a grave public scandal' and described his father-in-law as being 'totally blind to the inconvenience of the public scandal attaching to his conduct'.[44] Even the Colonial Chaplain, the Rev. W. D. Beard, who detested Pope Hennessy and believed that he was doing everything in his power to destroy Low, found the latter's action highly reprehensible and on McClosky's instigation extracted a written promise from him that nothing like it would ever happen again. McClosky then attempted through Beard to obtain from Low a public statement of his error but at this point the Colonial Chaplain realized that the exercise was being directed by the Governor himself and thus refused to cooperate any further.

Determined to dispose of Low, Pope Hennessy persuaded the more cooperative chief of police, Captain Hervey, to mount a careful watch on the Sagumau house where (as with most houses in Labuan) gambling was reputed to take place. For some time nothing could be detected, except that the inhabitants of the house sometimes spent their evenings singing *pantun* to musical accompaniment. However, on 17 June 1871 a Chinese man called Lee Ah Wee was arrested for illegally selling no less than five cents' worth of tobacco in the vicinity of the house. A police report was made which mentioned Low in association with the house and when he as Police Magistrate wrote a letter to the magistrates court protesting against this, Hervey, McClosky and a Chinese merchant refused to sit on the bench with him. Seizing on the letter, Pope Hennessy was then able to make a number of charges against Low and suspend him from office.

In his painstaking report on the charges,[45] Pope Hennessy's successor, Governor Henry Bulwer, exonerated him, although not without remarking on the impropriety of his letter to the court. Bulwer appears to have accepted Low's claim that all the charges against him had in fact arisen from the incident at the Sagumau compound and were aimed at establishing his guilt by association with alleged illegal activities there. Among other things, Pope Hennessy's charges had alleged that Dayang Nona Kamariah, who was then living at the Sagumau house with her sister, was a common prostitute. In reference to the police report's description of Nona Dayang Low as Low's 'concubine', Bulwer went to some trouble to clarify her actual status in the eyes of most Labuan people:

> The term 'Nona' it is said by Mr. Low is offensively translated into English as 'concubine'; and I am assured by those conversant with the Malay language that the term has been abused in the translation. If it were intended to translate the word 'concubine' into Malay the term used would have been 'purampuan' or 'gundik'; whereas the term 'Nona' while it signifies an unmarried woman is applied by the Malays as a term or title (and not one of disrespect) to women kept as mistresses by Europeans.

> In this way it has even come to be anglicized...[46]

Nor could he conclude that Low's relationship had in any way prejudiced his official responsibilities:

> ...while his connection with the woman Dayang Loya was well known throughout the Island, for in this small community it is impossible that such a connection, with whatever secrecy and precaution it be maintained, could be otherwise than well known, I cannot learn that he ever obtruded it upon the public observation or allowed it at any time to interfere with the proper discharge of his magisterial duties...[47]

From the point of view invoked by the Morels and by Pope Hennessy, Low's accidental bringing together of his legitimate and illegitimate daughters was similar to the earlier incident. By taking Kitty into the compound of his Malay mistress's house and allowing the two girls to see each other, he was thereby conferring on Kitty her illegitimate Eurasian half-sister's low status. Indeed, there was also a threat to the status of Pope Hennessy's sister who was visiting him at the time and apparently egged on her brother in his campaign against Low. It would be interesting to know how Kitty herself felt about Lucy, especially since her own mother had been in a similar position when William Napier married his European wife.

-III-

The status system implicit in the Labuan incidents is not difficult to define and one obvious element is race superiority. The McDougalls, the Morels and the Pope Hennessys would have had no doubt as to where they stood in the hierarchy of mankind, whether they thought in terms of the Great Chain of Being, or of the Social Darwinism soon to be expounded by Herbert Spencer. Another element is the political fact of colonial subjection which would have allowed Europeans to think in terms of power and authority and the unchallengeable position of their own institutions and conventions.

Status was also inextricably linked up with sexuality. In order to compete successfully with native women, European women had to emphasize social differences, racial differences and a higher and purer sexual morality. They could not emphasize their own superiority as sexual partners because this would have weakened the moral argument - and because they probably did not believe it anyway. They accepted the mystique of Asian feminine super-sexuality (which, incidentally, French novelists of the colonial scene were already beginning to challenge) and believed that it was licentious, dirty, degrading and even bestial.[48]

Possessing no economic or political rôle, European women in Borneo depended very much on monopolizing their husbands' sexual needs in order to achieve a sense of security. In a very real sense they were competing with native women who often sought the material and status benefits of an association with a European man and who were not constrained by conventional European proprieties.

In Sarawak and Labuan, native women were attracted by the material benefits and enhanced status that association with European men brought. For Dayak women, it represented an escape from a career of child-bearing and physical drudgery which promised a foreshortened lifespan. For Malay women, it represented a greater degree of security than could be obtained from a system which made unilateral divorce common and maintenance exceptional. There were positive advantages to be gained from a relationship with a European man and it would be surprising if some women did not seek this. Power and status, together with the strong element of novelty, must also have endowed the European colonial male with a certain sexual charisma.

It is unfair to suggest that the European 'mems' single-handedly constructed the status system of colonial Borneo, to emphasise 'the part played by such English women as Mrs. Slade in spreading racial prejudice throughout the mid-Victorian empire...'.[49] Before their arrival, European men, by virtue of their political and economic power, had created a hierarchical system which, among other things, gave them relatively free access to native women. Into this situation came European women who were acutely aware of the need to protect the benefits which association with European men bestowed on them against competition from native women. Their response was to invoke more explicitly the ideology of racial superiority on which the system was based and to use it as a means of demarcating social distance. They explored and exploited the full potential of the system and also acted as its principal agents of enforcement and perpetuation. There were times, however, when the politics of colonial life meant that European men such as Morel, Slade and Pope Hennessy could exploit that system of their own creation for their own specific ends.

POSTSCRIPT

After Sarawak became part of Malaysia in 1963, miscegenation took on a new dimension in the observable pattern of educated and high status Malays and Dayaks marrying European women, in most cases after contacts made during university education in Australia, New Zealand or Britain. When these relationships were translated into the local context, they may have conferred a certain cachet insofar as the women were still seen to reflect something of the status enjoyed by Europeans in the Brooke and British colonial eras. Nevertheless, the social position of the women has been largely defined by that of their husbands.

Although this trend represented a nice fulfillment of Charles Brooke's views on the desirability of unions between European women and Asian men, his thinking was informed, not by notions of racial equality, but of animal breeding and the superiority of the hybrid in an environment which was believed not to be conducive to European reproductive success.

NOTES

1. J. Butcher, The British in Malaya: The Social History of a European Community in Colonial South-East Asia, Kuala Lumpur: Oxford University Press, 1979, pp. 193-222.

2. R. Hyam, Britain's Imperial Century 1815-1914: A Study of Empire and Expansion, London: Batsford, 1976, p. 135.

3. N. Tarling, The Burthen, The Risk, and the Glory: A Biography of Sir James Brooke, Kuala Lumpur: Oxford University Press, 1982, p.

4. E. Hahn, James Brooke of Sarawak, London: Arthur Barker, 1953, p. 16.

5. D. Brown, 'Another Affair of James Brooke?', Brunei Museum Journal, Vol. 2, No. 4 (1972) p. 206.

6.	Cited by Hahn, op. cit., p. 16.

7.	Hyam, op. cit., p. 146.

8.	Annie Brooke to Lucy Grant, January 1858, Rhodes House, Oxford [RH], Mss.Pac.s. 90, Vol. 10, ff. 266-71. I am indebted to Dr. G. Saunders for this reference.

9.	Spenser St. John to Charles Grant, 5 September 1878, ibid., Vol. 15, ff. 104-9.

10.	H. Keppel, The Expedition to Borneo of H.M.S. Dido..., 2 Vols. London: Chapman & Hall, 1846, I, p. 66 (my emphasis).

11.	James Brooke to Emma Johnson, 2 June 1858, RH Mss.Pac.s. 90, Vol. 1, f. 230. See also, letters from James Brooke to Alfred Brooke, 1860-67, RH Mss. Pac.s. 83, Box 29, ff. 5-15.

12.	H. Keppel, A Sailor's Life under Four Sovereigns..., 3 Vols., London: Macmillan, 1899, II, 75.

13.	James Brooke to Thomas Williamson, 26 January 1846, in J. C. Templer, ed., The Private Letters of Sir James Brooke, 3 Vols., London: Richard Bentley, 1853, II, p. 116.

14.	This undated circular is preserved in Hugh Low's collection of Borneo Pamphlets, RH.

15.	H. Low, typescript journal, 1844-46, Pope Hennessy Papers, RH Mss. Brit. Emp.s. 409.

16.	C. Brooke, Ten Years in Sarawak, 2 Vols., London: Tinsley, 1866, I, p. 66.

17.	'List of Europeans on the Sarawak Territory', n.d., RH Mss. Pac.s. 90, Vol. 16, f. 116.

18.	2 Vols., London: Smith, Elder & Co., 1862.

19.	F. T. McDougall to T. F. Stooks, 2 May 1849, RH, U.S.P.G. Archives, [USPG], Borneo, Vol. I.

20.	F. T. McDougall to W. T. Bullock, 29 May 1856, ibid.

21.   Brooke, op. cit., II, p. 29.

22.   Harriette McDougall to Brooke Brooke, n.d., RH Mss.Pac.s. 90, Vol. 14, f. 154.

23.   A. Horsborough to E. Hawkins, 11 June 1859, USPG, Borneo, Vol. I.

24.   The Borneo Mission of the Propagation of the Gospel in Foreign Parts..., London, 1862.

25.   Spenser St. John to Charles Grant, 5 September 1878, RH Mss.Pac.s. 90, Vol. 15, ff. 104-9. In his thesis 'The Anglican Mission and the Brooke Raj' (University of Hull, 1989), G. Saunders recounts in considerable detail the dispute between McDougall and St. John.

26.   Charles Brooke to Brooke Brooke, 23 November 1862, RH Mss.Pac. S. 90, Vol. 8, ff. 179-184.

27.   Brooke, op. cit., I, pp. 129-130.

28.   W. J. Moore, Health in the Tropics; or, A Sanitary Art Applied to Europeans in India, London, 1862.

29.   Brooke, op. cit., II, p. 338.

30.   Ibid.

31.   Ibid

32.   Ibid. A fuller discussion of Charles Brooke's views on miscegenation and their relevance to his rajahship can be found in R.H.W. Reece, 'A "Suitable Population": Charles Brooke and Race-Mixing in Sarawak', Itinerario, Vol. IX (1985), No. 1, pp. 67-112.

33.   Margaret Brooke to Charles Willes Johnson, 29 June 1927, RH Mss. Pac.s. 83, Vol. 18, f. 10.

34.   Ibid.

35.   Margaret Brooke to Charles Willes Johnson, 10 August 1927, ibid., f. 15.

36.   Margaret Brooke to Charles Willes Johnson, 25 June 1927, ibid., f.8.

37.　Brooke, op. cit., II, p. 79.

38.　The Ranee of Sarawak, My Life in Sarawak, London: Methuen, 1913.

39.　H. H. The Rajah's Order Book, Sarawak Museum.

40.　John Pope Hennessy to Lord Kimberley, Despatch No. 9222, 20 June 1871, Public Record Office, Kew [PRO], CO 144/34.

41.　Ibid.

42.　J. Pope-Hennessy, Verandah: Some Episodes in the Crown Colonies 1867-1889, London: Allen and Unwin, 1964, p. 80. My account of the incidents on Labuan owes a good deal to this fine book by the governor's grandson.

43.　J. D. Ross, Sixty Years: Life and Adventure in the Far East, 2 Vols., London: Hutchinson, 1911, I, p. 37.

44.　John Pope Hennessy to Lord Kimberley, Despatch No. 9222, 20 June 1871, PRO CO 144/34.

45.　Ms. report by Governor Bulwer, ibid. 34.

46.　Ibid.

47.　Ibid. For more details of Low's Borneo career, see R. H. W. Reece, Introduction to H. Low, Sarawak: Its Inhabitants and Productions..., Singapore: Oxford University Press, 1988, pp. v-xlii [London: Richard Bentley, 1848].

48.　See H. Ridley, Images of Imperial Rule, London: Croom Helm, 1983.

49.　Pope-Hennessy, op. cit., p. 85.

KELING AND KUMANG IN TOWN:
DIFFERENTIAL EFFECTS OF URBAN MIGRATION ON
IBAN MEN AND WOMEN

VINSON H. SUTLIVE, JR.
The College of William and Mary

The migration of Iban into the city of Sibu and other urban centers in Sarawak has resulted in the elaboration and exaggeration of differences between men and women. The overwhelming success of Iban in their "socialization for achievement (aggression)" (DeVos 1973) is attested to in the pride of person and strength of character noted by even the most casual observer.[1] Both men and women carry themselves with an air of presence and confidence. These personal qualities are evident in the entrance of Iban into the modern institutions of education, business, and state politics. The disproportionate number of Iban men to women in the last two categories, however, is indicative of the traditional inequities in Iban society made more apparent by the differential effects of urban migration.

The purpose of this paper is threefold: (1) to summarize the sex role models of men and women in rural areas, that is, roles as they have been stereotyped based upon gender differences; (2) to examine egalitarianism as it has been described for traditional Iban; and (3) to describe and analyze the lives of urbanizing Iban.

489

1.   <u>Traditional Sex Role Models: Fact in Fiction</u>

In Iban folklore, the prototypical culture hero and heroine are Keling and Kumang. Keling is everything an Iban man should be: handsome, strong, and daring. Kumang is everything an Iban woman might be: industrious, clever, impetuous, and jealous.

In published stories of Keling and Kumang, these traits appear again and again. For example, in *Limau Senaman*, Kumang violates a taboo on bathing and is whisked away by a cyclone to the top of a mythic tree from which Keling rescues her after numerous battles with demons and spirits. In other accounts, Kumang works her magic on rivals for Keling's affections, and only the gracious Keling prevents her jealousy undoing their relationship. In *Kumang Betelu'* ("Kumang Lays Eggs"), a story with a clear Oedipal theme, the two are childless until Kumang lays eggs in the rice bin. When Keling discovers what she has done, he takes his spear and pierces each egg. Rather than killing the embryos, he merely pokes out their eyes and when they hatch, the couple have seven blind boys. Keling grows tired of taking care of the boys and when they reach adolescence, takes them into the forest where he abandons them. They encounter an *Antu Gerasi Papa'* ("Father Figure") but, being blind, they do not recognize him for the monster he is. Moved to compassion, the *antu* gives them a salve which they apply to their eyes, and gain their sight. The next time they meet the *antu*, they see him for what he is, and kill him. After lengthy wanderings, marriage, and starting their own families, they return to Keling and Kumang and live happily ever after.

Kumang always comes off second best to Keling. Despite her industry and other virtues, she is caricatured as inept, impatient, jealous, and given to acts with no thought of their consequences. There are many faces of Kumang (cf. Sutlive 1977), who can be strong-willed, naive, resourceful, determined, yet dependent.

The stories of Keling and Kumang contain a number of themes about female-male relations.

> First, the person and role of Kumang help set the stage for the remarkable feats of Keling (just) as the personhood and role of Iban women set the stage for the accomplishments of Iban men
> . . .
> Second, not only do the person and role of Kumang and the Iban woman set the stage for the activities of Keling and Iban men, they <u>require</u> the remarkable abilities of the male figures.

Third, the character of Kumang and Iban women is of such a nature as to make the correctives (and interventions) of males constantly necessary.

Fourth, Kumang, other female characters in oral literature, and women in general are said to be more naive and gullible than are males.

Finally, Kumang and Iban women are alleged to be impetuous, impatient, to act without thought to consequence (Sutlive 1977:158-160).

Jealousy is the trait most commonly attributed to Iban women by Iban men. The Iban word for jealousy, *ninding*, is instructive, because it derives from *dinding* or "wall". The inference I draw from the word is that women in traditional Iban society attempted to secure or "wall" in their outgoing men, but with little apparent success. There was the expectation--indeed, the legitimization by men--of husbands philandering while on *bejalai*,[2] certainly one of the motives for men undertaking their travels. According to some of my informants, husbands reverted to the status of bachelor and might take another wife in addition to the one he left behind. This happened in the extended travels of Tun Jugah[3] between 1918 and 1921. Though he was married, both Jugah and his brother Tedong took wives in a Kenyah community. Upon their return to their home community, they left their Kenyah wives and Jugah returned to find that his own young bride had divorced him and had gone back to her parents.[4]

2. The Problem of Egalitarianism, Female Status, and Actual Role Behavior

For three decades, Iban society has been described as "classless and egalitarian" (Freeman 1955:10).

A. J. N. Richards is technically correct when he writes

that (for Iban) the sexes are equal but different, opposite but matching (personal communication, April 3, 1990).

And on the same point, Freeman is right in concluding that

There is no institutionalized subordination or superordination in Iban social structure in Iban social structure; a child at birth can belong to either his mother's or his father's bilek family, and residence can be with either the husband's or wife's kin group (Freeman 1970:15).

A problem in the description of Iban society as "egalitarian" is that the term is rarely if ever defined. The principle of equity is apparent in

> the bilateral kinship system and the "utrolateral" . . patterns of residence . . ., the even distribution of jural rights and obligations . . . (and due consideration of the views of men and women in) decision-making (Davison and Sutlive, this volume, p. 163).

Inferences which have been drawn from the term "egalitarian" include an absence of class distinctions among pre-colonial Iban, which it apparently did, and the existence of equal opportunities for achievement by all, which I consider below. It has been applied as an ideal type, and once applied, anthropologists have accepted the term uncritically. Additionally, we probably have assumed more than was intended in Freeman's use of the term "egalitarian". If the textbook definition of "egalitarian" is used, viz. a society in which no one may tell another what to do, the definition has some validity and utility for understanding the Iban:

> Item: All Iban, men and women, have had relatively equal access to resources. Though men predominated as pioneers, they frequently were accompanied by women and both men and women might inherit rights to land. Such access has been qualified by circumstances of descent, with descendants of pioneers and warriors often having claims to more and better lands.

> Item: All Iban, men and women, have had relatively equal opportunities to succeed as farmers. Such opportunities have been conditioned, however, by a host of imponderabilia, most significant of which have been different attitudes towards the values of industry and stewardship. Many men have disdained farming, preferring the romance of the hunt. It is somewhat ironic, but not unpredictable, that many of those men who have applied themselves to what more traditional Iban men consider "women's work" have prospered far more than have the adventurers[5] (see life histories below).

> Item: All Iban, men and women, have had relatively equal privileges of participating in longhouse decision-making

meetings, including annual meetings to decide upon farm sites to trials.[6] Women as well as men may influence the decisions in all such meetings. That such privileges have often not been activated is due to the persuasive eloquence and strength of personality of more fluent (or merely voluble) men and women over less verbal community members.

If "egalitarian" implies equality of opportunity in all affairs, it simply is not true of Iban in previous generations and is becoming increasingly uncharacteristic of contemporary Iban society. For example, more perceptive Iban quickly perceived the resolve and the superior force of arms of the Brookes and British, and just as quickly allied themselves with the colonial administration.[7] The Second Rajah helped create a hierarchy of political offices which has become ever more divisive. Just as women were excluded from the prestige system based upon headhunting and warfare, so they were excluded from the political structure created by Charles Brooke, as, in fact, were most men.

Iban women have been the principal enculturators of their society. They have provided stability and continuity, in contrast to the destabilizing and discontinuous behaviors of many men. Michael Heppell's research (1975), describes the absolutely crucial role Iban women play in socialization of the young and in the quality of life--and even the survival--of their society. Heppell

> explores how consistent mothering behaviour in particular and consistent treatment by other attachment figures seem to elicit in an infant confidence and trust in other people's behavior so that he will approach the world with confidence and when faced with difficult choices or potentially alarming situations, he is likely to tackle them effectively and in an approved way. (Heppell) also examines the inconsistent mother and suggests that such early experiences are likely to elicit anxiety and little confidence in the child which results in his seeing the world as comfortless and unpredictable and his responding to it either by shrinking from it or by doing battle with it (1975:10).

Heppell's analysis is significant also because the role of the father is not mentioned. Some Iban fathers were respected, even revered, for their accomplishments, but the mother ensured the survival and stability of the family.[8] Nonetheless, as several of the brief life histories which follow will indicate, the presence or absence of a father could make a crucial difference in the life of a son.

Iban women never have been socialized to the non-responsible--not irresponsible[9]--self-indulgences of their men: They have never had the freedom to travel, and those women who assumed it did so at the cost of their names and reputations. They have had the major responsibilities for their families for months or even years while their husbands, brothers, or fathers have been away. They never have received the acclaim or adulation enjoyed by Iban men on festive occasions. By circumstances created by their quite independent men, Iban women have had to live with an equally high degree of independence. When men undertook the initiate's journey in early to middle adolescence, and every year in their adult life, their wives got by "with a little help from their friends." For example, the late *Manang Biga'*, a close personal friend of mine, claimed to be "called" by his familiar spirit annually just after the farm was planted to to on a healing tour. His arthritic wife was left to weed and manage as best she could. His adolescent children were forced to assume a major responsibility for the family until they were old enough to marry and move out. They continued to help provide for their parents until their death.

Some women who resented the lengthy absence of months or years and were not happy living with their husbands' families, divorced the travellers who as often as not returned to find the bride they left now the wife of another.[10] Resentments grew into antagonisms between men and women, expressed in what Freeman has described as female jealousy of males (1968), Sather as the warfare of coitus (1978), and the identification of members of the opposite sex as "the enemy" (Sutlive 1991, in press).

So capable were most women as primary producers, and so dominant in the symbolic activities of sowing seed, initiating the harvest (*matah padi*), setting the pace (*ngindu'*), and storing the threshed rice (*besimpan*) that, other than for the rituals they performed--and for doing the heaviest work--one must ask, Did Iban women really need men (cf. Davison and Sutlive, this volume)? Except for the heaviest work of clearing the farm, women were quite able to perform all the activities of agriculture, even to carrying home to heavy harvest baskets.

Freeman correctly observes that

> . . . it is not unusual for women to be completely responsible for farming because of the extended absence or sickness of their menfolk (1955:75)

Freeman seems to suggest that women have a harder work load than the remaining men in the community, in his observation that "(a) woman's day is more equal than a man's day" (1955:89).[11]

If the concept of egalitarianism implies an absence of status distinctions among men or between men and women, it is doubtful, if not wholly untrue. Whatever the source (cf. Rousseau 1980; Freeman 1981), Iban have long recognized distinctions of status based upon performance. The consummate coalescence of accomplishments was in the *raja berani* ("rich brave") (see Davison and Sutlive, this volume), who succeeded as pioneer, warrior, and farmer. Less prominent, but no less significant, was a set of roles (positions <u>existed</u> and were not created anew each generation) for the shaman, the bard, and the augur, and for women, the weaver. As Mashman and Drake (this volume) make abundantly clear, there existed a parallel process for recognition of the skills of the woman who mastered weaving and created innovative techniques or designs in the production of fine Iban fabrics. But in all truth, the successful weaver never eclipsed or even approximated the acclaim and approbation accorded outstanding Iban men.

The Formative Years

It is an hypothesis of this paper that differentiation between Iban boys and girls traditionally has begun by age seven or eight, or even earlier. By middle childhood, Iban girls have been given far greater responsibilities than their brothers ever would have to assume. While boys remain more carefree and playful, often to the annoyance of their parents, girls wash and cook, collect firewood and learn the highly disciplined work of weaving. Iban girls learned early that they did more that their brothers might do less.[12]

As recently as the 1960s, many Iban parents refused to send their daughters to school. (For that matter, many refused to send their sons, but there were more boys than girls in school.) Fearful that their children, who represented their only form of social security, might leave them, they forbade them to go to school and insisted that they work the farm, hunt, fish, and collect.

Maturation has been accompanied by an ever-widening gap in responsibilities, recreation, and ritual, reaching climax at puberty. We already have discussed the expectations that young girls aged 5 to 8 years will assume increasingly large shares of domestic chores. Boys have been much freer than girls to play games of tops, race boats, and join in cockfighting. There is no equivalence for girls to the elaborate life-crisis rituals by which boys become men and men become great men. Upon entering the host longhouse during festivals (*gawai*), adolescent girls and young women slip quietly into the *bilik* of relatives or friends, to reappear later in their ceremonial finery, while boys walk the "liquid gauntlet".[13]

The *gawai* system appears to have been created for and by men, to the virtual exclusion of females. As prelude to each festival, only men participate in cockfighting, the sport of the gods. Only men are received and moved along the verandah, finally to be seated against the outer wall, the place of highest honor, in the longhouse. Only men are protected by having a cock waved over their heads, and only certain men receive the adulation of young women who ply them with rice wine. It is important to remember, however, that women have been the principal providers of the rice from which the rice wine is manufactured. Women have woven the blankets for the ceremonial shrines, physically fabricating Iban culture. And during funeral rituals, the same women who embody the passage for birth and life escort the dead through death, by literally "crying them" (*nyabak*) to the next phase of existence.

3.   Iban in Town

Just as the *gawai* system has been dominated by men, so, too, the cities of Sarawak and their institutions have been created for and by men (cf. Sutlive 1988:141-170). The riverine markets and later the fort system, which was established for the suppression of headhunting, were dominated by males. This is not to suggest that women are not influential, for there are numerous examples of wives who either are active in state politics or business. But even today there is no woman who holds the position of state minister or who is head of a state department.[14]

In 1984, 12 years after completion of my initial research on the Iban of the Sibu District, I returned to Sibu to study the urbanizing Iban, supported by a Fulbright grant provided by the Malaysian-American Education Foundation. In comparing the sense of culture shock in 1984 with that my wife and I had experienced in 1957 when we first arrived in Sarawak, the impact some 27 years later was much greater. Perhaps it is a matter of age, but I think not.

The city of Sibu grew up around Fort Brooke which was built in 1862. The original inhabitants were Malays and Melanaus, joined at the beginning of this century by thousands of Chinese. By 1950 fewer than 500 Iban lived in Sibu. But the past three decades have seen the number of Iban city-dwellers grow to more than 10,000.

Determining the exact (or even an approximate) number of Iban residents in Sibu is problematic. As a Filipino sociologist once commented to me, "There are few things more easily collected than incorrect statistics." In the 1980 Census, 6,797 Iban were enumerated in the Sibu Urban District population. Extrapolating to 1984, a government statistician estimates the Iban population to have been 8,100 during the research period. My estimate places the number much higher, between 10,000 and 15,000.[15] There are approximately 400,000 Iban in Sarawak, of whom 20 percent, or 80,000, now live in the state's towns and cities. These urban migrants, probably to be joined soon by tens of thousands of others, are among the least studied members of Sarawak's societies. Yet the processes and effects of migration into Sarawak's cities have been neglected almost completely by social scientists.

I have summarized elsewhere the major changes urban migration is producing in settlement patterns, occupations, roles, and relations elsewhere (Sutlive 1988:192-199). In Sarawak's cities, traditional prescriptions and opportunities for achievement, dominated by warring for men and weaving for women, have given way to economic and political systems with uneven advantages for males. The parity of the sexes has given way to new adaptions with the development of new relationships. These new adaptions and relationships are much too complex to analyze within the space of this chapter. They are based upon controls exercised by state and federal governments over land, forests, oil, and other resources, all in the hands of men. Access to top level posts in ministries and departments is restricted almost exclusively to men.

Here I want to examine the life stories of Iban men and women in Sibu to dramatize the reality of differentiation.

Rich Man

Unchat anak Chok was born in 1922 at Bawang Assan. Bawang Assan is a large community comprised of seven longhouses with over 2000 residents. Its proximity to Sibu, and ease of access by public transport, has contributed to the rapid assimilation and acculturation of its members to city life. Most young people have left, first for school, subsequently for work. During the daytime, most of the houses are practically empty except for older people.

His real father was the late Tuai Rumah ("Headman") Saung, but he was adopted by Chok, his father's first cousin. Chok was exceptional in his commitment to farming and rubber gardening. While other men travelled, Chok and his family dedicated themselves to the production of rice and rubber.[16]

At the beginning of the century, Chok had become friendly with two Chinese,[17] who counseled him in the work of trade. Unlike some men who might have taken advantage of Chok, the two took him into their business, buying and selling rubber and jungle products. Scarcely had he begun to trade when the market area of Sibu burned to the ground in 1902.

Chok and his Chinese associates rebuilt. They rode out the fluctuations of the world market prices for rubber, and they prospered.

> We were the only ones with lots of rubber, along with the father
> of the late Temenggong Banggau.

Chok was encouraged to buy a shophouse at Number 6, Island Road, in Sibu. He said he didn't know how to make arrangements for the purchase, but a Malay, Abang Menteran, reassured and helped him consummate the purchase. From the purchase of one shophouse, Chok was able to acquire two more, which he rented to Chinese merchants.

Like many parents, Chok was suspicious of formal education, fearful that if his adopted son Unchat learned to read and write, he would abandon his parents. He relented, and when Unchat was 10, he entered Primary One and studied for three years. At age 12, Unchat dropped out to work full-time with his parents on the farm.

> I didn't travel as most other young men did. I took care of my
> family, because I was the only child, and my father didn't want
> me to leave home.

The Japanese Occupation delayed but did not destroy Chok's drive to prosperity. All the family returned to farming, but the market for rubber and other products collapsed. Unchat was recruited by the Japanese for a para-military or "police" force, <u>Keed Way</u>,[18] but Chok refused to allow him to join.

Unchat was married just before the Occupation, and remained part of his father's family. With the defeat of the Japanese, he and his wife established their own *bilik*. The first daughter, Pillor, was born in 1947, and subsequently, two sons, Manggang and Uat, and two more daughters, Helen and Herita.

The poor performance of their two oldest children in their first test scores convinced Unchat and his wife that they must move them from the rural school and enroll them in school in Sibu. In time, all were to study in Methodist or Roman Catholic schools, and three went abroad for university education. With his father's death and recognizing that the monthly rental of the family's shophouses was inadequate, Unchat sold the properties to fund his children's study abroad. Pillor studied to Form 3 before marrying a man from Bawang

Assan. Manggang unsuccessfully studied medicine, and became a medical technologist. Helen also attempted a degree course in medicine but settled for a diploma in biochemistry. Uat studied law, but returned to Sarawak without a degree and worked with Radio-Television Malaysia before taking up business studies.

Unchat and his wife built a house on Archer Road, but still maintain their *bilik* in Bawang Assan. For a decade after all the family members had moved to Sibu, they hired people to tap their rubber garden. But the yield dropped along with the price of rubber, and Unchat abandoned the tapping as he had farming. He and his wife are able to live off income from investments,[19] and with his children, have become members of Sarawak's "middle class".

And Wealthy Woman

The story of Indai Tamoh of Sungai Aup represents the entrepreneurial skills of Iban women, and the resolve they make to succeed on their own or ensure that their children will succeed. Married to a school teacher, also a native of Sungai Aup and a noted genealogist, Indai Tamoh was employed as hostel mother at the Nanga Selangau school where her husband was appointed headmaster. She was an excellent manager, maintaining oversight of her family's *bilik* in Rumah Nyala, Aup, a full day's journey from Nanga Selangau, while acquiring land near the school. During a visit to the school in 1964, I was surprised to discover that, in anticipation of a profit, she was buying up land, which local Iban were only too willing to sell. When a road was cut through near the land she had acquired, her speculation was rewarded.

Her husband was transferred back to Sibu, and she returned to Sungai Aup to farm her family's land. Though a woman, she employed men from her longhouse to prepare, plant, and maintain her rice fields. When her husband died, she moved into Sibu and purchased a house. She retains her *bilik* at Aup, and lives with her son and his family as matriarch of a successful family.

Poor Man

The story of Ansi[20] is representative of many Iban men who have moved to Sibu. Ansi and his family left Bawang Assan for Sibu in the early 1980s, when he was offered a low-paying job as a caretaker. They live rent free in modest quarters provided by his employer. He and his wife have three daughters, one of whom is employed by the government, another by the church, and the third who helps Ansi and his wife manage a guest house.

Ansi was born in Bawang Assan in 1940, just before the Japanese Occupation. His family moved downriver, delaying his attending school until he was about 13. His parents divorced, and his father left the family. Of his parents' divorce, Ansi recalls,

> We really suffered because my mother was left alone with us children. I asked my mother, "What's the advantage of divorce?" Even now, I cannot comprehend it. I am still angry at my father (for abandoning us).

His parents remarried each other, but Ansi would not accept his father. When he was 13, his family moved to Darau, below Bawang Assan, where there was a school.

> I knew that I wanted to go to school. I knew that I knew nothing. I couldn't read, I couldn't write, I couldn't add (or subtract).

Ansi attended school for two years, acquiring basic skills in reading, writing, and arithmetic. He had to drop out to help support his family when his father abandoned them a second time. He hired on as a laborer for a Chinese businessman, and extended his education, becoming proficient in Foochow and Malay. He quit that job to work on a motor launch. Impressed by his industry, his employer offered him a monthly salary of M$450 to supervise a sawmill operation.

> That was a generous salary in 1958. In addition, he would provide my living quarters with utilities. That was my chance.

But Ansi had married by then, and his father-in-law didn't want him to leave Bawang Assan. His parents-in-law had rubber, and Ansi and their daughter were the principal tappers. The father-in-law insisted that it would be more profitable for all if they tapped rubber, rather than taking the supervisory position in the sawmill.

> That was my chance, and I lost it. Instead of a good-paying job, my wife and I got up at two o'clock every morning, tapped and collected until eight, then processed the rubber until one in the afternoon. After we had lunch, we had to go back and clear the grass from the rubber trees. Eventually, I got fed up and quit.

I resent my father-in-law's interfering with my opportunity to be somebody.

Lawyer

Christopher Sawan is an attorney. He was born on August 19, 1946. In contrast to Heppell's emphasis upon "consistent mothering" (above), the strongest influences in Christopher's life apparently were men: the headman of the longhouse into which he was born, Imang; his grandfather; his father; and an English educator, Mr. Robert Nicholl.

The Iban custom of *bejalai* (see Kedit, this volume) was critical in his personal and family history: his grandfather, who still lived with Christopher's father at the time of the interview,[21] was born to an Iban travelling in Sabah. The same grandfather married while on *bejalai* to Skrang.

> The year I was born, my father followed the tradition of his grandparents (actually, only his grandfathers) by going on *bejalai* to Brunei, to Serian, and there he was offered a job as a Police Constable by the Brunei Government, but (was) particularly attached to the British Shell Co.

Christopher's grandparents protested vigorously to the traveller, so convincingly that Christopher's father returned to live with his family in the longhouse.[22]

> . . . From then on, I was a "longhouse boy". Basically, the concern my real grandparents and the people in the longhouse had was, they didn't want to see their children educated. They felt (correctly) that we wouldn't come back to work in the farms with them. . . The fact that we went back to the longhouse jeopardized my two sisters' chances of having (an) education. They are younger than I. And when I went to school, it was not the "in" thing for girls to go to school (in the rural areas), especially with boys. There were no facilities for girls . . .

Despite the disadvantages his sisters suffered, Christopher is convinced that his family's return to the longhouse was the best for all. He and his sisters learned to work and to appreciate the hardships their parents endured for them.

Had he stayed in Brunei, life would have been easy, my father would have made sufficient money, and it might have had a deleterious influence on my desire to study. I might have been satisfied just to hang around and do nothing, after finishing Form 3. I saw that happen to other boys my age. . . Going back to the longhouse, one can become a real Iban.

Christopher excelled in his studies, in effect was double-promoted, and in 1959, was sent to Tanjong Lobang School where he was to spend the next nine years. It was there he met Robert Nicholl who impressed upon Christopher that he could be just as good as any other student. Nicholl helped support Christopher at Tanjong Lobang and bought his first suit when he graduated from the University of Malaya in 1971. He joined the civil service and worked until 1975 when he left to read law. He qualified, and was called to the English Bar in 1978.

Christopher's analysis of the strengths and weaknesses of the longhouse is instructive:

The basic longhouse attitude is not really conducive to the modern concept of career-orientation or career goals. Thus, there is a tendency to think too much of others, and (longhouse people) expose themselves too much to others, so that other people are in a better position to take advantage of them. That is basically what is wrong with the longhouse mentality. It may be a mixture of naivete, it may be a mixture of ingenuousness, built on respect for others . . .

Domestics

The relatively lower status and longer days of uneducated women in rural areas are dramatically converted into the low-paying drudgery of domestic servants. A large number of Iban women work as domestics, with long hours and low pay. The story of Joyce[23] is representative of scores, even hundreds, of Iban women. She moved from her rural community to Sibu in the early 1980s, convinced that her life held nothing for her except grinding poverty and an inescapable routine of farming, cooking, and the domestic chores which fall to wives and daughters. Her relocation was part of a mass exodus from her community, from where practically all young to middle-aged adults have moved away. Only the old remain to care for one another, and to receive the remittances Joyce and others send them. Younger people return only for holidays or major festivals.

Joyce starts her chores as early as 6 a.m., and finishes work about eight o'clock in the evening, or even later if her employers entertain. By her own calculation, however, her work-day is no longer than it was in the longhouse. She does miss the sense of freedom and the latitude she enjoyed in scheduling her own work. She does the washing and after hanging it on the line to dry, prepares breakfast for the family. Eating on the run, or after she has cleaned up the dishes, she leaves for the market to buy fruit, vegetables, fish and meat. Upon returning at mid-morning, she cleans, dusts, mops, and prepares lunch. If there are children, she has to keep watch on them.

After washing up the lunch dishes, she may have time to take a brief "power nap". By two o'clock, she begins the ironing, minding the children, and starting the evening meal. Only after serving and cleaning up after dinner can she relax.

Most domestics earn M$40 to M$50 (about US$20) per month and many have only one day off each month. Often the objects of verbal abuse, more by their mistresses than their masters, some quit to take up prostitution.

The Second Oldest Profession (After Shamanism)

On my flight to Sibu in early June, 1984, I was seated next to an acquaintance who said that if I were going to study Iban urban migrants, I must study prostitutes. Within 24 hours of my arrival in Sibu, another long-term friend gave me similar advice.

Therefore, three nights later I went with two Chinese to the Hideaway, a darkened pub in what then was the New Capitol Hotel. We had drinks and waited for about half-an-hour when two Iban girls came in. They seated themselves in a corner booth, and after a few minutes I asked them if they would like to join us for drinks. They introduced themselves as "Jacqueline" and "Nancy", one from Song, the other, from a longhouse near Sibu. The girls assumed that I knew no Iban and one of the Chinese took the lead in talking with them. I spoke only in English. Jacqueline had no education and Nancy had finished Primary 6. Both indicated that they intended to stay in Sibu. They described life in the longhouse as boring, with limited opportunities, and said they would not return except for an occasional visit to see their families and friends.

About two hours after we met, I decided it was time to use Iban and to reveal the fact that I understood everything that was being said, much at my expense. Nancy particularly looked surprised, and after a moment's embarrassed laughter, recovered her composure. We then agreed to set up an appointment for lunch the next day when I interviewed both.

Each girl earns between M$600 to M$1000 a month,[24] considerably more than a domestic's pay. Each spends about half of her salary on herself, and sends the balance to her parents and, in Nancy's case, to support her child. The two recognized each other, often had coffee together, but worked alone, each one for herself.

Nancy was born and grew up in a longhouse near Sibu. Upon completing the sixth grade, she worked on her parents' farm for two years before marrying a young man from Bawang Assan. Her husband was not from her kin-group. She had met him when her sister had married a man from the same community. Sleeping in her brother-in-law's *bilik*, she was awakened by the young man who had come to talk with her. She repulsed his initial advances, telling him that she wanted to continue in school and that she knew what he was after. "I know you are still young," the man said, "but I want to be with you" (*ka' amat enggau de*). He convinced Nancy, and he convinced his parents that unless they arranged the wedding, he would run away. Nancy extended her visit for two weeks, during which she received an engagement ring.

One month later, the young man's parents visited Nancy's family and made arrangements for the wedding. The groom was asked again about his intentions, which he declared to be serious. Following the festivities, Nancy and her husband returned with his family to Bawang Assan. He refused to visit her family, and it was six months before he permitted her to see them. A year after the wedding, Nancy gave birth to her daughter.

It was then that her troubles began. Her husband, whom she described as a "playboy", left her for other women (*Ia gila indu'*, lit., "He (was) crazy (about) women"). He gave her no money, though he was employed by the government as a mosquito exterminator. He seldom came home before one or two o'clock in the morning. His failure to support her and flaunting of his affairs convinced her that she must take her daughter and return to her parents. His mother asked her not to leave him, to give him a second chance. She stayed another two months, but his neglect turned to abuse. He refused to be alone with her: If she entered the *bilik*, he went out onto the verandah. If she went onto the verandah, he fled to the *bilik*.

> I could do nothing to please him. He refused to wear clothes I washed, saying they weren't clean. He refused to eat food I cooked, saying I was trying to poison him.

Nancy herself became inconsolable, wondering how things had gone so wrong. Her husband's brothers and sisters tried to reason with him, but he turned his anger on them. She remembered his courtship, and now suffered his rejection. She couldn't eat or sleep, and finally decided that her only choice was to return home.

Her husband pursued her, and tried to persuade her to return to Bawang Assan with him. She relented, but his abuse became even more intense. Though he did not hit her, his rejection had become complete.

After the second attempt at making the marriage work, Nancy returned and told her parents that she was going to divorce her husband. The parents arranged for a hearing before the Penghulu. Her husband accused her of having run off with another man (*berangkat*), and insisted that she return with their child.

> I refused. I said I had moved. I said I refused "to eat the banana twice" (*enggai makai pisang kedua kali'*). The crowd laughed when I said that. But I was really angry with him. I even refused to let him hold our child.

The Penghulu declared the couple divorced for the good of each. And Nancy began her life as a prostitute.

According to figures obtained from the GUM (Government) Clinic, there were approximately 400 Iban women registered as prostitutes in Sibu. The reader should not interpret this figure as implying that all 400 were in Sibu at the same time. A Police Lieutenant placed the figure even higher, at 700. In 1983, 304 girls were brought in for documentation. The Police record includes (a) a photograph, (b) personal particulars, (c) family background, and (d) place of practice. Of the 304, 200 were older than 21, 104 younger. The oldest was 45, and the youngest, 12. Most were active during week-ends, paydays, holidays, and the beginning and ending of each month. From my own observations, and from interviews conducted following Police raids, many worked the streets and hotels, and in the words of a Police Lieutenant, prostitution was "quite common . . . quite open."

There was no evidence of recruitment nor of any "syndicate", as alleged by some residents. Most, if not all, came on their own, or were influenced by the apparent prosperity of friends or relatives. Many reasons for prostitution included: (a) poor living conditions in the longhouse; (b) desire for more clothing and jewelry; (c) no education and low job skills; (d) fleeing a husband or parents; (e) refused to farm any more.

None admitted to being forced into prostitution. The Police Lieutenant, a Chinese, observed that Iban women were very independent and he did not think anyone could coerce them into anything.

During the first week I was in Sibu, I interviewed the Director of the Social Welfare Department. (For the full interview, see Appendix A below.) Her responses to questions about prostitution provide the attitudes of a government official and her perception on prostitution. In answer to my question about reasons for young women coming to Sibu, she said:

O: They come to Sibu because life in the longhouse is so dull for them. And it's especially so because they are only doing farming, subsistence-type farming, and gathering other fruit and jungle produce that they bring to the town to sell, and usually in the absence of any males around the longhouse, because the young males now are working in Bintulu or Brunei or Kuching, anywhere there's construction or labor-type work, where the income is so much more available or higher per day, and they think they can make very much more there, and it's quite more exciting than living in the longhouse and tilling the soil. But yes, these alternate occupations are probably much more dull, and we don't know how to make them more interesting or acceptable to them. I don't know how we could persuade them that it's a far better thing than what they are doing now.

Women seek welfare and some turn to prostitution because they are abandoned by fathers or husbands who may be on *bejalai* or may simply have left their families with no intention of returning. On these needs for welfare, the Director commented:

O: I haven't actually spoken to these women but we do get an awful lot of cases of women coming in here asking for public assistance because they just cannot make ends meet in the longhouse. So far, about 60 percent of our cases are very young and old ladies who have been left with their grandchildren. A lot of our cases are young ladies who are quite healthy and should have a good future, and they all tell us the same thing, that they don't know where their husbands are, they've just up and gone. They think (the husbands are in) Bintulu. They think he's somewhere working and he just doesn't show up and he doesn't send any money. So, you know, I'm sure the emotional period they go through of being deserted like that could make them very angry and upset and vengeful.

Under the law, we are protectors of any woman under the age of 21. So, it's a very high age actually that they are making it. We have had one girl, a 14-year old girl come in, and she looks younger actually, and a number, say they are 16 but they may not be. Yes, there would be very young girls, and they are coming in to see their aunts, so working for their aunts, working for their cousins, or other relatives.

The entry of so many young and older women into prostitution is itself a reason to re-examine the nature of development. The apparent successes of development are always subsidized by less apparent human costs of impoverishment, loss of culture and dignity, and very real suffering. Addressing the high cost of development, the Director concluded our interview by saying:

O: We talk of development and development, but I'm not sure it's development at all, because the psychological and emotional costs are so high, and needs are not being met. I feel angry that all this development is taking place and we in the Welfare Department are not being given enough staff and enough mandate and enough facilities to assist in this development. It seems as if we are here just to take care of all the casualties and to do the bandage work. And actually the casualties are so many that we can't cope with them. And I think it's terrible to wait for these casualties to happen instead of doing something to prevent them from happening. . .

In 1986, Dr. Winny Koster, a medical anthropologist from the Netherlands, interviewed 16 prostitutes in Sibu. The report of her interview is published in its entirety in Appendix B. Dr. Koster discovered that most of the women were forced into prostitution by circumstance,

because they did not see another way to solve their problems. . . . (M)ost of them (were) married, and probably would never have believed that they might become a prostitute one day.

Ten of the 16 prostitutes Dr. Koster interviewed are Iban. Of the remaining six, four are Chinese, one is Malay, and the other, Kadazan.

The Iban were generally younger than the others; 8 of them were under 23 years old, the youngest being only 17 years of age.

Only one woman had not been married, 13 were divorced, and half of Dr. Koster's sample had children for whom they had to provide support. Prostitution is not a get-rich profession, but it is one of the few ways women with limited education can earn an adequate income. One worked ten-hour days in a carpentry shop for M$4.00 (US$1.50) a day, but quit when she realized that she could not live on the low wages. Three-fourths disliked prostitution, but saw no other work available to them. One of the Iban women had worked as a domestic, but lost her job because her mistress was jealous of her.

Two of the Iban prostitutes took up the profession to get back at their husbands or men in general. In their words:

I married and got divorced two times now and I am only 21. I got really fed up and angry with men. That is why I just joined the other prostitutes in town.

Half a year ago, my husband left me and our two children of 11 and two and a half to marry another woman. He met her when he was posted in another town. I am still very angry and hot with him for what he did to me. To take revenge on him I work as a prostitute and will do so till I am cooled down.

Conclusions

We are not dealing with a question . . . of whether men have "formal" power and women have "informal" power, whether women's normative and actual roles are "domestic" and men's "extradomestic"; the question is rather, once we have assumed that such differences exist and have better identified them in field research, what do these differences mean in terms of the relative autonomy of men and women in the society to make decisions regarding the conduct of their lives and their social and economic relationships with the others, and their ability to influence the decisions and behaviour at all levels of society, in their own interest? (White 1980:10).

The modern cities grew up around native communities in which were located forts (for men) for the explicit purpose of suppressing headhunting (by men). Except for petty traders, men have dominated all institutions of business and government. Currently, Iban men are taking their places of leadership in these institutions with men of other ethnic groups.

Iban women maintain their control of the domestic sphere, whether in their own homes or as servants. As wives of the rich and famous, they also exert considerable influence in the careers, investment strategies, and decisions of their husbands. Further research should be done on the indirect roles and the authority of the wives of Iban officials in government and of Iban businessmen.

A disturbing development, as yet unstudied but certainly a topic for future research, is spouse abuse. I was first informed about this form of domestic violence in 1984. If this information is incorrect, the characterization of Borneo as free of domestic violence in its indigenous societies is still valid. If it does occur—and at this time hard data are unavailable—it would indicate that those pan-Bornean mechanisms of self-restraint which have eschewed physical abuse are breaking down and are being replaced by new techniques of control.

I conclude with one of the observations we made in the Introduction to this volume: Traditional Bornean societies have accorded a relatively high status to women and have been characterized by an absence of sexual violence. Contrary to a self-serving fiction that male dominance is universal in human societies[25] the women of Borneo have contributed to the development and elaboration of their societies fully as much as have the men. Regrettably, with few exceptions, their contributions have been underevaluated and little appreciated and, like Kumang, they have been "the second sex." With change and new opportunities, what has been need not be. What the women—and the men—of Borneo will become, is not a matter of biological differences alone, but of moral choice.

REFERENCES

Devos, George A.
1973   Socialization for Achievement: Essays on the Cultural Psychology of the Japanese. Berkeley, University of California Press.

Freeman, Derek
1955   Report on the Iban. London. Her Majesty's Stationery Office.

1968   Thunder, Blood and the Nicknaming of God's Creatures. The Psychoanalytical Quarterly 37:353-399.

1970   Report on the Iban. London. Athlone Press.

1981   Some Reflections on the Nature of Iban Society, Canberra, Occasional Papers, Department of Anthropology, Research School of Pacific Studies, The Australian National University.

Heppell, Michael
1975   Iban Social Control: The Child and the Adult, Ph.D. Dissertation, Australian National University.

Heyzer, Karl
1986   Working Women in South-East Asia. London. Open University Press.

Lepowsky, Maria
1990   Gender in an Egalitarian Society: A Case Study from the Coral Sea. In Peggy Reeves Sanday and Ruth Gallagher Goodenough, eds. Beyond the Second Sex: New Directions in the Anthropology of Gender. Philadelphia. University of Pennsylvania Press.

Pringle, Robert
1970   Rajahs and Rebels: The Ibans of Sarawak under Brooke Rule, 1841-1891. New York. MacMillan.

Rousseau, Jérôme
1980   Iban Inequality. Bidjragen tot de taal-, land- en volkenkunde. 136:52-63.

Sather, Clifford
1978   The Malevolent *koklir*: Iban Concepts of Sexual Peril and the Dangers of Childbirth. Bijdragen tot de Taal-, Land- en Volkenkunde. 134:310-355.

Sutlive, Vinson
1977   The Many Faces of Kumang: Iban Women in Fiction and Fact. Sarawak Museum Journal. Vol. XXV(46):157-164.

1988   The Iban of Sarawak. North Arlington Heights, IL. Waveland Press.

1991   Apai: The Life and Times of Tun Jugah of Sarawak. Kuala Lumpur. Penerbit Fajar Bakti.

White, Benjamin and Hastuti Endang Lestari
1980   Different and Unequal: Male and Female Influence in Household and Community Affairs in two West Javanese Villages. Working Paper on Project on Rural Household Economies and the Role of Women.

NOTES

1. Insofar as I am aware, the only researcher to examine the psychodynamics of the process of enculturation has been Michael Heppell (1975). George Appell (personal communication) raises the important question, Why don't women pass their resentments of men off to their sons?

2. Thus, the conquests of beauties by Keling, though fiction, has a firm basis in fact. Derek Freeman's account (1968) of the slaying of the incubus illustrates the affairs wives, who are left behind, may have while their husbands are on *bejalai*, and the convenience of the belief in the *antu buyu'* to account for unexplained pregnancies. Such pregnancies also may have contributed to the not uncommon practice of abortion.

3.   See Sutlive, 1991, Chapter Three.

4.   Subsequently, he took a third wife whom he divorced after she had born him a daughter, and then married his fourth wife who at this writing survives him in Kapit. There were many unconfirmable stories of the late Tun and his affairs with women during his travels throughout Malaysia and abroad. For example, a companion who visited Taiwan with him said that he went to see "the butterflies", a reference to Taiwanese hostesses. I never was able to document any of the stories, and attribute them in part to the numerous "Jugahisms" with which he is remembered.

5.   This is dramatically illustrated in the story of the late Tun Jugah, the subject of a biography in press (see Sutlive 1991).

6.   I well remember one of the most arduous trips undertaken by our mobile clinic during the extended dry season of 1958, when a party from Rumah Gaong, Sengan, led by a tiny, wiry woman with consummate verbal skills, convinced us that their longhouse was being ravaged by cholera. Within 24 hours we had loaded the boat with medical supplies, and the nurse, driver and I were off to meet the community leaders at the mouth of the Sengan River which was rendered impassable because of the low water. We spent almost 10 hours manhandling and at times lifting the thirty-six foot boat, before reaching Rumah Gaong, only to learn that there was no cholera at all, but only the now-achieved intention of the group to have a mobile clinic boat visit their house.

7.   Cf. Pringle 1970; Sutlive 1991.

8.   In the story of the late Tun Jugah, his mother, Menti, appears to have exerted the greatest influence on him. It is equally evident, however, that Jugah himself provided the discipline and focus by which his children have become eminently successful in business and, in the case of one son, politics.

9.   The distinction between "irresponsible" and "non-responsible" is an important one, and one made by Morris Massey in his now classic film, "What You Are Is Where You Were When." Non-responsible connotes an absence of expectations of responsible behavior, or situations in which children are not given responsibility for nor made to accept the consequences of their actions. Irresponsible behavior connotes the rejection of responsibilities which one should assume.

10.   The late Tun Jugah, the second and last Paramount Chief of the Iban, left his young bride and went on his initiate's journey which lasted three years. His wife, who had moved in with his family, divorced him during his long absence.

11.   The most characteristic feature of rural women is their long and arduous working day. Many case studies of South-East Asian societies show that housework, the fetching of water and fuel, the caring of animals with their direct participation, occupy the rural women fully (Heyzer 1986:12).

12.   This process and principle is identified as "schismogenesis" by the late Gregory Bateson.

13.   Iban are extremely generous people, and are expected to offer large amounts of drink and food at festivals as an indication of their generosity. During major festivals (*gawai*), men enter at one end of a longhouse, usually early in the afternoon, and move slowly to the other end, receiving a shot-glass of rice wine or whiskey from a member of each family. Thus, in an average sized longhouse with 30 apartments, each guest will receive 30 glasses of liquor. Reaching the far end of the house, the guests are directed to the outer wall of the verandah where they are given more to drink. It is small wonder that by early evening, many of the guests are thoroughly drunk and some pass out. In the Rejang, it has been axiomatic that the verandah must be covered with retch (*basah mutah*), or the guests were not treated well.

14.   For an analysis of the processes referred to here see G.N. Appell, editor, *Modernization and the Emergence of a Landless Peasantry*, Publication Number 33, *Studies in Third World Societies*, Department of Anthropology, The College of William and Mary, Williamsburg, VA 23185.

15.   The figures of 6,797 and 8,100 are based upon information from the Department of Statistics, and ones which I find problematic. Joseph Ko Tee Hock, Government Statistician, has correctly criticized both my methods for obtaining data and figures for the Iban population of Sibu (cf. *Borneo Research Bulletin*, April 1987, Vol. 19(1):57-60). On the basis of Iban who claimed to have been uncounted in the 1980 Census, I would contend that the actual population is somewhere between those reported by the Department of Statistics and those of 10,000-15,000 I reported in the *Borneo Research Bulletin*, September 1985, Volume 17, Number 2, pp. 93-95.

16.   The introduction of rubber had a dramatic effect on those Iban who planted it. In the words of one, "Our feet were stuck in it," that is, they were not as mobile as their ancestors had been. The conflict between shifting cultivation and rubber gardening was expressed in an apocryphal account of a man named Aing whose rice was consumed by rubber (see Sutlive 1988:128-129). On the basis of this story, it is alleged that many Iban cut down their rubber trees. Some did during the Great Depression, when rubber prices fell, but not nearly so many as one might be led to believe.

17.   The first advisor was Chiew Ping Ann, whom the Iban called Towkay Ah Lo. The one most often mentioned was the father of Datuk Amar Dr. Wong Soon Kai, currently Minister of Infrastructure for the Government of Sarawak. The friendship with the elder Wong began after Chok lost everything in the fire of 1902.

18.   Spelling is based upon the Iban pronunciation.

19.   I have described the importance of banks in the evolution of economic class distinctions among the Iban (1988:185-186). The confidentiality of modern banking procedures permits Iban to hide wealth which previously they would have had to share by sponsoring festivals for their communities.

20.   A pseudonym.

21.   Interview conducted in Christopher's home, 10 July, 1984.

22.   The length and circumstances of *bejalai* vary considerably, as Peter Mulok Kedit makes clear in his chapter in this volume. Some wanderers may leave home and family for years, while others travel for only a few months. Apparently, Christopher's father was pressured into going back to his longhouse to assume responsibilities for his family.

23.   Though the life stories are based upon interviews and observations, pseudonyms are used for all domestics and prostitutes.

24.   Although I was skeptical of this figure, it was confirmed generally by interviews and conversations with a Police Inspector (June 22, 1984, June 29, 1984):

>   . . . (A)bout their earning, we cannot quite say (with certainty). . . The high class will be the highest,

approximately M$300, or maybe M$500. Then for the middle class, M$100 over. . .

25.   For a critique of this indefensible position see Maria Lepowsky (1990).

APPENDIX A

Interview with Social Welfare Officer (Female), June 22, 1984
V = Vinson Sutlive, O = Government Officer

V: Several residents of Sibu have told me that there is a problem with prostitution. Last week, I interviewed two, and have followed that up with additional interviews of young and not-so-young women picked up in Police raids. Could you comment on the problem as you see it?

O: There has been a women and girls'problem, as we like to term it, from prostitution, or women being led into immoral behavior. Our country has been very concerned about it and is trying to extend the legislation. It has been extended and has been in operation in Semenanjung Malaysia for some time. . . The State of Sarawak is only just trying to implement it now. . . The Police in Miri and Bintulu are going to be instructed to go ahead and make the raids and arrest them, and charge them under the "Women and Girls' Protection Act."

After we have seen to their sanitary health procedures, we will give them vocational training and counseling help training to give them an alternative more suitable, or an alternative way of making a living. I envisage a tailoring course, maybe typing courses, maybe training in domestic work, so they can get jobs as domestic helpers, catering for large parties. Maybe other handicraft, homemaking, that sort of thing.

V: Wouldn't income from tailoring or working as a seamstress or caterer, be substantially less rewarding than they are earning now. Wouldn't the life be just a bit duller, more drab?

O: They come to Sibu because life in the longhouse is so dull for them. And it's especially so because they are only doing farming, subsistence-type farming, and gathering other fruit and jungle produce that they bring to the town to sell, and usually in the absence of any males around the longhouse, because the young males now are working in Bintulu or Brunei or Kuching, anywhere there's construction or labor-type work, where the income is so much more available or higher per day, and they think they can make very much more there, and it's quite more exciting than living in the longhouse and tilling the soil. But yes, these alternate occupations are probably much more dull, and we don't know how to make them more interesting or acceptable to them. I don't know how we could persuade them that it's a far better thing than what they are doing now.

V: Doesn't this have to do with a change of values? The two young ladies I interviewed are working on their own--there are no pimps or procuresses. And they seem to be doing quite well, sending $100 to $400 a month back to the longhouse. But what I want to lead up to is this: In the case of one of the young women, she had been a victim of what we might call abuse by her husband. The abuse was more emotional than physical. She had been left short-handed in terms of money, and after the third time, she divorced him.

O: Would you tell me a bit more about the emotional abuse? Does it constitute the husband's leaving and not sending any money home?

V: Sometimes, but at others, he was physically present but ignored her. When he did pay any attention to her, it was to criticize her. Then, he took up with another woman and, as a result of that, nothing that she did satisfied him. This was while the couple was living in Sibu. Then she returned to the longhouse where she took up farming, and after about four years of farming, she decided that life in the longhouse was not for her, that Sibu offered more, and she moved to town on her own.

        I wonder if some women are taking up prostitution because of what might be termed the "pre-adaptive" custom of *ngayap* in the longhouse, in which they feel put upon by men. Also, because prostitution gives them an independence they otherwise couldn't enjoy.

O: I haven't actually spoken to these women but we do get an awful lot of cases of women coming in here asking for public assistance because they just cannot make ends meet in the longhouse. So far, about 60 percent of our cases are very young and old ladies who have been left with their grandchildren. A lot of our cases are young ladies who are quite healthy and should have a good future, and they all tell us the same thing, that they don't know where their husbands are, they've just up and gone. They think (the husbands are in) Bintulu. They think he's somewhere working and he just doesn't show up and he doesn't send any money. So, you know, I'm sure the emotional period they go through of being deserted like that could make them very angry and upset and vengeful.

Under the law, we are protectors of any woman under the age of 21. So, it's a very high age actually that they are making it. We have had one girl, a 14-year old girl come in, and she looks younger actually, and a numbersay they are 16 but they may not be. Yes, there would be very young girls, and they are coming in to see their aunts, so working for their aunts, working for their cousins, or other relatives.

V: One of the changes that I have noticed after being away for 12 years is an urbaneness which previously was missing. This seems like a very dramatic change indeed.

O: We talk of development and development, but I'm not sure it's development at all, because the psychological and emotional costs are so high, and needs are not being met. I feel angry that all this development is taking place and we in the Welfare Department are not being given enough staff and enough mandate and enough facilities to assist in this development. It seems as if we are here just to take care of all the casualties and to do the bandage work. And actually the casualties are so many that we can't cope with them. And I think it's terrible to wait for these casualties to happen instead of doing something to prevent them from happening. . .

We hear a lot about projects, and helping our clients to undertake their projects. But I've seen so many other projects underway--agricultural projects, fisheries projects, etc., etc. What we actually need to do is help these people cope with their projects they've already started, and in other ways: Help them with investing their earnings, helping with their budgets, counseling them in their aspirations for their children, or helping their children get into the proper areas they want to, with completing applications for scholarships or even placement in jobs.

520

APPENDIX B

Prostitutes in Sibu[1]

Respectable people, and in particular women, generally look down on prostitutes. Prostitutes are supposed to have no sense of honour, to be rude, to want to earn cheap money easily, to be dirty and to carry diseases. Also women find them dangerous because prostitutes are seducing husbands and boyfriends. Respectable women think of prostitutes as belonging to another category of women than themselves with whom they do not with to mix.

I talked with sixteen prostitutes in Sibu, Sarawak. I found that most of them were more or less forced into the profession, because they did not see another way to solve their problems. Some years ago, they were ordinary women, most of them married, and probably would never have believed that they might become a prostitute one day.

This article would like to give you more understanding about the live(s) and backgrounds of prostitutes, by telling the stories of the sixteen in Sibu. Women should think of prostitutes as allies in the emancipation of women and not as enemies.

Sibu is a fast developing town with more than 100,000 inhabitants in 1986. The town is busy with government offices, schools, and trade, Sibu being the port for the hinterland where timber is cut. Around Sibu there are many timbercamps, camps of police, fieldforce and army, where many men stay alone, without their possible family. There are also many businessmen who have to spend some time in Sibu away from their homes. All of them are potential customers for prostitutes.

Many people argue that if there are more prostitutes there will be more men wanting to visit prostitutes, or likewise, with less prostitutes available there will be less men going to prostitutes. I would rather argue the other way round:

Because there are so many potential customers there are so many prostitutes in Sibu. It is an illusion if women think that their men would not visit prostitutes if there were less of them. The available prostitutes would just have more work. There will always be prostitutes, secretly or openly, as long as there is a demand for them and as long as women have so few ways to earn a living.

I talked with prostitutes who visited the clinic for venereal diseases, the GUM Clinic, in Sibu. The clinic is set up and run by RASCOM and Medical Services Sarawak. The clinic started operating in April 1984. The goal is to stop the spread of venereal diseases (VD) by checking prostitutes every two weeks. The GUM clinic is not only for prostitutes, but for all persons who wish to be checked for VD.

All prostitutes have to carry a yellow card, with their photo attached. If they are found to be free of VD, they get a stamp on their yellow card. When a prostitute is found to have VD, her card is withheld till she has finished her treatment and has been checked again. Customers should always ask for the yellow card when they visit a prostitute, so to be sure she is free of VD. (In practise, men seldom ask for the card.) Quite a few women of women-organizations in Sarawak were against the introduction of the yellow card system. "It will make visiting a prostitute easier for men," they said, "and it will give an air of approval and legalization of prostitutes, with the consequence that more women are likely to go into prostitution."

Women arguing like this fail to see that it is in their own interest if prostitutes are regularly checked on VD. No woman likes her husband or boyfriend to visit prostitutes. It will be even worse, though, if he contacts a venereal disease and then spreads the contagious disease to her. This happened to a Chinese woman I spoke to in the GUM clinic. She told me:

> I know my husband is going to prostitutes sometimes. I don't like it, but I cannot do anything about it. He won't listen to me if I ask or beg him not to go. Now it is worse, because he has passed on a venereal disease from the prostitutes to me. I have to endure the humiliation and trouble of going to this clinic and getting a treatment for this disease.

Prostitutes meet their customers in the street, in hawkerstalls, in bars, in coffeehouses, in hotels and in barber and massage salons. I talked to prostitutes who work in hotels and barber and massage salons. They gave me an impression of their work environment.

In many barber salons there is a room available for massage and this room can also be used for having sex with customers. The woman can use the room for half an hour and has to pay a fixed amount of money (around $11 for half an hour) to the owner of the barber salon. Whatever she earns above that amount, for massage or for having sex, is for her. The women told me that they had started as a hairdresser, then did massage, and only later also had sex with customers who asked for it. The line between massage and having sex is quite easily crossed. And it is tempting to be able to earn so much more money which is urgently needed.

There are prostitutes-hotels in Sibu. Women rent a room per day, the cheapest being $19. The customers go to the hotel and make their choice, walking in the corridors and peeping in the rooms, or they have already made an appointment with a prostitute they knew before or had met on the street. The whole day and night the women are available for work, which means waiting for customers in their rooms. Customers are not abundant and they (the prostitutes) need all the money they can possibly earn.

Chinese prostitutes work almost exclusively in barber and massage salons, where the work conditions are a bit better than in hotels. Only the young and beautiful Iban women can find work in barber and massage salons. Iban usually work in hotels. Prostitutes who cannot earn enough money to pay for the hotel rent, have to work on the street to pick up customers.

The following are the stories of the sixteen prostitutes I interviewed in the GUM clinic. After I had explained to them what I was doing and why and that I was not connected with the police, most women were not shy to tell their stories. Of course I cannot generalize for all prostitutes in GUM clinic and in the whole of Sarawak, after having talked to only 16 of the 495 registered prostitutes in the GUM clinic. From their files they do not seem to be atypical, though.

There were 10 Iban prostitutes, 4 Chinese, 1 Malay and 1 Kadazan. The Iban were generally younger than the others; 8 of them were under 23 years old, the youngest being only 17 years of age. The Chinese were older, 28, 35, and two of them 38. This fits in with the general picture of prostitutes registered in the GUM clinic, that the average age of Iban is lower than that of the other ethnic groups.

Only 1 woman had not been married yet. Thirteen women were divorced and two were widows. Iban marry at a young age. Often the men leave the longhouse alone, to work elsewhere and they may meet other women and interests. They leave their wives at home and later divorce them. So in general the Iban women are divorced at a younger age than Chinese and Malay women because the last two also marry at a later age.

Half of the prostitutes have one or more children they have to take care of without a husband, either because the husband left them or because he passed away.

The majority of the women, 14, come from outside the Sibu District, from other districts and divisions, as far away as Sabah. This is because there is not much work for prostitutes at home and because they would not like their family and acquaintances to know how they are earning their money. Most of the women go home to their families or children when they have saved some money and go back into prostitution in Sibu once the money has run out. This point to the fact that the prostitutes do not do this work to get rich easily, as other people say. For them it is one of the few available ways to earn an income, if not the only way. I cannot trust the figures the women gave me about what they earn, because the figures vary extremely from $120 a month up to $2000. Their clothes and cheap ornaments gave me the impression that they do not earn much, though.

Only four prostitutes told me they liked the work they were doing. They were the younger Iban, 17, 19, 19, and 21 years old, who had been in the profession only for a short time, two for less than one year, the other two for only a year. Their circumstances did not force them to go into prostitution, like the other prostitutes. They were feeling bored in their longhouses, three of them after their husbands had divorced them. From other women in the profession they had heard about the townlife and the way to earn a living in the town. Three said they were happy with this work and would not like to have other work. One said that other work was impossible to find. All the women work in hotels and said they could earn enough money with prostitution.

The remaining 12 did not like being prostitutes, but they went into this profession because they did not see another way to solve their problems. Seven women had to earn money for a family and saw prostitution as the only work available to them to earn enough money. The following stories of the women illustrate this.

What can I do but earn my money with prostitution? Three years ago I divorced my husband. In a way I am relieved that we are not living with him anymore, because he is an unfriendly and hot-tempered man. But now I have to earn an income for myself and my three schoolgoing children. They are 11, 13, and 16 years old. I have only been to school for three years and I haven't learnt any profession. When I was married I just stayed at home and did the housekeeping for my family. After I was divorced I started working in a barbersalon, doing hairdressing and massage only. But I could not earn enough money from this work, only $800 a month. The house we live in costs $360 a month and the children need a lot of money. So that is why now I also have sex with the customers. I can earn $1000 extra per month and that is enough. I would like to have another job, because I don't like this work at all, but there is no other work I could do that pays enough. (Chinese, 35)

I am a divorced woman and I have two children to take care of. I have never been to school. The only way to earn enough money is by being a prostitute, although I don't like the work at all. (Malay, 33)

After my husband died I tried for one year to earn a living by cooking mee, but the income was too low. I looked for another job and ended up in a barbershop. First I only washed hair and did massage. Now I also have sex customers because I can only work half days since I have a baby at home and cannot earn enough washing hair and doing massage only. I don't like the work, but I have no choice. (Chinese, 38)

I married young and had a child, who is 12 years old now. My husband divorced me a long time ago. I had several jobs as an 'amah' ("domestic"). The last one was in Sibu, before that in other towns. I lost my last job, because the wife of the family was jealous. My parents have both died and I have to take care of my child and my older brother who is always sick and cannot work. They both stay in the longhouse. With this work as a prostitute I can work two months and then have enough money to go back to the longhouse for one or two months. Although I do not like the work, it is the best solution I can think of. (Iban, 30)

I was divorced ten years ago. I have to take care of my 18 year old daughter, my mother and my younger brother who is mentally ill. I send money back home and sometimes I go back myself. (Chinese, 38)

My husband died one and a half years ago. I do this work to earn money for my children, two and four years old. I worked as a barber before. I only earned $200 and I needed $1000 a month. I have only had three years of primary school. I don't see another way to earn enough money than by being a prostitute, so I just have to do it, although I don't like it. (Kadazan, 29)

After I was divorced, I did not want to stay in the longhouse anymore. With a girlfriend I went to Sibu to find work. We worked in a carpentry workshop for three months. We had to work from 7 a.m. till 5 p.m., and earned only $4 a day. My friend quit this job before me and started working as a prostitute. After a few weeks I followed my friend, because the money in the carpentry-workshop was not enough to live on and the work too hard. I don't like being a prostitute, but I have no other choice at the moment. (Iban, 19)

The last story, especially, but also some of the others, shows that there were no other ways for the women to earn enough money to live on, alone or with a family. There are just not enough well-paying jobs in Sibu for women. Except for these economic reasons, there were women who went into prostitution because they were angry or upset with a man, because he had left them either by divorce or by death. All three of these women did not like what they were doing, but saw this as a way to work off their anger and impotence.

When my husband died I was very angry and hot. I felt left by him, leaving me behind with nothing. Out of anger I went to another town and worked in a coffeehouse. When men asked me out and wanted to have sex with me and pay for it, I agreed. (Chinese, 38)

I married and got divorced two times now and I am only 21. I got really fed up and angry with men. That is why I just joined the other prostitutes in town. I don't feel very hapy though, about doing this work. I feel shame and guilt. Maybe nobody wants to have me for other work anymore. (Iban, 21)

Half a year ago, my husband left me and our two children of 11 and two and a half to marry another woman. He met her when he was posted in another town. I am still very angry and hot with him for what he did to me. To take revenge on him I work as a prostitute and will do so till I am cooled down. My children stay in the longhouse with my parents for the time being. My mother knows what I am doing and she understands me. (Iban, 28)

There was only one woman who more or less by chance came into prostitution. She does not like the work, but she sees it as a means to earn money now to start her business later. The following is her story:

> Three years ago I divorced my husband. He asked me for a divorce because he wanted to marry his girlfriend. I had no choice and agreed. I didn't have any children, so I was alone again. I had to find myself a job to earn a living. First I worked as a servantgirl with a Chinese family for $100 a month. The pay was too low and I didn't like the work. Then a friend asked me to come to Sibu and work in the barbersalon where she was also working. I had to wash hair and faces and also cut hair, for $200 a month. I never realized there were customers who came to barbersalons to have sex. Now I also have sex with customers, because I can earn so much more. I have decided to do it for a short time only, to earn money to open my own barbershop in my home town. I want to prove to the prople who look down upon me that I can earn a proper living with a shop of my own. (Chinese, 28)

The live of a prostitute is troublesome and sometimes dangerous. The women were complaining about men being aggressive and using force, not wanting to pay, not wanting to use condoms if they asked them to. In the hotels the women have no protection at all. They say that sometimes they have to call for a friend prostitute to help them get rid of a troublesome customer. Many of the prostitutes have often felt threatened and afraid. These are some of their stories:

> In Miri I had problems with a gang of Chinese boys I had reported to the police, because they had threatened me with a knife to rob my money. The gang heard of this and came after me. Then I felt very scared and I left Miri. (Chinese, 38, four years in prostitution)

> There are many customers who want to have sex without paying. Or they give me money first and then, after having sex, threaten me and force me to give it back to them. (Iban, 30, three years in prostitution)

> I have had many problems with the customers. They are using force on me. Drunkards become aggressive when I refuse to have sex with them. There are men who want to have sex continuously for the same money; they don't stop using me.

Some men have problems and cannot become satisfied, the sperm doesn't come out. They they blame me for it and want to have their money back. (Chinese, 38, ten years in prostitution)

Many times men come to me who want to have sex without paying. One time, when I refused, I was beaten up by a drunken man. I was very afraid. There was nobody to help me. (Iban, 19, two months in prostitution)

With such experiences you can expect the women to become rude, as a way of self-protection. They will also react rudely if they feel that other people look down upon them.

I hope that the stories of these women have made you understand that most of them, three-quarters, do not like being a prostitute. They would like to find other work, but for women other work is hardly available. If there is any work, the pay is very low. From the salary one surely cannot take care of children. The only choice the women have is to take advantage of the high demand for prostitutes in Sibu.

Women of Sarawak should fight together for more job opportunities, for better payment and for social welfare for women who are left by their husbands and who do not have a family to take care of them. When these conditions are fulfilled, less women will have to become prostitutes because they need the money.

The first thing women can do is to try to understand prostitutes and not look down upon them. The supportive understanding of other women will help prostitutes to try to find other solutions for their problems.

NOTE

1.   Winny Koster, Drs. Medical Anthropology, No. 71, 7346 AE Hoog Soeren, The Netherlands. Study was conducted March - May, 1986.